THE ROUTLEDGE INTERNATIONAL HANDBOOK OF DISABILITY HUMAN RIGHTS HIERARCHIES

Disability is defined by hierarchy. Regardless of culture or context, persons with disabilities are almost always pushed to the bottom of the social hierarchy. With the advent of the Convention on the Rights of Persons with Disabilities (2006), disability human rights seemingly provided a path forward for tearing down ableist social hierarchies and ensuring that all persons with disabilities everywhere were treated equally. Despite important progress, the disability human rights project not only remains incomplete but has also created new hierarchies among persons with disabilities themselves or across the human rights it promotes. Certain groups of persons with disabilities have gained new voices while others remain silenced, and certain rights are prioritized over others, depending on what states, international organizations, or advocates want rather than what those on the ground need most.

This volume was inspired by the continued need both to expose human rights violations against persons with disabilities and to explore the nuanced role that hierarchies play in the spread, implementation, and protection of disability human rights. The enjoyment of human rights is not equal nor is the recognition of specific individual and group rights. In order to change this situation, inequalities across the disability human rights movement must be explored.

Divided into five parts:
Who counts as disabled?
Political, social, and cultural context
Which rights on top, whose rights on the bottom?
Pushed to the periphery of the disability rights movement

Containing representations of disability comprising 34 newly written chapters including case studies from the Anglophone Caribbean, Bangladesh,

Bosnia-Herzegovina, China, Ghana, Haiti, Hungary, India, Israel, Kenya, Latin America, Poland, Russia, Scotland, Serbia and South Africa, and other countries, this book will be of interest to all scholars and students of disability studies, sociology, human rights law, and social policy.

Stephen J. Meyers is director of the Center for Global Studies at the University of Washington, Seattle, USA. He is the author of *Civilizing Disability Society: The UN Disability Convention Socializing Grassroots Disabled Persons Organizations in Nicaragua*. Cambridge University Press, 2019.

Megan McCloskey is senior fellow, Disability Inclusive Development Initiative, International Policy Institute, Henry M. Jackson School of International Studies at the University of Washington, Seattle, USA.

Gabor Petri is postdoctoral researcher at the Democracy Institute, Central European University, Budapest, and honorary lecturer at the Tizard Centre at the University of Kent, Canterbury, UK.

ROUTLEDGE INTERNATIONAL HANDBOOKS

ROUTLEDGE INTERNATIONAL HANDBOOK OF MULTIDISCIPLINARY PERSPECTIVES ON DESCENDANTS OF HOLOCAUST SURVIVORS
Edited by Judith Tydor Baumel-Schwartz and Amit Shrira

ROUTLEDGE INTERNATIONAL HANDBOOK OF VISUAL-MOTOR SKILLS, HANDWRITING, AND SPELLING
Edited by Yanyan Ye, Tomohiro Inoue, Urs Maurer, and Catherine McBride

ROUTLEDGE HANDBOOK OF ENVIRONMENTAL POLICY
Edited by Helge Jörgens, Christoph Knill and Yves Steinebach

THE ROUTLEDGE HANDBOOK OF SOFT POWER (2nd Edition)
Edited by Naren Chitty, Lilian Ji, Gary D Rawnsley

THE ROUTLEDGE HANDBOOK OF URBAN LOGISTICS
Edited by Jason Monios, Lucy Budd and Stephen Ison

THE ROUTLEDGE HANDBOOK OF COMPARATIVE GLOBAL URBAN STUDIES
Edited by Patrick LeGalès and Jennifer Robinson

THE ROUTLEDGE HANDBOOK OF TRANSATLANTIC RELATIONS
Edited by Elaine Fahey

THE ROUTLEDGE INTERNATIONAL HANDBOOK OF DISABILITY HUMAN RIGHTS HIERARCHIES
Edited by Stephen J. Meyers, Megan McCloskey and Gabor Petri

THE ROUTLEDGE INTERNATIONAL HANDBOOK OF DISABILITY HUMAN RIGHTS HIERARCHIES

Edited by Stephen J. Meyers, Megan McCloskey and Gabor Petri

Routledge
Taylor & Francis Group
LONDON AND NEW YORK

Designed cover image: Getty Images

First published 2024
by Routledge
4 Park Square, Milton Park, Abingdon, Oxon OX14 4RN

and by Routledge
605 Third Avenue, New York, NY 10158

Routledge is an imprint of the Taylor & Francis Group, an informa business

British Library Cataloguing-in-Publication Data
A catalogue record for this book is available from the British Library

Library of Congress Cataloging-in-Publication Data
Names: Meyers, Stephen J., 1976– editor. | McCloskey, Megan, editor. | Petri, Gabor (Postdoctoral researcher), editor.
Title: The Routledge international handbook of disability human rights hierarchies / edited by Stephen J. Meyers, Megan McCloskey and Gabor Petri.
Description: Abingdon, Oxon ; New York, NY : Routledge, 2024. | Includes bibliographical references and index.
Identifiers: LCCN 2023018139 (print) | LCCN 2023018140 (ebook)
Subjects: LCSH: People with disabilities—Civil rights. | People with disabilities—Social conditions. | Discrimination against people with disabilities. | Social status.
Classification: LCC HV1568 .R69 2024 (print) | LCC HV1568 (ebook) | DDC 323.3/7—dc23/eng/20230509
LC record available at https://lccn.loc.gov/2023018139
LC ebook record available at https://lccn.loc.gov/2023018140

ISBN: 978-1-032-53083-3 (hbk)
ISBN: 978-1-032-53084-0 (pbk)
ISBN: 978-1-003-41008-9 (ebk)

DOI: 10.4324/9781003410089

Typeset in Sabon
by Apex CoVantage, LLC

CONTENTS

FIGURES

TABLES

CONTRIBUTORS

Stephen Baranyi is a professor at the University of Ottawa's School of International Development, where he teaches and does research at the intersection of development and security. Before moving to the University of Ottawa in 2008, he was a practitioner with non-governmental and governmental agencies in Canada, Central America and Europe.

Dr. Kosana Beker holds a PhD from the Centre for Gender Studies of the Association of Centres for Interdisciplinary and Multidisciplinary studies of the University of Novi Sad (Serbia). Her work focuses on human rights and intersectional (gender-based) discrimination. Dr. Beker has been a member of the Academic Network of European Disability Experts (ANED) since 2017.

Diane Bell is an honorary associate professor at the University College of London through her role as head of Accessible Assistive Technology & EdTech at the Global Disability Innovation (GDI) hub. She is also a research fellow at the University of Stellenbosch Business School. Her research focuses on disability, education and assistive technology.

Adrian Brown is a dedicated self-advocate who speaks up for the rights of people with learning disabilities, medical conditions and profound disabilities. Adrian is a trustee of the Elfrida Society and has advised on research projects and the education of trainee clinical psychologists at University College London for the past six years.

Celia Brown is a long-term self-advocate who speaks up for the rights of people with learning disabilities, profound disabilities and medical conditions. Working for the Power and Control group at the Elfrida Society, Brown has provided support to University College London, advising researchers about the rights of people with learning disabilities.

Ricky Buchanan an assistive technology expert user and disability advocate from Melbourne, Australia. Passionate about disability and chronic illness, she thinks and writes a lot about assistive technology and how it fits into people's lives. Buchanan has been disabled and usually homebound/bed-ridden for her entire adult life.

Karen Bunning, PhD, is a reader in developmental disability at the University of East Anglia, UK. Karen's research interests are centred around the themes of empowerment, inclusion and participation for people living with disability.

Christine Burke is the director of the Foundation for People with Learning Disabilities (FPLD). FPLD works to ensure people with learning disabilities have the same opportunities as other people through carrying out research, policy, development and consultancy work. For the STORM programme, Christine was co-chair of the expert advisory panel.

Jean Cathro is studying for an MA in Art and Social Practice at the University of Highlands and Islands. She works for the University of Edinburgh supporting disabled students and is the founder of Crossing Countries, a social enterprise that (before the pandemic) offered opportunities for disabled and non-disabled people to volunteer in Durban, South Africa, and in Scotland.

Megan E. Cartier, MEd, worked as a high school special education teacher for 12 years in central Kentucky before coming to Syracuse University, where she is now a doctoral candidate in inclusive (special) education. She has earned a certificate of advanced study in disability studies. She is now an assistant professor at the College of Saint Rose.

Julie Jaye Charles is chief executive and founder of Start Change CIC Limited, an organisation seeking to empower disabled people of colour to drive changes that are meaningful to them and their communities. Start Change CIC is the culmination of Julie's 30-plus years' experience as an advocate and catalyst for change for Black and minority ethnic communities and disabled people.

Stephanie Côté (she/her), MA CYC, is a research and policy analyst with CASDA. Stephanie's work at CASDA has been informed by her academic focus on anti-oppressive practice in child and youth care and on the social model of disability as it relates to services for young autistic people.

Csilla Cserti-Szauer has been a service developer in the field of disability issues for more than 20 years. She has extensive experience as a special needs educator and an economist in network building, strategic planning and co-transforming ideas to projects. She is currently an assistant lecturer at ELTE Bárczi Gusztáv Faculty of Special Needs Education.

Eileen Davis, BsocSc, H Dip Ad & Comm Ed, M. Ed Guidance & Counselling, Dip in Life & Career Coaching. Eileen is a lecturer on the Professional Master's in Education (PME) programme for professionals in further education in Marino Institute of Education, Dublin.

Karuna Davies works as an assistant psychologist in the NHS. For the Standing Up for Myself (STORM) project, she was a research assistant. She has supported the digital adaptation and production of accessible materials.

Paul Davies is a long-term self-advocate and advises research and healthcare professionals on providing accessible support for people with learning disabilities. Working with the Elfrida Society, Paul also provides mutual support to people with learning disabilities.

Amita Dhanda is professor emerita at NALSAR University of Law, Hyderabad, where she continues to engage with questions of disability studies and rights as the head of the Centre for Disability Studies.

Panagiotis Diakakis is executive for employment requests by recipients/users of mental health services, working in Structure of Rehabilitation Psychosocial (PEPSAEE) and treasurer of the board of directors of the Association of Recipients/Users of Mental Health services Aftoekprosopisi.

Judith Drake is a disabled PhD candidate in European Theatre at the University of Edinburgh. Her thesis focuses on Scottish disability theatre and incorporates interdisciplinary approaches, including theatre and performance studies, disability studies and medical humanities.

Annie Fergusson has been family carer and the main advocate for her brother, who has profound intellectual and multiple disabilities, for 20 years. Now retired from a long career as a practitioner and university academic within the special education and learning disabilities field, Annie is a longstanding editor of the journal PMLD LINK.

Micah Fialka-Feldman is a self-advocate, teaching assistant, outreach coordinator, national speaker and pioneer who fights for disability pride, justice and inclusion. He is currently an outreach coordinator at the Lawrence B. Taishoff Center for Inclusive Higher Education.

Panagiota Fitsiou, Psychologist MSc, is the head of the EU Projects Department in the Society of Social Psychiatry P. Sakellaropoulos. Fitsiou is a psychotherapist in the Mental Health Institute for Children and Adults P. Sakellaropoulos and a member of the Standing Committee for Monitoring the Protection of the Rights of Persons with Mental Disorders.

Athina Fragkouli, PhD in speech and language therapy, psychology and applied social studies, is engaged in continuing education on issues of management and human resources; president of the board of the Society of Social Psychiatry P. Sakellaropoulos; and chairperson of the Institute of Mental Health for Children, Adolescents and Adults.

András Futár is a participatory teacher and researcher at ELTE Bárczi Gusztáv Faculty of Special Needs Education. He has been involved in several inclusive research projects and university seminars. In 2017, together with his colleagues, he was awarded the prize for International Development of Higher Education by the Tempus Public Foundation.

Beatriz Miranda Galarza holds a PhD in disability studies from Leeds University. She taught disability and development at the Athena Institute of the Vrije Universiteit Amsterdam and international public health at Amsterdam University College and was project manager of the SARI project about stigma in the lives of people affected by leprosy in Indonesia.

Chaya Gershuni is an activist and a doctoral student at the Meitar Center in the Faculty of Law at Tel Aviv University under the supervision of Professor Neta Ziv and Professor Dafna Hecker. She recently established a forum for disability researchers in ultra-Orthodox society on behalf of the Center for Disability Studies at JDC Israel and the Hebrew University.

Ewa Giermanowska is an associate professor and sociologist in the Institute of Applied Social Sciences at the University of Warsaw, Poland. Currently, she is engaged in a research project at Warsaw University Policies for independent living in Poland and Norway, dealing with personal assistance for people with disabilities.

Gabor Gombos was a world-renowned disability rights activist known for his radical advocacy of the rights of persons with psychosocial disabilities. Professor Gombos was the member of the United Nations Committee on the Rights of Persons with Disabilities from 2011 to 2013.

Rosemary Joan Gowran (PhD, MSc OT, BSc (Hons) OT), director of MSc Occupational Therapy (professional qualification) and post-graduate certificate in the Posture Seating and Wheelchair Mobility across the Life Course, University of Limerick, Ireland. She holds a visiting position at the Assisting Living and Learning Institute, Maynooth University.

Nicola Clare Grove, PhD, is a consultant and researcher in disability, communication and storytelling and a member of the Open University Social History of

Learning Disability group. She has been a schoolteacher, speech and language therapist and university lecturer, specialising in the field of intellectual disabilities.

Sahid Hadi is a researcher at the Center for Human Rights Studies of the Universitas Islam Indonesia (PUSHAM UII) and editorial staff for a national law journal, *Ius Quia Iustum*. He is completing his master of law at the Universitas Islam Indonesia and conducting a thesis on the human rights dimensions of business competition.

James Hardy is a PhD candidate at Nottingham Trent University, UK, and a learning and behaviour mentor for children with special educational needs and disabilities. Over the past six years, James has utilised his professional teaching experience to support non-governmental organizations across Africa, Asia and Europe.

Jason Harris is an autistic person who has been an advocate for about ten years. He has started his own non-profit and social media page called Jason's Connection, which reaches over 300,000 people. He is currently the director of strategic operations at Living Arrangements for the Developmentally Disabled in Cincinnati, Ohio.

Stéphanie Harvey is a researcher and guest lecturer, working primarily in the fields of disability and intersectionality, and an equalities policy maker with experience working both nationally and internationally. She was a member of the multidisciplinary research team for working on the D4D project on community and disability.

Elizabeth Hassler (she/her) is a writer and organizer based in Arcata, California. She hosts Disability Creativity Workshop, where she writes about being and longing.

Despan Heryansyah completed his doctorate in constitutional law in 2020 at the Universitas Islam Indonesia, focusing on regional autonomy in Indonesia and the idea of a federal state for Indonesia's future. Despan, together with his institution, the Center for Human Rights Studies of the Universitas Islam Indonesia (PUSHAM UII), advises on disability issues.

Naomi Hewardine is a speech and language therapist. After graduating from Manchester University in 2000, she worked in the NHS in Oldham for 11 years, based in community learning disability teams and special high schools. Since 2013, she has been part of L'Arche Manchester, a faith-based community of people with and without learning disabilities.

Njabulo Hlongwane is an artist and art educator from Durban, South Africa. He studied art at Johannesburg Art Foundation (1992–1994), where he also did courses in curatorship and teaching. He is currently teaching creative arts subjects, including visual arts, drama and music, at Mason Lincoln Special School, Umlazi Township, south of Durban.

James Ian is a working actor, singer and songwriter living in Los Angeles. He has auditioned for more than 50 roles over the past three years, but has only booked 6 roles. These included auditioning for the role of Theodore in the movie *Devil All the Time*, which went to non-disabled actor Pokey LaFarge, despite the character having a disability.

Jannatul Ferdous Ivy is a human rights activist, writer and the first woman with disability filmmaker of Bangladesh. Jannatul Ferdous was born on 1 July 1976. Ivy had a fire accident in 1997 that requires her to live with burn-related physical disability.

Abi James is a digital accessibility consultant and researcher specialising in supporting organisations to ensure that their content, websites and apps are accessible to all. With 20 years experiences in the assistive technology and accessibility field, she has led several projects to develop and deploy assistive technologies in the public and private sector.

Biljana Janjic holds an MA in international relations from the Webster University Vienna (Austria), and she currently works as an executive director at women's rights organization FemPlatz in Serbia.

Adetokunbo Johnson is currently a postdoctoral fellow at the University of the Free State, Bloemfontein, South Africa. She holds a DPhil in human rights and a masters of philosophy (MPhil) in multidisciplinary human rights from the Faculty of Law, University of Pretoria, South Africa.

Nicolas Joncour is a non-speaking autistic student. He was born in France, October 4, 1999, and has always been schooled in a regular school or by a correspondence course. In 2017, he became the first French non-speaking autistic student to pass the Baccalauréat exam, which is needed to go to university in France.

Sureshkumar Kamalakannan is an associate professor in public health disability and health systems research at the Public Health Foundation of India (PHFI) and the University of Northumbria. UK. He is a research fellow in public health and disability research for the India Alliance and LSHTM.

Alimata Abdul Karimu is an independent researcher and rights activist researching inclusive policies and disability rights. Abdul Karimu is currently a fellow with the Center for Inclusive Policy investigating the Disability Fund of the District Assemblies Common Fund in Ghana and other social protection frameworks to ascertain their inclusiveness.

Radoš Keravica is a disabled researcher from Serbia and a doctoral candidate at the University of Leeds, Centre for Disability Studies, in the School of Sociology and Social Policy and works as an EU Marie Sklodowska-Curie early-stage researcher in the Disability Advocacy Research in Europe (DARE) project.

Rebekah Kintzinger, diagnosed autistic in 2012, is a prominent autistic self-advocate from Kelowna, British Columbia (BC), Canada. Rebekah is a project officer at AIDE Canada and a director at the Canadian Autism Spectrum Disorder Alliance (CASDA) and is a founding member of the *Canadian Journal of Autism Equity*.

Natasha Layton, PhD, is an occupational therapist and senior research fellow with the Rehabilitation, Ageing and Independent Living Research Centre at Monash University in Australia and industry adjunct with Swinburne University. Layton is a longstanding member of the assistive technology community in Australia and internationally.

Sue Ledger, PhD, is a visiting research fellow at the Open University, UK. A member of the international Social History of Learning Disability Research Group since 2001, she has co-researched with people with intellectual disabilities on a range of projects, including institutional and community history, songs of resistance and life story work in practice.

Alena Levina (Alyona Lyovina) is an artist and feminist activist who fights for the rights of women with disabilities. She was born and lives in Moscow. She is one of the founders and an active participant in the Women. Disability. Feminism community.

Sarah Lewthwaite is a senior research fellow and UKRI Future Leaders fellow at the Centre for Research in Inclusion, Southampton Education School, University of Southampton, where she leads a five-year programme of research into the teaching of accessibility in digital disciplines as principle investigator.

Ilionor Louis is a professor at the faculty of ethnology of the Université d'État d'Haïti. His training is multidisciplinary, with a PhD in sociology from the Université de Montréal (Canada), a master's degree in social sciences from the Latin-American Faculty of Social Sciences (FLACSO) in Mexico, and a diploma a from the Université d'État d'Haïti.

Garyfalia Marini worked as a psychologist for SSP P. Sakellaropoulos in psychosocial rehabilitation units and is involved in community education projects using theatrical and improvisational techniques for the empowerment of children, adolescents and adults belonging to vulnerable groups.

Dominique Masson is a professor at the Institute of Feminist and Gender Studies and at the School of Sociological and Anthropological Studies of the University of Ottawa. She is a feminist social movement scholar whose work centers on the women's and feminist movements, intersectionality and solidarity building.

Jessica McLeod was a member of the Australian delegation to the Conference of States Parties 12 on the Convention on the Rights of Persons with Disabilities at the United Nations in New York. She is an early childhood and primary teacher.

Sharynne McLeod, PhD is a professor at Charles Sturt University in Australia and a life member of Speech Pathology Australia and received honors from the American Speech-Language-Hearing Association. She has co-authored 11 books and over 230 articles focusing on children's speech acquisition, speech sound disorders, multilingualism and communication rights.

Elizabeth Mestheneos, PhD, a UK-trained sociologist and academic, moved to Greece in 1983, becoming an independent social researcher in 1988. In 2005, she co-founded the NGO 50+ Hellas (www.50plus.gr) and was its MD for 10 years. Since 2003, she has served on the board of AGE-Platform Europe and was its elected president from 2008 to 2011 (www.age-platform.eu).

Senator Floyd Morris is a member and former president of the Senate of Jamaica, where he served two terms as senator from 1998 to 2007. Senator Morris is a member of the United Nations Committee on the Rights of Persons with Disabilities and special rapporteur on the Rights of Persons with Disabilities for the Caribbean Community (CARICOM).

Philippa Mullins is an assistant professor at the College of Humanities and Social Sciences of the American University of Armenia (AUA). She is core faculty on AUA's human rights and social justice master's program. She holds a PhD in social policy from the London School of Economics and Political Science.

Shubha Nagesh is a medical doctor and a public health physician, based out of Dehradun, Uttarakhand, the Himalayan state of India. She is presently the chapter development manager for Asia-Pacific and the Middle East at Women in Global Health. She is a senior Atlantic fellow in Global Health Equity at GWU.

Professor Deepak Nathan is a trained professional social worker with a master's in social work from Loyola College and a second master's in psychiatric research methods from King's College with a fellowship from the Paul Hamlyn Foundation London and King's College. Deepak teaches social work in Loyola College at present for post-graduate students pursing master's degrees.

Mildred Omino is a disability justice and gender justice activist based in Nairobi, Kenya, whose work is inspired by her lived realities as a woman with disability. Currently, she is the disability liaison officer at the University of Nairobi, Kenya.

Michaela Osborne is a trainee clinical psychologist at Newcastle University. She previously worked as a research assistant on the Standing Up for Myself (STORM) project at University College London. Part of her role is to support the inclusion of people with learning disabilities in research.

Maureen Phillip has worked with Promoting a More Inclusive Society (PAMIS) for over 20 years in a research, development and family-support capacity. She has an MA (hons) in English literature and a MSc in information science and research methods.

Rina B. Pikkel is a PhD candidate at the University of Haifa faculty of law, under the supervision of Dr. Sagit Mor. She earned her LLB and LLM in law and health from the University of Haifa. Her doctoral dissertation explores the socio-legal construction of sexuality and disability and the conceptualization of disability sexual rights.

Mariola Racław is an associate professor and sociologist at the Institute of Applied Social Sciences at the University of Warsaw, Poland. She is a member of the Government Population Council and the co-founder and vice president of the sociology of disabilities section of the Polish Sociological Association.

Lisa Richardson is a research associate at the University of Kent. Previously, she worked at the UCL Unit for Stigma Research and is study manager for the Standing Up for Myself (STORM) project, a psychosocial group programme to help people with learning disabilities manage and resist stigma.

Harry Roche is a passionate self-advocate working internationally to ensure that people with learning disabilities have equal opportunities, rights and treatment. Currently working in the communications team at Mencap and as a freelance self-advocacy consultant, Harry promotes Mencap's work on social media and campaigns for learning disability issues.

Ana María Sánchez Rodríguez holds a PhD in public policy from the University of Massachusetts Boston and a MSc in NGO management from the London School of Economics and Political Science. She is adjunct lecturer at the ALL Institute in Maynooth University. She has worked in human rights and social development at the federal and local governmental levels in Mexico.

Anikó Sándor graduated as a special needs teacher, therapist and economist. Her doctoral dissertation examined the self-determination possibilities and challenges of adults with high support needs. She is a founding member of Freekey and the Disability Studies and Social Innovation Lab.

Katrina Scior is professor of clinical psychology and stigma studies at University College London. She is passionate about challenging stigma and making sure that people with learning disabilities are treated more fairly and empowered to lead good quality lives.

Leonardos Skordos has worked in the Panhellenic Association for Psychosocial Rehabilitation and Vocational Rehabilitation (PEPSAEE) for people with psychosocial problems for the last 22 years. He has been president of the Association of Recipients/Users of Mental Health Services Autoekprosopisi since 2007.

Sara Jo Soldovieri, MEd, is a doctoral student in inclusive (special) education at Syracuse University. Prior to coming to Syracuse University, she ran the inclusive education program at the National Down Syndrome Society.

Armineh Soorenian is an independent researcher with research interests in inclusive education, disability arts and representations, disability and gender and disability hate crime. In November 2013, her book *Disabled International Students in British Higher Education: Experiences and Expectations* was published by Sense Publishing House.

Áine Sperrin, PhD, is currently a post-doctoral researcher with the Re(al) Productive Justice Project at the Centre for Disability Law and Policy, NUI Galway, Ireland. Áine lectures on independent living and nursing law. Áine was appointed to the Disability Stakeholders Group, an advisory group to the Irish government, in December 2021.

Pavithra Suresh (she/her) is a PhD candidate in cultural studies at George Mason University in Fairfax, VA, USA. Pavithra is currently working on her dissertation, which explores the crises of despair in the South Asian community in her hometown of Research Triangle, North Carolina.

Dorota Szawarska is a social anthropologist in the Institute of Applied Social Sciences at the University of Warsaw, Poland. She holds a BA from the University of Cambridge and a PhD from SOAS University of London in the UK. Her research interests include care, kinship, disability and medical anthropology.

Elizabeth (Liz) Tilley, PhD, is a senior lecturer in the School of Health, Wellbeing and Social Care, Faculty of Wellbeing, Education and Language Studies, at The Open University (OU). Liz co-chairs the Social History of Learning Disabilities Research Group at the OU, researching alongside people with learning disabilities, their families, supporters and allies.

Maria Tselovatova is a feminist activist and poet. She studies literature at the Russian State University of Humanities, where her specializations include narratology and American literature. She identifies as a lesbian and has disabilities. She was born and lives in Moscow. She is one of the founding members of the Women. Disability. Feminism community.

Gaye Tyler-Merrick is a senior lecturer at Nottingham Trent University, UK, where she leads the National Award for Special Educational Needs Co-Ordination. Gaye is a co-author of the Growing Children's Social and Emotional Skills: Using the TOGETHER programme (2022). She holds a PhD in education from the University of Canterbury in New Zealand.

Radina Ugrinova is a human rights researcher and disability rights activist. She has worked in various academic institutions in Europe, conducting socio-legal research in the field of disability studies and advocating for disability-inclusive workplaces.

Karin van Marle is a professor in the Department of Public Law, University of the Free State. Her research falls within the broad field of law and the humanities and involves critical theory, legal philosophy and jurisprudence. She is an adjunct professor at Southern Cross University, Australia, and a fellow at Stellenbosch Institute for Advanced Study (Stias).

Jan Walmsley has been working in the field of intellectual disability since 1985, when she created a course aimed at improving communication between staff and families. The course, called Mental Handicap: Patterns for Living, reached more than 30,000 people.

Jennifer Ward is a teacher for Deaf/Hard of Hearing children in San Diego, CA. She holds an EdD in international and multicultural education with a concentration in human rights education from the University of San Francisco. Dr. Ward is on the board for the Council of Exceptional Children's Division for Communication, Language and Deaf/Hard of Hearing.

Holly Wescott is a PhD candidate in the psychology department and Assisting Living & Learning (ALL) Institute at Maynooth University in Maynooth, Ireland. She also holds an MSc in global health from Trinity College, Dublin; a BA in disability studies and sociology from the University of Washington, Seattle; and a national interpreter certification (NIC) in ASL.

Gillian White is a children's book author and multi-sensory storyteller. She was a full time parent-carer to her son Leo, who was profoundly disabled, until he passed away in March 2022. Gill's first book – *Leo and the Lightning Dragons*, published in 2019 by Fledgling Press – was written for Leo, who had Ohtahara Syndrome.

INTRODUCTION

Disability is defined by hierarchy. Regardless of culture or context, persons with disabilities are almost always pushed to the bottom of the social hierarchy. With the advent of the Convention on the Rights of Persons with Disabilities (2006), disability human rights seemingly provided a path forward for tearing down ableist social hierarchies and ensuring that all persons with disabilities everywhere were treated equally. Despite important progress, the disability human rights project remains incomplete. Furthermore, a human rights lens has exposed new hierarchies in the ways specific states implement (or fail to implement) the convention, who and what rights the international disability movement prioritizes, and local inequalities that demonstrate that the rights of some persons with disabilities seemingly matter more than those of others.

In just the past few months that this volume has been under development, major international events have exposed how quickly progress in disability human rights can be reversed. At the advent of the global COVID-19 pandemic, the continued discrimination against persons with disabilities was highlighted by governments disseminating inaccessible information, hospitals instituting ableist triage policies, and community-based service providers suspending essential supports (Brennan, 2020). In many cases, these rights violations occurred in states that had signed and ratified the Convention on the Rights of Persons with Disabilities, which includes the right to access information (Article 21), the right to health (Article 25), and the right to live independently and be included in the community (Article 19). Furthermore, the impact of discrimination against persons with disabilities in relation to the pandemic has been uneven. Older persons with disabilities, for example, were often put at greater risk than younger persons with disabilities by discriminatory triage policies. Similarly, persons with disabilities dependent on assistance for the basic tasks of daily living were put in a life-threatening situations with the loss of services. Persons with disabilities around the world, however, have fought back. After

DOI: 10.4324/9781003410089-1

a disabled child died of starvation as the result of strict COVID quarantine policies in China, persons with disabilities in China and their families came together to forge self-help and advocacy networks to address access to basic needs and care (Huang, 2022). These stories of resistance are important, as they demonstrate how hierarchies can be attacked and, hopefully, someday dismantled.

The Russian invasion of Ukraine has similarly exposed the continued presence of a hierarchy. While much of the world came together to aid Ukrainians in fleeing violence and finding safe harbor, Ukrainians with disabilities faced barriers to travel, and many of those living in institutions found themselves trapped in conflict areas (Rosenthal et al., 2022; Mao, 2022), despite both international human rights and international humanitarian law that provides equal protection to persons with disabilities in situations of conflict. Thankfully, Fight for Right, a grassroots Ukrainian organization of persons with disabilities, has evacuated persons with disabilities one by one while also holding the UNHCR and other relief organizations accountable under Article 11 of the Convention on the Rights of Persons with Disabilities, Situations of Risk and Humanitarian Emergencies, which obligates states/parties to ensure the safety and protection of persons with disabilities in situations of risk (Fight for Right, 2022).

While failure to protect the rights of Ukrainians with disabilities unquestionably represents a human rights violation perpetrated by the international community, recent attention to the crisis in Ukraine also exposes an even greater inequality regarding refugees with disabilities from other parts of the world: The tens of thousands of disabled refugees from Syria, Sudan, Myanmar, and other non-Western countries have been ignored for more than a decade. Persons with disabilities with intersecting identities, such as women and girls with disabilities, indigenous and racial and ethnic minorities with disabilities, and persons with disabilities living in the Global South face greater barriers and are given less of a voice within the disability rights movement than majority ethnicity men with disabilities in the Global North, who often lead the international disability rights movement. Similarly, institutionalized persons with disabilities and individuals with psychiatric or intellectual disabilities are marginalized within the disability movement, which has historically focused on the rights of persons with physical or sensory disabilities.

This volume, which began at the beginning of the COVID-19 pandemic and well before the eruption of war in Ukraine, was inspired by the continued need both to expose human rights violations against persons with disabilities and to explore the nuanced role that hierarchies play in the spread, implementation, and protection of disability human rights. The enjoyment of human rights is not equal, nor is the recognition of specific individuals' and groups' rights.

The disability movement, for example, began with the imperative that persons with disabilities must come together and fight for the rights of *all* disabled persons equally. Persons with disabilities, however, are rarely equally represented in movements or equally protected under the law. Peipzna-Smarasinha (2019) argues that hierarchies in the disability rights movement made it necessary for "disabled people of color, queer and trans disabled folks of color, and everyone who is marginalized in mainstream disability organizing" to come together and form the alternative Disability Justice movement (p. 22) in order to ensure their voices were heard. Similarly, others have argued that the needs and interests of men with disabilities have consistently been prioritized over the needs and interests of women with disabilities in mainstream disability rights organizations (Banks & Mona, 2007; Sands, 2005). Age often plays an important role within movements, with youth with disabilities and older persons with disabilities being ignored by movements that emphasize the rights of working-age persons with disabilities (Meyers et al., 2014; McCloskey & Meyers, 2018; Meyers, 2020). In these ways, disability movements reflect social hierarchies across race and ethnicity, sexuality, gender, age, and myriad other intersecting identities despite their mission to promote equality.

In addition to social hierarchies ranking persons with disabilities on the basis of intersecting identities, persons with disabilities and their rights are often differentiated in law and culture on the basis of their specific type of impairment or the circumstance of their impairment. (See, for example, Deal, 2003; crippledscholar, 2015.) Legal regimes often differentiate persons with disabilities according to various hierarchies that imply that disabled ex-combatants or workers deserve greater protections and benefits than persons who have been disabled all their lives (see, for example, Aciksoz, 2019) or that the rights and freedoms of persons with physical or sensory disabilities deserve greater protection than those of persons with intellectual or psychosocial disabilities. (See, for example, Szmukler et al., 2014.) Mirroring this inequality in the implementation of rights, persons with intellectual disabilities or autistic people are often included in tokenistic ways in disability rights organizations and advocacy (Petri et al., 2017).

Geography often creates hierarchies in both knowledge production and global priorities. International scholarship relating to disability and the international disability movement often prioritize the needs, interests, and epistemologies of the Global North over those of the Global South (Grech, 2015; Meekosha & Soldatic, 2011; Meyers, 2019). Knowledge production and advocacy often go hand in hand because research publications often help define advocacy agendas. In a recent report on disability, bullying, and school-based violence, for example, of the 300 scholarly studies, only 2% were focused on experiences in low-income countries, and more than 230 out of 317 journal articles centered on North America and Europe. This means that despite the vast majority of children with disabilities living in the Global South, the international agenda to prevent school violence against children with disabilities is being defined by knowledge produced in the Global North (McCloskey & Meyers, 2021). Disability studies itself, despite being a critical discipline with an emancipatory research agenda, is similarly lopsided. Noting that virtually all disability studies theory emanates from Northern scholars, including when applied to the Global South, Meekosha (2008) warns that disability studies is perpetrating a form of scholarly colonialism.

Given the ongoing relevance of hierarchies in disability human rights, we decided to put together this volume as a means of confronting hierarchies within disability human rights by exposing inequalities in the enjoyment of disability human rights and in the varied ways that local groups of disabled persons have fought those inequalities. As part of that confrontation, we were particularly interested in contributions from people and perspectives not typically included in mainstream academic publications and in forms of expression not commonly published by academic presses, such as poetry, oral histories, and other creative works.

As editors, we are happy to report success in bringing together chapters that represent many dimensions of diversity. Contributions have come from Africa, Asia, and Latin America, as well as North America and Western Europe. Similarly, contributors include a range from disabled self-advocates through to established academic scholars. Finally, there are many dimensions of hierarchy explored and an important diversity in the mode of exploration. We have included poetry, oral histories, and other creative works as well as more traditional scholarly articles and research reports. Similarly, contributors discuss issues ranging from access to education and leadership in movements to the digital divide and gender-based violence.

Some of the cross-cutting questions contributors explore throughout this volume are:

- Whose rights are more likely to be violated?
- Where and in which contexts are disability human rights violated?
- Which rights are protected, and which are ignored?
- Who is represented by disability rights movements, and who is marginalized?
- What role does identity play in how persons with disabilities are represented?

On the basis of these common questions, we divided the volume up into the following thematic sections:

Who counts as disabled?

Disability is diverse, yet who counts as disabled, especially with respect to rights, is often a very narrow group of people. In this section, contributors to this volume explore "Who counts as disabled?" from a variety of perspectives. Jannatul Ferdous Ivy argues that disability policies and the larger culture systematically leave out women burn survivors in Bangladesh, despite the unique barriers they face. The Expert Advisory Panel for STORM (Standing Up for Myself) argues that persons with learning disabilities must be included disability rights research. Thus far, persons with learning disabilities are excluded from research and advocacy regarding issues that directly affect them. Radoš Keravica similarly explores an excluded population: children with disabilities. In their case, it is not the right to participate in human rights research that is in question, but the rights to participate in decision making and express their own views. Rebekah Kintzinger (with the support of Stephanie Côté and Ajay Gandhi) describes her lived experiences as an autistic woman. Her story includes the journey from diagnosis to advocacy. In a similar journey, Pavithra Suresh chronicles her lived experiences with Lyme disease, which was originally undiagnosed and, even when diagnosed, is rarely recognized as a disability. She further contemplates the racialized and classed elements of living with Lyme disease as a middle-class Tamil American woman. Julie Jaye Charles, a Black disabled British woman, and Stephanie Harvey, a white academic and civil servant, discuss the impact of intersectionality on discrimination and oppression. Of particular importance to them are labels, language, and the marginalization experienced by not identifying with the term "person with disabilities," which is used by the majority white, Anglo population in the United Kingdom. A diverse group of researchers and advocates from Greece discuss the history of Autoekprosopisi, a self-advocacy union representing mental health services users in Greece. One challenge experienced by members of Autoekprosopisi is that many people with psychosocial disabilities do not identify as disabled, much less as holders of disability human rights. Another diverse group of co-authors – academics, speech and language therapists, and family members of persons with disabilities in the UK – discuss ways that storytelling can be used to challenge barriers to inclusion to individuals with profound and multiple disabilities. Finally, Nicolas Joncour, a non-speaking autistic man in France, discusses the emergence of a civil rights movement in France representing his rights and the rights of other non-verbal autistic persons.

Context matters: political, social, and cultural context

Whether it is living in the midst of conflict in Northern Ireland or Bosnia Herzegovina or navigating the intersection of caste and disability in Nepal, the political, social, and cultural context of particular places matter. Local environments create novel hierarchies regarding whose disability human rights are recognized and what sort of rights violations specific groups of persons with disabilities face.

In this section, contributors explore the difference context makes in the lives of persons with disabilities. Conflict and its aftermath represent one major area of investigation. Áine Sperrin compares the experiences of adults with intellectual disabilities who participated in ethno-nationalist conflicts in Northern Ireland and Bosnia Herzegovina and the peace processes that followed, and Jennifer Ward explores the hierarchies created among refugees, including refugees with disabilities. Two of the chapters look specifically at higher education as a particular institutional context that determines the inclusion (and exclusion) of scholars with disabilities. Giermanowska et al. look at the relationship between independent living and access to higher education in Poland, and Heryansyah and Hadi study the barriers students face to higher education in Indonesia. More generally, Morris also looks at disability in the context of education, but in his case, he looks at primary and secondary education in the Caribbean.

Religion also creates specific contexts for persons with disabilities. Rina B. Pikkel and Chaya Gershuni discuss what it means to develop your sexuality as a person with an intellectual disability living in an ultra-Orthodox community in Israel. Finally, Holly Wescott and Rodríguez and Galarza explore civil society in Latin America as a specific political context. Rodríguez and Galarza look across Latin America, which has been a crucible for social movement over the past decades, and attempt to unearth the history of the disability rights movement within that context. Wescott, in a somewhat ironic chapter, explores the ways in which the United Nations in Uruguay creates a hierarchy among disability organizations in their attempt to include organizations of persons with disabilities in their consultation processes.

Which rights on top? Whose rights on bottom?

Human rights are indivisible and interdependent. This means that one set of rights cannot be fully enjoyed without the other. Human rights are also universal, meaning that everyone has the same human rights regardless of their identity or the context. Yet certain human rights and, in turn, the people they affect most directly get prioritized over others. Recognizing these inequalities and addressing them is important in ensuring that all people with disabilities enjoy all their rights.

In this section, contributors examine hierarchies in disability human rights from the perspective of rights that may be recognized in law but are largely ignored in practice and the role identity or context plays in determining who enjoys their rights. To that end, Sarah Lewthwaite and Abi James examine the growing divide in access to digital information, services, and education between the Global North and the Global South, which means, in effect, that the right to information for persons with disabilities who rely on screen readers and other adaptations are ignored. Similarly, Sharynne McLeod and Jessica McLeod compare the right to communicate for children with communication disabilities living in minority-language families with that of children with disabilities in majority-language families. Again, certain disability rights are found to be enjoyed by some and withheld from others. Sándor et al. research the vital role that being included in research plays in ensuring equal access to disability rights and go on to discuss the systematic exclusion of persons with intellectual disabilities from research, whereas persons with other disability types are more likely to participate. The intersection of gender and disability in Africa similarly creates barriers to specific rights. Adetokunbo Johnson and Karin van Marle explore this intersection in their research on reproductive rights for women with disabilities in Africa, many of whom encounter forced sterilization and other forms of violence. Finally, Hardy and Tyler-Merrick explore the urban and rural divide in China, which creates a profound difference in access to the right to education for children with disabilities on the basis of geography.

Pushed to the periphery by the disability rights movement

Creating a more equal and inclusive society is central to disability rights advocacy. Inequalities and exclusions, however, exist within the disability rights movement itself. Recognizing this injustice, especially from the perspective of those persons with disabilities who experience marginalization within the movement, is a prerequisite for change.

Armineh Soorenian reflects on her experiences participating in the UK and international disability movements as a disabled woman with a speech impairment from a non-Western country. Soorenian's autobiographical account shows that movements focused on inclusion can also be exclusionary spaces. Similarly, members of the Women Disability Feminist Collective in Russia (Lyovina et al.) provide auto-ethnographic pieces on violence and constructed vulnerability that are then followed by their own reflections on inclusive organizing, something that is necessary to address inequalities within the disability movement. Masson, Baranyi, and Louis similarly focus on the intersection of gender and disability. Together, they found that because women with disabilities were excluded by both the disability movement and the feminist movement in Haiti, they needed to embrace their identity as women with disabilities and mobilize under that banner in order to force their way into both movements. While gender and impairment type are important axes of exclusion, Karimu argues that formal education is equally, if not more, determinative of who speaks (and who is silenced) in the disability movement in Ghana. Even though access to education and poverty, which is often determined by access to education, represent some of the most important issues persons with disabilities face throughout the world, including in Ghana, persons with disabilities who have been excluded from education rarely have a seat at the table within the very organizations of persons with disabilities advocating for their rights.

Representations of disability

The adoption of the Convention on the Rights of Persons with Disabilities in 2006 and its broad dissemination around the world has meant the many more people with disabilities are being recognized as rights-bearing citizens and valued community members than ever before. In many cases, this recognition is due to persons with disabilities representing themselves through art and other forms of media, such as poetry. For example, James Ian and Elizabeth Hassler use poetry to express themselves. Some people with disabilities, however, continue to go unrecognized and unrepresented both in their local communities and on the global stage. Understanding and appreciating the diverse identities of persons with disabilities are key to addressing hierarchies around the world. Mestheneos uses drama to explore the way many older persons experience disability, an identity many are hesitant to use in the context of both an ageist and ableist society. Similarly, five scholars from Australia, India, Africa, Ireland, and Canada (Gowran et al.) and three scholar-activists from South Africa and

Scotland use conversation and creative dialogue to compare the lived experienced of disability across continents. Disability is also represented in the law, often in ways that treat some persons with disabilities differently from others. Radina Ugrinova compares tort cases in England and Wales to analyze the ways in which judges treat the claims of persons with physical disabilities differently from those of persons with psychosocial disabilities. In a similar transnational comparison, Omino and Nagesh look at the relative representation of women with disabilities in Kenya and India, especially women with disabilities from pastoral and nomadic communities and minority ethnic and regional identities, and the late Gabor Gombos and Amita Dhanda compare their experiences of both success and challenges in representing persons with psychosocial disabilities in efforts to build cross-disability solidarity in Hungary and India and the international community.

References

Aciksoz, S. C. (2019). *Sacrificial limbs: masculinity, disability, and political violence in Turkey*. University of California Press.

Banks, M. E., & Mona, L. R. (2007). Leadership and collaboration among women with disabilities. In J. L. Chin, B. Lott, J. K. Rice, & J. Sanchez-Hucles (Eds.), *Women and leadership: Transforming visions and diverse voices* (pp. 330–340). Blackwell Publishing.

Brennan, C. S. (2020) *Disability rights during the pandemic: a global report on findings of the COVID-19 Disability Rights Monitor*. Centre for Human Rights, University of Pretoria.

crippledscholar. (2015). Fighting my internalization of the hierarchy of disability. https://crippledscholar.com/2015/08/23/fighting-my-internalization-of-the-hierarchy-of-disability/. Accessed April 22, 2019.

Deal, M. (2003). Disabled people's attitudes toward other impairment groups: a hierarchy of impairments. *Disability & Society*, *18*(7), 897–910.

Fight for Right. (2022). News. https://ffr.org.ua/en/news-en/

Grech, S. (2015). *Disability and poverty in the global South: renegotiating development in Guatemala*. Springer.

Huang, S. (2022). Activating disability care: the formation of collective disability care networks in China's COVID-19 outbreak. *Disability & Society*, 1–22.

Mao, B. (2022) Ukrainians with disabilities are being left behind. It's time for concerted humanitarian action. *Davos 2022. World Economic Forum*. https://www.weforum.org/agenda/2022/05/ukraine-refugees-disabilities-humanitarian/

McCloskey, M., & Meyers, S. (2018). *Young persons with disabilities: global study on ending gender-based violence and realizing sexual and reproductive health and rights*. United Nations Population Fund (UNFPA).

McCloskey, M., & Meyers, S. (2021). *Violence and bullying in educational settings: the experiences of young people and children with disabilities*. UN Educational, Scientific, and Cultural Organization.

Meekosha, H. (2008, September). Contextualizing disability: developing southern/global theory. In *4th Biennial Disability Studies Conference*. Keynote paper given to 4th Biennial Disability Studies Conference, Lancaster University, UK 2nd–4th September 2008.

Meekosha, H., & Soldatic, K. (2011). Human rights and the global South: the case of disability. *Third World Quarterly*, *32*(8), 1383–1397.

Meyers, S. (2020). Allies, enemies, or indifferent? The disability and older persons movements in Jamaica. *Research in Social Science and Disability: Alliances, Allies, and Disability*, *12*.

Meyers, S., Karr, V., & Pineda, V. (2014). Youth with disabilities in law and civil society: exclusion and inclusion in public policy and NGO networks in Cambodia and Indonesia. *Disability and the Global South Journal*, *1*(1), 5–28.

Meyers, S. J. (2019). *Civilizing disability society: the convention on the rights of persons with disabilities socializing grassroots disabled persons' organizations in Nicaragua*. Cambridge University Press.

Petri, G., Beadle-Brown, J., & Bradshaw, J. (2017). More Honoured in the Breach than in the observance – self-advocacy and human rights. *Laws*, 6(4), 26.

Piepzna-Samarasinha, L. L. (2019). *Care work: dreaming disability justice*. Vancouver: Arsenal Press.

Rosenthal, E., Kurylo, H., Brown, M., Mathews, E., Ahern, L., Milovanovic, D. C., Rodriguez, P., & Biriukova, T. (2022, 5 May). Left behind in the war: dangers facing children with disabilities in Ukraine's Orphanages. *Disability Rights International*. https://www.driadvocacy.org/wp-content/uploads/DRI-Ukraine-Left-Behind.pdf?fbclid=IwAR2OJb-0zmy_gGzqFXnPo1UTzXSfJVVTE-UaE3OsvR55o-J1jLVGcbzI-W30

Sands, T. (2005). A voice of our own: advocacy by women with disability in Australia and the Pacific. *Gender & Development*, *13*(3), 51–62.

Szmukler, G., Daw, R., & Callard, F. (2014). Mental health law and the UN Convention on the rights of persons with disabilities. *International Journal of Law and Psychiatry*, *37*(3), 245–252.

PART I

Who counts as disabled?

1

KNOWING ABOUT THE HUMAN RIGHTS SITUATION OF WOMEN BURN SURVIVORS IN BANGLADESH

Jannatul Ferdous Ivy

I am a Bangladeshi woman with a burn-injury physical disability. I had a severe fire accident on 30 April 1997, which caused burns over 60% of my upper body. For the last 23 years, I have been under treatment to get back my mobility. Although I have gotten back almost 80% mobility in my body, the burn-affected areas of skin deformity still look ugly, and I have physical disability. This is the main cause of the lifelong insulting comments and inability to enjoy equal dignity in society that I face. Overcoming a very crucial chapter of struggles for my academic education, I have become a human rights activist to promote rights of women with disabilities, along with my passion for my profession. From my personal experience, I have noticed that burn-affected women and persons are absent in disability groups both nationally and globally. In 2015, I established Voice & Views, a small-scale human rights organization to raise the issues of persons who are severely affected by burn accidents. A study of 110 women burn survivors has been accomplished at the community level in the present socio-economic condition. We have gotten from the study that women with burn-related disabilities are harassed by males for sexual abasement. The survivors of burn accidents, victims of both acid violence and accidents, need almost lifelong treatment if the injury level of the individual is severe. Apart from the medical issues for burn survivors, victims of both violence and accidents face many kinds of social harassments, discrimination, and even more violence in their lives. They are not expected by society to be married and have happy families but are not left behind to be abused backstage. The women burn survivors face more. The social situation of burn survivors has never been identified in Bangladesh before. This study was designed to have empirical evidence of all types of burn victim survivors

DOI: 10.4324/9781003410089-3

through individual interviews. Women are more vulnerable to becoming burn victims than men because of their cooking responsibilities and because of domestic violence. Our experience from women rights–related works shows that domestic violence causes burn accidents many times. So the situation remains in a vicious cycle. Burn accidents are the cause of both physical and visual disabilities. The ultimate goal of this study is to incentivize governments and policy makers to form a policy ensuring the human right of burn survivors in Bangladesh.

Personal story

I am a Bangladeshi woman with physical disability due to burn injuries. I met with a severe fire accident on 30 April 1997, which caused burns over 60% of the upper half of my body. Since then, for the past 24 years, I have been undergoing treatment to get back my mobility. Although I have now gotten back almost 80% mobility, my burn-affected skin still looks deformed. My physical disability and my strange look are the main causes of the insults and crude comments I have faced all through my life, leading to injustice to my dignity in society and my professional life. Due to the fire accident, I was so traumatized that I could not complete the four-year undergraduate program in physics that I was pursuing at the time, as the study involved working in a lab with chemicals and fire. Hence, I shifted to a bachelor's program in social science and then did my master's in English literature and a master's in development studies. During my education years, I underwent a lot of hardships due to the disability that arose as a result of my burned skin. My neck area was so contracted and attached to my chin that it was extremely difficult for me to produce any kind of intelligible speech; the way I speak today was beyond my imagination on those days. During this time, I had only a two-inch neck because of the contracted skin, which made it difficult to lift my chin up to even see at eye level. It was also challenging even to write due to the scars and sores, which meant it was very difficult to do my exams.

Besides these physical challenges, many took the liberty of asking me awkward questions, such as whether I was an acid victim, in public places. Such questions and the related whispers surrounding them always made me feel more isolated. I then learned that, in the society I lived in, acid victim women were usually blamed; it was believed that she must have instigated such an act, thus making the victim the perpetrator of the incident. Such misconceptions always surrounded me, along with inhuman comments about the way I look. Sometimes, people also make inadvertent comments that are hurtful. On a particular day, during a call with one of the high-level cultural artists of my country, discussing one of my documentary film, she remarked that I should show my burned face in the video to gain sympathy and to manipulate people emotionally. Many times, I hear such painful remarks. However, my doctors are very kind and helped me accept the decision to restore my functional mobility rather

Figure 1.1 A photograph of the author, a burn survivor

than beautification. Now, most of my joints that were contracted by burns have been released through surgical intervention. During my struggles, my family was a source of inspiration and kept assuring me that I would get my mobility back and go on to help other burn-affected people. This inspiration has kept me going and helped me overcome all odds.

Jannatul Ferdous Ivy

Overcoming odds and Voice & Views

My professional journey began as human rights promoter in the organisation Action on Disability and Development (ADD) in 2005. Subsequently, I had the opportunity to work in national and international organizations like the National Council of Disabled Women (NCDW), Humanity and Inclusion (formerly Handicap International), and the Disabled Rehabilitation and Research Association (DRRA) in Bangladesh, gradually rising to higher positions in each organisation. My professional responsibilities involved facilitating the formation and empowerment of DPOs and the intervention of inclusive programs and to do advocacy for the disability movement in Bangladesh. I have worked with almost all DPO networks in Bangladesh, but I rarely found anyone with a burn-related disability in self-help groups or DPOs. These experiences made me worry about the rights of persons with burn-related disabilities.

I founded Voice & Views, a national level organisation in Bangladesh, with the aim of promoting the human rights of persons with disabilities and to address the human rights issues of women and children with burn-related disabilities in Bangladesh. The organisation was founded on 14 January 2014 and registered on 3 February 2015 with the Social Welfare Department of Bangladesh. The majority of board members are women and men with disability, and hence Voice & Views is a disabled people's organization (DPO).

The vision of Voice & Views is "a society where women with disabilities enjoy equal rights and dignity in society." Our mission is "to build up a resource-based organization and raise the voices of women with disability to achieve equal rights and establish potentialities in society."

The goals of Voice & Views are:

1. To increase awareness of the rights issues of women with disabilities using a rights-based approach
2. To empower the women with disabilities through capacity development
3. To increase awareness of climate adaptation, environmental justice, and the livelihood safety of women with disabilities
4. To increase awareness of environmental safety planning and for Bangladeshi local trees to play a strong role in mitigating global warming
5. To raise awareness of the rights issues of burn-survivor women with disability to establish social justice in society for women with burn-related disabilities.

Our work and our findings

By the grassroots raising of awareness and developing the capacities of women and women with disabilities as well as other persons with disabilities at the community and national levels, Voice & Views takes active part in achieving SDGs in national development of Bangladesh. We work in nine union parishads (UPs) in three districts in Bangladesh. With limited resources, the organization has been involved in raising awareness of gender equality and the rights of women with disabilities. To achieve the fifth goal of the organization, Voice & Views completed a situation analysis study in 2019 of the present socio-economic condition of burn-survivor women and how they are coping with the trauma in their everyday lives with seed grants of USD4,000 from Women's Fund Asia and the national charity organization Human Development Foundation (HDF). The study covered 116 individual interviews. We found that 55 women's burn occurred when they were under the age of ten. This means children are at the highest risk for burn accidents.

In our findings, out of the 116 women, 1 was an acid-violence victim, 3 were burned because of family conspiracy, and the remaining 114 were burned in fire accidents.

The literacy data of the 116 women was found to be as follows: 52 women were illiterate, 38 dropped out at the initial stage of their education, 12 dropped out of high school. Twelve were continuing their education. In terms of income and employment, out of 110 young and adult women, we found that 25 women were day labourers, worked in small businesses, did tailoring, or were rights activists. The remaining 85 were not earning.

The marital status of the 110 women depicts the social injustice as well. We found 98 married women among them: 25 women were left by their husbands, 2 marriage happened without dowries, and 96 marriage took place with dowries, but the in-laws' families were mentally cruel because of burn-related deformities and their contracted skin's different look.

The number of women who had inherited property was only 2. Almost all the respondents said they had been deprived by their siblings and relatives.

Medical and social approaches

In its Sustainable Development Goals, the WHO has stated that: "Injuries and Violence (including domestic violence against women and children) are the majorly neglected public health problems and lead to more than five million deaths a year." Injuries currently cause 14% of disabilities globally.

A study was conducted by Dhaka Medical College Hospital (DMCH) from January through December 2013 on the prevalence of burn patients admitted to DMCH. There were a total of 3,501 outpatients and 8,119 victims hospitalized due to burn injury during the study period. About 40% of them were due to burns occurring at homes, with kitchens being the main source. About 32% were victims of flame burns, which was the highest rate among burn victims. The second leading cause was hot water or the boiling of water during winter. Electrical burns constituted 28% among those who worked as electricians or in related fields. The study also showed that the majority of victims were children and women. So the identification of causes of burn injury and creating massive awareness of the causes of burn accidents are important to prevent violence against women and children, who may eventually acquire some form of disability.

In the medical approach to burn survivors, focus is on the physical condition of having a disability that limits one's performance of daily activities. Burn treatment is generally very expensive, and hence, it is difficult for those in low- and middle-income families to continue the treatment of a burn-affected member for a prolonged period of time. Treatment for those in remote areas is the most challenging aspect of the whole healthcare system in Bangladesh. Among those challenges, treatment of burn accident-related victims in remote areas is almost nonexistent.

The treatment of burns is a time-consuming process divided into two phases. In the first phase, first aid is provided to save the life of survivor, and the second phase involves the reconstruction of deformities of the burn-contracted areas of body. The second phase goes on for a prolonged period of time, which may put the victims in a vulnerable position, open to discrimination both at home and at work.

As the treatment of burn victims is expensive and time consuming, it causes a financial drain on low- and middle-income families. The situation is more serious if the patient is a woman. She then becomes an object of domestic violence. In the South Asian social context, women are mostly subject to homely chores and are responsible for preparing food and taking care of children and the elder members of the family. And, generally, women use fire every day, more than men. Domestic violence is another reason for the prevalence of women getting into fire accidents. So the situation remains in a vicious cycle: domestic violence causing burn accidents, and, on the other hand, women with disabilities due to burn accidents becoming victims of domestic violence by family members.

Another vicious cycle continues at labour-oriented factories, like ready-made garment (RMG) factories and chemical explosive factories that do not maintain the minimum occupational health safety standards. Workers at these factories are at risk of becoming burn accident victims, and those who are survivors hardly have any rights to work in labour-oriented factories. Such factories are among the major causes of burn accidents in Bangladesh.

The social approach of burn survivors focuses on the adversities faced by the victims because of burn deformities and lack of inclusion in society. Burn survivors are excluded and face many kinds of social harassments, discrimination, and even violence. No large-scale research has been done on the human rights situation of these burn-survivor women.

So prevention of burn accidents is important to minimize the rate of disabilities caused by burn injuries and burn-related issues. It may reduce violence against women and children as well. Raising awareness of the causes of burn accidents can lower accident rates and lessen the violence against women and children burn victims. Awareness of the rights of burn-accident survivors will also help achieve one of the goals of the SDG: that women and persons with burn-related injuries are not left behind.

UNCRPD and its relevance

In the United Nations Convention of Rights of Persons with Disabilities, "persons with disabilities" are defined as those "who have long-term physical, mental, intellectual or sensory impairments which in interaction with various barriers may hinder their full and effective participation in society on an equal basis with others" (UN CRPD, Art. 1). Burn-accident survivors have sensory impairment affecting their skin and limbs. So, either sensory or more than one type of disability can be found in burn-affected persons. For example, acid-burn survivors have lost their eyesight, and fire- and electricity-caused burn accidents cause physical impairments.

Apart from the definition, we should also be aware of the key principles of the CRPD that are stated across all its articles: respect for inherent dignity; individual autonomy, including the freedom to make one's own choices; independence of persons; non-discrimination; full and effective participation and inclusion; respect for difference and acceptance of human diversity and humanity; equality of opportunity; accessibility; equality between men and women; respect for the evolving capacities of children; and the rights of children with disabilities. To analyse the relationship between human rights and poverty, the first president of South African, President Nelson Mandela, delivered his famous speech at the Make Poverty History rally in London's Trafalgar Square in 2005 and called on world leaders to make poverty history:

> Like slavery and apartheid, poverty is not natural. It is man-made and it can be overcome and eradicated by the action of human beings. Overcoming poverty is not a gesture of charity. It is the protection of a fundamental human right, the right to dignity and a decent life.

UNESCO defined poverty in the following manner:

> Poverty may be defined as a human condition characterized by sustained or chronic deprivation of the resources, capabilities, choices, security and power necessary for the enjoyment of an adequate standard of living and other civil, cultural, economic, political and social rights. . . . Poverty is cited as violation of human rights in the Universal Declaration of Human Rights, in International Covenant of Economic, Social and Cultural Rights etc.

The UNCRPD combines civil and political rights with economic, social, and cultural rights under an overarching theory of non-discrimination. The concept of inclusion is the solution mentioned in UNCRPD, where we find that inclusion is a process of addressing and responding to the diversity of needs of all persons for active participation in communities and mainstream development programs. Going back to the situation analysis of burn-accidents survivors, we find the violation of rights as well as social harassment and discrimination.

The situation analysis study by Voice & Views found that women with burn-related were excluded from enjoying their rights. We found a message similar to Nelson Mandela's speech, in which human rights key principals are kept as "bookish words" or academic terms by the duty bearers. The situation analysis study of Voice & Views was designed to provide empirical evidence of all types of burn victim survivors through individual interviews. Burn accidents are causes of disability, and burn-affected women with disabilities are victims of all types of discriminations and violations of rights.

Voice & Views has been instrumental in forming self-help groups (SHGs) of women with burn-related disabilities in rural areas. Most of the women are from very poor families, while rest are from low-income families. Most of them hardly have any education, are not independent, and have experienced traumatizing situation all along. Gender-based violence is worse against women with burn-related disabilities.

All this has put me in a deep ocean of thoughts: how to change the view of the world towards us: the women who are burn-accident survivors? On days like International Women's Day, the International Day of Persons with Disabilities, and Human Rights Day, we hear so many ornamental words, such as "no one left behind," "no violence towards women," and many more. Though I appreciate these slogans, at the end of the day, we still remain excluded and prevented from enjoying our rights, making me think deeper: are we second-class citizens? Sometimes I think I am living in a fantasy where I am equal to everyone around me, but in reality, the world has never accepted me as an equal. Discrimination is not gender based and not a matter of men-women inequality. In many cases, women without disabilities also discriminate against burn-survivor women in our society.

I won't utter any ornamental words or slogans. I simply urge to whole world to recognize that burn-survivor women are also human beings. ***We are not different in our look; it is the mind-set and behaviour of the people around us who judge us by our burned look first and never respects our potentialities. We are beautiful in our minds, in our thoughts, and in our dreams. To change the whole society – a living planet for all of us, irrespective of caste and creed, to live with full dignity and meaning to life. Nothing about us without us!***

The ultimate goal of the sensitisation process is to form relevant policy ensuring the human rights of women burn survivors in Bangladesh.

Basic information about Voice & Views is available on our website, voiceandviews.org.

Reference

1. The official website of Voice & Views human rights based organization: https://voiceandviews.org.bd

2

CREATING A STORM

Working together to fight stigma and stand up for the rights of people with learning disabilities

Lisa Richardson, Michaela Osborne, Christine Burke, Karuna Davies, Adrian Brown, Celia Brown, Paul Davies, Harry Roche and Katrina Scior

Stigma and discrimination can be a harsh daily reality for many people with learning disabilities. This leads to poor quality of life and barriers to accessing employment, healthcare, relationships, housing and human rights. The Standing Up for Myself (STORM) research project at University College London aims to empower people with learning disabilities to feel good about themselves, challenge discrimination and exercise their rights. The project team includes researchers and expert advisors with learning disabilities, all working together. Our shared values are that it is important for people with learning disabilities to express their views, be listened to, and have influence over the things that matter to them.

This chapter has been written by researchers and the project's expert advisors. We met and discussed our thoughts and experiences of working together. We recorded these conversations and agreed that we (LR, MO, CB and KD) would turn these conversations into this chapter. What we have written is all our voices speaking up together. In this chapter, we share our experiences of working together on the STORM research, why the work is important to us and how we adapted during the COVID-19 pandemic. We will share what we have learned about making research accessible, inclusive and enjoyable. This chapter will be of benefit to other researchers (including those researching disability rights) to consider how they can and should involve people with learning disabilities in their work.

A virus called stigma

Stigma is like a virus. It spreads. The process of stigma is that groups get given negative labels called stereotypes and are discriminated against (treated unfairly) as a result (Link & Phelan, 2001). People with learning disabilities are one

DOI: 10.4324/9781003410089-4

minority group who are treated in this way; they are often negatively labeled as 'vulnerable' or 'not intelligent'. This is dehumanising. These negative attitudes are catching and can spread from one person to another and from one generation to another. Some things help keep stigma alive and spread it, like what people with power say and do. Many people with learning disabilities (but not all) are aware that they are stigmatised (Beart et al., 2005; Logeswaran et al., 2019). Stigma can affect how people think and feel about themselves. As four people with a learning disability, we (CB, AB, HR, PD) can feel judged, excluded and made to feel bad. This, in turn, can make us feel angry, frustrated and powerless; others have said the same as us (Jahoda & Markova, 2004). But having a learning disability is just one part of who we are. There are many other things that make us who we are. People with learning disabilities are individual human beings with lots of different stories to share. *Made Possible* (Salman, 2020) is a good example. It is a collection of eight stories from people with learning disabilities who talk about their achievements, showing what *is* possible. Perhaps if more people heard these stories, negative attitudes and unfair treatment might change. But stigma casts a long shadow, and the positive parts of who we are get hidden. These stories don't spread in the same way. This keeps stigma alive.

The power of stigma is strong, it means that people with learning disabilities don't have access to or get to enjoy their human rights. They experience unequal access to good health and social care (Emerson & Baines, 2011). It can also mean discrimination within the very systems that are meant to offer support. In reality, this means people are overmedicated (Branford et al., 2019) or deprived of their liberty and subject to abuse (Murphy, 2019). A new government white paper now sets out to change this so that only people with a learning disability who have a mental illness can be detained in hospitals (Department of Health and Social Care, 2021). Stigma can also mean that people with learning disabilities can end up with mental health problems (Ali et al., 2015) and poor self-esteem (Jahoda et al., 2010; Logeswaran et al., 2019; Paterson et al., 2012). Sadly, this means people come to accept and expect the poor treatment they receive from others (Richardson et al., 2016; Ali et al., 2016).

Like a virus, stigma needs something to slow it down and, ideally, eliminate it from society. There are a number of ways to tackle public attitudes and discrimination towards people with learning disabilities, written about elsewhere (Scior & Werner, 2016). This can mean changing attitudes but also changing the way power operates and who has it. It means making sure the human rights of people with learning disabilities are upheld, and discrimination is prevented and properly addressed. People with learning disabilities should be front and centre of this work to combat stigma, but we also want support from allies.

Creating a STORM against stigma

> Your solid unbending belief should be: '*. . . I matter. I matter equally. Not "if only". Not "as long as". I matter equally. Full stop.*'
>
> *Adichie (2017, p. 8)*

Making sure people with learning disabilities know they matter and matter equally is an important step in shifting power and changing attitudes. Only then will people with learning disabilities feel empowered to say no to negative attitudes and actions and to feel good about themselves. Using our voices to speak up and take a stand against stigma together is important. We all need to play a part to make a difference. When people *without* learning disabilities speak up, they are listened to; when we speak up about discrimination, people too often do *not* listen. This needs to change. People with learning disabilities have the right to have a say and to stand up for their rights. But we don't always know our rights, what the law says about our rights, and we don't all have access to the internet, education or the right support throughout our lives to learn these things.

This is where the Standing Up for Myself programme comes in. We call the programme STORM for short. People with learning disabilities can create their own personal STORM to fight stigma and the negative impact it has. The aim of the STORM programme is to offer people with learning disabilities support and a way to do this. They can find ways to manage unfair treatment when it happens or stand up to it, to actively resist stigma and its impact. Not accepting or believing the stigma means we can protect ourselves from negative feelings such as shame, anger and powerlessness. Instead, we can be self-determined, feel good about ourselves, have a sense of power and feel that we matter. Research has shown that for other groups who are stigmatised, this form of stigma resistance (Firmin et al., 2017; Thoits, 2011) can have a positive effect because people assert their rights and needs (Nabors et al., 2014).

It is our long-term plan to make STORM freely available for groups to use, but first, we are doing some research to make sure it is possible for groups to do, that people find it OK to do, and that it makes a difference to people's well-being, sense of power and self-esteem. Since 2017, we have worked together (there is a large team of us; please see our acknowledgements) to develop the STORM programme and resources. The STORM programme is designed for adults over 16 years of age with a learning disability who already meet together in a group. This can be a self-advocacy, educational or social group, for example. The STORM logo you see in the pictures later in this chapter was designed by Lester Magoogan, an artist with a learning disability. There are five sessions to STORM, each with a different focus. (See Table 2.1.)

Sessions 1 through 3 start with videos of people with learning disabilities talking about their experiences, followed by groups discussing their own experiences. The fourth session focuses on action planning: what people want to do or try to make sure they feel good about themselves, to stand up to stigma, to assert their rights or to educate others. The fifth session happens after a break of three to four weeks whilst people try putting their plans into action. In this last session, people share how they got on and what barriers they faced in carrying out their plan. At the end, they can have a celebration event. Peer support is a key part of STORM, through sharing experiences, supporting each other with carrying out actions and not giving up. Facilitators who run the sessions

Table 2.1 Key messages for the five STORM sessions

Session 1
My learning disability is only one part of me.
Session 2
It's not OK for people to treat me badly. I don't have to put up with it.
Session 3
I can stand up for myself when people treat me badly
Session 4
I can make a plan to help me stand up for myself. People I can trust can help me with ideas.
Session 5 (follow-up 3–4 weeks after Session 4)
Things can get in the way of my plan. Talking to others can help me decide what to do next and not give up.

with their groups receive brief training and support and access to the STORM resources. (See Figures 2.1 through 2.3.)

We ran a 'pilot', a test run in 2017–2018 with ten groups for people with learning disabilities (68 people altogether). To evaluate STORM, we interviewed group facilitators, participants and significant people in their lives to find out whether STORM was acceptable for people to do and the impact it had for people taking part. Questionnaires were collected before and after STORM and six months later. STORM was well received and apparent changes in self-esteem, psychological distress and sense of power before and after the intervention were encouraging. The good news was that these encouraging changes in how people felt about themselves were still present six months later. We couldn't be sure, though, that the positive changes we saw were down to STORM as we didn't have a control group (a group that didn't receive STORM) in our pilot.

From this work, we concluded that STORM may provide a good approach to well-being and stigma resistance for people with learning disabilities. We knew that more work was needed, and at the end of 2019, with funding from the National Institute of Health Research (NIHR), we set about the next steps evaluating STORM; we wanted to do a bigger, stronger piece of research. To be able to do this, we first had to find out whether it would be possible to do what is called a 'randomised control trial' for STORM. This way of doing research is considered the 'gold standard' when testing if something works. If this type of study were possible, it would mean we could be more certain about what effect the STORM programme had for people with learning disabilities. If it were safe and worked well, we could offer STORM freely and with confidence to more people.

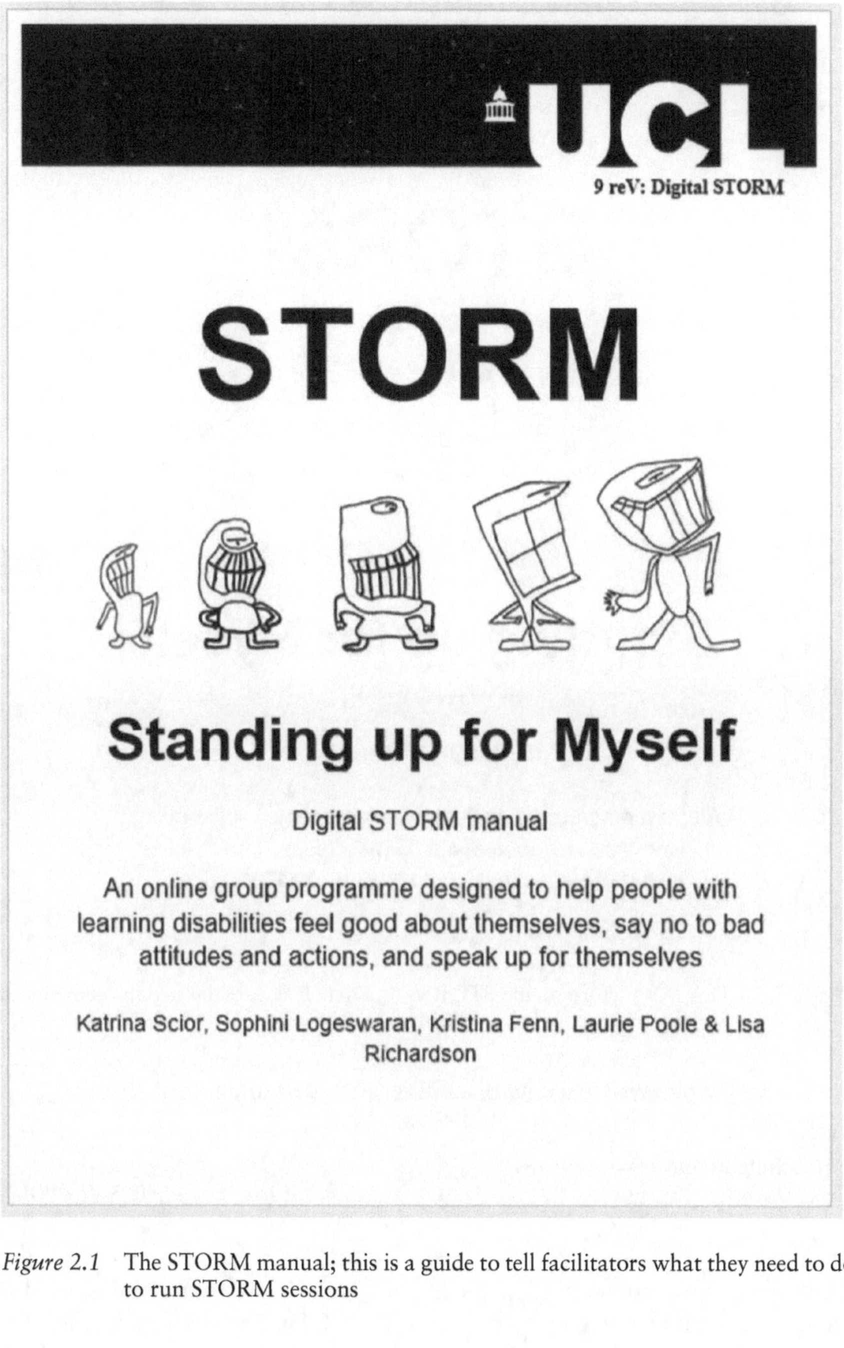

UCL

9 reV: Digital STORM

STORM

Standing up for Myself

Digital STORM manual

An online group programme designed to help people with learning disabilities feel good about themselves, say no to bad attitudes and actions, and speak up for themselves

Katrina Scior, Sophini Logeswaran, Kristina Fenn, Laurie Poole & Lisa Richardson

Figure 2.1 The STORM manual; this is a guide to tell facilitators what they need to do to run STORM sessions

Figure 2.2 This is a picture of the STORM booklet. It is used by group members to develop their action plans during STORM sessions

People with learning disabilities included in universities and research?

> Nothing about us without us.
>
> *Charlton (1998)*

These powerful words summarise the importance of representing often-excluded groups in decision making that affects their lives. It has become a mantra for disability activists. The conditions for social change to have access to equal human

Figure 2.3 This is a picture of the STORM Wiki, a website where all the videos and materials for running STORM groups are saved

rights and a life free from discrimination can be supported or hindered by the work of institutions such as universities. We see this from the history of ideas that are produced in universities and the influence these can have. In 2021, UCL issued an apology for its historical role in the eugenics movement, a set of ideas which suggest that different lives had greater or lesser value (University College London, 2021). These beliefs led to great harm as they justified crimes and oppression. For people with learning disabilities, these ideas led to policies such as institutionalisation (when people were sent to asylums or hospitals and locked away) and enforced sterilisation, which prevented them from having children (Richardson, 2005; Roy et al., 2012). UCL has acknowledged that these ideas have caused and continue to cause 'harm through racism, antisemitism, ableism and other stereotyping' and recognise that this affects people's lives by 'driving discrimination and denying opportunity, access and representation'. This is a fairly extreme example of why universities may not be welcoming to certain groups of people.

Historically, people with learning disabilities have been far from included in universities; we have been excluded from educational opportunities, teaching and research, where our voice needs to be heard. Researchers have been responding to funders' requirements for patient and public involvement in research, and the National Standards for Involvement (National Institute for Health Research, 2019) have set out clear expectations of how and what should be achieved. However, the National Institute for Health Research (2020) have recognised that researchers need to improve the inclusion of underserved groups in research. This includes stigmatised populations, such as people with learning disabilities. When we are included, this is not always as an inclusive part of decision making (Walmsley, 2001), although other, more positive accounts of involvement in research are emerging (Beighton et al., 2017; Tuffrey-Wijne & Butler, 2009).

The absence of people with learning disabilities in university teaching and research can mean the spread of negative and false ideas. One member of the team (LR) even had it suggested to them that it is not possible to involve people with learning disabilities in research because they don't have the necessary communication skills. These views were challenged, and through our work together, we prove these ideas and people wrong! The problem is that if research is only done about or for us, it will not benefit us or help us access our rights. Action amongst universities and researchers is crucial to breaking this cycle. We would like to see more research that makes the voices of people with learning disabilities central, and not just in places where they have a particular interest in learning disabilities.

Turning the tide with the STORM experts

Despite the traditional exclusion of certain groups from universities and research, the tide is turning, and positive changes are flourishing. The focus on including people with learning disabilities in research (Paul & Holt, 2017) means our voices must be heard so that we can shape research based on our experiences and understanding and ensure it is meaningful and relevant to our lives. Our inclusion will then be clear in the quality of the research and its findings.

The launch of the UCL Unit for Stigma Research (UCLUS), a new hub for research on stigma, seeks to produce high-quality research with a focus on involvement and co-production so that those who stand to benefit from the work are at the centre. It is here that our STORM research is hosted. The key to getting STORM and the research right has been working together from the very start. The STORM Expert Advisor's Panel is a patient and public involvement group who have been working with the researchers since 2017. As paid experts by experience, we (AB, CB, HR, PD) share our views about how people with learning disabilities *are* treated and *should be* treated in society. We also help make sure the research is acceptable and accessible for people with learning disabilities to take part in. (In Figure 2.4, you can see us at one of our meetings).

Figure 2.4 A photograph of the STORM Expert Advisor Panel following one of our meetings

As STORM experts, we are supported to be involved. Box 2.1 gives you some idea of the involvement we have had. Further on, we will share with you some of our tips for researching together. Through being part of the work at UCL, we have developed our own skills and confidence, and we can challenge others' negative ideas about what we can and cannot do.

Text Box 2.1 How we, as the STORM experts, have shaped the STORM research

- Advise researchers on what is important to people with learning disabilities
- Share ideas to help with decision making, including:
  - How to continue STORM in the context of COVID-19
  - How to adapt STORM for online meetings
- Present ideas to the research funder (NIHR)
- Co-chair research meetings (e.g. Inclusive Design Team meetings)
- Wider consultation work, including:
  - Finding people with learning disabilities to consult
  - Interviewing people with learning disabilities about their experiences of online groups
  - Telling the research team when more opinions were needed
- Advise researchers on how to make questionnaires accessible for people with learning disabilities; for example:
  - Wording of questions/response scale
  - Use of pictures and photosymbols
  - Accessible ways to deliver a questionnaire
- Finding ways to communicate complex ideas to other people with learning disabilities to help them decide about taking part in research (e.g. we produced a video).

Continuing our fight against stigma during a pandemic

There is a twist in the journey of our STORM research. Just as we set about finding people to take part in the next stage of the research, the coronavirus (COVID-19) was spreading across the world, creating a global pandemic and restrictions on everyone's usual way of life. Groups for people with learning disabilities stopped meeting in person, and many schools and colleges closed. This affected our ability to do the STORM research as we planned and to work together in the ways we were used to.

Uncertainty, fear and isolation became common feelings for many, including for people with learning disabilities. (See *Peter and Friends*, Cronin et al., 2020, for stories of the pandemic narrated by people with learning disabilities.) These feeling are not surprising when one considers that deaths from

COVID-19 have been six times higher for people with learning disabilities due to health inequalities (Public Health England, 2020). The UK Equality Act (2010) says that reasonable adjustments or changes should be made to ensure that people with disabilities can access services. Yet reasonable adjustments were rarely made during the pandemic in the way the law said they should be. Frequent changes to rules were communicated to the public through TV news briefings and a letter from the prime minister; both used complicated and unfamiliar language. Shockingly, despite increased risk from the virus, people with learning disabilities were not prioritised for vaccines, and when they were, this was only after vulnerability and pity narratives were employed (Scior et al., 2021). Perhaps the most concerning discrimination faced by people with learning disabilities has been the inappropriate use of 'Do Not Resuscitate' (DNR) notices (Bloomer, 2021; Tromans et al., 2020). Overall, the COVID-19 pandemic served to highlight the inequalities and stigma that people with learning disabilities face from the government, public services and the general public.

Given the developing situation described here, the STORM team had to think carefully about what to do next. We knew groups had stopped meeting in person, but some had started to meet online instead. We could pause the research or find a way to adapt. As experts by experience, we (AB, CB, PD, HR) felt that support around stigma was more important than ever. We hoped people could benefit from the opportunity to take part in a STORM group. We were clear that the research should continue by delivering STORM to those who can use digital technology now, but when people can meet face to face again, this should remain an option. We understood that this might affect the research (it might not work as well online), but there was the possibility that it could be a positive option. We also felt very strongly that we did not want the funding or all the effort and time spent on STORM so far to go to waste.

As a research team, we listened to everyone's views and discussed concerns but ultimately agreed with our STORM experts that the important work should continue, both despite and because of the pandemic. When we looked into whether other interventions had been adapted for digital online delivery, we found very little for people with learning disabilities. This seemed to support the idea of a digital divide (Elahi, 2020), another way in which people with learning disabilities are excluded and not afforded the same opportunities. We also felt doing this work might even teach us how we could include more people in research using digital approaches, and STORM could be offered to more and different people across the country: for example, people living in more diverse cities or in remote communities. Before we could go ahead with our plans, we had to seek permission from our funders. The STORM experts wrote a letter about why it was important to continue with STORM despite the pandemic, and one of us (AB) attended a meeting with the research team and funder too.

To make sure the STORM programme was successfully adapted for online delivery, we set up a Digital STORM Inclusive Design Team. (We all voted on this name.) This team consisted of the STORM experts, facilitators of groups for people with learning disabilities, STORM researchers and digital inclusion experts. The STORM experts had the role of co-chair, on rotation alongside a researcher (LR/MO). As co-chair, we (AB, CB, PD, HR) welcomed Inclusive Design Team members to the meetings, outlined meeting rules and attended to time keeping, whilst ensuring discussions were kept focused. The co-chair was provided with an Easyread annotated agenda in advance of the meeting, prepared by the other co-chair researcher, with time to practice ahead of the meeting. As part of the adaptation work, we (AB, CB, PD, HR) found people with learning disabilities whom we knew and interviewed them to find out their experiences of accessing meetings online. We then presented what people told us to the wider team. The interview findings helped us make sure that the adaption of STORM was guided by the experiences of people with learning disabilities, supporting Digital STORM to be inclusive and accessible to all.

In order for everyone to continue working as a team during the pandemic, we all met via online video calls and individual phone calls to prepare for the work and discuss ideas. The preparation for consultation interviews involved discussions about the skills and techniques used to conduct interviews in research: for example, how to ask questions and listen with interest and when/how to prompt for more information. We also discussed what support we wanted in taking on new roles like interviewing people. Because this was new to us, we felt most comfortable with a researcher present to assist with any technical issues and as back-up support if needed. We developed an Easyread interview guide to follow when talking to people. We (AB, CB, HR) enjoyed interviewing people with learning disabilities about their experiences and would feel even more confident to do this again in the future.

Lessons from the STORM project

Drawing on our experiences of working together on the STORM project, we have compiled a list of tips on how to create an inclusive and enjoyable research environment:

- **Experts in our own lives** – First and foremost, remember we are the experts in our own lives.
- **'Walk a mile in our shoes'** – Spend time with people with learning disabilities to get our views and find out why we want to get involved. Get to know and value our perspectives and strengths. Ask us about having a learning disability
- **Agree on clear roles** – Be clear about what is possible and what is not possible. Help us understand what involvement in research is all about – a good way to do this is to have an accessible role description that we negotiate, agree and sign. This should include our responsibilities and your responsibilities, how long the work is for and how we will be paid.

- **Make it accessible** – Ensure that all information is accessible in Easyread format (e.g. agendas, minutes). You may need to provide information in other ways too (e.g. Braille). Use worksheets to support different styles of thinking and communication. Importantly, be consistent in how you do this.
- **Explain new ideas** – There are a lot of jargon words in research. Explain things simply, and when we need to learn what a new word or idea means, take the time to explain it. Create a way to record these: for example, a 'Jargon Buster' folder to keep a shared Easyread glossary.
- **Be positive and speak up** – Support people to feel welcome. Focus on what people can do. Be positive. Correct negative and incorrect ideas about people with learning disabilities, and help people speak up about bad attitudes and stigma. You can promote positive stories and representations.
- **Tailor your support** – We are all individuals; make time to give us one-on-one support and mentoring to learn new skills. Talk to us about:
  - How to structure meetings (e.g. duration, breaks, timings, use of agenda)
  - How best to communicate information (e.g. verbal, presentation slides, Easyread summary documents)
  - Role and responsibilities of the chair/co-chair, who will take on this role and how they will prepare (e.g. using an accessible annotated agenda, meeting earlier with researcher)
- **Involve us in decisions** – If you have a problem or need to make a decision, we can help you find a solution.
- **Keep us informed** – We really want to hear how you are using what we tell you. You can provide feedback in a 'you said, we did' format. If you couldn't do something, we'd like to understand why!
- **Have fun** – Most of all, research should be enjoyable, so make time to be social, to be relaxed and to share a joke.

Conclusion

It is important that we keep fighting against the stigma that people with learning disabilities experience, to change attitudes and shift who has power. People with learning disabilities are leading this fight, but we also want support. The STORM programme offers a way for people with learning disabilities to acknowledge together the injustice they face and find a way to take action. These actions collectively can help ensure more positive stories about people with learning disabilities are shared and, importantly, help us access and enjoy our rights on an equal basis.

Being involved in research is important to us, but this requires commitment and resources to make sure our involvement is meaningful. More guidance for researchers who want to involve people with learning disabilities could be helpful, similar to those developed for involving Black, Asian and minority ethnic groups (National Institute for Health Research, 2020). This would benefit a wide range of researchers, especially those not experienced at working with people with learning disabilities, who might feel uncertain about where to start. We hope this chapter provides some ideas to help other people get started. Remember, it's 'nothing about us without us'.

Acknowledgements

Funding

We are grateful to Baily Thomas Charitable Fund for their support funding the development and initial pilot of the STORM programme.

Our current study is funded by the National Institute for Health Research (NIHR) Public Health Research programme (NIHR PHR Project 17/149/03). The views expressed in our work are those of the author(s) and not necessarily those of the NIHR or the Department of Health and Social Care.

Project team

STORM is the product of a large team of people working together. Our work is led by Professor Katrina Scior, who had the initial idea of working with groups to help them stand up against stigma. Recognition for the work is also shared with our collaborators and steering group who have helped develop STORM and the research. They include Richard Hastings, Andrew Jahoda, Afia Ali, Jason Crabtree, Liz Randell, Rachel McNamara, Dave Gillespie, Melissa Wright, Sean Johnson, Harriet Bird, Carla Barret, Laura Kerr, Jane Menzies, Lisa Bush and Eva Bonin. We are also grateful to past collaborators, including Sophini Logeswaran, Kristina Fenn, Laurie Poole, Adelle Havard, Sandra Baum, Sophie Doswell and Richard Maxfield.

We thank the Rix Centre, University of East London, for working with us to develop the STORM Wiki (our website where the STORM resources are hosted): in particular, thanks to Andy Minnion and Ajay Chotsky. Finally, we'd like to acknowledge Justin Spooner and Neil Mosley of Unthinkable Digital for their work helping the team develop the approach for Digital STORM, allowing us to provide an online offering following the COVID-19 pandemic in 2020.

References

Adichie, C. N. (2017). *Dear Ijeawele, or a Feminist Manifesto in fifteen suggestions.* Harper Collins.

Ali, A., King, M., Strydom, A., & Hassiotis, A. (2015). Self-reported stigma and symptoms of anxiety and depression in people with intellectual disabilities: Findings from a cross sectional study in England. *Journal of Affective Disorders, 187*, 224–231.

Ali, A., King, M., Strydom, A., & Hassiotis, A. (2016). Self-reported stigma and its association with socio-demographic factors and physical disability in people with intellectual disabilities: Results from a cross-sectional study in England. *Social Psychiatry and Psychiatric Epidemiology, 51*(3), 465–474.

Beart, S., Hardy, G., & Buchan, L. (2005). How people with intellectual disabilities view their social identity: A review of the literature. *Journal of Applied Research in Intellectual Disabilities, 18*(1), 47–56.
Beighton, C., Victor, C., Carey, I.M., Hosking, F., DeWilde, S., Cook, D.G., Manners, P., & Harris, T. (2017). 'I'm sure we made it a better study. . .': Experiences of adults with intellectual disabilities and parent carers of patient and public involvement in a health research study. *Journal of Intellectual Disabilities, 23*(1), 78–96.
Bloomer, A. (2021, January 25). Do not resuscitate orders and learning disability: Where are we now? *Learning Disability Today*. https://www.learningdisabilitytoday.co.uk/do-not-resuscitate-orders-and-learning-disability-where-are-we-now
Branford, D., Gerrard, D., Saleem, N., Shaw, C., & Webster, A. (2019). Stopping over-medication of people with intellectual disability, Autism or both (STOMP) in England part 1 – History and background of STOMP. *Advances in Mental Health and Intellectual Disabilities*, *13*(1), 31–40.
Charlton, J. (1998). *Nothing about us without us: Disability oppression and empowerment*. University of California Press.
Cronin, P., Hardy, S., Roberts, M., Burke, C., Mahon, D., & Chaplin, E. (2020). *Peter and friends talk about COVID-19 and having a learning disability and/or autism*. Penge Publishers.
Department of Health and Social Care. (2021). Reforming the mental health act. https://www.gov.uk/government/consultations/reforming-the-mental-health-act/reforming-the-mental-health-act
Elahi, F. (2020). Digital inclusion: Bridging divides. https://www.cumberlandlodge.ac.uk/read-watch-listen/digital-inclusion-bridging-divides-cumberland-lodge-report
Emerson, E., & Baines, S. (2011). Health inequalities & people with learning disabilities in the UK. *Tizard Learning Disability Review, 16*(1), 42–48.
Equality Act. (2010). UK public general acts. https://www.legislation.gov.uk/ukpga/2010/15/contents
Firmin, R. L., Luther, L., Lysaker, P. H., Minor, K. S., McGrew, J. H., Cornwell, M. N., & Salyers, M. P. (2017). Stigma resistance at the personal, peer, and public levels: A new conceptual model. *Stigma and Health*, *2*(3), 182.
Jahoda, A., & Markova, I. (2004). Coping with social stigma: People with intellectual disabilities moving from institutions and family home. *Journal of Intellectual Disability Research, 48*(8), 719–729.
Jahoda, A., Wilson, A., Stalker, K., & Cairney, A. (2010). Living with stigma and the self-perceptions of people with mild intellectual disabilities. *Journal of Social Issues, 66*(3), 521–534.
Link, B. G., & Phelan, J. C. (2001). Conceptualizing stigma. *Annual Review of Sociology, 27*, 363–385.
Logeswaran, S., Hollett, M., Zala, S., Richardson, L., & Scior, K. (2019). How do people with intellectual disabilities construct their social identity? A review. *Journal of Applied Research in Intellectual Disabilities, 32*(9).
Murphy, G. (2019). Whorlton Hall: A predictable tragedy? *British Medical Journal, 366*(14705). https://www-bmj-com.libproxy.ucl.ac.uk/content/366/bmj.l4705
Nabors, L. M., Yanos, P. T., Roe, D., & Lysacker, P. H. (2014). Stereotype endorsement, metacognitive capacity, and self-esteem as predictors of stigma resistance in persons with schizophrenia. *Comprehensive Psychiatry*, *55*, 792–798.
National Institute for Health Research. (2019). National standards for public involvement. https://www.invo.org.uk/posttypepublication/nationalstandards-for-public-involvement/
National Institute for Health Research. (2020). Improving inclusion of under-served groups in clinical research: Guidance from the Nihr include project. www.nihr.ac.uk/

documents/improving-inclusion-of-under-served-groups-in-clinical-research-guidance-from-include-project/25435

Paterson, L., McKenzie, K., & Lindsay, B. (2012). Stigma, social comparison and self-esteem in adults with an intellectual disability. *Journal of Applied Research in Intellectual Disabilities, 25*(2), 166–176.

Paul, C., & Holt, J. (2017). Involving the public in mental health and learning disability research: Can we, should we, do we? *Journal of Psychiatric and Mental Health Nursing, 24*(8), 570–579.

Public Health England. (2020). Deaths of people identified as having learning disabilities with COVID-19 in England in the spring of 2020. https://assets.publishing.service.gov.uk/government/uploads/system/uploads/attachment_data/file/933612/COVID-19__learning_disabilities_mortality_report.pdf

Richardson, L., Beadle-Brown, J., Bradshaw, J., Guest, C., Malovic, A., & Himmerich, J. (2016). "I felt that I deserved it"–Experiences and implications of disability hate crime. *Tizard Learning Disability Review*, *21*(2), 80–88.

Richardson, M. (2005). Critiques of segregation and eugenics. *Learning Disabilities: A Life Cycle to Valuing People*, 66–90.

Roy, A., Roy, A., & Roy, M. (2012). The human rights of women with intellectual disability. *Journal of the Royal Society of Medicine*, *105*(9), 384–389.

Salman, S. (2020). *Made possible: Stories of success by people with learning disabilities – in their own words*. Unbound.

Scior, K., Brown, A., Brown C., Davies, P.W., & Roche, H. (2021, March 18). People with learning disabilities are equal members of society, not vulnerable burdens. *BMJ Opinion*. https://blogs.bmj.com/bmj/2021/03/18/people-with-learning-disabilities-are-equal-members-of-society-not-vulnerable-burdens/

Scior, K., & Werner, S. (2016). *Intellectual disability and stigma: Stepping out from the margins*. Palgrave Macmillan.

Thoits, P.A. (2011). Resisting the stigma of mental illness. *Social Psychology Quarterly*, *74*(1), 6–28.

Tromans, S., Kinney, M., Chester, V., Alexander, R., Roy, A., Sander, J. W., Dudson, H., & Shankar, R. (2020). Priority concerns for people with intellectual and developmental disabilities during the COVID-19 pandemic. *BJPsych Open*, *6*(6).

Tuffrey-Wijne, I., & Butler, G. (2009). Co-researching with people with learning disabilities: An experience of involvement in qualitative data analysis. *Health Expectations: An International Journal of Public Participation in Health Care and Health Policy, 13*(2), 174–184.

University College London. (2021). UCL makes formal public apology for its history and legacy of Eugenics. https://www.ucl.ac.uk/news/2021/jan/ucl-makes-formal-public-apology-its-history-and-legacy-eugenics

Walmsley, J. (2001). Normalisation, emancipatory research and inclusive research in learning disability. *Disability & Society, 16*(2), 187–205.

3

RETHINKING THE CAPACITIES OF DISABLED CHILDREN FROM THE PERSPECTIVE OF NEW MATERIALISM

Radoš Keravica

Introduction

This chapter seeks to highlight the challenges disabled children are facing in an attempt to be recognised as the bearers of human rights and, in particular, of the right to be heard, as opposed to their portrayal as children in need of protection. Disabled children tend to be viewed as inherently vulnerable and in need of special protection due to their age and impairments. Such views contribute to the creation of an artificial hierarchy of disability rights in which the priority is given to interventions aimed at the provision and protection of disabled children over their participation rights. As a result, disabled children's participation, in both individual and collective decision-making processes, including within the disability movement, is sidelined.

The UN Convention on the Rights of the Child (UNCRC), brought into force in 1989, incorporates civil, political, economic, social, and cultural rights. The child rights stipulated in the UNCRC are broadly referred to, in what has become known in the context of UNCRC, as 3 Ps – provision, protection, and participation (Vandenhole, 2017). The introduction of participation rights of the child clearly marks the intention of the drafters to posit the child as the social actor whose views ought to be respected and balanced against the need to afford them special protection due to the vulnerabilities inherent in childhood.

The core of the participation rights of children is encapsulated in UNCRC Article 12, which is elevated to the status of general principle, along with three other general principles: namely, non-discrimination (Article 2); best interests of the child (Article 3); and the right to life, survival, and development (Article 6) (Hanson & Lundy, 2017; Lundy & Byrne, 2017). Being both a substantive

 DOI: 10.4324/9781003410089-5

right and a general principle, Article 12 is to be applied across all other substantive rights set out in the UNCRC, meaning that children's views ought to be respected in all areas of life. Colloquially known as the right to be heard, Article 12 entitles all children, including disabled children, to the opportunity to express their views in all matters that affect them and to have those views taken into account by adults when decisions are being made. That being said, it requires a profound shift in attitudes towards children and corresponding changes in laws, policies, practices, and culture adopting a view of the child as an agent rather than an object of adults' concerns (Parkes, 2013).

I will argue that disabled children are facing multiple layers of socially produced dependencies which all act to limit their participation in decision-making processes that affect them. Shedding light on barriers to participation disabled children face because of both their age and disability will reveal the low priority society affords to their participation rights. Thus, I will argue that the challenges in the implementation of disabled children's right to be heard caused by disableism and intergenerational power struggles construct the form of a hierarchy of disability rights in which the participation rights of disabled children appear subordinate to their welfare and protection.

In the second part of this chapter, the key requirements and human rights standards concerning the participation of children enshrined in the UNCRC and the UNCRPD will be examined, in order to set the scene for further analysis of the factors which afford disabled children's participation relatively low priority.

The third part will lay out the arguments for why we should be paying attention to disabled children's participation as much as we pay attention to their protection. The positive influence of participation in decision-making processes will be explored, charting the argument that allowing disabled children to exercise or share the responsibility with adults contributes to an increase in their confidence, self-efficacy, and self-worth. The benefits of respecting and supporting a disabled child's autonomy in childhood are likely to play a vital role in the disabled child's empowerment and successful transition to adulthood and independent living throughout the life course. The barriers to participation disabled children face will be closely examined, using the participation in the domain of healthcare as a case study pointing out the pitfalls of child-development theories that overemphasize the importance of normal development and thus construct disabled children as abnormal or developmentally delayed and lacking the capacity to participate in decision-making processes.

The potential of new materialism as a theoretical tool that breaks dichotomies of nature and culture, disability and impairment, or childhood and adulthood will be examined to help us rethink the disabled children's capacities to participate in decision-making processes without sliding back into essentialism. It will be argued that that the onus should shift from an assessment of disabled children's capacities to participate to an assessment of the competence of adults to provide age-appropriate and disability-related supports to disabled children and maximise their capacities in that way.

The international human rights law and two paradigms of children's rights

The significance of UNCRC Article 12 is reflected in the fact that it recognises children as human beings in their own right, endowed with integrity and personality which ought to be respected and supported by adults. The right to which children are endowed by virtue of Article 12 has been commonly referred to in abbreviated forms as the *right to be heard*, the *right to participate*, and the *right to be consulted*, each falling short of capturing the entirety of its requirements (Lundy, 2007). Before I elaborate further on the core requirements of Article 12, let us take a look at its full text:

1. States Parties shall assure to the child who is capable of forming his or her own views the right to express those views freely in all matters affecting the child, the views of the child being given due weight in accordance with the age and maturity of the child.
2. For this purpose, the child shall in particular be provided the opportunity to be heard in any judicial and administrative proceedings affecting the child, either directly, or through a representative or an appropriate body, in a manner consistent with the procedural rules of national law.

(UNCRC, Article 12)

While it is not my aim to engage in full legal analysis of UNCRC Article 12, I will reflect on the core obligations it requires from the states parties. First, it is worth noting that not all children are entitled to the right to express their view – only those who are capable of expressing it. This means that the right is not an absolute one but a qualified one, and I will argue later that this provision poses particular challenges for disabled children. Secondly, children have the right to express their views freely in all matters that affect them and to receive all information needed to exercise the right in a child-friendly and accessible manner. This encompasses decisions in both public and private spheres, including in the family (Parkes, 2013). Furthermore, the UNCRC Committee, in its General Comment no. 12, reiterated that *all matters* cover a broad range of actions in which the best interests of children as a group or an individual child are at stake (Committee on the Rights of the Child, 2009, para. 72). It follows that the right to be heard is conferred to each child in individual decision-making processes but also to children as a group. Collective participation of children as a group should be supported: for example, in the processes of preparation of laws and policies when the law or policy is likely to affect the best interests of children as a class. Thirdly, it is not enough only to allow children to express their view; once they express it, it should be given due weight and seriously considered by adults. That means that adult decision-makers are not obliged to follow a child's wishes, but if they assess that the wishes of a child are not in his/her best interests, they should provide feedback to the child explaining why his/her wishes cannot be pursued (Committee on the Rights of the Child,

2009, para. 45). When deciding how much weight should be given to a child's view, decision-makers are to be led by the child's age and maturity. While the UNCRC committee acknowledged the difficulties associated with the attempts to define maturity, it does offer its own interpretation of what maturity is by saying that 'it is the capacity of a child to express her or his views on issues *in a reasonable and independent manner*' [emphasis added] (Committee on the Rights of the Child, 2009, para. 30). The committee adds that it is 'an obligation for States parties to assess the capacity of the child to form an autonomous opinion to the greatest extent possible' (Committee on the Rights of the Child, 2009, para. 20). This represents a rather narrow view of maturity, placing an emphasis on the individualistic and isolated notion of autonomy.

The individualistic and isolated notion of autonomy is understood as a capacity of individuals to act independently (James, 2012), or as Christman puts it: 'the ability to act upon one's own authentic values, desires, and motives' (Christman, 2018), poses a particular challenge for children as their evolving capacities indicate that they still have not acquired sufficient capacities to act independently and thus be autonomous. It follows that the link between capacity and autonomy is said to be such that the capacities serve as a gatekeeper to autonomy (Ruhe et al., 2016), and those children who can exhibit traits such as rationality, reasonableness, and independent thinking and expressing would be considered mature. Tobin and Cashmore (2020) point out that the concept of rights associated with ideas of autonomy, independence, and rationality reflects the Western liberal masculinist conception of rights and is not the concept of rights that underpins the UNCRC. They argue that the concept of children's rights is relational, emphasizing the interdependence and reciprocity between children and adults and the embeddedness of children in the local community and culture. While this argument opens up the possibility of challenging the view of children as immature and lacking capacity, it does not seem that it has been fully grasped and taken up by the UNCRC committee as I have demonstrated. The practice of children's participation in decision-making processes at the national level further proves that the individualistic notions of capacity and autonomy have a stronghold among adult decision-makers, causing the exclusion of all children and disabled children in particular from participation. The UNCRC committee's emphasis on the reasonableness and independence of manner of a child's expression has potentially discriminatory effects for disabled children, and I will revisit this argument in the following sections.

The second paragraph of UNCRC Article 12 underlines that the right to be heard applies in 'any judicial and administrative proceedings', and the UNCRC committee listed some examples of judicial proceedings, which include, among others, separation of parents; custody, care, and adoption; victims of violence and abuse; healthcare; and asylum-seeking and refugee children while administrative proceedings may include 'decisions about children's education, health, environment, living conditions or protection' (Committee on the Rights of the Child, 2009, para. 32). It is clear that many of these types of proceedings bear particular relevance to disabled children, not least because of the increased risk of violence and abuse, separation from family and institutionalization, segregation in education, and higher rates of hospitalization compared to their non-disabled peers (United Nations Children's Fund, 2021).

Besides Article 12 of the UNCRC, the participation rights are set out in Article 7 of the UN Convention on the Rights of Persons with Disabilities (UNCRPD). Its third paragraph draws from Article 12 of the UNCRC and reads as follows:

> States Parties shall ensure that children with disabilities have the right to express their views freely on all matters affecting them, their views being given due weight in accordance with their age and maturity, on an equal basis with other children, and to be provided with disability and age-appropriate assistance to realize that right.
>
> *(UNCRPD, Article 7(3))*

At the first glance, the text of UNCRPD Article 7 (3) is very similar to the text of UNCRC Article 12. However, the standards of children's participation embodied in these articles still differ in one seemingly important aspect for disabled children. While the text of UNCRC Article 12 clearly stipulates that the right to be heard is qualified rather than an absolute, meaning that not all children are entitled to the right to express their views but only a child 'capable of forming his or her own views', this conditionality is absent from UNCRPD Article 7.

The second novel feature of Article 7 of the CRPD is the extension of the right to be heard by virtue of the requirement to provide disability and age-appropriate assistance to disabled children in order to maximize 'their capacities for autonomous decision-making' (Della Fina et al., 2017). This requirement bears relevance for understanding children's capacities, making it unjustifiable to preclude children from participation in the decision-making process based on presumed immaturity and lack of capacity without offering and providing assistance. The CRPD, in its General Comment No. 1 on equal recognition before the law, warned against mental capacity assessments discriminatorily applied to persons with disabilities as they cannot 'accurately assess the inner-workings of the human mind' (Committee on the Rights of Persons with Disabilities, 2014, para. 15). As a result, they are used as the reason to prevent disabled people from enjoying their human rights. This is important as it raises the following question: if it is discriminatory to use mental capacity assessments as the reason for limiting the enjoyment of human rights of adults with disabilities, then how could it be legitimate to rely on the assessments of children's mental capacities/cognitive abilities when deciding whether to give them an opportunity to express their views and what weight to attach to those views?

Disabled children and the right to be heard – what is at stake?

Ever since the adoption of the UNCRC, the implementation of Article 12 has been fraught with challenges, not least because of the resistance of adults to accepting the possibility that a child might have valid views deserving to be considered (Parkes, 2013). Multiple studies conducted across different life domains have consistently pointed out that children's views are often not solicited at all, and when they are, they easily get discarded by adult decision-makers, resulting in tokenism, often due to adults' perceptions of children as inherently vulnerable and in need of protection (Berrick et al., 2015; Daly, 2018; Lundy, 2007; Stahl, 2007). In Lundy's (2007) view, the reasons for faltering implementation of UNCRC Article 12 can broadly be classified into three groups: a belief that children do not possess the capacity to contribute meaningfully to the decision-making process, a worry of adults that their authority will be undermined if a child is given more control, and the concern that the implementation requires too much effort. I will argue that these three groups of challenges to the implementation of children's right to be heard are even more accentuated when it comes to the participation of disabled children and in the following paragraphs, I will analyse these challenges in turn.

Discriminatory effects of overreliance on assessment of children's capacity to participate

Disabled children are facing at least a two-fold risk of being excluded from decision-making processes – due to their age and child status and because of disability. In some areas of law, specific age limits are prescribed under which the children are not allowed to exercise the right and over which a child can exercise the right independently (e.g. voting age, the age for legal marriage, and the age of consent to medical treatment). For example, most countries in Europe have introduced a statutory age of consent to medical treatments, which varies between 12 and 18 (Day et al., 2015). Such provisions correspond to the status approach, whereby children are excluded from independent decision-making on the basis of their age and status as a child.

However, the age itself is not a marker of maturity but a proxy for it as 'individual children reach maturity at different ages' (Committee on the Rights of the Child, 2016), so using the age classifications can always be either over-inclusive or under-inclusive, meaning that some children who are not yet mature enough will be entitled to exercise the right as they reach the prescribed age while some younger children who are mature and would potentially be able to exercise it are prevented from it by the fact that they are still young (Godwin, 2011).

Bearing in mind these difficulties of using the age as a proxy for maturity, in some countries or the areas of law, a move was made away from set age limits and towards assessments of the child's capacity or maturity in order to decide whether a child is competent to exercise the right freely (Elizari Urtasun, 2019). The ruling in the landmark Gillick case from 1985 in England (*Gillick v West Norfolk and Wisbech AHA [1985] 3 W.L.R. 830*[1986] *A.C. 112*, 1985) entitled children under 16 to consent to medical treatment if they exhibit 'sufficient understanding and intelligence'. The Gillick case ruling represented understanding that age as a sole criterion may not be enough to justify restrictions of a child's participation in healthcare decision making (Freeman, 2006, p. 201). It intended to move away from a status-based to a functional approach by focusing not on a child's age but on a child's competence for decision making. However, the more recent case law in England implies that even a competent child may not be allowed to refuse life-saving treatment (Cave, 2014). In such cases, the paternalistic interventions are justified using the outcome approach – the child should not be allowed to make a decision which would evidently pose serious harm, so the best-interests principle trumps the decision of a competent child (Elliston, 2007).

However, in the analysis of normative content of UNCRC Article 12 outlined in the previous section, we have seen that Article 12 is not about giving the children full adult-like autonomy and the unlimited possibility to make independent decisions. Consent to medical treatment refers to being a primary decision-maker, but this is only the end of the spectrum of participation. The right to be heard rather obliges adults to ensure that children are given the chance to participate, to be informed of what is at stake in decisions, and to express their views and have those views seriously considered by adults. It is about careful considerations of the limits of adults' paternalistic interventions towards children rather than a complete elimination of all forms of paternalism (Campoy Cervera, 2017a).

I have explained that there are two ways in which the text of CRC Article 12 makes reference to the capacities or maturity of children. First, it endows children who are capable of forming a view with the right to express their views, and secondly, it prescribes that the adult decision-makers should be guided by the child's age and maturity when deciding how much weight they will assign to child's views (Daly, 2018). It should be noted here that concepts such as capacity, competence, and maturity are vague, rarely explicitly defined, and highly contested, which opens the possibility of different interpretations (Borgne & Tisdall, 2017; Jonathan Todres, 2012; Tisdall, 2018).

Much of the understanding of the concept of children's maturity applied in the legal context draws from the strands of developmental psychology (cognitive-developmental theory from the mid-20th century, as proposed by Jean Piaget) and an understanding of a child's development as universal and linear (the ages and stages approach, in which children's chronological age sets the expectations for a certain level of capacities or cognitive abilities) (Griffin, 2011; Shute & Slee, 2015). Even though Piagetian cognitive development theory has been criticised for biological determinism and new theories of child development sensitive to social context (notably the socio-cultural theory of Lev Vygotsky and the psycho-dynamic theory of Erik Erikson) pointed out the importance of exposure to experience and responsibilities and the role of the environment, culture, and relationships with peers and adults (Mercer, 2018; Shute & Slee, 2015), it is still prevalent to assess child's capacities in relation to the set expectations regarding the cognitive and physical abilities considered typical for certain age indicating normal development (Daly, 2018; Priestley, 1998).

The courts are regularly referring to children's alleged lack of capacity as the reason to deny their wishes or even not to engage in ascertaining their wishes altogether without even attempting to specify what capacity is (Buss, 2009; Daly, 2018). Preoccupation with capacity, placing the focus of adult decision-makers on assumed developmental stages, can lead to what has been described as competence bias (Hinton, 2008; Tisdall, 2018). Disabled children are facing an increased risk of being judged as incompetent due to the presence of impairments understood as developmental delays (Davis & Watson, 2000; Tisdall, 2018).

Consequently, they may be deemed abnormal, immature, or particularly vulnerable, and adult decision-makers may give little weight to their views and wishes, if they're ascertained at all in the first place (Cooper, 2013; Davis & Watson, 2000). In fact, the development of disabled children may be compromised by the lack of opportunities to acquire experiences that are available to their non-disabled peers due to environmental barriers, overprotection and increased surveillance by adults, long periods of hospitalization, or segregated education and life in residential care settings (Anaby et al., 2013; Davis & Watson, 2000; Priestley, 1998; Watson et al., 1999). Associating the child's impairment with incapacity and failing to recognise that the source of disablement lies in socially constructed barriers to participation (Oliver, 2009; Oliver & Barnes, 2012) renders it way too easy for adults involved in decision making to justify paternalistic interventions towards disabled children and undermines the human rights standards of children's participation.

Participation as a process of sharing power between adults and children

The participation of children is contingent on the recognition of and support for a child's autonomy and agency by adults and their willingness to share or confer decision-making powers to children (Coyne & Harder, 2011; Sandland, 2017). As power is 'multidirectional and alinear' (Sandland, 2017), it is embedded in the relationships between all the actors included in decision-making processes: child-parent, parent-professional (e.g. service provider, child protection worker, healthcare professional, judge, teacher, etc.), professional-child. Thus, examining the attitudes of all these actors and their professional or parenting practices contributes to an understanding of the contextual factors of children's participation in decision making that reside outside their individual decision-making capacities.

The participation rights of children entail a positive obligation for parents to support the child towards autonomy and gradual acquisition of responsibilities (Betzler, 2015; Ruhe et al., 2016). As it is up to adults to create the environment and provide support to children to exercise their decision-making capacities, the issue of children's participation becomes the issue of the power imbalance between adults and children.

Dillen is referring to possible tension between the caring responsibilities of parents and the participation rights of children. She advocates that the resolution of this tension may lie in the 'theory of responsibility through and for the other', whereby parental responsibilities extend beyond care and protection to support for the child's increasing responsibilities (2006). She further advocates for an alternative view of parent-child relations which is not based on the struggle for power and autonomy but centres on human connectedness and 'heteronomous appeal to responsibility', in which the child, as an active agent, sends the ethical appeal to their parents and calls for their responsibility while they, in turn, provide not only the care and protection but also a stimulus for child's responsibility (Dillen, 2006).

While the rights discourse may regard children as non-autonomous and incapable of independent decision making, the idea of human connectedness and interdependence reveals the importance of parental guidance and, at the same, the importance of partnership and trust between parents and a child. The participation of the child is not an obligation but a matter of the child's choice, and parents have the responsibility to be proactive and engage the child in deliberations in important matters to the extent the child feels comfortable with. Alderson's study on children's consent to surgery (1993) showed that even very young children expressed the preference to be informed on the medical treatment and wanted to be included in decision making to some extent, and the majority of them wanted to share those decisions with their parents.

Disabled children are rarely given the opportunity to voice their concerns in the matters that affect them, and it is a common occurrence that their views are solicited through parents or carers as proxies (Bantekas, 2018; Garth & Aroni, 2003). Pervasive paternalism towards disabled children creates a serious impediment to their right to be heard and privileges the voices of adults in all actions taken for disabled children.

On the other hand, the positive impact of participation on a child's development has been well documented. The studies have shown that participation of children in decision-making processes contributes to their development, well-being, confidence, resilience, self-worth (Cavet & Sloper, 2004; Cossar et al., 2016; Daly, 2018), adherence to treatment, and reduction of fear and anxiety in the context of healthcare decisions (Alderson, 1993; Brady, 2020; Coyne & Harder, 2011; Kate Martin & Feltham, 2020). Therefore, overprotection in childhood has tremendous potential to represent a serious obstacle to independent living in adulthood and to extend socially produced dependency throughout the life course of a disabled person.

The exclusion of disabled children and young people is also evident within the disabled people's movement and disability advocacy organisations, and it is only a fairly recent development that the inclusion of young disabled people has started receiving more attention among international disabled people's organisations (DPOs).[1] However, these scattered initiatives mainly target young people over 18, and disabled children have yet to find their voices within the disabled people's movement, both nationally and internationally. The disabled people's movement has been struggling against the infantilization of disabled adults, especially adults with learning difficulties who were are often classified through medical discourse as infants at the level of development considered normal for a certain chronological age (Safta-Zecheria, 2018). In her critique of medical diagnostic categories which classify adults with intellectual impairments as children, Safta-Zecheria claims:

> [W]hat is problematic about the way in which the classification is presented is not only the progressive degrees of development (and not areas of development) considered relevant for assessing the person's abilities, but also the fact that those scoring less on IQ tests are likened automatically to children of different ages. The political consequence of this discursive move is easy to anticipate, people are considered child-like, therefore politically immature and de facto incapable of autonomous decision making.
>
> *(Safta-Zecheria, 2018)*

Safta-Zecheria further writes that infantilization happens not only through medical discourse and diagnostic categories but also in everyday life, especially in care settings. Disabled people over 18 are sometimes referred to as children when others or even they themselves want to emphasise the position of vulnerability and need. Disabled adults are then effectively placed in a depoliticised position of inferiority in relation to other, more powerful members of society (Safta-Zecheria, 2018).

In their effort to fight against the infantilisation of disabled adults, the disabled people's movement fails to question the justification of political marginalisation of all children, including disabled children. The core of this argument revolves around the claim that there is something intrinsic in children which renders them inherently vulnerable and justifies paternalism towards them, while the same cannot be said about adults with intellectual impairments as they ought to be considered as beings in their own right. The danger of such argument is the further exclusion of disabled children from the disability movement and their silencing as the disability movement accepts that adults are defined by what children are not – mature, competent, and autonomous.

Griffiths, in his research on young disabled people's experiences and views of the disabled people's movement, documented barriers to participation in disability activism young disabled people face. One of the young interviewees claimed:

> Especially because of the way that our, if you're a disabled child, the way you are treated is still so heavily dependent on making sure you can walk, making sure you can hear, making sure you can talk and various other things, so it feels as if there's still a medical model constraint on children,

> whereas, I dunno, yeah, I think that once you get to a slightly older age and once you realise that the barriers that are created are created by society, it's a bit different.
>
> *(Griffiths, 2018, p. 207)*

This quote illustrates that the position of disabled children is marked by the dominance of the medical model of disability, whereby the focus of interventions towards disabled children is fixing to get as close as possible to an ideal of normality (Mclaughlin & Coleman-Fountain, 2014). The social model as a 'big idea' of the disability movement (Beckett & Campbell, 2015) has certainly contributed to the emancipation of disabled people globally, but for disabled children, it still remains a distant idea. Arguably, the more useful strategy for the disability movement would be to strengthen efforts towards disabled children's emancipation and to make this 'big idea' accessible to disabled children. It should recognise that both adults and disabled children are interdependent and that disabled children's lived experiences represent a valued and important contribution to the disability movement and consequently should be listened to. For that to happen, it is necessary to consider the effort that needs to be taken to make the right to be heard a reality for disabled children.

The effort needed to guarantee the right to be heard to disabled children

In order to achieve full implementation of the right to be heard for disabled children, it is not enough only to allow children to express their views. A series of proactive actions needs to be taken by adults to make this right effective. Participation is not an obligation of the child but a choice. However, the role of adults is to invite, encourage, and support a child's participation in order to make this choice meaningful (Parkes, 2013).

The first step in the implementation of the right to be heard is to help a child prepare for participation by informing them that they have a right to express their view. A child should also know what the decision-making process will look like, where it will take place and how, who will be present, and to what extent their opinion will matter (Committee on the Rights of the Child, 2009). All the information should be given in an age-appropriate and child-friendly manner, and it is of particular importance for disabled children who may not communicate verbally or have other communication needs to receive the information in an accessible manner, including through communication devices or other assistive technologies if needed (Roulstone & McLeod, 2011). For example, in the domain of healthcare, what matters to children when they experience hospitalisation are child-friendly spaces for leisure and entertainment, which should be mainstreamed into the hospital environment as a whole (Lambert et al., 2014). Such an environment renders the hospital a less intimidating place and helps reduce fear and anxiety in children, thus encouraging participation. Providing information and communication support to a child – and in particular to disabled children – may require time, and time can be a scarce resource in some settings, such as social care or healthcare, where the staff may operate under time pressure (Franklin & Sloper, 2009; McNeilly et al., 2015; Runeson et al., 2001). It is also important that staff members who are involved in the decision-making process have received adequate training to develop skills to communicate with disabled children since a lack of communication skills may lead to the exclusion of disabled children from participation opportunities (Beresford & Sloper, 2003; Cavet & Sloper, 2004; Olli et al., 2012). Children may not be able to understand complex medical information, especially when communicated using unfamiliar medical terms. Examples of child-friendly and age-appropriate interventions in healthcare settings may include audio-visual interventions like animated films which depict the experience of hospitalisation or a particular medical procedure, a tour of an operating room or hospital ward, use of a preoperative playroom, a booklet with graphic images of medical procedures, or medical play dolls with medical instruments and similar (Bartik & Toruner, 2018; Chow et al., 2016; Hosseinpour & Memarzadeh, 2010). Such interventions help children understand what they can expect during their treatment and hospital stay and may help them form a view or ask further questions. Such interventions should take into account the access needs of disabled children and be designed to accommodate children with a different types of impairments. For children with hearing impairments, communication with health professionals may require additional time dedicated to a child patient to explain the information in writing or to provide sign language interpreters or subtitles to animated films used in preoperative programs. For those children with visual impairments, health professionals would do well to explain verbally what is happening during an examination or a medical procedure or to provide the toy models of medical instruments or dolls that children can touch and get acquainted with when receiving the information on proposed treatments. This means that child participation needs to be embedded in organisational cultures and fostered throughout professional practices and in social care, healthcare, and judicial systems, for example, rather than depending on committed individuals (Brady, 2020; Franklin & Sloper, 2009).

I have already mentioned that once a child is supported to express their view, adults involved in the decision-making process should give it due weight, meaning that they should consider it seriously and balance it against their judgment of what is in the child's best interests (Archard & Skivenes, 2009). Various authors pointed out the lack of operationalisation of the concept of due weight and the problems associated with the best interests principle, questioning the ability of adults to determine with any level of certainty what the child's needs are and whether a decision would truly be in their best interests (Campoy Cervera, 2017b; Daly, 2018; M. Freeman, 1997; Woodhead, 2015). While space limitations prevent me from engaging in this matter further, it is worth noting that the child's needs are socially constructed and vary across times and places (Woodhead, 2015), and adults should have strong justification if they take action contrary to the child's views and provide feedback to the child, explaining why a certain course of action was taken in a child-friendly and accessible manner.

By shedding light on the efforts needed to guarantee disabled children the right to be heard, reflecting on the examples of participation in healthcare settings, I painted a picture that successful participation does not depend only on discursive practices in terms of the attitudes of the adults involved in the decision-making process towards disabled children and the assessment of their capacities but on material realities as well, such as communication devices, assistive technologies, spaces in which participation happens, time available for participation, support workers involved, or similar. That being said, in the next section, I will explore the new materialistic perspective of disabled children's capacities, which allows considering how the material and discursive factors I described earlier work together to produce disabled children's capacities.

Contribution of new materialism to changing the understanding of disabled children's capacities

The adoption of the UNCRC in 1989 marked a period of increased interest in children's rights and childhood research. The academic interest in childhood research had previously been reserved for the discipline of developmental psychology, but the end of the 80s and the 90s saw an emerging interest by sociologists, which emphasised the child as a social actor and childhood as a permanent social structure varying across time and geographical locations, to be later superseded by a social constructionist view of childhood, privileging a discourse in social analysis (James, 1998; James & Prout, 1990).

Over the last three decades, the concept of children's agency has become a central one in the field of childhood studies (Oswell, 2013). The concept of agency denotes the shifting views of children – they are now regarded as social actors who actively shape the world around them rather than the objects of adults' concerns (James & Prout, 1990; James, 1998; James, 2012). The restrictions of their agency are said to stem from a flawed understanding of childhood as a state of dependency contingent on biology. Thus, the new sociology of childhood challenged the view of children as inherently vulnerable, lacking skills and competence, for whom the goal was to outgrow this stage of dependence through the process of development and maturation and reach fully independent adulthood. It emphasized that a child should be considered a being in their own right with valuable contribution to present society rather than a human in becoming (James & Prout, 1990). Uprichard warns against the claim of a child as *being* because it places too much focus on proving the competence of a child, while it might be more useful to consider both adults and children as *being and becoming* at the same time: interdependent and all competent in some things while incompetent in others (Uprichard, 2008). This is a useful step in breaking down a dichotomy between childhood and adulthood, particularly challenging the notion of adults as fully competent and children as incompetent.

Allan Prout has been claiming that the sociology of childhood has to move away from false dichotomies characteristic of modernity, such as those between nature and culture, agency and structure, and material and discursive and points out that discursive analysis of childhood has to be combined with the analysis of the materialities of children's bodies, built environment, and technology, which all extend children's capacities and agency (Prout, 2005, 2011). The idea is that children are social actors able to influence and shape the environment while, at the same time, being influenced by the social world consisting of human and non-human actors (such as technology, built environment, and other material spaces and things). Such a reciprocal relationship is indicative of the flat ontology espoused by new materialism, which rejects dichotomies between nature and culture, human and non-human, and material and discursive (Fox & Alldred, 2016). Thus, instead of claiming the ontological position of children as *human beings*, the ontological assumptions of new materialism rather regard both children and adults as beings that are in a permanent process of becoming, relational and in constant flux: i.e. *humans-in-becoming* (Fox & Alldred, 2016). Disabled children's participation in decision-making processes would be considered from such an approach in terms of decision-making events, drawing from assemblage theory. The decision-making event is formed by the assemblage consisting of human actors such as professionals, disabled children, and their parents producing and reproducing the social reality through their actions and meanings they attach to their actions, the actions of others, and various material and non-material artefacts (e.g. laws, policies, cultural understandings of childhood and disability, assistive technologies, material spaces and artefacts, etc.).

The new materialist view of children's capacities moves away from an essentialist notion of children's capacities and autonomy determined by biology and the stage of cognitive development and instead focuses on disabled children's capacities afforded to them by the heterogeneous assemblages which form at particular times to enable or constrain what they can be (Spyrou, 2019). It focuses on the exploration of relations between disabled children and adults and non-human entities (including but not limited to laws, welfare system features, assistive technologies, and material spaces in which participation happens) in the social-material practice of participation in decision making, acknowledging situational perspective and relationality and interdependence in disabled children's lives (Spyrou, 2019). Such a view is closely associated with distributed methodology, which analyses disabled childhoods by examining the role of significant adults in children's lives such as professionals and parents, along with those of children (Curran & Runswick-Cole, 2014).

Therefore, there cannot be any ontological assumptions of a disabled child as lacking capacity. Capacity or maturity is not something inherent to a child, disabled or not, at one point in time, but from a new materialistic perspective, the child's capacity to participate in healthcare decision making, for example, or any other type of proceedings whatsoever is situational (Coyne & Harder, 2011) and socially produced through networks of assemblages consisted of human and non-human entities, each affecting the other. Those can be supporting adults who help the child understand relevant information, child-friendly spaces and procedures for participation, assistive technologies and communication devices, or laws and policies which regulate access to assistive technologies or prescribe the obligation for professionals to listen to children's views.

All these human and non-human entities, from a new materialistic perspective, have agentic potential and operate in an assemblage to produce or maximise a child's capacities. This corresponds with the argument that children's capacities should not be regarded in individualistic and essentialist terms but relational, situational and context-dependent ones (Ruhe et al., 2016). The question should not be what capacities a child has, but what capacities a child would have if provided with the right supports. Again, if we look at the example of the healthcare domain, for effective participation of the disabled child, an array of different components in participation assemblage would need to be considered. For some children, but also for parents, exposure of a child to surgical treatments may be traumatising and lead to post-traumatic stress disorder (Ben-Amitay et al., 2006; Turgoose et al., 2021). Disabled children who develop some forms of psychosocial disabilities due to the traumatising experiences of medical treatment may require psychological counseling and support after the treatment or as part of their preoperative program in future treatments (Bartik & Toruner, 2018). Material artefacts such as tablets with animated films of medical procedures, medical play dolls, and booklets on children's rights in the hospital in alternative formats may play a crucial role in boosting children's understanding and helping facilitate the expression of their views. On another hand, discursive components such as a hospital's procedures, training on communication with child patients that healthcare professionals received, or parenting style may also act as enablers of or impediments to disabled children's participation (Jeremic et al., 2016).

Therefore, the assemblage of material and discursive components which all have an agentic potential creates a more or less conducive environment for disabled children's participation and renders children's decision-making capacities situational and relational.

Conclusion

Despite the human rights standards enshrined in UNCRC Article 12 and UNCRPD Article 7, disabled children are in many ways excluded from participation in both individual and collective decision-making processes. On one hand, they are facing the risk of exclusion because of their age and deeply rooted attitudes of adults which marginalize and silence the views of children. However, disability adds another layer of exclusion. Disabled childhood is often understood as the site of vulnerability and need, leading to the depoliticisation of disabled children. This mechanism of exclusion operates both at the level of society as a whole and within the disability movement. In this way, an artificial hierarchy of disability rights is established in which the right of disabled children to be heard is given relatively low priority compared to the corpus of rights pertaining to provision and protection.

Disabled children's participation is further constrained by the overly paternalistic attitudes of adults. Service provision systems are characterised by risk aversion, prioritising disabled children's protection at the expense of their participation. As a result of paternalism and the dominating medical model in the context of disabled childhood, disabled children are seen but not heard. The focus on the capacity or competence of children to participate contains the risk of competence bias, and exclusion of disabled children in the presence of impairment may wrongly lead to an assumption of incapacity.

Defining disabled children by a vulnerability may obfuscate their integrity, personality, and potential for independent living. Tobin (2015) challenges the notion of childhood as the site of inherent vulnerability as opposed to adulthood. He emphasises that no human being can be considered invulnerable and that there is a need for adults to recognise and foster children's resilience:

> Protective measures are therefore necessary to mitigate against the myriad of threats to children's (and indeed adults') health and well-being. But a protective paradigm that emphasises a child's vulnerability at the expense of their evolving capacity will do little to increase children's resilience and capacity to protect themselves from harm. The challenge for adults, therefore, is to commit to this broader conception of children as being both vulnerable and resilient, and where appropriate, work with children to enable them to maximise their capacities for self-protection and interdependence.
>
> *(Tobin, 2015, p. 182)*

The new materialist view of disabled childhood challenges boundaries between childhood and adulthood and between capacity and incapacity. By doing so, it concedes that both children and adults are *humans in becoming*, meaning that all people, children and adults alike, are continually developing and learning and are in need of support in decision-making processes. New materialism does not privilege the importance of discourse or materiality. Instead, it posits the concepts of childhood, disability, and impairment without sliding back to essentialist views of the materialities of childhood or impairment (Feely, 2016; Fox & Alldred, 2016; Monforte, 2018). In that way, the focus of analysis is on relational 'context-dependent capacities, rather than essential identities' (Feely, 2016, p. 10) of disabled children in the context of participation in decision making. Such a move reduces the risk of disabled children being assessed as incompetent and incapacitated because it shifts the focus from assessing the capacity of the child to the competence of adults to provide age-appropriate and disability-related supports and, in that way, maximise the capacity of disabled children. This is more in line with the UNCRPD and the social model of disability, which identifies socially constructed barriers as a true source of exclusion and oppression.

The interpretations of the UNCRC committee of the meaning of maturity, which implies that the indicators of maturity are the ability of a child to express the view in a reasonable and independent manner, represent a serious obstacle to the participation of disabled children. The UNCRPD, as a newer human rights treaty, offers, arguably, a more progressive view of autonomy. Instead of regarding it in individualistic terms conditioned by possession of inherent capacity, the UNCRPD emphasises the interdependence of disabled people and the importance of the provision of supports aimed at maximisation of opportunities to participate. In the context of children's rights, that includes the right to information in an accessible and child-friendly manner, the right of a child to decide whether they want to participate and in which manner, the right to access age-appropriate and disability-related supports needed to express the views, and the obligation of adults to give due weight to child's views. Age or disability should never be the reason to deny to a child the right to participate or to discard the child's view.

Adults, including family members, service providers, and the disability community as a whole, have an ethical responsibility to disabled children to support them to assume responsibilities gradually. Only by acknowledging the harm that may befall a child if their views are not respected will we be able to take a step towards the recognition of disabled children as social actors and agents. Ultimately, independent living is not about being self-sufficient and living in isolation from others. Independent living philosophy recognises the interdependence of all people and stresses the importance of autonomy, choice, and control in disabled people's lives. Having an opportunity to exercise some choice and control in childhood with the support of adults will pave the way for disabled children to live independently in adulthood. Disabled children should be seen and heard now if the artificial hierarchy of disability rights is to be dismantled.

Disclaimer

This chapter has been produced under the Disability Advocacy Research in Europe (DARE) project that received funding from the European Union's Horizon 2020 research and innovation programme under the Marie Skłodowska-Curie grant agreement No 814249. The content of this publication represents the views of the author only and is his/her sole responsibility. The European Commission does not accept any responsibility for use that may be made of the information it contains.

Note

1 European Network on Independent Living (ENIL) established its Youth Network in 2015, gathering young disabled people aged 15 to 35. See more at https://enil.

eu/enil-youth/about-the-enil-youth-network/. European Disability Forum (EDF) has established the Youth Committee, which includes young members aged 18 to 35. See more at https://www.edf-feph.org/group/youth-committee/. International Disability Alliance (IDA) also established the Youth Committee in 2021 and a global ListServ through which young people with disabilities can meet and exchange experiences. See more at: https://www.internationaldisabilityalliance.org/youth-with-disabilities.

References

Alderson, P. (1993). *Children's consent to surgery*. Open University Press.

Anaby, D., Hand, C., Bradley, L., DiRezze, B., Forhan, M., DiGiacomo, A., & Law, M. (2013). The effect of the environment on participation of children and youth with disabilities: a scoping review. *Disability and Rehabilitation*, *35*(19), 1589–1598. https://doi.org/10.3109/09638288.2012.748840

Archard, D., & Skivenes, M. (2009). Balancing a child's best interests and a child's views. *The International Journal of Children's Rights*, *17*(1), 1–21. https://doi.org/10.1163/157181808X358276

Bantekas, I. (2018). *The UN convention on the rights of persons with disabilities: a commentary*. Oxford University Press.

Bartik, K., & Toruner, E. K. (2018). Effectiveness of a preoperative preparation program on children's emotional states and parental anxiety. *Journal of Perianesthesia Nursing*, *33*(6), 972–980. https://doi.org/10.1016/j.jopan.2017.09.008

Beckett, A. E., & Campbell, T. (2015). The social model of disability as an oppositional device. *Disability & Society*, *30*(2), 270–283. https://doi.org/10.1080/09687599.2014.999912

Ben-Amitay, G., Kosov, I., Reiss, A., Toren, P., Yoran-Hegesh, R., Kotler, M., & Mozes, T. (2006). Is elective surgery traumatic for children and their parents? *Journal of Paediatrics and Child Health*, *42*(10), 618–624. https://doi.org/10.1111/j.1440-1754.2006.00938.x

Beresford, B. A., & Sloper, P. (2003). Chronically ill adolescents' experiences of communicating with doctors: a qualitative study. *Journal of Adolescent Health*, *33*(3), 172–179. https://doi.org/10.1016/S1054-139X(03)00047-8

Berrick, J. D., Dickens, J., Pösö, T., & Skivenes, M. (2015). Children's involvement in care order decision-making: a cross-country analysis. *Child Abuse & Neglect*, *49*, 128–141. https://doi.org/10.1016/j.chiabu.2015.07.001

Betzler, M. (2015). Enhancing the capacity for autonomy: what parents owe their children to make their lives go well. In A. Bagattini & C. Macleod (Eds.), *The nature of children's well-being: theory and practice* (pp. 65–84). Springer. https://doi.org/10.1007/978-94-017-9252-3_5

Borgne, C. L., & Tisdall, E. K. M. (2017). Children's participation: questioning competence and competencies?(Report). *Social Inclusion*, *5*(3), 122–130. https://doi.org/10.17645/si.v5i3.986

Brady, L.-M. (2020). *Embedding young people's participation in health services – new approaches*. Policy Press. https://policy.bristoluniversitypress.co.uk/embedding-young-peoples-participation-in-health-services

Buss, E. (2009). What the law should learn from child development research. *Hofstra Law Review*, *38*(1), 13.

Campoy Cervera, I. (2017a). Legal analysis of article 7 of the convention on the rights of persons with disabilities: children with disabilities. *Age of Human Rights Journal*, *9*, 116–141. https://doi.org/10.17561/tahrj.n9.6

Campoy Cervera, I. (2017b). Ideas for the construction of a human rights model for children, with and without disabilities. In C. O'Mahony & G. Quinn (Eds.), *Disability law and policy: an analysis of the UN Convention*. Clarus Press.

Cave, E. (2014). Goodbye gillick? Identifying and resolving problems with the concept of child competence. *Legal Studies*, *34*(1), 103–122. https://doi.org/10.1111/lest.12009

Cavet, J., & Sloper, P. (2004). Participation of disabled children in individual decisions about their lives and in public decisions about service development. *Children & Society*, *18*(4), 278–290. https://doi.org/10.1002/chi.803

Chow, C. H. T., Van Lieshout, R. J., Schmidt, L. A., Dobson, K. G., & Buckley, N. (2016). Systematic review: audiovisual interventions for reducing preoperative anxiety in children undergoing elective surgery. *Journal of Pediatric Psychology*, *41*(2), 182–203. https://doi.org/10.1093/jpepsy/jsv094

Christman, J. (2018). Autonomy in moral and political philosophy. In E. N. Zalta (Ed.), *The Stanford encyclopedia of philosophy* (Spring 2018). Metaphysics Research Lab, Stanford University. https://plato.stanford.edu/archives/spr2018/entries/autonomy-moral/

Committee on the Rights of Persons with Disabilities. (2014). *General comment No. 1 (2014) Article 12: equal recognition before the law* (CRPD/C/GC/1). Committee on the Rights of the Child.

Committee on the Rights of the Child. (2009). *General comment No. 12 on the right of the child to be heard*. Committee on the Rights of the Child.

Committee on the Rights of the Child. (2016). *General comment No. 20 (2016) on the implementation of the rights of the child during adolescence*. Committee on the Rights of the Child.

Cooper, H. (2013). The oppressive power of normalcy in the lives of disabled children: deploying history to denaturalize the notion of the "normal child". In *Disabled children's childhood studies: critical approaches in a global context*. Palgrave Macmillan.

Cossar, J., Brandon, M., & Jordan, P. (2016). "You've got to trust her and she's got to trust you": children's views on participation in the child protection system. *Child & Family Social Work*, *21*(1), 103–112. https://doi.org/10.1111/cfs.12115

Coyne, I., & Harder, M. (2011). Children's participation in decision-making: balancing protection with shared decision-making using a situational perspective. *Journal of Child Health Care*, *15*(4), 312–319. https://doi.org/10.1177/1367493511406570

Curran, T., & Runswick-Cole, K. (2014). Disabled children's childhood studies: a distinct approach? *Disability & Society*, *29*(10), 1617–1630. https://doi.org/10.1080/09687599.2014.966187

Daly, A. (2018). *Children, autonomy and the courts: beyond the right to be heard*. Brill.

Davis, J., & Watson, N. (2000). Disabled children's rights in everyday life: problematising notions of competency and promoting self-empowerment. *The International Journal of Children's Rights*, *8*(3), 211–228. https://doi.org/10.1163/15718180020494622

Day, L., Percy-Smith, B., Ruxton, S., McKenna, K., Redgrave, K., Ronicle, J., Young, T., European Commission, Directorate-General for Justice and Consumers, Ecorys United Kingdom Ltd, University of the West of England, B., & Child-to-Child Trust, I. of E. (2015). *Evaluation of legislation, policy and practice of child participation in the European Union (EU): final report*. Publications Office.

Della Fina, V., Cera, R., & Palmisano, G. (Eds.). (2017). Article 7 children with disabilities. In *The United Nations convention on the rights of persons with disabilities a commentary* (First edition). Springer.

Dillen, A. (2006). Children between liberation and care: ethical perspectives on the rights of children and parent-child relationships. *International Journal of Children's Spirituality: Children's Spirituality and Children's Rights*, *11*(2), 237–250. https://doi.org/10.1080/13644360600797230

Elizari Urtasun, L. (2019). Conflict between children's autonomy and protection in healthcare (Comparative Study between Spanish and Belgian Law). *European Journal of Health Law*, *26*(4), 289–307. https://doi.org/10.1163/15718093-12264429

Elliston, S. (2007). *The best interests of the child in healthcare* (First edition). Routledge-Cavendish.

Feely, M. (2016). Disability studies after the ontological turn: A return to the material world and material bodies without a return to essentialism. *Disability & Society*, *31*(7), 863–883. https://doi.org/10.1080/09687599.2016.1208603

Fox, N. J., & Alldred, P. (2016). *Sociology and the new materialism: theory, research, action*. Sage Publications Ltd. https://doi.org/10.4135/9781526401915

Franklin, A., & Sloper, P. (2009). Supporting the participation of disabled children and young people in decision-making. *Children & Society*, 3–15.

Freeman, M. (1997). The best interests of the child? Is the best interests of the child in the best interests of children? *International Journal of Law, Policy and the Family*, *11*(3), 360–388. https://doi.org/10.1093/lawfam/11.3.360

Freeman, M. D. A. (2006). *Children's health and children's rights*. Brill. http://ebookcentral.proquest.com/lib/leeds/detail.action?docID=468076

Garth, B., & Aroni, R. (2003). "I value what you have to say". Seeking the perspective of children with a disability, not just their parents. *Disability & Society*, *18*(5), 561–576. https://doi.org/10.1080/0968759032000097825

Gillick v West Norfolk and Wisbech AHA [1985] 3 W.L.R. 830[1986] A.C. 112, AC 112 (House of Lords 1985).

Godwin, S. (2011). Children's oppression, rights and liberation (SSRN Scholarly Paper ID 1803459). *Social Science Research Network*. https://papers.ssrn.com/abstract=1803459

Griffin, M. (2011). Developing deliberative minds – Piaget, Vygotsky and the deliberative democratic citizen. *Journal of Public Deliberation*, *7*(1), 30.

Griffiths, M. (2018). *These days are ours: exploring young disabled people's experiences and views of the disabled people's movement*. Liverpool John Moores University.

Hanson, K., & Lundy, L. (2017). Does exactly what it says on the Tin? *The International Journal of Children's Rights*, *25*(2), 285–306. https://doi.org/10.1163/15718182-02502011

Hinton, R. (2008). Children's participation and good governance: limitations of the theoretical literature. *The International Journal of Children's Rights*, *16*(3), 285–300. https://doi.org/10.1163/157181808X311141

Hosseinpour, M., & Memarzadeh, M. (2010). Use of a preoperative playroom to prepare children for surgery. *European Journal of Pediatric Surgery*, *20*(6), 408–411. https://doi.org/10.1055/s-0030-1265172

James, A. (1998). *Theorizing childhood*. Polity.

James, A. (2012). *Key concepts in childhood studies* (Second edition). SAGE.

James, A., & Prout, A. (1990). *Constructing and reconstructing childhood: contemporary issues in the sociological study of childhood*. Falmer.

Jeremic, V., Sénécal, K., Borry, P., Chokoshvili, D., & Vears, D. F. (2016). Participation of children in medical decision-making: challenges and potential solutions. *Journal of Bioethical Inquiry*, *13*(4), 525–534. https://doi.org/10.1007/s11673-016-9747-8

Jonathan Todres. (2012). Maturity. *Houston Law Review*, *48*, 1107–1241.

Kate Martin, & Feltham, A. (2020). Shared decision-making with young people in mental health services. In L.-M. Brady (Ed.), *Embedding young people's participation in health services – new approaches*. Policy Press.

Lambert, V., Coad, J., Hicks, P., & Glacken, M. (2014). Social spaces for young children in hospital. *Child: Care, Health and Development*, *40*(2), 195–204. https://doi.org/10.1111/cch.12016

Lundy, L. (2007). 'Voice' is not enough: conceptualising Article 12 of the United Nations Convention on the Rights of the Child. *British Educational Research Journal*, *33*(6), 927–942. https://doi.org/10.1080/01411920701657033

Lundy, L., & Byrne, B. (2017). The four general principles of the United Nations Convention on the Rights of the Child: the potential value of the approach in other areas of human rights law. In E. Brems, E. Desmet, & W. Vandenhole (Eds.), *Children's Rights Law in the Global Human Rights landscape: Isolation, inspiration, integration?* Routledge and Taylor & Francis Group.

Mclaughlin, J., & Coleman-Fountain, E. (2014). The unfinished body: the medical and social reshaping of disabled young bodies. *Social Science & Medicine*, *120*, 76–84. https://doi.org/10.1016/j.socscimed.2014.09.012

McNeilly, P., Macdonald, G., & Kelly, B. (2015). The participation of disabled children and young people: a social justice perspective. *Child Care in Practice: Northern Ireland Journal of Multi-Disciplinary Child Care Practice*, *21*(3), 266–286. https://doi.org/10.1080/13575279.2015.1014468

Mercer, J. A. (2018). *Child development: concepts and theories*. SAGE.

Monforte, J. (2018). What is new in new materialism for a newcomer? *Qualitative Research in Sport, Exercise and Health*, *10*(3), 378–390. https://doi.org/10.1080/2159676X.2018.1428678

Oliver, M. (2009). *Understanding disability: from theory to practice* (Second edition). Palgrave Macmillan.

Oliver, M., & Barnes, C. (2012). *The new politics of disablement*. Macmillan Education UK and Palgrave Macmillan.

Olli, J., Vehkakoski, T., & Salanterä, S. (2012). Facilitating and hindering factors in the realization of disabled children's agency in institutional contexts: literature review. *Disability & Society*, *27*(6), 793–807. https://doi.org/10.1080/09687599.2012.679023

Oswell, D. (2013). *The agency of children: from family to global human rights*. Cambridge University Press.

Parkes, A. (2013). *Children and international human rights law: the right of the child to be heard*. Routledge.

Priestley, M. (1998). Childhood disability and disabled childhoods: agendas for research. *Childhood*, *5*(2), 207–223. https://doi.org/10.1177/0907568298005002007

Prout, A. (2005). *The future of childhood: towards the interdisciplinary study of children*. RoutledgeFalmer.

Prout, A. (2011). Taking a step away from modernity: reconsidering the new sociology of childhood. *Global Studies of Childhood*, *1*(1), 4–14. https://doi.org/10.2304/gsch.2011.1.1.4

Roulstone, S., & McLeod, S. (2011). *Listening to children and young people with speech, language and communication needs*. J and R Press.

Ruhe, K., Clercq, E., Wangmo, T., & Elger, B. (2016). Relational capacity: broadening the notion of decision-making capacity in paediatric healthcare. *Journal of Bioethical Inquiry*, *13*(4), 515–524. https://doi.org/10.1007/s11673-016-9735-z

Runeson, I., Enskär, K., Elander, G., & Hermerén, G. (2001). Professionals' perceptions of children's participation in decision making in healthcare. *Journal of Clinical Nursing*, *10*(1), 70–78. https://doi.org/10.1046/j.1365-2702.2001.00433.x

Safta-Zecheria, L. (2018). The infantilization of intellectual disability and political inclusion: a pedagogical approach. *Journal of Educational Sciences*, *19*(2), 104.

Sandland, R. (2017). A clash of conventions? Participation, power and the rights of disabled children. *Social Inclusion*, *5*(3), 93–103. https://doi.org/10.17645/si.v5i3.955

Shute, R.H., & Slee, P.T. (2015). *Child development: theories and critical perspectives*. Routledge. https://www.routledge.com/Child-Development-Theories-and-Critical-Perspectives/Shute-Slee/p/book/9781848724525

Spyrou, S. (2019). An ontological turn for childhood studies? *Children & Society*, *33*(4), 316–323. https://doi.org/10.1111/chso.12292

Stahl, R. M. (2007). "Don't forget about me": implementing article 12 of the United Nations Convention on the Rights of the Child. *Arizona Journal of International and Comparative Law*, *24*(3), 803.

Tisdall, E. K. M. (2018). Challenging competency and capacity?: due weight to children's views in family law proceedings. *The International Journal of Children's Rights*, *26*(1), 159–182. https://doi.org/10.1163/15718182-02601003

Tobin, J. (2015). Understanding children's rights: a vision beyond vulnerability. *Nordic Journal of International Law*, *84*(2), 155–182. https://doi.org/10.1163/15718107-08402002

Tobin, J., & Cashmore, J. (2020). Thirty years of the CRC: Child protection progress, challenges and opportunities. *Child Abuse & Neglect*, *110*(Pt. 1), 104436–104436. https://doi.org/10.1016/j.chiabu.2020.104436

Turgoose, D. P., Kerr, S., De Coppi, P., Blackburn, S., Wilkinson, S., Rooney, N., Martin, R., Gray, S., & Hudson, L. D. (2021). Prevalence of traumatic psychological stress reactions in children and parents following paediatric surgery: a systematic review and meta-analysis. *BMJ Paediatrics Open*, *5*(1), e001147–e001147. https://doi.org/10.1136/bmjpo-2021-001147

United Nations Children's Fund. (2021). *Seen, counted, included: using data to shed light on the well-being of children with disabilities*. UNICEF.

Uprichard, E. (2008). Children as 'being and becomings': children, childhood and temporality. *Children & Society*, *22*(4), 303–313. https://doi.org/10.1111/j.1099-0860.2007.00110.x

Vandenhole, W. (2017). Distinctive characteristics of children's human rights law. In E. Brems, E. Desmet & W. Vandenhole (Eds.), *Children's rights law in the global human rights landscape: isolation, inspiration, integration?* Routledge and Taylor & Francis Group.

Watson, N., Shakespeare, T., Cunningham-Burley, S., & Barnes, C. (1999). *Life as a disabled child: a qualitative study of young people's experiences and perspectives* (vol. 34). University of Leeds.

Woodhead, M. (2015). Psychology and the cultural construction of children's needs. In A. James & A. Prout (Eds.), *Constructing and reconstructing childhood: contemporary issues in the sociological study of childhood*. Routledge.

4

A JOURNEY TO REALIZE AN AUTISTIC'S RIGHTS

Rebekah Kintzinger, Stephanie Côté and Ajay Gandhi

Author's Note

The content presented in this chapter is based on original work by Rebekah Kintzinger, *Educating the Underdiagnosed*, a video that was published by CASDA in October 2020. The video can be accessed at https://www.youtube.com/watch?v=myrTyXcEKv8. Kintzinger's is the first voice of the narrative. The co-authors, Stephanie Côté (manager of policy initiatives at CASDA) and Ajay Gandhi (student at McMaster University), have provided support by working jointly with Kintzinger to further integrate scholarly references, citations, and academic research into this narrative. We hope that this narrative, told from Kintzinger's perspective, will highlight the importance of centering autistic voices and will immerse the reader in the real-life experiences of autistic people.

A journey to realize autistics' rights

I did not always know I was autistic. That is the thing about knowing something. When it comes to knowing, we only have access to the resources we are exposed to. We learn more about ourselves as we learn more about the world. I lived in a particularly small town in a Canadian province in a decade when autism was not as forefront a topic as it is today. My parents were not exposed to knowledge of Asperger's syndrome,[1] which is what I would later be diagnosed with.

Certainly from my personal experience, no professional during any of my school years ever suggested autism as a cause of some of my strengths in class or the reason for any of my challenges. Looking back, however, is a lot different because now I have been exposed to a greater understanding of autism throughout adulthood, especially for autistic[2] women[3] and the challenges they

 DOI: 10.4324/9781003410089-6

face with accessing support. In reflecting on my upbringing, there is no scenario where I do not recognize my younger self as autistic. The traits and signs of autism were there the whole time and present in all my interactions with people and the world.

Some of my early indicators of autism include my early childhood play style, where I lined up toys and organized them a lot rather than engaging in "typical" imaginative play (American Psychiatric Association, 2013). When I chose to read books, I only read books from specific authors or series. One of my specialized interests was in a strategy computer game I played called Sid Meier's Civilization, from its inception in 1991 to its current version. No other computer game have I played to that extent. The repetitive behaviour playing Sid Meier's Civilization and neglect of other games could have given clues to indicate autism. I could not stand the sound of specific things, like the sound a vacuum makes or my sister eating her food. The smells of bacon and perfumes agitated me so much that I verbalized my frustration in unusual ways that often confused or upset my family members, instead of just asking for an accommodation for the sensitivity. I wore the same clothes over and over because it was agonizingly uncomfortable if I didn't. When I wore clothes or was in a situation that went beyond my comfort, my skin hurt, and I stimmed a lot more to compensate. I would also talk less and have a harder time focusing. I did not look at people in the face all the time, certainly not enough for them – my lack of eye contact was regularly mentioned.

I often experienced echolalia as a child, which is described as the immediate or delayed repetition of the speech of another person (Arciuli & Brock, 2014). Research suggests that echolalia may serve an important function for language development, although it is commonly referred to as a non-functional self-stimulatory behaviour (Kapp et al., 2019), or stimming, a core feature in the diagnosis of autism and often serves as a useful coping mechanism that helps soothe or communicate intense emotions or thoughts. Stimming, as it turns out, is not that "non-functional" after all, especially for autistic people. My echolalia as a child stood out to my mother mostly because I would repeat something that she said over and over in the car as we were driving to school in my elementary years, and it would easily annoy her. My mother did not understand how pleasing it was for me to repeat the phrases she was saying. My other repetitive behaviours were often redirected because they did not fit function or the social situation. I had selected topics I was interested in and liked to talk about them for a very long time. Some of my specialized interests included rocks and gemstones, trees, the Mafia, and the periodic table of elements. Still, when it came down to other people's interests, I was not so talkative and eager.

So how did I grow up without a diagnosis? I wish that I had not grown up without a diagnosis – part of me is still unsure how I got through it. However, another part of me has some ideas. In 1987, when I was taking kindergarten for the second time – because I "was not ready" the first time – there were few, if any early-intervention programmes and screening tools available for autism, especially in my community of fewer than 4,000 people. My teachers had a minimal understanding of the autism spectrum, and most of what they knew would have fallen under *classic autism*, another term for *autistic Disorder*, which is what autism was referred to as in the older editions of the *Diagnostic and Statistical Manual of Mental Disorders* (DSM) (American Psychiatric Association, 2000). There is no doubt that most of my teachers and family members considered me unique – I remember hearing that word used a lot when adults described my personality. I have kept a lot of report cards dating back to elementary school remarking on behaviours and characteristics that stood out from what was considered typical behaviour for children my age at the time. Still, no one knew enough about the autism spectrum to connect my traits, inside or outside school, to an autistic diagnosis.

Today, awareness of autism and diagnostic processes have changed, and autism is often reported in Canada as one of the most prevalent developmental disabilities (Statistics Canada, 2015). Better and earlier detection and diagnosis mean that autism will only become increasingly common and better known (Gillberg et al., 1991; Gillberg & Wing, 1999). This means better support for autistic children in ways that promote their learning and growth, both at school and within their community. If I had been diagnosed in my childhood, much of my life would have been different because of the access to support and services I would have received at an earlier age. I did not know at the time that my experience is a common one for girls and women on the spectrum.

Navigating the world as an autistic

As a young girl, growing up without a diagnosis put a lot of pressure and stress on me to figure things out for myself. The things I was trying to learn by myself were things that are extremely difficult for a child to accomplish alone. Essentially, I was navigating domestic life, educational life, and social life without a lot of the skills that came naturally to my family members, peer groups, and non-autistic people around me at any given time and in many different contexts. This frustrating experience did not change too much after my diagnosis because I still needed to learn the things that do not come naturally for me, although having a diagnosis of autism helps explain a lot of the reasons I struggle with these things when other people do not.

In addition to there being much confusion for others when these "natural skills" were absent, for myself, it felt like a race to catch up on something everyone else had already learned that I was constantly erring in. I struggled with trying to correct the "inconvenient" timing of things I said to others by choosing words that wouldn't make them feel uncomfortable, waiting appropriately for my turn, and constantly monitoring what I was sure was awkward body language. I was also slow at processing jokes and would often not understand jokes at all. I had to actually teach myself to become aware of all these things. These were not things I knew right off the bat, and these social tensions changed the ways I felt I could fit into social situations. In fact, all these struggles made fitting into any peer group difficult for me. To cope, I very quickly learned in my life as an autistic woman to mimic others and camouflage myself to fly under other people's radars. Women on the spectrum tend to copy non-autistic people's social behaviours more than autistic men; this is referred to as camouflaging (Attwood, 2007; Hull et al., 2017). For me, camouflaging is a series of instinctual unconscious behaviours that allow me to appear less autistic to others, behaviours that are typically picked up or learned through existing in a non-autistic world. For example, I am camouflaging when I unconsciously begin to act from a script while in a social setting to better fit in. autistic women also tend to be much more successful at masking, which is defined as disguising autistic traits as a method of coping (Bargiela et al., 2016). In my life, I define masking as the deliberate and specific actions that I take to hide my autistic traits. When I do things I would not normally do, like stuff my hands in the pockets of my sweatshirt so that others do not see that I am stimming with my hands. These two strategies – camouflaging and masking – are used in order to come across as neurotypical to others (Attwood, 2007; Wing, 1981). For example, in order to fit in, I engaged with my peer group by mimicking dialogue and body language that I had seen in TV shows and movies or had read about in books. Oftentimes, these attempts set me even further apart from my peers. As an autistic advocate and adult, there are times I am still masking and camouflaging. I do this because not all spaces are safe to "be autistic". There continues to be a stigma attached to many of the characteristics and traits of autism. Until society becomes more supportive of diverse minds such as those of autistic people, even people who have higher autistic identity will continue to camouflage and mask and to be affected by its many drawbacks. This is despite research suggesting that the more a person identifies as autistic, the less likely they are to camouflage (Cage & Troxell-Whitman, 2020). It is exhausting to always put effort into trying to hide my natural impulses and expressions, without apparent success.

Autistic individuals who are able to mask their disability's characteristics may more easily make friends, improve their social support, and perform better in job interviews. However, masking and camouflaging can impact mental health and exacerbate symptoms of anxiety and depression, with the most prominent consequence reported by autistic individuals being exhaustion (Hull et al., 2017). Many autistic people feel stress from the constant monitoring of themselves, others, and the environment, and this stress is felt during and after the interaction occurs (Hull et al., 2017, 2020). Autistic people who mask and camouflage also often report that their perception of themselves gets misconstrued: in particular, their sense of authenticity towards the outside world (Hull et al., 2020). Motivations for masking and camouflaging are the desire to fit in with others and avoid bullying or negative treatment and wanting to form connections with others who are not autistic. Forming relationships with people who are not autistic sometimes does not feel possible when autistic people present their authentic selves (Cage & Troxell-Whitman, 2019; Hull et al., 2020).

Up to 70% of autistic individuals have at least one other mental health condition during their lifetime, a much higher percentage than the general population, with common conditions being anxiety and depression (Buck et al., 2014). These can be perpetrated by autism being undetected in childhood (Aggarwal & Angus, 2015). Camouflaging and masking are usually quite mentally draining tasks for the autistic person to perform. Anxiety is common among autistic children and may worsen during adolescence and adulthood (White et al., 2009). Social anxiety in particular appears to occur at higher comorbidity rates, with approximately 20 to 57% of autistic youth exhibiting symptoms (Wood & Gadow, 2010). For me, the challenge of navigating social relationships caused me a lot of anxiety that was masked with meltdowns, shutdowns, and camouflaging. My meltdowns usually consisted of me crying or having outbursts of verbal negativity and occasionally wrecking my personal belongings, which I regretted terribly afterwards. Typically, the shutdowns followed my meltdowns. Shutdowns were when I displayed a lack of verbal expression, experienced physical and mental exhaustion, and had an inability to focus on the tasks at hand. Because of the camouflaging, no one in my family knew I had anxiety. I started experiencing headaches early in school, which have continued until now in situations where I am processing too much and trying very hard to camouflage or pass as neurotypical. I also had stomachaches during my school years, which I now recognize were attributed to anxiety. Anxiety is a tricky emotion, in that you might experience anxiety and not realize it because it comes out in many ways. Depression is similar in that way, and looking back, I can now recognize the times I may have been depressed in school and not have known it. As an undiagnosed autistic woman, school was a real challenge for me.

I did not experience my first panic attack until I was in grade 12, in English class. I was just beginning a book presentation in front of the class for which I had over-prepared. That is right: I had over-prepared for a presentation on *Alice in Wonderland*! I was supposed to give a brief presentation on the book and its symbolism in ten minutes or less, which I could not manage to do. In fact, I had prepared overhead sheets, an intro song ("White Rabbit" by Jefferson Airplane), and many pages on what I considered levels of symbolism in the book. It was unlikely I would do the presentation in ten minutes and more likely that I might need more than double that time. The fact that I had done all this and not thought twice about it had immediately set me apart from my peers. Being set apart from my peers was a common occurrence for me.

At some point during the introduction song, while I was preparing the overhead sheets, I started to feel disoriented. I was feeling light headed, and the room felt really bright. I could hear myself talking, but I did not feel like I was in control of the talking. I could just hear my voice. I was so disoriented, and all this really stressed me out – so I ran! I ran right out of school, off the property into the public library and hid there until the school day was over. Something else had also happened. I could not speak. I became non-verbal for an extended period of time after this experience. I probably should have told my parents about all of it – about the presentation, the running out of school, the not being able to speak for hours, and how the whole time I felt locked inside my head.

The reality was that I did not tell my parents about this for years because I did not understand the situation I was in at the time, and it was hard to talk to people about things I did not understand. I now know that my not being able to express emotions and articulate them to others was because of alexithymia, a condition where a person lacks terms to express emotions and moods (Lesser, 1981). A common trait people with alexithymia have is the inability to verbalize their emotions, either due to the inability to identify their own emotions or a confusion between emotional and bodily feelings (Poquérusse et al., 2018). Unsurprisingly, alexithymia often overlaps with autism, and it is estimated that 50% of autistic people experience alexithymia (Kinnaird et al., 2019; Poquérusse et al., 2018) like I did that day when I came home from my class presentation and wanted to explain what happened to my parents but couldn't.

My anxiety in that situation was real and visceral, but it still felt so out of the blue, even to me, because I had been masking other forms of it for years and not addressing it. This expression of anxiety caught me off guard and shook my confidence in public speaking for over two decades. This poem I wrote when I was 11 captures some of the feelings I experienced from elementary school:

After the Storm

15/09/1994
The storms may come
And limbs may break
Yet others bend
Beneath the weight
Of heavy rain
And windy breeze
A storm can mark
The strongest trees
Life sometimes deals
With us this way
In unseen trials
We meet each day
It's not how much our bodies break
Or how much they bend
It's our outlook in our own life
That helps our spirit mend.

Barriers such as alexithymia can prevent autistic people such as myself from having a voice in many situations. For meaningful and accessible inclusion in policy, different forms of expression, including autistic expression, must be seen as valid. To me, writing poems is empowering in expressing how I feel, but to someone else who is autistic, expressing themselves in videos, with pictures, or even virtually on social media may be how they best convey their message. If I could go back and have a redo of that day, I would have liked to see accommodations in place in the classroom so that I would not have experienced such dysregulation when it was my turn to give a presentation. For example, at that time in my life, I had no idea of the positive impact that stimming toys have in reducing stress and may have used one during the presentation. In addition, I may have worn clothing that was sensory friendly. I would have dimmed the lighting in the classroom, asked to present to fewer people if possible, and perhaps even have had a quiet room to go to before and after the presentation to decompress. A diagnosis would have helped me know sooner the accommodations that I need.

A diagnosis

I think if I had a diagnosis of autism back in my developmental years, I could have been more prepared for an event like this, and the fallout from it would have been a lot less impactful on my life and health. This, and reasons like this, are strong motivators for me to advocate every day.

You have probably heard that boys are four times more likely than girls to be autistic, and I think that this number could be even lower for autistic people who are gender non-conforming. This disparity in diagnosis is because when girls or other minoritized genders meet the current criteria for autism, they tend not to be diagnosed (Loomes et al., 2017). This is because the criteria for autism is based on preconceived behaviours studied predominantly among boys and men (Kirkovski et al., 2013; Kopp & Gillberg, 2011; Mattila et al., 2011), creating a diagnostic gender bias. The first studies on autism by Leo Kanner and Hans Asperger were male dominant, with diagnostic criteria being built around the male phenotype (Haney, 2016). Women have been observed seeking and receiving an autism diagnosis in adulthood to a greater extent than men (Happé et al., 2016) and, thus, are receiving services and support contingent on a diagnosis much later in life (Milner et al., 2019; Tint & Weiss, 2018).

Most autistic children grow up to be autistic adults and therefore require ongoing support into adulthood. Autism being less recognized in adulthood is a significant barrier when women and gender non-conforming people try to get a diagnosis later in life. The older an autistic person is, the more difficult it is for them to get a diagnosis (Pellicano et al., 2014), receive autism-related services (Lake et al., 2015), and gain access to mental health support (Croteau et al., 2019; Lake et al., 2015; McMorris et al., 2019). This causes a "lifetime of difficult transitions" (p. 636) because of fewer available resources and more restrictive service, which impacts overall inclusion and available funding for older autistic people (Milen & Nicholas, 2017). This is unfortunate because as people on the spectrum age, rates of psychiatric hospitalizations can also increase (Croteau et al., 2019).

Accessing services and supports are even harder for autistic people who do not live in cities (Hoogsteen & Woodgate, 2013; Tsiplova et al., 2019), as was my case growing up. Getting diagnosed so late in my life meant that it was difficult for my family members to see me as an autistic person because, for my whole life, they had just thought of me as someone else. They decided I was different, quirky, easily frustrated, and very rigid but could not recognize my autism. Even though my autistic traits can be plain as day, like many people, my family members understood only a pamphlet amount about autism, and the traits I have as an autistic person did not really show up on their pamphlet. If they had had more information at hand to understand the autism spectrum, I would have been accepted more than I am now. It is easier for some of my family to accept my misdiagnosis than the fact that I am autistic. That really hurts, and I find it uncomfortable.

Unfortunately, there is a vast array of misinformation online about autism that does not help with this gap in general knowledge. Parents tend to face the diagnosis process by searching for themselves what autism is (Gentles et al., 2020). They can feel dissatisfied with medical and associated professionals, uninformed, and that the process is both long and delayed (Wong et al., 2017), and so they tend to look for autism-related support before even receiving a diagnosis (Gentles et al., 2020; Wong et al., 2017). How parents explain autism might influence their choice of support for their children (Shyu et al., 2010), and sadly, many parents still think that environmental factors such as vaccines and diets cause autism (Millau et al., 2018). Parents of autistic people also report that information on complementary and alternative medicine and therapies is complex and confusing (Smith et al., 2020), and "fads" or treatments that have little to no empirical support, such as chelation therapy, can be extremely harmful for autistic people (McDonald et al., 2012). These situations leave me especially worried when thinking about how little we know about autistic girls and women (Milner et al., 2019).

A woman on the spectrum

There are a lot of ways to journey through life, but right now, there are a lot of girls and women on the autism spectrum who do not have the correct diagnosis but are instead under- and misdiagnosed, making their journey even more challenging. Often, we are diagnosed with a mental health condition instead of autism, which can have consequences that affect our well-being. In my case, prior to receiving my autism diagnosis, I was misdiagnosed with bipolar disorder and prescribed medication for this condition, which had no positive effect for me. Misdiagnosis is common for autism (Luciano & Keller, 2014), and because of the lack of information on autistic girls and women, we are especially at risk. I find that the mental health industry is not usually assessing neurological developmental abilities alongside mental health issues, and being pharmaceutically treated for something you do not have can have a tremendous impact on your health and happiness. Further, perhaps we instead go without a diagnosis because we fly under professionals' radar, not receiving any help at all, and are left without access to any support that would likely really help us thrive in the world.

Both camouflaging and masking contribute to the underdiagnosis of autistic girls and women (Milner et al., 2019). Our ability at better applying social skills and camouflaging in social situations means we tend to be less likely to be referred for treatment and are more prone to misdiagnosis (Haney, 2016). Because of this, women often report negative experiences with the diagnosis process but feel relieved once they receive the diagnosis (Milner et al., 2019). Early diagnosis is especially important because we report more difficulty in initiating and maintaining relationships. This missed diagnosis or late diagnosis leads to less access to an appropriate range of resources for autistic girls and women across our lifetime, therefore leading to a decreased quality of life (Aggarwal & Angus, 2015). We are also more prone to sexual abuse, and this introduces even more vulnerabilities that autistic women and girls experience (Bargiela et al., 2016; Cridland et al., 2014).

What would make a lot of difference in the way we address this problem is including more girls and women in studies about autism. Specifically, if those studies were about what the female phenotype of autism looks like in comparison to the male phenotype and then the results of those studies were incorporated into diagnostic material. Clinicians and diagnosticians need to become more aware of the differences in presentation of autism between females and males so that we are not going most of our lives without a diagnosis of autism and missing out on the value of what that diagnosis could mean to us and our families. Increased attention needs to be focused on the diagnostic process for autistic girls and women, and increased training would improve teachers' and clinicians' recognition of autism spectrum conditions which may lead to more timely identification, risk mitigation, and well-being promotion (Bargiela et al., 2016). This is why I advocate for us to get the diagnosis we need so that we have access to the information and resources that will help us succeed and experience better health in our lives.

Finally, let's not forget that there are more autistic people than people without autism who experience gender dysphoria (Dewinter et al., 2017; van Schalkwyk et al., 2015). There is a need for better support, understanding, and practices for LGBTQIA2S+ people who are autistic. Not only is the research and information on autistic girls and women minimal, but this knowledge gap exists despite the high rate of autistic people who are gender diverse (Hillier et al., 2019), further perpetuating the gaps in services and diagnoses the autism community faces.

Advocacy to realize the rights of autistics

Gender, age, mental health, and invisible disability are just some of the intersecting factors that define the disability rights hierarchy for autistic people, but these are the ones that most impacted me growing up. It is not surprising that these experiences have led me to become an advocate for disability and, more specifically, autistic rights. I am involved with a national autistic alliance in quite a major way, being on the board of directors, although that doesn't mean that the alliance is made up of only autistic people, as it's not. Getting autistic people and non-autistic people who want to be involved in autism advocacy together and aware of each other's roles and needs is crucial to the success of such an alliance. Sometimes this means autistic people have to refocus or reframe a lot of what is going on inside an alliance because the perspectives of actually autistic people are invaluable. This is the same in the neurodivergent community. The perspectives and lived experiences of the neurodivergent community cannot be taken for granted and must be considered openly by groups and organizations working alongside them. This looks like having neurodivergent minds giving their opinions on media statements, social media posts, and the general direction that an organization they're involved with wants to go. These small changes can shift the entire organization to a more inclusive and neurodivergent-centric approach. One area in which I feel a difference can be made is policy, and something that is lacking in this area is the representation of disabled people among decision-makers. Autism is an invisible disability, meaning that right from the start, the disability is a further disadvantage by not being easily discernible to others (Davis, 2005). When we are not "seen" as disabled, it is more difficult for us to secure the assistance or accommodation that we need (Davis, 2005). Autism is not only an invisible disability in terms of the behavioural definition; the "autistic voice" is made invisible within the current process of how knowledge about autistic people is produced, often excluding empowered autistic self-advocates from the process (Milton, 2012).

The importance of people with lived experience developing the policies and strategies that impact them cannot be overstated. Unfortunately, the autistic population is often considered not "capable" of making life decisions, leading to the creation of guides on shared decision making that may not even be necessary for people who have disabilities that are not developmental (Autistic Self Advocacy Network, 2016). In my experience, autistic people are often seen as unable to take on such power and responsibility as informing policy. Often, I would find myself the only autistic person in a room of non-autistic individuals talking about recommendations and policies that directly impact autistic lives, always leading me to ask myself whether I was being tokenized. When I see a small number of members of an underrepresented group (such as autistic people) being used in a supporting role rather than a prioritized one, I think that this is to give the appearance of equality being maintained, and I think of tokenism. Autism organizations and groups need to be consciously aware of the way they are utilizing autistic voices so that they are not just symbolically represented, potentially harming the autistic community that they serve. When I advocate and I am asked to present, speak, or otherwise represent an autistic voice, I am always thinking, *Is my representation authentic or symbolic?* As a woman who is autistic in a community that is still male dominated, my voice is often a priority to be heard. I like to give most organizations the benefit of the doubt that their desire for representation is authentic and not purely to prevent criticism and appear to treat these groups fairly. But in this industry, many autistic voices are wary of being tokenized. Autistic advocates have the potential to create lasting change in policy development as well as in society, as long as we are not being tokenized, and our voices have a true seat at the table.

One way of effecting change in this domain is moving away from seeing autism as a debilitating neurological condition and towards seeing it as a neurodivergent difference. The shift away from using person-first language is a way to effect that change. Person-first language was meant to be used universally across able-bodied and disabled people, but this ended up not being the case (Gernsbacher, 2017). For example, it is less likely a child without a disability is referred to with person-first language than a child with a disability (Gernsbacher, 2017). In my experience, most organizations and people want to acknowledge the person and not the disability that the person has, so this is why person-first language has been used in the past, with good intention. Person-first language continues to be used across the world in government documents, but advocates want this to change because of the obvious stigma that it can cause (Collier, 2012). Identity-first language offers the distinctions that person-first language cannot. You cannot be separated from your autism, as person-first language suggests that you can. You also cannot acknowledge all the worth and value of an autistic person if you are just being referred to as a "person with autism" rather than an "autistic person". While the nuance of "person with autism" is an unfortunate circumstance, I can be proud of being an "autistic person" and the traits that come with this disability. Being autistic is who I am and cannot be separated from me. Using identity-first language to refer to my disability recognizes that, affirms who I am, and validates my identity as a person who is autistic.

Advocating for autistic people and their families across Canada is something I can do pretty endlessly at this point in my life. It gives me real happiness and a sense of purpose. I am working with a visionary organization (the Canadian Autism Spectrum Disorder Alliance), which focuses on guiding the development of a national autism strategy (NAS) in Canada, a strategy we hope will ensure that all autistic Canadians have full and equal access to the resources they need, regardless of where they live. Personally, I want to make sure that autism is thought about at a national level so that the current disparities between provinces and territories as well as rural and urban communities, such as access to diagnosis, do not continue to inhibit the successes of the autistic community. There is another component of a national autism strategy I think is important, and it is the way that we acknowledge all we know about the autism spectrum and share that with others in our country so that people are not feeling ignorant of such a large community of Canadians. There are a lot of people out there who do not know enough about autism, and even less about autism as experienced by girls and women, but they want to learn. They need access to accurate and timely information so that they can relate to, employ, and otherwise engage with the autistic people in their lives without unintentionally harming them. A national autism strategy should improve upon the methods currently being used to communicate the autistic community's needs throughout the country. I also think we need as many voices from the autistic community as possible to build a healthy national autism strategy because, as we say, "Nothing about us without us" – a statement that the United Nations referred to in the elaboration of the Convention on the Rights of Persons with Disabilities (United Nations, 2004).

I have high hopes that a national autism strategy will better enable Canada to bridge the aforementioned gaps and hierarchy of rights described. Sharing information, such as with a public national acceptance campaign, would allow for the normalization of autistic traits like echolalia and stimming. This may help create a better sense of inclusion among autistic individuals, especially girls and women, who may feel less inclined to mask or camouflage their autistic traits, hopefully reducing their risks of mental health challenges. Additionally, a national autism strategy could include providing educational materials and tools for healthcare providers in Canada, which would be helpful in reducing delays in autism diagnosis. Earlier recognition and diagnosis of autism would allow for a better quality of life overall, as individuals would be able to access the resources they need at an earlier point in life, plus it would allow professionals to be knowledgeable of conditions that are often concurrent with autism, such as anxiety, depression, and alexithymia (Buck et al., 2014; Poquérusse et al., 2018; White et al., 2009). Earlier recognition of mental health conditions would lead to earlier intervention, increased quality of life, and a reduced burden on hospitals in Canada, which currently have high rates of psychiatric hospitalizations of its autistic population (Croteau et al., 2019; Office of the Ombudsman of Ontario, 2019). As mentioned previously, there is a diagnostic gender bias for autism (Loomes et al., 2017), and so the current information on how autistic people use services and what services they need may not reflect those of the entire autistic population.

National strategies can help researchers across a nation work together and stay informed on each other's work, which would help advance studies about autism in female and LGBTQIA2S+ populations, further improving the diagnostic and service system for autism. Advancing our understanding of autism as well as training teachers and clinicians would improve the recognition of autism, mitigating risks and promoting the well-being of the female autistic population (Bargiela et al., 2016). Personally, an earlier diagnosis would have better prepared me for the obstacles in my life, as I would have had a better understanding of my behaviours and personal feelings.[4]

Conclusion

I did not always know I was autistic. When I found out I was autistic, my life changed. I needed help from some people in areas I wanted to grow in and to be told about autism, especially about the experiences of people who received their diagnosis later in life and who are women, like me. I eventually found my true diagnosis, and I am a much, much healthier person for it. On my life's journey, you could say a fork in the road formed when I found out I was autistic. A new path opened up that gave an understanding of autism and how it was connected with my own personal experiences.

Through facing the barriers that misdiagnosis, gender, and an invisible disability have placed in my life, I have emerged a stronger advocate today. I have also had to face more struggles than some of my autistic peers have, as there is a hierarchy in this disability. The hierarchy of gender bias exists in the autistic world, as it does outside it, and many women struggle to be seen and heard in the same way that men are. Some women need to work harder to be taken seriously in their advocacy, to feel heard in their work, or to gain meaningful employment; there exist all the needs that come with being autistic, as well as all the challenges of being a woman in a male-centric world (Milner et al., 2019). This has left some trauma and hurt in my life that was unnecessary. One way to make sure that gender bias is addressed in autism advocacy is to include more experiences of other genders who are autistic in the media we are exposed to and in employment opportunities and to speak up when this is not being done. Through more awareness and acceptance and putting policy into practice, we can hope to dismantle both the obvious and the subtle hierarchies that currently exist and protect other autistic people from having similar negative experiences.

I am not someone who does not look back, I reflect on my life and my journey often. But when I turn around to look back and then keep moving forward, I know I am in the right shoes, on the right path, going in the right direction. There are a lot of people out there who are still trying to find their path, and I want to help them if I can.

Acknowledgements

I would like to acknowledge the psychologists and people who specialize in the field of autism who were there to give me guidance and who were oftentimes my mentors: Cayley Burton, Jonathan Lai, Margaret Whelan, and Mackenzie Salt, whose attention to detail made these pages what they are today. I would also like to thank the friends I have who stayed by me throughout my assessment and diagnosis and remain my friends today. We have an even stronger bond now than ever before.

Notes

1 Asperger's syndrome (AS) was previously included in the *Diagnostic and Statistical Manual* (DSM) as a pervasive development disorder (PDD) separate from Autistic disorder (American Psychiatric Association, 2000). AS, Autistic disorder, and other PDDs have been removed from the DSM in its fifth edition and replaced with autism spectrum disorder (American Psychiatric Association, 2013).

2 With respect to the Autistic population, this chapter was written using a disability interpretive lens, characterized by viewing individual differences as ways of being rather than as deficits, which is usually reflected in the language used by the authors (Creswell, 2013). Where possible, I used identity-first language. This may appear unusual; however, the diagnosis of autism is often liberating to Autistic people (Dunn & Andrews, 2015; Marshall et al., 2017; Powell & Acker, 2016) and taking claim of one's disability has long been argued to be empowering in disability studies (e.g., Chalk et al., 2020; Shakespeare, 1996; Singh & Chopra, 2021).

3 The chapter uses "girls and women" to refer to people who identify as female and uses "female" in instances where it highlights other authors' writing that refers to biological sex.
4 We recognize that the issue of diagnosis is not uncomplicated. The experience may not be the same for all Autistic people and may even be harmful in certain situations: for instance, in the context of misdiagnosis, as the author Rebekah Kintzinger demonstrates in the introduction to this chapter.

References

Aggarwal, S., & Angus, B. (2015). Misdiagnosis versus missed diagnosis: diagnosing autism spectrum disorder in adolescents. *Australasian Psychiatry*, *23*(2), 120–123. https://doi.org/10.1177/1039856214568214

American Psychiatric Association. (2000). *Diagnostic and statistical manual of mental disorders* (Fourth edition). American Psychiatric Association.

American Psychiatric Association. (2013). Neurodevelopmental disorders. In *Diagnostic and statistical manual of mental disorders* (Fifth edition, vol. 1). https://doi.org/10.1176/appi.books.9780890425596.dsm01

Arciuli, J., & Brock, J. (2014). *Communication in autism*. John Benjamins Publishing Company.

Attwood, T. (2007). *The complete guide to Asperger's syndrome*. Jessica Kingsley Publishers. http://catdir.loc.gov/catdir/toc/ecip0616/2006020065.html

Autistic Self Advocacy Network. (2016). The right to make choices: international laws and decision-making by people with disabilities. https://autisticadvocacy.org/wp-content/uploads/2016/02/Easy-Read-OSF-For-Families-v3.pdf

Bargiela, S., Steward, R., & Mandy, W. (2016). The experiences of late-diagnosed women with autism spectrum conditions: an investigation of the female autism phenotype. *Journal of Autism and Developmental Disorders*, *46*(10), 3281–3294. https://doi.org/10.1007/s10803-016-2872-8

Buck, T. R., Viskochil, J., Farley, M., Coon, H., McMahon, W. M., Morgan, J., & Bilder, D. A. (2014). Psychiatric comorbidity and medication use in adults with autism spectrum disorder. *Journal of Autism and Developmental Disorders*, *44*(12), 3063–3071. https://doi.org/10.1007/s10803-014-2170-2

Cage, E., & Troxell-Whitman, Z. (2019). Understanding the reasons, contexts and costs of camouflaging for autistic adults. *Journal of Autism and Developmental Disorders*, *49*(5), 1899–1911. https://doi.org/10.1007/s10803-018-03878-x

Cage, E., & Troxell-Whitman, Z. (2020). Understanding the relationships between autistic identity, disclosure, and camouflaging. *Autism in Adulthood*, *2*(4), 334–338. https://doi.org/10.1089/aut.2020.0016

Chalk, H. M., Barlett, C. P., & Barlett, N. D. (2020). Disability self-identification and well-being in emerging adults. *Emerging Adulthood*, *8*(4), 306–316. https://doi.org/10.1177/2167696818812604

Collier, R. (2012). Person-first language: noble intent but to what effect? *Canadian Medical Association Journal*, *184*(18), 1977–1978. https://doi.org/10.1503/cmaj.109-4319

Creswell, J. W. (2013). *Qualitative inquiry and research design* (Third edition). SAGE.

Cridland, E. K., Jones, S. C., Caputi, P., & Magee, C. A. (2014). Being a girl in a boys' world: Investigating the experiences of girls with autism spectrum disorders during adolescence. *Journal of Autism and Developmental Disorders*, *44*(6), 1261–1274. https://doi.org/10.1007/s10803-013-1985-6

Croteau, C., Mottron, L., Dorais, M., Tarride, J.-E., & Perreault, S. (2019). Use, costs, and predictors of psychiatric healthcare services following an autism spectrum diagnosis: population-based cohort study. *Autism*, *23*(8), 2020–2030. https://doi.org/10.1177/1362361319840229

Davis, N. A. (2005). Invisible disability. *Ethics, 116*(1), 153–213. https://doi.org/10.1086/453151.

Dewinter, J., De Graaf, H., & Begeer, S. (2017). Sexual orientation, gender identity, and romantic relationships in adolescents and adults with autism spectrum disorder. *Journal of Autism and Developmental Disorders, 47*(9), 2927–2934. https://doi.org/10.1007/s10803-017-3199-9

Dunn, D. S., & Andrews, E. E. (2015). Person-first and identity-first language: developing psychologists' cultural competence using disability language. *American Psychologist, 70*(3), 255. https://doi.org/10.1037/a0038636

Gentles, S. J., Nicholas, D. B., Jack, S. M., McKibbon, K. A., & Szatmari, P. (2020). Coming to understand the child has autism: a process illustrating parents' evolving readiness for engaging in care. *Autism, 24*(2), 470–483. https://doi.org/10.1177/1362361319874647

Gernsbacher, M. A. (2017). Editorial perspective: The use of person-first language in scholarly writing may accentuate stigma. *Journal of Child Psychology and Psychiatry, and Allied Disciplines, 58*(7), 859–861. https://doi.org/10.1111/jcpp.12706

Gillberg, C., Steffenburg, S., & Schaumann, H. (1991). Is autism more common now than ten years ago? *The British Journal of Psychiatry, 158*(3), 403–409. http://dx.doi.org.proxy3.library.mcgill.ca/10.1192/bjp.158.3.403

Gillberg, C., & Wing, L. (1999). Autism: Not an extremely rare disorder. *Acta Psychiatrica Scandinavica, 99*(6), 399–406. https://doi.org/10.1111/j.1600-0447.1999.tb00984.x

Haney, J. L. (2016). Autism, females, and the DSM-5: Gender bias in autism diagnosis. *Social Work in Mental Health, 14*(4), 396–407. https://doi.org/10.1080/15332985.2015.1031858

Happé, F. G., Mansour, H., Barrett, P., Brown, T., Abbott, P., & Charlton, R. A. (2016). Demographic and cognitive profile of individuals seeking a diagnosis of Autism Spectrum Disorder in adulthood. *Journal of Autism and Developmental Disorders, 46*(11), 3469–3480. https://doi.org/10.1007/s10803-016-2886-2

Hillier, A., Gallop, N., Mendes, E., Tellez, D., Buckingham, A., Nizami, A., & O'Toole, D. (2019). LGBTQ + and autism spectrum disorder: experiences and challenges. *International Journal of Transgender Health, 21*(1), 98–110. https://doi.org/10.1080/15532739.2019.1594484

Hoogsteen, L., & Woodgate, R. L. (2013). Embracing autism in Canadian rural communities. *Australian Journal of Rural Health, 21*(3), 178–182. https://doi.org/10.1111/ajr.12030

Hull, L., Petrides, K. V., Allison, C., Smith, P., Baron-Cohen, S., Lai, M.-C., & Mandy, W. (2017). "Putting on My Best Normal": Social camouflaging in adults with autism spectrum conditions. *Journal of Autism and Developmental Disorders, 47*(8), 2519–2534. https://doi.org/10.1007/s10803-017-3166-5

Hull, L., Petrides, K. V., & Mandy, W. (2020). The female autism phenotype and camouflaging: a narrative review. *Review Journal of Autism and Developmental Disorders, 7*, 306–317. https://doi.org/10.1007/s40489-020-00197-9

Kapp, S. K., Steward, R., Crane, L., Elliott, D., Elphick, C., Pellicano, E., & Russell, G. (2019). 'People should be allowed to do what they like': Autistic adults' views and experiences of stimming. *Autism, 23*(7), 1782–1792. https://doi.org/10.1177/1362361319829628

Kinnaird, E., Stewart, C., & Tchanturia, K. (2019). Investigating alexithymia in autism: A systematic review and meta-analysis. *European Psychiatry, 55*, 80–89. https://doi.org/10.1016/j.eurpsy.2018.09.004

Kirkovski, M., Enticott, P. G., & Fitzgerald, P. B. (2013). A review of the role of female gender in autism spectrum disorders. *Journal of Autism and Developmental Disorders, 43*(11), 2584–2603. https://doi.org/10.1007/s10803-013-1811-1

Kopp, S., & Gillberg, C. (2011). The Autism Spectrum Screening Questionnaire (ASSQ)-Revised Extended Version (ASSQ-REV): an instrument for better capturing the autism phenotype in girls? A preliminary study involving 191 clinical cases and community controls. *Research in Developmental Disabilities*, *32*(6), 2875–2888. https://doi.org/10.1016/j.ridd.2011.05.017

Lake, J. K., Vogan, V., Sawyer, A., Weiss, J. A., & Lunsky, Y. (2015). Psychotropic medication use among adolescents and young adults with an autism spectrum disorder: Parent views about medication use and healthcare services. *Journal of Child and Adolescent Psychopharmacology*, *25*(3), 260–268. https://doi.org/10.1089/cap.2014.0106

Lesser, I. M. (1981). A review of alexithymia concept. *Psychosomatic Medicine, 43*(6), 531–543. https://doi: 10.1097/00006842-198112000-00009

Loomes, R., Hull, L., & Mandy, W. P. L. (2017). What is the male-to-female ratio in autism spectrum disorder? A systematic review and meta-analysis. *Journal of the American Academy of Child & Adolescent Psychiatry*, *56*(6), 466–474. https://doi.org/10.1016/j.jaac.2017.03.013

Luciano, C., & Keller, R. (2014). Misdiagnosis of high function autism spectrum disorders in adults: An Italian case series. *Autism-Open Access*, *4*(131), 2. https://doi.org/10.4172/2165-7890.1000131

Marshall, N., Wilton, F., & Weinroth, S. (2017). It is our turn! Autistic young people inform praxis and policy. *Relational Child and Youth Care Practice*, *30*(3), 36–50.

Mattila, M.-L., Kielinen, M., Linna, S.-L., Jussila, K., Ebeling, H., Bloigu, R., Joseph, R. M., & Moilanen, I. (2011). Autism Spectrum Disorders according to DSM-IV-TR and comparison with DSM-5 draft criteria: an epidemiological study. *Journal of the American Academy of Child & Adolescent Psychiatry*, *50*(6), 583–592. e11. https://doi.org/10.1016/j.jaac.2011.04.001

McDonald, M. E., Pace, D., Blue, E., & Schwartz, D. (2012). Critical issues in causation and treatment of autism: why fads continue to flourish. *Child & Family Behavior Therapy*, *34*(4), 290–304. https://doi.org/10.1080/07317107.2012.732849

McMorris, C. A., Baraskewich, J., Ames, M. A., Shaikh, K. T., Ncube, B. L., & Bebko, J. M. (2019). Mental health issues in post-secondary students with autism spectrum disorder: experiences in accessing services. *International Journal of Mental Health and Addiction*, *17*(3), 585–595. https://doi.org/10.1007/s11469-018-9988-3

Milen, M., & Nicholas, D. B. (2017). Examining transitions from youth to adult services for young persons with autism. *Social Work in Health Care*, *56*(7), 636–648. https://doi.org/10.1080/00981389.2017.1318800

Millau, M., Rivard, M., & Mello, C. (2018). Immigrant families' perception of the causes, first manifestations, and treatment of Autism Spectrum Disorder. *Journal of Child and Family Studies*, *27*(11), 3468–3481. https://doi.org/10.1007/s10826-018-1180-7

Milner, V., McIntosh, H., Colvert, E., & Happé, F. (2019). A qualitative exploration of the female experience of autism spectrum disorder (ASD). *Journal of Autism and Developmental Disorders*, *49*, 2389–2402. https://doi.org/10.1007/s10803-019-03906-4

Milton, D. E. M. (2012). On the ontological status of autism: the 'double empathy problem.' *Disability & Society*, *27*(6), 883–887. https://doi.org/10.1080/09687599.2012.710008

Office of the Ombudsman of Ontario. (2019). 2018–2019 Annual report. https://www.ombudsman.on.ca/Media/ombudsman/ombudsman/resources/Annual%20Reprts/2018-19AR-EN-accessible.pdf

Pellicano, E., Dinsmore, A., & Charman, T. (2014). What should autism research focus upon? Community views and priorities from the United Kingdom. *Autism*, *18*(7), 756–770. https://doi.org/10.1177/1362361314529627

Poquérusse, J., Pastore, L., Dellantonio, S., & Esposito, G. (2018). Alexithymia and autism spectrum disorder: a complex relationship. *Frontiers in Psychology*, *9*. https://doi.org/10.3389/fpsyg.2018.01196

Powell, T., & Acker, L. (2016). Adults' experience of an Asperger syndrome diagnosis: analysis of its emotional meaning and effect on participants' lives. *Focus on Autism and Other Developmental Disabilities*, *31*(1), 72–80. https://doi.org/10.1177/1088357615588516

Shakespeare, T. (1996). Disability, identity and difference. In C. Barnes & G. Mercer (Eds.), *Exploring the divide* (pp. 94–113). The Disability Press.

Shyu, Y.-I. L., Tsai, J.-L., & Tsai, W.-C. (2010). Explaining and selecting treatments for autism: parental explanatory models in Taiwan. *Journal of Autism and Developmental Disorders*, *40*(11), 1323–1331. https://doi.org/10.1007/s10803-010-0991-1

Singh, R., & Chopra, G. (2021). Evolution from negative identity to affirmation of 'disability identity': life story of a woman with Spina Bifida in India. *Disability, CBR & Inclusive Development*, *32*(1), 81–100. https://doi.org/10.47985/dcidj.409

Smith, C. A., Parton, C., King, M., & Gallego, G. (2020). Parents' experiences of information-seeking and decision-making regarding complementary medicine for children with autism spectrum disorder: a qualitative study. *BMC Complementary Medicine and Therapies*, *20*(4), 1–13. https://doi.org/10.1186/s12906-019-2805-0

Statistics Canada. (2015, December 3). Developmental disabilities among Canadians aged 15 years and older, 2012. *The Daily*. https://www150.statcan.gc.ca/n1/daily-quotidien/151203/dq151203b-eng.htm

Tint, A. & Weiss, J.A. (2018). A qualitative study of the service experiences of women with autism spectrum disorder. *Autism*, *22*(8), 928–937. https://doi.org/10.1177/1362361317702561

Tsiplova, K., Ungar, W. J., Flanagan, H. E., den Otter, J., Waddell, C., Murray, P., D'Entremont, B., Léger, N., Garon, N., Bryson, S., & Smith, I. M. (2019). Types of services and costs of programs for preschoolers with autism spectrum disorder across sectors: a comparison of two Canadian provinces. *Journal of Autism and Developmental Disorders*, *49*(6), 2492–2508. https://doi.org/10.1007/s10803-019-03993-3

United Nations. (2004). *"Nothing about us without us": international day of disabled persons*. International Day of Disabled Persons. https://www.un.org/esa/socdev/enable/iddp2004.htm

van Schalkwyk, G. I., Klingensmith, K., & Volkmar, F. R. (2015). Gender identity and autism spectrum disorders. *The Yale Journal of Biology and Medicine*, *88*(1), 81–83.

White, S. W., Oswald, D., Ollendick, T., & Scahill, L. (2009). Anxiety in children and adolescents with autism spectrum disorders. *Clinical Psychology Review*, *29*(3), 216–229. https://doi.org/10.1016/j.cpr.2009.01.003

Wing, L. (1981). Sex ratios in early childhood autism and related conditions. *Psychiatry Research*, *5*(2), 129–137. https://doi.org/10.1016/0165-1781(81)90043-3

Wong, V., Yu, Y., Keyes, M. L., & McGrew, J. H. (2017). Pre-diagnostic and diagnostic stages of autism spectrum disorder: a parent perspective. *Child Care in Practice*, *23*(2), 195–217. https://doi.org/10.1080/13575279.2016.1199537

Wood, J. J., & Gadow, K. D. (2010). Exploring the nature and function of anxiety in youth with autism spectrum disorders. *Clinical Psychology: Science and Practice*, *17*(4), 281–292. https://doi.org/10.1111/j.1468-2850.2010.01220.x

5

"TO TREMBLE, ELSE BREAK"

Dismantling normative hierarchies of chronic Lyme

Pavithra Suresh

Pre-diagnosis

I was described as sensitive for as long as I can remember: sensitive to food, to texture, to sound. Bright lights or strong odors would set off debilitating headaches. My *pati* would say to cover my head when it was raining, for I was sickly, claiming that the moment a raindrop touched my head, I would fall ill. As a child, I would cry in pain from what my doctor insisted were growing pains despite swollen, bruised joints that creaked as I moved.

When I wasn't in bed, I was outside. The mild North Carolina climate meant I could be found outdoors no matter the season, with the sun out past eight p.m. on summer evenings. I traipsed through our forested backyard, swinging on saplings, studying earthworms, and catching fireflies right up until bedtime. My well-intentioned Tamil mother would chide me for letting my golden skin deepen to a rich copper tone after hours spent in the sun. The contradiction of my childhood doesn't escape me. It barely escaped any of us: how could a child spend hours outdoors and barefoot, playing in piles of leaves and shallow streams, only to spend the next week in bed? It was not until my young adulthood that we began to piece together the story of my mysteriously sickly nature.

Every summer, I would be horrified to find at least one or two deer ticks attached to my flesh. We would recoil in horror as my older sister or a childhood friend would pluck them out, flicking the tiny things to the ground. *Eww*. Even in the 2000s, it was commonplace to brush off tick bites, at least in North Carolina. One particularly gnarly bite and an *ABC World News* report on Lyme disease led my mother to take me to a pediatrician, with a deer tick–containing Ziploc bag in hand. "Don't worry," my pediatrician consoled her. "We don't have Lyme around here – plus, she doesn't have a bulls-eye rash.

DOI: 10.4324/9781003410089-7

I know I had dozens of tick bites, only in hindsight realizing that each represented the weakening of my immune system little by little. However, I graduated from sickly to sick quickly. Upon reflection, I can identify the tipping point as a beautiful, crisp fall day in 2002 – the kind of day we would enjoy late into October in North Carolina. We had gone to the state fair with family friends, all of us children rolling in hay and playing in petting zoo pens. I had convinced my parents to let me stay the night at my childhood friend's house close to the fairgrounds. We played in piles of leaves all evening. I could feel myself covered in insect bites, some of them getting inflamed and blotchy after I showered that evening. Exhausted from the day's activities, we quickly fell asleep – only for me to awaken in what felt like a paralysis at five a.m. I cried out, unable to move, an achy pain radiating through my body. My mother came to pick me up. "I can't move!" I wailed. She consoled me, telling me I had overexerted myself. "There's lots of pollen out. It's probably allergies." Getting out of bed and into the car was the worst pain I had ever experienced. I had always been sick, but not like this.

When I trace the timeline of my illness, I know things seemed to get worse for me around that time. At some point during Operation Iraqi Freedom, I developed debilitating anxiety and agoraphobia. I would cry at the prospect of attending school. Chalked up to separation anxiety – and possibly a touch of childhood post-trauma from 9/11 – my parents did what they thought was best and taught me to meditate. I learned to ask God to relieve my suffering as I felt my skin on fire with anxiety and panicky impulses to harm myself.

I find it difficult to remember much of my life before age 20. I do not discount the ways in which the fugue state of my childhood limited my capacity to understand what was going on around me. I struggled academically. I found myself ill with every seasonal flu and virus. I missed weeks of school. I was diagnosed with a rare gut infection. I developed pernicious anemia, unable to maintain normal iron levels. My body remained emaciated and childlike, not reaching puberty until 15 and only hitting 100 pounds at 17. My stiff joints were deemed clinically arthritic by my teen years, with my knees and ankles swelling painfully with every cold front. I was told my allergies were mild, but I was sensitive. I was told my fevers were mild, but I was sensitive. I was told my pain was mild, but I was sensitive. I was told most kids were resilient to childhood anxiety, but I was sensitive.

It wasn't until March 2015 that a specialist asked me, masking her tone but with worry in her eyes, "You haven't *ever* been tested for Lyme disease?"

Diagnosis

After a month of comprehensive testing, I received a diagnosis of "late-disseminated Lyme disease" – a big phrase I had almost no schema for interpreting. While my diagnosis did not meet criteria set forth by the notoriously imprecise enzyme-linked immunosorbent assay (ELISA, or Western blot) testing recommended by the CDC, my medical history, clinical presentation, and results of more detailed experimental testing suggested I was indeed sick with Lyme. Lyme disease is caused by pernicious Borrelia burgdorferi spirochete bacteria – deemed "The Great Imitator" in a xeroxed copy of a 1990s *New York Times* article given to me by my doctor due to its nefarious ability to mimic the symptoms of countless other disorders. With the Lyme bacterial infection often comes a host of other common co-infections, including anaplasma, bartonella, Ehrlichia, and babesia. I learned I tested positive babesiosis, a life-threatening blood infection similar to malaria but caused by the *Babesia microti* protozoa. I learned that due to the *Babesia* infection, I had developed hemolytic anemia – a condition in which red blood cells are depleted faster than they can be produced. My hours-long appointment ended with my Lyme specialist outlining her recommended treatment protocol, which included a cocktail of antibiotics, immune-supporting supplements, and an antidepressant for the neurological symptoms. She cautioned me that I had likely had these infections for over a decade, so the goal of treatment was to stabilize my severe immune deficiency. I would likely always live with this disease but could hopefully strengthen my immune system enough to render the infections dormant. I left the appointment with a small packet of prescriptions in hand, weeping as I drove away with relief from finally receiving a diagnosis, fear of this new normal, and grief for the person I was before I knew the extent of my illness.

In her memoir *Sick*, author Porochista Khakpour (2018) reflects on her experience with late-stage Lyme, particularly the difficulty of getting diagnosed. She writes, "In the end, every Lyme patient has some psychiatric diagnosis too, if anything because of the hell it takes to getting a diagnosis" (p. 166). I was by no means an exception. I had been on unstable ground psychologically for some time now, in part due to the neurological symptoms associated with the disease, but diagnosis unleashed a new understanding of the extent to which I had internalized the belief that my illness was my fault. Khakpour notes that the hardest parts of Lyme were not always the pain or symptoms, but loneliness: "How could I recognize myself if no one else could?" (p. 167). At the time of my diagnosis, I was midway through my junior year at a tiny women's college in Virginia. Beginning my medication protocol unleashed the full extent of my symptoms, rendering me unable to leave my bed most days. I had been a precocious overachiever, and now, suddenly, I could not perform – and I felt the impact. The group of ambitious women I was used to having around began to thin. I heard whispers in the dining hall and occasionally from a gossipy peer about my flakiness, about how I was "faking it," about how someone's sister once had Lyme and got better right away so what was wrong with me?

In the famously complex opening line of her essay "On Being Ill," Virginia Woolf (1930) muses that despite the ubiquity of illness in human life, we somehow cast it out as something discrete from other human experiences. Almost a century later, and in the midst of a global pandemic, illness is still cast out of public view and stigmatized. My experience of Lyme forced me to reckon with overwhelming loss: loss of agency to live unencumbered by cocktails of prescriptions, dietary restrictions, and planning daily life around rest; loss of my trustworthiness, both in how others perceived me and in how I perceived myself; loss of bodily autonomy, losing control of my body to doctors' orders, to medical protocols, and to itself. In her last published work prior to succumbing to complications of rheumatoid arthritis at the age of 82, Adrienne Rich explored the turbulence to be expected with life, the things we drop to steady ourselves: "The plane's/supposed to shudder, shoulder on/like this./It's built to do that./You're designed to tremble too./Else break" (2011, p. 24). Mostly bedridden, I lost track of time and turbulence, immersed in online spaces for people with Lyme, endlessly scrolling through forums and community spaces. Soon, I started to observe that Lyme patients all seemed to resemble me – not only in symptoms, but in positionality as thin, middle-class women; however, they were almost all white. Quickly, my lament of "Why me?" turned into an intellectual "*How* me?" The science is clear: Lyme is an underdiagnosed epidemic. What particularities did I possess that led me to diagnosis and treatment? More interesting to me was "Why did others go undiagnosed and untreated?"

The politics of diagnosing Lyme

Through an attempt to explore the social construction of Lyme disease, Dr. Robert A. Aronawitz (1991) incidentally also exposes the social construction of medical diagnostics. When discussing Lyme diagnostics, he notes that "[d] octors often bemoan the faddishness of Lyme Disease and the growing number of patients who aggressively pursue the diagnosis" while "[p]atients with chronic Lyme Disease are angered by the ambivalent way they are treated by doctors" (p. 107). While all parties involved seek out a "technological fix for the dilemma of diagnosis," Aronawitz suggests that the "textbook prototypes" of Lyme disease often do not "match the particular clinical encounter" of it (p. 107). Aronawitz laments that "medicine fixes on its canonical descriptions as the rationale for the doctor-patient encounter" (p. 107), essentially relying on the social negotiation of Lyme symptoms and clinical presentation to inform how the disease is treated in the future. Challenges with diagnosis vary from the inconsistent accuracy of the widely used Western blot test to many medical professionals being unfamiliar with the disease pathology and thus unable to effectively diagnosis it.

Medical student and practitioner LaShyra Nolen (2020) drew attention to the politics of Lyme disease in her opinion piece for the *New England Journal of Medicine* entitled "How Medical Education Is Missing the Bull's-eye." Through the article, Nolen traces how clinical diagnosis of Lyme disease relies on the appearance of the hallmark *Erythema migrans* bulls-eye rash; however, as is standard in medical education, depictions of the rash appear almost always on white skin. Nolen continues: "The current standardized, homogeneous representation of white males in medical education is exclusionary and puts patients of color and women at risk for adverse health outcomes" (p. 2491). She argues that "these exclusionary practices are pervasive throughout medicine and are indicative of a larger problem: the systemic exclusion of these patients from clinical trials, like their underrepresentation in anatomy courses, affects the quality of care we provide to these populations" (p. 2491). Until visiting this article recently, I never believed I had a bulls-eye rash from a lifetime of tick bites; however, my heart sank upon seeing the image of *Erythema migrans* on a deep-complexioned patient Nolen had included, as I recognized the mark from my own childhood body.

Aside from the racialized social construction of Lyme disease, the legacy of its treatment is heavily informed by the socio-economic forces that intersect with its diagnosis and treatment. When I was diagnosed with Lyme disease, the CDC recommendation for treatment was a two-week course of doxycycline. Upon completing the course, my symptoms continued to manifest; at the time, the prevailing medical perspective was that there was no such thing as "chronic Lyme disease," despite clinical studies suggesting the legitimacy of long-term symptoms for many Lyme disease patients. Recent changes to CDC standards of Lyme disease diagnostics have led to the introduction of a new diagnostic syndrome called post-treatment Lyme disease syndrome (PTLDS). Still, treatment of patients with this pathology continues to be hotly debated, with many doctors who choose to continue to treat symptomatic patients being characterized as pseudoscientific, "alternative," or irresponsible. On the other hand, doctors who refuse treatment to symptomatic patients are perceived as ignorant and uninformed about the disease. The challenge of living with Lyme disease long term manifests in material ways at the nexus of this debate. Treating my disease is deemed "experimental" by insurance companies, meaning the costs of care are astronomical. Going without treatment for many means an increasing loss of functionality, with many symptomatic individuals self-reporting unemployment or underemployment due to the debilitating effects of the disease. Getting a diagnosis is itself challenging, with epidemiologists estimating Lyme disease is underdiagnosed, considering the increasing population of Lyme-containing ticks throughout the Northern Hemisphere due to habitat loss and climate change. Even once a patient receives a diagnosis, treatment becomes cost prohibitive should symptoms continue following the two-week course of antibiotics, leaving many symptomatic people from low-wealth communities untreated and debilitated by the persistent infection.

My diagnosis and treatment of what the CDC calls PTLDS – what I have come to call late-disseminated Lyme disease – is a reflection of both the privileges and the oppressions that find a home in my body and positionality. Despite having what I now believe to have been *Erythema migrans*, the assumption of whiteness in medical education and epistemologies – as well as existing regulation in North Carolina surrounding diagnosing Lyme – led doctors to other diagnoses of the marks on my brown skin: allergies, eczema, spider bites. In not receiving the requisite antibiotic course upon first infection, I spent my childhood suffering silently, believing it was all in my head. Yet my Tamil American upbringing was one of privilege: I grew up caste privileged and upper middle class. I was sick, but my family could afford regular trips to the doctor. I struggled in school, but my family could afford an after-school tutor.

The extra support I received paid directly into my eventual diagnosis. It was at my private women's college – a college I could have never ended up at without those specific privileges – that I learned about Lyme disease and began to suspect I may have been infected. Thanks to the 2008 passage of the Affordable Care Act, I was able to afford initial doctor's appointments and prescriptions though coverage under my parents' insurance in my early 20s. The cultural value of generational closeness – and the structural casteism that enabled my family to generate wealth – meant my family was able to support me financially while I sought treatment. I spent two summers living at home to recover from its brutal side effects. While my initial diagnosis was delayed in part because of the color of my skin and my state of birth, my eventual treatment is a testament to the privileges of my positionality.

Lyme as disability, deviance, destruction

In exploring the privilege of diagnosis and treatment of Lyme, it is not my intention to diminish the difficult physical, mental, and spiritual effects of living with a "controversial" diagnosis. Epidemiologists and social scientists alike have sought to explore the different interpretations of disease from the perspective of diagnostics; however, little attention is paid to the people living with the incapacitating effects of Lyme, PTLDS, and co-infections, particularly those who do not have the privilege or legitimation of diagnosis and treatment. It proves necessary to theorize the social and medical epistemologies that inform how Lyme disease is understood and where Lyme disease patients find belonging. When looking for community, I found myself considered disabled by the able-bodied world and still somehow not at home within the dominant disabled community.

Materialist Katherine Ott (2014) argues that "disability is . . . dynamic and contextual" and that "no one is always disabled for all things; disability depends on the person, the environment, and the activity" (p. 121), placing emphasis on the role of material culture – particularly the use of "disability things" (p. 121), like a wheelchair, a cochlear implant, or a prosthetic limb – in defining someone's socially lived experience as "disabled." Within the social model of disability made popular through prior decades of disability activism, specific emphasis is placed on the social perception of disability, which is overwhelmingly determined by able-bodied fantasies of "the material culture of disability." Disability scholar Bill Hughes (1999) remains critical of the social model for this reason, arguing "the oppression of disabled people is also umbilically linked to the visual constitution of impairment in the scopic regime of modernity" (p. 155) and that disability is constituted through an abled-bodied gaze. Hughes focuses his critique on what he deems the erasure of the role of aesthetics in constructing disability – that impairment is deemed disability when it is visible, despite the fact that disablement constitutes moments in which impairment is not visible but still exists. In spite of the violent pain in which I found myself, the debilitating neurological symptoms, and the constant anxiety about my ability to exist in an able-bodied world, others did not "see" me as disabled based on the parochial, able-bodied idea of disability. In fact, following treatment-induced weight loss, I found myself on the receiving end of compliments: "What did you do to lose the weight?" they would ask earnestly. "Contracted Lyme disease," I would retort.

I looked to find myself in theory; however, in part due to the historical violence of pathologizing disabilities like deafness or autism spectrum disorder, a recurrent attitude among scholars who utilize the social model implied that any individual in part served by medical discourse should not be included in the discourse about disability. This attitude undergirds much of the foundational disability studies discourse and fails to account for the very real challenges faced by disabled people at the hands of neoliberal medical and state institutions – encompassing but not limited to a lack of affordable healthcare, antiquated medical literature resulting in physiological illness being misattributed to psychosomatic response, and insufficient pain management resources. These structural challenges run analogous to the structural violence experienced by disabled people prior to the disability activism of the 1980s and 1990s that led to disability accommodation legislation. It is clear that these two concurrent and intersecting critiques of the social model – its failure to highlight the role of the neoliberal state in the construction of oppression and its failure to incorporate non-fixed definitions of disability – are integral to recognizing the structural constraints placed on the non-visible facets of disability, particularly for those who exist outside normative notions of disability.

In his 2001 article "Disability in Theory," Tobin Siebers reconsiders the way in which the social construction of disability often erases the material realities of disability; while we can see how social systems can create and compound disability, we must also recognize that theoretical discourse on disabled bodies rarely involves the individuals experiencing the most marginalization because of disabilities. He continues,

> The central issue for the politics of representation is not whether bodies are infinitely interpretable but whether certain bodies should be marked as defective and how the people who have these bodies may properly represent their interests in the public sphere.
>
> *(p. 742)*

Siebers notes grimly, "We have not even begun to think about how these bodies might represent their interests in the public sphere for the simple reason that our theories of representation do not take account of them" (p. 742). He raises a key concern within disability activism that those whose needs are most marginalized are often unable to access institutions which allow them to advocate for meeting those needs.

In particular, Siebers highlights pain – partially in opposition to *pleasure*, on which social constructionism within body politics often fixates, and partially because a significant experience of disability is pain. As a politically isolated group, disabled people, particularly those in pain, are not represented in the mainstream social constructivist theories that seek to replace the term "disability" with "differently abled." Siebers continues,

> I stress the importance of pain not because pain and disability are synonymous but to offer a challenge to current body theory and to expose to what extent its dependence on social constructionism collaborates with the misrepresentation of the disabled body in the political sphere.
>
> *(2001, p. 743)*

Moreover, he notes that when social constructivists of the body include pain in their analysis, "[t]hey present suffering and disability either as a way of reconfiguring the physical resources of the body or of opening up new possibilities of pleasure" (p. 745). Siebers cautions against "[mythologizing] disability as an advantage," (p. 746), calling instead for a restoration of a realism of the disabled body, taking into account the ways that social systems compound disability while also recognizing "the physical realities of the disabled body" (p. 749). To Siebers, this helps us to realize that "the most urgent issue for disability studies" is political representation and advocacy for disabled people, which necessitates a "realistic conception of the disabled body" (p. 750).

Accepting the useful critiques put forward by the social model of oppression while also rightly cautioned against mythologizing disability, I encountered a different perspective on my body through queer and crip readings of disability. Rosemarie Garland-Thomson's *Extraordinary Bodies* (1997) presents an early queering of existing tropes of disability. In her text, Garland-Thomson develops a critical methodology for examining cultural scripts of disability in the US. Similar to many of the ideas of performativity and identity formation put forward by queer theorists, Garland-Thomson argues that while disability is pervasive in American media, it often rests on stereotypes or metaphors that come to inform how disabled people see themselves. Garland-Thomson seeks to uncover "how representation attaches meanings to bodies," also exploring the normalization of able bodies as benign non-factors in relation to the types of bodies that "culture calls deviant" (p. 63). She defines disability through what is seen as able bodied: the "cultural complement to the acquisitive and capable American who claims the normate position of masculine, white, non-disabled, sexually unambiguous, and middle class" (p. 6). The normate individual is not only a banal antithesis to disabled bodies but also an ideal type of the body itself. Such a theoretical vantage point brings together seemingly disparate oppressed groups who are all considered antitheses to the normate. Garland-Thomson cites that "many parallels exist between the social meanings attributed to female bodies and those assigned to disabled bodies," since both are "cast as deviant and inferior; both are excluded from full participation in public as well as economic life; both are denied in opposition to a norm that is assumed to possess natural physical superiority" (p. 29). Additionally, Julian Carter's *The Heart of Whiteness* (Carter, 2007) adds contexts to Garland-Thomson's concept of the normate. Tracing the emergence of eugenics in the United States, Carter looks to how the "normal" body was constructed as a monogamous, heterosexual, and white body tasked with maintaining white civilization in the face of increasing racial, ethnic, and bodily diversity. Under this framework, queer people were coded as sexually deviant, even disabled, and racialized peoples could legitimize their proximity to whiteness and normalcy by practicing heteronormativity. According to Robert McRuer (2006), able-bodiedness exists along the same vein as heteronormativity: as a compulsory facet of the lived experiences of all people within a neoliberal capitalist system. He continues, "In a nutshell, you either have an able body or you don't" (p. 7).

Disability as queer coded, deviant, and the binary opposite of "good" finds resonance in work by Susan Sontag (1978, 1989) around illness as a metaphor. Discussing the use of both cancer and tuberculosis as metaphors for societal ills, Sontag writes, "Modern disease metaphors specify an ideal of society's well-being, analogized to physical health, that is as frequently anti-political as it is a call for a new political order" (1989, p. 108). In framing social issues as illness, Sontag argues that we begin to assume a belief that "disease [is] not . . . a punishment but . . . a sign of evil, something to be punished" (1989, p. 115). In her memoir *The Cancer Journals,* Audre Lorde (1997) chronicles her experiences with breast cancer and the ways she endured victimization as a Black woman cancer patient. Recalling the experience of mastectomy and a push from her healthcare team to use prosthetic breasts, Lorde identifies an attempt to erase her experience with cancer so as to make her body more palatable to a disease-phobic and misogynistic world. She declares:

> I refuse to have my scars hidden or trivialized behind lambswool or silicone gel. I refuse to be reduced in my own eyes or in the eyes of others from warrior to mere victim, simply because it might render me a fraction more acceptable or less dangerous to the still complacent, those who believe if you cover up a problem it ceases to exist. I refuse to hide my body simply because it might make a woman-phobic world more comfortable.
> *(p. 53)*

Both Sontag and Lorde recognize the impacts of cancer narratives producing harmful, stigmatized, and shame-filled experiences for those who experience cancer.

Moreover, the metaphors surrounding cancer evoke a sort of decentralized, depersonalized evil; this conjures memories of the dominant virus metaphors during the COVID-19 pandemic. Early in the pandemic, eco-fascist memes circulated illustrating the positive impact of stay-at-home orders on the natural environment, bearing the phrase "We are the virus." In the wake of racist police brutality and the rise of anti-Asian hate crimes, protest signs and Twitter activism declared racism and hate "a virus." Disability justice commentators have been quick to critique this school of thought, for not only does it diminish the experiences of COVID-19 patients, it also suggests that somehow racism permeates society with no one bearing responsibility for it, therefore erasing the structural reality of white supremacy.

COVID-19-related metaphors differ in many ways from the existing dominant discourse about viruses. Sontag points to the narrative surrounding HIV/AIDS, particularly during the HIV/AIDS epidemic:

> With AIDS, the shame is linked to an imputation of guilt; and the scandal is not at all obscure. . . . It is not a mysterious affliction that seems to strike at random. Indeed, to get AIDS is precisely to be revealed, in the majority of cases so far, as a member of a certain "risk group," a community of pariahs. The illness flushes out an identity that might have remained hidden from neighbors, job-mates, family, friends. It also confirms an identity and, among the risk group in the United States most severely affected in the beginning, homosexual men, has been a creator of community as well as an experience that isolates the ill and exposes them to harassment and persecution.
>
> *(1989, pp. 154–155)*

Narratives surrounding HIV/AIDS are far more explicit in naming and shaming the individuals responsible for their diagnosis: namely, the patients themselves. Furthermore, underlying the blame of patients is a disgust towards homosexuality and a tacit acceptance of heteronormativity, seeing AIDS as a harbinger of the destruction of society as we know it. Some of these ways of framing viruses have manifested during COVID-19, as viral tweets have circulated blaming citizens of Republican-controlled states in the US with their high rates of infection. It is clear that the AIDS epidemic, as well as the neoliberal and individualistic turn during the Reagan era, set the course for reframing virus-induced disease as a destructive personal choice rather that a structural reality under a market-oriented, heteronormative, and white supremacist system. In response to this framing, Lennard Davis articulates in *Enforcing Normalcy* (1995) that "the 'problem' is not the person with disabilities; the problem is the way that normalcy is constructed to create the 'problem' of the disabled person" (p. 24).

Rejecting eugenics

Underlying existing schemas of wellness, ability, disability, and disease emerges the violence of eugenics. Eugenicist thinking relies on hierarchical scripts of whose bodies matter, applying a narrow window of "humanness" to those with bodies deemed "normal" and deeming all other bodies disposable. Moreover, these schemas are upheld individually, interpersonally, and institutionally, manifesting through metaphors of illness to tacit acceptance of poor global health outcomes in the name of preserving the free market. However, the COVID-19 pandemic has rendered this reality visible to many previously untouched by illness and disease. As COVID-19 has rocked communities around the world, proximity to disease, unemployment, and feelings of abandonment seem to have enabled a wave of resistance to existing institutional violence. In an era defined by eugenicist and market-oriented sensibilities, the impetus for widespread networks of mutual aid and community care emerged.

Much of the disability advocacy of the past countered the pathologizing of bodies brought on by medical institutions, trading a medical model for a social model of disability. Yet, in my experience, it was only the legitimation of my illness through medical diagnosis that countered the doubt and discrimination I faced. Nonetheless, we must expand our understanding of the social model of disability to encompass the social formations of oppression produced by an asymmetrical, highly politicized, and often inaccessible medical establishment. The repressive pathologizing of some disabilities runs parallel to the violent neglect of others, particularly in historical marginalized communities that have experienced the legacy of eugenics framed as medicine. Ultimately, whether one's experience of disability does not benefit medical intervention or if it does, frameworks of disability as a social oppression prove useful in identifying how powerful institutions produce the circumstances in which we experience disablement. Disability justice is not harmed by those who benefit from medical frameworks of legitimation; rather, all disableds can articulate the complicate hierarchies of power that produce lack of access, neglect, and harm.

Prophetically, Johanna Hedva's "Sick Woman Theory" (2016) anticipated anarcho-communist resistance during the pandemic, wherein normative hierarchies of both ability and disability are collapsed: "The most anti-capitalist protest is to care for another and to care for yourself . . . [practicing a] radical kinship, an interdependent sociality, a politics of care." Hedva imagines a politics rooted in care, anticipating the shared experience and proximity to disease:

> Because, once we are all ill and confined to the bed, sharing our stories of therapies and comforts, forming support groups, bearing witness to each other's tales of trauma, prioritizing the care and love of our sick, pained, expensive, sensitive, fantastic bodies, and there is no one left to go to work, perhaps then, finally, capitalism will screech to its much-needed, long-overdue, and motherfucking glorious halt.
>
> *(np)*

As I write this chapter, my kith and kin are experiencing the horrors of a mass disabling event in India, made more horrific for those with a lack of economic mobility, for the caste oppressed, and for those who do not benefit from global resource networks that privilege the Global North. Vaccine hoarding and neoliberal approaches to healthcare – with billionaires and intellectual property proponents like Bill Gates being propped up as experts on the topic – have condemned millions to succumb to disease, illness, and neglect. As I write this chapter, people around the world are angry, devastated, and bearing witness to the horrors not only of disease but also of the oppressive systems that compound it. But, as I write this chapter, we are one step closer to capitalism's "motherfucking glorious halt."

I do not know how a post-COVID world, should we ever reach it, may influence how we think about illness, disease, viruses, and disability. But I see in my colleagues, peers, students, and community a deeper understanding of the structures that influence, produce, and condemn many to poor health outcomes. Maybe we will start to make healthcare more accessible. Maybe we will start to develop better diagnostics and treatments for Lyme disease. Maybe we will believe people when they are in pain. Maybe we will recognize the trauma of having to choose health or economic stability, health or employment, health or housing. Adrienne Rich told us that we should expect turbulence, that we are "designed to tremble/Else break" (2011, p. 24). We are at a breaking point; it's time to shake things up.

Epilogue

I order my supplements on Amazon. I know I should source them more ethically, but on a grad student salary, it is not always possible to be an ethical consumer. It is almost never possible to be an ethical consumer when our economy relies on exploitation.

I pop a cocktail of supplements in my mouth as I think about concluding this chapter, ruminating on what it means to exist in the in-between: disputed diagnoses, privilege and lack of access, neither healthy nor as sick as I once was. What it means for the HIV-positive people who have managed their viral load to an undetectable level. What it means for COVID long-haulers. What it means for cancer survivors, organ donors, transplant recipients, colostomy bag users. What it means for all of us once deemed sensitive, all of us who went without diagnoses, all of us who lost a part of ourselves when we got sick, all of us who do not fit within normative hierarchies of what constitutes disability.

We have to navigate not only the traits and symptoms of disability and disease but also a hostile, ableist world. And increasingly, our communities are waking up to the oppressive reality we have been gaslit into accepting, the supposed "choices" we have no agency to reject. We find ourselves in each other, and in community, we find the strength to resist.

References

Aronawitz, R. (1991). Lyme disease: the social construction of a new disease and its social consequences. *The Millbank Quarterly*, *69*(1), 79–112. https://doi.org/10.2307/3350122

Carter, J. B. (2007). *The heart of whiteness: normal sexuality and race in America, 1880–1940*. Duke University Press.

Davis, L. J. (1995). *Enforcing normalcy: disability, deafness, and the body*. Verso.

Garland-Thomson, R. (1997). *Extraordinary bodies: figuring physical disability in American culture and literature*. Columbia University Press.

Hedva, J. (2016). Sick woman theory. *Mask Magazine*. http://www.maskmagazine.com/not-again/struggle/sick-woman-theory

Hughes, B. (1999). The constitution of impairment: modernity and the aesthetic of oppression. *Disability & Society*, *14*(2), 155–172. https://doi.org/10.1080/09687599926244

Khakpour, P. (2018). *Sick: a memoir*. Harper-Perennial.
Lorde, A. (1997). *The cancer journals*. Aunt Lute Books.
McRuer, R., & Berube, M. (2006). *Crip theory: cultural signs of queerness and disability*. New York University Press.
Nolen, L. (2020). How medical education is missing the bull's-eye. *New England Journal of Medicine*, *382*(26), 2489–2491. https://doi.org/10.1056/NEJMp1915891
Ott, K. (2014). Disability things: material culture and American disability history, 1700–2010. In S. Burch & M. Rambis (Eds.), *Disability histories* (pp. 119–135). University of Illinois Press.
Rich, A. (2011). *Tonight no poetry will serve: poems 2007–2010*. W.W. Norton.
Siebers, T. (2001). Disability in theory: from social constructionism to a new realism of the body. *American Literary History*, *13*(4), 737–754. https://doi.org/10.1093/ALH/13.4.737
Sontag, S. (1978). *Illness as metaphor*. Farrar, Straus, and Giroux.
Sontag, S. (1989). *AIDS and its metaphors*. Farrar, Straus, and Giroux.
Woolf, V. (1930). *On being ill*. Hogarth Press.

6

THE BALANCING ACT

Disability at the intersection of minority ethnicity

Stéphanie Harvey and Julie Jaye Charles

This chapter presents a discussion between two people working at the intersection of disability and racialisation, minority ethnicity and migration on the topic of additional barriers to human and disability rights that people at this intersection in the UK experience. We have, in this discussion, focused primarily on how language and labels designed to be empowering to disabled people can have the opposite effect for some intersectionally located people. We highlight specific ways in which imposing the label of 'disability' can act to further marginalise people from minority ethnic backgrounds and the particular impacts for some people of colour. Minority ethnicity in this chapter is understood as minority ethnicities within the UK context, which might otherwise be understood as the global majority.

Though we both work in the disability space in one way or another, we are two women with very different backgrounds and life experiences. Put us down on paper, and a casual reader might conclude that we have very little in common. Julie identifies as disabled; Stéphanie only recently found a home in the label of neurodivergent. Julie identifies as Black, and Stéphanie as white. Julie works as a board advisor lead on co-design and advocacy and is an advocate and the founder of a number of charities. Stéphanie is a researcher with a background in policy making.

Perhaps more parallels of experience emerge around our shared experiences of mixed-cultural backgrounds, our relationship to nationalities. Both of us are British nationals with migrant backgrounds, brought up with multiple cultural influences and languages. Raised with three cultures, Julie was born in the East End of London to a French Caribbean (Dominican) mother and Dutch Caribbean (Aruban) father. Upon becoming ill, Julie saw firsthand how the three cultures in her life approached serious ill health differently. Stéphanie's Scottish father and French mother raised her in a bilingual household. Spending part of her childhood in the Middle East, Stéphanie has both first- and

 DOI: 10.4324/9781003410089-8

second-generation migration experiences, which inform her work at the intersections of migration and cultural difference with disability. Lastly, but no less importantly, both have experienced forms of ableist discrimination that have led us to have complicated relationships with the label of 'disabled'.

These complexities in our individual identities have exposed both of us to the very real ways in which labels can misrepresent and deny identity as much as they can be used to create community and unity. Both of us have been touched in some way, both professionally and personally, by the complexities that surround labels of disability, ethnicity and nationality. Both of us have witnessed time and again the balancing act that Western societies require of people in these intersectional spaces: that of navigating and trading labels to access rights, support and acceptance. And both of us recognise that richer understandings of these different experiences are necessary for the evolution of anti-oppression movements and the creation of more inclusive societies. It is this conviction that has led to this chapter.

This is not a traditional interview but rather an edited discussion between two people with different experiences, knowledge and perspectives on the topic. In this discussion, we do not seek to correct the other or impose our own views, but rather to enrich the other's understandings and to find ways forward.

Identifying with 'disability' at the intersection of minority ethnicity

Julie: Let's start how we mean to go on. People of colour very rarely identify with being a disabled person. Sometimes that could feel like an embarrassing word, and sometimes it's a word that they just do not relate to. For some people, disability is not actually a word in their language. I want to say this bit; it's important. What may be in their language are words that are no longer used by what we in the UK call the 'disability movement'. The word that is used is 'handicapped'.

Now, a lot of people in the English-speaking world who relate to or identify with being a disabled person and have that lived experience of disability would say 'handicapped' is a terrible word: a terrible way of actually identifying. However, if within your culture . . . if your language does not have the word 'disabled' in its dictionary, how else do you actually identify? It is a concept and a way of thinking about certain life experiences that sits outside of the community or a culture's terminology.

Stéphanie: I'm thinking . . . I'm actually thinking of my mother tongue, French. The nearest translations are 'incapacité', 'infirimité' or 'handicapée'. The dictionary gives 'infirmité' as the closest translation, which also directly translates to the state of being 'infirm', which doesn't align with the concept of 'disability'. Most people tend to use 'handicapée'. . . . So does the UN in its French translation of the treaty.[1] There isn't a separate word for the concept of 'disability', not in the way we mean it in the equality and human rights context, I mean: i.e. 'disability' as the experiences created by ableist attitudes and systems in society.

J: Yes. In Greece also they would say 'handicapped', or that someone's got a sickness. They will name an illness. It's the same in the Caribbean, in my culture. That's how we identify with things. We know that a condition makes us very sick. Take myself. I remember when I got really ill. 1996. I had lupus. I collapsed. I spent nine months in hospital. My parents had to fly back from the Caribbean to look after my children. I then came home from hospital into a home that was in no way fitting for me anymore, and there the fight began.

There the fight began because I would not say that I was disabled. I saw myself as someone with lived experience of long-term conditions who needed support since getting ill. Disability was a white person thing. I was ill. That's how I used to identify before I read up on disability.

S: It's interesting because this issue of not identifying with the label of 'disability' definitely came up as something I had to negotiate in my own research. As you know, Julie, I worked with people with long-term mental health issues/distress who have minority ethnic backgrounds, identify as people of colour, and migrants. Coming from a disability studies and policy background, at the start of the research, I was using the word 'disability'. But I quickly had to stop because the people I was working with – the participants – just did not identify with that term. They had either had a 'mental illness' or 'mental health issues' or were very 'sad', 'anxious', 'distressed' or 'mentally distracted'.[2]

The terms participants tended to use either related to illness or named a specific emotion or mental state. Sometimes, the rejection of illness labels [was] linked to the sorts of cultural and linguistic differences we talked about [earlier]. For example, a Swazi lady who participated in my research spoke of having a very different understanding of mental health to the Western understanding when she arrived in the UK. She said that in Swaziland, either you were stressed or sad, or you were 'mad', which could include being possessed by 'djinn'. A few other participants who migrated to the UK from across different African countries described similar understandings in their countries of birth.

'Samantha' in the research described her discomfort with the label of 'mental illness' multiple times to me. And for her, a big part of that discomfort was feeling forced to accept a version . . . a description of 'mental distraction' and 'mental problems' that didn't fit with her understanding of the world. It meant for her that she found it more difficult to engage with support services, partly because she felt there was no attempt by the services to meet her halfway and offer support that corelated with her understanding of what was going on for her. Sorry, bit of a tangent, but I think there's a bit of a parallel.

J: There is a parallel there.

S: And conversations like this, along with participants' reactions or use of the word 'disability', made me really reflect on the language I'd use in the research write-up. In the end, although I acknowledged the influence of disability studies scholars on my thinking and much of the analysis takes a more social model-esque approach, I didn't apply the label of 'disabled' to any participants unless they themselves used it – which was only ever in relation to physical conditions they had. It felt wrong to put a label on the participants when they themselves reject it or, at the very least, reject it in relation to the mental health issues/distress they experienced. Especially when it seemed to make many of the people I was working with feel additionally disempowered, when they already experienced that as a result of other aspects of their life or identity.

J: I do think this issue of feeling disempowered from many angles is important. We'll come back to that, but I just wanted to say that there's the cultural differences, but there's also a perceptions issue. You started hinting at it before. That 'disability' was understood by some participants as just being about physical conditions. It's also that when you say 'disability', people of colour from a minority group often relate to that as a white person. A white disabled person.

S: With the image of the white disabled person also usually being someone with mobility issues.

J: Yes. Or somebody who has a visual impairment and uses a stick to give them that independence. S you have this barrier for people of colour or from minority ethnic groups in the UK identifying with the term 'disabled' because it doesn't fit with ideas in their communities or in their language. But in some communities, there's also something else. . . . You know, it can be really difficult for people within some Asian communities to reply positively to questions like 'Are you a disabled person? Do you identify as being a disabled person?' Because disability is a huge, huge word that can be offensive to some communities.[3] In some communities, admitting to being disabled or having a disabled family member can have a lot of repercussions for the whole family.

S: It didn't come up in my own research so much, but I read other research and testimonials about marriage prospects being harmed or a reduction in social status in the local community. A really complex and nuanced area, but in communicates where these dynamics were playing out, there were often links to fears of impairments being hereditary or a sign of being punished by God or possessed by demons. Are these the sorts of issues you're talking about?

J: It is. We have to understand that when this label of 'disability' is put on people because it's the only word that is used within institutions in English-speaking Western countries like the UK, the US, Canada . . . how can I put it? It's problematic for many people at the intersection of disability and minority ethnicity. It's just not a word that is accepted by all. But people are forced to use it to access support and their rights.

For example, if you wanted to use the UK's Equality Act, 2010 to challenge an employer who is refusing to make reasonable adjustments for your chronic illness, you have to challenge them under the disability section. Which means you have to first identify yourself as disabled. And that might be even more difficult for people from backgrounds where taking on that label has repercussions for your family, your status in the community or that sits uncomfortably with your cultural identity. And I think that that's important to recognise.

S: So, are you saying that forcing people to adopt the label of 'disabled' so that they can get access to protections or access to services, for many minority ethnic communities – particularly racialised ethnic communities – it's almost like a form of colonisation again?

J: That's the word I was looking for. Yes. It is a colonisation. And it reminds people of being put into an ancestral box that reminds them of slavery, being given a name, a label, which is not chosen by themselves but by someone else.

S: In what way?

J: I'll explain. And I'm speaking here from my own lived experience and that of other people I've worked with throughout my time as an advocate for people of colour and disabled people.

Racial and colonial complications with the 'disability' label

J: When you're a Black person, there's a lot of things that you have to accept. For example, that discrimination isn't always someone calling you a name. It can be that you work as a cleaner in a hospital, and you see doctors that are all white. And that lack of representation can say a lot about the place of race in that institution and about power relations in society. A lot of people relate to Black people as 'once upon a time, we were slaves'. And disability can be a slave language.

S: OK. I'm really interested in that. I've never thought about it in that way.

J: It can be a slave language because of the way that it's used by some to undermine people or support people's rights being taken away from them. On the rights front, you and I and the disability movement know that the label 'disabled' is meant to empower people because it relates to the social model. But, in reality, disability gets used to take people's rights away. Just look at some of the practices in the UK during the pandemic. Do not resuscitate [orders] being put against the charts of people with learning disabilities without any consultation with them or their families. For people who already have histories of being denied support because of other aspects of their identity or lives, being forced to take on another label to get some support feels extra risky because they know it can also end up denying them rights.

But it's also a slave language in that you're made to feel inferior if you don't use the terms accepted by the Western institutions and disability or human rights movements and charities. So we talked before about cultural and language differences that mean many people of colour in the UK don't use 'disability' but use the word 'handicapped' instead. But the disability movement, when they rejected the word 'handicapped' to take on the word 'disability', would position people using the word 'handicapped' as less educated, less enlightened . . . that sort of thing.

S: So it's like there's a hierarchy that's been placed on the terminology. Is that what you mean?

J: Yes.

S: So, is it a feeling that the disability movement's excepted terminology is heralded as better? More informed? More educated? I suppose the implication would be that the use of terminology that many people from certain minority ethnic backgrounds are comfortable with is interpreted as demonstrating a lack of understanding. A lack of education. That they lack the understanding and education to use the term 'disability' properly. And there's an added layer when this judgement is placed on people from minority ethnic backgrounds or people of colour, I suppose. Because accusations like that sound very similar to racist narratives of the 'uncultured' and 'primitive' peoples of colonised countries.

J: Yes, exactly.

S: And that links not only to ideas of cultural deficit, but also those of individual intellectual superiority and inferiority as well.

J: Yes, it does. That's what I mean. It is the intellectual superiority. I understand the term 'disability', and I relate to it now because I don't believe that it's my fault that I experience many of the barriers I do. I do believe that society can be disabling to some people with conditions. But that's a discussion that hasn't been had in many minority ethnic communities. We've not had that space.

S: And that's important for anyone working in the disability rights space to recognise. Especially because something that I feel is not often talked about is the way that racism and ableism have been interwoven historically. There's something *really* fundamental in the history of racialisation that plays to the heart of the way that disabled people were oppressed as well.

J: Oh, you did quite a bit of reading on this, didn't you? Go on. I know what I think, but I'm interested in what you've read.

S: So it's not something I've seen explored a lot in disability studies. That said, I'm starting to see more as academics from the Global South are more and more included as part of the conversation and as ideas from critical race theory are brought in as a lens to use when thinking about disability and ableism. What gets highlighted is that ideas of racial inferiority – which were used to justify slavery and colonisation – were often legitimised with claims of intellectual, moral or physical inferiority.

So, for example, claims that Black people had smaller brains [were] brought in as the so-called physical proof of intellectual and moral inferiority. Both of which made them – in the eyes of a deeply ableist society – closer to animals than humans. This was used to justify slavery and the dehumanisation of entire peoples. That's one way that ableism propped up racism and colonial ideas.

J: Absolutely.

S: This idea was also used to undermine shows of physical strength which might have been supported narratives of the physical 'superiority' of some Black people over some white people if left unchecked. Putting physical strength together with the false claims of smaller brains and intellectual and moral deficit allowed the really harmful stereotype of the 'big, bestial Black man' to emerge. So, basically, 'Well, you might be really big and strong, but you're feebleminded. More like an ox than a man'. 'Feebleminded' was the actual term that got said.

J: Yes. Yes.

S: This is a hugely oversimplified explanation of the interplay between racism/colonialism and ableism, I know.

J: That's all right. It gets the main points across. And it shows another layer . . . another reason why people of colour might not want to associate with the label of 'disability' or why they feel it's for white people and not them. Accepting the label is accepting the white man's label for how we should understand ourselves. Like we had to in slavery. In colonies. There's nowhere to turn because you're not allowed to use your own identity or what it is that is your reality. And this is where – I'll go back to what I was saying before about using the term 'handicapped' being associated with being less educated.

You know, there's a long history in the UK and other Western countries of people of colour and indigenous people having lower educational attainment. And that was always put down to intellectual and cultural inferiority. You know, 'primitive people'. It took a long time – a lot of fighting – to change that view. To show that the lower grades in school were more to do with structural issues and oppression than your genes, your race, your culture.

Then you've got people saying you have to use the word 'disabled' because 'handicapped' is immoral and shows lack of education on what it is to live with conditions and on your rights. You're back to being told that the way you and your community view the world is primitive. No wonder so many people of colour find the disability space too risky.

S: Were these issues for you when you first started looking for support related to your chronic illness?

J: For me, disability was white people in wheelchairs or blind people on the telly chained to Parliament gates with placards. I couldn't bring myself to relate to that. That was my view when I started trying to get support.

The balancing act when claiming rights

J: I really struggled to get what I needed, even though I was eligible. Like I said, it was a fight. And I just thought, 'You know what, they're discriminating against me because I'm a Black person'. I thought I was being discriminated against because when I spoke to an organisation called the Family Service Unit about my difficulties getting support, they said 'A stairlift is nothing. Why aren't they giving you a stairlift?' They said that I should be entitled to one by law. And I said, 'Well, I'm struggling here. I'm sleeping downstairs. I can't get up the stairs'. Because my legs were numb. I was semi-paralysed. They agreed to take my case on and fight.

So it took a white-led organisation to fight for me to get a stairlift. For everything that I needed to get, I had to go through this UK kind of white process. I was trying to understand why there were so many barriers to getting any services, to getting equipment, so that I can live a life that suited me and my children. I started realising that the reason I wasn't getting support wasn't as straightforward as me being a Black woman. It also had to do with identifying as disabled. I didn't, and that was a problem. And people in the system didn't seem to understand why that would be more difficult for some people of colour or from other cultural backgrounds.

For some of us, it goes back to what we talked about before about the links between ableism and racism and our collective memory of slavery and colonisation. It makes some of us warry of terms like 'disability' that come from white spaces and don't fit with our own cultural heritage or languages. So then you're in the business of trading off parts of your identity. Saying to yourself, 'What's more important to me right now? Getting support, or my own idea of myself? My understanding of myself in my community?'

S: Yes, I saw similar patterns among the people in my research when they navigated mental health–related terminology. I wonder, because you mentioned it a bit earlier, the Equalities National Council. You founded and ran the ENC for 25 years. Whilst there was a focus on supporting people of colour, actually you supported anyone with a minority ethnicity, regardless of racialisation. I remember you telling me that you also saw a lot of people with Gipsy or traveller backgrounds and people from countries like Poland, who would also struggle a lot with getting the services that they needed.

J: Because of the identification, Stéphanie, it was difficult for people to identify with that word 'disabled'. It was really hard. Like I said before, there wasn't always a word for disability in people's first language. So they might not have the complications of colonialism and racism to deal with, but they have the cultural and language differences. I know that there are a lot of white British disabled people who struggle to get the support they need. And a lot of white British people who are chronically ill or who are neurodiverse and who don't identify as being disabled. But I think what I'm trying to point out is two things that make this experience different when you are a person of colour or from a minority ethnicity.

First, there is a level of discrimination that white British disabled people experience trying to get heard and their requirements met, but it's not anywhere near the level of discrimination that people from racialised groups go through. And that's because of things like we were saying before about how ableism and racism [come] together. The second thing I would say is that you have to remember that people who are British or white British, white American, white Canadian, they have this kind of privilege – whether they're working in service provision or whether they're like in a disability organisation – that comes from their whiteness and their nationality.

S: Yes, they have credibility coming from other aspects of their identity. Some parts of their identity fit with the majority or the privileged parts of society, which then gives them some credibility when speaking up or out. So for white British disabled people in the UK, their whiteness and nationality give them more grounds to be taken seriously by those in power or our institutions. Or less grounds on which they can be marginalised. Is that what you mean?

J: Yes. They *are* part way up the hierarchy. They already have that.

S: So, if people are discredited when they have stigmatised labels or labels that open them up to forms of oppression, then more labels can equal less credibility. I think this relates again to what we were saying about how being coerced into taking on the label of disability can feel like another way that people are colonised. I wonder whether this goes back to what you were talking about before with your view that 'disability' is a 'slave language' in the way it's used. I guess what I'm thinking about here is ideas around epistemological injustices. So what I mean by that is the injustices that happen when a minority or marginalised group is forced or coerced to accept or work with the understandings and knowledge upheld by a majority or privileged group in ways that demean their own knowledges.

J: Yes! I have felt more oppressed taking on the label as a disabled person than I did being a non-disabled Black woman.

S: And do you think that's because of the two coming together?

J: Yeah. Yep, I've felt more oppressed. It was my choice to go one way and one way alone years ago when I adopted the label of disabled person. I did it because I have long-term conditions, and society does disable me. But why did I have to use the word 'disabled' to identify myself before I can get a service?

S: When actually that was itself a traumatising act.

J: A traumatising and demoralising act, yeah.

As somebody born in the UK and who has followed the development of UK disability law, I now identify as a disabled person because I know that there are laws that actually protect disabled people. I have made sure that I understand those laws and can use them for my protection. However, those laws don't particularly work for me because I feel that the law does not pick up on racialised disabled people. What it picks up on is a disabled person and the type of disability discrimination that is purely about conditions or illness. It doesn't pick up on discriminations that are a combination of ableism and racism, let's say. And then there's the gender factors, etc.

S: Oh, Julie. We're straying into our favourite place here, I think. Intersectionality. The need to recognise it and learn from it.

Intersectionality and finding ways forward

J: Didn't you put something on intersectionality in your research conclusion? That policy making on mental health inequalities could be hugely improved if intersectional approaches were taken?

S: I did, yes. And Crenshaw – who coined the term 'intersectionality' – her starting point was the law. She saw how certain areas of American law were not protecting Black women from discrimination because the law took a single-issue approach. So judges could only recognise forms of sexism that were based purely on the type of sexism and stereotypes that white middle-class women experienced. In one of her essays, Crenshaw writes with a caution to people advocating single-issue approaches to identity politics and rights issues. She essentially says that you will never significantly reduce, much less get rid of, certain forms of oppression until you understand all of the ways that it manifests. If you ignore sexism as it's experienced by Black women, then you're not eradicating sexism. You're just shifting the issue to a sub-set of people.

J: Sounds very similar to the issue I find here in the UK.

S: Absolutely. And if the oppression you're experiencing in the way you experience it [isn't] being talked about, it's more difficult to identify with that form of oppression. So when you're approaching a service and you're told to identify with a label that links you to a form of oppression that doesn't feel like the oppression you've experienced – even if you can see links to it – that's dangerous. Not only are you accepting a label that doesn't sit right, but also you know that in identifying with that label, you're accepting another set of types of oppression.

J: Yes, and it's got an impact on your life for the rest of your life.

S: That's very difficult to accept, I think. It certainly seemed to be an issue for several participants in the research I did. And this is important because it can either retraumatise or put up massive barriers to claiming rights and support.

J: Exactly. I've seen it for myself. And I've seen it for all the people who came to the Equalities National Council looking for support. And with other people in my community. It's a big issue. So we need to build understandings that are more inclusive and more intersectional. Intersectionality should be the key word when we're actually identifying as people: as human beings that are not in a homogeneous group. People can fit within a group, but we're not a homogenous group. It's the same whether you're talking about women, people of minority ethnicity, disability . . . take whatever identity label, and you'll find incredible diversity in each grouping.

Intersectionality for me as a person of colour, as a woman, as a disabled woman of colour is so important. It opens up the doors to pushing for more understanding, and more understanding can lead to being able to claim rights more easily. With all those parts of my identity opening me up to forms of discrimination, society can be very discriminative against me. It's important that the disability movement opens up to people who might experience ableism but don't identify specifically with the term 'disabled'.

S: Yes, it's similar to the point I make in my research. That policy making on such issues can only be enrichened by intersectional understandings. Understanding this diversity and designing around that can surely only lead to more inclusive approaches. But it may also require letting go of certain traditional approaches. Our focus in this discussion has been around identifying with the label of disability. So perhaps finding ways to hold on to the 'Nothing about us without us' mantra of the disability movement whilst also not requiring everyone to self-identify as 'disabled' to have a voice? But accepting other ways of identifying, even if on the surface it looks like accepting that terminology is counter to the change you are seeking. Because not doing that is just silencing and excluding parts of society.

I wonder, at the grassroots, because you know my area is more the academic and policy side of things. You're really at the grassroots of that lived experience understanding and how the services work and all of that. I kind of feel like the benefit of a [real] understanding of intersectionality at the grassroots level is essentially to say, 'We understand that concepts like disability and the social model are important and useful. *But*, they are one form of lived experience. They're one form of understanding. And we have a more diverse population'.

J: Yes. We have more diversity! It's huge. The diversity of experience. The diversity of language, which reflects different parts of our experience. If you're down there at the grassroots level, and you are a being, all you do is try to live. Never mind taking on a label. So let that person live with what they understand. Sure, try sharing your understandings. But don't force them on others. We may not know their reasons for thinking and seeing things differently. And even if we do know, still doesn't give us the right to force a label on someone who doesn't identify that way. And that's what happens when people have to self-identify as disabled to have a say or to access rights and support. We need to think and act with intersectionality in mind if we want a disability movement, disability policies and disability research that is properly representative and inclusive.

S: You put that so beautifully.

J: Done. [Laughing]

Notes

1 See the United Nations Convention on the Rights of Persons with Disabilities.
2 See Harvey, 2021. *Moving beyond the cheapest kind of understanding: enriching policy responses to BAME mental health inequality.*
3 *Over-looked communities, over-due change.*

References

Equality Act 2010. https://www.legislation.gov.uk/ukpga/2010/15/introduction [Accessed 10 November 2018].

Harvey, S. (2021). *Moving beyond 'the cheapest kind of understanding': enriching policy responses to BAME mental health inequality*. Bath Spa University. http://researchspace.bathspa.ac.uk/14351/

7

MENTAL HEALTH SERVICE USERS CLAIMING THEIR RIGHT TO SELF-ADVOCACY

The journey of Autoekprosopsi

Leonardos Skordos, Diakakis Panagiotis, Garyfalia Marini, Athina Fragkouli and Panagiota Fitsiou

Internationally, human rights legislation has become a powerful tool to combat injustice and violence against human beings, especially vulnerable groups such as people with mental health issues. For a long time, people with mental health issues have been excluded from society, and their rights have been violated. They have been deprived of significant basic rights of a civil, political, social and economic nature (Sayce, 2001). Discrimination and stigma, inability to access healthcare, involuntary treatment and denial of self-determination on various matters are only few of their rights deprivations. In addition, their voices could not be heard and, they did not have access to self-advocacy.

For the aforementioned reasons, many reforms have taken place concerning mental health policies, professionals' training and networking of institutions so that people with mental health problems can enjoy their rights. In this chapter, we will address the importance of self-advocacy among persons with psychosocial problems by examining the journey of Autoekprosopisi (meaning "self-advocacy" in Greek), a union that represents mental health service users around Greece and whose seat is in Athens. We will also examine the issue of the exclusion of people with mental health problems from the disability movement.

Evolution of the Greek mental health care system

To thoroughly understand the journey of Autoekprosopisi, a short overview of the Greek mental health care system will be provided. It is known that until the end of 1970s and the early 1980s, the Greek mental health care system was

 DOI: 10.4324/9781003410089-9

asylum-centered, based on "closed care" services. Up to a point, social care and especially housing protection for people with psychosocial disabilities was provided by families. This informal solidarity network was filling the gap in mental health and social care service provision in the previous years (Fitsiou & Kourachanis, 2019). Maybe this is why Greece delayed, compared to the rest of Europe, the creation of asylums.

After 1981, when Greece joined the European Economic Community, the National Health System Law 1397/83 became active (1983) for the first time, giving equal access to health services and setting a new basis for psychiatric care.

Soon after the Leros scandal, which exposed Greece as an extreme expression of institutional misery (Mitrossili, 1995), the country received the support of the European Union through EEC Regulation 815/84, which was amended by Regulation 4130/88. Under this support, a network of community-based, preventive and therapeutic psychiatric services was developed, and the number of long-term patients in public psychiatric hospitals was reduced (Mastroyannakis et al., 2015). Important national legislation, Law 2071/1992 and mostly Law 2716/1999, described a modern community mental health system (prevention, primary, secondary and psychosocial rehabilitation) with an emphasis on the protection of the rights of people with mental health problems.

To ensure the continuity of the mental health reform, the Ministry of Health in late 1995 produced a long-term project for psychiatric reform called Psychargos. The initial planning involved two phases (Phase I: 1997–2001 and Phase II 2001–2006), and then a third phase was developed in 2010–2020, which aimed at deinstitutionalisation and the transformation of psychiatric hospitals, the development of a network of community-based services in sectorised areas, vocational training and upgrading of skills (of both professionals and service users), social integration and labor inclusion for people with psychosocial problems, and community awareness raising. In addition, great emphasis was given to the users' satisfaction and the upgrading of the quality of services (Mastroyannakis et al., 2015).

The structure of the mental health care system consists of the public sector (psychiatric hospitals, general hospital psychiatric wards and their associated outpatient units), non-profit organisations (primary care structures such as day centres and mobile units, tertiary care structures, residential houses, apartments and occupational rehabilitation structures) and the private sector (private psychiatric clinics and private practitioners) (Mastroyannakis et al., 2015). Also, mental health services are provided by social security funds, local government, the church and the armed forces.

It is important to say that at this moment that there have been significant steps towards the improvement of the psychiatric care system, though the reform remains uncompleted (Loukidou et al., 2013). We still lack primary services (day centres, mental health centres, mobile units) and secondary services, while the existing services are unevenly distributed among sectors (Mastroyannakis et al., 2015).

Regarding the rights of people with psychosocial problems, there is still a high rate of involuntary admissions in psychiatric clinics, along with a high rate of re-admissions, known as the phenomenon of the "revolving door" (Stylianidis et al., 2017).

In recent years, several users' and families' associations emerged, and the legislation, up to a point, enhances their participation in the planning, monitoring and evaluation of mental health services: i.e. they participate on mental health sector committees and on the Standing Committee for Monitoring the Protection of the Rights of Persons with Mental Disorders. However, more progress needs to be made concerning the equal and substantial participation of users in the process of evaluation of services. That is why the development and strengthening of the users' movement is particularly important.

Self-advocacy and activeness of mental health service users

It is certain that many steps have been made, as the mental health care system adopted a model of service provision that promotes empowerment and social integration, leading to deinstitutionalised community services. However, the institutional and asylum-centered culture had been long established. The impression that mental health service users are unable to be in control of their opinions, let alone speak up for their rights, needs and desires, has followed the institutional culture and the common narrative for many years. The media, films etc. have also, contributed to this impression. Traditionally, the approach to mental health matters is not based on human rights principles, and people are mostly subjects of interventions and seem passive recipients of services.

On the other side, there is the human rights–based approach to mental health, according to which mental health service users have an active role in claiming their rights, have a say in their personal treatment and take part in the planning of services and the decision-making processes on corresponding matters (Curtice & Exworthy, 2010). Such an approach facilitates the empowerment of people, which is now one of the main goals along with the full exercise of human rights (McGuire, 2009). That way, objectives and indicators can be formed based on human rights principles while transparency and accountability systems become key elements in the designing of mental health services.

Along with these reforms, focusing on the self-advocacy and empowerment of people with psychosocial problems could amplify our efforts to achieve human rights–compliant and community-based services (Williams & Lindley, 1996). Autoekprosopisi is working on exactly those axes so as to raise awareness and advocate for improvement in policies.

The foundation of the Autoekprosopisi

The union of Autoekprosopisi, which represents mental health service users around Greece, by creating a growing network of members and supporters, has started to deliver its main message: "Nothing about us without us". As members of the union, we acknowledge that the voices of individuals with lived experience of psychosocial problems are not taken enough into consideration. Also, we support that the opinions and interests of the people with psychosocial problems should never be excluded from the decision-making process on mental health matters or the designing of services.

Indeed, the formulation of a union or an association can be challenging, especially for people who do not have the opportunity to be trained on matters around self-help and self-advocacy. However, with limited help from professionals and supporting organisations, such initiatives can arise. At least, that was the case with the union of Autoekprosopisi.

In November 2001, a self-help group was formed in the Panhellenic Association for Psychosocial Rehabilitation and Work Integration (PEPSAEE) under the support of Athina Fragkouli. The group was active until October 2006, and during that time, a wide range of activities and training meetings took place to create a quarterly newspaper called *Charissis* 6 (the former address of the PEPSAEE Day Centre of Social Dialogue. During that process, the editing group of the newspaper, now members of Autoekprosopisi, undertook the translation of the *Guidelines for Self-Help* from the European Network of Users and Survivors of Psychiatry (ENUSP), from which many ideas emerged concerning our empowerment. We started to acknowledge the consequences of the hierarchy people with mental health problems suffer from, inside both communities and the human rights movement. Therefore, we found self-advocacy to be the answer to all hierarchies.

What started as a self-help group became a dynamic group that started to expand. With limited support from professionals, our activities started to become much more socially interactive so as to include more people facing similar difficulties. The sole action of speaking up was not only empowering to us, as members of the group, but it also started to have an impact on others. A member of ENUSP, Clemens Huitnik, influenced the group and enhanced the idea of creating a movement – a union. This idea started to grow while the group was organising conferences, seminars and more focus groups about self-help. The first steps were made with the help of professionals from various organisations. With the financial support of the EU and the help of Mental Health Europe, PEPSAEE, the Society of Social Psychiatry P. Sakellaropoulos and the National Confederation of Disabled People in Greece (ESAMEA), we managed to visit multiple psychosocial care structures around Greece.

The first elections took place in 2007, when members elected the administrative council of the union. Although the seat of Autoekprosopisi was in Athens, our active presence in multiple cities led to more members all around Greece. We tried to share the empowering experience of belonging to Autoekprosopisi and to encourage the formation of multiple unions. As a result, we had already started to convey the message of "Nothing about us without us" in central city points and mental health centers. These first meetings with the new members seemed to be the precursors of the seminars that Autoekprosopisi would launch some years later.

Activities and interests of Autoekprosopisi

The administrative council of the union has a monthly meeting, in which the main activities are discussed. These mostly revolve around participating in conferences and trainings and the organising of our yearly seminar. All activities aim at raising awareness within the community, recruiting new members, partnering with other organisations and advocating for changes in laws and policies. It is highly important for us to stay connected and continue to exchange knowledge and good practices. Autoekprosopisi members are often asked by mental health organisations and collectivities to contribute to conferences and meetings so as to present our project. Also, we take part in trainings held by mental health organisations, which mostly focus on matters of resilience and recovery.

In addition, we get involved with various Erasmus+ programmes/trainings, such as the Erasmus+ programme European Profile for Peer Support Workers, which aims to create European professional standards for peer support work. The peer support specialist is a mental health professional who works based on his/her personal recovery experience in order to support and empower other people in their own recovery process. Peer support is evolving into a new profession, gradually joining the interdisciplinary mental health teams. Work based on the principles of recovery and peer support is inextricably linked to the current policy of the European Union. In our country, there is still no formal education or formal framework qualification for this profession, even though there is an ever-increasing interest in this field of work.

Seminars. The main activity of the union and the most effective way to expand our ideas and grow our network has been the yearly seminar of Autoekprosopisi. Since 2017, Autoekprosopisi has implemented four annual seminars (Amfissa-Fokida, 2–3/12/2017; Athens, 25–26/1/2019; Alexandroupolis-Thraki, 29/11–1/12/2019; online seminar 23/1/2021). The innovation of the seminars is based on the concept of being organised by mental health service users for mental health service users. The organisational and implementation processes are carried out by members of our union, as the carers and mental health professionals provide limited support and supervision.

To be more specific, as members of the administrative council, we agree on the seminars' themes and the times and space in which they will take place, and we share responsibilities throughout the days of the events. After being trained, we undertake to coordinate the participant groups and to give instructions and clarifications throughout the event. It was important for us to create an effective methodology on how to conduct the seminars. Using experiential techniques and focus groups, we manage to create a safe space for persons with mental health problems to share personal experiences, ideas and needs. In addition, carers and professionals who participate in the seminars hold their own group to facilitate the unhindered expression of mental health service users' experience and proposals, while offering their valuable input.

The first seminar, which was conducted in Amfissa-Fokida on 2–3/12/2017, with the financial support of Mental Health Europe, was the necessary connection that helped cultivate hope and vision for the next activities of the union. In this first meet-up, participants had the opportunity to share their experiences, beliefs and wishes concerning mental health matters and their personal condition. By creating drawings, sharing poems and exchanging ideas, they managed to encourage each other and envision ways to have their desires and needs fulfilled. This meeting seemed to be the seed participants laid to cultivate a community of sharing in the next seminars.

The second seminar, which took place in Athens on 25–26/1/2019, was characterised by a deeper review of specific issues that are important for people with psychosocial difficulties. The matters of stigma, self-stigmatisation, involuntary hospitalisation and the recovery process were addressed. After a theoretical approach provided both by professionals and mental health service users, the participants broke in smaller groups, discussing questions such as "What is the meaning of the term 'recovery' for you?" "What can mental health services do to facilitate this process?" "What can each of us do, individually, to facilitate our own personal path to 'recovery'?" The same pattern was followed for the rest of the topics so that participants could share personal experiences with stigma, self-stigmatisation and involuntary treatment and think about alternative solutions to these problems.

The third seminar was held in Alexandroupolis-Thraki on 29/11–1/12/2019 and followed a structure similar to the previous one. The participants examined the violation of rights in relation to the cases in which people with mental health problems cannot make decisions or exercise their rights independently. In such situations, the legal system provides mechanisms that intervene to substitute or support the person in need. In addition, the Convention on the Rights of Persons with Disabilities was reviewed and analysed to distinguish the forms of rights' marginalisation among people with psychosocial problems.

Furthermore, the concepts of "recovery" and employment were analysed, as they are among the topics that often come up in the seminars. The model of "recovery" is a widely used approach for psychosocial rehabilitation (Jacobson & Greenley, 2001). It emphasises the personal potential of each individual with mental illness to live a satisfactory and meaningful life. Rather than focusing on a set of specific results, "recovery" refers to a personal journey of development focusing on the creation of hope and self-sufficiency, on the formation of a supportive network of relationships, on continuous empowerment and the individual's social integration. Complementary to this model of psychosocial rehabilitation is vocational rehabilitation, which seems to strongly concern persons with mental health problems. After all, employment is one of the key factors for the improvement of life quality, and it is necessary for meeting basic needs. Quite often, minimal financial support from the state is not enough for the individual's financial independence, which is significant for all human beings.

A participant of the seminar mentioned, "We need to acquire skills in order to find a job and be competitive in the market". An answer to this problem has come from the growth of social entrepreneurship, which comprises the third sector of the economy, after the private and the public sectors. Social-solidarity entrepreneurship manages to confront the rigid competitiveness of the private sector and the bureaucratic base of the public sector. While creating jobs for socially vulnerable groups of the population, social entrepreneurship is organised on a real business base with real working conditions. Major progress has been made as many cooperatives of this kind, called Social Cooperatives of Limited Liability (Koi.S.P.E.) (Law 2716/1999), aim for the socio-economic and professional integration of people with serious psychosocial problems, contributing to their treatment and possible financial self-sufficiency. In Greece, as in other countries of the EE, the operation of Koi.S.P.E. has established visible and positive results.

Autoekprosopisi's latest seminar was organised via an online meeting platform on 23 January 2021. In spite of the current COVID-19 situation, the change of plans and the challenges of digital media, we decided to implement the seminar and not miss the opportunity to meet. Professionals and mental health service users attended the seminar and shared opinions and remarks on the current situation and on how COVID-19 had become a pretext for violation of human rights among people with psychosocial difficulties. About the violation of human rights, a participant highlighted, "There are still people inside psychiatric hospitals that are 'drowning'. I have lost contact due to COVID. I want to help them. I won the battle, but they are still fighting".

One advantage of cyberspace was that it allowed us to have a view of the inside of rehabilitation centers where people with experience of mental health problems reside. For many of those people, it was a needed and meaningful interaction which was not only a comforting way out but also an empowering experience. This can be confirmed by the decision of the participants to meet again not at the next yearly seminar but sooner, to work on the plans and aspirations expressed in the seminar.

In the case of Greece, people are experiencing extensive lockdowns, and measures have been taken restricting mobility. This has had a major effect on the daily lives of all citizens, especially mental health service users. For most people, levels of employability, supportive networks of relationships and general quality of life have been affected, but the inequalities that vulnerable groups are experiencing seem to be intensified during the COVID-19 pandemic. For example, when a person with psychosocial problems loses his/her job, there is a risk of recurrence. As a participant mentioned, "Work seems to function as a personal compass in order to lead a life of dignity and morality".

In addition, a significant number of participants said that alternative therapeutic activities – other than pharmaceutical treatment – are hard to continue in times of lockdown. Gardening, being outdoors and volunteer work are activities that have a therapeutic effect on their mental and physical health and are part of the mental health services offered to people in need. As a result, many people with mental health issues face additional struggles these days, due to the disruption of their treatment. Also, many participants expressed alarming feelings about their rights to freedom, privacy and choice in treatment.

Participants chose various ways to express their thoughts and feelings, including through works of art. The poem that follows, written by a service user named Theonas Charatsis, is about his interpretation of the meaning of liberty.

LIBERTY
Liberty for me is the smell of a recently printed book.
The human relationships in all their dimensions.
The complexity of this world but also its phenomenal simplicity.
Liberty is when I have the courage to choose
Without feeling guilty
Without feeling inferior
Without feeling ashamed.
Liberty is
A ladder I climb stair by stair
A road I walk step by step
A bridge I cross over a river.
Liberty is
The vast, starry sky
The deep, blue sea
The infinite, endless universe.
Liberty for me is to live, to love, to share truly and fearlessly!
Charatsis Theonas, Greece

The seminar helped the participants process feelings of loneliness and fear. We managed to exchange methods of self-help in these challenging times and discussed the prevention measures taken for our physical and mental health. However, it was noted that many mental health service users still do not have the opportunity to connect to such platforms and "get together" due to lack of equipment. The exclusion seems to be even greater for the users treated in hospitals as they are often not allowed to use their phones for long periods of time, let alone have internet connections. In addition, due to COVID-19, visiting people in need in shelters or hospitals is limited or not allowed, amplifying feelings of loneliness and exclusion.

In the last seminar, it was expressed that perhaps the confinement everybody is experiencing triggered more feelings of unity as it showed how all people, including mental health professionals, can be exposed to dangers to overall health, physical and mental. It may offer new perspectives on the designing of mental health services on behalf of carers, service users and policy makers. However, the results of this situation are expected to unfold in the future.

In general, the seminars, which are among our central activities, benefit the union and its members in various ways, due to the valuable exchange of information and ideas. In this context, we can help each other by raising awareness of important matters and standing up against rights violation. By feeling empowered, we can deliver more input in our treatment and address our collective and subjective needs. Furthermore, we are able to nurture empathy and understanding as we are connected by our common lived experiences.

Mental health service users' place in the disability movement

It is shown that treatment, housing, education and entertainment are areas that have turned out to be more accessible for people with psychosocial problems than employment, active citizenship and activities in the community (Yotsidi & Kounenou, 2018). The act of creating or belonging to a union is the epitome of active citizenship, which can benefit all the other neglected areas. Participating in such unions can benefit the members in multiple ways. Members of the Autoekprosopisi have said that just the process of organising and conducting a seminar, a meeting or a training (apart from being only a participant) has made a major difference in their empowerment and recovery. The process of communicating our ideas can be demanding, but only through practice will we build our capacities and skills. This way, we have a chance to contribute to an important task using all our knowledge, such as university education or any past training. The union of Autoekprosopisi and the expansion of similar initiatives can be major steps towards the empowerment and self-advocacy of people with psychosocial problems, who still have a great personal potential. This potential can turn out to be precious for the advocacy movement in mental health and the wider disability movement on human rights.

In the case of Greece, the matter of hierarchy in the disability rights movement and the marginalisation of the voices of individuals with psychosocial problems have some specific features. The collectivities formed by individuals with psychosocial problems who are voicing their interests have been instituted only in the last years. We are mostly witnessing the emergence of such a movement in the field of mental health. Therefore, it is logical to still have this population underrepresented in the disability movement and not have any mental health service users in leadership positions within national cross-disability organizations.

Many people with mental health issues are still unfamiliar with the terms "human rights" and "advocacy", reflecting a lack of awareness and information. In addition, among professionals, institutions and decision-makers, there is still difficulty in including human rights perspectives in clinical practice and policies. The later remarks highlight the need to have educational programmes which aim to inform interdisciplinary groups of users, professionals and policy-makers.

An example of this methodology is shown by Poulopoulos and Tsiboukli (2016), in which groups of mental health professionals, service users and administrative staff were trained together following the "action research" methodology (Lewin, 1946), based on theories of transformative learning and group dynamics. Using the action research allowed all members to offer their knowledge and experience in the training, while questioning matters of hierarchy and authority between trainees and trainers. That way, the interdisciplinary group managed to de-learn dysfunctional assumptions about each other and to equally take part in the decision-making process concerning changes in mental health organisations. Similar methodology could be applied in other mental health organisations or even cross-disability organisations to facilitate the integration process.

Concerning the integration of persons with psychosocial issues into the disability movement, more progress needs to be made. One of the main goals of the National Confederation of Disabled People in Greece (ESAMEA) was to encourage individuals with lived experience of any form of disability to create local groups that can be included in larger associations, unions and ultimately a federation. Multiple federations can be later included in ESAMEA. Surely, this is a challenging ongoing project, especially in the case of users of mental health services. After all, it is quite common for people with psychosocial problems not to identify as disabled and for the disability rights movement not to include this population. It is usual to have a misconception on the term "disability", even though it ultimately includes consequences of both physical and mental difficulties. Legally, it may be established, but it is not yet widely accepted within society. More efforts need to be made so that people with psychosocial problems can feel represented by the disability movement. After all, the United Nations Convention on the Rights of Persons with Disabilities offers a privileged field of consolidation of mental health rights and is a valuable tool for advocacy and self-advocacy.

By joining forces with other federations under the umbrella of "disability", all collectivities could have their requests be voiced more powerfully and heard more efficiently. Thus, collaboration among initiatives of active citizenship from multiple groups can benefit the human rights disability movement, bringing real changes to policies and everyday life. Feelings of unity serve both the movement of self-advocacy in mental health and the wider disability movement.

Strong networking between associations, unions and federations can make the movement's responses more structured, systematic and coherent. Thus, individuals can have access to support and legal aid in cases of emergency, such as the involuntary treatment, in a more effective way.

Networking between federations can be just as important as networking between institutions. Such reforms can lead to a stronger and more inclusive disability movement on human rights. An inclusive disability movement can inspire initiatives of creating unions of people with other intersecting identities. Diversity and multiplicity in identities do not change the fact that all initiatives are working for the same cause. Self-expression, self-advocacy and protection of the human rights of people with disability are the common ground that connects all initiatives.

Inside the disability movement, the union of Autoekprosopisi highlights the importance of self-advocacy among people with psychosocial difficulties. Getting together in a union and making decisions for ourselves becomes the alternative we propose to the hierarchy imposed on us in our communities. The journey to claiming the right of self-advocacy might be a challenging one, but, for sure, it is a fair way to battle stigma and the common narrative on mental illness. Also, it is important that mental health professionals and carers support such initiatives while trying to stand next to the people voicing their needs. The mental health community should be prepared to listen, in the context of a human rights–compliant approach on mental health, and avoid "overprotection" when collaborating with persons with psychosocial difficulties. The sole action of speaking up is part of the recovery process, and it can change dramatically the scenery of the human rights disability movement.

References

Curtice, M. J., & Exworthy, T. (2010). FREDA: a human rights-based approach to healthcare. *The Psychiatrist*, *34*(4), 150–156.

Fitsiou, P., & Kourachanis, N. (2019). Social policy challenges for homeless people with mental illness: views of Greek mental health professionals. *European Journal of Homelessness*, *13*(2).

Jacobson, N., & Greenley, D. (2001). What is recovery? A conceptual model and explication. *Psychiatric Services*, *52*(4), 482–485.

Lewin, K. (1946). Action research and minority problems. *Journal of Social Issues*, *2*(4), 34–46.

Loukidou, E., Mastroyannakis, A., Power, T., Thornicroft, G., Craig, T., & Bouras, N. (2013). Evaluation of Greek psychiatric reforms: methodological issues. *International Journal of Mental Health Systems*, *7*(11), 1–8.

Mastroyannakis, A., Nikolakopoulos, I., Markatou, A., Braoudaki, E., Braoudakis, G., Power, T., Graig, T., Thornicroft, G., & Bouras, N. (2015). *Final evaluation report of the implementation of the psychiatric reforms for the period 2011–2015*. Ministry of Health.

McGuire, M. (2009). Dignity, equality, freedom and respect: a human rights-based approach to mental health. *Health Issues*, *101*, 13–16.

Mitrossili, M. (1995). *Study on the social and legal status of the patients in the state mental hospital of Leros*. Printed in Greece by Edition Aivalis. (The European Commission supported financially the research project and the publication).

Poulopoulos, C., & Tsiboukli, A. (2016). *Group dynamics and change in organizations*. Topos Books.

Sayce, L. (2001). Social inclusion and mental health. *Psychiatric Bulletin*, *25*(4), 121–123. https://doi.org/10.1192/pb.25.4.121

Stylianidis, S., Peppou, E., Drakonakis, N., Douzenis, A., Panagou, A., Tsikou, K., Pantazi, A., Rizavas, Y., & Saraceno, B. (2017). Mental health care in Athens: are compulsory admissions in Greece a one-way road? *International Journal of Law and Psychiatry*, *52*, 28–34.

Williams, J., & Lindley, P. (1996). Working with mental health service users to change mental health services. *Journal of Community & Applied Social Psychology*, *6*(1), 1–14.

Yotsidi, V., & Kounenou, K. (2018). Experiences of mental health service users on their empowerment and social integration in the community. *The European Journal of Counselling Psychology*, *7*(1), 165–180.

8

DEVELOPING CULTURAL CAPACITY WITH PEOPLE WHO HAVE PROFOUND INTELLECTUAL DISABILITIES

Nicola Clare Grove, Annie Fergusson, Gillian White, Naomi Hewardine, Karen Bunning, Maureen Phillip, Sue Ledger and Elizabeth Tilley

This chapter is dedicated to the memory of Leo White, who taught us all so much. Here we explore cultural participation by a low-incidence population who remain largely unnoticed and unmentioned within academic literature or elsewhere: people with profound intellectual and multiple disabilities (PIMD). They are amongst the most marginalised and isolated groups in the modern world.

Article 27 of the Universal Declaration of Human Rights[1] states that "everyone has the right freely to participate in the cultural life of the community" and is further strengthened by the intentions laid out in the UN Convention on the Rights of Persons with Disabilities.[2] These include taking part on an equal basis with others in cultural life, with access to varied activities in accessible formats, as well as the opportunity to develop their creative, artistic and intellectual potential, not only for their own benefit but also for the enrichment of society. However, the voices and stories of those with PIMD remain unheard, and consequently, they have little impact on their own lives or the world around them.

Profound and multiple disabilities and cultural participation

The term "profound intellectual and multiple disabilities" details a set of distinct but common characteristics describing the complex and interrelated needs of this population. These include severe cognitive, neuromotor and/or sensory disabilities (IASSIDD).[3] They frequently have other disabling conditions including physical or sensory impairments, sensory processing difficulties, complex

DOI: 10.4324/9781003410089-10

medical needs, 'coping behaviours' (which may challenge others) and mental health difficulties. Communication is primarily non-verbal and prelinguistic. Ongoing prejudice, discriminatory practices and pervasive low expectations have resulted in a lack of personalised services and meaningful opportunities; they suffer from poorer health status and preventable early mortality (Harflett et al., 2015; LeDeR, 2019; Mansell, 2010), largely due to neglect by policy makers and inequities in service provision.

A key factor is that they are highly dependent on others for all aspects of their lives, including the interpretation of their emotions, interests and wishes. Those who know them well – families/carers/advocates/friends and involved professionals – act as their communication partners to advocate with and for them in ways that need to be creative, innovative and flexible (Doukas et al., 2017). It is notable that families too can feel isolated and ostracised (Fergusson, 2019; Harflett et al., 2015). Quality of life for persons with PIMD is too often judged (directly and indirectly) by those with no understanding or awareness of their lives, aspirations and potential or of the contributions they can make (Boyd, 2020). They are frequently invisible within their own local communities, often marginalised amongst people with learning disabilities (Palmer & Walmsley, 2020) and living by default on the fringes of society.

Participation for people with PIMDs

> Given the barriers they face, what kind of participation in culture is feasible? *Participation* has been defined as 'involvement in the life situation' (World Health Organization, 2001). A multi-dimensional concept, it involves two related constructs: *attendance/presence* (being present in the here and now) and *involvement*, (the subjective personal experience of taking part whilst attending.
>
> *(Imms, 2020)*

Presence is often reported as an indicator of participation, with measures of frequency and duration derived from surveys and observational schedules. Just being amongst others can enable visibility. This may seem a minimal requirement but is often difficult to achieve because of the need for adequate transportation, physical access, the sensory challenges presented by diverse environments and the fearful or uncomprehending reactions of others (de Haas, 2020; Nind & Strnadova, 2020). However, parallel occupation of space and time does not necessarily imply active engagement or social and emotional connection. These are critical to a consideration of the more complex construct of *involvement*. Involvement interacts with the individual's 'activity competence', 'sense of self ' and 'preferences' (Adair et al., 2020;129) across the life course.

Going beyond presence means creating opportunities for what Simmons (2020, p. 31) calls "active participation in culturally specific ways of engaging with the material environment" (and, we would add, the social environment). Cultural participation is not only important for enriching the lives of people with PIMD but also has benefits for society at large. Active representation of persons with disabilities in the cultural sector can challenge stereotypes (Graham et al., 2019); demonstrate the realities of translating policy into practice, allowing a fuller historical understanding to emerge (Welshman & Walmsley, 2006); and contribute to a discourse of diversity and inclusion. This is increasingly critical in a world where people are often perceived in terms of a 'single story' (Adichie, 2009): in this case, one of physical and mental deficit (Ledger, 2012). Yet all our lives consist of many overlapping stories, and people with PIMD are no different. To be included as a citizen, you need to be seen and heard. Only thus can individuals gain influence and contribute to society (Duffy, 2018; Nind & Strnadova, 2020). Cultural experience must relate to our own lived experiences. So what is the lived experience of people with PIMD, and how do they take part in the cultural life of their communities?

Lived experience

Here we present two accounts of lived experiences: a small boy and a young woman, both with PIMDs, one by a parent and one by a support worker.

Living with Leo: a parent's testimony

My son Leo is non-verbal. He has Ohtahara syndrome, a rare form of intractable epilepsy characterised by seizures and severe developmental delay. As much as I wish I could read his mind, I cannot. I don't pretend to understand the fullness of the difficulty that my son faces every day of his life. Yet I am his advocate. I am his voice.

That is no easy thing – being the voice for someone when you don't truly know what it is that they would want to say.

To the average onlooker, Leo does not have much to say. He does not show his emotions in ways that a lot of people can understand. He does not yet smile, nor does he laugh. Instead, Leo lets us know when he is unhappy. He does so initially by using small gestures and vocalisations, which are easily and often misinterpreted by others.

He does have things to say, though, and we do our best to listen.

As a family, we have always tried to give Leo as many experiences as we can. We pay attention to his reactions, and when we repeat the experience, we pay attention again. When a reaction is consistent, we gain an understanding of what he does and does not like.

Some of these reactions can be surprising, and we are learning all the time. I was moved recently by his reaction to a cello, an instrument which I was concerned that he would not enjoy. When he vocalised, the cellist responded by playing a note in a similar key and so on. This continued for seven or eight vocalisations. It was wonderful for me to watch him discover something new and interact with another person in this way.

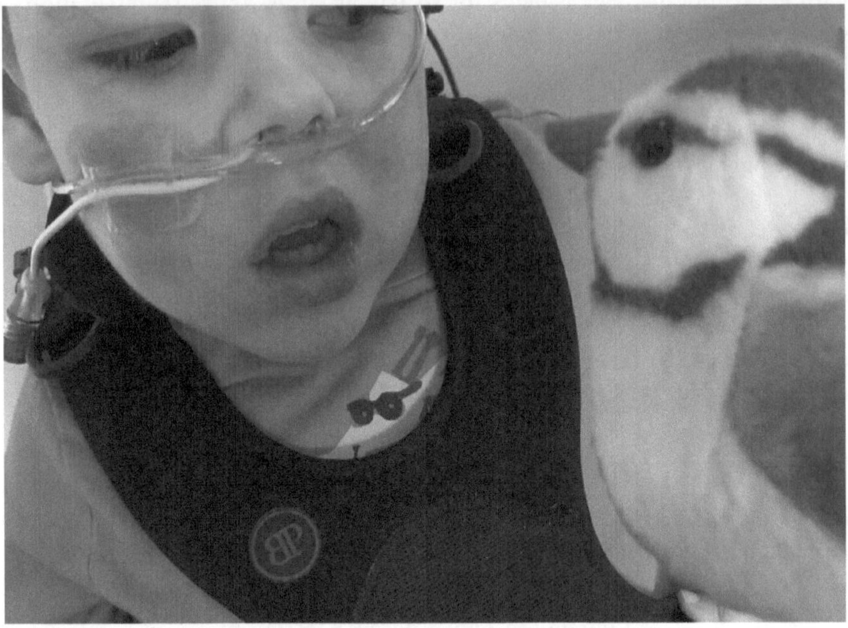

Figure 8.1 Leo and his bird

Sometimes medication, poor sleep, seizure activity or pain can make a previously enjoyable experience rather unpleasant. When we place a lot of significance on an experience, or if we are perhaps overly focused on development or progress, an off day can be disheartening.

On those days, it pays to remember that sometimes less is more.

I learned this lesson one warm afternoon in our garden. I was trying hard to engage Leo in a sensory story. He wasn't responding well, so I tried using his wind chimes and music, then herbs from his sensory garden. Everything served only to increase his agitation level and seizure activity. Eventually, worn out and feeling like a failure, I gave up.

Sitting there in silence, I noticed the tension relaxing in Leo's face and hands. He was clearly comfortable and looked so peaceful that I just left him to it. I sat alongside him, and as I listened to the birdsong, the bees and the occasional barking of the neighbour's dog, I began to relax also.

It was one of those perfect moments in which we experienced the same things together, and it only became possible when I stopped trying to force him into my moment and instead sat with him in his. Being able to adapt has always been key to living with Leo. There is no 'one size fits all' approach, and something that he seems to enjoy one day may not work the next. We need to pay attention and be sensitive to his needs and how he experiences things. I always try to keep in mind that day in our garden and remember that the most important thing is to meet Leo where he is.

Leo now has a collection of toy birds which sing when pressed. He enjoys the sound of water, learned from watching his reactions on our many walks along the river and the seafront. I incorporate the things I know he finds enjoyable into sensory stories. By doing this, I am able to gently introduce new sensory elements alongside ones we know soothe him. My focus is on trying to recreate in some way these shared moments or happy memories, rather than simply providing a range of sensory experiences. This process has so much more meaning for us, particularly when these will be repeated often. When event organisers understand this and can adapt and provide some degree of personalisation in how they provide cultural activities, it enriches the whole experience and makes it more meaningful. Organised events allow us to get out and have fun and inclusive experiences which not only allow us the opportunity to find out something new about our son but can also form the basis for new memories. As a family, these shared experiences build a connection, with both Leo and his wider community. That's what we want: to feel connected to our child and our locality, to understand him better and, in turn, to make his difficult life as enjoyable as we can.

Lived experience in adulthood

As people with PIMD grow older, they should be provided with an increasing range of opportunities to develop their interests and experience. An example is provided by Eve, who lives in a L'Arche community. L'Arche is an international federation of intentional communities in 35 countries worldwide that exists to 'make known the gifts of people with learning disabilities' in many creative ways. Eve is a woman in her mid-20s with PIMD and a connoisseur of classical music. Her mother and brothers are all professional musicians, and she grew up hearing them practise. Eve beats her foot in exact time to whatever piece she is listening to. The better the music, the more she vocalises, and far from being put off by this, local people have invited her to observe their rehearsals to see if they pass the 'Eve test'. She is known in local churches as 'the lady who likes concerts' (not the disabled lady), and her team is always informed about organ recitals and visiting choirs that might interest her. It is when that local community really does care that people with PIMD can be their true selves.

Cultural access for Eve means listening to music, attending concerts and participating in other communal events. For example, in 2020, L'Arche Canada organised the world's first international lip sync competition hosted by people with learning disabilities, which was an amazing experience for all involved. Communities from around the globe were pitted against each other on Facebook and YouTube, so they had huge exposure as well as some celebrity endorsements. Viewing a video of a person with PIMD portraying an artist like Taylor Swift (UK winners L'Arche Manchester)[4] challenges the public's assumptions and prejudices.

Leo and Eve are both living full lives within their own immediate circles. For the wider community to be involved, we need to find ways of enabling not only community presence but also active participation in cultural and civic life. One tried and tested avenue is through storytelling, both fictional and personal.

Access to culture through multi-sensory storytelling

Cultural access is the first step to participation – both in terms of managing to get into and stay in locations (adequate toilet facilities needed, as well as ramps and lifts) – and in enabling the audience to engage with the experience and materials. One of the first considerations in developing channels of engagement is the need to use a multi-sensory approach. We need to recognise that for people with PIMDs, access to experiences must be tailored to their needs as 'sensory beings' (Grace & Silva, 2017). Because they function largely at the level of sensori-motor reactions, their ability to monitor and instigate actions in the world beyond their immediate personal space is limited. They are likely to rely more on proximal senses of movement, touch, smell and taste than the distal sense of vision – although many will be highly responsive to sounds, whether environmental, music or familiar voices and tones. Such approaches come into play with multi-sensory storytelling, which encompasses the essence of the story, accompanying text with appropriately selected (and selective) props, smells, images and sounds, with both fictional and personal stories. (See Fuller, 2022; Grove & Park, 1996.) People participate both as audience and as creators of culture through these stories.

Audience participation

PAMIS in Scotland have been developing a rich programme of cultural storytelling, related both to landscape and to heritage sites and museums. Oral stories and literature provide a doorway into our cultural heritage and provide us with a sense of identity, connection and belonging. The portrayal of people with disabilities in stories provides an insight into the thinking of society at the time. It is a doorway to understanding how society viewed people with disabilities, and stigmatised representations are, of course, common in folklore and legend (Schmiesing, 2014), although redemptive narratives are also to be found. (See, *inter alia*, Grove et al., 2016.) Their absence and subsequent portrayal in children's picture books over time also conveys attitudes towards disability. However, that is slowly changing, and today we are beginning to see picture books and literature that celebrate people with disabilities from diverse backgrounds for who they are[5]. Two examples of culturally located practice are stories created in landscape and stories created in museums and arts or heritage centres.

Stories of the land

The natural world supports people with PIMD to immerse themselves in the land, its stories and its heritage. For example, when the journey of a river is followed from source to sea, its smells, sights and sound become a playground brimming with cultural information. The lives of people who lived along the route and the creatures who live in the river are woven into folklore, myths and legends of giants, kelpies,[6] fairies and magic, brought to life through a multi-sensory approach. Art, music, spoken word, poetry, film, sound, sight, smell, taste and touch can be woven together to create a vibrant and relevant learning experience of the river, which also provides a therapeutic space for connection with the personal story, meeting people, chatting to people, listening to natural sights and sounds, all reminding people with PIMD that they are a part of a wider society. This enables engagement with local culture. A trip to the river can be enjoyed as a day out and then be recreated on return. For example, his mother re-enacts Leo's excursions into nature, using a consistent set of massage strokes[7] props to represent memories of wind, speed, water and birdsong. Community celebrations of the story of the river are great ways of including everyone in the event.

Museums and heritage sites

Museums and heritage sites brim with stories. They are vibrant cultural hubs that people with PIMD can access and enjoy through multi-sensory storytelling and also expand our understanding of what cultural heritage means and its reach. For example, collaborating with authors and the Edinburgh International Book Festival to produce accessible versions of texts ensures full inclusion for people with PIMD. In Scotland, there is dedicated funding for access, with mandatory provision of appropriate toilets and consultation about transport with families. The V&A in Dundee[8] have customised displays for access and visibility, providing accessible information and designating quiet times.

Accessing the creative arts, culture and heritage through forms of storytelling provides opportunities for lifelong learning and opens doors to other worlds offering exploration, imagination, enjoyment, fun, excitement, learning and development. Through storytelling, people with PIMD become visible and included in their communities.

However, for the kind of active participation envisaged by Simmons (2020), people with PIMD need to make their voices heard. Again, storytelling offers a valid route, this time through the sharing of personal life experiences.

But in order to be truly accepted, people with PIMD are now changing the story from one of being excluded to one of being accepted in society for who they truly are. As our next topic demonstrates, they can be creators as well as consumers of culture.

As tellers of their own stories

Personal stories are the way we build communities, sustain relationships and understand our world. They are an essential tool in developing a shared culture with others both at the micro-level of social circles – friends, families, workplaces and lived environment, where 'small stories' are exchanged (Bamberg & Georgapoulou, 2008) – and at the macro-level of society, where life events are writ large, framed and fashioned into the stories we tell ourselves about who we are and which form our cultural identities. A personal story is one that actually happened to me or to someone I know. (We can and do incorporate the experiences of others into our repertoire.) Our memory of the event inescapably takes the form of a narrative – when and where we were, with whom, what occurred, the reactions, how it began and ended. Emotion is the driving force for sharing these stories – we seek an audience to confirm our account of ourselves, to empathise, explain, applaud or recoil in shock. Without the ability to do this, we are trapped in a solipsistic present, with no means of understanding our past or looking to our future. This, in fact, is reality for many persons with PIMDs. It is hard for us to enter their world and to see it from their perspective. We cannot "know" what they make of the experiences they have. This, as we have seen, can lead to exclusion; they seem to operate in a parallel universe where concepts of citizenship and community participation have little meaning. We can, however, change this situation by putting shared experiences and their retelling at the heart of provision, using appropriate conversational strategies and multi-sensory presentation.

The process of sharing a personal story

Stories of personal experience always cohere around a significant meaningful event. To engage people with PIMD in narrative means enabling them first to have experiences worth sharing, then to register the event as it happens, to have someone who shares the experience and to recall it for an empathetic audience. One approach we use is Storysharing[9] (Bunning et al., 2017; Grove & Harwood, 2022), which draws on social constructionist theories of anecdotal narrative, teaching partners to distinguish between fact finding and shared telling. Rhythmic qualities of everyday speech are emphasised, recapitulating the structure of early interactions (Trevarthen, 2015). Through repeated co-telling, partners learn to build the story together and make space for each other. For example, in one home, staff and residents shared a memory of taking the cat to the vet and how everyone cared for each other. In Eve's case, a house excursion to see Eve's mum play in the orchestra for *The Snow Man* was retold using Storysharing techniques to help everyone recall and celebrate the event. Thus, shared culture is integrated into Eve's own life story.

These small stories of everyday life feed into life stories, which are increasingly regarded as vital in understanding a person's history and their identity (e.g. Ledger et al., 2022; Middleton & Hewitt, 1999; PMLD Link, 2019; Terjavjainnena, 2020; Campaign 4 Change, 2020.)[10] Life stories and experiences can be shared face to face but also recorded using a range of different options – digital media (e.g. McCormack, 2020), personalised story boxes (Lambe et al., 2022) and artwork. However, to enable these stories to have the wider currency they deserve, further barriers need to be overcome.

Participating as an artist: the negotiation of consent

In the UK, artists with PIMD have begun to share their work in leading artistic venues, both locally and nationally.[11] This raises questions about access to exhibition space, permanent collections and the archives that are the continuing record of a culture for the opportunity to be represented in history is an important part of belonging in society (Tilley et al., 2020), a point recognised by the National Archives, UK:

> Our collections will reflect all of society, so that whether an individual, community or organisation, archives can tell us who we are and how we got here.
>
> *(2017, p. 4)*

Such a process involves addressing complex historical, legal, ethical and practical issues that have to be navigated by the institutions that document and preserve our history and heritage. But who is referred to by the ambiguous *our*? This question raises fundamental issues about representation, rights and legacy. Whose accounts, experiences and memories are captured? Whose voices count; whose lives are considered to have value? As a result, it is vital to explore the mechanics of how people with PIMD can be supported to be 'part of history' through the archives.

However, a major barrier to the inclusion of PIMD in archives and history is that of their perceived capacity to consent to sharing and depositing materials, experiences and artefacts. Hunt et al. (2015) describe how confusion about the law prevented the inclusion of photographs of people with complex disabilities in their oral history exhibition. Consultation with heritage sector staff (Tilley et al., 2020) identified that one of the most significant barriers is the necessity to evidence consent from a potential depositor with PIMD. In this section, we explain how one artist and her family worked with researchers to build a decision-making pathway that addresses the barrier of capacity to consent as part of the Inclusive Archive of Learning Disability History Research Project, led by the Open University (2014–2017).[12] This research was divided into two stages: *consultation* and *co-production* of an archive depositing pathway.

Consultation

As this was such a new and under-researched area, it was critical to begin with a consultation to establish if participation in public archives was of genuine interest and potential benefit. A series of national and inclusive events brought together people with PIMDs, their families, paid supporters, advocacy groups, social care providers, health and social care practitioners, archivists, heritage specialists, disability arts and theatre groups, academics and technologists. Findings confirmed that people with PIMDs and those closely involved in their lives did have stories and materials to share through archives. Families felt that this could contribute to improved understanding and inclusion in society more generally, in addition to reducing the social isolation they so often experienced. A very strong message was that having someone who cared a great deal about the person and knew them well would support really good communication and decision making. Families also made the point that many of them were already collating their own informal archives and sharing photos using online platforms and that this was beneficial, enabling the gifts and contributions of individuals to be acknowledged and shared. Potential risks to inclusion were also identified, such as exposure to negative comments or online trolling and tracing, but the consensus was that these could be tackled through existing legislation and adjustment of local systems rather than presenting insurmountable barriers to participation in archive collections.

To overcome the barriers associated with understanding and consent, the overriding preference was a clear, step-by-step and legally compliant decision-making pathway, co-developed with people with PIMD, that families, care staff and archivists could follow. Such an 'archive depositing pathway' would provide guidance for archivists inexperienced in communicating with people with profound intellectual disabilities and unfamiliar with the application of legislation such as, in England and Wales, the Mental Capacity Act (2005). The first step was to find a potential depositor with PIMD. The research team opted to work closely with one individual with PIMD and their circle of support, alongside an archivist, to co-produce the pathway.

Co-production with artist Cherry Lane

We got to know Cherry Lane and her mother, Angela, as part of a research project exploring people with intellectual disabilities' participation in – and contribution to – heritage.[13] Cherry lives with her family, supported by a team of personal carers. First, we spent time at Cherry's home, where she was able to share some of her artworks with us and where we met members of her family and heard the story of her development as an artist. Angela explained that Cherry was first introduced to working creatively with different materials when an experienced artist from a collective visited her school. Cherry was given the space, time and encouragement to express herself using different media and colours.

In her family's view, the opportunity for Cherry to express and communicate her world and feelings through art has been life changing. Since that first visit, she has consistently chosen to make art. Through this interest, she is part of a wider artistic community where she is welcomed and where her talents and multi-sensory approach to working with paint are clearly recognised and respected. Art has enabled Cherry to share her perspective on the world and aspects of her own story. Now a longstanding member of the same art collective, with her own studio space, she has contributed as a visual artist to several local public exhibitions and to a national show at the Tate Gallery in London (see Figure 8.2) and an international conference (Adams, 2019). In 2021, her art collective were finalists in the Turner Prize with an installation that includes Cherry Lane's catalogued work.[14] A copy of a ground-breaking publication

Figure 8.2 Self-portrait, by Cherry Lane with Project Art Works[15]

Source: Photo credit Layton Thompson, www.laytonthompson.com

showcasing her artwork was identified by Cherry's family as a possible item to deposit in their local public archive (Adams & Shaw, 2009).

Cherry's family and carers all felt that Cherry had enjoyed sharing her art work at previous events. She had also participated in a multimedia project to document her life story and had a collection of photographs, films and objects linked to this work. She therefore had items that were of confirmed interest to her local archive, The Keep in East Sussex,[16] whose staff were keen and available to work with us. Over a period of a few months, the research team worked alongside Cherry and her mother to enable Cherry to find out more about The Keep and to gauge her reactions to it. This involved a series of visits, enabling Cherry to hang out in the building, experience the environment, meet a learning and outreach specialist and view other items that had been deposited, including donations from other local artists.

Cherry seemed to enjoy being in the archive – she appeared interested in viewing and touching materials made by other artists. She was enthusiastic about being shown around the archive's strong-rooms, where precious material is held. Cherry also seemed happy to 'try out' the process of depositing by putting her own things in a box and to share her art work with strangers. We therefore embarked on a decision-making process to determine whether or not her art work should be deposited at The Keep.

The decision-making pathway

The process we used is documented in detail by Tilley et al. (2020). In England and Wales, the legislation covering decision making with adults who may lack mental capacity is the Mental Capacity Act (2005), which requires an assessment to be completed if doubts arise about an individual's capacity to understand, retain, weigh up information or communicate a specific decision. If a person has been assessed as lacking capacity, then any action taken or any decision made for or on behalf of that person must be made in his or her best interests. The Act provides a non-exhaustive checklist of factors that decision-makers must work through during this process.

The completed online pathway shows Cherry and her supporters moving through the stages:

1. Considering and identifying possible deposits
2. Learning about what an archive is and making a series of visits
3. Weighing up the pros and cons of Cherry sharing her story in a public archive – including the issue of sharing with strangers
4. Completing a mental capacity assessment
5. Making a best-interests decision with Cherry's full involvement
6. Cherry depositing in her local archive

Photographs and film clips of Cherry were embedded at each pathway stage (see Figure 8.3) in addition to links to simple pro forma templates, designed

Figure 8.3 Cherry Lane visiting The Keep. (The learning and outreach officer had prepared a collection of work from other local artists for Cherry to view and handle)

to enable easy evidencing of compliance with legislation (Graham & Cowley, 2015). A key function of the pathway was to demonstrate how people with profound disabilities can be supported to explore what depositing in an archive might involve and to express their views and reactions about taking part: for example, monitoring assent and providing information using a range of media.

The pathway also contains guidance for archivists in preparing for a person with profound disabilities to visit. Interestingly, the archivist observed that the steps she took to prepare and engage with Cherry as a potential depositor were the same as for any other visitor to the archive.

In Cherry's case, it was determined that a 'best-interests' decision was the optimum way to proceed, and Cherry's mother weighed up potential risks and benefits, leading to the deposition of the publication at The Keep. At last, the work of an artist with profound intellectual disabilities would become part of the historical record: her contribution to culture recorded for posterity. Another artist may well have been deemed to have the capacity to consent or to refuse. And, of course, the right of an artist to decline opportunities is just as important as their right to accept.

An important step forward has been the confirmation that the pathway is legally compliant (Lee, 2017), thus addressing one of the critical barriers in this arena. Our discussions with the QC also confirmed that the concept of 'best interests' was expanding with emerging case law to encompass elements of public benefit – notably notions of altruism and concern for others (Lee, 2017). This was critical to discussions that were unfolding in our research about the role of PIMD and their families in matters of legacy, representation and using history for social change. The legal advice also addressed the 'emotional dimension' of best-interests decision making: i.e. the significance of relationships and a sense of belonging, which we argue are highly relevant for decisions relating to one's participation in history and heritage.

Moving forward, we hope that this pathway will enable people with profound disabilities, their families and their carers to feel a greater sense of their lived experiences and contributions being confidently welcomed in public archive collections and to consider adding their own stories to the historical record.

Conclusion: Beyond inclusion

Despite rights and entitlements being well detailed in international agreements and enshrined in law, access to cultural provision and opportunities for meaningful inclusion and participation vary considerably. For this PIMD group of individuals, we see diversity and inequities by age (especially between children and adults), geographically (as illustrated in examples shared here from Scotland compared with England) and attitudinally, where a sliding scale of prejudice is mapped to an individual's level of cognition/intellectual impairment.

Although much remains to be done, some societies have enacted legislation to address these barriers, and people with PIMD are now educating communities about what is needed to ensure we are a fully inclusive society. This population have much to contribute and lead lives in which they don't just survive; they thrive. However, we need to go beyond an extension of access to ensuring that the needs and abilities of the most excluded individuals are the starting point for designing provision.[17]

The dimensions of cultural participation that we have discussed in this chapter are an inclusive, positive and welcoming attitude on the part of providers; accessibility (both physical and information related); representation; and the opportunity to contribute, both as audience and as artists.

Hearing their authentic and personal stories offer valuable insights into the important minutiae of their real-world set, they demonstrate firsthand how we can develop more creative, outside-the-box thinking and an appreciation for living in the moment. Where people are enabled to have a voice and draw on their lived experiences, they can act as advocates and activists, campaigning for change (Terjavjainnena, 2020); they can take on roles in their local communities[18] or as expert advisors and consultants (Fergusson, 2019; Frozen Light Theatre[19]; The Sensory Projects[20]) and even proactively contribute to and influence national health services (CBF/Tizard21).[21] They can engage in cultural arenas as artists, players, storytellers and musicians (Numata, 2016). Above all, they are our best educators. People with PIMD are changing the story from one of being excluded to one of being accepted in society for who they truly are.

Acknowledgements

We would like to thank all the individuals and families mentioned in this chapter for generously sharing their experiences. We are grateful also for the work of influencers in the field, including Loretto Lambe, founder of PAMIS, and Kate Adams, founder of Project Art Works.

Notes

1 http://www.unesco.org/culture/culture-sector-knowledge-management-tools/10_Info%20Sheet_Right%20to%20Culture.pdf
2 UN convention on the rights of persons with disabilities. https://www.un.org/development/desa/disabilities/convention-on-the-rights-of-persons-with-disabilities/article-30-participation-in-cultural-life-recreation-leisure-and-sport.html Accessed 23 March 2021.
3 https://www.iassidd.org
4 https://www.ross-shirejournal.co.uk/news/video-larche-highland-rocks-the-lockdown-with-disney-classic-224893/
5 Looking for Someone Like Me: Representation in Picture Books – Learning | Edinburgh International Book Festival (edbookfest.co.uk)
6 Kelpies are shape-shifting aquatic spirits of Scottish legends. These malevolent creatures are found in rivers and streams and usually take the shape of a horse.
7 https://storymassage.co.uk
8 https://www.vam.ac.uk/dundee
9 www.storysharing.org.uk
10 https://www.youtube.com/watch?v=8hS2WK5l7t0&t=26s
11 See, *inter alia*, https://projectartworks.org, https://intoart.org.uk
12 The Inclusive Archive of Learning Disability History Project was funded by the UK's Arts and Humanities Research Council, grant number, AH/K007459/1, between 2014–2017.
13 The Inclusive Archive of Learning Disability History Project, led by the Open University, was funded by the UK's Arts and Humanities Research Council, grant number AH/K007459/1, between 2014–2017.
14 https://coventry2021.co.uk
15 Cherry worked with Project Art Works. The technique of filming Cherry with a mini camcorder and projecting it on a wall for her to watch before freezing and painting over the projected image is one that Project Art Works have used often with artists with profound intellectual disabilities.
16 https://www.thekeep.info
17 See http://www.universaldesign.com/what-is-ud/
18 https://dimensions-uk.org/get-involved/campaigns/covid-leaders-list/
19 https://www.frozenlighttheatre.com.
20 http://www.thesensoryprojects.co.uk/the-sensory-being-project
21 https://www.challengingbehaviour.org.uk/driving-change/seldom-heard.html

References

Adair, B., Majnemer, A., & Imms, C. (2020). Measuring participation as an outcome: attendance and involvement. In C. Imms & D. Green (Eds.), *Participation: optimising outcomes in childhood-onset neurodisability* (pp. 129–142). MacKeith Press.

Adams, K. (2021, November). Introduction to awareness raising. In [Conference presentation] *Explorers Conference Art, Rights and Representation Conference.* Milton Keynes Art Gallery.

Adams, K., & Shaw, P. (2009). *Art in transition.* Project Art Works.

Adichie, C. N. (2009, July). The danger of a single story [Transcript]. *TED Conferences.* https://www.ted.com/talks/chimamanda_ngozi_adichie_the_danger_of_a_single_story/transcript. Accessed 20 April 2021.

Bamberg, M., & Georgapoulou, A. (2008). Small stories as a new perspective in narrative and identity analysis. *Text & Talk – An Interdisciplinary Journal of Language, Discourse Communication Studies, 28,* 377–396.

Boyd, C. (2020). Fury over NHS 'coronavirus scoring system' which treats learning disability patients like a 'sub-class of the population'. https://www.dailymail.co.uk/news/article-8214689/Fury-NHS-coronavirus-scoring-discriminates-against-learning-disability-patient.html. Accessed 14 April 2020.

Bunning, K., Gooch, L., & Johnson, M. (2017). Developing the personal narratives of children with complex communication needs associated with intellectual disabilities: what is the potential of Storysharing®? *Journal of Applied Research in Intellectual Disabilities, 30,* 743–756.

Campaign 4 Change. (2020). We are people (film). https://www.youtube.com/watch?v=8hS2WK5l7t0&t=26s. Accessed 12 April 2021.

de Haas, C. (2020). Singing together: friends and families' perspectives of possible ways to be included in society. In M. Nind & I. Strnadová (Eds.), *Belonging for people with profound intellectual and multiple disabilities: pushing the boundaries of inclusion* (pp. 176–195). Routledge.

Doukas, T., Fergusson, A., Fullerton, M., & Grace, J. (2017). Supporting people with profound and multiple disabilities. *Core and Essential Service Standards.* http://www.pmldlink.org.uk/wp-content/uploads/2017/11/Standards-PMLD-h-web.pdf. Accessed 23 April 2021.

Duffy, S. (2018, November 28). Everyone, yes, everyone can be a citizen [Conference presentation]. In *Citizen network: raising the bar II, PMLD LINK Conference.* https://www.pmldlink.org.uk/national-conference/

Fergusson, A. (2019). Raising the bar through inclusive theatre. An evaluation of the isle of Brimsker by Frozen Light – a multisensory theatre performance for adults with profound and multiple learning disabilities. https://www.frozenlighttheatre.com/resources. Accessed 24 April 2021.

Fuller, C. (2022). Multi-sensory story packs. In N. Grove (Ed.), *Storytelling, special needs and disabilities: practical approaches for children and adults* (pp. 112–119). Routledge.

Grace, J., & Silva, A. (2017). Refining the guidance for sensory storytelling with individuals with PMLD: a move towards improved research and practice. *PMLD Link, 29*(3), Issue 88, 11–15.

Graham, H., Brownlee-Chapman, C., Chapman, R., Eardley, C., Forster, S., Green, V., Harkness, E., Headon, K., Humphreys, P., Ingham, N., Ledger, S., May, V., Minnion, A., Tilley, E., & Townson, L. (2019). The public and the relational: the collaborative practices of the inclusive archive of learning disability history project. In S. Popple (Ed.), *Communities, archives and new collaborative practices* (pp. 219–234). Policy Press.

Graham, M., & Cowley, J. (2015). *A practical guide to the Mental Capacity Act 2005.* JKP.

Grove, N., & Harwood, J. (2022). Storysharing® Personal narratives for identity and community. In N. Grove (Ed.), Storytelling, special needs and disabilities: practical approaches for children and adults (pp. 159–167). Routledge.

Grove, N., & Park, K. (1996). *Odyssey NOW*. JKP.

Grove, N., Takano, M., Udo, M., & Mitsudo, Y. (2016). Heroes with a difference: legends and personal stories with Japanese school children. *SLD Experience*, pp. 3–5.

Harflett, N., Turners, S., & Brown, H (2015). *The impact of personalization on the lives of the most isolated people with learning disabilities. A review of the evidence.* NDTI.

Hunt, P., Pickard, S. & Harris, L. (2015, June 19). The 'hidden now heard' project [Conference presentation]. In *Biography, life stories and life histories*, The Open University, Milton Keynes.

Imms, C. (2020). The nature of participation. In C. Imms & D. Green (Eds.), *Participation: optimising outcomes in childhood-onset neurodisability* (pp. 5–11). MacKeith Press.

Lambe, L., Miller, J., & Phillip, M. (2022). Sensitive stories: tackling challenges for people with profound intellectual disabilities through multi-sensory storytelling. In N. Grove (Ed.), *Storytelling, special needs and disabilities: practical approaches for children and adults.* (pp. 143–151). Routledge.

LeDeR. (2019). *Learning disability mortality review (LeDeR) programme. Annual Report 2018.* University of Bristol.

Ledger, S. (2012). *Staying local: support for people with learning difficulties from inner London 1971–2007.* (Unpublished PhD Thesis). The Open University, Milton Keynes.

Ledger, S., McCormack, N., Walmsley, J., Tilley, E., & Davies, I. (2022). "Everyone has a story to tell": a review of life stories in learning disability research and practice. *British Journal of Learning Disabilities*, *50*, 484–493. https://doi.org/10.1111/bld.12388

Lee, A. (2017). In the matter of The Open University and a proposal to establish a learning disability archive (Legal advice received from 39 Essex Chambers, private correspondence).

Mansell, J. (2010). *Raising our sights: services for adults with profound intellectual and multiple disabilities.* University of Kent, Tizard Centre.

McCormack, N. (2020). A trip to the caves: Making life story work inclusive and accessible. In M. Nind & I. Strnadová (Eds.), *Belonging for people with profound and multiple disabilities: Pushing the boundaries of inclusion* (pp. 98–112). Routledge.

Middleton, D. & Hewitt, H. (1999). Remembering as social practice: identity and life story work in transitions of care for people with profound learning disabilities. *Narrative Inquiry*, *9*, 97–121.

Nind, M., & Strnadova, I. (Eds.) (2020). *Belonging for people with profound intellectual and multiple disabilities. Pushing the boundaries of inclusion.* Routledge.

Numata, R. (2016). The Otoasobi project: improvising with disability. *Music & Arts In Action*, *5*(1), 45–51.

Palmer, C., & Walmsley, J. (2020). Fellow traveller account 3: are people with profound and multiple learning disabilities and their families welcome in the wider learning disability community? In M. Nind & I. Strnadova (Eds.), *Belonging for people with profound intellectual and multiple disabilities: pushing the boundaries of inclusion* (pp. 129–132). Routledge.

PMLD Link. (Eds.). (2019). Celebrating lives – living life to the full. *PMLD LINK*, *31*(3), 35–36.

Schmiesing, A. (2014). *Disability, deformity and disease in Grimm's Fairy Tales.* Wayne State University Press.

Simmons, B. (2020). Exploring the situated social being of children with profound and multiple learning difficulties across educational contexts. In M. Nind & I. Strnadová

(Eds.), *Belonging for people with profound intellectual and multiple disabilities: pushing the boundaries of inclusion* (pp. 27–40). Routledge.

Terjavjainnena, E. (2020) Samir, Frankie and Brad from Campaign 4 change present at the Learning Disability England (LDE) conference. *PMLD LINK, 32*(2), 49–50.

The National Archives (2017). *Archives unlocked*. OGL.

Tilley, E., Ledger, S., & de Haas, C. (2020). Enabling people with profound and multiple learning disabilities to belong in public and community archive collections. In M. Nind & I. Strnadová (Eds.), *Belonging for people with profound intellectual and multiple disabilities: Pushing the boundaries of inclusion* (pp. 176–195). Routledge.

Trevarthen, C. (2015). Infant semiosis: the psycho-biology of action and shared experience from birth. *Cognitive Development, 36*, 130–141.

Welshman, J., & Walmsley, J. (Eds.). (2006). *Community care in perspective: care, control and citizenship*. Palgrave Macmillan.

World Health Organization. (2001). International classification of functioning, disability and health (ICF). https://www.who.int/standards/classifications/international-classification-of-functioning-disability-and-health. Accessed 22 April 2021.

9

FIGHTING FOR THE RIGHTS OF THE NON-SPEAKING

Typing words to be heard

Nicolas Joncour

Life for autistic people is difficult enough, but it becomes even harder for a non-speaking person.

I am an autistic student, and I am 21 years old. I have dyspraxia, which prevents me from speaking, and I need full-time help. I have passed the baccalaureate (the exam in France that is required to go to university), and I am now studying law at the University of Rennes.

Today I am a member of several associations defending the rights of disabled people, autistic people, and non-speaking people: the European Network for Independent Living (ENIL), a group for autistic people's freedom of expression (CLE-Autistes), and the International Association for Spelling as Communication (I-ASC).

I don't speak, but I communicate by typing on a computer keyboard or iPad and pointing to letters on a communication board.

People think that the involuntary gestures and sounds I make render impossible my participation in any conversation and that I am unable to communicate. Yet I write essays on constitutional law, I am interested in the history of political cultures, I read books on economics, and I am wondering what future we are building together by continuing down the neoliberal path.

Mostly, I am not seen as a capable being but as a strange animal that has no access to the outside world. For neurotypical people, the mere fact that I can express myself through typing seems impossible. Most people see me as a person who doesn't understand what is being said. I am often referred to in the third person as if I am not there, even though I can communicate. I am aware that I am perceived by most people as a being devoid of any intelligence, understanding of others, or even any form of thought or desire.

DOI: 10.4324/9781003410089-11

I have long had the secret strength to endure poor evaluations of my abilities. As a child, I despaired of having a happy life without being assimilated into the stereotype of the little alien in his protective bubble. I am a human being who has faith in the creative power of societies and social progress. I want a world that allows everyone to be accepted as a being with dignity, dreams, knowledge, singular perceptions, and a will of their own.

Then I realized that the source of my suffering and that of my peers was mainly ignorance and that the best way to break down discrimination was to use law and education.

After becoming interested in the history of the Holocaust and particularly Aktion T4,[1] I decided that rather than just showing the horrors of the past, I would denounce the eugenic and ableist practices that are very trending through the world today. I seriously believe that my desire to storm the national assembly is greater every day! The law is a source of understanding for me of political and institutional mechanisms and helps me build hope for a better life based on federative and solidarity struggles.

In fact, a discriminatory hierarchical structure has usurped the universal feature of human dignity.

Unfortunately, I must inform you of my observations. The value of a human being is massively based on their capacity to correspond to norms: productivity, verbal communication, having a standardized body and behavior, showing the power of their physical or mental strength.

I also have experienced prejudice and stigma from disabled people who are not autistic. In fact, it is not just belonging to a group that makes sense, but a real awareness of the problems created by a system that denies the value of our differences. I do believe that a person experiencing oppression can reproduce that same oppression if he or she has integrated certain norms without violating or questioning them. For example, I have noticed that people can be highly ableist while they have a disability and are being denigrated as well. I, for my part, think people can have one or more disabilities and frankly make fun of a person among passersby on the street for having an unusual gait or a stylistically different body language. Many people stigmatize those with neurodifference or autism because we are seen as lacking intelligence.

We are constantly associated with severe deficiency or insanity. For a part of the population, people with unusual mental systems do not even deserve to live, even if the Nazi regime collapsed in 1945. I cannot say that the community has prioritized the rights of non-speaking autistic people because we are massively burned on the altar of pathologization and are a minority within the minority. That is to say, in the end, very few of us are able to express ourselves – to write, for example – in a complex way by ourselves, with adapted communication supports and really talented people we trust in to assist us. And above all, the enormous majority of non-speaking autistic people – I am revolted by this situation – are in institutions and cannot live independently. Indeed, it is also the way we are perceived that often prevents our rights from being respected. From the moment we are looked at as intellectually deficient or ill-suited to the world, we have definitely remained subhuman in many people's minds. There is no denying that the disability rights community, of which I am a member, is mostly made up of people with motor disabilities. What is important is to reconsider the perspective of opening up the anti-disability struggle to neurodivergent people and to people with mental disabilities as well. I think it's nonsense to decide that the right to dignity is granted according to the appreciation of intelligence. I have struggled since I was a child to prove that I have an opinion and a will of my own, and I am worn down by the disregard. Many of us experience this unacceptable stigma.

I would like to have an aspiration for more consideration, more decisions that I initiate. My body does not obey my will, and I have to do a lot of work to be always in control of myself. I can't always act in a direct way as my body doesn't do everything I would like it to do. I am used to writing down my desires and sharing the plans I have in mind with my personal assistant because I can't initiate on my own. I make plans for myself, however, to start moving: all I need is a good personal assistant to listen to me and act as a "supporter". This means that with each person who assists me, and in each different context, I have to rework my typing skills, and this is very difficult. I feel like I have to start typing all over again as if I had to relearn everything, and I need a lot of time to have effective communication. Sometimes my wishes are not listened to very quickly. Because I sometimes have difficulties in writing them, people will do it for me, or really decide for me, because they want to do things quickly, whereas I ask for my legitimate desire for self-determination to be respected.

As I read, watched movies, reviewed the news, and grew up, the world seemed especially built on segregated principles. People whose ways of expressing themselves, communicating, and perceiving are different are systematically devalued and discriminated against. It is a terrible mistake for society to remain in a state of exclusion that risks standardizing the human being.

If the neurodiversity[2] movement has made it possible to break the absurd laws established by the ableist doctrine, its liberating value goes unnoticed in many countries like France.

It is a model that allows us to get out of the pathological vision of people who, like me, comprehend the world differently. In France, the medical model takes a decidedly virulent place and muzzles the social struggles of autistic people and disabled people considerably. I believe that what prevents this new wave of thought from flourishing lies in the antagonistic positions that have been established within the autistic community.

On the one hand, we have representatives of a model focused on our social adaptation that aims to modify our behaviours so that they correspond to the acceptable norm for an allistic person.[3] On the other hand, there is a vision that asserts that we have modes of communication, perception, and thought that belong only to us and that it is therefore society that must respect our rights and needs.

Recently, the neurodiversity movement has been growing in Europe, but it is often perceived as radical. We deserve to be considered as persons of interest with dignity, and we want the world to stop reducing us to maladjusted individuals. This is not to dispute the fact that we have special needs to help us live well, such as appropriate support in our schooling and studies, tools to manage our emotional and sensory difficulties, alternative communication supports, and trusted people who see us as their equals.

I had a fabulous experience at a ENIL youth summer session in 2018. We were very attentive to each other, and all the friends really allowed me to express myself by giving me a real space to type. There was a beautiful care, respect, and solidarity. I have never felt so good in my life. This was of one week of my life, and one of my happiest dreams would be for my daily life to be like this all the time. I'm truly blessed to be a part of the independent living movement, and I have faith in a better scenario than the one of the evil eugenics touted by the state.

I am sorry to see that some people believe that the independent living movement is only for people with a so-called "minimal" disability, just as those who believe that neurodiversity only includes Asperger's. This is totally false. The truth is that it is institutional logic that prevents free choice. Most people think that an institution is the necessary answer for people with significant disabilities. By entering an institution, we lose our freedom for so-called protection. Yet we are subjects of law, just like non-disabled people. France ratified the International Convention on the Rights of Persons with Disabilities in 2010. However, the last report of the UN committee (August 2021) was very critical of France. There is no will among politicians for deinstitutionalization. Although international law, in principle, supersedes domestic law, the government seems to remain in a certain archaism of charitable culture, which blandly serves the meritocratic ableist tyranny. In reality, France does not respect the Convention. They are not even in conformity with 2005 law on the compensation of disability, even its definition of disability. New projects of inclusive homes or residential units do not correspond to Article 19 of the CRDP on the right to independent living. A process of deinstitutionalization must begin for France, and we want to have a better representation. Rome was not built in a day, but I keep the faith.

France is also in violation of Article 12 of the CRPD concerning equal recognition of legal personality before the law. The current French government gave the right to vote to protected adults in 2019 (reform of March 23), but it is the whole system of legal protection that must be questioned. Guardianship must be replaced by supported decision making. With guardianship or curatorship, we are deprived of our rights since the legal representative or guardian decides for us, in our place. Society gives us an illusion of autonomy. It is important to keep our legal capacity: regardless of our disability, we have desires and preferences.

I never knew what it was like to live under guardianship because my parents always fought for me so I could make my own choices and be accompanied in my administrative adventures and my life projects. Indeed, without self-determination, I would not have arrived in a faculty of law after one year in physics,

Neither could I have gone to church and then gotten baptized, even though my parents are atheists. Even if I have my legal capacity, I do know, however, that our rights are easily taken away. Anyone can try to put me under guardianship against my will because some people doubt my intellectual capacities. I would then no longer be able to exercise my rights as a citizen.

If my parents had not been there to encourage me to express my views and wishes for my life, and also to support the cause of autonomy for disabled people, I would never have been able to exercise my legal capacity. I would surely be in an institution, chained to a wall of silence, without political involvement or the possibility to study, without being free to make my life choices, either. This unchangeable destiny would have jeopardized my freedom, and I would have had only crumbs of it.

Accepting these conditions of existence would have turned this fabulous dream of autonomy, this heritage of years of struggle, into a forgotten and denied history. Nevertheless, most people do not know about the struggle for disability rights because they have never been told about it, and others are unaware of our experiences because it seems easier for them not to feel guilty.

I am looked at as a "retard", but I continue my journey to freedom by believing in justice and in God's love.

Let's make this future society a world where our rights are respected, regardless of our differences.

Cle-Autistes: https://cle-autistes.fr/

ENIL: https://enil.eu/

I-ASC: https://i-asc.org/

My YouTube channel: @joncournicolas7646

Notes

1 The Nazi regime's campaign of extermination of people with physical and mental disabilities from 1939 to 1941, which killed 70,000 to 80,000 people.

2 The term "neurodiversity" was first used by Australian sociologist and Autistic person Judy Singer and first published in an article in *The Atlantic* in 1998.

3 Non-Autistic person.

PART II

Political, social, and cultural context

10

EXPLORING THE NOW AND THE PROSPECTS OF THE DISABILITY RIGHTS MOVEMENT IN LATIN AMERICA

Ana María Sánchez Rodríguez and Beatriz Miranda Galarza

Introduction

Latin American social movements have constantly been a reference in the universal search for political liberation and a democratic system. A varied and vast literature about the history of social movements in the region highlights the social, economic, and political struggles of marginalized and oppressed groups (peasants, workers, students, migrants, indigenous, women, Black people) as the main cause for people organizing themselves around a political project and fighting for social change. Paradoxically, while people with disabilities are clearly a marginalized and oppressed group, their way of resisting and mobilizing is not counted in such literature as a social movement. Why? Is it related to the overwhelming medical and individual approach (Oliver, 1984) to disability that ends up moralizing and medicalizing that group's social fights?

Yet the purposes of contemporary Latin American social movements are the "production of an alternative conception of citizenship" and multiplying the public spaces where socio-cultural, gender, ethnic, and economic exclusion can be questioned and redefined (Revilla Blanco, 2010, p. 54). These social movements are seen as an alternative to a single ideology and offer new meanings to those representing "pluralistic societies, global, post-racist, post-colonial and, maybe, post-modern [ideologies]" (Bruckmann & Dos Santos, 2005, p. 17).

DOI: 10.4324/9781003410089-13

When viewed through this paradigm, a disability social movement is there to counteract ableism, understood as:

> a network of beliefs, processes and practices that produces a particular kind of self and body (the corporeal standard) that is projected as the perfect, species-typical and therefore essential and fully human. Disability then is cast as a diminished state of being human.
>
> *(Campbell, 2001, p. 44)*

In this regard, the history and contribution of the disability social movement in Latin America needs to be explored.

The history of the disability movement in Latin America is fragmented, not explicitly documented (Samaniego de García, 2006, pp. 46–47; Gutiérrez Rodríguez, 2019; Kirakosyan, 2016; Benvenuto et al., 2019 and Zubiría-Mutis, 2012), and its written sources are limited. A narrative is somehow built by civil society organizations, but in that narrative, the voices of disabled people and the families that support them are not visible. The disability social movement is also absent from the literature of the social theory of Latin American social movements.

For this chapter, the authors conducted a descriptive literature review to identify significant works on the disability movement in Latin America, which includes some relevant evidence about its history. Due to the limited amount of information found, we opted to reach out to key informants, people known in the disability field. Interviews were conducted in Spanish, via Zoom, between February and May 2021, with previous written consent from the participants. The interviewees were selected for their role in and knowledge of the disability movement across Latin America. Eight practitioners and disability researchers from Ecuador, Mexico, Argentina, and Colombia were interviewed: one male and seven female (six out the seven with a known disability.) They are not intended to be representative of Latin America. The purpose of the interviews was to provide an overall view of the history of the disability movement.

The authors also included 11 radio interviews between March and September 2021 with advocates and founders of disability organizations in Mexico implemented by the 17, Instituto of Critical Studies through the radio program *Dis-locaciones*.[1] The interviews were analyzed using grounded theory, starting with the raw data to develop more abstract conceptual categories and themes (Charmaz, 1996).

The chapter is organized in three sections. The first part explores social movement approaches to defining disability mobilization as a social movement. The second part addresses the context of social movements in Latin America and analyzes the disability social movement. This section also addresses the disability movement's relationship with other movements such as the feminist and the LGBTIQ+. The third and final section discusses the paradoxes of the disability movement in Latin America. The chapter ends by addressing the disability movement's challenges.

What are social movement approaches to the disability movement?

There are different approaches to studying social movements (Morris, 1984). A resource mobilization approach highlights the processes in which a group takes control over the resources for collective action (Jenkins, 1983). Furthermore, the formation of the movement depends on the availability of the resources and the political environment. Scotch (1989) used the RM to analyze the disability social movement in the United States, which comprises a few organizations of persons with disabilities, individuals, and networks with goals focused on empowering and promoting the rights of persons with disabilities (1989, p. 383). Scotch further argued that it is essential to have an adequate organizational apparatus and a rights-oriented consciousness to constitute a disability movement. Economic and political resources are the basis to build linkages and network connections for the movement.

The new social movement (NSM) approach differentiates among old movements and new movements; the latter emphasize social conflict beyond the realm of work and identity formation. The disability social movement as a "new movement" is identity based (Edelman, 2001), formed to fight against pitying views about persons with disabilities. Shakespeare (1993, pp. 262–263) and Beckett (2006) interrogate whether the NSM approach explains the formation and the characteristics of the disability social movement in the United States and the United Kingdom (UK). They argue that the disability social movement is not a new movement. The disability concept is, as Shakespeare explains, "less of a unitary concept", taking the experiences of people living with different disabilities (1993). Similarly, Becket found that there was not a representative unique identity or a "disability culture" among the people he interviewed (Beckett, 2006, p. 743).

Oliver (1997) argues that the disability movement is a new social movement because it arises from an "emerging consciousness of disabled people who were beginning to recognize that the problem of disability was externally located and that our exclusion from society was a human rights issue" (p. 245). Oliver further contends that the disability movement is a new movement that promotes change to improve the lives of persons with disabilities through political involvement. In defining a disability social movement, Oliver addresses Barbara Lisicki´s definition of a social movement as

> a set of ideas that presents a challenge to the dominant ideology that says disabled people are burdens on society and that they should be taken care of, but the disability movement is also about people who believe that they have the right to a life.
>
> *(1997, pp. 245–246)*

Meanwhile, Beckett (2006) summarizes four key areas of discussion regarding the UK disability social movement. The first one refers to whether the term "movement" is the right one to describe the political activities of groups of persons with disabilities. The second area goes to question if the disability movement is a new social movement and if it has indeed formed a "disability culture". The third area addresses the intersections between disability and other categories, such as gender and ethnicity. The fourth and final area refers to the focus given by the movement to its organization and how it has been structured (2006, p. 736). We consider these four areas relevant for a discussion of the disability movement in Latin America, and by exploring its history, we expect to find some paths for its better understanding. However, we believe that there is more to the disability movement in Latin America that can be explained by the RM and NSM used to analyze the US and UK disability movements.

The history of the social disability movement in Latin America: A brief account

It is essential to underline that while the term "Latin American social movements" is used as an umbrella, their organization, structure, goals, and ways of action vary from country to country, and their history has followed complex and heterogenous paths (Veltmeyer, 2019). In Latin American countries, the process of organization and development of a disability movement responds to a different time frame and a variety of factors related to the political, social, and cultural system of each country. For instance, in most countries the decades prior to the 1960s, the welfare of people with disabilities and their families rested completely in the hands of the same families and religious and charity organizations (Kingman, 1996). The latter ran and supported hospitals and hospices that were built in an alliance between the Church and the state (Kingman, 1996). However, in countries like Mexico, it could have been some variants. In fact, the creation of the first public Mexican school for Deaf people in 1867 would have prompt the first organized Deaf community around sports and vocational workshops (Jullian, 2018), which served as spaces of economic and social support. As a result, soccer clubs were founded in some states of the country that reclaimed the rights of Deaf people to leisure and sports, though they did not obtain support from the government until 1995. In Brazil and Argentina, the dictatorships in the 60s and 70s were characterized by a slow but differentiated progress in disability policies (Brégain, 2013). During those decades, Argentina approved an act to protect persons with disabilities; that was not the case in Brazil. Unfortunately, there are a few historical records that indicate that in these countries, some important political mobilizations led exclusively by disabled people happened during the 1970s and the 1980s (Brégain, 2013), which could have meant that the negotiation with governments was left in hands of organizations for disabled people with a few disabled activists involved.

In general, it could be said that the period between colonization and the beginning of the 19th century, religious institutions and wealthy families became the benefactors of disabled people, among other marginalized groups. However, with the introduction of modern medicine and statistics in the world of public governance at the end of the 19th century, disability became a public issue to be solved by scientific methods, welfare, and institutional approaches (special schools and psychiatric hospitals, for instance) (Apráez Ippolito, 2010). Here, it is important to underline the impact of the worldwide eugenics movement and its practices during the decades of the 1920s through the 1940s. Organizations and leagues that were founded in Latin American countries like Argentina, Chile, Mexico, Brazil, and Peru promoted what was called "preventive eugenics" (Vallejo, 2005), "providing a framework for contextualizing matrimonial eugenics and prenuptial certificates, as well as the commensurability of eugenics and public health campaigns against 'racial poisons' (Stern, 2016, p. 8). There are historical records of cases of women labeled "retarded" or mad or whose relatives were subjected to involuntary sterilization and forced institutionalization (Yupanqui-Concha & Ferrer-Pérez, 2019).

Furthermore, by the end of the 1940s, the world had inherited the effects of two wars that brought an enormous migration from Europe to different parts of the world, including Latin America, and the responsibility passed to the state to deal with those citizens who became disabled due to the wars. Europe and the United States saw a growing number of projects and programmes to support the rehabilitation of disabled people. Their aim was to integrate them socially and economically (Bryan, 2010). Some of these organizations were led by religious groups, among them the *Fraternité catholique des malades*, founded by a French priest who promoted that "ill people" have to liberate themselves from the paternalism of those who are "healthy" (Brégain, 2013). This movement expanded to other countries including Argentina, Brazil, and particularly Peru, under the influence of the Spanish Jesuit Vicente Masip (Brégain, 2013, p. 4). Led by people who were chronically ill or had visual or physical impairments, some of the fraternities in Brazil and Argentina adopted a political stand that responded to Marxist and theology of liberation postulates. According to Brégain, these groups implemented a variety of actions that included street demonstrations, occupation, hunger strikes, and other actions. They occurred between 1980 and 1982 in Brazil and in 1973, 1977, 1978, and 1981 in Argentina (interrupted by a dictatorial government). The main goal of such events was to reclaim the right to work or to access the compensation benefits implemented by the government in the case of Argentina. The historical documents do not register these events as subversive as the governments did not consider them "dangerous groups". Their mobilization diminished during the 1980s.

While relevant emancipation revolts were taking place in Latin America and around the world in the decades of the 1960s and 1970s, the UK and the United States saw the emergence of a new type of social movement demanding the deinstitutionalization of people with disabilities and overall placing themselves as citizens who might be recognized by the state (Tremain, 2006). The reflection and discussions around the political character of disability in the UK gave birth to the social model of disability coined by Mike Oliver in 1983 (Oliver, 1984). In the United States, the Independent Living Movement founded by Ed Roberts together with other activists with disabilities on the Berkeley University Campus in California (Carson, 2013) was behind the advent of an unusual movement. These two scenarios represented a novel and challenging response to a medical approach to disability that questioned the very core of how disability and the disabled individual were defined by society and by the state.

Meanwhile, in Latin America, the prevalence of a medical and pedagogical understanding of disability determined that between the 1960s and the 1990s, the groups leading the work in the field were those founded by middle- and upper-class families; by individuals with acquired physical impairments; or by non-governmental organizations under the direction of professionals like psychiatrists, psychologists, pedagogues, and physiotherapists (Zubiría-Mutis, 2012). In the years since, these groups have been impacted by international changes that happened in the field, and a group of them became responsible for the spread of a human rights discourse and the negotiation with governments of social policies and programs to improve the lives of disabled people. A former director of one of the first Mexican organizations addressing the rights of people with intellectual disabilities to an educations mentioned in a broadcast interview that

> understanding the changes that were happening in countries like the United States or Canada and the visit of unorthodox professionals due to invitations by non-governmental organizations helped to spread the wind of the rights of disabled people not only in Mexico but in Latin America.
> *(March 18, 2021)*

In this sense, the history of the movement of disability organizations in Latin America can be pictured as a complex process by which disabled people and organizations supporting them were equipped with discourses of medicalization, institutionalization, and rehabilitation. In parallel, these organizations have coexisted with those promoting discourses of rights and citizenship. That is the case today (Griffiths et al., 2009).

The narratives offered by people interviewed from Ecuador, Argentina, Colombia, and Mexico characterize the mid-1970s through the 1990s as a very productive time in terms of expansion of disability organizations promoting education, rehabilitation, and leisure, especially for children with intellectual disability, autism, and cerebral palsy. In Colombia, for example, Andrea, a Colombian lawyer and human rights activist, recalled that the first organizations for Blind and Deaf people influenced disability policies and created two institutions in the 1980s (personal communication, March 1, 2021). Also, in most Latin American countries, a few associations and other social groups led by physically disabled people had appeared by the end of the 1970s. However, the opening of some special private schools that ran parallel to the public ones could have been seen as the beginning of a fight for the rights of disabled children to access good education. In Brazil, for instance, one of the achievements of parents of disabled children was the introduction of the Pestalozzi system in some special schools led by the Pestalozzi associations together with the *Associações de Pais e Amigos dos Excepcionais* (Association of Parents and Friends of the Exceptional) (APAE) (Mendes, 2010). A similar assertation was made in a broadcast interview by one of the Mexican activists for the rights of children with intellectual disabilities, who maintained that

> the growing number of special schools run by private organizations in Latin America should be considered as one of the few first steps given between the 1960s and the 1970s to defend their rights to have equal access to optimal educational services.
>
> *(April 8, 2021)*

As mentioned earlier, associations of Deaf people in Mexico were organized between the mid-19th century and the mid-20th century. This would have been the case in countries such as Argentina, Uruguay, and Brazil, where schools for the Blind and the Deaf were opened due to the influence of French and Italian professionals who either migrated to the continent or were brought by the governments especially for this purpose (Jullian, 2008). Most of the interviewees underlined that the only spaces where disabled people met before the 1970s were the special schools and the rehabilitation centres they attended (Maior, 2017). Nevertheless, Jullian (2018) found in his research that, for Deaf people in the city of Mexico, besides soccer clubs, Catholic and Christian temples have been spaces where they could express their cultural identity in the past decades, resisting in this way social exclusion from the dominant culture. A well-known anthropologist who has closely followed the historical process of the Deaf movement in Mexico mentioned in a broadcast interview that in Latin America, there is the tendency to exclude the history of Deaf people from the history of disability, perhaps because "the Deaf have never felt disabled and organized themselves earlier than those identified as disabled" (September 30, 2021).

Relevant international events had given impulse to the creation of organizations leading the field of educational integration by the end of the 1970s and the middle of the 1980s. The year 1981 marked the beginning of a new era of rights for people with disabilities with the invitation by the United Nations (UN) to implement a world plan of action at the regional, national, and local levels. There were three essential axes of work: prevention, rehabilitation, and equalization of opportunities (United Nations, General Assembly, 1982). This plan was part of the declaration by the UN General Assembly of 1981 as the International Year of Persons with Disabilities (IYPD) and the International Decade of Persons with Disabilities between 1983 and 1992, ending the decade with the adoption in 1993 of the Standard Rules for Equalization of Opportunities for Persons with Disabilities (Mji et al in MacLachlan & Swartz, 2009). These 22 rules refer to education, employment, rehabilitation, medical care, research, public policies, planning, monitoring of actions, and equal opportunities, among others.

The pressure exerted by national and international organizations at the global, national, and local levels generated remarkable changes at the political level, such as the creation of national programmes and policies related to disability and the opening of national government bodies to address the demands of disabled families regarding education, labor integration, and rehabilitation/medical services (García-Ruiz, 2014; Maior, 2017). The years between 1980 and 2000 are seen by García-Ruiz as decades of paradoxical developments. On the one hand, the creation of National Councils of Disability (CONADIS is the acronym in Spanish and CONADE in Brazil), governmental institutions, often at the national level, took place in most Latin American countries, as did the organization of federations of disabled people. These federations grouped organizations for people with disabilities and a few associations of people with physical, intellectual, and sensorial impairments in countries like Ecuador, Peru, and Colombia and advocated for the implementation of national disability laws (García-Ruiz, 2014). National disability laws and integral systems of protection for people with disabilities were implemented in most Latin American countries (García-Ruiz, 2014). Rosangela Berman writes that from 1986 to 1988, representatives of disability organizations in Brazil were involved in rewriting the national constitution after the military coup (Humanity & Inclusion, 2018). She refers to a group of disabled people who attended university, which was unusual at that time. On the other hand, these were also times of telethon activities, a charity chain that perpetuated an ideology of seeing people with disabilities as objects of charity. In countries like Chile, the telethon started in 1978 (Humeres, 2019), and it was rapidly followed by other countries in the region. Telethons involved activities that, as Humeres writes, included funding rehabilitation centres and sheltered occupational workshops for people with intellectual disabilities who were accommodated by many social foundations in countries like Peru, Argentina, Uruguay, Ecuador, Venezuela, Colombia, and Mexico.

The emergence of national associations and federations of organizations led by disabled people resulted from the spread of actions by international organizations (Jelinek-Mendelsohn 2018; Maior, 2017) like Disabled People´s International (dpi.org), Inclusion International (inclusion-international.org), International Disability Alliance (www.internationaldisabilityalliance.org), CBM (formerly Christian Blind Mission, www.cbm.org), and Humanity & Inclusion (formerly Handicap International, hi.org), among others. In addition, in 1999, the Inter-American Institute on Disability and Inclusive Development (iiDi), formerly the Inter-American Institute on Disability,[2] was created as a catalyst and information centre to influence the development of disability policy in the Americas (Mill Neck International, n.d.). The variety of activities organized by these groups, such as conferences; seminars; and meetings about disability rights, leadership, accessibility, and inclusion, offered the ideal space for people and groups from different countries to meet and exchange information and knowledge (MacLachlan & Swartz, 2009). However, those opportunities for training and building social capital also revealed the inequalities, hierarchies, and frictions that existed within a fragile disability movement in which leadership was marked by class and gender (Griffiths et al., 2009; Zubiría-Mutis, 2012). This argument was supported by many of the people interviewed for this chapter.

The implementation of community-based rehabilitation projects (CBR) in Latin America in 1994 aided in the creation of small organizations and associations of people with different types of disabilities (Díaz-Aristizabal et al., 2012). These organizations are concerned with the social inclusion of people with disabilities, their access to medical and rehabilitation services, and their and their families' economic empowerment (Anau et al., 2014). According to Anau, one of the fundamental contributions of the CBR strategy is the creation of small associations of parents and people with disabilities in rural areas as well as in indigenous communities.

In 2001, Mexico successfully introduced a resolution to discuss a draft for an international convention at the United Nations General Assembly and encouraged other countries to join the request, thus creating an Ad Hoc Committee of the General Assembly (Parra-Dussan, 2010). An essential feature of this period was lobbying work carried out by activists and organizations supported by human rights experts and academics committed to disability studies and disability rights.[3] In 2002, this led to international organizations such as Amnesty International, Handicap International, and Human Rights Watch meeting with organizations of persons with disabilities to create the International Disability Caucus (IDC) (Reina, 2008). The IDC provided a space for collaboration but also for the knowledge exchange that gave birth to a project called South Project to promote the participation of disabled people from countries of the so-called South. The director of *Piña Palmera*, a CBR project in Oaxaca-Mexico, who participated in the negotiation of the CRPD, highlighted in a broadcast interview that the limited participation by representatives of regions like Latin America reflected the inequalities experienced by disabled people, such as restricted access to education, lack of English skills, difficulties in obtaining visas to travel to the United States where the discussions were taking place, and the feeling that representatives had little knowledge about international affairs in the fields of disability law and disability rights (April 14, 2021). These limitations determined the profile of the disabled activists who were involved and informed the discussion and the negotiation process. They were, in general, leaders of large organizations because of their university education; knowledge of international affairs, human rights, and law; and English skills. Participation of persons with disabilities, especially in relevant international events, is still limited to disability practitioners and a privileged group of disabled leaders and activists which responds to the inequality and social exclusion that most disabled people experience.

Since 2006, organizations for and of people with disabilities have shifted their goal to fight for the implementation of the Convention on the Rights of Persons with Disabilities (CRPD), leaving behind the discussion on structural problems (Zubiría-Mutis, 2012). Gonzalo, an Argentinean PhD student of anthropology with disability who is researching the disability movement in Ecuador, explains that the social model promoted by the CRPD "in Latin America is not understood from its foundations . . . the political point is rooted but is not the founding reason for a movement that needs to understand the social model as political" (personal communication, March 17, 2021). Griffiths et al. (2009) argue that while large organizations of disabled people are concerned with the implementation of the CRPD demands at all levels, small disability associations and groups are addressing advocacy and empowerment goals at the subnational level. Interviewees highlighted that people with disabilities and their families, who are not related to academia or to the main organizations' movement, do not know what the CRPD is about or its implications for their daily life. Bubulina, a Colombian artist and disabled activist, leader of one of the premiere organizations of feminists with disabilities in her country, underlines that pressure from international disabled people's organizations to promote the implementation of the CRPD in the region has been accepted by national organizations without proper reflection on how the Convention centers the demands made by disabled people in the past decades. She also identifies the differences encountered between urban and rural organizations on this matter. People in rural areas, she adds, are even less aware of what the CRPD conveys and continue lobbying for their daily demands (personal communication, March 1, 2021).

Some of the interviewees commented that disability organizations seized the opportunity raised after the adoption of the CRPD when there was an urgent reason for them to convene, but afterwards, "the movement is dissolved". For instance, in 2007 the Mexican state filed an Interpretative Declaration to paragraph 2 of Article 12 of the Convention, which precisely established the full recognition of the legal capacity of persons with disabilities. This act was received with anger by the leaders of different organizations, and their pressure provoked its withdrawal by the government (Avilés, 2011). Something similar would happen in Colombia with the Colombian Coalition for Disability with the support of international disability non-governmental organizations (INGOs). In countries like Peru and Costa Rica, an alliance between some representatives of organizations of disabled people and human rights organizations resulted in the adoption of laws to eliminate all forms of guardianship for people with disabilities (Bregaglio & Constantino, 2020).

Some organizations had their genesis in the CRPD adoption and the meetings and networking that came resulted (Zubiría-Mutis, 2012; García-Ruiz, 2014); La Red[4] (Iberoamerican network of physically disabled people) was created in 2001; RIADIS[5] (Latin American network of NGOs and families) was created in 2002; *Red Interuniversitaria de Latinoamérica y el Caribe sobre discapacidad y Derechos Humanos* (Latin American and the Caribbean Inter-University Network on Disability and Human Rights)[6] was created in 2009; the Iberoamerican Network on Social Studies and Disability (RIESDIS)[7] was created in 2010; *Red de RBC de las Américas*[8] (CBR Network of the Americas) was created in 2011; the Indigenous Persons with Disabilities Global Network was created in 2013 (IDA, 2023). Andrea commented that while some of these regional organizations have faded and others are working on specific themes such as the *Red Regional por la Educación Inclusiva* (Regional Network of Inclusive Education) (RREI)[9] and *La Redesfera Latinoamericana De La Diversidad Psicosocial* (Latin American Net-sphere of Psychosocial Disability),[10] disability groups' demands are rising (personal communication, March 1, 2021).

The decade from 2010, as García-Ruiz heralds, saw the awakening of new forms of networking. The spread of disability studies programmes in different universities in Colombia, Argentina, Mexico, and Brazil has opened a variety of discussions about new topics in the region, such as critical disability studies, feminisms, coloniality, and Crip theory (Gutiérrez Rodríguez, 2019; Murillo & Sherry, 2021). For instance, Sandra, one of the founders of the *Red Latinoamericana Interuniversitaria* (Latin American Inter-University Network) from Argentina said in the interview that the creation of transnational university networks started from the need to explore what everyone was doing on disability in the region but that somehow stayed unknown. She said, "The network growth with the desire to expand and being supportive and six countries in Latin America, including Argentina and Mexico, have committed to the work on inclusion of students with disabilities" (personal communication, March 17, 2017).

There is also the emergence of groups of young disabled people who differ in their goals and ways of working. *Movimiento estamos tod@s en acción*[11] (Movement We All Are in Action) (META), created in 2012, is a project of the Inter-American Institute on Disability & Inclusive Development that includes disabled and non-disabled members from Costa Rica, the Dominican Republic, Uruguay, Panama, Mexico, Peru, Honduras, Brazil, and Colombia. It promotes sexual and reproductive rights and inclusive education. There are also groups of young disabled women, LGBTIQ+ activists, and artists developing a sort of digital activism in countries like Mexico, Ecuador, Chile, Argentina, and Brazil (Murillo Lafuente, 2020). They seem to be engaged in academic and political discussions through the promotion of podcasts, Zoom sessions on specific topics, and digital radio interviews. In Mexico *SinColectivo* (Without Collective) and *Mexicanas con Discapacidad* (Mexican Women with Disabilities) are engaged in political activities that pursue social inclusion of people with psychosocial disabilities and disabled women in the country.

A few organizations are challenging and addressing intersections such as gender non-conforming people and are encouraging the opening of new protest venues in alliance with other social movements. *Polimorfas*[12] is a Colombian collective that includes lesbian and transexual women with disabilities and led the 2020 Women's march in Bogota, Colombia. The collective *Torceduras y bifurcaciones* (Twists and Bifurcations) gathers Argentinean queer and queer disabled artists. In Chile, small groups that identify themselves as Crip and feminists are involved in the reformation of the Chilean National Constitution. In respect to this, Mercedes, an Ecuadorian disabled activist who acquired a disability from an accident in her early twenties and founded a disability organization in her country, underlined the importance of the inclusion of diverse groups in the disability movement, saying, "As people with disabilities, we are not isolated. One realizes that we can be disabled and be indigenous or gay; we are inclusive" (personal communication, March 3, 2021).

According to Inguanzo (2020), the new venues available for a social movement in the disability arena respond to the creation of transnational networks that have been made possible thanks to technology and the accelerated use of social media, taking as an example the creation of the Indigenous Persons with Disabilities Global Network. Regarding technology as one of the means to promote new approaches to the disability movement in Latin America, it is important to notice that the COVID-19 pandemic has somehow made visible another paradoxical phenomenon. On the one hand, many disabled people – those who live in poor and marginal – areas, have been isolated as the digital era has not reached them or has done it partially. Sandra, an Argentinean psychologist, physical education teacher, and member of the Latin American and the Caribbean network on disability and human rights, explains that "The pandemic aggravated inequalities" and mentions as an example the case of Deaf students connecting online to attend classes with a cell phone and having to follow a sign language interpreter (personal communication, March 17, 2021). Regarding this, MaryAngel, a disabled feminist who leads a group of disabled women in Mexico mentioned that "the majority of people with disabilities in Latin America live in poverty, and despite disability organizations promoting their participation via digital platforms there is still a gap between disability leadership and the population of people with disabilities" (personal communication, May 7, 2021). She identifies more people with disability using digital platforms nowadays, but only privileged groups have access. She adds that there is more communication across disability activist groups, but this number is far from representing the overall number of people with disability in the census. On the other hand, international seminars, conferences, and forums such as the CRPD Conference of State Parties (2020 and 2021), which takes place in New York, are becoming accessible digitally, and this has opened access to more activists and disabled people who otherwise would not have been able to attend them.

The pandemic has also made visible the fact that disability organizations have a heterogeneous and complex character. In the corridors, there is a growth of discussions about considering as part of the movement those who advocate for conservative actions such as sterilization, institutionalization of disabled people, or even the elimination of the CRPD. A Mexican journalist committed to the rights of persons with disabilities argued in the broadcast interview, "Why wouldn't the disability organizations have their conservative and right-wing sector?" (May 12, 2021). She highlighted that in countries like Mexico, Brazil, and some Central American countries, there are groups of professionals and parents, as well as some organizations of people with physical impairments, promoting the sterilization of people with intellectual disabilities. She also observed that while there are talks and discussions among activists, there is the need for research that makes these arguments public. A report presented by *Colectivo Chuhcan* and Disability Rights International on the sexual and reproductive rights of disabled women in Mexico could support such arguments (DRI & Colectivo Chuhcan, 2014).

Discussing the Latin American disability social movement: A paradox

In the following section, we discuss the disability movement in Latin America, its assertions, and its contradictions, and we point out the challenges ahead. The previous section included a brief account of the history of the disability movement in Latin America. We found similarities across the region that characterize a movement. However, we are unsure whether there is a disability social movement in Latin America or a movement of organizations, associations, and federations working on disability. The NSM theory, for example, focuses on identity-formed social movements; however, in Latin America, it appears there are distinct organizations addressing specific disabilities rather than one disability identity or culture (Beckett, 2006). Many of the interviewees herald the complexity of the disability movement in Latin America and say that naming it as such is problematic. MaryAngel, for instance, recognizes that there are different perspectives on disability: those who think that there is a disability culture and those who don't (personal communication, May 7, 2021). The RM theory explains social movements through resource mobilization and political opportunity; in the case of the Latin America, much of the advancement of the movement has been possible through organizations that have access to resources: for example, regional networks and national disability federations with the support of INGOs.

The history of the disability social movement in Latin America is paradoxical and characterized by 1) a diverse compound of organizations (charities, federations, centres of education, non-governmental organizations (NGOs), associations of parents and professionals); 2) a predictable relationship between predominant disabled leaders and government authorities; 3) a multiplicity of agendas according to the type of disability; 4) a CRPD social model approach which has not been implemented, and 5) an activism that attempts to change policies but has not outlined and adopted a political project. We therefore cannot conclude there is a disability social movement as such.

Even with the diversity of organizations and networks, the multiplicity of agendas, we conclude that many of the disability organizations in Latin America have advanced their agendas. However, in terms of including all disabilities in the movement, people with intellectual and psychosocial disabilities have come last. An example is the gap in organizations representing people with psychosocial disabilities to advocate for their right to equal recognition before the law (Molina Toledo et al., 2017). The CRPD has been, for disability-led organizations, a benchmark to advocate before the state. Even if the CRPD was a success for the disability rights movement (Sabatello, 2013) and some of the interviewees mentioned it, it has not represented a collective agenda.

With the creation of different regional disability networks, tensions arise, and addressing power and leadership is important. Interviewees have commented on the underrepresentation of organizations concerning intellectual disability and psychosocial disabilities as well as the divided agenda as each organization fights for a specific issue, but as Sandra mentioned, "There is no a comprehensive disability agenda". She also invited advocates "to be honest about the hierarchies that exist within the disability movement because those who have the power, and the spokespersons are clearly white male that acquired a disability or blind men" (personal communication, March 1, 2021).

The organizations of persons with disabilities are not experiencing a change in their relationship with the state. We mentioned earlier that the political understanding of the social model has not permeated the structures. Virginia, a young Argentinean woman with a disability who works in an international organization that advocates for the rights of women and girls with disabilities and has experience working in the region with META, expressed that "the social model has been embraced by the disability organizations, but not by the rest of the population" (personal communication, May 7, 2021). Even though the disability movement and its organizations have advanced disability policies, in countries like Ecuador, the disability federations depend financially on the state, thus lacking autonomy to represent their interests. Regarding the creation of the national councils of disability and other government disability bodies, Gonzalo holds that these "reflect the way that politics is understood in most of the countries, based on lobbying and arrangements made between leaders that have access to political circuits" (personal communication, March 17, 2021).

When the CRPD was adopted, it created momentum for organizations of and persons with disabilities. However, people with disabilities and their families who are not connected to the organizations' movement do not know what the CRPD is about and its implications for their daily live. Small disability people's organizations and organizations located in rural areas are left behind by the advocacy agenda of large urban disability organizations. These circumstances have marked the way that discussions are conducted and the type of agendas that run within either the movement or the organizations. Most of the leaders have access to information and are the ones who make decisions about the topics that will be included in the agenda. These arguments were presented by many of the people interviewed, who added that the problem of the disability movement in Latin America being considered as such is that power is centred in a few hands, and there is little support for young leaders. Also, it has been mentioned that there is an important gap in the dialogue between the new generation of activists and leaders and those who have been "in charge" of the disability agenda.

The Latin American disability social movement and its organizations have become more visible. This raises new challenges. The first challenge is building a comprehensive agenda that recognizes diversity within disability. This will require alliances to advocate fighting for causes that reflect the needs of each group: for example, legal recognition of national sign languages and the legal capacity of people with psychosocial and intellectual disabilities, amongst others. The CRPD represented a road map for the organizations and their networks, but, as María, a disability advocate and a woman with a disability, mentions,

> It is painful that having a Convention that provides not only the theoretical and philosophical foundations to achieve change, there is neither the culture nor the will to adopt it as a bible . . . there is greater awareness of rights but this is not enough to become a political force as it is needed"
> *(personal communication, February 27, 2021)*

The disability movement comes from a long tradition of charities and family and professional organizations, some of which have turned into a movement that seeks the recognition of the rights of people with disabilities; however, a movement led by disabled people is relatively new. Some of the next challenges include achieving social protection schemes that allow political participation because the struggle continues to be access to basic needs, such as education and work, As Andrea states (personal communication, March 1, 2021), changing power hierarchies within the disability organizations has also been demanded, as well as building bridges between the academia and the grassroots.

Conclusions

The disability social movement in Latin America has a history on its own, but it needs to be recovered from the voices of people with disabilities and the disabled leaders who initiated the struggle. In telling the story of the movement, we tried to locate the differences amongst Latin American countries, but extensive research is needed.

The movement was characterized from the beginning by groups of upper-class families and the influence of the church, with some variations regarding some of the organizations for the Blind and the Deaf that were first advocating for state policies. We also discussed the relationship of the movement and its organizations with the state and the governments, sometimes compliant and others defiant, but not taken as disrupters of the status quo. In this regard, we ask in what ways the state is recognizing a disability social movement.

The disability social movement in Latin America does not have a single agenda, and in recent years, the struggle has focused on creating a unitary discourse followed by the adoption of the CRPD. We addressed the influence of NGOs and INGOs promoting a disability approach, and we mentioned the CBR strategy and some local disability foundations and associations as examples. However, we must further analyze the influence of the international disability movement promoting a disability approach (Meyers, 2014).

New disability organizations are amplifying the voices of women with disabilities and disabled youth. They have found a way to communicate and advocate via digital networks. Moreover, they are promoting some narrative changes, encouraging people to become more critical of the hierarchies experienced in the disability organizations, accounting for intersections such as indigenous people, women, and gender non-conforming persons with disabilities. It is important to notice that such a new wave could be also the result of a visible development of disability studies university programmes and university education being more accessible for certain groups of disabled students.

The last section highlighted the challenges and the limitations of the disabled movement, emphasizing inequalities in the movement, from urban to rural areas, organizations for persons with disabilities, and grassroots groups led by disabled people. The disability knowledge promoted in academia is far from communicating with families and people with disabilities facing ableism and discrimination. A personal anecdote shows this. One of us was participating in the 2019 Women's March along with activists and allies who shouted slogans such as "*Abajo el capacitismo*" (Down with ableism). A mother of a young boy with autism asked, "What does ableism mean? I want equal opportunities for my son, and I don´t understand what you mean by ableism".

To conclude, due to the limited information we have found about the history of the movement of organizations of disabled people in Latin America, the urgent need to recover the voices of people who have been involved in the complex process that fighting for social justice and equity involves becomes clearer. Alliances between academia and the disability organizations would be a potent way to implement a collective historiographical reflection to build a transformed society for all. This process could lead to a profound and critical joint reflection on whether there is a social movement of disability or a movement of disability organizations. Creating a solo identity in a movement that has different claims has proved to be challenging, and the understanding is that there is not a movement like others such as the feminist or the environmental. The CRPD has attempted to create synergy across disability groups through a common understanding of rights but does not take into account the hierarchies and the inequalities that existed long before. Perhaps we need to analyze through different lenses what a movement is constituted in the case of disability in Latin America as we move along recognizing the asymmetries amongst different disabilities and other intersecting identities.

Notes

1 Radio program about the history of the disability movement in Mexico. It takes place every other Thursday via 17, Radio and is conducted by Beatriz Miranda Galarza.
2 https://www.facebook.com/iiDienred/?tn-str=k*F
3 The website Voices on the CRPD (http://crpd.hi.org), supported by Humanity & Inclusion, keeps an archive of interviews with some of the main disability activists involved in the CRPD project, among them Luis Fernando Astorga (Costa Rica), Silvia Quan (Guatemala), Rosangela Berman (Brazil), and Pamela Molina (Chile).
4 http://www.laredliberoamericana.com/la-red/
5 http://www.riadis.org/

6 http://red-universidadydiscapacidad.org/
7 http://www.um.es/discatif/RIESDIS.htm
8 https://www.facebook.com/groups/428926710473999/
9 https://rededucacioninclusiva.org/tag/articulo-24/
10 https://www.redesfera.org
11 https://metajuvenil.wordpress.com
12 http://polimorfas.com/en-que-creemos/

References

Anau, F., Matías, P., Enríquez, M., & Jarquín, A. R. (2014). Discapacidad y prácticas educativas comunitarias. En R. Reygadas & R. Vega (Eds.), *Caminos de lucha y esperanza*. Once relatos por la justicia, la inclusión y todos los derechos humanos.

Apráez Ippolito, G. (2010). *La medicina social y las experiencias de atención primaria de salud (APS) en Latinoamérica: historia con igual raíz* (p. 27). Revista Latinoamericana.

Avilés, E. (2011, October 13). Declaración Interpretativa de Discapacidad. Comunicado de Prensa. Urgente retirar declaración interpretativa sobre personas con discapacidad: ONG. https://cmdpdh.org/2011/10/14/declaracion-interpretativa-de-discapacidad/

Beckett, A. E. (2006). Understanding social movements: theorising the disability movement in conditions of late modernity. *The Sociological Review*, *54*(4), 734–752.

Benvenuto, A., Brégain, G., & Meziani, M. (Eds.). (2019). Perspectivas comparadas sobre discapacidad: Francia-América Latina. Estudios Sociológicos Editora.

Brégain, G. (2019). Comparar las trayectorias nacionales de las políticas públicas de rehabilitacion a través del prisma de las circulaciones transnacionales. Argentina-Brazil, 1920's-1980's.

Bregaglio, R., & Constantino, R. (2020). Un modelo para armar: La regulación de la capacidad jurídica de las personas con discapacidad en el Perú a partir del Decreto Legislativo 1384. *Revista Latinoamericana en Discapacidad, Sociedad y Derechos Humanos*, *4*(1).

Brégain, G. (2013). An entangled perspective on disability history: the disability protests in Argentina, Brazil and Spain, 1968–1982. In S. Barsh, A. Klein, & P. Verstraeten (Eds.), *The imperfect historian. Disability histories in Europe* (pp. 133–153). Peter Lang Edition.

Bruckmann, M., & Dos Santos, T. (2005). Los movimientos sociales en América Latina: un balance histórico. *Semináro Internacional REG GEN: Alternativas Globalização, 8*.

Bryan, W. V. (2010). *Sociopolitical aspects of disabilities: the social perspectives and political history of disabilities and rehabilitation in the United States*. Charles C Thomas Publisher.

Campbell, Fiona AK. (2001). Inciting legal fictions-disability's date with ontology and the ableist body of the law. *Griffith Law Review*, *10*, 42.

Carson, D. (2013). *Ed Roberts: father of disability rights*. Dog Ear Publishing.

Charmaz, K. (1996). The search for meanings-grounded theory. In J. A. Smith, R. Harré, & L. Van Langenhove (Eds.), *Rethinking methods in psychology* (pp. 27–49). Sage Publication.

Díaz-Aristizabal, U., Sanz-Victoria, S., Sahonero-Daza, M., Ledesma-Ocampo, S., Cachimuel-Vinueza, M., & Torrico, M. (2012). Reflexiones sobre la estrategia de rehabilitación basada en la comunidad (RBC): la experiencia de un programa de RBC en Bolivia. *Ciência & Saúde Coletiva, 17*, 167–177.

DRI & Colectivo Chuhcan. (2014). *Abuso y Negación de Derechos Sexuales y Reproductivos a Mujeres con Discapacidad Psicosocial en México*. DRI. https://www.driadvocacy.org/wp-content/uploads/Informe-México-Mujeres-FINAL-Feb2415.pdf

Edelman, M. (2001). Social movements: changing paradigms and forms of politics. *Annual Review of Anthropology, 30*(1), 285–317.
García-Ruiz, S. (2014). Construyendo historias y soñando con utopías: a propósito de la Red de Rehabilitación Basada en Comunidad (RBC) de las Américas. *Disability & The Global South, 1*(1), 161–171.
Griffiths, M., Mannan, H., & MacLachlan, M. (2009). Empowerment, advocacy and national development policy: a case study of disabled peoples' organizations in Bolivia. In *Disability & international development* (pp. 105–117). Springer.
Gutiérrez Rodríguez, V. H. (2019). Movimiento asociativo de personas con discapacidad: su impacto en la universidad y en la sociedad. *Acta Sociológica, 80*, 49–77.
Humanity & Inclusion (HI). (2018). Voices on the CRPD. Interview with Rosângela Berman Bieler. http://crpd.hi.org/#interviews
Humeres, M. (2019). "Gane usted y ayude a la Teletón": mecanismos neoliberales en la gestión del bienestar. *Convergencia, 26*(81).
Inguanzo, I. (2020). Construcción de marcos-puente en el movimiento de personas indígenas con discapacidad. *Andamios, 17*(42), 357–385.
International Disability Alliance (IDA). (2023). Indigenous persons with disabilities global network. https://www.internationaldisabilityalliance.org/content/indigenous-persons-disabilities-global-network#:~:text=IDA%20supports%20the%20Indigenous%20Persons,and%20regional%20human%20rights%20and
Jelinek-Mendelsohn, R. (2018). La inclusión y los derechos de las personas con discapacidad y su incidencia en las políticas públicas. *Revista de Administración Pública INAP, I-III*(1), 119–131.
Jenkins, J. C. (1983). Resource mobilization theory and the study of social movements. *Annual Review of Sociology*, 9(1), 527–553.
Jullian Montañez, C. G. (2008). *Quitando el velo de la oscuridad: La Escuela Nacional de Ciegos* (Ciudad de México, 1870 a 1928). Tesis de maestría en historia, México, Universidad Nacional Autónoma de México, Programa de Posgrado en Historia, 2008. Recuperado de. http://132.248.9.195/ptd2008/julio/0629375/Index.html
Jullian Montañez, C. G. (2018). Haciendo "hablar" a una historia muda. Surgimiento y consolidación de la comunidad sorda de Morelia. *Relaciones. Estudios de historia y sociedad, 39*(153), 261–291.
Kingman, E. (1996). De la beneficencia de antaño a la auténtica caridad. *Procesos: revista ecuatoriana de historia*, 83–98.
Kirakosyan, L. (2016). Promoting disability rights for a stronger democracy in Brazil: The role of NGOs. Nonprofit and Voluntary Sector Quarterly, 45(1_suppl), 114S-130S.
Maclachlan, M., & Swartz, L. (Eds). (2009). *Disability & international development towards inclusive global health*. Springer Science & Business Media.
Maior, I. M. (2017). Movimento político das pessoas com deficiência: reflexões sobre a conquista de direitos. *Inclusão Social, 10*(2). http://revista.ibict.br/inclusao/article/view/4029
Mendes, E. G. (2010). Breve historia de la educación especial en Brasil. *Revista Educación y pedagogía, 57*, 93–109.
Meyers, S. (2014). Disabled persons associations at the crossroads of two organizational environments: grassroots groups as part of an international movement and local civil society. In Barbara M., Altman & Sharon N. Barnartt (Eds.), *Environmental Contexts and Disability (Research in Social Science and Disability, Vol. 8* (pp. 3–31). Emerald Group Publishing Limited. https://doi.org/10.1108/S1479-354720140000008002
Mill Neck International. (n.d.). IIDI and META: disability inclusion in inter-American region. https://millneckinternational.org/resources/iidi-meta-disability-inclusion
Mji, G., Gcaza, S., Melling-Williams, N., & MacLachlan, M. (2009). Chapter 5. Networking in disability for development: introducing the African network for

evidence-to-action on disability (AfriNEAD). In M. Maclachlan & L. Swartz (Eds.), *Disability & international development towards inclusive global health* (pp. 69–89) Springer Science & Business Media
Molina Toledo, P., Astorga Gatjens, L. F., & Gómez Motta, S. (2017). *Informe de Mapeo acerca del Ejercicio de la Capacidad Legal de las Personas con Discapacidad Psicosocial en Seis Países Latinoamericanos*. Fundación para las Américas.
Morris, A., & Herring, C. (1984). Theory and research in social movements: a critical review. https://deepblue.lib.umich.edu/bitstream/handle/2027.42/51075/307.pdf?seq
Murillo, E., & Sherry, M. (2021). Disability in Bolivia: a feminist global south perspective. In *Disability in the Americas* (pp. 135–165). Palgrave Macmillan.
Murillo Lafuente, I. E. (2020). Experiences of Bolivian disabled activist women [Master's thesis, University of Toledo]. Electronic Theses and Dissertations Center. http://rave.ohiolink.edu/etdc/view?acc_num=toledo1588613995048859
Oliver, M. (1984). The politics of disability. *Critical Social Policy*, *4*(11), 21–32.
Oliver, M. (1997). The disability movement is a new social movement!. *Community Development Journal*, *32*(3), 244–251.
Parra-Dussan, C. (2010). Convención sobre los derechos de las personas con discapacidad. Antecedentes y nuevos enfoques. *International Law: Revista Colombiana de Derecho Internacional*, *8*(16).
Reina, M. V. (2008, February 6). How the international disability caucus worked during negotiations for a UN Human Rights Convention on Disability. *Global Action on Aging*. http://globalag.igc.org/agingwatch/events/CSD/2008/maria.htm
Revilla Blanco, M. L. (2010). América Latina y los movimientos sociales: el presente de la «rebelión del coro». *Nueva sociedad*, *227*, 51–67.
Sabatello, M. (2013). A short history of the international disability rights movement. In *Human rights and disability advocacy* (pp. 13–24). University of Pennsylvania Press.
Samaniego de García, P. (2006). Aproximación a la realidad de las personas con discapacidad en Latinoamérica. CERMI. ISBN 8461115023, 9788461115020
Scotch, R. K. (1989). Politics and policy in the history of the disability rights movement. *The Milbank Quarterly*, 380–400.
Shakespeare, T. (1993). Disabled people's self-organisation: a new social movement? *Disability, Handicap & Society*, *8*(3), 249–264.
Stern, A. M. (2016). Eugenics in Latin America. In Caulfield, S., Schettini, C., & Beezley, W. (Eds.), *Oxford research encyclopedia of Latin American history*. Oxford University Press.
Tremain, S. (2006). *Foucault and the government of disability*. The University of Michigan Press.
United Nations, General Assembly. (1982). Resolution adopted by the General Assembly 37/52. *World Programme of Action Concerning Disabled Persons*. http://www.un-documents.net/a37r52.htm
Vallejo, G. (2005). Las formas del organicismo social en la eugenesia latina. En M. Miranda & G. Vallejo (Eds.), *Darwinismo social y eugenesia en el mundo latino* (pp. 233–272). Siglo XXI.
Veltmeyer, H. (2019). Resistance, class struggle and social movements in Latin America: contemporary dynamics. *The Journal of Peasant Studies*, *46*(6), 1264–1285.
Yupanqui-Concha, A., & Ferrer-Pérez, V. A. (2019). Análisis de la producción científica mundial sobre esterilización forzada de mujeres con discapacidad entre 1997 y 2016. *Gaceta Sanitaria*, *33*(4), 381–388.
Zubiría-Mutis, B. (2012). Ciudadanos invisibilizados: discapacidad y política pública en Barranquilla (Colombia). Reflexión sociológica sobre los movimientos. *Revista Colombiana de Sociología*, *35*(2), 141–160.

11

ON THE MARGINS WHILE IN THE MIDST OF CONFLICT

Adults with intellectual disabilities in Northern Ireland and Bosnia Herzegovina

Áine Sperrin

Introduction and methodology

This chapter will discuss the experiences of adults with intellectual disabilities during and after the conflicts in Northern Ireland (1970 onward) and Bosnia Herzegovina (1992 onward).

Qualitative research is analysed alongside legislative and policy provisions to determine the hierarchal structures of disability experienced in the aftermath of conflict. The theoretical framework of the UNCRPD is used to assess the impact of conflict and peace processes on adults with intellectual disabilities.

This chapter highlights the hierarchy of disability in the social welfare supports in Bosnia Herzegovina and the siloed delivery of disability supports in Northern Ireland based on origin of disability.

This chapter explores the experiences of adults with intellectual disabilities who were formal combatants, informal participants in conflict-related activities, and civilians. Experiences of both institutionalization and community-based living during and after the conflicts are examined from the perspectives of ten adults with intellectual disabilities and ten professionals in the disability services and human rights sectors in each jurisdiction.

Hierarchy has often been the catalyst for social unrest and rightly so, as hierarchy innately infers superiority of one group over another (Thompson, 1961). This unrest can vary from temporal disruption, such as isolated riots, to more prolonged periods of intra-country conflict or civil war, as is the focus of this chapter about Northern Ireland and Bosnia Herzegovina. The atrocities committed by all sides of these conflicts – nationalist Catholics

 DOI: 10.4324/9781003410089-14

and loyalist Protestant populations in Northern Ireland; Bosnian Muslims, Catholic Croats, and Orthodox Serbians in Bosnia Herzegovina – were based on perceived hierarchies of ethnicity. However, these ethnic groups are not homogenous groups within themselves – they comprise multiple and intersectional identities. There is a dearth of the experiences of adults with intellectual disabilities during the conflicts and peace processes of Northern Ireland and Bosnia Herzegovina. This chapter focuses on the impact of the hierarchy within the disabled population during and after the conflicts. While the UNCRPD was not formalized during the conflicts discussed in this chapter, the correlating human rights principles of equality, non-discrimination, and basic standards of living were recognized in other international human rights law instruments.

Disability hierarchy is defined by Kim Sanders (2015) as a social construct that makes certain kinds of disabilities more acceptable than others. Discussing periods of conflict, this chapter considers the notion of disability hierarchy in terms of origin of disability as allocating a higher status within post-conflict social structures. As the social model of disability recognises that people are disabled by their environments and society, this chapter considers how the two societies of Northern Ireland and Bosnia Herzegovina allocate levels of acceptability to disability based on origin in the aftermath of conflict.

Northern Ireland and Bosnia Herzegovina were selected for study as both jurisdictions experienced ethno-nationalist conflict during the early 1990s. Both jurisdictions' current status of social deprivation and internal partitions based on ethnicity are comparable, as are the bureaucratic nature of governance and UNCRPD ratification status. While both conflicts attracted international attention and investment in the aftermath of the wars, the nature of the conflicts and peace processes differed vastly. The Northern Ireland conflict was a prolonged conflict with targeted violence against members of the armed forces and paramilitary actors in both Catholic nationalist and Protestant loyalist communities. Members of the public were not primary targets, although they were often were killed and injured. The conflict in Bosnia Herzegovina was much shorter but more extreme in the out-and-out violence inflicted, including genocide against Bosnian Muslims by Bosnian Serb forces. The characteristics – both similarities and differences – of these jurisdictions provide an opportunity to consider how the differing nature of the conflict and the peace processes has had an impact on the post-conflict societies for adults with intellectual disabilities.

Methodology

Desk-based literature review was complemented by qualitative research in both jurisdictions.

The qualitative research involved two categories in each jurisdiction – five people with lived experience of intellectual disabilities and five professionals in the fields of law, policy, academia, disability advocacy, and services.

Lived experience participants were born before 1970 and lived in the jurisdiction in the years prior to and during the conflict through the present day. The different lengths of the conflicts – 30 years in Northern Ireland and three years in Bosnia Herzegovina – meant that the participants were at different stages of the life cycle for the pre-conflict and partially during the conflict periods. In Northern Ireland, the childhood years of lived experience participants would have coincided with the beginning of the Troubles, whereas in Bosnia Herzegovina, the participants' childhoods coincided with the pre-conflict period. All the lived experience participants were adults during the 1990s when the conflicts escalated and the peace processes were furthered.

The qualitative interviews were conducted on the basis of anonymity, and each participant was allocated an identifier based on their jurisdiction (Northern Ireland – NI or Bosnia Herzegovina – BIH), participant group (lived experience – LE, professional – P), and the order of their interview (1–5). For example, the first participant I interviewed from the lived experience group in Northern Ireland is referred to as NILE1. The first participant from the professional group in Bosnia Herzegovina is referred to as BIHP1. The researcher questions and comments are denoted by 'R', with 'Supporter' clarifying support contributions as separate from the person with lived experience of disability.

Where individuals, towns, cities, organisations, or services are identified in the qualitative research, these have been anonymised and a brief description of the place mentioned for clarity: e.g., 'X residential institution'. Also, I provide additional information in square brackets in order to clarify the meaning of participants from the context of the quote or to explain local dialect in the Northern Ireland contributions. All participants with a lived experience were accompanied to their interviews by a support person. Support persons' contributions are recorded separate from the participants' statements. The transcripts of the five Bosnian interviews were verified by a translation service in Ireland for accuracy. No significant errors were highlighted. Where there was a discrepancy in the original translation, the most accurate version is included and the inaccurate translation discounted.

The chapter will first outline the social movement which progressed disability rights and the unintended hierarchy of disability which has arisen from it. Section 3 will explain the context of the conflict, the legislative and policy provisions governing the lives of adults with intellectual disabilities during and after the conflict, and the qualitative research contributions for Northern Ireland during the same period. Section 4 outlines the context of the conflict, the legislative and policy provisions relating to adults with intellectual disabilities during and after the conflict, and the qualitative research contributions for Bosnia Herzegovina during the same period.

Section 5 offers a discussion of the evidence of hierarchy within both jurisdictions and the impact that hierarchy has on the daily lives of persons with intellectual disabilities.

Historical context

The rights abuses suffered by persons with disabilities related to every aspect of their lives – their place of residence, their access to education, employment, health services, interaction with friends and relatives, and limitations on choices surrounding relationships (Kempton & Kahn, 1991). Whether maliciously or benignly pursued, these actions had the effect of relegating persons with disabilities to a category of charity, from whom little could be expected and whose deviant behaviour warranted criminal sanctions rather than rehabilitation or support. Charleton (2000) use of the phrase 'sick, abnormal and pathetic condition' succinctly narrates the prevailing attitude towards persons with disabilities before the grassroots revolution, which would become known as the Independent Living Movement. This movement emerged to challenge everything that had been denied to people with disabilities throughout history.

Hierarchy within the disability rights movement

Shakespeare (1993) describes numerous factors that contributed to the development of the Independent Living Movement in the US. These included the American dream of self-reliance, a lack of a coherent welfare systems and labour forces, commercialism, and the increasing numbers of war veterans. Ed Roberts is considered the 'father of independent living'. Karp (2017) outlines the activism starting as Roberts contracted polio as a teenager and became a wheelchair user. Personal assistance for Roberts to attend college at UC Berkeley in California was provided through a state programme, Aid to the Totally Disabled (McDonald & Oxford, 2005). Following Roberts's admission, increasing numbers of students with disabilities enrolled at the college. Encouraged by this accomplishment and alongside community members who were supportive of independent living, the first Centre for Independent Living (CIL) was established at Berkeley in 1972 (Centre for Independent Living Berkeley). The Independent Living Movement continued to grow from strength to strength internationally (Wehmeyer & Gragoudas, 2004). While much has been written about the protests to secure legislation to enable independent living (Heuman), the primary advocates and beneficiaries of the movement have been persons with physical impairments for whom adjustments to the built environment would remove disabling barriers in society. For adults with intellectual disabilities, the fact that they have had to challenge persistence of residential supports in institutional settings with limited interaction to this day demonstrates that a hierarchical structure has inadvertently emerged. While many efforts were made to make the Independent Living Movement inclusive, for adults with intellectual disabilities, a much-delayed and separate self-advocacy movement has been necessary (Johnstone, 2004). What has emerged in society is a hierarchy placing those with more easily realised accommodations at the top and those with the most intense accommodations towards the bottom. This chapter will discuss how a hierarchical structure based on origin of disability emerged in the post-conflict jurisdictions of Northern Ireland and Bosnia Herzegovina.

Northern Ireland

Northern Ireland context

There is much written about the ethno-nationalist conflict 'the Troubles', which has become synonymous with Northern Ireland. To place this chapter in context, the delivery of disability services in Northern Ireland during the conflict will be briefly outlined. While there is a long history of political discontent in the region, the Troubles are recognized as originating during the 1960s. The failure of the governance structures to serve the entire community in Northern Ireland was heavily linked to the alignment of Unionist-dominated political agendas with judicial enforcement (Bosi, 2008). The Northern Ireland Civil Rights Association was established in January 1967. The aims of this organisation were predominantly social justice based, and its efforts focused on obtaining unbiased and transparent voting mechanisms, allocation of housing, availability of employment and, the enactment of anti-discrimination legislation in government for the betterment of the lives of Catholics (Edgerton, 1986). While disability was not referenced in the objectives of the movement, improving socio-economic conditions for Catholics as a whole would benefit their disabled community members. It is under this banner that peaceful protests were organised, and one such protest on 5 October 1968 serves as a starting point for this research (O'Dochartaigh, 2005). Interviewees gave an example of a similar incident which escalated violence by police forces against civilians who were unconnected to peaceful protests during this period.

> Because two people [the police] were looking for went into the house, [the police] went in and killed an innocent man in the house. That's when the conflict started between . . . People took up guns then to defend themselves, thinking, you know . . . And they brought the army in then, and the whole thing escalated then after Bloody Sunday.
>
> *(NILE2's support worker)*

More concentrated episodes of the Troubles resulted in the Ulster Parliament being suspended in 1972 (Kennedy, 1973). Lynn (2021) notes that the efforts to overhaul the governance structures that determine the status of Northern Ireland began almost immediately with the establishment of the Northern Ireland Assembly from 1973–1974. These proposals were outlined in the 1973 'Northern Ireland Constitutional Proposals', a UK government white paper. The fundamental argument contained therein asserted that a government in Northern Ireland could no longer continue to comprise representatives from only one community. The arguments of the Northern Ireland Civil Rights Association were being recognized, however blighted by the violence.

Disability experiences in Northern Ireland

Segregation based on the grounds of disability was the norm internationally for education, employment, and general support services. In Northern Ireland, many public services involving congregations of people were delivered along religious lines, such as education. However, this was not the case for services delivered to persons with disabilities. It would have been excessively onerous to provide segregated disability services which were also segregated by ethnicity as the population of persons with intellectual disability across both communities was relatively small. This meant the environment in which disabled children were educated was very different from that of their non-disabled peers. Negative experiences were recounted of being transferred from religiously aligned mainstream education to a non-denominational disability-specific school.

> Aw, I didn't mind the religion but what I did mind at the time, through my own ignorance and perceptions, from a primitive mind at the time was when I found out later on that I had a disability, I didn't accept that I had a disability. I didn't want to accept it and I was called names for going to a special needs school . . . outside and inside [the special needs] school as well. . . . I was bullied physically and verbally but naw, I didn't want to go to school with special needs at the time. I remember that well.
>
> *(NILE2)*

NILE2 recognised, in hindsight, that the smaller class sizes and education tailored to his ability were the best setting for him at the time. Outside school, NILE2's interactions with local children were further marked by hostility towards English people as there were perceptions of involvement with the oppressive armed forces. NILE2 identified how he was excluded from what were for other young people comradery-building activities.

> Well my friends down in (townland), they were throwing stones as well. Ah, aye there was people in my area, very bitter because my dad was from Liverpool, whatever they'd see the soldiers they'd say '[NILE2] is that your father down there, call him down.' You know . . .
>
> *(NILE2)*

NILE1 was born in Northern Ireland but sent to a Catholic convent in a neighbouring jurisdiction until she reached young adulthood. The terminology and attitude used about her learning skills are indicative of the prejudicial attitude towards people with intellectual disabilities. The casual manner in which NILE1 describes her education indicates there was no hiding these terms from students.

NILE1: Aye, I couldn't pick up with the rest of the children in (local institution) and that's why I had to go to (neighbouring jurisdiction). A backwards school.
R: And did people use that word 'backwards school'?
NILE1: Very slow picking up, you see. I learned then when I was there. I knew everything when I left it . . . . We had to make our own fun. Life was hard, you know.

Despite the religious orders being entrusted with the education and care of young people with disabilities, NILE1 did not receive an educational qualification and described knowing how to tell the time as the peak of her learning. She returned to Northern Ireland as a teenager at the start of the Troubles and resided in long-stay hospitals and institutions throughout her life. NILE1 worked in local factories, and with her consent, a support worker outlined how her daily routine was disrupted by the conflict.

Supporter: Her experience of the Troubles would have started when she moved to (second named institution).
NILE1: Aye.
Supporter: 'Cause these streets would have been blocked off, there was no buses on. (Townland) was a war zone, and (named factory) was 50 yards away from a no-go area. Any buses went in were hijacked and burned.
NILE1: I walked up (to the factory).
NILE1 Supporter: (Employees) would have been sent home because (paramilitary forces) would have just thrown a petrol bomb in the middle of (named workplace), and they'd have been sent home.

Later in the interview, NILE1 described the lack of knowledge about the Troubles but recognised at the time that speaking about it could lead to trouble in her own life.

R: Did you ever feel like it wasn't safe to say some things to people?
NILE1: No, you didn't want to say something that you would regret it.
R: So how did you know what you could say and what you couldn't?
NILE1: I didn't know what to say.
R: So there was a lot of confusion about what you could talk about?
NILE1: Aye. [Yes.]

NILE1's supporter linked their current advocacy around criminal procedures involving adults with intellectual disabilities in Northern Ireland to historical practices in which policy would have taken advantage of them to gain information improperly.

> 'Cause things have happened over the years that people with learning disabilities were involved in. With their brother, cousin, nephew in the house involved in the Troubles, and (the disabled person) would have signed documents that would have gotten someone arrested. And what would have happened then was because the Special Powers Act, they weren't allowed to testify, that was taken carte blanche, he's been in the Troubles. And there's been people put away (imprisoned) for that.

The concern about the repercussions of involvement in covert activities by adults with intellectual disabilities – knowingly or not – was highlighted as well by professionals.

> [People with intellectual disabilities] may have been involved perhaps as look out people. You can imagine how attractive that might be, being part of a gang and a group, all the excitement that's going on as part of that group so that desire to belong and be part of something. But it did also mean that I may be more easily caught, I may not be as good I guess at using the system, or knowing what my rights are and those kind of things.
>
> *(NIP1)*

These concerns are not relegated to the past, although the repercussions would have been much more significant during the Troubles.

> Yeah, the problems they would have gotten into in those days would have been much more serious, you know, sort of looking out for people or whatever. Now I guess it's more petty crime sort thing . . . . But probably more so it's about people seeking the approval of others and maybe not having ready-made friendship groups. So you know they want to be part of a group and they're willing to do things to be part of that group.
>
> *(NIP4)*

The professionals reinforced the disconnection experienced between adults with intellectual disabilities and the restrictions experienced within their own communities as a result of having a disability.

> Well, first of all, my parents, if I'm a person with a learning disability, my parents are going to be more protective about me, so they're going to be more anxious. I'm going to have less freedom and also because of the nature or uncertainty that came with that conflict. So I didn't know if that bus was going to travel from A to B, it could be going from A to Z to C, so those uncertainties and my family's natural desire to be protective about me meant that I was probably even more restricted in my movements, who I saw and what I did. And therefore it was probably more home based and more linked into my family. So it had that impact on people with a learning

> disability that I think is different to the rest of the population. While there was always no-go areas, or you couldn't mix there and go there, there was still a path of freedom within a community to move around and I don't know if that was the same for people with disabilities.
>
> *(NIP1)*

Socialising in the community was more difficult when families worried that the young person with an intellectual disability couldn't navigate political sensitivities or remove themselves from danger in the way non-disabled young people adapted to quickly.

> But just going back to the impact on the people with a learning disability. What I have described in terms of people travelling around meant that people with a learning disability were prevented from becoming independent. Because there were real fears and there were genuine risks. I knew people who were beaten up because they were wearing the wrong school uniform in the wrong area. Having a disability or not, you just got beaten up.
>
> *(NIP3)*

This lack of connection to their peers did not mean the participants were immune to the daily disruptions of the conflict. Interviewees described the intimidating nature of armed police forces setting up checkpoints at the entryway to cities and commercial areas and tolerance of segregated education along disability lines and not religious lines. However, when it came to awareness of the Troubles, interviewees reported that their knowledge was limited to media reports at the time. NILE3 was reluctant to speak about the Troubles, and it emerged during a discussion of the peace process that her sister had been killed. The qualitative research I have briefly outlined here indicates that persons with intellectual disabilities definitely experienced the Troubles in a unique way compared to their non-disabled counterparts. The provision of non-denominational education and day services assumed that adults with intellectual disabilities did not have political identities. Connected to this, they were not equipped with the knowledge around local politics and activities to enable them to stay safe in their communities and were restricted in their movements to a greater extent than their non-disabled friends and family. While the communities in which they resided were under attack, the interviewees did not enjoy the same level of community participation the non-disabled community cultivated during the crisis. The chapter will now briefly discuss the post-conflict context for disability rights.

Post-conflict context

Across Northern Ireland, the peace process created a shift in attitude to recognising the rights of all citizens from 1998 onwards. The peace process in the North was negotiated by politicians who were recognised and supported by their constituencies, and the Good Friday Agreement was accepted in a referendum. NILE2 took pride in telling me about voting for the Good Friday Agreement, and while he did not concern himself with the details concerning government administration, he was happy to participate in a democratic process which recognised that people in Northern Ireland did not want the Troubles to continue. There was a considerable shift towards monitoring human rights as the Northern Ireland Human Rights Commission was established, and the rights of persons with disabilities is under their remit. Section 75 of the Northern Irelandl Act 1998 also set out requirements for state bodies to consider the equality impact of their work on their own staff, service users, and the public. This duty had the potential to ensure that human rights and equality, which would benefit persons with intellectual disabilities, would be embedded in the policies and programme activities of statutory bodies. However, NIP2 and NIP3 indicated that this has become merely a tick-box exercise lacking potential for any substantive change.

> Where [Section 75] ended up being is a tick-box exercise so I think there, people got very stuck on the policy.
>
> *(NIP3)*

Hierarchy in disability in post-conflict Northern Ireland

While a formal disability rights movement has not occurred in Northern Ireland, the development of social services was not immune to the hierarchy arising in other jurisdictions. Kerr (2013) suggests that the health and medical focus of serving people who acquired physical disabilities through the Troubles has contributed to a lack of social movement in the jurisdiction. The impact of the conflict on social issues has only recently begun to emerge in Northern Ireland with the LGBTQI and poverty among the issues which have been marginalised (Byrne et al., 2017). The professionals in the research are critical of the lack of recognition of disability rights due to the focus having been on the conflict over the last two decades.

> I think it's because the focus here has always been on the conflict. And now post conflict, anything else is seen as secondary. It's quite similar if we look at children and young people. If we look at other groups, women's groups, LGBT groups have now started to have a much stronger voice in terms of protesting. For disabled people, I think there is a general lack of awareness of the social model of disability because of the role of the church and the role of health organisations and services. The role of family. They're very protective here compared to other parts of the UK. So I guess disabled people tend to be wrapped up in cotton wool a lot more here than in other jurisdictions, and that has had an impact.
>
> *(NIP2)*

NIP2 rejected the idea that disability was recognised as a cross-party issue and pointed to the lack of supports available to people who have sustained disabilities through the conflict to highlight the lack of joined-up thinking at government level. NIP1 indicated that there is no acknowledgement of the interrelatedness of the issues and needs of victims of the Troubles and persons with disabilities in Northern Ireland. Different supports are available depending on whether an individual identifies as a 'victim' or a 'person with a disability', despite the potential for both groups to benefit from similar initiatives instead of being siloed.

> It just hasn't been considered in the context of the conflict. Even though a lot of people who are now disabled were disabled as a result of the conflict that hasn't been on the agenda with politicians and policymakers. Their focus has been on victims and there has been no recognition of the relationship between some individuals who have been injured during the Troubles and what that means in disability terms. The disability unit for example have no contact with the victims and survivors chapter, the victims unit/strategy – all these post conflict issues that have emerged, disability sector or unit have not engaged with that at all and vice versa. The victims sector hasn't engaged with the disability sector. The two issues have been very siloed even though it would seem to be logical. . . . They see themselves as victims rather than as disabled, and in that language, even though if you think of yourself in both those terms, you open yourself up to a broader range of services and potential opportunities that just haven't been explored.
>
> *(NIP1)*

This is reinforced by another contribution.

> With the conflict being the preeminent force – issue – because it matters then with bread-and-butter issues, and people with disabilities were pushed to the side. Although in saying that, we have now, in the last few years, we have seen a growth of advocacy for persons with disabilities who are disabled as a result of the conflict. And they are arguing for pensions for their members and other points, so I think that's flagging up the challenges that persons with disabilities face. They would have a – they'd be more for people disabled as a result of a conflict more so than disabled people in general, but they're certainly flagging up the issues that persons with disabilities face. And a person disabled as a result of the conflict here, they'll likely face the same challenges as someone who has another acquired disability. That's not to undermine; I'm sure there's impacts of the circumstances that it occurred, but the challenges, possibly, would be similar to those faced by another person with an acquired disability.

R: **In relation to learning disability?**
NIP5: I suppose its they've not had the same sort of attention that they should have had.

NIP1 highlighted the hierarchy within the disabled population, in which persons with intellectual disability were the lowest rank.

> That's a general issue in NI. We don't have a real disability movement of individual disabled people. So we're having to start to identify individuals or there's a few individuals who keep doing the same thing again and again. . . . [P]articularly people with intellectual disability; they tend to be at the bottom when it comes to these kinds of things.
>
> *(NIP1)*

The professionals also lamented the lack of a culture of advocacy in Northern Ireland and that where disability is considered, intellectual disability is considered too cumbersome to effectively engage with in terms of consultation on national policies.

> In the North it is very tokenistic involvement. I suppose there is more now than has ever gone on before. . . . We don't have much of an independent advocacy scene here. . . . I think people, when they think about disability, they think about people in wheelchairs first of all. And then they think about people with health conditions maybe, maybe blind, visually impaired, people with hearing loss. But I really think people don't think about learning disabled people unless they're really quite sophisticated in their thinking. And then you've got the difficulty of how do you involve those people. I mean, it's hard enough for organisations: how do you involve the visually impaired and blind community, how do you involve people with complex needs or whatever. So I think it's maybe too much of a challenge for them; they'd like to do it. I'm not sure they'd even like to do it. For some people, it is on their agenda. The peace process, I'm not sure, I don't think it is. I've never heard of anybody (with an intellectual disability) who was involved in that.
>
> *(NIP4)*

The issue of funding within the disability sector also pits service organisations against each other, but where services are provided by organisations with a community ethos, there is potential for consensus building on issues important to independent living.

> I would say in the – there's some organisations money tends to be the main issue of dispute. So there would be some voluntary organisations very money orientated, and they might be driven by that agenda. And the

> private sector would be driven by that agenda. So here, most recent issues have been about the national living wage, equality law around talking about European law on sleep over times. That, it hasn't driven a wedge, but obviously the focus of some organisations has been about the money side of things. I'd say probably [in] the voluntary community sector, there is generally a lot of consensus around things.
>
> *(NIP4)*

Connected to the issue of finance for disability inclusion, NILE2 recounted an experience of being denied a place on an education course due to lack of resources. It is difficult to think that had the disability been physical in nature, such an attitude would have been permissible.

> I went out to try and do a course. I think it was something in (educational company) with essential skills, and they said I couldn't do that course because I have a disability. Because I didn't know anything about rights at the time, I sort of just walked away, put my head down, and accepted it. But in hindsight, I should have challenged it. . . . Naw, there's a [technical college], right. They have a service that gives help to people with disabilities. They give you forms, and they ask you to tick if you have a disability. And then if you do request the extra help, you find that you don't get it. And then when I asked about it, they said, 'Look, our hands are tied; we don't have the money'. That's what their response was.
>
> *(NILE2)*

It is evident from the research that, during the Troubles, there was a hierarchy of experiences, with persons with intellectual disabilities experiencing curtailments on their lives to a much greater, yet unrecognized, extent than their non-disabled peers. The conflict placed broader social issues much lower in priority by public governance since the peace process. The segregation of persons with intellectual disabilities from their peers during and since the Troubles has relegated them to peripheries of the marginalized disabled population, as difficulties in resources and inclusive consultation practices prevail.

The next section will consider the corresponding experiences in Bosnia Herzegovina.

Bosnia

Bosnia Herzegovina context

Pre-conflict social services hierarchy

Bosnia Herzegovina, like Northern Ireland, has been directly detrimentally impacted by conflict over the last century. The city of Sarajevo in particular has played a hugely important role in international conflict (History, 2018).

In the wake of World War II, the communist dictator, Tito, was successful in administering a constitutional structure of governance which satisfied the various national identities within the then–Socialist Federal Republic of Yugoslavia (SFRY), albeit through the abolition of free speech and suppression of criticism of government (Forsythe & Rieffer-Flanagan, 2016). Archer (2016) acknowledges the emphasis in the literature on the economic system within the SFRY during this period but highlights that significant social inequality was experienced by the population at this time. Jansen's (2014) research on everyday life in the SFRY recounts that citizens were satisfied once basic employment and accommodation needs were met. Residents of SFRY experienced a more moderate form of socialism than that implemented in other communist states (Stokes, 2005).

After the dissolution of the Socialist Federal Republic of Yugoslavia, the EU and the US recognized Bosnia as an independent state (Gunneriusson, 2017). Efforts to establish local governance structures known as cantons were unsuccessful due to objections from all three ethnically aligned political groups. Sariv and Rodwin are sceptical of the idea that a multitude of religious and ethnic groups were cohabiting peacefully in SFRY before the conflict (Sariv & Rodwin, 1993). However, there was no indication of ethnic tensions from the qualitative research. Participants referred to schoolmates and living in the community with people of different ethnicities peacefully before the war.

In April 1992, Bosnian Serbs, supported by the Yugoslav Army, initiated armed conflict against areas with significant Bosnian Muslim populations. Due in part to the extremity of the violence perpetrated by all armed forces (Ruigrok et al., 2005), the Bosnian war received intense media coverage at the time and has been subject to significant academic, policy, and legal scrutiny since then. A wide variety of sources from the desk-based research documented the disruption to fundamental services, food, and essential supply shortages. There is also considerable focus on the conflict as a cause of physical disability, but it was not possible to locate accounts of experiences of persons with intellectual disability.

BIHLE2 is a Muslim woman who recounted having her education curtailed. Among factors such as safety in the locality (drug use was described) and the religious attitudes towards education for girls, she also suggest that her family attempted to hide her disability.

> Her parents from an early age – maybe that was why they didn't allow her to go to school; they perceived that she had minor disability, minor intellectual disability.
>
> *(BIHLE2)*

Pre-conflict social services hierarchy

A hierarchy of disability was more explicitly embedded in Bosnian social structures than in Northern Ireland. The charity Every Child (2014) explains that in the Central and Eastern European Region, communism brought about a prioritisation of institutional care over parental care of children with disabilities with the aim of alleviating the pressures on families experiencing poverty after WWII. Phillips (2009) outlines the former USSR's welfare system, which would have been influential in the former SFRY. Priority was given to those injured in military service, depending on which armed activity the individual had engaged in. Persons who acquired disability through the workplace or due to the actions of another person were next in the hierarchy while persons with disabilities from birth, under which classification persons with intellectual disabilities would be categorised, are the lowest tier of the hierarchy. This categorisation was not based on medical terms but rather on the perceived potential for contribution to society, an extremely important element of socialist societies. Those disabled during military service or at work received higher benefits and do to this day in Bosnia, as praise for their contribution to society. The impact of the demarcation of disability categories resulted in differences in treatment by the state depending on individual circumstances. The welfare system did not acknowledge society as creating a disabling environment; instead, it focused on the cause of the disability at an individual level, stifling recognition of persons with disabilities as a significant section of society. This was encouraged by the socialist state rather than a collective or societal attitude which could lead to a social movement of persons with disabilities. Initiatives to encourage participation in the workforce were individualised and sought to restore perceived absence of ability (Rassell and Iarskaia-Smirnova, 2013). Sutton (1988) provides a similar overview of the reliance of social protection institutions, which were regarded as beneficial services provided by the state for vulnerable citizens in the USSR. Segregated education was provided, but some children were considered uneducable in the USSR, so persons with intellectual disabilities were further excluded within already-segregated settings.

The OECD (2003) provides only a brief reference to children with disabilities being 'screened' in pre-conflict Bosnia Herzegovina, but there are no details as to the nature of disabilities being screened. There is acknowledgement of the segregation of children with disabilities within institutions and that conditions in these institutions were poor.

Disability experiences of the conflict

All the male participants in the Bosnian research were engaged in the conflict with their respective ethnic armed forces. Their descriptions of witnessing violence, death, and civil unrest are reflective of the wider reporting of the atrocities of the war, but the added dimension of having an intellectual disability resulted in more trauma for these men. BIHLE1 retrospectively considered how he appeared to be fit for armed service.

> So in that time, the army was fighting with other armies. In 1993, he was in third brigade, like professional army, and he spent there for seven

> years. He was on the weapons – you know, where you shoot big, big hard weapons – he was trained for that. I was healthy at that time. They accepted me in that school for army because I was healthy. I didn't have problems in that time with my hearing, eyes, or psyche. . . . And seemingly, I was OK. . . . Psyche, mentally healthy.
>
> *(BIHLE1)*

Civilians experienced severe disruption to vital supplies, such as food and electricity. One participant described his interactions with civilians while he was serving in the Croat army.

> They were confused and didn't know what to think, what to do in that time. Very scared – they needed to run from their houses and left everything. The animals like cows, sheep, and pigs, what they had in their villages, were just walking around. . . . €50 was one packet [of] cigarette[s]. People were selling their cows to buy nuts.
>
> *(BIHLE1)*

Residing in an urban area, BIHLE4 explained the measures that her family took to maintain their safety.

> She was mostly talking to her mother about the Bosniak forces fighting the Serb forces. They were also hiding in basements. That was a common case in (city) – if their neighbourhoods were being bombed, they would usually take refuge or shelter in the basements. She is talking about the lack of electricity; she didn't have electricity. There were many occasions they were very frightened. [S]omebody was knocking on their doors, and they didn't have the electricity, so they thought that the Serb forces came. Towards the end of the war, in 1993, the electricity came back. Without electricity, you don't know.
>
> *(BIHLE4)*

Only one professional I spoke to had worked in the disability service sector during the war. The other professionals had gleaned information from their own experiences during the war and from longer-serving colleagues.

> So if they lived with their families, their status and situation remained unchanged. However, throughout the war, all these DPOs* [sic] were very active in providing support, providing disability services from psycho social support and others sorts of supports. They were never left aside or on the road. It was only when they were totally on their own without any family members and when their lives were jeopardized; [in] those specific cases, they were placed in institutions where they could be cared for.
>
> *(BIHP2)*

During the period of crisis, there was a sense of community and identity connected to the conflict. There was negativity towards members of the community who were perceived to not be upholding those values.

> Because they were seen that they were not contributing to the struggle. There was that. There was also intersectional discrimination. A few examples that I'm aware of, where they were members of minority groups in wherever. So this friend of mine whose brother is in (named institution) – the mother is a Croat, the father is a Serb – so in addition to being a person with a disability, he was also a member of a different ethnic group, so there was that element as well. Plenty of bullying, not to mention anything more serious. It was really difficult for anyone, but for persons with intellectual disability also.
>
> *(BIHP5)*

All participants were grateful for the end of the war as it brought an end to violence and death, but BIHP5 was critical of the manner in which the future of their country was decided behind closed doors.

> Twenty years after the war (the Dayton Peace Accords) has never officially been translated from English, so our constitution is only in English. Its accessibility to the population in general [is low], not to mention there is no easy to read or any other attempt to make it accessible to persons with any kind of disabilities, not to mention persons with intellectual disabilities. The process was not inclusive for the majority of population. It was just a few warlords who sat down and put their signature on a piece of paper that was prepared by the Americans. So no one had much to say about it.
>
> *(BIHP5)*

Post-conflict hierarchies of disability

Having attracted international attention to the atrocities of violence and rights abuses, the recovering state of Bosnia and Herzegovina received funding from the World Bank (World Bank Operations Evaluation Department, 2004). This collaboration resulted in the identification of disability as a priority issue and the need to reform the national rehabilitation and health services to include quality community-based care (Edmonds, 2005). While this strategy was intended primarily to address the physical disabilities inflicted on citizens during the war, the ethos of the Independent Living Movement was not incorporated. BIHLE1 and BIHLE5 indicated that the attention they received in the aftermath of their armed service was medically focused and not readily available to all participants. BIHLE1 described experiencing homelessness and being at risk of losing his leg due to cold weather exposure before availing themselves of medical attention. BIHLE5 claimed the care he received in Croatia was superior to that in Bosnia. The bureaucracy and organisation involved in prioritising armed service staff was complex for BIHLE5 as he had served both in Bosnia and Croatia, but his Croatian service was not recognised. This indicates that the health and social service system was not user friendly on many levels, not just for persons with intellectual disabilities. BIHLE5 did not have a unique experience of discrimination based on military service. The Republic Srpska had limitations on the entitlements of veterans who served for armies other than their own in the aftermath of the war (European Commission, 2008), which has been highly detrimental to populations who returned after ethnic cleansing. The focus and prioritisation of rewarding military service continues beyond immediate post-conflict health and social services. BIHP1 explained how the inherent inequality of the social protection system is reinforced by legislative provisions within each of the entities that determine eligibility criteria separately. Within Bosnia Herzegovina, each of the individual 14 cantons determine eligibility criteria for social protection.

The International Federation of Persons with Physical Disability highlights the momentum during and after the war to establish organisations of, and for, persons with disabilities. In terms of advancing physical disability services, civil society and voluntary organisations established norms and benchmarks and worked to pilot successful programmes in line with state structures in order to fill a gap in disability service provision (Hope87, 2014). Discussing the post-war social protection system in Bosnia and Herzegovina, UNICEF (2003) highlights that there is no institution at state level responsible for social protection. There were more centralised social protection services, especially in relation to children with disabilities, in the Republica Sprska, but despite this, international aid organisations still had to pilot social protection projects. Milosavljevic indicates that the current social protection system in the Federation of Bosnia Herzegovina, under which disability services are provided, is based on an ethos of helping (Europe Aid, 2015), rather than addressing the causes of disabling factors in society.

Disability services followed a similar structure to the pre-war era with services available based on individuals' perceived social contribution and source of the impairment, rather than need. In this sense, the source of the individual's impairment influenced the degree and type of supports, including financial assistance, that could be received. More beneficial treatment was afforded to war veterans than to civilians injured in the conflict, who, in turn, received better conditions than those with a disability not connected to the conflict. Memisevic et al. (2017) indicate that persons with intellectual disabilities therefore continue to experience the lowest quality of life within the category of persons with disabilities in Bosnia Herzegovina. BIHP1 was critical of these differences in support throughout the country and of the categorisation of support need being linked to the perceived source of the individual's impairment.

> In terms of where people live, in terms of them having different rights, not equal rights. What is the cause of disability? Whether it is war or not, civilian victims of war or not, it is not defined. If we take that into

> consideration, there are three different groups of disability. [I]t is people who become disabled in the war like soldiers – military. Second group is civilian victims of war. Third group is those who have nothing to do with the war, and they have the worse status, and we see they have direct discrimination.
>
> *(BIHP1)*

One participant outlined his attempts through his role as a politician to eliminate discrimination based on origin of impairment.

> After he left the ministry, there was this unfinished law that he was trying to promote. A law on the equalisation of rights for all persons with disability, whether they're civilian victims of war. However, he left the ministry, and it hasn't been finished yet. Civilian victims of war and war victims, they're being discriminated. . . . Non-war persons with disabilities – they have the worst status compared to victims of the war. They have the best status, actually; they receive more fees.
>
> *(BIHP4)*

BIHP3 outlined the frustrating bureaucratic nature of governance in Bosnia, which results in inadequate resourcing of disability initiatives and the potential for corruption, further restricting the potential for reform.

> So a smaller portion of people receives the highest amounts of money. Only certain individuals – this is again the difference between civilian victims of war of, for example, the deaf, blind or persons with intellectual disabilities. They have the worst status. Civilian victims of war receive more money. So it's not a proper or transparent or equal allocation of money. Corruption exists, especially in terms of institutions. They actually receive a lot of money. 20 million KM are allocated towards these institutions, of public funds, 20 million annually, every year, and the beneficiaries still live in catastrophic, terrible conditions. (Named staff member) showed you the photographs from the institutions. And how many square metres are actually available to a particular beneficiary. So you receive the money, but it's not visible when you see it, worse than a prison. So they're probably corrupt. That's another, entirely different story. There should be some agency dealing with corruption.
>
> *(BIHP3)*

BIHP5 describes the obstacles facing organisations representing and advocating for persons with disabilities" 'There are some attempts. The thing is that the disability movement is quite segmented, as is everything else. The country is divided so the disability movement is divided and then also the competence of different levels of government will be different.'

The extent of the problem of institutionalisation was recognised by the Institution of Human Rights Ombudsmen of Bosnia Herzegovina (2009) in what they termed 'Social Care Institutions'. The report highlights shortcomings in education, health protection, isolation from families, and low standards of accommodation due to significant overcrowding. The lack of regard for the safety and mental health of both staff and service users was also highlighted as a systemic issue. Overall the ombudsman's report suggested investment in community-based programmes, oversight of institutions, and improved standards within institutions.

The hierarchy of disability is part of a wider complex system of bureaucracy which BIHP5 suggests is suited to the retention of power by a minority of political actors, which had devastating impacts on the lives of persons with intellectual disabilities.

> Bosnia is just so hopeless (laughing). . . . I guess by now you know about the obstacles that are now being created in the aftermath of the Dayton peace agreements. Simply because it is being seen as a tool for existing political structures to stay in power for as long as possible. I mean it's just, this is so far away from any of the priorities that they might. I'm definitely not optimistic about the country's future. I'm trying to imagine a point where they have a disability strategy or prioritise needs. Or rights, not to mention needs, just rights of persons with disabilities. And I really am having difficulty seeing that moment. Because they are just so self-centred, everything is about power, it has nothing to do. It is not a social government; it is just completely screwed up.
>
> *(BIHP5)*

The chapter will now discuss the impact of hierarchical structures on the lives of adults with intellectual disabilities in Northern Ireland and Bosnia Herzegovina.

Discussion

Hierarchies

While the qualitative research involved only a small cohort of individuals with professional and lived experiences in Northern Ireland and Bosnia Herzegovina, the discussion of intellectual disability during the periods of conflict was novel to all participants and goes some way to addressing a significant gap in literature on the issue. Hierarchy was not a theme the research participants were questioned explicitly on, but their comments, particularly those of the professionals, suggest that it has been intricately woven into the services which disabled people avail themselves of in each jurisdiction. The impact of the conflict on the landscape of current disability services in both jurisdictions cannot be overstated. For the research participants with lived experiences of intellectual disability, their lives are very much influenced by hierarchical structures, from how they are perceived by the public to the funding allocated to their support and the accessibility of services in their communities. This section will examine two emerging hierarchical structures which have also impacted the lives of research participants.

Gender hierarchies

Within the experiences discussed, both during and since the conflict, disabled women and men had very different experiences. None of the women with intellectual disabilities participated directly in the conflict in either jurisdiction. For those in Bosnia, their contributions related to work in the home to survive – domestic chores, setting up comfortable shelter spaces, and experiencing the stress of having male family members involved in the armed forces. The harmful perceptions that men should take up arms for their respective ethnic groups led to men with intellectual disabilities being harassed, whereas little was expected of women with intellectual disabilities. Neither woman was in employment at the time of the interviews, and their networks remained limited to their immediate families and disability support staff. At the time of interviews, the men were all living independently and engaging in further education or employment based on their trade.

In Northern Ireland, only one female participant described working outside the home during the Troubles. Even this freedom of employment was frequently curtailed by outbreaks of violence, and socialising was kept to a minimum. The other Northern Ireland female participants who were younger than NILE1 described attending education or youth training courses. Unlike NILE2, who described throwing stones at soldiers and witnessing buses being hijacked, none of the women had the freedom for or, arguably, interest in youthful misbehaviour. When speaking about their current lives, they described busying themselves with arts, crafts, and stereotypically female activities such as hairdressing, bingo, and dance classes. Two of the women were residents in institutional settings while one resided with her sister's family. One of the men resided with his sister with a large degree of independence, and the other man lived independently. It is difficult not to link the protectionist attitudes towards women which may have served to protect them during the conflict as restricting their potential to live independent lives in later years.

Combatant versus civilian hierarchies

The contributions from male Bosnia participants with lived experiences that they had served in the armed forces was an unexpected revelation during the research. The lack of sufficient screening of potential army candidates for intellectual and mental health disabilities painted a picture of last-minute scrambling for resources to defend from attacks. Were the situation to arise today, it would be difficult to see that a national armed force would not exempt them from armed duty due to safety concerns. The participants themselves indicated that their intellectual disabilities were only identified while receiving medical treatment for physical injuries, and that acquiring post-traumatic stress disorder and periods of institutionalization exacerbated their disability. Ironically, the impact of their participation in conflict ultimately led to them receiving preferable, but far from ideal, disability supports. However, as their physical injuries were addressed and they progressed to relying on intellectual disability services, they were subject to the same system which has failed to invest in intellectual disability supports, albeit with their own financial situation stronger due to army pensions. One male participant described how he was forced to sign over his legal capacity in order to be eligible for a pension linked to his deceased parents' social welfare. There were questions raised about how legal this was, but the system for challenging this is difficult to navigate, and the individual was just relieved to have financial security. One participant had only recently secured freedom from an institution and was excited about the prospect of living independently in the community. His description of being institutionalized, initially for PTSD and then for more prolonged period (upwards of 20 years) due his intellectual disability, demonstrates the tapering off of intellectual disability services compared to combat-related disability.

In Northern Ireland, only one participant described actively engaging in anything that could be construed as connected to the Troubles – childhood stone throwing – although the professionals outlined the potential for manipulation by paramilitary actors on both sides of the conflict. Due to the conflict itself, other social justice issues were placed much lower on the public governance agenda, and even when a human rights approach was embraced, the focus was on anti-sectarianism and avoiding a return to violence. The lack of literature and evidence which reflects the experiences of persons with intellectual disability does suggest that they were not perceived as participants in either combatant or civilian roles. It is important to recognize that adults with intellectual disabilities who lost family members and friends in the violence potentially lost a supporter or advocate who could promote their independence, will, and preferences, whereas those who acquired physical disability could still advocate for themselves.

Conclusion

Neither jurisdiction experienced a disability rights movement on a par with the activism outlined in Section 2, and this was even slower to impact persons with intellectual disabilities.

The issue of disability has been siloed from the discourse on victims of the Troubles, whereas it has been more to the fore in the re-establishment of social services in Bosnia Herzegovina. Arguments that integrated services across conflict and disability would concentrate on acquired physical and psychosocial disabilities fail to recognise that persons with intellectual disabilities can hold multiple identities and experience multiple disabilities at a time.

While the qualitative research involved only a small cohort of individuals with professional and lived experiences in Northern Ireland and Bosnia Herzegovina, the discussion of intellectual disability during the periods of conflict was novel to all participants and goes some way to addressing a significant gap in literature on the issue.

The conflicts in Northern Ireland and Bosnia Herzegovina were devastating to individual, community, and national levels but had the potential to completely reform the affected societies and to challenge hierarchies within disability and broader civil society. Funding from international development organisations was essential for the reestablishment of governance structures and public services. However, the investments failed to adequately address structural inequalities across the populations they sought to serve. The conflicts have shaped the fabric of the societies and distracted political attention from social justice issues which have progressed much more successfully in other countries.

The hierarchy of disability is much more pronounced in Bosnia than in Northern Ireland – the individual's impairment and origin of impairment influence the degree and type of supports, including financial assistance, that could be received. More beneficial treatment was afforded to war veterans than to civilians injured in the conflict, who in turn received better conditions than those with a disability not connected to the conflict. In contrast, in Northern Ireland, many people who have acquired physical disability through the Troubles identify as 'victims' rather than as disabled persons. The lack of cohesion within the health and social services to connect and integrate services across 'victims' and disabled people is a missed opportunity to address the disability hierarchical structure in Northern Ireland.

Ultimately, the hierarchies in place in both jurisdictions pit already marginalized populations against each other and undermine the solidarity across impairment type, which was an aspiration of the original independent living movement.

*The organisations referred to by the interviewee do not meet the standards required for a DPO, and the concept of DPO had not been formalised during the period of the war.

References

Archer, R. (2016). Social inequalities and the study of Yugoslavia's dissolution. In Bieber, F., & Galijaš, A. (Eds.), *Debating the end of Yugoslavia*, (pp. 135–152). Routledge.

Bosi, L. (2008). Explaining the emergence process of the civil rights protest in Northern Ireland (1945–1968): insights from a relational social movement approach. *Journal of Historical Sociology*, *21*(2), 242–271.

Center for Independent Living, Berkeley. CIL's History. http://www.cilberkeley.org/history/

Charleton. (2000). *Nothing about us without us: disability oppression and empowerment*. University of California Press.

Edgerton, L. (1986). Public protest, domestic acquiescence: women in Northern Ireland. In R. Ridd & H. Callaway (Eds.), *Caught up in conflict. Women in society*. Palgrave. https://doi.org/10.1007/978-1-349-18380-7_4
Edmonds. (2005). *Disabled people and development*. Poverty Reduction and Social Development Division Regional and Sustainable Development Department, Asian Development Bank.
Europe Aid. (2015). Development of social service at the local level in Bosnia Herzegovina. http://iris-see.eu/wp-content/uploads/2016/03/PolicyPaper-BiH.pdf
European Commission. (2008). The country of return information project, Country Sheet, Bosnia and Herzegovina. http://www.refworld.org/pdfid/49afa139d.pdf
Forsythe, D. P., & Rieffer-Flanagan, B. A. (2016). *The International Committee of the Red Cross: a neutral humanitarian actor*. Routledge.
Gunneriusson, H. (2017). The events in 1992. In *Bordieuan field theory as an instrument for military operational analysis. New security challenges*. Palgrave Macmillan.
History.com. (2018). Outbreak of world war one. http://www.history.com/topics/world-war-i/outbreak-of-world-war-i
Hope 87. (2014). Bosnia and Herzegovina: support for persons with disabilities. htp://www.hope87.at/galleries/bosnia-and-herzegovina-support-persons-disabilities
Institution of Human Rights Ombudsmen of Bosnia Herzegovina. (2009). Special report on the situation of human rights in the institutions for accommodation of mentally disabled persons. http://www.ombudsmen.gov.ba/documents/obmudsmen_doc2013020401071133eng.pdf
Jansen, S. (2014). On not moving well enough: temporal reasoning in Sarajevo yearnings for 'normal lives. *Current Anthropology*, *55*(S9).
Johnstone, J. (2004). Disability and identity: personalised construction and formalised supports. *Disability Studies Quarterly*, *24*(4).
Karp, G. (2017). 'Ed Roberts. The father of independent living. *Ability 360*. http://ability360.org/livability/advocacy-livability/ed-roberts-independent-living
Kempton, W., & Kahn, E. (1991). Sexuality and people with intellectual disabilities: a historical perspective. *Sexuality and Disability*, *9*(2), 93–111.
Kennedy, E. K. (1973). Ulster is an international issue. *Foreign Policy*, *11*, 57–71.
Kerr. S. (2013). Disability and conflict: exploring how the peace process in Northern Ireland assesses and addresses the needs of persons with disabilities. *Disability & Society*, *28*(6), 826–838.
Kim, S. (2015, August 22). Fighting my internalization of the hierarchy of disability. *Crippled Scholar.com*. https://crippledscholar.com/2015/08/23/fighting-my-internalization-of-the-hierarchy-of-disability/
Lynn, B., (2021) Northern Ireland assembly (November 1982 to June 1986) – Summary of main events. *Cain Webservice 1996–2021*. http://cain.ulst.ac.uk/events/assembly1982/summary.htm
McDonald, & Oxford. (2005). History of independent living. *Independent Living Research Utilization*. https://www.accessnorth.net/contact/contactResources/HistoryOfIndependentLiving.pdf
Memisevic, H., Hadzic, S., Biscevic, I. & Mujkanovic, E. (2017). Quality of life of people with disabilities in Bosnia and Herzegovina – is there a moderating effect of the health status? *Scandinavian Journal of Disability Research*, *19*(4).
O'Dochartaigh. (2005). *From civil rights to Armalites-Derry and the birth of the Irish Troubles*. Palgrave Macmillan.
Organisation for Economic Cooperation and Development. (2003). *Reviews of national policies for education reviews of national policies for education: South Eastern Europe* (Vol. 1). Albania, Bosnia-Herzegovina, Bulgaria, Croatia, Kosovo, OECD Publishing.

Phillips, S. D. (2009). "There are no invalids in the USSR!": a missing soviet chapter in the new disability history. *Disability Studies Quarterly*, *29*(3).
Rassell & Iarskaia-Smirnova. (2014). *Disability in Eastern Europe and the former Soviet Union: history, policy and everyday life*. Routledge.
Ruigrok, N., de Ridder, J. A., & Scholten, O. (2005). News coverage of the Bosnian war in Dutch newspapers. In P. Seib (Eds.), *Media and conflict in the twenty-first century*. Palgrave Macmillan.
Sariv, M., & Rodwin, V. G. (1993). The once and future health system in the former Yugoslavia: myths and realities. *Journal of Public Health Policy, 14*(2), 220–237.
Shakespeare, T. (1993). Disabled people's self organisation: a new social movement? *Disability, Handicap and Society*, *8*(3).
Stokes, G. (2005). From nation to minority: Serbs in Croatia and Bosnia at the outbreak of the Tugoslav wars. *Problems of Post-Communism*, *52*(6).
Sutton, A. (1988). Special education for handicapped pupils. In J. Riordan (Ed.), *Soviet education: The gifted and the handicapped*. Routledge.
Thompson, V. A. (1961). Hierarchy, specialization, and organizational conflict. *Administrative Science Quarterly*, *5*(4), 485–521.
UNICEF. (2003). Bosnia Herzegovina, Legal aspects of social protection for children in Bosnia Herzegovina. https://www.unicef.org/spanish/evaldatabase/files/BH_2003_Leg_Aspects_Social_Protection.pdf
Wehmeyer & Gragoudas. (2004). Centers for independent living and transition-age youth: Empowerment and self-determination. *Journal of Vocational Rehabilitation*, *20*(54).
World Bank Operations Evaluation Department. (2004). Bosnia and Herzegovina post conflict reconstruction and the transition to a market economy. An OED evaluation of world bank support. https://openknowledge.worldbank.org/bitstream/handle/10986/14900/302270PAPER0Bi1flict0reconstruction.pdf?sequence=1&isAllowed=y

12

PERSONAL ASSISTANCE SERVICES IN POLAND DURING THE PERIOD OF HIGHER EDUCATION

Paving the way for independent living

Ewa Giermanowska, Mariola Racław and Dorota Szawarska

Introduction: The problem and background

The Polish official statistics register legally disabled persons (with an appropriate certificate) and biologically disabled persons (who define themselves as disabled). However, we do not have current data for both categories. The results of national censuses provide the most information, but only those from a decade ago are available. According to the data of the last National Census of Population and Apartments in 2011, 46,975,000 people with disabilities lived in Poland, which constituted 12.2% of the country's population – including 4.1% of people with only biological disabilities, 6.9% with legal and biological disabilities, and 1.2% disabled only legally (GUS, 2012 – Narodowy Spis Powszechny Ludności i Mieszkań 2011. *Raport z wyników*). More recent data will bring the results of the next national census, which ended in September 2021. However, information on people with disabilities will not be obtained until September 2022. The Polish Central Statistical Office, using the registers of the Social Insurance Institution, publishes yearly data on people with a certificate of incapacity for work or disability (legal disability). In 2019, there were 2.4 million such people. On the other hand, the group of young people ages 20 to 24 with a certificate of incapacity for work or disability amounted to almost 42,000 (Osoby niepełnosprawne w 2019r2020/People with disabilities in 2019–2020).

The rights of people with disabilities to inclusive education, higher education and academic development are now unquestionable. They are sanctioned by the UN Convention on the Rights of Persons with Disabilities, which Poland

DOI: 10.4324/9781003410089-15

signed in March 2007 and ratified in September 2012. UN CRPD in Poland has been in force since 25 October 2012 (Dziennik Ustaw Rzeczpospolitej Polski, dnia 25 października 2012 r. Poz. 1169).

Journal of Laws of October 25, 2012, item 1169). However, this does not mean that the aspirations of all those who are in need and have the appropriate abilities are respected. Article 24 of the UN CRPD specifically mentions that state parties of the Convention are obliged to ensure that all people with disabilities have access to inclusive education at all levels, which means that the state parties have to ensure that reasonable accommodation is provided to persons with disabilities. These accommodation vary depending on the needs of a person with disability in education, but they may include the services of an assistant. The services of an assistant appears also as an element of implementing the idea of independent living in Article 19 of the UN CRPD. Indeed, the full implementation of Articles 19 and 24 contribute markedly to freedom, inclusion, contribution and fulfilment of the personal potential of people with disabilities, which the article deals with in the context of higher education.

In Poland, for people with disabilities, access to higher education widened only after the political transformation in 1989, when round table talks took place between the communist government and the leaders of the solidarity movement. Following the elections in June 1989, a new government was formed, and transition towards democracy and free market commenced. Modernisation of economy, society and culture brought Poland closer to the West (Zofia Kinowska-Mazaraki, 2021), which also included a transformation of attitudes towards people with disabilities. This was further strengthened after Poland joined the European Union in 2004 and participated in a number of initiatives and projects at various levels related to equal opportunities and rights of people with disabilities.

Still, equal access to institutions and the enjoyment of rights by all persons with a disability is an unfinished process. This is the result, among other things, of historical and political conditions characteristic of the countries of the former Eastern Bloc. In Poland, people who are not involved in activism rarely refer to the concept of citizen's rights. In particular, in relation to people with disabilities, the language of welfare provisions dominates.

Referring to the specificity of the countries of the Eastern European bloc, it is also worth referring to the issue of inequality in access to higher education in the period of the socialist state. Despite the dominant ideology of equality in Poland in the times of "real socialism", the distance between the most privileged and the most disadvantaged categories of pupils and students has not changed (Białecki, 1998). The state undertook many corrective actions, but still, social background and economic and cultural capital had a decisive influence on graduating from higher education. On the other hand, there was a clear equalization of educational opportunities between men and women. As a result, an increasing proportion of women attained higher levels of education, and in the tertiary category, their share became distinctly higher than that of men (Białecki, 1998).

After the political change in Poland, there was an educational boom at the tertiary level, which also included students with disabilities. Back in 1999, the number of students with disabilities at Polish universities did not exceed 2,000. In the 2017–2018 academic year, 23,828 people with disabilities (including foreigners) studied at universities and constituted 1.8% of a total of 1,291,870 students. Among students with disabilities, Deaf or hard of hearing people accounted for 7.4%, Blind or visually impaired students 8.4%, and people with motor disabilities accounted for 30.5%. More than half the students were people with other types of disabilities (53.7%), (GUS, 2018, Szkoły wyższe i ich finanse w 2017 r.).

It should be emphasised that students with disabilities at Polish universities are an elite group among people with disabilities. According to the Ministry of National Education, in 2017, there were 35,078 schools of different types in the education system (covering primary and secondary schools) in Poland, including 30,273 mainstream schools; 2,895 special schools; 1,554 mainstream schools with integrated branches; 175 integrated schools; 110 mainstream schools with special branches; and 71 mainstream integrated schools. In these schools, there were 239,438 students with disabilities who had a certificate of need for special education (Strategia na rzecz Osób z Niepełnosprawnościami, 2021–2030, 2021, p. 39/Strategy for Persons with Disabilities 2021–2030, 2021, p. 39). Despite the measures taken to increase the chances of people with disabilities to participate in education together with non-disabled people (in inclusive education) and the possibility of continuing education at subsequent levels of education, there are still many barriers that hinder the education process (see also Stumbo *et al* 2011). People with disabilities are still, on average, less educated than people without disabilities, which also affects their chances of continuing education at the university level. In 2018, 9.4% of people with disabilities and 26.0% of people without disabilities had higher education in Poland (Strategia na rzecz Osób z Niepełnosprawnościami, 2021–2030, 2021, pp. 39–40/Strategy for People with Disabilities, 2021–2030, 2021, pp. 39–40/). It is worth noting, however, that the lower education levels of people with disabilities is correlated with age; older groups have not had the opportunity to continue their education and are significantly less educated than non-disabled people. Also, living in rural areas still limits the participation of students with disabilities in higher levels of education. An important factor limiting the development of the potential of students with disabilities is that recommendations made in decisions on the need for special education are not always followed at every level of education, including recommendations concerning the requirement to individualise the course of education.

Access to higher education as well as doctoral studies for people with disabilities remains elitist and is the result of a complex process of conditions that are largely independent of the individual. The very process of studying also creates new hierarchies among people with disabilities. Personal assistance services at universities were supposed to equalise opportunities for people with different types of disabilities, but this was not always so.

When using the term "personal assistance services at universities," we are aware of definitional differences. According to the spirit of the UN Convention on the Rights of People with Disabilities of 2006, personal assistantship (Article 19) is the support provided to a person with a disability, carried out under the person's direction by another person, with the aim of enabling independent living (Asystent osobisty osoby z niepełnosprawnością, 2017, p. 5). The obligation to provide personal assistant services stems directly from the Convention ratified by Poland in 2012. Personal assistance has not yet been introduced into the Polish system of support for people with disabilities, but various legal acts provide for some forms of support similar to personal assistance, although they are not always called as such (ibidem. 6).

In Poland, assistance services at universities (defined as educational, research and transport services) are intended to ensure the independence of persons with disabilities in the process of studying and are carried out under their supervision and should be in accordance with their needs. They are similar in concept to personal assistance services but limited to the educational process, although in practice, they often extend beyond these areas. One reason for this is the lack of access to personal assistance services outside the university. Such services are sporadically available through project activities of local governments or NGOs. On the other hand, the local network of care services (social workers) is relatively well developed in terms of the number of social welfare centers and the variety of services offered. Also, very often family members assist persons with disabilities. The prevalence and strong rooting of care (assistance) services in Poland have their consequences in language used. The use of assistance services is still sometimes defined as care, help or asking for help, rather than a right that a person with a disability has. Despite the observed increase in awareness of rights among students, descriptive language sometimes remains in the area of help and care, which is evident in the interviews cited.

Previous research results concerning the use of personal assistants' services at Polish universities

The presence of assistants for people with disabilities at universities is one of the instruments supporting the process of education of people with disabilities. Their role is to support people with disabilities by enabling them to fully participate in social life: in fulfilling social roles and developing according to their potential. The presence of assistants at universities is varied. At some universities, the service is unknown, and personal assistants are absent. Sometimes, students with disabilities do not want to disclose their disabled status or are unaware of such an accommodation as personal assistants. There are several to several dozen assistants at other universities (Chrząszcz, 2018, p. 175).[1] As in Stodden and Conway (2003). US study support and programs for students with disabilities are fragmented, ineffective and varied across the country. The model of educational assistantships at universities fulfills many important functions for the aforementioned group of people in the university environment, enabling them to participate more fully in the educational process.

> He/she performs both supporting and compensating functions. Satisfactory completion of assistant's tasks, permit one to study, follow the program of the studies, develop one's own interests, obtain material and financial support, taking advantage of various forms of student activities, establishing social contacts and participation in student social life.
>
> *(Chrząszcz, 2018, p. 172)*

Based on the literature and research findings, a variety of functions of an assistant of a student with disability have been identified: communicative, supportive, integrative, inclusive, didactic, mobility, administrative and basic needs assistance (ibidem: 173–174).

Research among students with disabilities at Polish universities, conducted in the 2015–2016 academic year, showed that young people expect their assistants to both "prosthetise" them in terms of their own fitness limitations (e.g. help in taking notes, help in moving around, pushing a wheelchair, translating didactic materials for students with sensory disabilities, helping organise work or translating into sign language), as well as accompanying them in social situations (e.g. when establishing contacts with a peer group or support in conflict situations) (Chrząszcz, 2016). This means that students need personal and sometimes supportive assistance in social relationships. Hence, the question arises whether the presence of an assistant with a large range of supportive assistance components does not create a barrier to the development and maintenance of students' own resourcefulness.

The idea of support at the level of higher education gives rise to ethical problems related to the "phenomenon of assistance" and its institutionalisation, which results in many negative phenomena, such as loss of contact with those in need, disproportionate or unjust distribution of support combined with growth of controversy around forms of assistance, suspected lack of competence, waste and dishonesty (Filek, 2015). Student support activities, due to their complexity, are exposed to possible ineffectiveness and many other negative consequences. Difficulties and risks that might appear in the context of assistance, for example, include reverse discrimination, violation of the dignity of a person with a disability, limitation of their developmental opportunities and the risk of assistance turning into violence (ibidem).

The purpose of the present study and methodology

The aim of this chapter is a critical analysis of the functioning of assistantship services at Polish universities, based on empirical material: that is, qualitative interviews with students using such services. We want to find out to what extent the functioning system of assistance increases students' independence in the process of studying, whether it is flexible and adapted to diverse individual needs or whether it creates new inequalities and social hierarchies.

When describing the hierarchies and inequalities related to personal assistance services at universities, due to the word limit of the chapter, we had to select the material. In the analyses, we want to focus on institutional rules (law on personal assistance services), organisational practices (universities) and behaviours of individual actors (persons with disabilities and assistants). We are interested in the relationships produced in the process of studying in relation to the use of personal assistance services present in the narratives of students with disabilities.

The perspective of people with disabilities and consumers of services and their depiction of institutional rules, organisational practices and behaviours of individual actors will provide us with an indicator of the process of respecting human rights in relation to disability. We will consider whether the implemented system of assistant services at universities is known to people with disabilities, whether it meets their needs and the consequences of its implementation. The concluding remarks will concern the dilemmas related to the dissemination of personal assistance services in the field of education and professional work as well as the actual possibilities of implementing the postulates of independent living.

The empirical material used in the article consists of 25 qualitative interviews. Interviews were conducted with learners at all three levels of academic education (bachelor's, master's and doctoral studies), from all modes of education (full-time, evening and extramural studies) at various universities in Poland (including University of Warsaw, University of Białystok, UMCS in Lublin, SWPS in Gdynia, University of Rzeszów, University of Gdansk, the Pontifical University of John Paul II in Krakow, Jagiellonian University in Krakow, Music Academy in Gdansk and Medical University of Lodz). Participants with various types and degrees of disability, including movement, sensory (hearing, vision) and neurological disabilities, were recruited for the interviews.

The interviews were conducted by five trained interviewers recruited from among young researchers from various university centers in Poland. Due to the pandemic, the interviews were carried out remotely or by phone. In two cases, due to the type of disability, the interviews were asynchronous (in one case, a respondent with a hearing impairment answered the questions in writing; in another, for technical reasons, only a telephone conversation was conducted). The selection of respondents for the research was carried out using the snowball method, through the Support Offices for People with Disabilities at universities, the section of the Sociology of Disability of the Polish Sociological Society and contacts with academics and doctoral students dealing with the phenomenon of disability. We interviewed 19 women and 6 men, of whom 14 were undergraduate or graduate students and 11 were doctoral students.

The scenario of the interview included about 25 questions focused on the following issues: the experience of using personal assistance services during studies; perceptions and opinions about the functioning of the system of personal assistance services at universities and in the future workplace; the role of personal assistance in the realisation of the demands of independent living, especially in the areas of education and professional work; the impact of the COVID-19 pandemic on the possibility of using personal assistance services; quality of life; and course of studies.

Interviews were recorded and transcribed. All respondents gave their signed consent to the interview and to share the results of the analyses. The empirical material was analysed using the Nvivo-12 program.

Results

In reporting the results of the research, we will consider three levels of analysis. We will discuss the institutional rules for the operation of the personal assistance service system in universities (macro level). We will present organisational practices at universities (mezzo level). We will then focus on the individual experiences of students and their relationships with assistants (micro level). Referring to students' narratives, we will try to capture the factors of hierarchy and inequality associated with the use of personal assistant services. We assume that hierarchies and inequalities are produced at all three levels and that their co-occurrence may be cumulative. Imperfect solutions at the institutional level influence limitations in organisational practices and result in tensions in service provision and in the relationship between the person with disability and the assistant.

Macro level

In describing the functioning of personal assistance services at universities, students pointed to the general lack of systemic solutions in Poland concerning the availability and financing of such services outside the walls of the university. They emphasised that these college services were something "unique" and "temporary" and not a "systemic" solution, a "standard". The theme of transition from school to work was particularly strongly emphasised. Students highly valued the opportunity to study and the conditions that universities created for them: e.g. through access to assistance services. However, they were well aware that after graduation, they would have to rely only on themselves or their relatives for support. As one of our respondents put it, "End of studies, end of support" (W16). For those with communication issues, remote work or family transportation remained the only option.

> It would be good to have any kind of remote work, as I have no one to commute with. So it's also a bit like clipping our own wings. So what that the state finances our studies [and assistance services during studies] if later on, there are problems with employment, due to logistic and other kinds of exclusion, so assistants are needed here to compensate for that. *(W1)*

> In my place of residence this [assistance services] does not exist, because I live in a small village. . . . I am at the stage of looking for a job. . . . At the beginning my mother will help me, and then I will look around.
>
> *(W16)*

> Being disabled, we study in order to go to work after our studies, and since we can't move or leave home by ourselves, it [assistance] should be extended further; it is kind of logical. And, well, more and more cities, local governments, people perceive this problem. However, it is hardly functioning and also is being developed at a tortoise's pace.
>
> *(W1)*

Shortcomings at the level of macrostructure determined the behaviour of particular students who individually solved the problems resulting from them. A paradoxical result of the lack of personal assistance services beyond the period of education was the practice carried out by one of our respondents, which can be described as "abuse of the support system" – that is, the maintenance of the status of "eternal student".

> Currently, there is no adapted workplace for me in Poland because the employer would have to hire a personal assistant along with me. That is why I have been a student for so many years. I have impaired hands and speak inarticulately, so I need an assistant at the workplace.
>
> *(W21)*

> The solutions in place are well [off] the mark. On the one hand the state, through PFRON [State Fund for the Rehabilitation of the Disabled], through various measures, or even through education at universities, which is what we're talking about, provides us with such or other conditions for studying. On the other, hand after defending our thesis and receiving our diploma, we can hang it on the wall, and in 90% of cases, not much happens with this diploma, with this knowledge. No, we are not going any further, because we have no way, because in 90% of the cases these are not the choices of disabled people: that I'll get one degree, and I'll go on to another, and another.
>
> *(W1)*

Students' concerns about their ability to function in the labour market are not unfounded. Earlier, researchers in Poland identified a phenomenon called "unfinished emancipation" in relation to university graduates with disabilities (Giermanowska et al., 2015). It consists in "opening up" to them educational pathways at universities without institutional and cultural preparation of labour market actors. Society has made higher education institutions accessible but blocked access to work institutions, preventing independent living for young educated people with disabilities. Unlike in the USA (Stodden & Conway, 2003), university education in Poland did not significantly increase the probability of employment for students with disability.

Hierarchies and inequalities resulting from the lack of systemic solutions were perceived during the course of study and also applied to support outside the walls of the university. Personal assistance services were generally limited to activities related to the educational process, making it difficult or often virtually impossible for students to lead active, reasonably independent lives. Students with complex disabilities or those who required the presence of an assistant sought such services from non-governmental organizations (project-based or pilot programs) or relied on the assistance of relatives.

> From my experience of working with some students, I know that especially those with complex disabilities, mobility impairments, these students do not have the opportunity to benefit from a "care" assistant: that is, an assistant specifically related to everyday life. And here, unfortunately, a very large role often has to be played by their parents, siblings and loved ones.
>
> *(W20)*

> I rate the teaching assistants very well, while with respect to the personal assistants in Poland [outside the university], it looks pretty bad. I actually don't have funding for either a caregiver or an assistant, except for insufficient hours of community caregiver from community care center.
>
> *(W21)*

Meso level

Within the university, inequalities in the treatment of students with disabilities, especially in the early days of support services for persons with disabilities, resulted from a narrow understanding of assistance applied to all students, without taking into account the special needs of those with complex disabilities. As in the case of the USA (Bolt, 2004), disability services available at the university were insufficient to remove or radically decrease the barriers experienced by students with severe physical disability in the context of higher education. Applying the same rules to all students using assistants led to gross neglect of students' needs and even harassment and conflict. The assistance services offered at universities are mainly didactic assistance – help with taking notes, adapting materials: that is, tasks strictly related to the process of studying and logistical assistance related to moving to and within the university premises. However, students with profound motor disabilities also require assistance in so-called self-service matters.

> I don't recall such situations [conflicts], apart from defining what the assistant's duties are and what they're not, because, for example, in a private conversation, for example I asked for help with the toilet, someone simply said that for one reason or another they couldn't help me with that, and the subject was sort of dropped, but there were also people who were able to complain about it in the support office. And that it went the official way, so de facto, I, having an equal right to support and education but having such and such disability, had problems because of things independent of myself.
>
> *(W1)*

The purpose of Support Offices for Persons with Disabilities is to deal with narrowly understood educational needs of students with disabilities. This approach, given the lack of systemic solutions regarding personal assistance, leaves students with so-called severe disabilities in a difficult situation. Part of the educational experience of university is being a member of a student community, whether as part of formal study groups, set team projects, or informal arrangements. Students who cannot, without assistance, take care of their basic needs (toilet, eating etc.) or, in some cases, communicate are left stranded. Thus, we have two groups of students with disabilities: those for whom the existing provision is sufficient, and those for whom it is lacking.

At the university level, activities related to the operation of personal assistance services were handled by the Support Offices for Persons with Disabilities, which provided standardised information to newly admitted students.

> When I came to the university, I also immediately found out about the Office for Disability Issues, I found out that there was a possibility of such support there, so I immediately took advantage of it, and it turned out that it is actually helpful, and there are a lot of different reasons why you should take advantage of it.
>
> *(W5)*

Evaluation of service delivery at the universities was mixed. Positive feedback indicated that the service was accessible and procedures were understandable to students and met their expectations. Negative opinions focused on the insufficient number of hours in relation to the needs, lack of choice of assistant, frequent turnover of assistants and lack of information about the service at the university.

The experience of assistantship, as the respondents say, depended on the rules implemented at the university (specified in the adopted university regulations), the funds they had at their disposal, and the flexibility of employees of the Disabled Persons' Offices and their ability to individually respond to the reported needs of students. The main problem for most of the universities is the lack of a sufficient number of assistants in relation to the reported needs. As a result, the provision of the service was uncertain and carried out randomly, putting the person with disability in an awkward situation of having to ask for help:

> One assistant was sometimes assigned several people that he was supposed to assist, and it was also physically impossible for him. . . . Sometimes there were such discrepancies that in two rooms, the same assistant had to take two people to the lecture. And when this happened . . . then I said that I would manage, asking random people for help.
>
> *(W1)*

> During the day, when I had, for example, five hours of classes, the assistants changed every hour, they were often late, and this was usually not due to their bad will, but when helping another person with disability, they missed my classes. This was due to the distance between the places where the classes were held. Several times, the assistant simply did not turn up to the classes without informing me, and I was then left without help.
>
> *(W24)*

> I have fallen victim a few times to precisely this kind of underestimation of needs. For example, when classes were cut short, I could ask will you take me back to the dorm? Somebody said I'll take you, somebody said no, and I sat there for two hours waiting for the bus, and I didn't even call the driver because I knew I wasn't the only one who had to be driven, which meant that my assistant from municipality who came to help me get to bed, have supper etc. left after the curfew, at ten past ten, because I came back from university at half past ten, and we couldn't eat dinner, go to bed, and use the toilet within an hour. It was not possible to overcome the fact that simply for people who use an assistant and are physically dependent, even if the assistant is only part time, only for the person who uses him, she should not be the subject to penalties for the assistant going out after ten pm. Within a month, if there were ten such fines of 50 PLN each; it's easy to count.
>
> *(W1)*

Due to staff shortages, universities often recruited people who were unprepared to perform the functions of assistants, and the students with disabilities themselves initially did not have the appropriate competences to prepare work schedules for their assistants. This raised further problems related to the quality of assistant services.

> And first of all, strange things happened here regarding the scope of duties or the assistant's work, because the lady told the assistant to work out what I needed. And secondly, then there was a strange flow of

> information about salary. This person told me something different. . . . I mean. I felt I was treated very objectively.
>
> *(W4)*

> I had to learn how to organise my time. I also had to learn that I choose my own people because I don't have to agree to everything.
>
> *(W22)*

As in the case of the lack of systemic solutions, students perceived imperfect solutions at universities and the creation of hierarchies and inequalities among students using assistance services. It is also worth noting that during the period of their studies. they increased their awareness of their rights enshrined in the UN CRPD.

> I do not agree that, as a citizen of the Republic of Poland, I should worry about it from the grassroots level [access to personal assistance services], because from the top down, so to speak, the so-called systemic solutions should be implemented.
>
> *(W1)*

> I started my studies and I didn't know if I could manage on my own and I found out in the Support Office for Persons with Disabilities that there is such an option that you can use. And so I decided to take advantage of that sort of right.
>
> *(W3)*

Micro level

The next level of analysis concerns the experiences of individual, direct relationships of people with disabilities with their assistants. Here, we have obtained a wide spectrum of statements reflecting the emotional and individualised nature of these relationships, resulting from the provision of paid work in conjunction with the interdependence of the person with disability and their assistant and the formation of hybrid/cross-border, formal-informal, service-social ties. This was further complicated by the fact that, not infrequently, the assistants were recruited from among fellow students at the university, sometimes even from the same year and subject.

The experiences of students were varied: from friendly, cordial relations connected with the fulfillment of the necessary needs by the assistant to situations that gave rise to conflicts, a sense of being treated objectively or even rejection.

> The assistants, the girls who always did everything in such a way with me that I didn't feel that I couldn't do something, they just knew what

I couldn't handle and they just complemented me like that, so it was very pleasant for me.

(W10)

Well, yes, we talked to each other sometimes, but with the other women assistants – because they were usually ladies – *sensu stricto*, I didn't have any relationship beyond a business relationship.

(W3)

We had a quarrel, and it affected our relationship later on, somewhere in the group, and the student group is not large, so I just had to be the nicest person possible and patiently put up with the fact that she [the assistant] had no time for me.

(W13)

The situation became ambiguous when the relationship between the student with disability and their assistant went beyond supporting the education process. This concerned, for example, the situation of going to the cinema and other forms of spending free time, which were not included in the duties of an assistant. Some assistants wanted to treat this time as working time for which they receive remuneration while people with disabilities wanted to make friends. This situation is reflected in the account of one of our respondents:

We were even at the cinema together; well, she's [the assistant] going to write it in [the time sheet], so I said to her, "Do you take money for friendship?", and of course, she started laughing. And that's what I mean by separating the two – not everyone can do it; not everyone understands it.

(W9)

Conflict situations also arose when students and assistants had different opinions about what the assistant's duties were. This could be due to the occurrence of unusual situations, as well as the lack of prior arrangements regarding the scope of duties:

In these eight years, there's only been one conflict, and it was in the first year, and it concerned the fact that I needed help with something; my computer broke down, and I wanted to take it to the shop, and somewhere in there the rules didn't cover that, and I asked the assistant to do it. It's like, here's a little conflict, but it was – it's like this one only.

(W16)

This friend of mine was such a less independent person, and, for example, she wanted the assistant, I don't know, to put on her jacket, and she is

> not a person with a physical disability, but a visually impaired person. And it spoils their relationship a bit, right, because the requirements get a little bigger.
>
> *(W13)*

Or the assistance provided was of low quality:

> She did not really fulfil her obligations there. It looked like that these notes were not really full, and I had to ask others; I usually found out from others that something was missing when I was studying for the exams. And the assistant [who was also a student of the same year and subject] claimed that she didn't have more because she had as much as she had, so she also didn't keep track of the list, which had to be signed, carried, and delivered to the office every month. I usually did it myself, and it's not a problem because it's just a matter of agreeing, whether it's the assistant or the person you're helping, whether they're the one who fills in the list and the range of subjects where you help with the notes.
>
> *(W18)*

The experience of a conflict in the relationship with the assistant was not unequivocally negative. It allowed students with disabilities to learn to deal with this type of situation and assert their agency. They were supported in this process by the employees of the Offices for Persons with Disabilities.

> However, when I talked to Maria [at the office], she told me to tell her directly what I didn't like and to clarify some misunderstandings; it was the assistant who admitted directly that Maria had told her not to help me as much as she could and that she took her words to heart too much, and when we clarified this, later everything went smoothly between us.
>
> *(W10)*

> When I saw that she writes down the hours when she does not accompany me, when she is not there, even when I need it, when it is very slippery, she writes me in the morning that she overslept, or I saw that she calculates the number of hours to make the most of them, then I went with my colleagues, who also noticed this, to the team for students with disabilities. I told about the whole situation, and the ladies terminated her contract, and I got an assistant assigned by the team right away.
>
> *(W9)*

Students were divided in their views regarding who should have the right to a personal assistant from the university. Students believed that because there are finite resources, there should be a definite criteria for granting an assistant. Some argued that the service should be offered primarily to students who are certified disabled.

> Well, as far as accessibility is concerned, it is well known that a certificate is a kind of indicator because what defines us as disabled people? It is the certificate. So, imagine that everyone would have assistants; it would be twice as many people at the university! Somehow it's hard to imagine.
>
> *(W2)*

However, some argued that even in that case, it should be somehow verified if the student really needed an assistant. And, indeed, the need for assistance was the second criteria listed by some students as a key criterion for granting assistance.

> Not everyone with a disability certificate, exactly. It just depends on the disability, on the degree of disability, on the needs really.
>
> *(W18)*

> It is mainly those people who cannot cope. Who, for example, are in wheelchairs, well . . . who are dependent to some extent. In my opinion.
>
> *(W3)*

Those who argued for the importance of certification were not always sure about the status and needs of students who did not possess such certification but had a need. And whilst they granted that need should justify access to assistance, this lack of awareness about people who live with a disability but, for whatever reason, do not possess a certificate indicates yet another demarcation line among students with disability.

> I haven't thought so far that it could be somehow different than going with a certificate, so I don't know what other needs, for example, people who don't have a certificate could have, but if only there is a need that really makes this assistance necessary, and they justify it in a sensible way, well then OK, well, I won't – I can't – we can't deny this to anyone, and neither can we discriminate such cases, but if there is a need, well, then why not [grant assistance]?
>
> *(W13)*

In fact, according to one of our informants who, in addition to being a post-graduate student, was also employed at the Offices for Persons with Disabilities, universities are obliged to provide support regardless of certification:

> According to the law from the year two thousand and eighteen, we, as a bureau, are obliged to support people with disabilities and special needs regardless of whether they have a certificate or not. And therefore, it is not the certificate that determines whether a given person is entitled to this assistant, or whether we are obliged to provide him or her at this

> point, but, in fact, the individual situation, the health situation or the situation connected with a particular dysfunction of a particular person, of a particular individual.
>
> *(W20)*

This is an interesting theme, in which the standard perception of the system – exclusive organisations-inclusive beneficiaries/recipients – is reversed. In this case, the representative of the university unit points to the inclusive legal provisions and the openness to provide support by the office while the potential recipients of the service perceive the necessity to apply selection based on "hard" verification of the occurrence of a need. Access to a "rare good" such as an assistance service, in the social perception of young people, should be limited. This perception of young people with disabilities should not come as a surprise in a society in transition to a social model; however, to reiterate Ayesha Vernon (2008, p. 67), "It is not enough merely to acknowledge that, because inequality is rife in society at large, it is inevitable that disabled people will have absorbed these practices too. To do so is to condone and perpetuate all forms of inequality". It is therefore important to reflect on the origins and consequences of this type of thinking.

Discussion

For many young people acquiring education in Poland, the opening of universities to admit students with disabilities is already an obvious right connected with the implementation of the principle of equal opportunities. However, the implementation of the idea of independent living, whose indicators are relative control over the life course and free choice, is hindered by the need to submit to the rigours of bureaucratic provision and settlement of services for which students are unprepared. Although personal assistance services have taken firm root at Polish universities, the lack of systemic solutions makes this service imperfect, fragmentary, and not a comprehensive solution to the situation of many students, especially those with complex disabilities requiring support not only during the educational process but also in everyday life. Many shortcomings related to the functioning of the service result from the relatively short experience of the Support Offices for Persons with Disability, as well as insufficient knowledge and preparation of persons with disability and assistants themselves. As in Holloway's study (2001, p. 612), our study also indicates that "students experienced a model of provision that individualised disability and failed to recognise the social factors that determine the experience of disability."

One of the problems appears to be that the introduced solutions are not driven by the desire for a diverse student body but by the need to fill bureaucratic and legal obligations resulting from the ratification of the UN CRPD and elements of the Polish constitution. (See also Bolt, 2004.) Although efforts are made to introduce new elements driven by the idea of independent living that are behind much of the UN resolution, the approach to disability in Polish legislation is based on the medical understanding of disability. Consequently, this is the approach that dominates the implemented solutions. Disability is treated as a problem resulting from impairments of individuals that needs to be tackled by relevant accommodation and not as an opportunity to enrich the learning experience (Ainscow, 2007, p. 148). Note that accommodations for students with disabilities are administered through the Support Office for People with Disabilities, which somehow institutionally sets people with disabilities apart, rather than through, for example, the more inclusive Teaching and Learning Unit, as in some British universities.

Rigid procedures and time schedules to control work and expenses make the service easier to manage for the Support Offices for Persons with Disability, but it often become an obstacle to flexible adaptation of the service to student needs These structural conditions listed create hierarchies and inequalities among people disabilities. They divide the student community into those whose needs are fully or significantly met and those who are marginalised by the system and feel treated as objects or even rejected.

Although the service was meant to reduce inequalities between students and make higher education accessible for all, the way it operates, unintentionally, perpetuates and makes more visible existing hierarchies between students with disabilities.

Having a disability makes any other inequalities more acute. Studying is a privilege. In the case of students with disabilities, as is the case with able-bodied students, young people from rural areas and periphery, as well as people whose families are disadvantaged, are even less likely to enter higher education, especially in the more prestigious universities, as it requires a considerable effort and resources for a person with disability, especially a complex one, to complete middle education at the appropriate level. But it is the prestigious universities that have better developed support and assistance services for students with disabilities. So students with disabilities studying there are more likely to take fuller advantage of their studies and better develop their potential, which, despite the complaints students voice, increases their chances of employment in the future. Moreover, having to manage one's assistant (schedule, etc.) develops skills useful for pursuing independent living. The experience of the successful completion of studies also may give one a sense of achievement, self-confidence, and agency. Thus, it is known in the sociological literature as the Matthew effect (Merton, 1968), describing the tendency to accumulate once-gained advantages and to deepen once-suffered degradation or marginalisation as a result of the mechanism of "self-fulfilling prophecy". Students from better socio-demographic backgrounds may receive a better quality education and support services than their peers from backgrounds described as disadvantaged and/or with complex health conditions.

Still other divisions arise from the direct work exchange relationship between the person with a disability and his or her assistant. The ability to schedule the service, manage time, and plan expenses requires specific competencies that young people with disabilities often do not yet possess. The situation is also made more difficult by the proximity of the relationship between the PA and the person with disability, the co-existence of formal and informal contacts. The emotional nature of the relationship related to the performance of work by the assistant in situations of different expectations and perceptions of the person with disability and their assistant often cause misunderstandings and even conflicts. Being able to use the service and being prepared for it allow people with disabilities to avoid many disappointments, perpetuating their self-marginalization and sense of exclusion. The hierarchies created in the relationship between the assistant and the student with disability, related to the use of power, are not at all obvious. Sometimes the dominant party is a person with a disability, who exceeds the agreed scope of tasks in his/her demands, and sometimes the assistant subordinates the student with a disability to himself/herself and tries to take control over him/her. Hence, when the same (equal) procedures are applied, a difference arises due to the degree of preparedness of the service recipient to receive the service and the preparedness of the service provider to provide the service.

Conclusion

Independent life is not only a noble idea but also a set of social practices that should be put into practice. As a social practice, it can be understood as the implementation of the principle of social equality among people of diverse capabilities. Rulers tend to pursue equality as the ultimate goal because it is an important stake among the governed, with the caveat that equality as a goal can only be realised if inequality is used as an instrument (Kozłowski, 2016, p. 47). This inequality in instrumental terms is, for example, the establishment of services that, financed by public funds, are addressed to selected social categories. The point is that not every service, and not at every time, will turn instrumental inequality into equality, understood as the ultimate goal of action. In Poland, researchers analysing the relationship between disability and public policies addressed to people with disabilities point out that these policies stem from a medical model of understanding disability (which contradicts the provisions of the CRPD ratified by Poland) and can hardly be called "intelligent" (Gąciarz, 2014). The postulate of an intelligent social policy towards disability was introduced by the Polish sociologist Barbara Gąciarz (2014), who enumerated such features of the policy as optimal adjustment of instruments to diverse groups of recipients, flexible organisation of social services, and evaluation of policy effects from the point of view of their results for recipients of activities. Starting from this postulate, smart services should be tailored to the needs of the specific recipient, given to them in a timely manner, and complementary to each other (in order to gain synergies accumulated over time) in a way that respects their dignity. Their outcome and main measure in evaluation should be the improvement of well-being and prosperity of individuals in their social roles (cf. Racław, 2018, p. 69).

Analysing the empirical material gathered in our research, we see that assistance services have the potential to be described as "smart", but the way they are delivered needs improvement. The procedures used lead to further differentiation of students with disabilities. And here we come to the relationship of equality and difference, which forces the resolution of the so-called "dilemma of difference" (Minow, 1991). Martha Minow (1991) highlights the unreliability of focusing on difference itself, on a particular difference. She recommends considering first of all the relations in which it is perceived or described. Contextualising difference means that laws working towards equality will either highlight or ignore it, whereby – as critical sociologists in turn note (cf. Sztobryn-Giercuszkiewicz, 2017, p. 30) – the rejection of difference can lead to the marginalisation of people with special needs. According to them, the solution is to introduce the principle of diversity. In other words, equality as an ultimate goal, using inequality instrumentally, should see diversity, because a solution (e.g. assistance) introduced as a mechanism for establishing equality will not work if procedures limit its flexible adaptation to the different functioning of people belonging to one group of addressees of specific inclusive measures.

The principle of equality is difficult to apply. It is also difficult to gain consensual support for it. For it is beneficial to those who are inferior/subordinate; for the superior/subordinate it is not beneficial or at any rate they do not see it as beneficial: " in this context <in the last instance>, the fate of equality depends on efforts and favourable circumstances on the part of those who are disadvantaged in the distribution of social resources" (Kozłowski, 2016, p. 224).[2]

This gives hope that young people with disabilities, by gaining knowledge of their rights as university students and acquiring their first experiences and skills in managing themselves and the services to which they are entitled, will become agents of change. The empowerment of the dominated may eventually lead to the completion of the process of emancipation of people with disabilities in Poland. As noted by Oliver and Barnes (2010), there is a positive link between people with disabilities in academic settings and activism leading to change, but what is evident from this chapter, and in agreement with Oliver and Barnes (2010), large-scale systemic changes are required for the emancipation and equality of and among people with disabilities.

Notes

1 Translated from Polish by D. Szawarska for the purpose of this publication.
2 Ibid.

References

Ainscow, M. (2007). From special education to effective education for all: a review of progress so far. In L. Florian (Ed.), *The Sage handbook of special education* (pp. 146–159). Sage Publications.

Asystent osobisty osoby z niepełnosprawnością – zapotrzebowanie na miarę Konwencji o prawach osób z niepełnosprawnościami (2017). [A personal assistant for a person with disabilities - a demand that meets the needs of the Convention on the Rights of Persons with Disabilities.]: Biuletyn Rzecznika Praw Obywatelskich, nr 5.

Białecki, I. (1998). Merytokracja i równość szans. In I. Białecki & J. Sikorska (Eds.), *Wykształcenie i rynek* (pp. 107–127). Wydawnictwo Tepis.

Bolt, D. (2004). Disability and the rhetoric of inclusive higher education. *Journal of Further and Higher Education*, *28*(4), 353–358.

Chrząszcz, K. (2016). Asystent edukacyjny – pomoc czy droga w kierunku bezradności studentów z niepełnosprawnością?, *Niepełnosprawność – zagadnienia, problemy, rozwiązania, Nr III*(20), 23–35.

Chrząszcz, K. (2018). *Funkcje asystenta studenta niepełnosprawnego w polskich uniwersytetach*. Rozprawa doktorska napisana pod kierunkiem naukowym prof. dra hab. Zenona Gajdzicy oraz promotora pomocniczego dr Doroty Prysak, Uniwersytet Śląski w Katowicach Wydział Etnologii i Nauk o Edukacji.

Convention on the Rights of Persons with Disabilities, adopted in New York on 13 December 2006. (Journal of Laws of the Republic of Poland Warsaw, 25 October 2012 Item 1169).

Dziennik Ustaw Rzeczpospolitej Polski, dnia 25 października 2012 r. Poz. 1169

Filek, J. (2015). Rozważania wokół form wsparcia studentów niepełnosprawnych. In W. Bernadeta Szczupał & K. Kutek-Sładek (red.), *Wielowymiarowość integracji społeczno-zawodowej studentów z niepełnosprawnością* (pp. 15–31). Uniwersytet Papieski Jana Pawła II w Krakowie, Kraków.

Gąciarz, B. (2014). W kierunku nowego modelu polityki społecznej. *Polscy NiePełnosPrawni*, 377–392.

Giermanowska, E., Kumaniecka-Wiśniewska, A., Racław, M., & Zakrzewska-Manterys, E. (2015). *Niedokończona emancypacja. Wejście niepełnosprawnych studentów szkół wyższych na rynek pracy*. WUW.

GUS (2012). Narodowy Spis Powszechny Ludności i Mieszkań 2011. *Raport z wyników. Warszawa: Zakład Wydawnictw Statystycznych.*

GUS (2018). Szkoły wyższe i ich finanse w 2017 r., Warszawa 2018, https/stat.gov.pl/obszary-tematyczne/edukacja/edukacja/szkoly-wyzsze-i-ich-finanse-w-2017-roku,2,14.html

Holloway, S. (2001). The experience of higher education from the perspective of disabled students. *Disability & Society*, *16*(4), 597–615.

Kinowska-Mazaraki, Z. (2021). The Polish paradox: from a fight for democracy to the political radicalization and social exclusion. *Social Sciences*, *10*(3), 112.

Kozłowski Michał. (2016). Znaki równości. O społecznym konstruowaniu stosunków egalitarnych, Scholar, Warszawa.

Merton, R. K. (1968). The Matthew effect in science the reward and communication systems of science are considered. *Since*, *159*(3810), 56–63.

Minow, M. (1991). *Making all the difference: inclusion, exclusion and American law*. Cornell University Press.

Oliver, M., & Barnes, C. (2010). Disability studies, disabled people and the struggle for inclusion. *British Journal of Sociology of Education*, *31*(5), 547–560.

Osoby niepełnosprawne w 2019 r. Informacje sygnalne (2020). GUS.

Racław, M. (2018). Rodzice, instytucje, organizacje: czy potrzeby jednostek wytworzą inteligentne usługi społeczne? In D. Wiszejko-Wierzbicka, M. Racław, A. Wołowicz-Ruszkowska Byliśmy jak z kosmosu (EDS.), *Między (nie)wydolnością środowiska a potrzebami rodziców z niepełnosprawnościami* (pp. 69–94). Instytut Spraw Publicznych.

Stodden, R. A., & Conway, M. A. (2003). Supporting individuals with disabilities in postsecondary education. *American Rehabilitation*, *27*(1), 24–33.

Strategia na rzecz Osób z Niepełnosprawnościami 2021–2030, uchwała NR 27 Rady Ministrów z dnia 16 lutego 2021 r.[Strategy for Persons with Disabilities 2021–2030, Resolution NR 27 of the Council of Ministers of 16 February 2021.]

Stumbo, N. J., Hedrick, B. N., Weisman, C., & Martin, J. K. (2011). An exploration into the barriers and facilitators experienced by university graduates with disabilities requiring personal assistance services. *Journal of Science Education for Students with Disabilities*, *14*(1), 1–24.

Sztobryn-Giercuszkiewicz, J. (2017). Krytyczna teoria niepełnosprawności jako rama teoretyczna w badaniach nad niepełnosprawnością [in:] Jakub Niedbalski, Mariola Racław, Dorota Żuchowska-Skiba, red., Oblicza niepełnosprawności w teorii i praktyce. Łódź: Wydawnictwo Uniwersytetu Łódzkiego, s. 23–39.

United Nations Convention on the Rights of Persons with Disabilities. (2006). *Signed in New York*, December 13. https://www.ohchr.org/en/hrbodies/crpd/pages/conventionrightspersonswithdisabilities.aspx

Vernon, A. (2008). Multiple opression and the disabled people's movement. In B. Bytheway, V. Bacigalupo, J. Bornat, J. Johnson, S. Spurr (Eds.), *Understanding care, welfare and community. A reader* (pp. 64–68). Routledge – The Open University.

13

THEORIES OF SOCIAL DOMINANCE IN GROUP-BASED HIERARCHIES

Reflections from the United Nations Partnership on the Rights of Persons with Disabilities (UNPRPD) project in Uruguay

Holly Wescott

This chapter brings together three related frames to contextualise the process of change within a project which aimed to promote the rights of people with disability. First, we briefly consider theoretical frames of social dominance and group-based hierarchies. Then census data from the country on which we focus – Uruguay – is presented to understand disability and demographics at the national level; to inform the 'field' targeted for change. We then describe the change project, which was a component of the larger United Nations Partnership on the Rights of Persons with Disabilities (UNPRPD). We explore the structural dynamics and changes that have taken place through the application of the UNPRPD in Uruguay. Finally, we review how our frames contribute to our understanding of the implementation of the UNPRPD in Uruguay.

The UNPRPD was established to create the sort of structural changes – that is, changes in social institutions – required to make realisation of the Convention (United Nations Convention on the Rights of Persons with Disability) (UNCRPD) possible. The UNPRPD works through a tripartite relationship between a number of collaborating United Nations agencies (minimum three), a government department or departments, and one or more civil society organisations (UNDP, 2016). Clarke (2016) notes, for implementation of a new law or regulation or, in this case, a Convention, "historical behaviours are required to change in line with the expectations underlying the regulation. . . . [O]ften, behaviours of more than one group need to change" (p. 32).

 DOI: 10.4324/9781003410089-16

Theoretical frames

Social dominance theory (SDT) (Sidanius et al., 1994) has gained much empirical support in the last two decades. It argues that there is an evolved human tendency to form and maintain group-based social hierarchies. These hierarchies may reflect any social designation, such as ethnicity, caste, class, or disability; where dominant social groups (e.g. those without disability) have disproportionate social advantages (e.g. high status or political power), and subordinate groups (e.g. those with a disability) experience disproportionate social disadvantages (e.g. poorer access to education, justice, or healthcare), even if their objective needs may be greater. SDT sees such social hierarchies as often "in large part created, preserved, and recreated by social institutions, or organizations" (Haley & Sidanius, 2005). Such social institutions "can powerfully promote or suppress existing social hierarchies based on how they allocate positive resources (e.g., prestige, wealth, healthcare) and/or negative resources (e.g., disdain, poverty, endangerment)" (p. 189).

Kurt Lewin (1890–1947) pioneered work relating to social change, including the concept of planned change, and provides an extensive range of valuable tools to understand and initiate change (Swanson & Creed, 2014). His basic theory of change posits a three-stage process: "unfreezing" of the current situation; "moving", when the change actually takes place; and "refreezing", when the new habit or norm is espoused or institutionalised (Bargal, 2014).

Lewin did not consider the importance of power relations, symbolism, different forms of capital, or the general idea that the privileged often prefer to maintain things as they "naturally" are (Lewin, 1939, 2013; MacLachlan et al., 2019). The work of Pierre Bourdieu does, however, address these issues. While his sociological scholarship was largely focused on social class, it has also been applied to the area of disability (Byrne, 2018; Wescott et al., 2021). This perspective is represented by Pret and Carter (2017) (Figure 13.1), which illustrates how the "field" is dominated by different forms of capital.

Extending Marx's ideas of the importance of economic capital in shaping one's position and opportunities, Bourdieu (1986) considered other types of capital too. For instance, cultural capital can be embodied (one's accent), objectified (the type of car you have), or institutionalised (having a degree or title), all symbolising competence, authority, or status, allowing us to identify "people like us". Bourdieu's concept of habitus refers to individuals learning how to "play the game" that forms the repetitive behaviours of their social niche (Bourdieu, 1984), often seeing such a position as part of a "natural order". For Bourdieu "the field" was where habitus was practiced and capital expended, with different rules applying in different fields: people with disabilities might have improved access to transport but not political office, for instance (Bourdieu, 1986; Bourdieu, 1990).

Sidanius and colleagues have demonstrated a range of ways and contexts in which people have a psychological propensity – they argue an evolutionary drive – to form group-based hierarchies, which imbue prejudicial attitudes.

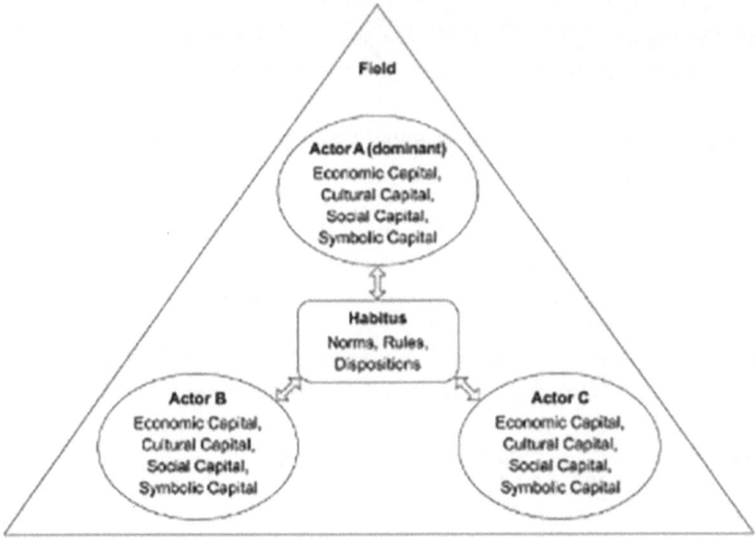

Figure 13.1 Illustration of capital forces in a field
Source: Adapted from Pret and Carter (2017)

Bourdieu recognises the social power dynamics of privilege and position, which groups often wish to protect: implicitly, if not always explicitly. Lewin's field theory has spawned the Theory of Change (ToC) movement, in which participatory methods are seen as central to being the change. This chapter therefore seeks to bring together theorising related to individual and institutional experiences of change (Breuer et al., 2016; MacLachlan & McVeight, 2021) through analysis of the implementation of the UNPRPD programme in Uruguay. Uruguay was a particularly compelling country to focus on because it is geographically interesting as a small South American country nested between much larger countries, was recently reclassified as a high-income country (The World Bank, 2019), is known for a progressive government, and is high on the development index (The World Bank, 2019). These conditions can serve as an interesting case study for a global programme designed to adapt to diverse development contexts, particularly as disability exclusion is not limited to countries traditionally found in development projects.

UNPRPD country project in Uruguay

Background

The United Nations is an intergovernmental organisation containing dedicated thematic agencies such as UNICEF focusing on children, WHO for health, and

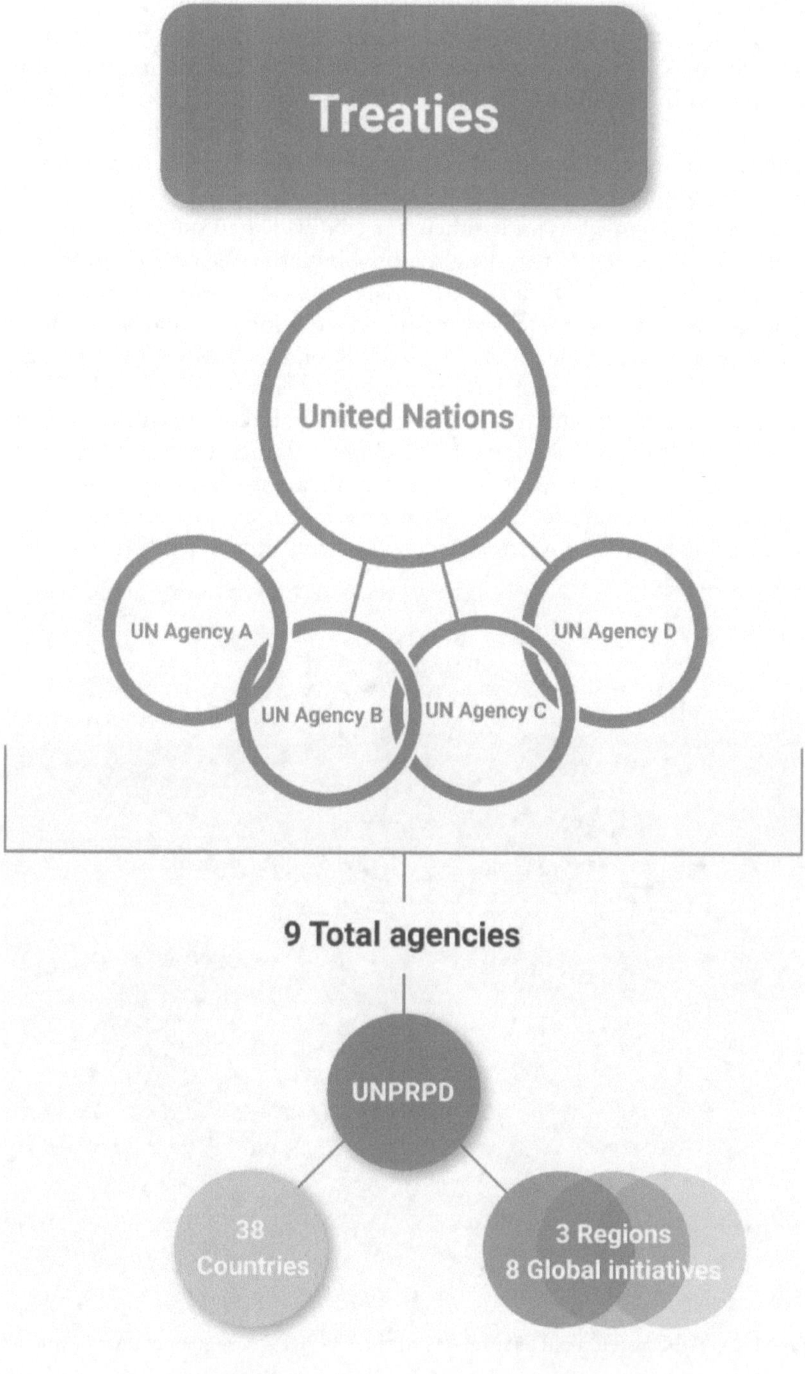

Figure 13.2 Conceptual diagram of the UNPRPD within the UN system

UN Women for gender equality within the larger UN system (United Nations, n.d.). Of the agencies and programmes within the UN system, nine participate in the interagency initiative called the United Nations Partnership on the Rights of Persons with Disabilities (UNPRPD). While there is no UN agency that focuses solely on disability inclusion, the UNPRPD promotes intersectoral participation from various sectors to mainstream disability rights as a component of directives within the existing bodies (United Nations, n.d.; UNDP, 2016). By 2019, when this work was undertaken, the UNPRPD had supported projects in 38 countries, three regions, and eight global initiatives around the world since its inception in 2011 (UNPRPD, 2019). One of these countries was Uruguay.

The United Nations system also supports the implementation of international treaties enacted for a range of populations such as Convention on the Elimination of All Forms of Discrimination against Women (CEDAW), the Convention on the Rights of Persons with Disabilities (CRPD), and more generally, the Universal Declaration of Human Rights. Each of these treaties outlines specific rights afforded to the individuals it serves to protect and is governed by UN committees to oversee government compliance through periodic reporting between governments, civil society, and United Nations country teams (UNCTs).

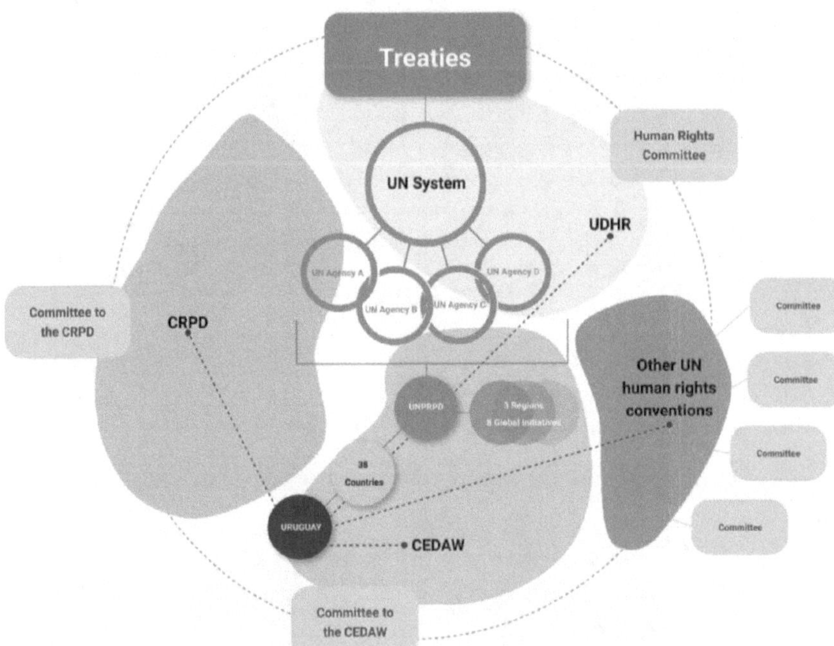

Figure 13.3 UN system field as it relates to the UNPRPD Uruguay country project

Table 13.1 Legend of acronyms

Diagram term	*Description*
CRPD	Convention on the Rights of Persons with Disabilities
CEDAW	Convention on the Elimination of All Forms of Discrimination against Women
UDHR	Universal Declaration of Human Rights

Uruguay adopted the CRPD on 3 April 2007, eventually ratifying it on 11 February 2009 (OHCHR, 2014). Uruguay, which is surrounded by upper-middle-income countries, has enjoyed sustained economic growth since 2003 (The World Bank, 2019) and a progressive government for 15 years, before the 2019 election (The Economist, 2019). In 2013, the World Bank reclassified Uruguay as a high-income country (2019). National poverty, extreme poverty, and inequality have remained low according to various measures (e.g. human development index, human opportunity index, economic freedom index) (The World Bank, 2019). Although political and economic stability have improved the living conditions of Uruguayans, and the CRPD was formally adopted, disability exclusion persists in the country as evidenced in the concluding observation reports from the Committee on the Rights of Persons with Disabilities (UNCRPD, 2016) and the Committee on the Elimination of Discrimination against Women (CEDAW) (UNCEDAW, 2016). The Uruguayan UNPRPD project sought to address this disparity by aligning the national frameworks previously enacted and the United Nations Conventions Committee recommendations.

In response to the committee recommendations, the United Nations Office of the Resident Coordinator applied for project funding to the UNPRPD programme to initiate a multi-partner project. The proposal was accepted in 2018 for a one-time project cycle of 24 months, concluding March 2020.

The UNPRPD project comprised three pillars of work: 1) to advance universal access to health through sexual and reproductive health rights of young persons with disability, 2) the prevention and response to gender-based violence (GBV) among persons with disability, and 3) improving the systematised collection and use of disability data. Each of these pillars held working group meetings with representatives of each stakeholder group, followed by a monthly plenary session with all key actors for ongoing project discussions. Some actors who were involved in multiple pillars attended more than one thematic meeting. For example, the Ministry of Public Health assigned one representative as liaison to the UNPRPD on behalf of the institution, who engaged with all three pillars for the project duration.

Methods

This study initially followed a traditional qualitative case study approach with 22 semi-structured interviews among United Nations, government, civil society, and consultancy representatives of the UNPRPD project in Uruguay in 2019. Data was collected using the most significant change technique (MSCT) (Davies & Dart, 2005; Quilliam & Wilson, 2011), a semi-structured appreciative enquiry method. Open-ended questions were designed to prompt reflection while maintaining the scope of distinct responses within the UNPRPD project. Following the data collection, interviews were analysed using interpretive phenomenological analysis (IPA) to better understand how the key UNPRPD focal points make sense of the project goals and implementation process (Smith et al., 2009).

During the site visit during which interviews were conducted, several participants wondered out loud, 'We know disabled people are excluded, but to *where*? *Where* are they?' This question lingered as the project sought the participation of persons with disabilities, aiming to amplify those voices above all else. Engagement was challenging for many reasons discussed in depth later in the chapter; however, it led the researchers on a quest to better understand the tension of local disability exclusion and efforts to increase participation.

The UNPRPD project proposal noted the 2011 census results citing that 16% of Uruguayans have some form of disability (Ines Núñez, 2014), providing a quantitative data set to explore the concerns expressed by project participants. GIS software and statistical analysis revealed noteworthy demographic distributions that bring light to the question project participants continued to ask themselves in search of persons with disabilities: '*Where* are they?'

Demographics were only part of the story. While the UNPRPD global programme provides guidance for project development, there are contextual forces unique to each country that are difficult to anticipate in full before decisions have to be made. Activities must be determined and partnerships engaged very early on when implementing a two-year fixed timeline, revealing many key insights only later upon reflection.

The MSCT questions are designed to engage participants in reflection on their experience and connect the events of a story with the *how* and *why* it illustrates something significant. The questionnaire is designed as an appreciative inquiry, engaging key focal points in exploring the positive events generated by their work to better understand what promotes successful implementation of disability rights in structural development. Responses were unexpected as participants were not able or willing to provide a story illustrating the 'most significant change' since the project began and instead shared concerns. The MSCT still provided tools to reflect on their concerns. For example, the following questions ask the participant to think about how that concern came to happen. In other words, the questions prompted a retrospective field analysis of processes in specific terms (e.g. contextual factors, power differences). These responses provided the data to code inductively as the results were unexpected and fit no predetermined framework.

A case study is used to understand different perspectives of a shared phenomenon and removes the guise of a neutral researcher. Measures are taken to reduce bias and overinterpretation through systematic data handling. IPA looks at the full scope of a phenomenon by incorporating the diverse participant perspectives of a shared experience first by reading all transcripts in full for clear understanding, then coding interviews for themes, connecting the themes as they relate to each other, and repeating the same protocol with all interview transcripts in the same fashion before proceeding with the analysis (Smith et al., 2009). Interpretation of participant responses takes place at only two points in the data-handling process: identifying themes and conducting the written analysis. The emergent themes often use the terms given by participants as seen in the illustrative quotations; however, the interpretive synthesis of the collective responses provides the meaning derived from the study. IPA identified the following themes; these will be discussed in turn.

Participants

Each UNPRPD project partners with UN agencies, government ministries, and civil society organisations relevant to the priorities set for implementation. Some projects have several ministries involved and one national disability organisation (or vice versa), varying the distribution of partners in each stakeholder group. For the purposes of this case study, gathering interview data from each of the three main stakeholder groups was essential to capture data

Table 13.2 IPA superordinate and subordinate themes

Superordinate themes	*Subordinate themes*
Programmatic barriers	Managing participation
	• Project coordinator
	• Civil society engagement
	• Representation
	Hierarchical positionality
	Project priorities
	• Theory over action
	• Determining capacity
	• Individual representation
	Capital capacity
External forces	Field changes
	• Status implications
	Theories of change
Internal forces	Awareness
	• Paradigm shift
	Increasing structural stability
	• Building partnerships

across hierarchies that interact in multiparter projects. The distribution of focal points per stakeholder group varied in each country; thus, some groups offered fewer individuals to select from for interviewing. Despite the variation in focal points per stakeholder group, all three institutions (UN, government, and civil society) were represented in the interview data for this study. Representatives from 12 major institutions participated. The National Institute for Women in the Ministry of Social Development (Inmujeres) was the only major institution involved in the project from which the researcher (HW) was unable to secure an interview; nonetheless, coverage of all other partners provided broad perspectives surrounding the UNPRPD Uruguay project.

The United Nations

Six representatives from UNFPA, UN Women, WHO, the Office of the Resident Coordinator, and the UNPRPD project coordinator participated in interviews for this study. These representatives take part in several United Nations projects in addition to the UNPRPD (with the exception of the UNPRPD project coordinator) and act as focal points for the UNPRPD with their respective agencies.

Civil society

Member states and UNPRPD projects commit to the CRPD in pursuit of realising the rights outlined across all 50 Convention articles. One key piece of the Convention (United Nations, 2006) is Article 4.3, stating

> In the development and implementation of legislation and policies to implement the present Convention, and in other decision-making processes concerning issues relating to persons with disabilities, States Parties shall closely consult with and actively involve persons with disabilities, including children with disabilities, through their representative organizations.

In practice, Article 4 mandates direct participation with populations of persons with disabilities, either individuals or their representative organisations, in disability development efforts.

The primary partnership for civil society representation is the Uruguayan Alliance of the Organization for the Rights of Persons with Disability (also referred to as Alianza, or the Alliance). Established in 2016 to produce a shadow report to the Committee on the Rights of Persons with Disabilities, the Alliance is an umbrella organisation of various disability and service-specific civil society groups. Initially, the Alianza comprised 6 member organisations located in the capital, Montevideo, but it has grown to roughly 27 organisations with recent expansion to the interior of the country. The umbrella group's membership varies as organisations enter and exit the Alliance. As of July 2019, the Alianza was a civil society umbrella organisation with no OPD membership.

The Alianza was asked to join the project during the initial planning and recruitment phase based on their participation in the Convention reporting system and UNPRPD programmatic criteria for representing a broad range of disabilities. According to participant reports, other well-established OPDs or disability organisations align with the longstanding medical model of disability, making the Alliance a natural fit for the UNPRPD's rights-based programme.

Participation in the Alliance is on a volunteer basis, with the exception of grants and hired consultancy. The organisation has no funding stream or central body for coordination. Service providers or parents of persons with disabilities head the various member organisations, conducting most of the Alliance's work outside business hours without compensation. The project hired a consultant to support participation from the Alianza, attend meetings on their behalf, assist in coordinating the variety of organisations, and help develop an operational structure that would grow and continue beyond the scope of the project.

Government

Several government institutions were invited to participate in the project, including the Administration of Health Public Services (ASSE), Uruguayan Agency for International Cooperation (AUCI), Social Provision Service (BPS), Ministry of Social Development (including the national disability program PRONADIS and National Institute for Women, Inmujeres – MIDAS), the National Statistical Institute (INE), and the Ministry of Public Health (MSP). A focal point from each institution was selected to represent their department within the UNPRPD project and channel expertise to and from the project.

Results

Census data

> The metaphor of fractal geography suggests that wherever, in whatever space you look for disabled people, study us as a social group, as a community, you should cast your eye on the outer fringes, regardless whether that space of inquiry is Manhattan, rural Japan, the industrial zones of Sao Paolo, or the shanty-towns of Lagos. I am not saying that all peripheral space is the same.... What I am suggesting is that wherever we [disabled people] are located, we are on the outside looking in.
>
> *(Charlton, 2010, p. 197)*

Located in South America between Brazil and Argentina, Uruguay declared its independence in 1825. The total population of Uruguay is 3.449 million (The World Bank, 2019). Of these, roughly 1.3 million residents live in the capital, Montevideo (Ines Núñez, 2014). While the capital is a small region of the country, it is a highly populated urban area based on the 2011 census.

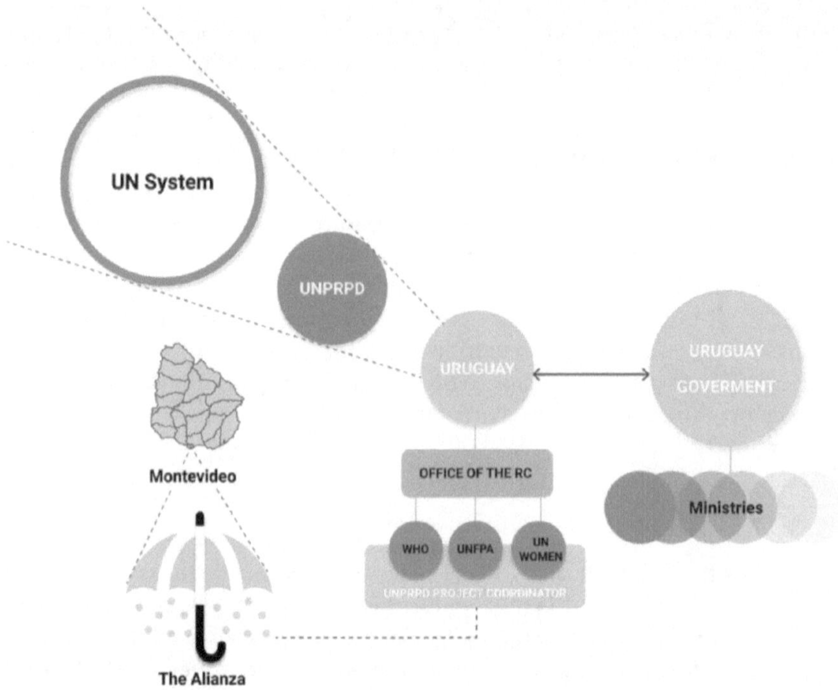

Figure 13.4 UNPRPD Uruguay country project-partnering entities

Table 13.3 Legend of acronyms

Diagram term	*Description*
UNPRPD	United Nations Partnership on the Rights of Persons with Disabilities
Office of the RC	Office of the Resident Coordinator
WHO	World Health Organisation
UNFPA	United Nations Population Fund
Ministries	Represents seven participating Uruguayan government ministries
The Alianza	Participating civil society organisation

Disability data was also collected in the census of 2011. A survey called the Washington Group Questions were developed as a set of general disability measures to standardise and compare disability data internationally (Madans et al., 2004). Since implementing the use of the Washington Group Questions on the 2011 national census, 16% of Uruguayans have reported having a disability (Ines Núñez, 2014). Of this 16%, 60% were women, reporting higher absolute percentages across all categories of mild, moderate, and severe disability (Ines Núñez, 2014). Although the interior of the country is much less densely populated than the urban areas, the 2011 Uruguayan census reports a disproportionate amount of disability in rural municipalities. While the raw number of Uruguayan persons with disabilities residing in the country's urban areas is high, the proportion of disability is significantly lower in the cities and significantly higher in some of the most rural regions of the country. The three municipalities with the highest ratio of disability to population are clustered on the east side of the area that borders Brazil and have relatively low populations (Ines Núñez, 2014), as shown by the "hotspot" analysis (Anselin, 1995) in Figure 13.5. Many disability-related resources and services are centred in the capital, Montevideo, where proportionality few persons with disabilities reside, including the engagement for the UNPRPD project. In contrast, the municipalities with the highest proportion of persons with disabilities are, as Charlton describes, on the periphery.

Interview data

The Uruguayan case study affirms the abstract and lived implications of the group stratification he described. The census data in 2011 uncovered disability 'hotspots' and 'cold spots' whereby persons with disabilities live on the fringes

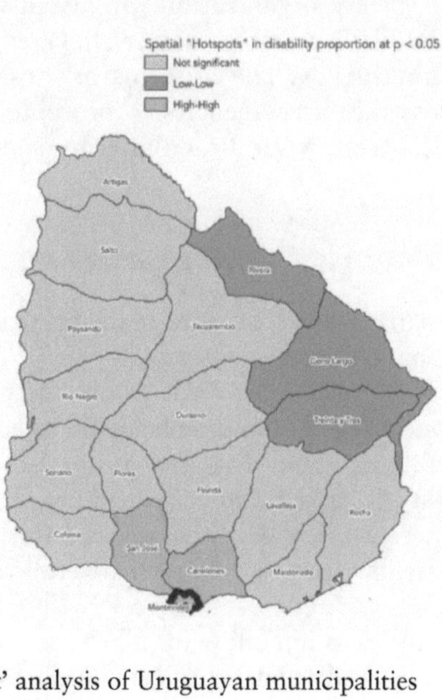

Figure 13.5 'Hotspot' analysis of Uruguayan municipalities

of social action far outside the capital, Montevideo. The literal manifestation of persons with disability on the periphery was mirrored by the lack of meaningful participation reported by the interview participants in the UNPRPD project. The challenge for initiatives such as the UNPRPD is not how to recognise differentials in power, position, and privilege, which have historically marginalised people with disability, but to prevent these from dominating the process of change which seeks to empower marginalised groups. We now consider this by reviewing our results in relation to the key theoretical frame introduced at the beginning of this chapter: 1) group-level behaviour is rooted in historical hierarchical positions in a multistakeholder initiative such as the UNPRPD, 2) different forms of capital operate within and between groups that can facilitate or hinder efforts towards implementing change, and 3) theories of change are rooted in contextual forces that must be embraced to implement targeted outcomes.

Programmatic barriers

Managing participation

The UNPRPD project in Uruguay was proposed by the Office of the Resident Coordinator and implemented by three UN agencies: UNFPA, WHO, and UN Women. The project team assigned a focal point for each agency, or a point of contact for meetings, technical support, and operations. Noting the complexity of multiple UN agencies, multiple government ministries, and an umbrella civil society organisation (discussed in more detail later in this chapter), the UNPRPD country project allocated funds for a project coordinator from within the UN. The coordinator's residence was designed to be split evenly across the three agencies to promote neutrality (autonomous from any one UN agency) and facilitate implementation across the partnerships.

Project coordinator

The role of the coordinator was valuable to many participants. For example, one government participant shared,

> [Without a coordinator] [t]hat would replicate the exact same thing that is happening now. Talking about disability in isolated sectors. What we want is that disability is talked about everywhere, because the life of disability is everywhere, so they need to come together. This work is demanding for all actors, but they have quite an overall vision.

The UNPRPD programme does not allow for a project coordinator, according to the UNCT. Despite this regulation, a project coordinator was appointed as a 'technical assistant' to work around the UNPRPD global programme design. A UNCT representative shared:

> One of the conditions of the proposal . . . you are not authorized to have a project coordinator. It is impossible to have a project coordinator in the budget. So we have to [them] as technical assistance. All the countries did the same, I can imagine. It was impossible to have 30 different agencies in one room without some coordination. [The coordinator] was hired after the development of the project. There is no way – it doesn't make sense to not have a project coordinator. [There are] a lot of joint projects where you can apply for some money, but they put in some conditions that are ridiculous. For this project, the time was very short. If this is a new agenda in the country – it is impossible in some months to do something. This is not an issue that is much more mature in the country – this is a new topic. And they don't allow a project coordinator like that. So we camouflage that.

While the UN recognised the necessity of project coordination and was able to modify procedure appropriately, civil society engagement was similarly selected by *technical* capacity, which resulted in those organisations most represented by persons with disabilities being least likely to participate.

Civil society engagement

One of the primary challenges to the project was a lack engagement with persons with disabilities. According to several research participants, the UNPRPD programme requires an umbrella or national disability organisation for the purpose of including diverse and state-wide representation. Unfortunately, this became a barrier to entry for local representation. A participant from the government explained, '[It is] not that there are no OPDs – just not in the Alianza, and not in an umbrella or national configuration'. In the case of Uruguay, a national DPO was not operational (see Participants). The Alianza was selected in response to the shadow report issued in 2016 for the Committee to the CRPD, having gained previous experience interacting with disability rights through an international framework. Technical expertise in developing a shadow report and previous engagement with the UN system were not UNPRPD programmatic requirements; however, it became the criteria for participation, despite the lack of disability membership. According to many project representatives, the Alliance had two capacity issues: 1) Alianza is not an OPD, and 2) Alianza functioned as a group of individual organisations without a central body.

Representation

Reflections on the absence of disability representation was the most common overall theme across all interviews. One government participant shared: 'The

Alliance was born in controversies – some OPDs don't recognize the Alliance as a legitimate organisation of representation – by the time I joined, the Alliance was already signed in.' Another participant from the UNCT perspective shared,

> The issue is there is no person with a disability. The voice is from their parent. They are very involved family, but there is no people with disability. There is always something that is in the middle – people who are in the middle – the family, the social leader. Their voices have to be here, have to be expressed. . . . The project was organized to help them be the main actors.

Some participants felt most Uruguayan disability organisations were led by parents or providers, whereas others recognised the availability of local OPDs that were not formally enlisted in the project due to being single-disability issue organisations. Some participants sought opportunities to gather the expertise of persons with disabilities for input where the Alliance was unable to support the ongoing activities. A project consultant shared,

> Many Alianza organisations won't meet. [We] had meetings with OPDs outside the Alianza. Alianza is not enough, but they were selected for this project. There *are* DPOs, just not in the project because of the agreements. And they [outside OPDs] did answer their calls.

Another participant explained, '[There are] about 600 organizations focusing on disability, including DPOs (OPDs), only 28 are in Alianza – mostly family representation. No other major federation – no other intuitive place to go'. The Alliance was the only group to meet the programmatic need for an organisation serving a range of disabilities, but it did not bridge the project closer to persons with disabilities. Mitigating the local hierarchy between decision-makers and rights holders was an ongoing effort by the UNCT, made more difficult by the regional distribution of persons with disabilities and the umbrella organisation requirement.

The absence of coordination to unify the roughly 27 separate organisations was a challenge in the face of providing a structural proxy for Uruguayans with disabilities. The Alliance membership was made of working professionals advocating for disability rights during their off hours or parents of individuals with disabilities of all ages who had to divide their time between professional, family, and advocacy obligations. One UNCT participant asserted,

> I cannot blame them. They are full of everyday challenges. Everyday obstacles. Everyday needs. But they are losing the strategic opportunity that is this project. It is not a question of blaming them. It is a question of talking with them and help them to realise what this means for Uruguay and for the life of persons with disabilities. It is the first project, and it will be the last one.

Hierarchical positionality

Sidanius's work on SDT explores the evolutionary tendency to group and situate into hierarchies. Further, these groups may operationalise dominance in different ways depending on the institutional socialisation. The UNCT serves a central role by bringing the UN system to local settings and are the technical expertise offered by the UN to country governments. There remains a hierarchy within the UN system whereby the UNCT operates within the larger UNPRPD inter-agency programme, nested within the larger UN framework. Thus, the UNCT implements the UNPRPD programmatic rules by way of UN institutional approaches. While the UNCT in Uruguay was tasked with framing the project around the overarching UNPRPD programmatic operational framework, they also determined which rules to break. One of the issues exerting influence on the project was the need for disability representation in their tripartite partnership. The programmatic requirement for an umbrella or representative national organisation was identified by focal points as a major barrier in Uruguay to realising the thematic objectives in a meaningful way. Several respondents noted being aware of the mismatch but lacked an alternative organisation that met the required criteria. While this rule was upheld despite the impact on the project, the UNCT found a way to hire a coordinator under a different title. This coordinator role is known as such and found in other country projects, recognising some rules are openly negotiated while others were upheld.

Unlike some of Sidanius's work around in-group solidarity, there is little evidence of participants trying to protect their group status; rather, UNCT representatives were forthright in their responses. The data showed active recognition of the missing voice of persons with disabilities as an impediment to implementing 'real change'. Many of the respondents made efforts to include persons with disabilities via consultancies or informal engagement yet often thought out loud, 'Where are they?', wishing to minimise the distance between groups rather than preserve it.

Project priorities

Significant effort went into cultivating the partnerships after the focal points were selected; however some key decisions were determined by UN capacity during the project proposal phase prior to engagement.

In practice, requests for project proposals are sent internally to the United Nations and submitted by UNCTs. Projects originate from the United Nations, rather than civil society or government, and then the UNCT proceeds with the partnership approach outlined in the UNPRPD programmatic framework. One government participant who joined the project after the proposal was approved for funding reflected,

> I asked myself, '[W]hy were these components chosen over the many issues that are pending or are a priority on the disability rights agenda

> in Uruguay?' [It has] more to do with the UN agencies' willingness and capacity for the project. Started with UN and their 'capacity and willingness', *then* a dialogue with the government. The government said they were involved and chose the priorities together. It really doesn't add up to me.

Another statement from civil society revealed this sentiment:

> I haven't had the opportunity to explain this. They already have the agenda decided. Sometimes I can give my opinion, but many of them are interested in the Alliance . . . but I am not very appointed sometimes, because I am not formally appointed. But I always attend because you have to listen to everybody.

While consensus and dialogue were fundamental tools in the project, this aspect was reported to be true only after priorities were chosen based on the availability of the UN. Additionally, there were perceived differences between official and unofficial appointments to the project. The previous participant quote was from a member organisation of the Alianza, though neither was, or felt like, a formal focal point with decision-making authority.

Theory over action

One area of focus came up several times – the desire to have included rehabilitation in the project. This was particularly true as focal points from the Ministry of Health recognised the collaboration with WHO and UNFPA. Rehabilitation felt like a more pressing need than GBV and involved the same institutions engaged in the project. A government representative had a practical consideration, stating,

> The project in the UN has helped with the sexual and reproductive health [and] concepts for diagnostic training, but it doesn't cover the more specific aspects of rehabilitation in the Ministry of Public Health . . . We made theoretical progress without having real things to offer [such as] rehab in health. [We] can have all the theory, but it is not only about the technical support.

The UNCT considered the need for rehabilitation in disability development for Uruguay; however the project sought a different direction, explaining,

> Rehab is not involved in this project. . . . [W]e strongly defined that rehabilitation will not be included in the project because it is strongly based on the medical model. This main objective of this project is to promote the social model of disability.

The UNCT wanted to emphasise the need to change social structures, rather than intervene at the individual level. As a result, the option to address rehabilitation was not prioritised for the project.

Determining capacity

The UNCT was aware that priorities were selected for the project based in part on capacity, stating, 'This project could have been very different if it were focused on education with UNICEF, or labour and ILO, but the results of the capacity to advance were these 3 agencies.' The same participant wrestled with the process, sharing, '[We] had to make critical choices – for example, not to include education – that is a very critical issue. But we had to choose.' Capacity of the United Nations was the first line of decision-making to ensure the project had support within the UNCT. The thematic decisions were felt throughout the project by many participants; however, civil society engagement was widely considered the primary barrier to the overall strength of the project.

The perception of civil society's capacity was rooted in the absence of direct representation and familiarity with UN systems to interact on project terms. Some issues led to disheartening experiences for project actors. One participant candidly shared their unmet expectations regarding the Alianza: 'At first, [the project sought] more representation to make decisions, now they are trying just to make it work.' Partnership with the Alliance came with barriers to engaging some additional OPDs, as well as inter-organisational competition, as described by one participant, who said:

> [We] wanted to give civil society some independence to come up with their own activities: [a significant amount of funding] to civil society to create workshops on gender-based violence, and they have only reached six women with disabilities. Some organisations left Alianza because for funds – set off conflict in the Alliance regarding who would receive the funds and why – the grants weakened the Alliance.

The Alliance runs on a volunteer basis; thus, they were given funds to support two organisations. They recognised the difference in stakeholder resources and aimed to reduce barriers and increase engagement in the project. Introducing a small amount of economic capital to an environment without a financial structure made fair distribution difficult and resulted in internal conflict with small-scale results.

The perspectives from within the Alianza (including consultancy) were much more optimistic about the growth of the Alliance, having expanded organisational membership from being limited to Montevideo to adding a few groups from the interior of the country – increasing their capacity. Representatives from the Alliance attributed their progress to the UNPRPD support. For example, one interviewee said,

> The [UNPRPD] project allowed the Alianza to organise its work. And make it possible to show its work with a wider audience (because we are the) only organisation representing disabled people recognised by the state. The Alianza is too young, just started in 2016.

Despite the growth of the Alliance, participants outside civil society felt the challenges were still too significant to engage in the project as planned. One participant reported, 'We feel impotent, trying to find the real mechanism to give them a voice and protect and empower them. It's hard.' Most notably, in an interview with a Spanish-English interpreter in the session, one participant spoke directly in English to the researcher, saying, 'It's not working. The Alianza is not working.' While participants acknowledged what was feasible for each of the stakeholders to deliver, the ghosts of what could have been lingered in conversation through statements such as: 'It is a bit sad we are not embedding that participation into the project. It was a unique single opportunity', and 'I think we lost in quality . . . on what could have been'.

Individual representation

The project did have key individuals with disabilities assisting in various roles that proved to be very powerful in the interviews with participants. When reflecting on the capacity limitations of the Alliance, many recalled the impact that individuals with disabilities had when invited to the inception phase or during training sessions. The initial intent of having a representative organisation was to avoid narrowing a diverse population of people into a few consultants or other individuals. This possibility was a known risk to participants. They continued to encourage engagement from the Alianza while several select individuals with disabilities brought the power and representation that many participants sought. One response noted,

> [T]here is an incorporation of a disabled person in the team of teachers. Very independent woman, and she has been fighting for the rights of disabled people, and that is a strength when you think about reaching people with a message. Especially for health teams.

This impact was particularly true of the inception phase that publicly launched the project to stakeholders in Uruguay. Several participants reflected on this event as a major success for the project. One government participant stated,

> It is so very few times that persons with disabilities were heard, and have the chance to speak to government officials, to public, policy makers, and we created an environment. That was something that we – that gave these people the chance to think or be confronted with exclusion or with a different image. One girl was talking about all her achievements, and that helped break barriers of the vision of disability that is current. Charity

> and that. But I think that moment was very moving. . . . It was a big ceremony, and everyone was listening. So it was worth the risk. That doesn't change the life of anybody, but that was something. It was important.

The UNPRPD designed projects to include persons with disabilities in all stages of work. Special events such as the inception created the opportunity to reach outside an official partnership to highlight the strengths of representation from persons with disabilities. Those individuals were fewer than the team aimed to engage and solidify as partners, yet they played a significant role in guiding the vision for the project.

Capital capacity

Bourdieu's habitus describes the modification of historical behaviour practiced by individuals as a feedback loop for change between agent (historical behaviours) and state (laws or regulations). This begins to give shape to enacting change. Based on Bourdieu's work on embodiment and structural behaviour, programming should recognise the role of capital in the different positions and influence of partners engaged in the project. Further, Lewin outlines a five-step force field analysis to manage change at the group level by defining the desired change and mapping strategies to create a path forward, and while the UNPRPD did not explicitly use or cite in their process, they followed a similar approach. The Uruguayan case study seen through Lewin's work highlights a key force missing from his framework that Bourdieu examines in depth. For example, Lewin's field analysis begins by defining the problem space, which is highly dependent on who is doing the defining. Each step that follows would vary greatly based on which persons are conducting the analysis. For Bourdieu, the capital underpinning the power distribution in a hierarchy is essential to a field and was a major point of tension in the UNPRPD Uruguay project.

Forms of capital were evident in the participant responses with some awareness of their implications. For example, the UNCT recognised a volunteer organisation's limited capacity without a governing body or funding stream. Importantly, both the UNCT and government focal points recognised the impact of symbolic and cultural capital and the inability to replace the engagement of persons with disabilities or a representative OPD with civil society that does not possess disability membership. These were meaningful barriers to change in the project. While participants were aware of these issues, there were fewer comments on the relational aspect whereby capital is relative. As a result, an absence of power in some areas has a relationship to dominance in others. Many participants reported feeling limited by decisions that had been made early on in the project, such as thematic priorities, even if the decisions came from within. More dominant structures exerted small amounts of authority in contracting individuals with disabilities in any role possible but did not alter the internal procedures that led to those barriers when applied to the Uruguayan context. Likewise, government focal points agreed the priorities of the project did not reflect more urgent local needs but felt the opportunity to pivot was outside their authority. So, while some forms of capital in partnering structures were recognised, a structure's own power and dominance to make changes were not felt when encountering roadblocks.

External forces

Field changes

Structures have relational implications that demonstrate the hierarchical dynamics in disability development projects, such as UNPRPD regulations for an umbrella or national OPDs mismatched with the availability of such a structure in the country. These hierarchies operate in country contexts that also respond to social dynamics. Two of the changes in social space that were seen as impactful to the project were the reclassification of Uruguay to a high-income country in 2013 and the change of government in 2019. Both these external conditions began to define the participants' perception of project success. Participants could acknowledge positive outcomes from the project, but the successes were shadowed by the social changes underpinning their work. For example, a member of the UNCT said,

> I believe the two or three studies we have produced from this project are really an advance to measure and assess disability. The access to social benefit. The guide on sexual & reproductive health. I think they are very good. They have a strong quality. And so based in scientific information, so I feel they are a smart contribution. It is a very valuable output, but the government have no real time to implement them.

The elections were seen as a deadline to secure the project changes, knowing the government would likely be replaced by a more conservative body. The same UNCT representative described a dual project timeline – one for the UNPRPD and one for the period of government:

> The different groups may propose, and they – each official or group may propose some changes, but there is no time to produce those changes. That is a fact. There is no time to propose to the Parliament, to the government, to produce those changes. But it will remain updated and documented for promoting the changes in the future – in the short future, in the near future. Now there is no political time.

Prior to the elections that November, which did result in a change of political party, participants felt the likelihood of change was a direct concern for the project. One government participant worried, '[There is a] real risk all the hard work they have done stays in a limbo. Risk of having to do it all over again'. Another from the UNCT shared, 'I don't know how the future will be when the project finishes. Because there are these elections. But certainly political change. That may be a threat for the project'. While the team was trying to 'make it work' with civil society, the looming political climate made the project feel increasingly dependent on external factors to achieve substantial change for persons with disabilities in Uruguay.

Status implications

Additional pressure from the country classification to high-income status made the UNPRPD project feel like the last opportunity Uruguay would receive of that magnitude. One participant explained,

> It is not a competition. In a country like Uruguay, the agencies have to justify the reason they are here, there is a pressure – or syndrome of the winner – is a little bit present. They are cooperating pretty well, but I mean, that is present.

The need to prove the value of the work as funded projects become redirected to low- and middle-income countries leaves little room for error in a tight, two-year timeline. One participant from the UNCT shared, 'This was the biggest opportunity to let people know disability is here in Uruguay, and we have not done that'. Another explained the urgency for increasing the capacity of civil society before the end of what felt to some like their final opportunity: 'That is why it is important to strengthen the Alliance. The project will end and the Alliance will end'. Participants spoke with finality in their responses over the changes happening around them, many of which were not the changes they imagined going into the project.

Theories of change

Reflecting on Lewin's field analysis, the case in Uruguay surfaces the question: what if some restraining forces are self-imposed by varying structures within a hierarchy – particularly those structures with the most resources to exert force? Bourdieu's concepts of multiple, overlapping fields expand the scope of analysis to include hierarchical power such as locating the authority to choose how mismatched rules are handled and the implications of structural authority. There were several layers of analysis to consider in addition to the scope of work aiming to take something created by the project and alter the external environment or their ToC. The project had a traditional, outward ToC whereby a tripartite partnership would collaborate to improve sexual and reproductive health, gender-based violence, and systematised disability assessments. There was a larger programmatic framework to follow, which, on occasion, created barriers to what participants called 'real change'. The programmatic framework, operations, and authority within each stakeholder group, the demographic distribution of persons with disabilities in the country, local needs, and preexisting capacity were all under analysis; however, the analyses did not come with an internal (reflexive) ToC. Neither the UNPRPD project nor any partnering stakeholder was intentionally perpetuating the peripheral role of persons with disabilities; rather, the tripartite partnership reflected the preexisting social hierarchies. The participants did not report an established action plan for what to do if the broader UNPRPD framework created barriers – a ToC for their own internal process.

Finally, the participants expressed an urgent need to 'refreeze' the changes made by the project before elections would change government power. Bourdieu's field theory is helpful to visualise forces coming from multiple directions with varying degrees of importance. There are limitations to what the biggest actor in a system can do when another field force encompasses the project. Meaning that even with all the power of the UNCT and participating government focal points, if the Uruguayan public voted for a new party that destabilized the project's work, there was little control the project could exert to push their desired outcomes forward. The project was hosted within the Uruguayan context, and that context could suddenly shift in a different direction than the project was designed to operate within. Ultimately, the participants reported concern over the longevity of project outcomes as a new government took office, and the project approached the end of its funding.

Internal forces

Awareness

The external forces shaping the project were significant to the participants in this study. That being said, there were several positive changes within the project, particularly the individual changes that extended into their structural role. Beginning with an example of individual change, a UNCT participant described the growth in their personal awareness stating,

> As a personal experience, I learned a lot about persons with disabilities and how to act when you are [with them]. . . . all my instinctive actions are not always right. With blind people, I have to talk and not just act. That has increased my capability to have relations with persons with disabilities.

These actions were not limited to the internal process. One other UNCT participant was compelled to order new business cards with Braille embossed onto the material. She shared, 'You are called to action, you are touched by it. . . . [T]hat is the way this project touched me, I changed some part of my life – my (business) cards. This is the personal change I have made.' She continued to describe how the disability rights paradigm from the project changed her approach to work within the UNCT:

> For the first time, I had to be very sincere. For the first time, we at the office rethink the issues that [come up at] our public events: for example, if they were accessible for everyone. . . . But for me, it was a project that made me ask me questions about what we are doing every day from [the UN agency].

Paradigm shift

Internal changes were found in all three partnering structures according to interview reflections. A UNCT participant reflected on a shift in government dynamics toward fostering future progress as a result of the UNPRPD:

> It is not easy that actors convince themselves to take steps that can really change their structure. Those steps we are talking about from the economic point of view, the human resources, to the vision also. The institution is questioning itself and admitting that something that it has been doing for a long time, they are not doing the right way. There can be a better way to do it. I think this – taking this awareness is a super big step. It's the key to be open to the change. If you don't do this step, all the changes you can achieve are just temporary.

A representative from a government ministry shared a similar sentiment, stating, 'We are coordinating about real things instead of talking about what we don't have. That is new and a change'. Structures previously unfamiliar with disability rights became more open and willing to change from within to become more inclusive and move priorities forward.

Increasing structural stability

The Alianza also noticed internal changes as a result of the UNPRPD project. For example, one participant on behalf of civil society noticed,

> One very positive point, thanks to the project and thanks to the activities, the Alianza could go into the interior of the country. Lack of funds, so it couldn't do that before. Used to be only concentrated in Montevideo – now met very receptive groups to join Alianza.

Crucially, a member of civil society reported increased engagement with persons with disabilities: 'Participating in the project allowed the Alianza to include activities to the disabled, and include disabled people in activities, and reflect the needs of disabled people'. While the capacity of the Alliance presented challenges for this project, it did work towards deepening the role of persons with disabilities in the existing umbrella organisation.

Building partnerships

Changes within individuals extended to their respective structures and, further, between structures partnered by the UNPRPD.

> I think there are, you know this project has one successful achievement. That is to join, to put at the same table some of the public actors that don't speak to each other about this subject about human rights of persons with disabilities. It is a success to see them speaking together about these common matters. Because each one has one perspective in one function in terms of political or social action. They have one piece of the picture. And the project, joined them – put them in the situation to dialogue.

The same UNCT representative explained the value of dialogue across partnerships: 'This allows or provides structure to make it work'. The participants in this study, nearly all key focal points in the project, ended with optimism for the future of disability in Uruguay. The UNPRPD inspired progress outside the initial scope of the project, led by the internal growth of the people within government ministries. They requested support from the UNCT for their discussions, initiating an ongoing relationship beyond the two-year UNPRPD timeline:

> There have been movements within people that when we share real situations of the weaknesses, the feedback we get from them; it's like, OK let's get together to find the best way. I think even though it may seem like something small, I think that some situations are being put on the agenda that had no visibility in the past at all. I do believe there is intention and political will to think about how to go about it. I don't know when, but at least we do have the will.
>
> From the very beginning of the project, the same actors said we are working together, but we don't want to go beyond some of the rules we have. Some of the policies we have. And now they are working at least to discuss these policies – the tools we have to measure – for example – the disability [determination assessment]. So it is very interesting. The dialogue – to set up the dialogue [was] productive, not just to share.

The UNPRPD project engaged external partners spanning a range of hierarchical positions and set out to address sexual and reproductive health and gender-based violence and improve systematised disability data in Uruguay; however, the UNPRPD focal points ended up undergoing a paradigm shift towards disability rights as a result of the project. The shifts reported as significant were largely internal, seen as the foundation from which to build external change, such as securing the importance of disability inclusion in policy and future programming among powerful actors. Dialogue between structures began as a practical communication tool for the defined project pillars and led to a working group of several government ministries extending an invitation to the UNCT on a supplementary line of work. This line of work was initiated between government sectors and the UNCT as a result of the UNPRPD project, passing down the absence of disability representation from one project to the initiation of another. The maintenance of hierarchical relationships is a durable force, even in projects designed to be participatory. Many participants felt internal growth was important but too abstract to have achieved 'real change' for Uruguayans with disabilities: highlighting the divide between the collective impact of key individual's paradigm shifts, the structural operations of affiliated institutions, and the social conditions facing persons with disabilities.

Conclusion

Scholars have theorised about creating intentional change over the years, and similar frameworks have been applied within organisational frameworks called programmatic Theories of Change. In the case of the UNPRPD, the design aims to leverage the strengths of existing hierarchies by including CSOs/OPDs in the same conversations with government and UNCTs. The aim is that hierarchies can be useful to implement targeted changes to social systems. The case study in Uruguay provides a real-world example of the theoretical implications of group-based hierarchies, the effectiveness of ToCs, and role capital plays in identifying and 'unfreezing' restrictive forces to implement social change. Each theory has strengths and weaknesses, which were explored in the UNPRPD Uruguay project, distinguishing theoretical change from what happens in practice.

Limitations

Change is dynamic, and this data was collected during a one-month period. Further case studies over time will provide deeper context to the participant responses during various stages of project implementation. Additionally, census data is known to be imprecise, particularly the enumeration of persons with disabilities. This study provides only one case example of theory in practice from the UNPRPD global programme and cannot claim to reflect the broader phenomenon.

Acknowledgements

The authors would like to thank Mr. Damjan Tatic for his thoughtful comments on this chapter. We would also like to dedicate this work to Dr. Martin Charlton, who generously helped during the early stages of brainstorming and cartographic exploration.

References

Anselin, L. (1995). Local indicators of spatial association (LISA). *Geographical Analysis*, *27*(2), 93–115.
Bargal, D. (2014). Lewin, Kurt. In D. Coghlan & M. Brydon-Miller (Eds.), *The SAGE Encyclopedia of action research* (pp. 500–503). SAGE.
Bourdieu, P. (1984). *Distinction: a social critique of the judgment of taste*. Harvard University Press.
Bourdieu, P. (1986). The forms of capital. In J. Richardson (Eds.), *Handbook of theory and research for the sociology of education* (pp. 241–58). Greenwood.
Bourdieu, P. (1990). *The logic of practice*. Stanford University Press.
Breuer, E., Lee, L., De Silva, M., & Lund, C. (2016). Using theory of change to design and evaluate public health interventions: a systematic review. *Implementation Science*, *11*(63). https://doi.org/10.1186/s13012-016-0422-6
Byrne, B. (2018). Dis-equality: exploring the juxtaposition of disability and equality. *Social Inclusion*, *6*(1).
Charlton, J. (2010). *Nothing about us, without us: disability oppression and empowerment*. University of California Press.
Clarke D. (2016). Chapter 10. Law, regulation and strategizing for health. In G. Schmets, D. Rajan & S. Kadandale (Eds.), *Strategizing national health in the 21st century: a handbook*. World Health Organization.
Davies, R., & Dart, J. (2005). The 'Most Significant Change' (MSC) technique: a guide to its use. https://www.mande.co.uk/docs/MSCGuide.pdf
Haley, H., & Sidanius, J. (2005). Person-organization congruence and the maintenance of group-based social hierarchy: a social dominance perspective. *Group Processes and Intergroup Relations*, *8*(2), 187–203.
Ines Núñez, L. (2014). Personas con discapacidad en Uruguay: Algunas cifras del censo 2011. *Asesoría General en Seguridad Social*. https://www.bps.gub.uy/bps/file/8195/1/44._personas_con_discapacidad_en_uruguay._algunas_cifras_del_censo_2011._nunez.pdf
Lewin, K. (1939). Field theory and experiment in social psychology: concepts and methods. *American Journal of Sociology*, *44*, 868–896.
Lewin, K. (2013). *Principles of topological psychology*. Read Books.
MacLachlan, M., Mannan, H., Huss, T., & Scholl, M. (2019). Macropsychology: challenging and changing social structures and systems. In D. Hoggets & K. O'Doherty (Eds.), *Handbook of applied social psychology* (pp. 116–182). Sage.
MacLachlan, M., & McVeight, J. (2021). Macropsychology: definition, concept and scope. In M. MacLachlan & J. McVeigh (Ed.), *Macropsychology – a population science for sustainable development goals*. Springer.
Madans, J. H., Loeb, M. E., & Altman, B. M. (2004). Measuring disability and monitoring the UN Convention on the Rights of Persons with Disabilities: the work of the Washington group on disability statistics. *BMC Public Health*, *11*(S4).
OHCHR. (2014). Status of ratification: interactive dashboard. https://indicators.ohchr.org/. Accessed April 21, 2020.
Pret, T., & Carter, S. (2017) The importance of 'fitting in': collaboration and social value creation in response to community norms and expectations. *Entrepreneurship and Regional Development*, 29, 639–667.
Quilliam, C., & Wilson, E. (2011). *Literature review – outcomes measurement in disability services: a review of policy contexts, measurement approaches and selected measurement tools*. Deakin University.
Sidanius, J., Liu, J., Pratto, F., & Shaw, J. (1994). Social dominance orientation, hierarchy-attenuators and hierarchy-enhancers: social dominance theory and the criminal justice system. *Journal of Applied Social Psychology, 24*, 338–366.

Smith, J. A., Flower, P., & Larkan, M. (2009). *Interpretative phenomenological analysis: theory, method and research*. Sage.

Swanson, D. J., & Creed, A. S. (2014) Sharpening the focus of force field analysis. *Journal of Change Management*, *14*, 28–47. https://doi.org/10.1080/14697017.2013.788052

The Economist. (2019). Power shifts in Uruguay, without much fuss: riding the waves. https://link.gale.com/apps/doc/A624582224/AONE?u=nuim&sid=AONE&xid=054681c5. Accessed November 19, 2020.

The World Bank. (2019). The world bank in Uruguay: overview. https://www.worldbank.org/en/country/uruguay/overview. Accessed July 14, 2020.

UN Committee on the Elimination of Discrimination against Women (UNCEDAW). (2016). Concluding observations of the committee on the elimination of discrimination against women: Uruguay. CEDAW/C/URY/CO/8–9.

UN Committee on the Rights of Persons with Disabilities (UNCRPD). (2016). Concluding observations on the initial report of Uruguay. https://documents-dds-ny.un.org/doc/UNDOC/GEN/G16/222/12/PDF/G1622212.pdf?OpenElement. Accessed October 20, 2018.

United Nations. (2006). Convention on the rights of persons with disabilities and optional protocol. http://www.un.org/disabilities/documents/convention/convoptprot-e.pdf. Accessed December 15, 2009.

United Nations. (n.d.). UN system. https://www.un.org/en/about-us/un-system. Accessed February 10, 2021.

United Nations Development Programme [UNDP]. (2016). UNPRPD strategic and operational framework. mptf.undp.org/document/download/15036. Accessed November 2, 2020.

UNPRPD. (2019). Who we are: we work towards a society for all. http://www.unprpd.org/who_we_are. Accessed January 15, 2021.

Wescott, H., MacLachlan, M., & Mannan, H. (2021). The macropsychology of disability rights and structural change: using Bourdieusian analysis to understand stakeholder power relations. In M. MacLachlan & J. McVeigh (Eds.), *Macropsychology: a population science for sustainable development goals* (pp. 175–187). Springer.

14
INTELLECTUAL DISABILITY AND SEXUALITY IN ULTRA-ORTHODOX JEWISH COMMUNITIES

Rina B. Pikkel and Chaya Gershuni

Introduction

This chapter explores the construction of sexuality and sexual rights of intellectually disabled people within the social, cultural, and political setting of the Ultra-Orthodox (Haredi) community in Israel. Haredi Jews are a religious separatist community that follows strict conservative practices and has unique traits and a complex relationship with their surrounding society. The concept of human rights, and thus disability and sexual rights, is foreign to the Haredi way of life, and they favor familiar religious and moral principles (Gershuni, 2018a; Orr et al., 2021a, 2021b). This unique social context requires a novel approach. Therefore, we will interrogate the conceptualization and construction of sexuality of intellectually disabled persons by identifying the underlining norms and values and their interpretation by the Haredi community and the distinct practices and solutions they yield.

Disability scholars and advocates first turned the spotlight to the missing discourse on sexuality approximately 25 years ago (Shakespeare, 2000; Shakespeare et al., 1996; Shuttleworth & Mona, 2002). Traditionally, disabled persons were portrayed and perceived as asexual, undesirable, and childlike. In addition, intellectual disability was often associated with sexual vulnerability and abuse (Perlin & Lynch, 2016; Shildrick, 2007; Tepper, 2000). The rise of a social-critical approach to disability changed the way we understand the sexuality of disabled persons. It emphasized sexual autonomy and pleasure, acknowledging previously overlooked sexual needs and wishes. Disability studies focused on social barriers that make sexuality inaccessible for intellectually disabled persons and the importance of education and accommodations as possible solutions (Shakespeare & Richardson, 2018; Shildrick, 2007; Tepper,

DOI: 10.4324/9781003410089-17

2000). In recent years, new rights-based understandings of disability emerged as the struggle for inclusion and equality shifted towards legal recognition and action (Perlin, 2008; Shakespeare, 2000; Shakespeare & Richardson, 2018; Shuttleworth, 2007). Respectively, claims regarding the sexuality of disabled people adopted a conceptualization of sexual rights over sexual needs and desires.

Ultra-Orthodox Jews have distinct characteristics and traits. Haredi communities are usually homogeneous and separatist; they have specific social structures congregated around religious leadership. The central common denominator is their rigorous adherence to Jewish law (Halacha) and rabbinical dictates (Friedman, 1991; Malach & Cahaner, 2019; Leon, 2016; Zicherman & Cahaner, 2012). Haredi society often views disability negatively and demonstrates beliefs that coincide with medical-individual approaches to the matter. The Ultra-Orthodox perceive disability as an unwanted trait that can hinder the family's position in the community (Gershuni, 2018a; Lifshitz & Globerman, 2006). In recent years, we have seen slow yet significant changes in Haredi acceptance and treatment of disabled persons (Vardi, 2019). Haredi society demonstrates greater tolerance, compassion, and awareness of disability rights (Gershuni, 2018a).

The Haredi understanding of sexuality is relatively narrow and influenced by their devotion to Halachic rules (P. Feldman, 1992; Nahary & Hartman, 2020). Thus, sexuality is a concept that refers almost exclusively to the intimate relationship between heteronormative married spouses, who conduct all their sexual practices according to Jewish law and within the marriage. Other types of sexual expression, orientation, or relationships are forbidden (P. Feldman, 1992; Hoffman, 2020; Ribner, 2003). Nonetheless, in a pronatalist society that encourages procreation, sexual relations between spouses are considered essential for the institute of marriage and an inseparable part of the Jewish home (P. Feldman, 1992; Tal, 2016).

We used qualitative research methodology and conducted semi-structured in-depth interviews. We interviewed family members of couples with disabilities, therapists, caregivers, rabbis, and matchmakers who work with disabled families. We then performed a textual analysis of all interviews. The starting point of our research was that in the absence of a rights discourse, the Ultra-Orthodox would address the sexual needs and desires of intellectually disabled people through a different perspective. We performed a four-stage analysis: first, we looked for the religious concepts and values that underline Haredi's understanding of sexuality and disability. In the second stage, we used these values to create a thematic organization of social perceptions, constructions, and mechanisms. In the third stage, we identified what practical applications and solutions these values and perceptions have. Finally, we applied a disability studies perspective to adapt our findings to promote change in perceptions of disabled sexuality in general society. Consequently, this chapter offers a broader understanding of critical-social theory in a conservative, dogmatic setting as it explores the relationship between human rights, community values, and public resources.

Disability and sexuality: the emergence of sexual rights

The advancements of disability studies over the last few decades have brought about perceptual changes. The understanding of disability shifted from medical-individual models that considered it a personal misfortune or tragedy to critical-social ones that placed it in a broader context and emphasized social construction and the significance of social barriers over bodily and mental limitations (Drum et al., 2009; Linton, 1998; Oliver, 1990, 1996; Shakespeare, 2006, 2013a). Later models included rights-based conceptualizations of disability that addressed disabled persons as a minority group or a legal category worthy of protection (Bagenstos, 2009; Degener, 2017; Heyer, 2015; Stein & Stein, 2007). Scholars introduced sexuality to disability studies later in this theoretical development, first considering it a relatively marginal issue (Shakespeare, 2000; Shakespeare et al., 1996; Shakespeare & Richardson, 2018; Shildrick, 2007; Shuttleworth, 2007; Tepper, 2000). The individual-medical models viewed people with disabilities as asexual, either unable or unwilling to participate in intimate relationships or sexual acts; their bodily and mental limitations contradict sexual needs and desires (Shakespeare, 2000; Tepper, 2000). Thus, the dominant approach was paternalistic and focused on protecting disabled persons from sexual assault and harm (Foley, 2019; Nosek et al., 2001; Perlin, 2008). The changing understanding of disability also changed the meaning of disabled sexuality; the new critical models of disability acknowledged sexual pleasure and choice and the role of society in excluding disabled persons from the sexual realm (Shakespeare, 2000; Shakespeare et al., 1996; Shakespeare & Richardson, 2018; Shildrick, 2007; Shuttleworth, 2007; Tepper, 2000).

Despite many significant achievements of disability scholars and activists over the years, perceptions of disabled sexuality are still primarily negative, ranging from childlikeness and vulnerability to danger and deviation. In many cases, the sexual needs of disabled people are ignored by family members, caregivers, and professionals as they are considered disgusting and repulsive. Disabled persons, especially women, are often described as vulnerable, susceptible to abuse and assault, and lacking the ability to consent or enjoy sex. At the same time, intellectually or mentally disabled men are considered perverted and dangerous, lacking control over their sexual drive and desires (Cook, 2000; Foley, 2019; Nosek et al., 2001; Perlin et al., 2017; Shakespeare & Richardson, 2018).

According to the critical-social models, intimate relationships are not accessible for disabled people not just because of objective limitations entailed by the disability but primarily due to a variety of social barriers. Among these barriers, one can encounter economic obstacles, physical inaccessibility of public spaces, social exclusion, insufficient self-confidence resulting from social attitudes, and inadequate social skills (Shakespeare & Richardson, 2018; Shildrick, 2007; Shuttleworth & Mona, 2002). Some of the most significant barriers are prevailing social perceptions regarding disabled sexuality and a social structure that excludes disabled people from the public sphere, cultural events, social gatherings, etc. (Emens, 2009; Shakespeare & Richardson, 2018). The most overt exclusion occurs with disabled people living in sheltered residences, where their very home denies them vital connections and encounters with others, especially non-disabled people (Emens, 2009; Perlin & Lynch, 2016). Yet, the objective difficulties that drive from one's limitations are particularly valid when discussing sexuality, a realm where a person's physical experience is remarkably present. Ability or disability to perform and consent to sexual acts is critical (Shakespeare, 2013b; Shakespeare & Watson, 2001). Questions of consent and capacity are dominant in the case of people with intellectual disabilities. The fear of exploitation and the lack of ability to understand the various aspects of sexuality and intimacy and give affirmative consent are highly significant (Boni-Saenz, 2015; Perlin et al., 2017).

As the disability struggle for equality took on a legal rights–based approach, a similar shift occurred in the discourse on sexuality and disabilities: from needs and desires to sexual rights and citizenship (Mor & Pikkel, 2019; Sanders, 2007; Shildrick, 2007, 2013). The Convention for the Rights of People with Disabilities (CRPD) (United Nations, 2006) is considered the main comprehensive international instrument for promoting disability rights. The CRPD was signed and ratified by many countries and states, adding an international human rights law layer to domestic disability legislation (Harpur, 2012; Heyer, 2015). The CRPD. includes both normative declarative articles, anchoring primary principles of disability theory (such as access and choice), and a robust list of specific rights (such as housing and education). It acknowledges the importance of intimate relationships; it protects and respects the home and family: hence, the right to form a family (Article 23). The convention also protects the right to enjoy good health (Clause 25) and the right to privacy within one's family (Article 22). However, the CRPD does not directly tackle sexuality. The terms "sexual rights" and "the right to sexuality" do not appear in the CRPD; instead, one can identify different elements of sexuality within existing generalized articles (Foley, 2012; Ruiz, 2017; Sabatello, 2014; Schaaf, 2011).

The absence of an article specifically dealing with sexual rights is not accidental, as it was suggested in an early draft and later excluded from the text (Ruiz, 2017; Sabatello, 2014; Schaaf, 2011). It is rooted in political occurrences that shape the world of international law. The standing of the right to sexuality as an independent right – separate from the right to family life and parenthood – is controversial and has not yet been recognized as a human right by international law. Only several aspects of sexuality (particularly sexual health and protection from sexual harm) are present in international charters, conventions, and treaties. The CRPD follows these convictions and does not expand the scale of rights beyond those already recognized, thus refraining from including an explicit article on sexual rights (Sabatello, 2014; Schaaf, 2011). Religion is another substantial justification for the absence of sexuality from the CRPD, which is most relevant to this research. Islamic states, the Vatican, and conservative Christian organizations based in the USA argued that official recognition of sexual rights, especially sexual autonomy, encourages intimate relationships outside of marriage, considered taboo in many religious societies. The objection to signing the original drafts on these grounds led to the later accepted version, which covertly incorporated sexuality in other articles (Ruiz, 2017; Sabatello, 2014; Schaaf, 2011). This way of articulating sexuality and sexual rights, which considers religious limitations and influences, can provide insights into the dilemmas, challenges, and solutions presented in this chapter.

Haredi Jews in Israel: Characteristics and perceptions of disability

The Haredi community is a conservative Jewish community comprising various groups, all maintaining strict adherence to the Jewish Halacha (Friedman, 1991; Stadler, 2019b; Zicherman & Cahaner, 2012). They are considered part of Orthodox Judaism; 12.5% of Jews (and 15% of Israelis) define themselves as Haredi (Cahaner & Malach, 2019). Their essential trait is their religious piety; they strictly follow Halachic commands in every aspect of life. Ultra-Orthodox Jews live in tight communities organized around rabbinical leadership (Friedman, 1991; Leon, 2016).

Haredi society has a unique structure. The rabbi, the religious community leader, is the center and focal point of his community. The inner ties in Haredi communities are solid; mutual help and assistance are prevalent as even the poorest of Haredi are volunteering and donating to their friends and neighbors (Malach & Cahaner, 2019; Leon, 2016). Haredi sanctify childbirth, and families usually have a relatively large number of children; family planning is highly controversial and often forbidden (Friedman, 1991; Malach & Cahaner, 2019).

Haredi devotion and obedience to Jewish law and rabbinical dictates also manifest in their tendency to often alienate themselves from liberal concepts and ideas (Barzilai, 2013; Gershuni, 2018a). The human rights discourse is liberal and foreign to Orthodox existence and society (Gershuni, 2018a; Orr et al., 2021a, 2021b). Despite being a community that differentiates itself by creating a counterculture and group cohesion, the politics and values of general Israeli society influence the Ultra-Orthodox community (Gershuni, 2018a). Ideas and concepts (such as human rights) are not fully adopted; yet, there is a slow graduate diffusion, and adaptation of norms says that research into the allocation and localization of human rights must consider context and particular cultural circumstances (Orr et al., 2021a, 2021b). In the case of Haredi Jews, there is a complex process in which the rights terminology undergoes transformation and adaptation using local concepts and terms. This process occurs as Haredi adopts a new understanding of disability and disability rights from the general society and adapts them into familiar religious values (Orr et al., 2021a, 2021b). Critical and rights-based conceptualizations take on a different shape; compassion, care, and solidarity substitute for equality and access (Gershuni, 2018a).

The Ultra-Orthodox have a negative tragic perception of disability compared to the general population (Lifshitz & Globerman, 2006). Yet there seems to be a certain improvement in the inclusion and acceptance of disabled individuals (Vardi et al., 2019). A study that examined attitudes towards disabled people in Israel found no differences between the various Israeli sectors (secular, religious, and Haredi Jews) (The National Organization for People with Mental Disabilities and thier Families [AKIM], 2013). We can now identify progressive trends in their perception of disability (Gershuni, 2018a). Haredi parents of intellectually disabled children demonstrate a greater sense of growth than non-Haredi parents (Manor-Binyamini, 2012). It appears that faith, religion, and community support positively affect the quality of life of Haredi families raising a disabled child (Taub & Werner, 2016). Yet having a disabled child or sibling might hinder one's position in society. It influences the attractiveness of family members in terms of marriage due to concerns regarding possible hereditary and genetic aspects (Raz & Vizner, 2008; Whiteley et al., 2017). This multifaceted and contrasting understanding of disability stems from a difference in attitudes towards containment, compassion, and human rights, perceived differently by the Haredi community (Gershuni, 2018a).

Intimacy and sexuality in Haredi communities

The Halacha dictates every aspect of life for Haredi Jews, including family life, marriage, and childbirth. Sexuality is considered taboo and is absent from the Haredi discourse. When addressed, it is usually spoken of in great privacy in the intimate female or male sphere (Nahary & Hartman, 2020; Taragin-Zeller & Kasstan, 2021). However, within the framework of marriage, sexuality is a vital component of the Jewish home (Ribner, 2003; Tal, 2016).

An elaborate scheme of commands controls the private lives of community members at every stage. One of the most central values that dictate Haredi conduct is modesty before marriage and later in any setting outside the family home. The Haredi dress code requires maximum coverage of one's body (Hoffman, 2020). All sexual expressions and aspects are considered immodest in this setting. Among immodest practices are sexual relationships with others and autoerotica; masturbation is forbidden and considered "extracting semen in vain" (P. Feldman, 1992; Hoffman, 2020; Ribner, 2003). There is an almost absolute separation between the sexes from infancy and throughout life. For example, all Haredi education systems are separate from preschool onwards. Physical contact and socializing with the opposite gender are allowed only within the family between parents, children, and spouses (P. Feldman, 1992; Hoffman, 2020). Young adults of the proper age for marriage cannot freely meet potential partners. Therefore, marriages depend on a third party's involvement; family members and matchmakers are responsible for finding the young men and women an appropriate match (Bokek-Cohen, 2018; Heilman, 2021; Stadler, 2019a).

Marriage is the entrance key into society and a mandatory rite of passage for young individuals (Friedman, 1991; Rosenbaum et al., 2013; Stadler, 2019b). Haredi get married at a relatively young age, as 85% of the Haredi marry before reaching 20 (Cahaner & Malach, 2019). Marriage is the gateway to an independent life, especially for young women. The separation from their parents' home happens concurrently with their marriage. Married life provides a first-time introduction to the sexual realm that is off limits beforehand (Cohen & Tsuria, 2019).

Upon marriage, the commands of family purity[1], *Nida Ve Tahara*, regulate intimate relations. They forbid intercourse and physical contact, including kissing or holding hands, between the husband and wife during menstruation (P. Feldman, 1992; Ribner, 2003). After menstruation ends, the couple waits an additional week. Then, the woman dips into the "mikveh" (the purity bath). Only then is the couple allowed, encouraged, and obligated to have intercourse. This ritual usually coincides with ovulation, contributing to increased conception and birth rates, a central value in the Haredi community (Guterman, 2008; Rosenbaum et al., 2013).

Judaism sanctifies and empowers sexuality when it adheres to the Halacha. Sex is a powerful tool that allows the ongoing fertility and continuity of the Jewish people. Therefore, Haredi discourse on sexuality focuses on sexual practices that facilitate procreation (P. Feldman, 1992; Taragin-Zeller & Kasstan, 2021; Wenger, 1999). In the Haredi community, marriage and sexuality are bound in an inseparable tie involving Halacha, cultural values of procreation, and emotional experiences of sexual intimacy. For the Haredi individual, marriage and childbearing are necessary for personal fulfillment, communal belonging, and religious obedience (Heilman, 2021).

Marriage and family life of Haredi Jews with disabilities

As marriage and sexuality are tightly connected, an additional significant layer is marriages among disabled people and the effect of disabilities on arranging marriages. Disabilities affect the marital prospects of disabled people and their families considerably (Orr et al., 2021a; Raz & Vizner, 2008; Whiteley et al., 2017). The candidates' physical and mental health play a central role (Greenberg et al., 2012; Raz & Vizner, 2008). Therefore, much information about candidates' background, health, and prominent traits is revealed. Having a disabled family member negatively influences and can potentially hinder one's chances of finding a match (Orr et al., 2021a; Raz, 2015; Raz & Vizner, 2008).

The marriage of disabled persons is acceptable in parts of the Haredi society (Gershuni, 2018b; Rabbis of the Beit Hillel Beit Midrash, 2016), yet some oppose such unions. Opposers raise concerns about the hereditary aspect of disability (Gershuni, 2018b). The complexity of matchmaking increases when the candidate has a disability since there is some reluctance to arrange matrimony in these cases (Gershuni, 2018b; Greenberg et al., 2012). The matchmaking of disabled people requires extra sensitivity, and it needs to be a match that will satisfy the families of both sides. The disabilities of the young couple need to be considered "equal" (for instance, both have Down syndrome) (N. Feldman, 2015). There is tension between the centrality of family life and marriage (as late bachelorhood can make one feel excluded from the community) and the suspicion and hesitation towards the union of disabled persons (Gershuni, 2018b).

Halachic commands concerning the Jewish home and intimacy are binding for disabled and non-disabled persons alike. At the time of engagement, the couple must have the ability to observe the complex Halachic laws of family purity (Gardin, 1988). Marriage counselors who specialize in working with disabled people assist couples in understanding these commands and their meanings as they strive to make the complex purification procedures accessible (Rabbis of the Beit Hillel Beit Midrash, 2016).

Most disabled married couples live in the community, with or close to their families. However, despite strong family ties, not all disabled persons can live independently with little assistance, and some require supported housing. There are various housing projects throughout Israel, suiting different types of disabilities, function levels, and other traits of their residents, such as their religious affiliation (Katzav & Nieman, 2015; Lerner, 2008). Due to the distinct characteristics of the Haredi society, Ultra-Orthodox have separate housing. Most state-sponsored sheltered housing (contrary to institutions) house approximately six tenants of mixed genders and rarely allow romantic socializing. The facilities that accept couples do not offer much privacy, as there are usually three to four other roommates in the apartment (Lerner, 2008). In comparison, the specialized Haredi housing projects provide the following options: all male or all female apartments for unmarried tenants and private accommodations for couples not available to the non-Haredi population.

Methodology

This research applies qualitative methodologies to explore the relationships, sexuality, and intimacy of disabled people in the Haredi community. We performed semi-constructed in-depth interviews with individuals who take an active role in the lives of disabled Haredi persons. We then performed deductive content analysis to uncover the values underlying the construction of sexuality and disability, their meaning, and the practical solutions they generate.

During the first stage of the research, we interviewed individuals engaged in the intimate lives of disabled Haredi couples. We interviewed twenty-six participants, eight therapists and social workers, eight workers and professionals in the housing projects, three family members, three bride counselors, two rabbis, two matchmakers, and two social activists. Due to ethical limitations, we could not interview the disabled couples themselves. We recruited participants mainly through a personal acquaintance with the community, and additional participants were recruited through the "snowball" method, as one interviewee referred another.

One of the limitations of this study was the relatively small pool of potential participants as there are a limited number of people who specialize in and work with young people with disabilities. Also, due to the strong community ties and connections, most of the potential participants know each other; this benefited us in reaching additional interviewees and, at the same time, limited their number. This setting raised different concerns of anonymity; in addition to participants knowing each other, it was easy to identify who the participants were in these closed communities, as only a few people work with this population.

The first part of the interview dealt mainly with clarification and questions related to the role the participant fulfills and their connection to the research. In the second part, we focused on specific topics not yet addressed in the first part. The issues were challenges facing disabled adults in the Haredi community, sources of support, the participant's approach to relationships and marriage of disabled people, the factors affecting decision making, the place of the Halacha in decision making, etc. Before being interviewed, the participants signed consent forms, and the interviews were recorded and fully transcribed with the participants' consent.

We changed identifying details and names of all participants as much as possible. Due to the prevalence of stigmatic perceptions of disability in the Haredi community, we chose to offer anonymity to all participants to avoid any potential harm.

During the second stage of the study, we performed a deductive qualitative content analysis (Bengtsson, 2016; Elo & Kyngäs, 2008; Forman & Damschroder, 2007; Patton, 2014). We sought to test preexisting theoretical assumptions regarding the construction of rights in the Ultra-Orthodox community. We followed Gershuni (2018a), who suggested that the liberal individualistic discourse of rights is foreign to the Haredi understanding of the social structure, favoring traditional community-oriented discourse. Orr et al. (2021a, 2021b) found that the localization of disability rights in Haredi society takes place by adapting them into familiar traditional values. Based on this previous research, we articulated our basic assumption that the construction of sexuality and sexual rights of disabled persons in Haredi society will be based not on a human or disability rights discourse but rather on adapting conventional Haredi values. Therefore, our research illustrates the construction of disabled sexuality by identifying these values, their meaning, and their implementations.

Our deductive content analysis allowed us to code our data into categories based on previous theoretical and empirical findings (Bengtsson, 2016; Elo & Kyngäs, 2008; Patton, 2014). The analysis was carried out based on categorization, disassembling, and classifying the data. In addition, we closely examined each category to identify its meaning within the theoretical framework and research questions. We used the Nerlaser software to compile the data while maintaining a balance between the methodological specifications (Shkedi & Shkedi, 2005).

We coded our findings in three steps. First, we searched for terms that described traditional Haredi values relevant in this context. We traced three central values that recurred throughout the data: 1) importance of marriage, 2) family purity, and 3) modesty. Second, we coded the meaning given to these values by the participants in the context of our research. Finally, we realized our participants referred to the real-life implementation of the values. Thus, during the third step of coding, we coded the practical solutions associated with these values. To conclude the analysis, we applied disability studies theory to understand how this value-based conceptualization of the sexuality of disabled persons can be interpreted in other cultural settings.

Findings

The interviews yielded detailed accounts of social perceptions and regulation of disabled sexuality and intimacy in Haredi society. We found that most participants refrained from openly discussing sexuality, especially the physical aspect of sexual relations. The words "sexuality" and "sex" were not mentioned as they are not part of the Haredi vocabulary, as it is immodest to discuss such issues. When they brought up sexuality, they used obscure terminology such as "intimacy," "relations," and "need." Participants we interviewed in their professional capacity were more open to an explicit discussion. Despite their unwillingness to openly discuss sex, the participants were open to answering questions and offering insights regarding marriage, weddings, and disabled couples.

The participants did not use rights terminology or turn to disability rights or sexual rights as a conceptual framework. Instead, they favored religious reasoning and talked about values and duties. We identified three central values that our participants referred to: 1) importance of marriage, 2) family purity, and 3) modesty. These traditional religious values are at the heart of Haredi existence and are significant in the sexuality-related discourse. We further identified the meanings assigned to these values and their practical applications.

The importance of marriage

Sexuality is an inseparable part of marriage; it is essential for procreation and childbirth. The importance of marriage derives from its institutional significance, community values, duties, and religious commandments. It is one's obligation to marry and form a Jewish home. Matrimony is a key to being a full member of society and part of the social norm.

The centrality of marriage is vital to understanding the motives of those who support the marriage of disabled people, despite possible reservations.

Therefore, the participant often opened the talk with a statement underscoring the centrality of marriage and the Jewish home.

"Rabbi Padot" (rabbi at a rehabilitation center for people with disabilities) emphasized the importance of forming a family: "First of all, we need to know that we are talking about an ideal. The ideal is that everyone should get married. Everyone who can get married should get married. That is the ideal. "

"Shoshana" (the rabbi's wife, works in a Haredi high school for disabled girls and acts as a matchmaker for her students) stated that working with disabled persons requires courage and effort. She told us of a father to an adult intellectually disabled son who wished to consult her husband about his son's marriage. The rabbi explained that it is the father's Halachic duty to arrange the marriage considering intellectual and mental disabilities:

> So, my husband told him unequivocally that it is your duty to marry your son and help him in whatever way you can . . . but it is your duty as a father to find a match for your son.

"Nurit" (parental advisor for parents with high-functioning autistic children) advocates for the marriage of young adults with intellectual disabilities, as she believes that one's marital status is important; she also believes it is beneficial for one's well-being: "We want them to get married because couples can't live out of wedlock. And we want them to be a couple. And we think that being in a relationship is a good thing for the soul and your life."

The meaning of marriage is so great that it extends to disabled Haredi persons; participants stated it is a religious duty and a command to help them get married.

Some addressed the needs of disabled persons themselves. They referred to a need for intimacy, including sexual intimacy, using the term "need." The proper way to fulfill these needs is through marriage.

"Nehama" (a manager of a housing project) consulted the rabbi about whether to encourage unmarried residents to find a match. The rabbi accentuated that marriage could answer the need for intimacy, and that is a *mitzvah* (a religious commandment):"So, he told me – if you identify people who have a need, it is a mitzvah to get them married."

"Simha" (head of the housing project) made a similar statement. Simha shared the answer she received from a Rabbi: "So he [the tabbi] told me: if you identify people who need it, then it is right to get them married . . . that means that you have solved half of their problems. It is a basic need."

"Shira" (a matchmaker whie specializes in disabled Haredi people) is highly encouraging of these marriages. She was somewhat surprised with our questions, as the answers were evident in her eyes. She emphasizes the emotional aspects and benefits of marriage and addresses the difficulties of solitariness:

Q: What does marriage contribute to disabled people?

What does marriage contribute to *you*? Because he limps? Or because they have learning disabilities? Or because he cannot hear?

Q: What if they cannot lead an independent life?

Especially in these cases! God has said that man should not be alone. This need is for closeness, understanding, affection. One of the hardest things in life is loneliness.

Despite the participants' general support of disabled persons' matrimony, this is an intricate, delicate process in a social setting where the negative medicalized view of disability is prevalent. Many still express hesitation regarding such weddings. A specialized matchmaking system was created to provide a solution. The matchmakers we interviewed explained that their work requires cautiousness, courage, and additional efforts. Their caution is essential in promising that disabled persons will meet potential partners.

Shira explains that her work involves a rigorous examination of the candidates' medical and familiar backgrounds to find a suitable partner with a compatible disability (for example, a couple with Down syndrome). She can never pressure the families (unlike in non-disabled matches) and makes do with offering names for both sides.

> When I have an offer, I first turn to the parents discreetly . . . and if they are receptive to the offer, then I turn to the other side, again, without any mention of a name. Then if they say that yes, they are ready, I ask permission to say the name and how to call, and then I get out of the picture. I get out of the picture, and the parents will talk to each other. I have already given them the information. The parents want to talk to each other. What do I need to get involved? If they have a question if they need my help – that's something else.

The participants described the importance of marriage and establishing a Jewish home as a Halachic command and addressed some emotional aspects. Yet they did not resort to human rights terminology.

Family purity

Some of the most important commands in the Halacha that address private lives are the complex and detailed commands of family purity. Haredi youth marry young and do not have contact with the opposite sex before their engagement; thus, they require guidance and advice on what married life entails. The couple usually receives thorough instruction on these commands from bride and groom counselors before their wedding (Lehmann & Siebzehner, 2009).

When the bride and groom are disabled, their ability to marry is determined by their capability to maintain family purity. Understanding these commands is a necessary condition for marriage. "Tamar" (a disability activist) explains the essential difference between marriage and sexuality in Haredi communities compared to the secular population. For Haredi, marriage is the only way to have intimate relations; in the general society, casual relationships outside matrimony are allowed and accepted. She believes the need to make sure that the engaged couple will be able to keep family purity adds an additional burden:

> It doesn't exist in the secular population. It is much easier there for people with disabilities to have intimate relations. No one checks whether you understand or not [how to maintain family purity]; it does not interest them. The very fact that you want it [intimate relations and sex] is enough. In our community, you need to be sure that you are not violating a command. You need to prove that you can withhold the restrictions of the Halacha, and that's a lot more difficult.

As disabled couples are expected to uphold the commands, they receive close guidance and supervision from either family members or counselors when they struggle to do so. Marriage is contingent upon this external assistance in understanding when it is past the date suitable for the *Mikveh*.

"Rabbi Rubinstein" (a Halachic counselor to supported housing) clarifies that the practitioners involved with arranging the couples' marriage must ensure proper Halachic supervision of family purity; lack of such control jeopardizes the union: "Whoever marries off the couple must be responsible. If they are married, and they do not know how to heed the Torah, then they are forbidden to marry, for it is like the marriage of brother and sister."

Rabbi Rubinstein also stresses the heavy responsibility of parents:

> Parents really have a very big responsibility . . . [t]o know that they live [according to the Halacha]. It is written in the Gemara. In the Gemara as well. So, a woman who does not know so, ah . . . there are those who check them, check her to see that she is pure.

Family life and purity regulation have taken different shapes over time, particularly in supported housing projects. These projects provide a meticulous system in which all aspects of sexuality are supervised and conducted under the Halacha, and therefore, they constitute a fascinating research arena.

"Ayala" (a bridal counselor) explains that the Haredi supported housing scheme was designed to facilitate couples' leading a proper Jewish lifestyle:

> When such a couple lives independently in the community, and they do not have our supervision, it may look as if they are managing on their own, and it will look perfect to you. So, you might ask why they need supported housing. But when you get down to the details, you will discover all the gaps, and you will see all the sad mishaps. . . . That's a couple that has sex freely even when they are forbidden from doing so. Simply free, completely free.

We asked Ayala about birth control that prevents menstruation and can spare some Halachic scrutiny. Ayala was vigorously opposed and stated that there is no need for such measures and that proper guidance is sufficient. She emphasized the importance of the *Mikveh* in the couple's intimacy:

> To deprive them of it. What do they have in life? They do not have children. . . . [W]hat do they have? Do they have a house? Can they cook food? They have intimacy! And the *Mikveh* enriches them and makes it more interesting for them!

This statement is fascinating, as it acknowledges sexual needs and desires at the same time as it demonstrates negative assumptions regarding disability and parenting. Despite the pronatalist nature of Haredi society, there are severe reservations regarding the parenting abilities of disabled couples. For disabled persons, there is a detachment between marriage, intimate relations, and parenting. Supporting unions of disabled couples rests on the value of marriage itself. At the same time, for other Haredi youth, these are two inseparable aspects of family life, as marriage is also the means to have children and fulfill the command of procreation. Though interesting, this discussion goes beyond the scope of this chapter.

The welfare authorities support and finance the Haredi housing projects and subject them to policies, procedures, and guidelines regarding placement and management. For example, in apartments assigned to couples, additional criteria are intended to ensure the ability to observe family purity. Ayala explains how a couple was denied entrance to the facility based on this criterion:

> We didn't receive them. We do not just receive anyone . . . because, from the Halachic viewpoint, Rabbi Rubinstein says we can only accept someone who can exercise discretion and the ability to resist [sexual] gratification. He said that we couldn't use our judgment; resisting gratification is a must.

"Mika" (a mother) has an adult daughter with intellectual disabilities. Mika described her daughter's wearisome journey. The daughter and her husband were denied supported housing due to a false claim of their inability to observe family purity:

> They called me to a meeting and told me that they had decided not to accept her. . . . [T]o this day, I cannot tell you for sure what their reason was; the reason according to them was that they were concerned that they couldn't maintain family purity commands. It wasn't even relevant because she was getting an injection [for birth control] every three months, so there was no question of menstruation.

Mika did not challenge the general decision to condition entry upon observing the Halacha. However, she opposed the factual decision in her daughter's case.

Tamar, the social activist, believes the scrupulous intervention and regulation in the name of family purity is excessive and harmful. She contends that this rigorousness stems from the structure of the housing project, which imposes a heavy Halachic responsibility on its owners and workers:

> If she does not go to the *Mikveh*, then you're in trouble. You are responsible if they cross the street dangerously or overeat chocolate and if they keep their house clean. You must get into their life, know when she purifies, if she takes a purification break, and when. You know if she did her check-ups properly or not, and that can create impossible situations. Impossible. It creates situations where people cannot consummate their relationship because they're constantly being examined.

Tamar, Haredi herself, suggests giving the couple more choice in the matter:

> I would like Hannah Levy [a counselor in the housing project] to be there, but without the responsibility, understand? She will be an option. She'll be such a nice and pleasant option that most of the people will want to meet with her once a week and will want her help on matters of Halacha and relationships in general.

There may be rabbis who will support Tamar's approach. However, as Rabbi Rubinstein clarified, others believe they cannot trust the couple due to their disabilities.

The housing projects in this context exhibit two supposedly contrasting principles. On the one hand, there is the possibility of intimate personal relationships and sexuality. But, on the other hand, it is subject to even stricter regulation, which interferes with the couple's independence and subjugates their sexual lives to constant Halachic supervision.

Modesty

Modesty, the third value we identified, is closely associated with privacy; all aspects of sexuality and intimacy are considered part of the private sphere; hence, public discussion or mentioning is immodest and forbidden. Indeed, the first finding of this research was the marginality of sexuality and the fact that participants knowingly avoided any explicit mentioning.

"Rasie" (a bridal counselor) describes how Haredi brides are reluctant to ask questions and talk about sex: "One says to me, 'What?! I will have to tell him I am in menstruation?! It is not nice! To say that?"

Or a bride who worries about the relative openness of her future husband's family to what she perceives as intimate details:

> I had a bride who said, "I made a mistake. . . . [T]he groom's family is talking too openly.' "

Q. On intimate matters?

Yes. Let us say someone says I'm five months pregnant. . . . [S]he says that in her family, they don't mention it at all.

These descriptions are more relevant when it comes to disabled persons. "Ahuva" (who runs an advocacy group for intellectually disabled Ultra-Orthodox women) encountered a problem discussing intimacy:

> When the conversation arose within the group about who would get married and who would not, there were parents who just really took it very hard. How can I bring such matters, and how can I call myself an Ultra-Orthodox woman that I allow them to talk about whether to get married or not get married? You must understand that the whole conversation was about marriage, and marriage it was not something . . . beyond that. And there was nothing very, very. . . . [I]t was not at all about intimate things."

The religious value of modesty played a central role in forming the unique Haredi supported housing projects. When it was suggested to open designated housing, Haredi representatives explained to welfare authorities that residents must lead a modest Jewish lifestyle; as "Bracha" (head of a housing project) describes:

> In that conference, they presented the project with three couples in an apartment for six. So, we said that it does not suit us in terms of the Halacha. It damages family values. We said that we could only agree to have each couple living separately. Within the community but separately. That's it.

Tamar, the disability activist, adds:

> In the secular sheltered housing, there are couples in the same house. Did you know that? According to the Ministry of Welfare, the size and budget of the apartments obligate six people in an apartment, so they put three couples in one place. This cannot be done in our community since it doesn't work in terms of the Halacha, modesty, etc.

This successful demand was based on a religious reasoning rather than a liberal one that failed to make a similar impact.

Discussion

This chapter interrogates how the sexuality of intellectually disabled persons is constructed and understood in Ultra-Orthodox communities in Israel. In recent years, disability studies and advocacy have embraced human rights terminology. Sexuality is also a part of this change, with emphasis on sexual rights over sexual needs. Yet the liberal conceptualization is often insufficient to comprehend the practices and customs of non-liberal societies, such as Haredi Jews. Following Gershuni (2018a) and Orr et al. (2021a, 2021b), we identified the values that underpin the construction of the sexuality of disabled people. The values determined to be central in the context are 1) the importance of marriage, 2) family purity, and 3) modesty.

Marriage is a powerful institution and one of the anchors of the Haredi understanding of sexuality and disability. Matrimony is an unavoidable rite of passage and a condition of being a full community member. Life as a single individual is not a suitable option for young people, disabled or not. Thus, the Haredi community created a specialized matchmaking mechanism to arrange suitable marriages for persons with disabilities. In a society that encourages sexual relations between the husband and wife, the support of marriage also signifies recognition of disabled persons' sexuality. It appears that in this setting, disabled people get an unexpected advantage. The religious duty to wed leads to marriages of people who might otherwise encounter significant barriers on their way to finding a partner. Consequently, being married allows Haredi access to some aspects of sexuality and intimacy while disabled persons in the general society often struggle to be considered sexual beings.

Family purity is one of the basic commands in Judaism that dominates and dictates how the Haredi conduct their intimate lives. The complex rules raise concerns regarding the couple's ability to understand their practical and religious meaning. Specialized support and guidance systems were designed to verify that disabled people follow these essential commands. The counselors accompany them before and after marriage, providing accessible information on all aspects of sexuality, both physical and spiritual, allowed under the Jewish law.

The importance of modesty is evident in linguistic choices and the content of Haredi discourse. For example, it is improper and immodest to discuss intimate topics such as sexuality with others. Modesty also created the need for unique housing solutions, which offer optimal privacy to the married couple. Consequently, the Haredi community articulated a demand for better quality supported housing, funded and supervised by the state. Making this claim on the grounds of modesty, contrary to relying on a right to privacy as done by non-Haredi organizations and advocates, proved successful.

We identified a model that enables the realization of the sexuality of Haredi disabled people within the boundaries of the Halacha. This is a relatively progressive scheme considering the conservative nature of the Ultra-Orthodox and their traditionalist views of sexuality and disability. They recognize disabled persons' sexuality, support and assist them in meeting a potential spouse, and provide extensive sexual education and appropriate spaces where couples can engage in sexual acts. Yet, as we will elaborate, there are significant reservations one should be aware of when evaluating or applying this model elsewhere.

Applying disability theory to the social construction in Haredi society provides an opportunity to examine the relationship between religious values and human rights. It reveals options and solutions that are foreign to the human rights framework and can provide new insights. Furthermore, these findings can be adapted to suit other cultural settings (Ingstad, 2007), as is seen in Table 14.1.

Table 14.1 Central values, their meaning and practical implementation, and their reevaluation using disability theory

	Importance of Marriage	*Family purity*	*Modesty*
Meaning	Marriages of disabled adults are accepted, and their sexual needs are acknowledged	Concerns regarding the couple's capacity to understand the commands and their ramifications	No open discourse or explicit terminology. Intimacy between spouses requires privacy in residence.
Implications	Marriages are arranged by designated matchmakers who specialize in working with disabled persons	Close supervision and receive extensive guidance regarding family purity and proper sexual practices	Designated supported housing programs financed by the welfare system, accommodating each couple in a separate apartment
Disability theory perspective	Acknowledging disabled sexuality, creating spaces and opportunities for making connections	Providing adequate sexual education and support. Attentiveness to one's capacity to understand and consent to sexual acts.	Redesigning supported housing, preferring community housing, using public resources to respect and promote disability rights

Supporting marriage and intimate relationships contradicts deeply rooted assumptions regarding the capacity of disabled people to engage in meaningful relationships. It also challenges the portrayal of disabled people as asexual or childlike. In a non-Haredi setting, such an understanding can support various sexual expressions, identities, and relationships. It is essential to keep in mind that some people in the Haredi community, including those working with disabled people, have voiced their opposition to arranging such marriages. Therefore, this research does not aim to fully represent the Ultra-Orthodox society as there is no unanimous agreement on these matters. However, this study provides a window into the intimate lives of Haredi disabled people.

Haredi attitudes towards the sexuality of disabled persons may vary depending on gender, as sexuality carries different meanings, duties, and obligations for Haredi men and women, yet this didn't come through significantly enough in our data. We focused on the couple and the institute of marriage in this study, yet we believe that further research should address possible gender biases.

A central barrier disabled people face in search of sexual partners is the inaccessibility of public and social spaces that prevent them from making acquaintances, especially for romantic or sexual purposes (Emens, 2009). The Haredi matchmaking model shows the importance of creating accessible spaces and opportunities to realize one's sexuality. The Halachic requirement of rigorously supervising the ability of disabled couples to observe family purity led to the creation of a counseling system for young couples. The need to cope with the challenge of purity created an opportunity for accessible sexual education and guidance. The services provided by the Haredi community shed light on this and call for a reevaluation of the scope of sex education and counseling available for intellectually disabled people nowadays.

The Haredi housing projects enable couples to enjoy the advantages of state-financed residence while maintaining their privacy. It is an example of what public assisted-living solutions can and should be and what welfare services can offer when they are willing and attentive. The housing projects are relatively new; however, it is unclear whether this results from the diffusion of new norms or simply outsourcing services previously offered by the community. As we know, disabled Haredi couples also live independently in their communities with the close assistance of their families.

Applying disability theory in adapting elements of the Haredi conceptualization can assist in promoting disability sexual rights in other social settings. It is a circular process in which a critical rights-based discourse adapts new ideas and conventions from a traditionally conservative environment. The Haredi will then absorb norms and notions of disability sexual rights and defuse and adapt them into Orthodox discourse.

There are significant reservations to be considered in such a process. Haredi people with disabilities have a chance to realize their sexuality, but they do so under strict regulation, with very little autonomy and choice. We may identify statements that correlate with a critical-social approach and supposedly reveal progressive trends, yet this is not necessarily the case. Liberal thinking is foreign to the Ultra-Orthodox way of life, and these seemingly progressive ideas are rooted in tradition and religious law. The Haredi demonstrate a narrow definition of sexuality; they do not recognize same-sex relationships, premarital sex, autoerotic practices, or non-heteronormative identity. The supervision of sexual lives and practices extends to all community members. This heavy regulation exists throughout the lifespan, with explicit rules that differ in every stage of life. Hence, when we discuss the possibilities of Haredi disabled persons, we must understand the restrictive setting in which they arise.

Conclusion

Ultra-Orthodox Jewish communities in Israel demonstrate a unique understanding and conceptualization of the sexuality of intellectually disabled persons. Our research revealed a complex social structure built around three central values: 1) importance of marriage, 2) family purity, and 3) modesty. These values are essential to the Haredi way of life; they are at the heart of the Jewish home. In the context of intellectually disabled persons, these values have specific meaning and interpretation. The social significance of marriage has cleared the path for the marriage of disabled persons, with sexual intimacy being a vital component of married life and regulated by commands of family purity. A comprehensive counseling system assists disabled couples in observing Halachic commands. This support is offered both in the community and in specialized, state-sponsored assisted living solutions.

Our research reveals that the general conservatism that characterizes traditional and highly religious societies can present itself differently in some cases. Haredi have severe limitations, strict rules, and a narrow definition of what proper sexuality is. They often have negative stigmatic perceptions about disabled people and what it means to live with a disability. Despite this starting point, the juxtaposition of sexuality and disability in this setting reveals progressive elements. Nonetheless, the Haredi social structure raises major reservations to consider when examining our results elsewhere.

While rights discourse is foreign to the Haredi society, its existence within the general population enables the allocation and localization of new norms, adapted and intertwined with preexisting values and beliefs. The specific combination of community values, religious duties, and the impact of the general Israeli society has allowed Haredi communities to develop an innovative conceptual and practical conceptualization of disability and sexuality.

It is unclear what level of impact the general society has and to what extent the allocation of disability rights influences this social construction. There is very little research into disability rights in Haredi culture. It does not offer a comparative historical account of how sexuality and disability were addressed before introducing disability rights. We should cautiously say that it is possible that parts of this scheme relied on traditional Haredi thinking and existed before changes in the general understanding of disabled persons' sexuality. Yet, while previous research focused on interpreting disability rights into Haredi values, our study suggests a way to adapt the Haredi values back into the disability rights discourse.

Our study illuminates several important aspects that require further research. First, a study focused on intellectually disabled persons' voices that illustrates how they perceive their sexuality and social setting. Second, other aspects, such as employment and education, should be thoroughly examined to trace the adaptation of disability rights into Haredi values and vice versa. Third, additional research into how disability rights are understood and utilized in deeply religious communities, such as Haredi Jews, is required. Finally, as the disability cause is a global, transnational one, we must map the different interpretations and adjustments for non-liberal cultures.

Note

1 The term "family purity" refers to a set of religious laws that deal with the ritual purity and impurity of the Jewish couple. They regulate the intimate relationship of the couple according to the woman's menstrual cycle. Any physical contact between the couple is forbidden during menstruation and the following days as she is considered impure (the Halachic term is *Niddah*). Then the woman must submerge in the ritualistic purity bath called *Mikveh* to purify herself; from that point onwards, the couple is allowed to have intercourse, touch, and be intimate until the next menstruation begins (Gardin, 1988; Feldman, 1992; Ribner, 2003).

References

AKIM – The National Organization for people with Mental Disabilities and thier Families. (2013). The inclusion index of people with mental disabilities in Israeli society. https://www.kshalem.org.il/wp-content/uploads/2020/12/45%D7%94%D7%A2%D7%AA%D7%A7-%D7%A9%D7%9C-%D7%9E%D7%93%D7%93-%D7%94%D7%94%D7%9B%D7%9C%D7%9C%D7%94-%D7%94%D7%9E%D7%9C%D7%90-%D7%92%D7%A8%D7%A1%D7%94–26112020.pdf

Bagenstos, S. R. (2009). *Law and the contradictions of the disability rights movement*. Yale University Press. https://doi.org/10.12987/yale/9780300124491.001.0001

Barzilai, G. (2013). The different among us: law and political boundaries of religious fundamentalism. *Eyunei Mishpat*, 27(2), 587–625.

Bengtsson, M. (2016). How to plan and perform a qualitative study using content analysis. *NursingPlus Open*, 2, 8–14. https://doi.org/10.1016/j.npls.2016.01.001

Bokek-Cohen, Y. (2018). The dual role of jewish matchmakers: sympathetic helpers versus community boudaries policemen. *Australian Journal of Jewish Studies*, *31*, 27–52.

Boni-Saenz, A. (2015). Sexuality and incapacity. *Ohio State Law Journal*, *76*(6).

Cahaner, L., & Malach, G. (2019). *The haredi society yearbook 2019*. The Israel Democracy Institute. https://www.idi.org.il/books/29375

Cohen, Y., & Tsuria, R. (2019). A match made in the cloud: jews, Rabbis, and online dating sites. In A. Hetzroni & M. Tuncez (Eds.), *It happened on tinder: reflections and studies on internet – infused dating* (pp. 177–190). The Institute of Network Cultures.

Cook, J. A. (2000). Sexuality and people with psychiatric disabilities. *Sexuality and Disability*, *18*(3), 195–206. https://doi.org/10.1023/A:1026469832339

Degener, T. (2017). A new human rights model of disability. In V. Della Fina, R. Cera, & G. Palmisino (Eds.), *The united nations convention on the rights of persons with disabilities: a commentary* (pp. 41–59). Springer International Publishing. https://doi.org/10.1007/978-3-319-43790-3_2

Drum, C. E., Krahn, G. L., & Bersani, H. J. (2009). Models and approaches to disability. In C. E. Drum, G. L. Krahn, & H. Bershani Jr. (Eds.), *Disability and public health* (pp. 27–44). American Public Health Association.

Elo, S., & Kyngäs, H. (2008). The qualitative content analysis process. *Journal of Advanced Nursing*, *62*(1), 107–115. https://doi.org/10.1111/j.1365-2648.2007.04569.x

Emens, E. F. (2009). Intimate discrimination: the state's role in the accidents of sex and love. *Harvard Law Review, 122*(5), 1307–1402. https://doi.org/10.2139/ssrn.1694174

Feldman, N. (2015). *Health and medical culture in the ultra-Orthodox "society of matchmakers"* (Master's Thesis). Tel Aviv University [Hebrew]. http://primage.tau.ac.il/libraries/theses/humart/free/002533814.pdf

Feldman, P. (1992). Sexuality, birth control and childbirgh in orthodox Jewish tradition. *CMAJ – Canadian Medical Association, 146*(1), 29–33.

Foley, S. (2012). The UN convention on the rights of persons with disabilities: a paradigm shift in the sexual empowerment of adults with down syndrome or more sound and fury signifying nothing? *Sexuality and Disability*, *30*(4), 381–393. https://doi.org/10.1007/s11195-012-9279-z

Foley, S. (2019). *Intellectual disability and the right to a sexual life: a continuation.* Routledge.

Forman, J., & Damschroder, L. (2007). Qualitative content analysis. In L. Jacoby & L. A. Siminof (Eds.), *Empirical methods for bioethics: a primer advances in Bioethics* (Vol. 11, pp. 39–62). Emerald Group Publishing Limited. https://doi.org/10.1016/S1479-3709(07)11003-7

Friedman, M. (1991). *The haredi (Ultra Orthodox) society – sources, trends and processes – Jerusalem Institute for Policy Research.* The Jerusalem Institute of Israeli Studies.

Gardin, S. K. (1988). The laws of taharat hamishpacha: potential effects on fertility. *Journal of Biosocial Science*, *20*(1), 9–17. https://doi.org/10.1017/S002193200001720X

Gershuni, C. (2018a). The discourse of equal rights of people with disabilities in the Haredi community. In H. Zicherman & Y. Margaliyot (Eds.), *The law and the haredim in Israel* (pp. 323–359). Tel Aviv University [Hebrew].

Gershuni, C. (2018b). *The right to marriage of ultra-orthodox women with disabilities – critical aspects* (Master's Thesis). Tel Aviv University [Hebrew].

Greenberg, D., Buchbinder, J. T., & Witztum, E. (2012). Arranged matches and mental illness: therapists' dilemmas. *Psychiatry, 75*(4), 342–354. https://doi.org/10.1521/psyc.2012.75.4.342

Guterman, M. A. (2008). Observance of the laws of family purity in Modern-Orthodox Judaism. *Archives of Sexual Behavior*, *37*(2), 340–345. https://doi.org/10.1007/s10508-007-9261-5

Harpur, P. (2012). Embracing the new disability rights paradigm: the importance of the convention on the rights of persons with disabilities. *Disability and Society*, *27*(1), 1–14. https://doi.org/10.1080/09687599.2012.631794

Heilman, S. (2021). Passages: matchmaking, betrothal, and wedding. In *Defenders of the faith* (pp. 277–290). University of California Press. https://doi.org/10.1525/9780520354494-020

Heyer, K. (2015). Rights enabled. In *Rights enabled*. University of Michigan Press. https://doi.org/10.3998/mpub.5946811

Hoffman, S. (2020). *Standards of sexual modesty, gender separation and homosexuality: rabbinic and psychological views*. Mondial.

Ingstad, B. (2007). Seeing disability and human rights in the local context: botswana revisited. In B. Ingstad & S. Reynolds whyte (Eds.), *Disability in local and global worlds* (p. 255). University of California Press.

Katzav, M., & Nieman, C. (2015). *Best practices of social services in the State of Israel 2015*. The Ministry of Social Affairs and Services.

Lehmann, D., & Siebzehner, B. (2009). Power, boundaries and institutions: marriage in ultra-Orthodox Judaism. *Archives Europeennes de Sociologie*, *50*(2), 273–308. https://doi.org/10.1017/S0003975609990142

Leon, Nissim. (2016). The ethnic structuring of "sephardim" in haredi society in Israel. *Jewish Social Studies*, *22*(1), 130. https://doi.org/10.2979/jewisocistud.22.1.04

Lerner, N. (2008). The land of limited possibilities The right of people with intellectual disabilities to live in the community. www.bizchut.org.il [Hebrew]

Lifshitz, H., & Globerman, R. (2006). The attitude of ultra-orthodox society towards the exceptional person: from the stigma effect to the 13 adaptation effect. In M. Hovav & P. Gittleman (Eds.), *From differentiation to integration: dealing with disabilities in the community* (p. 147). Carmel Press.

Linton, S. (1998). Disability studies/not disability studies. *Disability and Society*, *13*(4), 525–539. https://doi.org/10.1080/09687599826588

Malach, G., & Cahaner, L. (2019). *The yearbook of ultra-orthodox society in Israel 2018 – The Israel Democracy Institute*. The Israel Democracy Institute. https://en.idi.org.il/publications/25651

Manor-Binyamini, I. (2012). Parental coping with developmental disorders in adolescents within the ultraorthodox Jewish community in Israel. *Journal of Autism and Developmental Disorders*, *42*(5), 815–826. https://doi.org/10.1007/s10803-011-1313-y

Mor, S., & Pikkel, R. B. (2019). Disability, rights, and the construction of sexuality in Tort Claims. *Law and Society Review*, *53*(4). https://doi.org/10.1111/lasr.12438

Nahary, G., & Hartman, T. (2020). Orthodox Jewish women's sexual subjectivity. *Sexual and Relationship Therapy*, 1–19. https://doi.org/10.1080/14681994.2020.1743972

Nosek, M. A., Foley, C. C., Hughes, R. B., & Howland, C. A. (2001). Vulnerabilities for abuse among women with disabilities. *Sexuality and Disability*, *19*(3), 177–189. https://doi.org/10.1023/A:1013152530758

Oliver, M. (1990). *The politics of disablement: a sociological approach*. Palgrave Macmillan.

Oliver, M. (1996). The social model in context. In *Understanding disability* (pp. 30–42). Macmillan Education UK. https://doi.org/10.1007/978-1-349-24269-6_4

Orr, Z., Unger, S., & Finkelstein, A. (2021a). The challenges and dilemmas of local translators of human rights: the case of disability rights among Jewish ultra-orthodox communities. *Journal of Human Rights*, 1–17. https://doi.org/10.1080/14754835.2020.1868294

Orr, Z., Unger, S., & Finkelstein, A. (2021b). Localization of human rights of people with disabilities: the case of Jewish ultra-orthodox people in israel. *Human Rights Quarterly*, *43*(1), 93–116. https://doi.org/10.1353/hrq.2021.0003

Patton, M. Q. (2014). *Qualitative research & evaluation methods: integrating theory and practice*. Sage Publications.

Perlin, M., Cucolo, H., & Lynch, A. (2017). Sex, sexuality, sexual offending and the rights of persons with mental disabilities. *Laws*, 6(4), 20. https://doi.org/10.3390/laws6040020

Perlin, M. L. (2008). Everybody is making love/or else expecting rain: considering the sexual autonomy rights of persons institutionalized because of mental disability in Forensic Hospitals and in Asia. *Washington Law Review*, *83*(4), 481–512.

Perlin, M. L., & Lynch, A. J. (2016). Sexuality, disability, and the law: beyond the last frontier? In *Sexuality, disability, and the law: beyond the last frontier?* Palgrave Macmillan. https://doi.org/10.1057/9781137481085

Rabbis of the Beit Hillel Beit Midrash. (2016). Marriage of people with developmental intellectual disabilities. In B. Lao (Ed.), *And there are no equal opinions about the status of a person with intellectual and developmental disabilities in the world of Israeli tradition* (pp. 220–231). Van Leer Institute.

Raz, A. (2015). Premarital carrier testing and matching in Jewish communities. In A. Shaw & A. Raz (Eds.), *Cousin marriages: between tradition, genetic risk and cultural change* (pp. 185–201). Berghahn Books.

Raz, A., & Vizner, Y. (2008). Carrier matching and collective socialization in community genetics: Dor Yeshorim and the reinforcement of stigma. *Social Science and Medicine*, *67*(9), 1361–1369. https://doi.org/10.1016/j.socscimed.2008.07.011

Ribner, D. S. (2003). Determinants of the intimate lives of Haredi (Ultra-Orthodox) Jewish couples. *Sexual and Relationship Therapy*, *18*(1), 53–62. https://doi.org/10.1080/1468199031000061263

Rosenbaum, T. Y., De Paauw, E., Aloni, R., & Heruti, R. J. (2013). The ultra-orthodox Jewish Couple in Israel: an interdisciplinary sex therapy case study. *Journal of Sex and Marital Therapy*, *39*(5), 428–435. https://doi.org/10.1080/0092623X.2011.644653

Ruiz, F. J. (2017). Committee on the rights of persons with disabilities and its take on sexuality. *Reproductive Health Matters*, *25*(50), 92–103. https://doi.org/10.1080/09688080.2017.1332449

Sabatello, M. (2014). Disability, human rights and global health: Past, present, future. In M. Freeman, S. Hawkens & B. Bennet (Eds.), *Law and global health current legal issues* (Vol. 16, pp. 244–263). Oxford University Press.

Sanders, T. (2007). The politics of sexual citizenship: commercial sex and disability. *Disability and Society*, *22*(5), 439–455. https://doi.org/10.1080/09687590701427479

Schaaf, M. (2011). Negotiating sexuality in the convention on the rights of persons with disabilities. *Sur International Journal on Human Rights*, *8*(14), 113–132. https://sur.conectas.org/en/negotiating-sexuality-convention-rights-persons-disabilities/

Shakespeare, T. (2000). Disabled sexuality: toward rights and recognition. *Sexuality and Disability*, *18*(3), 159–166. https://doi.org/10.1023/A:1026409613684

Shakespeare, T. (2006). *Disability rights and wrongs*. Routledge.

Shakespeare, T. (2013a). The social model of disability. In L. J. Davis (Ed.), *The disability studies reader* (4th ed., pp. 214–221). Routledge.

Shakespeare, T. (2013b). *Disability rights and wrongs revisited* (2nd ed.). Taylor and Francis. https://doi.org/10.4324/9781315887456

Shakespeare, T., Davies, D., & Gillespie-Sells, K. (1996). *Sexual politics of disability: untold desires*. Bloomsbury Academic.

Shakespeare, T., & Richardson, S. (2018). The sexual politics of disability, twenty years on. *Scandinavian Journal of Disability Research*, *20*(1), 82–91. https://doi.org/10.16993/sjdr.25

Shakespeare, T., & Watson, N. (2001). The social model of disability: an outdated ideology? *Research in Social Science and Disability*, 2, 9–28. https://doi.org/10.1016/S1479-3547(01)80018-X

Shildrick, M. (2007). Contested pleasures: the sociopolitical economy of disability and sexuality. *Sexuality Research and Social Policy*, *4*(1), 53–66. https://doi.org/10.1525/srsp.2007.4.1.53

Shildrick, M. (2013). Sexual citizcenship, governance and disability: from foucault to Deleuze. In S. Roseneil (Ed.), *Beyond citizenship?* (pp. 138–159). Palgrave Macmillan. https://doi.org/10.1057/9781137311351_7

Shkedi, A., & Shkedi, Y. (2005). *Narralizer: a software for qualitative research analysis (Version 1.01.001)*. Yazamut Yakum.

Shuttleworth, R., & Mona, L. (2002). Disability and sexuality: toward a focus on sexual access. *Disability Studies Quarterly*, *22*(4), 2–9.

Shuttleworth, R. P. (2007). Disability and sexuality: toward a constructionist focus on access and the inclusion of disabled people in the sexual rights movement. In N. Teunis & G. Herdt (Eds.), *Sexual inequalities and social justice* (pp. 174–207). University of California Press.

Stadler, N. (2019a). The new haredi family. In *A well-worn tallis for a new ceremony* (pp. 66–86). Academic Studies Press. https://doi.org/10.1515/9781618110664-007

Stadler, N. (2019b). *A well-worn tallis for a new ceremony*. Academic Studies Press. https://doi.org/10.1515/9781618110664

Stein, M., & Stein, P. (2007). Beyond disability civil rights. *Hastings Law Journal*, *58*(6), 1203–1240. https://doi:10.2139/ssrn.1552010

Tal, A. (2016). Be fruitful and multiply: Jewish procreation and Ultra-Orthodox fertility. In *The land is full addressing overpopulation in Israel*. Yale University Press. https://www-degruyter-com.ezproxy.haifa.ac.il/document/doi/10.12987/9780300224955-010/html

Taragin-Zeller, L., & Kasstan, B. (2021). 'I didn't know how to be with my husband': state-religion struggles over sex education in Israel and England. *Anthropology & Education Quarterly*, *52*(1), 5–20. https://doi.org/10.1111/aeq.12358

Taub, T., & Werner, S. (2016). What support resources contribute to family quality of life among religious and secular Jewish families of children with developmental disability? *Journal of Intellectual & Developmental Disability*, *41*(4), 348–359. https://doi.org/10.3109/13668250.2016.1228859

Tepper, M. S. (2000). Sexuality and disability: the missing discourse of pleasure. *Sexuality and Disability*, *18*(4), 283–290. https://doi.org/10.1023/A:1005698311392

United Nations. (2006). Convention on the rights of persons with disabilities. https://www.un.org/development/desa/disabilities/convention-on-the-rights-of-persons-with-disabilities.html

Vardi, M., Orr, Z., & Finkelstein, A. (2019). Civic engagement of students from minority groups: the case of ultra-orthodox students and communities in Jerusalem. In D. Y. Markovich et al. (Eds.), *Understanding campus-community partnerships in Conflict Zones* (pp. 261–292). Springer International Publishing. https://doi.org/10.1007/978-3-030-13781-6_11

Wenger, B. S. (1999). Mitzvah and medicine: gender, assimilation, and the scientific defense of "family purity". *Jewish Social Studies*, *5*(1–2), 177–202. http://www.jstor.org/stable/4467548

Whiteley, C., Coyle, A., & Gleeson, K. (2017). An idiographic analysis of women's accounts of living with mental health conditions in Haredi Jewish communities. *Mental Health, Religion and Culture*, *20*(3), 277–293. https://doi.org/10.1080/13674676.2017.1354820

Zicherman, H., & Cahaner, L. (2012). *Modern harediism an ultra-orthodox middle class in Israel*. The Israel Democracy Institute. https://www.idi.org.il/books/5737 [Hebrew]

15

ON THE HIERARCHY OF HUMAN RIGHTS OF PERSONS WITH DISABILITIES AND HIGHER EDUCATION

Capturing the fulfilment of the right to accessibility in Indonesia

Despan Heryansyah and Sahid Hadi

Introduction

The accessibility of higher education[1] for persons with disabilities is an important discourse in the contemporary context. In Indonesia, this is important because Thohari, for instance, revealed that 84% of educational institutions, specifically in Malang City, East Java, including universities, did not provide reasonable accommodation and were not in accordance with the needs of persons with disabilities, both in services and physical facilities and infrastructure.[2] Bullying of persons with disabilities also still occurs at the university level.[3] This indicates that most universities are not fully accessible for persons with disabilities.[4] As noted by Riyadi, "Universities have not been able to fulfill the right to access education for persons with disabilities"[5] in Indonesia.

Indonesia, in fact, has a strong commitment to the field of education to ensure and fully promote all categories of rights and freedoms for persons with disabilities based on the spirit of equality. Its foundational basis lies in the Preamble of the 1945 Indonesian Constitution (the Constitution) that the state formation was intended to educate the life of the nation.[6] That is the reason that Article 28C paragraph (1) jo. Article 31 of the Constitution stipulates that everyone, including persons with disabilities, has the right to self-development, to obtain education, and to benefit from science and technology.[7] Law Number 12 of 2012 on higher education strengthens it by affirming that higher

DOI: 10.4324/9781003410089-18

education is held with democratic, fair, non-discriminatory principles and upholds human rights.[8] Specifically, Law Number 8 of 2016 on persons with disabilities (the Indonesian Act on Persons with Disabilities) states that persons with disabilities have the right to education and the right to accessibility.[9] With the right to accessibility, persons with disabilities also have the right to take advantage of public facilities and get reasonable accommodation when accessing higher education.[10]

The fact that universities are not fully accessible to persons with disabilities makes us aware that the normative guarantee of the fulfillment of the right to accessibility in higher education for persons with disabilities has not been implemented properly. In this regard, this research was conducted to identify the barriers faced empirically by persons with disabilities in accessing universities and the implications of these barriers to the fulfillment of equal rights for persons with disabilities in the context of the right to accessibility and higher education.

Research questions

This study focuses on two research questions. First, how is the empirical portrait of the fulfillment of the right to accessibility for persons with disabilities in universities in the Special Region of Yogyakarta? Second, how does (in)accessibility of higher education affect the fulfillment of the right to accessibility for persons with disabilities in universities?

Research method

This was empirical research. The research locations consist of six universities in the Special Region of Yogyakarta, Indonesia: namely, the Atma Jaya University Yogyakarta (UAJY), Gadjah Mada University (UGM), Muhammadiyah Yogyakarta University (UMY), Yogyakarta State University (UNY), Sunan Kalijaga State Islamic University Yogyakarta (UIN Suka), and the Islamic University of Indonesia (UII). These universities were chosen because they represent adequately public, private, and religion-based universities.

The research data was primary in the form of direct assessments regarding the right to accessibility for persons with disabilities at the six universities by going directly to the field and conducting interviews. Interviews were conducted of 19 people as representatives of the six universities, of whom 3 were students with disabilities and 2 were lecturers with disabilities. In each university, our resource persons consisted of university leaders such as the chancellor, vice chancellor, secretary to the chancellor, and/or deputy dean as a faculty representative; head of sub-section for the facilities and infrastructure, equipment, and transportation; and representatives of the public relations section for universities, lecturer representatives, and students with disabilities. At the UIN Suka and UGM, interviews were also conducted with the head of the disability service center or unit at each university.

The primary data was supported by secondary data in the form of laws and regulations in Indonesia and primary legal materials related to disability and higher education, such as the Constitution and Law Number 8 of 2016 on Persons with Disability (Indonesian Act on Persons with Disabilities). Other secondary data in this research consists of books, journals, and other written documents related to disability and higher education and secondary legal materials.

The direct assessment of the right to accessibility for persons with disabilities at the research locations was conducted based on five categories of barriers for persons with disabilities (indicators) as developed by the Center for Human Rights Studies of the Islamic University of Indonesia (PUSHAM UII). As noted, this was constructed "using the approach of the social model as its methodological basis."[11] The indicators in question are as follows:[12]

1. Physical facilities and infrastructure barriers. Assessment based on this indicator was conducted by identifying, at least, 1) the unavailability of physical facilities and infrastructure in the research locations so that persons with disabilities will have difficulty accessing higher education and 2) available physical facilities and infrastructure at the research locations that make higher education accessible for persons with disabilities.
2. Behavioral barriers. Assessment based on this indicator was conducted by identifying acceptance or rejection as well as responses from universities regarding the presence of persons with disabilities.
3. Legal and procedural barriers. Assessment based on this indicator was conducted by examining university-level policies and/or procedures that are detrimental to persons with disabilities in accessing higher education and those that promote equality and fulfillment of the right to accessibility for persons with disabilities in the research locations.
4. Technology, information, and communication barriers. Assessment based on this indicator was conducted by identifying 1) the unavailability of technology, information, and communication facilities at the research locations so that persons with disabilities will have difficulty accessing higher education and 2) the availability of technology, information, and communication facilities that make higher education accessible for persons with disabilities.
5. Resource barriers. Assessment based on this indicator was conducted by identifying 1) the unavailability of certain resources in the research locations so that persons with disabilities would have difficulty accessing higher education and 2) the availability of certain resources that make education accessible for persons with disabilities.

Legal analysis of the Indonesian Act on Persons with Disabilities: a brief introduction

This sub-chapter provides a critical review of the Indonesian Act on Persons with Disabilities (the Act).[13] The study focuses on the approach used in the regulation, particularly the approach to understanding disability conditions.

This is intended to identify the hierarchy of human rights for persons with disabilities, particularly in accessing higher education, which originates from the legal recognition of persons with disabilities. To justify the analysis of the approach in the Act, its derivative regulations are also examined.

The analysis focuses on the significance of the Act and how it, and its derivative regulations, define barriers for persons with disabilities. Narratively, the provisions analyzed are as follows:

1. "Persons with disabilities" according to Article 1 point 1 of the Act refers to "any person who experiences physical, intellectual, mental, and/or sensory limitations in the long term who, in interacting with the environment, may face barriers and difficulties to participate fully and effectively with other citizens based on equal rights."[14] This significance is also adopted by the Act's derivative regulations.[15] In the context of education, Article 1 point 3 of the Government Regulation Number 13 of 2020 on Reasonable Accommodation for Students with Disabilities (GR No. 13/2020) also sets out the same significance as the Act regarding persons with disabilities.
2. The Act and GR No. 13/2020 do not provide explanations regarding barriers for persons with disabilities. In fact, in their definition, both regulations emphasize one element: barriers. However, other derivative regulations of the Act contain such provisions. This is regulated in Article 19 paragraph (2) of Government Regulation Number 39 of 2020 on Reasonable Accommodation for Persons with Disabilities in the Judicial Process (GR No. 39.2020). The stipulation is that persons with disabilities may have visual, hearing, speech, communication, mobility, memory, and concentration barriers; intellectual, behavioral, and emotional/self-care barriers; and/or other barriers determined by the results of personal assessments.

These aforementioned provisions show that the significance of the Act, including its derivative regulations, categorizes persons with disabilities as persons with limited physical, intellectual, mental, and/or sensory abilities, whose limitations are inherent in a person individually and who "may" face barriers in interacting with the social environment. In terms of barriers, GR No. 39/2020, as the derivative regulation of the Act, attaches it to the body of a person with disabilities, in which persons with disabilities may have visual, hearing, speech, communication, mobility, memory and concentration barriers; intellectual, behavioral, and emotional/self-care barriers; and/or other barriers determined by the results of personal assessments. Explicitly, all barriers are attached to the body and organ function of persons with disabilities. In its explanation section, the Act also elaborates that the condition of physical disability, for instance, occurs due to impaired body movement function. Intellectual disability occurs due to impaired thought function. Mental/psychosocial disability[16] occurs due to impaired function of the mind, emotion, and behavior. This shows that the Act and its derivative regulations still individualize the viewpoint of disability issues.

This approach to disability is identical to the medical model,[17] in which disability is believed to be damage to the body[18] and individual impairment problems that may be caused by illness, accident, or other health conditions.[19] In these terms, the medical model itself "understands disability as a problem located in the individual."[20]

This was widely accepted for a long time,[21] but in the late 20th century, around the 1980s and 1990s, it drew substantial criticism.[22] This model has been criticized because the medical point of view of impairment and deficiency in persons with disabilities individually disrupts the principle of equal rights.[23] This point of view has led to the categorization of "normal" or "not normal" and "perfect" or "imperfect" people, which has negative connotations and demeans human dignity. The medical model also reduces the knowledge of persons with disabilities about their bodies and experiences.[24] Iriarte added,

> The disproportionate expense made on technology and research to "cure" disability when, first, there is insufficient evidence of the effectiveness of such techniques, and second, investment in improving social conditions for disabled people may have an even greater quality of life benefits.[25]

This debate, in turn, shifts the approach to looking at disability from the medical to the social model.[26]

The social model is different from the medical model. The social model sees disability as a situation caused by environmental conditions that are not accessible to the diversity inherent in each person.[27] Disability is a problem that is located outside the individual; it does not exist in the individual. For instance, a Deaf person cannot communicate with other people, not because of hearing impairment in thier ears, but because the people around them are unable to use sign language. A wheelchair user is unable to go to the second or third floor of an educational building, not because of an impairment in their legs, but because the education building does not provide adequate ramps or an elevator that is wide enough. A person with schizophrenia is not unable to take education because of their limitations or mental damage, but because the education system does not provide reasonable accommodation according to their needs, in terms of services, facilities, and infrastructure.

The key commitment to addressing disability issues is no longer focused on the logic and responsibility to fix the person[28] but to remove the environmental barriers (external factors) faced by persons with disabilities to improve their opportunities and quality of life.[29] As Hawking emphasized in the 2011 World Report on Disability, "in fact, we have a moral duty to remove the barriers . . . to unlock the vast potential of persons with disabilities."[30] Chan and Zoellick also commented that the conditions experienced by persons with disabilities today exist because "persons with disabilities experience barriers in accessing services," so "we must . . . remove the barriers which prevent them participating in their community; getting a quality education, finding decent work, and having their voices heard."[31] For instance, a Blind person will find it difficult to follow the educational process if the materials are available in written format only. The education system must, therefore, remove the barriers faced by persons with disabilities, among others, by providing materials in audio or Braille format. Carey also provided an example: "[P]eople who processed information more slowly would not necessarily be 'disabled' in settings that did not require them to process complex information or that provided for them to do so."[32] Today, the social model has succeeded in replacing the medical model and has had a major impact on the global discourse on disability.[33]

Thus, the Act has a paradigmatic problem. It still considers that disability is caused by limited circumstances within each individual internally. This is represented by the phrase "people who have physical, intellectual, mental, and/or sensory limitations." The Act also still considers that the condition of disability occurs because of an impairment in a person, starting from impaired function of body movement, thought, emotion, behavior, and/or the five senses. External barriers are positioned as additional variables that persons with disabilities "may" face when they interact with their environment as asserted by the regulations. This explicitly indicates that, according to the Act, whether or not there are external or environmental barriers, persons with disabilities are indeed persons with disabilities due to their limited physical, mental, intellectual, and/or sensory functions.

The Act, in fact, was established based on a consideration that "every citizen, including persons with disabilities, has legal standing and has the same human rights as Indonesian citizens."[34] Its establishment was also aimed at realizing equal rights and opportunities for persons with disabilities.[35] These are the main reasons that this law replaces its predecessor, Law Number 4 of 1997 on Persons with Impairments. The Act emphasizes that "Law Number 4 of 1997 on Persons with Impairments is no longer following the paradigm of the needs of persons with disabilities so it needs to be replaced."[36]

The impact of the significance promoted by the Act and its derivative regulations regarding persons with disabilities is the strengthening of the categorization of "perfect" and "imperfect" people or "normal" and "not normal" people. The degree and dignity of those who are perfect or normal tend to be considered hierarchically higher than those of the imperfect and not normal. Thus, legal factors remain to contribute to a situation where the hierarchy of human rights for those without disabilities is higher than for those with disabilities.

Empirical portrait of fulfillment of the right to accessibility for persons with disabilities in higher education in the Special Region of Yogyakarta: Findings

1. Universities and their perspective on persons with disabilities

There are two groups of perspectives on persons with disabilities based on research data. First, UIN Suka, UNY, and UGM consider disability a diversity aspect inherent in everyone. UIN Suka, UNY, and UGM have the same commitment that persons with disabilities have equal rights and obligations due to humanity. At UIN Suka, for instance, we got an answer from a lecturer that "persons with disabilities are people with different abilities . . . [I]t could be from a physical aspect, for example, which causes them not to have the same performance as others."[37] According to him, if persons with disabilities are considered to have the same needs and abilities as non-disabled people, then injustice will happen for both parties.[38] He also explicitly stated that the UIN Suka Disability Service Center (DSC) understands the condition of disability based on the social model, that "disability is the result of an unfair and unenabled social construction."[39] At UGM, a lecturer understands persons with disabilities from the perspective of balance in the context of perfection. He understands that perfection and imperfection are a necessity for everyone. Therefore, the perfection that one has should be used to cover the imperfection that others have. For him, perfection and imperfection are inherent in every human being. Thus, making one's degree and dignity different from others because of the difference is inappropriate for him.[40] Another lecturer also has the same perspective; according to her, disability and non-disability are only differentiating variables for each person, and that distinction does not affect the equality of human dignity.[41]

> *Sudut pandang disabilitas sudah berubah dan berevolusi. Dulu, penyandang disabilitas pernah dianggap sebagai orang sakit sehingga pendekatannya adalah menyembuhkan penyakit yang diidap seorang penyandang disabilitas. Kemudian, ini bergeser menjadi pendekatannya sosial. Saya menjadi disabilitas karena lingkungan, bukan karena diri saya. Menurut saya, penyandang disabilitas itu juga sama seperti yang lain. Artinya, setiap orang memiliki perbedaan masing-masing.*
>
> (The way people see disability conditions have changed and evolved. In the past, a person with disabilities was considered to be sick, so the approach was to cure the disease suffered by that person. Later, this shifted to the social approach. I became disabled because of the environment, not because of myself. In my opinion, persons with disabilities are the same as others. This means that everyone has their own differences.)
>
> Other interesting answers need to be promoted, that:
>
> *[O]tak kita yang membuat adanya disabilitas. Misalnya, Anda atau Saya dianggap bukan disabilitas. Namun, ketika Anda atau saya akan mengganti sebuah lampu di atap, apakah bisa tanpa alat bantu? Ndak bisa. Kenapa? Karena kita sama-sama pendek. Saat itulah Saya dianggap disabilitas. Saat saya punya alat bernama tangga, Saya bisa dan tidak disabilitas lagi.*

([It] is our brains that create disabilities. For example, you and I are considered to be non-disabled persons. However, when I am about to replace a lamp on the roof, is it possible without any tools? I cannot do that. Why? Because I am short. That is the situation when I was considered to be disabled. When I have a ladder as the tool, I can do it and no longer have any disability.)[42]

Second, UAJY, UII, and UMY see persons with disabilities as persons with special needs. At UAJY, for instance, there was a response that persons with disabilities "*harus memiliki perlakuan khusus di kampus karena tidak bisa disamakan dengan mahasiswa biasa*" (should have a special treatment on campus because it cannot be equated with ordinary students).[43] At the UAJY, one response said,

[S]ejauh pemahaman Saya, penyandang cacat dan berkebutuhan khusus perlu kita samakan perlakuannya. Sebagai manusia yang memiliki keterbatasan fisik, mereka juga tidak bisa dianggap sebagai anak tiri atau disingkirkan tetapi harus disejajarkan.

([A]s far as I understand, persons with impairment and special needs need to be treated equally. As humans who have physical limitations, for example, they also cannot be considered as stepchildren or removed but must be equated.)[44]

At UMY, when we asked about persons with disabilities, the response we got was that persons with disabilities were not limited to those with limits in the five senses but also included those with physical limitations that could be caused by impairment or age.[45]

2. Sunan Kalijaga State Islamic University (UIN Suka)

a. In regard to physical facilities and infrastructure barriers

UIN Suka has provided accessible physical facilities and infrastructure for persons with disabilities. As commented by a student,

Kalau sarana dan prasarana di bidang akademik sudah membantu. Di perpustakaan, ada layanan difa repository. Jadi, buku-buku bisa discan untuk dibaca dengan pembaca layar. . . . Layanan informasi pendaftaran sudah aksesibel. UIN juga memiliki Pusat Layanan Difabel yang membantu untuk mengurusi berkas-berkas kami.

(The facilities and infrastructure in the academic field have been helpfull. In the library, there is a *difa* repository service. So, books can be scanned so that they can be read with a screen reader. . . . Registration information service is already accessible. UIN Suka also has a Disability Service Center that helps to take care of our files.)[46]

Available physical facilities and infrastructure include the following: 1) wheelchairs to help Blind people, wheelchair users, the elderly, and the obese; 2) computers equipped with screen readers and books in Braille in the library; 3) the Faculty of Economics and Islamic Business has elevator facilities, an accessible bathroom, and a fairly inclusive building design; 4) each faculty has provided lecture rooms on the lower floor of the building to make the teaching and learning process accessible for persons with (physical) disabilities; and 5) mosques, religious laboratories, and the convention hall are accessible to persons with disabilities because the entrance has a ramp, the division of spaces is quite wide, and there is a guiding block. In terms of services, physical facilities and infrastructure are accessible for persons with disabilities. The service desk has been designed to be accessible for wheelchair users.[47] However, accessibility is not comprehensive enough and does not cover the campus environment as a whole. In these terms, physical facility and infrastructure barriers are still identified in the UIN Suka campus environment. These barriers include unavailable road signs; minimal parking spaces some points that are not accessible to wheelchair users; sidewalk access for pedestrians is not friendly for persons with physical and sensory disabilities because they do not have guiding blocks and/or handrails; some buildings are not equipped with elevators to access the upper floors; the doors in all buildings aren't wide enough, particularly for wheelchairs; the majority of bathrooms in the UIN Suka lecture building are not reasonably accessible for persons with disabilities; and the pedestrian bridge between buildings is not accessible, particularly for wheelchair and/or crutches users, because it only has stairs.[48]

b. In regard to resource and behavioral barriers

The perception of and treatment by the academic community at the UIN Suka to persons with disabilities is good. Bullying, violence, and discrimination against persons with disabilities, for instance, have not been reported. As a student said, "*Ya, respon dosen dan teman-teman positif. Mereka selalu bersedia membantu ketika saya menghadapi kesulitan. Tidak ada tindakan bullying atau diskriminasi yang saya rasakan.*" (Lecturers' and friends' responses are positive. They are always willing to help me when I face barriers. I do not feel any bullying or discrimination.)[49] Another student also confirmed that there was no violence committed by either students or lecturers, even though there were lecturers and campus employees who were indifferent to several events "which may be because of their character."[50] He also added that during exams, he gets additional and intensive time so that he can carry out the exam well.[51]

The academic community at the UIN Suka is quite supportive and responsive to helping persons with disabilities when needed. From the perspective of seeing persons with disabilities, a lecturer at UIN Suka stated that disability is a diverse aspect of human beings, so campus services and facilities must adapt to their needs to reflect justice and equality.[52] As stated by the UIN Sukas's representative, "*[K]ami juga siapkan layanan penerjemah bahasa isyarat ketika sholat berjamaah, khususnya sholat Jumat, di laboratorium untuk mengakomodir orang tuli.*" (We also provide [a] sign language interpreter services during congregational prayers, especially for Friday prayers, in the laboratory to accommodate Deaf people.)[53]

UIN Suka has a disability service center (DSC). It was established on May 2, 2007. The DSC has become a structural institution under the Research and Community Service Institute (LP2M) of the UIN Suka. Since 2015, the DSC has provided services to 55 students with disabilities at the UIN Suka.

c. In regard to legal and procedural barriers

The UIN Suka has declared itself an inclusive campus, although there is no internal regulation that explicitly emphasizes the fulfillment of the rights of persons with disabilities.[54] To support this commitment, the UIN Suka has a standard operating procedure for services for persons with disabilities and established a DSC that is specifically tasked with managing and intensively supporting all activities related to persons with disabilities.[55] The UIN Suka has an open policy for students with disabilities if they need an examination and assessment scheme according to their personal needs. The UIN Suka, through its DSC, has routinely held training on disability issues for lecturers and education staff.[56] Dissemination of information on disability issues is also adequately organized. The UIN Suka also routinely and adequately conducts data collection for students with disabilities in its environment, although data collection is not carried out for employees.

d. In regard to technology, information, and communication barriers

The UIN Suka has provided reasonable technology to meet the needs of persons with disabilities in the library. In addition, the UIN Suka also prepares a sign language interpreter if there are persons with disabilities who need them to communicate. However, the availability of technology, information, and communication has not covered the entire UIN Suka campus.

3. Atma Jaya University Yogyakarta (UAJY)

a. In regard to physical facilities and infrastructure barriers

The UAJY has provided accessible physical facilities and infrastructure for persons with disabilities. However, the existing physical facilities and infrastructure are not evenly distributed throughout the UAJY campus. The available physical facilities and infrastructure are 1) elevators in some buildings, such as in libraries and faculties other than the law faculty; 2) transit places for wheelchair users; 3) pick-up corners that are friendly to persons with disabilities; 4) road signs that are quite complete; 5) handrails in several places; 6) parking spaces that are wide enough and close to the campus; 7) access for pedestrians that is friendly to persons with disability; and 8) available ramps at several buildings.[57] However, there are still barriers to physical facilities and infrastructure for persons with disabilities; for example, there are no elevators at the law faculty; guiding blocks are not available; the entrances to rooms are still too narrow for wheelchair users, so they tend to be inaccessible; toilets are not accessible and inclusive because the door and toilet room are narrow; and data on students, lecturers, and employees with disabilities are not available.[58]

b. In regard to resource and behavioral barriers

The academic community at the UAJY is friendly to persons with disabilities. There are no reports of bad treatment, violence, or discrimination.[59] The academic community at UAJY is always willing to help persons with disabilities in their campus environment if needed. However, there is one note: namely, that charity-based and medical views are still identified so that capacity-building related to disability issues still needs to be promoted.

c. In regard to legal and procedural barriers

The UAJY does not have reasonable policies for disability issues on campus. For instance, the curriculum is prepared without considering the diversity of persons with disabilities in the UAJY campus environment.[60]

d. In regard to technology, information, and communication barriers

The UAJY has provided reasonable technology to meet the needs of persons with disabilities in the library. In addition, the guiding signs for persons with disabilities in the UAJY campus environment are also quite good. However, the availability of technology, information, and communication has not covered the entire UAJY campus environment: for example, the availability of sign language interpreters.

4. The Yogyakarta State University (UNY)

a. In regard to physical facilities and infrastructure barriers

The UNY already has physical facilities and infrastructure that support accessibility for persons with disabilities. In some buildings – the rectorate building, for example – there is a specific parking space for persons with disabilities located close to the building. Access to the building has also been equipped with a ramp, but the design does not fit universal standards. Some buildings, such as the post-graduate program building and the library, have elevators. Toilets that are accessible to persons with disabilities are also available but do not fit universal standards; the toilet door is a push door, not a sliding one, and the sink height exceeds 70 cm. The toilet space is quite spacious, and handrails are available next to the closet and around the sink. In addition to physical facilities and infrastructure that do not meet universal standards, there are still physical facilities and infrastructure barriers faced by persons with disabilities. For instance, inter-building access is not adequate because guiding blocks are only provided at crossroads; guiding blocks are not available inside the building; the campus service desk is higher than 70 cm., so it is not accessible for persons who need a maximum table height of 70 cm.; and the prayer room is not equipped with a ramp, so it is not accessible for wheelchair users.

b. In regard to resource and behavioral barriers

The UNY has never organized training related to disability issues for students, lecturers, and employees. However, the response of the academic community at the UNY is friendly for persons with disabilities. There are no reports of bullying, violence, or discriminatory treatment against persons with disabilities at the UNY.

c. In regard to legal and procedures barriers

The existing policies related to campus accessibility for persons with disabilities have not been identified. However, as a good practice, the UNY facilitates lecturers who are experts in using sign language and understand Braille for the teaching and learning processes of persons with disabilities. In addition, the UNY does not yet have a data collection system to identify persons with disabilities in its campus environment.

d. In regard to technology, information, and communication barriers

There was no report regarding technology, information, or communication barriers at the UNY. Reasonable accommodation for persons with disabilities in the context of technology, information, and communication has not been identified in the campus environment.

5. The Islamic University of Indonesia (UII)

a. In regard to physical facilities and infrastructure barriers

The UII has physical facilities and infrastructure that support accessibility for persons with disabilities. At some university buildings, parking spaces are provided specifically for persons with disabilities, but they are not equipped with guiding blocks or directions to access the campus environment. Access between buildings is not equipped with guiding blocks either. Guiding blocks are available in the law faculty, but their designs do not fit universal standards. Some university buildings have been equipped with elevators. Toilets that are accessible for persons with disabilities are also available. However, physical facilities and infrastructure barriers are still identified at the UII. In addition to the discrepancy in the design of existing accessible facilities and infrastructure with universal standards, the existence of elevators is still limited in some buildings; in fact, buildings at the UII, such as the law faculty, generally have more than one floor. The service counter is not accessible because its height exceeds 70 cm., so it is difficult for wheelchair users to access it. There are still many buildings that are not equipped with guiding blocks and road signs.

b. In regard to resource and behavioral barriers

In general, there are no reports regarding bad treatment, violence, or bullying of persons with disabilities at the UII. However, the UII has never conducted socialization and capacity building for disability issues in its campus environment.

c. In regard to legal and procedural barriers

The UII does not have a specific policy on the rights and/or accessibility of persons with disabilities. The UII also does not have an adequate data collection system for persons with disabilities in its campus environment.

d. In regard to technology, information, and communication barriers

Reasonable accommodation for persons with disabilities in the context of technology, information, and communication has not been identified in the campus environment.

6. The Gajah Mada University (UGM)

a. In regard to physical facilities and infrastructure barriers

The buildings at the UGM are divided into old and new buildings. In general, the new buildings at the UGM are fairly accessible for persons with disabilities. All new buildings at the UGM have accessible toilets for persons with disabilities and are equipped with ramps. In the rectorate building, there is a specific parking lot for persons with disabilities, which is located close to the building. There is a spacious elevator. In the library, there is also a computer with a screen reader feature and a ramp at the entrance. However, the old buildings at the UGM do not have the same level of accessibility as the new buildings. Physical facilities and infrastructure barriers are still being identified, such as toilets that are not fully accessible. There are no guiding blocks, road signs, or handrails.[61]

b. In regard to resource and behavioral barriers

The academic community at the UGM has a good culture of acceptance of persons with disabilities. No bullying, violence, or discrimination has been reported. It was reported that the academic community at the UGM is helpful to students with disabilities.[62] As noted by a student, "*Walau pun UGM tidak punya strukutr tertentu yang memang mengoordinasikan layanan bagi penyandang disabilitas, kulturnya UGM sebenarnya sudah mendukung inklusivitas.*" (Although UGM did not have a specific structure that coordinates services for persons with disabilities, UGM's culture actually supports inclusiveness.)[63] He also said:

> *Kita punya beberapa, difabel mental. Mereka bisa kuliah dengan baik dan tidak ada bullying. Jadi, lingkungan sosialnya UGM memang sangat mendukung menurutku. Aku juga bisa kuliah lancar karena temen-temenku. Ketika aku kesulitan, aku minta bantuan, mereka tidak pernah menolak dan selalu bantu.*
>
> (We have several friends with psychosocial disabilities. They can study well, and there is no bullying. So, in my opinion, UGM's social environment is supportive. I can also study smoothly because of my friends. When I'm in trouble and I ask for help, they never refuse and are always helpful.)[64]

The UGM has organized training on disability issues, specifically for internal public relations, the UGM protocol, and all secretaries at UGM.[65] The UGM also organized socialization related to disability issues on campus. In this case, the UGM has made a seven-minute video that contains introductions from students with disabilities at UGM.[66]

The UGM has a working group to respond to disability issues in its campus environment. This group is in charge of compiling data collection instruments for persons with disabilities in the UGM campus environment and preparing the establishment of a disability service unit at the UGM.

c. In regard to legal and procedures barriers

The UGM has a data collection system on the needs of persons with disabilities for applicants, lecturers, and employees. As noted by a students, "*Kalau mendata keberadaan penyandang disabilitas, UGM sejak dulu sudah punya data.*" (If collecting data about the presence of persons with disabilities, UGM has that data.)[67] However, the data collection system still has a problem in terms of accuracy. The data collection problems occur because 1) data fillers (applicants, lecturers, and employees) understand the column of "specific needs" in a broad sense, beyond the meaning of disability; and 2) the applicants are not open/transparent enough to enter data.[68] As confirmed by a student:

> *Itu sebenarnya masih masalah. Makanya, ke depan, tugas kelompok kerja termasuk mendata dan memastikan instrumen pendataannya benar. Kalau instrument pendataannya salah, hasil datanya akan salah. Saat ini, jenis pertanyaannya adalah pertanyaan terbuka. Jadi, temen-temen yang tidak paham makna disabilitas atau kebutuhan spesifik mengisi sesuai dengan kebutuhan-kebutuhan yang menurut mereka spesifik di luar konteks disabilitas. Akhirnya, data itu ada tetapi berantakan. Aku harus mengakui, belum ada saat ini data yang terintegrasi.*

(That is actually still a problem. Therefore, in the future, the task of the working group will include collecting data and ensuring that the data collection instruments are correct. If the data collection instrument is wrong, the results will also be wrong. Currently, the types of questions are open questions. So anyone who does not understand the meaning of disability or specific needs fill in according to needs that they think are specific outside the context of disability. Finally, the data is there, but it is a mess. I have to admit, there is not any integrated data currently.)[69]

The same point was also asserted by a lecturer in UGM:

> *Kalau kita bicara masalah pendataan, UGM memang belum punya data yang mutakhir terkait dengan jumlah mahasiswa disabilitas atau jumlah mahasiswa yang tidak disabilitas. Sebenarnya, pada saat penerimaan mahasiswa baru, ada pendataan. Dalam kasus ini, maksud pertanyaannya adalah untuk menentukan yang bersangkutan disabilitas atau tidak itu, namun terkadang agak abu-abu. Kalau tidak salah, kata-katanya adalah apakah anda memiliki kebutuhan khusus? Sayangnya, ersepsi dari mahasiswa bukan ke disabilitas. Padahal, intensi pertanyaan lebih ke apakah di antara kalian mengalami atau dalam kondisi disabilitas?*
>
> (If we talk about data collection, UGM does not have up-to-date data regarding the number of students with disabilities or the number of students without disabilities. Actually, at the time of admission of new students, there is data collection. In this case, the purpose of the question is to determine whether the person has a disability or not, but sometimes, it is a bit in a gray area. If I'm not mistaken, the question is "Do you have any special needs?" Unfortunately, the perception of students is not only about disability. In fact, the question is more whether or not you have or are in a disability condition?)[70]

The UGM does not have a written policy that specifically regulates the rights or accessibility of persons with disabilities. However, practical attempts to respond to the needs of persons with disabilities are usually based on the discretion of the campus leader. In this case, faculty leaders are responsive to the needs of persons with disabilities.[71] As a student commented, "*Itu diskresinya fakultas saat ini.*" (Today, it is the faculty's discretion.)[72] In the context of policy, he also explained:

> *Kalau di fakultas hukum, tempatku kuliah, semua kebijakan disesuaikan dengan aku. Sebagai contoh, ketika aku masih dalam masa orientasi, setiap mahasiswa baru diwajibkan menulis dengan tanga. Tetapi, aku tidak bisa. Lalu, aku bertanya, bolehkah aku menulis pakai komputer? Aku diizinkan saat itu. Saat ujian, juga begitu. Aku dibolehkan membawa*

laptop sendiri. Soal ujiannya disediakan dalam bentuk soft copy sehingga aku bisa mandiri seperti temen-temen yang lain juga.

(In law school, where I studied, all policies were adjusted to me. For example, when I was in orientation, every new student was required to write by hand. But I can't. Then I asked the committee, "Can I write on a computer?" I was allowed then. During exams, too. I am allowed to bring my own laptop. The exam questions are provided in soft copy so that I can be independent like other friends too in carrying out the exam.)[73]

d. In regard to technology, information, and communication barriers

Technology, information, and communication facilities at the UGM are accessible for persons with disabilities, particularly in new buildings. In the faculty of economics and business, for instance, information in visual form has been available so that it is quite accessible. At the law faculty, apart from the availability of information in visual form, the library has been equipped with a computer that has a screen reader feature to make it accessible for totally Blind and/or low-vision students.

7. The Muhammadiyah University of Yogyakarta (UMY)

a. In regard to physical facilities and infrastructure barriers

The UMY has old and new buildings. For new buildings, physical facilities and infrastructure are quite accessible. The buildings have been equipped with ramps, flat entrances, elevators, and toilets that are accessible for persons with disabilities, and they include supportive technology facilities for persons with disabilities. However, in the old buildings, the UMY still has physical facilities and infrastructure barriers for persons with disabilities. For instance, the entrance to the faculty of medicine is still using stairs, and no ramp can be accessed by wheelchair users. In addition, in the faculty corridor, there are no guiding blocks or handrails. Also, the floor is not flat.[74]

b. In regard to resource and behavioral barriers

The UMY has started paying attention to disability issues in the last five years. Regarding physical accessibility itself, the UMY has been paying attention to it since five to ten years ago.[75] There are no reports regarding bad behavior, violence, or discrimination against persons with disabilities at the UMY. The UMY also organizes thematic Real Work lectures, whose programs are related to disability issues. Socialization and training on disability issues at UMY are still limited. As a result, some lecturers do not fully understand the correct learning methods, particularly for Blind and Deaf persons.[76]

c. In regard to legal and procedures barriers

The UMY does not have an adequate data collection system to detect persons with disabilities in its campus environment.[77] The UMY does not have a policy that specifically regulates disability rights and/or issues. However, the UMY applies the campus policy of "healthy, comfortable, orderly, and safe." The UMY considers that this includes the comfort, order, and safety of persons with disabilities.[78] Since 2020, the UMY has provided the *bidik misi* scholarships for two prospective new students with disabilities.

d. In regard to technology, information, and communication barriers

The availability of technology and information in UMY's new buildings is relatively accessible, given that the new buildings have been designed with reasonable accommodation for persons with disabilities, in the form of services, physical facilities, and infrastructure.

(In)accessibility of higher education: Detecting the hierarchy of human rights for persons with disabilities in fulfillment of the right to accessibility

1. The right to accessibility for persons with disability in universities

The constitutional basis for the fulfillment of the right to accessibility in universities in Indonesia lies in Article 31 of the 1945 Constitution of Indonesia. The Constitution is committed to every citizen having the right to education. The government is mandated to organize an education system to educate the nation's life. The Constitution uses the phrase "every citizen," which includes persons with disabilities. Indeed, the Constitution does not explicitly and specifically mention the right to education for persons with disabilities. However, this is understandable, given that the constitution is a law whose rules are general so that its reach includes all people and citizens, including persons with disabilities. In addition, the article is also supported by Article 28H paragraph (2) of the Constitution, where everyone is guaranteed to be entitled to facilities and specific treatment to obtain the same opportunities and benefits in order to achieve equality and justice. Of course, this provision includes aspects of education, particularly in higher education.

These aforementioned constitutional commitments are translated into the Indonesian Act on Persons with Disabilities. Although the Act can still be criticized paradigmatically, as elaborated in the earlier subsections, mainly because its substance has not fully accommodated the social model, it has asserted the rights of persons with disabilities quite completely, including the right to accessibility. The right to accessibility itself, in the context of higher education, refers to the right to services and facilities provided for persons with disabilities to realize equal opportunities in higher education.

Article 10 of the Indonesian Act on Persons with Disabilities reaffirms the normative guarantee of the right to education for persons with disabilities. There are four points of rights applicable to persons with disabilities in accessing higher education: namely, 1) obtaining quality education in all types, pathways, and levels of education in an inclusive and specific way; 2) equal opportunity to become a lecturer or education staff member in all areas, types, pathways, and levels of education; 3) equal opportunities as the organizer of quality education in all types, pathways, and levels of education; and 4) reasonable accommodation as students. Article 10 of the Indonesian Act on Persons with Disabilities promotes equal opportunities for persons with disabilities to obtain an education, become students, and become lecturers and staff members in universities. In addition, the article emphasizes the need for reasonable accommodation for students with disabilities. In the context of the right to accessibility, then, the responsibilities of higher education include improving the social environment and education system that is accessible for persons with disabilities.

The Indonesian Act on Persons with Disabilities promotes an institution that supports inclusive and accessible higher education for persons with disabilities: the Disability Services Unit. Higher education, according to Article 42 paragraph (3) of the Indonesian Act on Persons with Disabilities, is required to establish this institution. It is used for:

a. Improving the competence of lecturers and education personnel in higher education in dealing with students with disabilities
b. Coordinating every work unit in universities in meeting the needs of persons with disabilities
c. Supervising and evaluating the implementation of reasonable accommodation
d. Providing counseling services to persons with disabilities
e. Conducting early detection for students with disabilities
f. Referring students who are indicated as persons with disabilities to doctors, psychologists, or psychiatrists if necessary
g. Providing socialization on disability issues and inclusive education systems to academics in the campus environment

The Indonesian Act on Persons with Disabilities also complements its regulation with sanctions if higher education institutions do not establish a disability service unit and realize their main duties and functions. The sanctions are based on Article 42 paragraph (7) of the Indonesian Act on Persons with Disabilities: namely, 1) written warning, 2) termination of educational activities, 3) suspension of license to provide education, and 4) revocation of license to provide education.

2. Hierarchy of human rights for persons with and without disability

There is still a hierarchy of human rights between persons with disabilities and persons without disabilities in the context of the fulfillment of the right to accessibility in higher education. First, from the perspective of seeing persons with disabilities, some campuses still see persons with disabilities as "disabled" or persons with impairment and limitation who have shortcomings, are not normal, and are not perfect. There are still categories of "normal" or "not normal" and "perfect" or "imperfect" people in higher education. This means that not all universities have an understanding that the disability condition is caused by environmental or external factors. This shows that persons with disabilities have not been fully seen as equal to persons without disabilities because they are still considered persons who have damage, limitations, and impairment. Therefore, persons without disabilities are hierarchically higher in degree and dignity than persons with disabilities.

Second, in terms of reasonable accommodation for persons with disabilities, the available facilities and infrastructure still favor of the needs of persons without disabilities. Physical facilities and infrastructure that are accessible and fit the needs of persons with disabilities are not fully available. If accessible facilities and infrastructure as forms of reasonable accommodation are available, the procurement has not been based on a full awareness that inaccessible physical facilities and infrastructure are the main factors (barrier) that cause disability conditions in everyone. Thus, the provision of physical facilities and infrastructure seems to be a formality because there is no adequate policy as a legal basis for procurement and its incompatibility with universal standards. In addition, services as a form of reasonable accommodations in universities have relatively equalized persons with disabilities with non-disabled persons, given that there are no reports from any university regarding bullying, violence, and/or discriminatory services for persons with disabilities.

3. Hierarchy of human rights among categories of disabilities

There is a hierarchy of human rights between categories of disability in the context of the fulfillment of the right to accessibility in universities. Referring to the interpretative scheme on persons with disabilities, the research data shows that universities tend to understand the issue of disability in terms of physical and sensory disabilities only so that persons with disabilities seem to be the only ones who use wheelchairs or crutches or are Blind or Deaf. In this case, when we asked about the availability of accessible physical facilities and infrastructure, for instance, most universities reported that they, to a limited extent, are seeking to fulfill the requirements for physical facilities and infrastructure that fit the needs of persons with physical and sensory disabilities, such as providing guiding blocks, handrails, ramps, classrooms downstairs, street signs, sign language interpreters, elevators, and computers with screen readers. Meanwhile, the need for physical facilities and infrastructure for persons with intellectual and mental/psychosocial disabilities was not identified from the results of observations and interviews, such as the preparation of learning materials according to the needs of persons with intellectual and mental/psychosocial disabilities, the preparation of a curriculum according to the needs of persons with intellectual and mental/psychosocial disabilities, and procurement of a space to release tension or a relaxation room for persons with intellectual and mental/psychosocial disabilities.

To determine the presence of persons with disabilities in higher education, the majority of universities still rely on the physical appearance of a person in the absence of adequate data collection systems to identify them. This shows that, although a university is successful in detecting the presence of persons with disabilities in its campus environment, the probability of detecting persons with intellectual and mental/psychosocial disabilities is fairly small. Therefore, counseling rooms that provide psychologists or psychiatrists are important facilities and infrastructure that need to be promoted in higher education. In this case, the UNY even admits that persons with mental/psychosocial disabilities are not detected or identified in the campus environment.

Based on the Indonesian Act on Persons with Disabilities, a disability service unit can maximize this data collection role. However, the data shows that only two universities have a disability service unit: the UIN Suka and UGM. In fact, with the main tasks and functions that have been determined by law, the disability service unit can not only assist universities in collecting data on persons with disabilities but also may handle the problem of gaps in reasonable accommodation between categories of disabilities.

4. Factors causing the hierarchy of human rights for persons with disabilities in universities

Five factors cause the hierarchy of human rights for persons with disabilities in universities: both the hierarchy between persons with disabilities and persons without disabilities and the hierarchy among categories of disabilities. They are:

a. The absence of a specific disability service unit

The disability service unit, an institution that functions as a provider of services and facilities for persons with disabilities, has an important role in encouraging the fulfillment of the right to accessibility for persons with disabilities in universities. The Indonesian Act on Persons with Disabilities has established the minimum functions of the disability service unit: namely,

1) Improving the competence of lecturers and education personnel in higher education in dealing with students with disabilities
2) Coordinating every work unit in universities in meeting the needs of persons with disabilities
3) Supervising and evaluating the implementation of reasonable accommodation
4) Providing counseling services to persons with disabilities
5) Conducting early detection for students with disabilities
6) Referring students who are indicated as persons with disabilities to doctors, psychologists, or psychiatrists if necessary
7) Providing socialization on disability issues and inclusive education systems to academics in the campus environment

The minimum function is being able to handle the problem of the hierarchy of human rights for persons with disabilities in universities based on the spirit of equality, not only by providing adequate services but also by creating an inclusive environment so that persons with disabilities can access the university environment freely, independently, safely, and comfortably. Unfortunately, the existence of disability service units in universities is still minimal.

b. Inadequate data collection systems

The data collection system is a key aspect. In providing accessible higher education for persons with disabilities, a data collection system can be an adequate first step to map the variety of disabilities that exist in universities and the barriers faced by persons with disabilities. The mapping based on an adequate data collection system will be useful for universities to develop a policy framework and provide accessible physical facilities and infrastructure for persons with disabilities. However, only two universities have carried out data collection related to persons with disabilities in the campus environment. The UIN Suka already has an adequate data collection system, and UGM has carried out good practices in terms of data collection, but these data collection systems still have a problem with regard to accuracy, due to incomplete and different interpretations of "persons with disabilities" and the openness of data entry.

c. Limited knowledge and understanding of disability issues by human resources at universities

Knowledge of disability issues is an important basis in responding to disability issues in universities. With knowledge of medical models in viewing persons with disabilities, for instance, human resources at universities may see persons with disabilities as disabled, not normal, and imperfect human beings. On the other hand, with knowledge of social models in seeing persons with disabilities, human resources at universities can understand persons with disabilities as those whose potential is locked due to barriers created by their social and external environment. This significant difference, of course, has different consequences. The first interpretive scheme, the medical model, leads human resources at universities to focus on efforts to "fix" persons with disabilities so that reasonable accommodation is not a major concern. On the other hand, the second interpretive scheme, the social model, focuses on human resources in universities taking adequate measures to remove external and environmental barriers that make universities inaccessible to persons with disabilities.

Human resources in universities, including civitas academic, unfortunately, do not have adequate knowledge and understanding of persons with disabilities and the rights of persons with disabilities in higher education.

d. The minimal and limited dissemination and capacity building on disability issues

Knowledge related to issues of disability is an important aspect in realizing accessible universities for persons with disabilities so that every element of the university must be equipped with this knowledge. In these terms, the knowledge related to issues of disability, at least, can guide universities to fulfill the right to accessibility for persons with disabilities. However, only two universities were identified to have carried out socialization on disability issues in their campus environment: namely, the UIN Suka, which has done it regularly, and UGM, which has done it partially to some human resources on campus. The absence of dissemination, including campaigns, regarding issues of disability means the academic community in universities are not aware of issues of disability, so it can trigger resource and behavioral barriers for persons with disabilities in accessing campus.

e. The absence of regulations on rights or accessibility for persons with disabilities

Universities in Yogyakarta do not have specific regulations on the rights or accessibility of persons with disabilities. As a result, the provision of reasonable accommodation is not based on a measurable policy. In general, the provision of reasonable accommodation, in the form of services and physical facilities and infrastructure, is only carried out as a response to emergencies. For instance, a reasonable accommodation that previously did not exist is provided just because the campus has students with disabilities later.

Conclusion

The fulfillment of the right to accessibility for persons with disabilities at universities in the Special Region of Yogyakarta has not been realized adequately. This portrait shows that the universities have begun to fulfill the right to accessibility for persons with disabilities. However, there is still serious work for universities to remove physical facilities and infrastructure barriers; resource and behavioral barriers; legal and procedural barriers; and technological, information, and communication barriers to fulfilling the right to accessibility for persons with disabilities. This study identifies that, at the practical level, 1) in terms of the hierarchy of human rights for persons with and without disability, persons without disabilities are hierarchically higher in degree and dignity than persons with disabilities in the context of the fulfillment of the right to accessibility in higher education, and 2) in terms of the hierarchy of human rights among categories of disabilities, persons with physical and sensory disabilities are still hierarchically higher in degree than persons with intellectual and mental/psychosocial disabilities in the context of the fulfillment of the right to accessibility in higher education. This study has also identified five factors that cause the hierarchy of human rights for persons with disabilities in universities, both the hierarchy between persons with disabilities and persons without disabilities and the hierarchy among categories of disabilities. They are the absence of a disability service unit at the university, the inadequate data collection systems, the limited knowledge and understanding of disability issues by human resources at the university, the minimal socialization and capacity building on disability issues, and the absence of regulations on rights of accessibility for persons with disabilities.

Notes

1 The term "higher education" will be used interchangeably with the term "university" in this chapter. This is because the term "university" is more familiar among Indonesians.

2 Slamet Thohari identified 125 public facilities in Malang City; 25 of them are educational institutions, including higher education. See, Slamet Thohari, "Views on Disability and Accessibility of Public Facilities for Persons with Disabilities in Malang City," *Indonesian Journal of Disability Studies*, Vol. 1, Issue 1, June 2014, p. 27–37.

3 See, Didit Haryadi (Ed.), *Kasus Bullying Mahasiswa Digabel, Gunadarma Bakal Disomasi*, 19 Juli 2017, https://nasional.tempo.co/read/892515/kasus-bullying-mahasiswa-difabel-gunadarma-bakal-disomasi/full&view=ok. Accessed June, 10, 2021.

4 Andayani Muhrisun Afandi, "Empowerment and assistance of communities with disabilities in accessing higher education," *APLIKASIA: Journal of Applications of Religious Sciences*, Vol. 16, No. 2, 2016, pp. 153–154. See also Donny Michael, "Organization of higher education for persons with disabilities at Brawijaya University," *Jurnal HAM*, Vol. 11, No. 2, 2020, pp. 2001–202. See also Akhmad Sholeh, "Islam and persons with disabilities: A study of accessibility rights of persons with disabilities in the education system in Indonesia," *Palastren*, Vol. 8, No. 2, 2015, pp. 294–296. Policies related to the education of students with disabilities have not yet reflected an important aspect of the educational needs of persons with disabilities: namely, the accommodation aspect. Education policies have not shown sensitivity towards education for persons with disabilities. Akhmad Soleh, "Policy of Yogyakarta State Universities towards persons with disabilities," *Journal of Islamic Education*, Vol. III, No. 1, 2014, pp. 2 and 26–27. See also M. Syafi'ie, "Accessibility fulfillment for persons with disabilities," *Inclusion Journal*, Vol. 1, No. 2, 2014, p. 280.

5 This is based on three considerations. First, universities do not have regulations as the basis for organizing higher education to be accessible for persons with disabilities, both inclusive and specific. Second, administrative policies are also inadequate. Third, practical policies are merely a form of empathy and symbolism. See Eko Riyadi, "Implementation of the fulfillment of the right to accessibility of higher education for persons with disabilities in Yogyakarta," *Ius Quia Iustum*, Vol. 28, No. 1, 2021, pp. 71–93.

6 Fourth paragraph of the Preamble of the 1945 Constitution of Indonesia.

7 The same provisions can be found in Article 12 of Law Number 39 of 1999 on Human Rights. Indonesia has also ratified the United Nations Convention on the Rights of Persons with Disabilities (UNCRPD) with Law Number 19 of 2011. Article 24 Paragraph (1) of the UNCRPD affirms that the state party is mandated to recognize the right to education for persons with disabilities. It is based on the principle of equal opportunity. The state is also required to ensure an inclusive education system at all levels of education. Eko Riyadi, "Implementation of Fulfillment . . ." *Op.Cit.*, p.72. See also Delia Ferri, "Unveiling the challenges in the implementation of Article 24 CRPD on the right to inclusive education. a case-study from Italy," *Laws*, Vol. 7,

No. 1, 2018, pp. 2–5. See also Gauthier de Beco, "The right to inclusive education: Why is there so much opposition to its implementation?", *International Journal of Law in Context*, Vol. 14, No. 3, 2017, pp. 2 and 6. See also Peter Mittler, "The UN convention on the rights of persons with disabilities: Implementing a paradigm shift," *Journal of Policy and Practice in Intellectual Disabilities*, Vol. 12, No. 2, 2015, p. 83.

8 Article 6 Letter b of Law Number 12 of 2012 on Higher Education.

9 Article 5 Paragraph (1) Letters e and m of Indonesian Act on Persons with Disabilities.

10 Article 18 of Indonesian Act on Persons with Disabilities.

11 Eko Riyadi, "A process that respects the principle of 'nothing about us without us," in Puguh Windrawan (Ed.), *Aksesibilitas Peradilan bagi Penyandang Disabilitas*, PUSHAM UII, Yogyakarta, 2015, p. vii.

12 See Puguh Windrawan (Ed.), *Aksesibilitas Peradilan Bagi Penyandang Disabilitas*, PUSHAM UII, Yogyakarta, 2015. However, resource and behavioral barriers are combined in the display of field data in this research. This is because, when our resources persons were asked, they explained the two barriers together and did not separate the explanations.

13 Law Number 8 of 2016 on Persons with Disabilities.

14 This replaces the definition of persons with impairments based on Law No. 4/1997 on Persons with Impairments. Based on Article 1 Point 1 of Law No. 4/1997, "person with impairments" refers to any person who has physical and/or mental disorders that can interfere with or are obstacles and barriers to their doing something properly.

15 The derivative regulations are Government Regulation Number 52 of 2019 on the Implementation of Social Welfare for Persons with Disabilities (GR No. 52/2019); Government Regulation Number 70 of 2019 on Planning, Implementation, and Evaluation of the Respect, Protection, and Fulfillment of Rights of Persons with Disabilities (GR No. 70/2019); Government Regulation Number 13 of 2020 on Reasonable Accommodation for Students with Disabilities (GR No. 13/2020); Government Regulation Number 39 of 2020 on Reasonable Accommodation for Persons with Disabilities in the Judicial Process (GR No. 39/2020); Government Regulation Number 42 of 2020 on Accessibility to Settlements, Public Services, and Protection from Disasters for Persons with Disabilities (GR No. 42/2020); and Government Regulation Number 60 of 2020 on the Disability Service Unit in the Employment Sector (GR No. 60/2020).

16 The term "mental disability" is based on the provisions of the Indonesian Act on Persons with Disabilities, which categorizes four types of disabilities. According to Article 4 Paragraph (1) of the Act, the first type is physical disability, the second type is sensory disability, the third type is mental disability, and the fourth type is intellectual disability. The term "mental disability" itself is equivalent to psychosocial disabilities.

17 See, Srikala Naraian, Sarah Schlessinger, "When theory meets the 'reality of reality': Reviewing the sufficiency of the social model of disability as a foundation for teacher preparation for inclusive education," *Teacher Education Quarterly*, Vol. 44, No. 1, 2017, p. 82. See also Teryl L. Dobbs, "A critical analysis of disabilities discourse in the journal of research in music education, 1990–2011," *Bulletin of the Council for Research in Music Education*, No. 194, 2012, pp. 8–10.

18 Eko Riyadi, "A Process that Respects . . ." *Op.Cit., hlm.viii.*

19 German Federal Ministry for Economic Cooperation and Development, *A Human Rights-based Approach to Disability in Development. Entry Points for Development Organizations*, p. 10. See also Agustina Palacios, "The Social Model in the International Convention on the Rights of Persons with Disabilities," *The Age of Human Rights Journal*, Vol. 4, 2015, p. 93. To see how persons with disabilities are treated

when disability is viewed using this model, see Nick Watson, Alan Roulstone, Carol Thomas (Ed.), *Routledge Handbook of Disability Studies*, Routledge, Oxon, 2012, p. 70. Mike Oliver calls the medical approach to disability "the personal tragedy theory of disability." Mike Oliver, "A New Model of The Social Work Role in Relation to Disability," in Jo Campling (Ed.), "The handicapped person. A new perspective for social workers?", *Proceeding of a Conference held at the Royal National Hospital for Rheumatic Diseases*, 17 September 1981.

20 Edurne Garcia Iriarte, "Models of disability," in Edurne Garcia Iriarte, Roy McConkey, Robbie Gilligan (Eds.), *Disability and Human Rights. Global Perspective*, Palgrave, London, 2016, p. 13.

21 See Colin Barnes, "Understanding the social model of disability: Past, present, and future," in Nick Watson, Alan Roulstone, Carol Thomas (Eds.), *Routledge Handbook . . . Op.Cit.*, pp. 12–29.

22 The debate started with a discussion of the meaning of "impairment," which tends to be inhumane and degrading to human dignity. The medical belief that disability is an individual impairment and the construction of disabled people is closely related to the meaning of damage, uselessness, and imperfection. All of them have negative connotations. Suparman Marzuki, "The judicial process must ensure accessibility for persons with disabilities," in Puguh Windrawan (Ed.), *Aksesibilitas Peradilan bagi Penyandang Disabilitas*, PUSHAM UII, Yogyakarta, 2015, p. xiii. See also Michelle A. Travis, "Gendering disability to enable disability rights law," *California Law Review*, Vol. 105, No. 3, 2017, p. 842. One study identified that "persons with disabilities started to organize themselves in the 1960s and 1970s in various parts of the world." Hisayo Katsui, "Key Concepts and Theories," in Hisayo Katsui, Shuaib Chalklen (eds.), *Disability, Globalization, and Human Rights*, Routledge, New York, 2020, p. 8.

23 The term "impairment" is close to the meaning of damage, uselessness, imperfection. Suparman Marzuki, "The Judicial Process . . ." *Loc.Cit.*

24 Edurne Garcia Iriarte, "Models of . . ." *Op.Cit.*, p. 16.

25 Ibid.

26 Michelle A. Travis, "Gendering Disability. . ." *Op.Cit.*, p. 838. Models in understanding disability are not theories, but models represent concepts or approaches that can guide when interacting with and making decisions for persons with disabilities. Edurne Garcia Iriarte, "Models of . . ." *Op.Cit.*, p. 13.

27 Edurne Garcia Iriarte, "Models of. . ." *Op.Cit.*, p. 17.

28 Ibid., p. 16.

29 Allison C. Carey, *On the Margins of Citizenship. Intellectual Disability and Civil Rights in Twentieth-century America*, Temple University Press, Philadelphia, 2009, p. 16.

30 World Health Organization, "World Report on Disability," WHO Press, Geneva, 2011, p. ix.

31 Ibid., p. xi.

32 Ibid.

33 Hisayo Katsui, "Key Concept . . ." *Op.Cit.*, p. 10. See also Stephen Bunbury, "Unconscious bias and the medical model: How the social model may hold the key to transformative thinking about disability discrimination," *International Journal of Discrimination and the Law*, Vol.19, No. 1, 2019. DOI: 10.1177/1358229118820742. See also Anna Lawson, Angharad E. Beckett, "The social and human rights model of disability: Towards a complementarity thesis," *The International Journal of Human Rights*, 2020. DOI: 10.1080/13642987.2020.1783533. At the regulatory level, see also the United Nations Convention on the Rights of Persons with Disabilities.

34 Considerations letter a of the Indonesian Act on Persons with Disabilities.

35 Considerations letter c of the Indonesian Act on Persons with Disabilities.

36 Considerations letter d of the Indonesian Act on Persons with Disabilities.
37 Interview with DF, a lecturer at the UIN Suka, on November 19, 2019.
38 Ibid.
39 Interview with Ar, a head of UIN Suka Disability Service Unit, on November 20, 2019.
40 Interview with SAD, a lecturer at the UGM and coach of a student activity unit on disability at the UGM, on December 3, 2019.
41 Interview with WH, a lecturer at UGM and head of the UGM Disability Service Unit Working Group, on December 10, 2019.
42 Interview with AAB in the UGM Chancellor's Secretary Room on December 10, 2019.
43 Interview with NI, a lecturer at UAJY, on November 20, 2019.
44 Interview with T, a representative from a faculty at UAJY, on November 20, 2019.
45 Interview with GB, a UMY representative, on November 13, 2019.
46 Interview with Ah, a Blind student at UIN Suka, on November 19, 2019.
47 This data was obtained by direct observation of lecture and rectorate buildings at UIN Suka on November 18, 2019, and interviews with R, head of certain sub-sections at UIN Suka, on November 19, 2019.
48 Interviews with R, head of certain sub-sections at UIN Suka, and Ah, a Blind student at UIN Suka, on November 19, 2019.
49 Interview with Am, a student with a physical disability at UIN Suka, on November 18, 2019.
50 Interview with Ah, a Blind student at UIN Suka, on November 19, 2019.
51 Ibid.
52 Interview with DF, a lecturer at the UIN Suka, on November 19, 2019.
53 Interviews with R, head of certain sub-sections at UIN Suka, on November 19, 2019.
54 Interview with W, a UIN Sukas representative, on November 20, 2019.
55 Interview with Ar, a head of UIN Suka Disability Service Unit, on November 20, 2019.
56 Interview with W, a UIN Sukas representative, on November 20, 2019.
57 This data was obtained by direct observation of lecture and rectorate buildings at UAJY on November 20, 2019.
58 This data was obtained by direct observation of lecture buildings at UAJY and interviews with S, the head of a certain section at UAJY, and NI, a lecturer at UAJY, on November 20, 2019.
59 Interview with NI, a lecturer at UAJY; A, a student at UAJY; and S, head of a certain section at UAJY, on November 20, 2019.
60 Interview with S, head of a certain section at UAJY, and T, a representative from a faculty at UAJY, on November 20, 2019.
61 This data was obtained from direct observations of lecture buildings and rectorates at UGM on December 28, 2019. This was also confirmed through interviews with resources person from UGM.
62 Interview with WH, a lecturer at UGM and head of the UGM Disability Service Unit Working Group, on December 10, 2019. Also, interview with SAD, a lecturer at UGM and coach of a student activity unit on disability at the UGM, on December 3, 2019.
63 Interview with TTW, a Blind student at the UGM, on November 27, 2019.
64 Ibid.
65 Interview with N, a representative from UGM public relations and protocol, on December 10, 2019.
66 Interview with TTW, a Blind student at the UGM, on November 27, 2019.
67 Ibid.
68 Interview with WH, a lecturer at UGM and head of the UGM Disability Service Unit Working Group, on December 10, 2019. D also stated, "*[M]asih banyak juga*

temen-temen disabilitas yang malu untuk mengungkapkan kondisinya." (There are still many disabled friends who are embarrassed to reveal their condition.) Interview with SAD, a lecturer at UGM and coach of a student activity unit on disability at the UGM, on December 3, 2019.

69 Interview with TTW, a Blind student at the UGM, on November 27, 2019.

70 Interview with SAD, a lecturer at the UGM and coach of a student activity unit on disability at the UGM, on December 3, 2019.

71 Ibid. Also, interview with GK, UGM representative, on December 10, 2019.

72 Interview with TTW, a Blind student at the UGM, on November 27, 2019.

73 Ibid.

74 This data was obtained by direct observation of buildings at UMY.

75 Interview with AS, a lecturer at the UMY and head of the Center for Disability and Humanity Studies of UMY, on November 21, 2019.

76 Ibid.

77 Ibid.

78 Interview with GB, a UMY representative, on November 13, 2019.

Reference

Andayani, Muhrisun Afandi, "Empowerment and Assistance of Communities with Disabilities in Accessing Higher Education", *APLIKASIA: Journal of Applications of Religious Sciences*, Vol. 16, No. 2, 2016.

Barnes, Colin, "Understanding the Social Model of Disability. Past, Present, and Future", in Nick Watson, Alan Roulstone, & Carol Thomas (Eds.), *Routledge Handbook of Disability Studies*. Routledge, Oxon, 2012.

Beco, Gauthier de, "The Right to Inclusive Education: Why is There so much Opposition to Its Implementation?", *International Journal of Law in Context*, Vol. 14, No. 3, 2017.

Bunbury, Stephen, "Unconscious Bias and the Medical Model: How the Social Model May Hold the Key to Transformative Thinking about Disability Discrimination", *International Journal of Discrimination and the Law*, Vol. 19, No. 1, 2019. DOI: 10.1177/1358229118820742

Carey, Allison C., *On the Margins of Citizenship. Intellectual Disability and Civil Rights in Twentieth-century America*. Temple University Press, Philadelphia, 2009.

Dobbs, Teryl L., "A Critical Analysis of Disabilities Discourse in the Journal of Research in Music Education, 1990–2011", *Bulletin of the Council for Research in Music Education*, No. 194, 2012.

Ferri, Delia, "Unveiling the Challenges in the Implementation of Article 24 CRPD on the Right to Inclusive Education. A Case-Study from Italy", *Laws*, Vol. 7, No. 1, 2018.

German Federal Ministry for Economic Cooperation and Development, "A Human Rights-based Approach to Disability in Development. Entry Points for Development Organizations", in Haryadi Didit (Ed.), *Kasus Bullying Mahasiswa Digabel, Gunadarma Bakal Disomasi*, 2017. https://nasional.tempo.co/read/892515/kasus-bullying-mahasiswa-difabel-gunadarma-bakal-disomasi/full&view=ok

Iriarte, Edurne Garcia, "Models of Disability", in Edurne Garcia Iriarte, Roy McConkey, & Robbie Gilligan (Eds.), *Disability and Human Rights. Global Perspective*, Palgrave, London, 2016

Katsui, Hisayo, "Key Concepts and Theories", in Hisayo Katsui & Shuaib Chalklen (Eds.), *Disability, Globalization, and Human Rights*, Routledge, New York, 2020

Lawson, Anna, & Angharad E. Beckett, "The Social and Human Rights Model of Disability: Towards a Complementarity Thesis", *The International Journal of Human Rights*, 2020. DOI: 10.1080/13642987.2020.1783533.

Marzuki, Suparman, "The Judicial Process Must Ensure Accessibility for Persons with Disabilities", in Puguh Windrawan (Ed.), *Aksesibilitas Peradilan bagi Penyandang Disabilitas*. PUSHAM UII, Yogyakarta, 2015.

Michael, Donny, "Organization of Higher Education for Persons with Disabilities at the Brawijaya University", *Jurnal HAM*, Vol. 11, No. 2, 2020.

Mittler, Peter, "The UN Convention on the Rights of Persons with Disabilities: Implementing a Paradigm Shift", *Journal of Policy and Practice in Intellectual Disabilities*, Vol. 12, No. 2, 2015.

Naraian, Srikala, & Sarah Schlessinger, "When Theory Meets the 'Reality of Reality': Reviewing the Sufficiency of the Social Model of Disability as a Foundation for Teacher Preparation for Inclusive Education", *Teacher Education Quarterly*, Vol. 44, No. 1, 2017.

Oliver, Mike, "A New Model of The Social Work Role in Relation to Disability", in Jo Campling (Ed.), *The Handicapped Person. A New Perspective for Social Workers? Proceeding of a Conference held at the Royal National Hospital for Rheumatic Diseases*, Radar, 17 September, 1981.

Palacios, Agustina, "The Social Model in the International Convention on the Rights of Persons with Disabilities", *The Age of Human Rights Journal*, Vol. 4, 2015.

Riyadi, Eko, "A Process that Respects the Principle of 'Nothing about us without us'," in Puguh Windrawan (Ed.), *Aksesibilitas Peradilan bagi Penyandang Disabilitas*. PUSHAM UII, Yogyakarta, 2015.

_________, "The Implementation of the Fulfillment of the Right to Accessibility of Higher Education for Persons with Disabilities in Yogyakarta", *Ius Quia Iustum*, Vol. 28, No. 1, 2021.

Sholeh, Akhmad, "Islam and Persons with Disabilities: A Study of the Right to Accessibility for Persons with Disabilities in the Education System in Indonesia", *Palastren*, Vol. 8, No. 2, 2015.

_________, "Policy of the Yogyakarta State Universities towards Persons with Disabilities", *Journal of Islamic Education*, Vol. III, No. 1, 2014.

Syafi'ie, M., "The Fulfillment of Accessibility for Persons with Disabilities", *Inclusion Journal*, Vol. 1, No. 2, 2014.

Thohari, Slamet, "Views on Disability and Accessibility of Public Facilities for Persons with Disabilities in Malang City", *Indonesian Journal of Disability Studies*, Vol. 1, No. 1, 2014.

Travis, Michelle A., "Gendering Disability to Enable Disability Rights Law", *California Law Review*, Vol. 105, No. 3, 2017.

Watson, Nick, Alan Roulstone, & Carol Thomas (Ed.), *Routledge Handbook of Disability Studies*. Routledge, Oxon, 2012.

Windrawan, Puguh (Ed.), *Aksesibilitas Peradilan bagi Penyandang Disabilitas*. PUSHAM UII, Yogyakarta, 2015.

World Health Organization, *World Report on Disability*. WHO Press, Geneva, 2011.

The 1945 Constitution of Indonesia.

The Indonesian Law Number 4 of 1997 on Persons with Impairments

The Indonesian Law Number 8 of 2016 on Persons with Disabilities

The Indonesian Law Number 12 of 2012 on Higher Education

The Indonesian Law Number 19 of 2011

The Indonesian Law Number 39 of 1999 on Human Rights

The United Nations Convention on the Rights of Persons with Disabilities.

16

VIOLENCE AGAINST WOMEN AND GIRLS WITH DISABILITIES IN RESIDENTIAL INSTITUTIONS IN SERBIA

Kosana Beker and Biljana Janjic

Introduction

Women in Serbia have the same rights as men, but their overall position in the public and private sphere is worse than that of men (Beker et al., 2021). Women are discriminated against on the grounds of their sex and gender, and they are exposed to discriminatory gender stereotypes and violence (Commissioner for Protection of Equality [CPE], 2015). Even though women are more educated, they are less employed, work in lower paid jobs, are burdened with household work and childcare more than men and participate less in decision making (Beker et al., 2021). Some groups of women are at risk of multiple discrimination: for example, elderly women, rural women, Roma women, LBT women,[1] women with disabilities, etc. (CPE, 2015). They are exposed to specific forms of violence and are disadvantaged compared to both women in the general population and men in their groups. In Serbia, persons with disabilities make up 8% of the total population, and 58% of them are women (Marković, 2014). Due to their higher exposure to multiple discrimination, women with disabilities encounter numerous obstacles in exercising their rights. As stated by the Committee on the Rights of Persons with Disabilities (CRPD), women with disabilities are not recognized in gender policies because of their disability, while they are also not recognized in disability policies because of their gender (CRPD General Comment No. 3, 2016). The areas in which discrimination against women with disabilities are particularly evident are access to healthcare, education, and employment; social benefits; exercising the right to family life and parenthood; and protection from violence (Beker et al., 2020).

DOI: 10.4324/9781003410089-19

The patriarchal and stereotyped roles of men and women in Serbia negatively affect the already difficult position of women with disabilities (Mitanovski et al., 2009). They are invisible in public life, and they are poorer and more often unemployed than men with disabilities (Beker et al., 2021). Women with disabilities experience of all forms of violence, including institutional violence, and there are stereotypes and prejudices related to their gender roles, especially regarding marital and family relationships and parenting (CPE, 2015). Additionally, women with disabilities are faced with barriers to access to healthcare services, especially when it comes to their sexual and reproductive health (Beker & Baćanović, 2018). Women with disabilities placed in residential institutions are among the most marginalized groups in the society. They are at higher risk of intersectional discrimination on the grounds of gender, disability, and place of living (Beker & Milošević, 2017). They have the least power, and their voices tend to be completely silenced.

Having that in mind, the aim of this chapter is to present the position of women with disabilities in residential institutions, as well as the violence they are exposed to, including special forms and manifestations of violence against this category of women.

In this chapter, we present data collected from different sources, but it is mainly based on the interviews and focus group discussions conducted with women with disabilities who live in residential institutions or have a history of institutionalization. Interviews and focus group discussions were conducted in the period from 2018 to 2020. In 2018, 13 individual interviews and five group interviews (approximately 20 women) were conducted, with the main aim of collecting and publishing testimonies (life stories) of women with disabilities who live in residential institutions or have a history of institutionalization, especially on the violence they survived in the institutions. In 2019, an additional 19 individual interviews were conducted, while in 2020, due to the COVID-19 pandemic, several group discussions with 15 women were conducted online. The women we interviewed were between 24 and 60 years old and, at the time of the interviews, resided in six different institutions. On average, they had spent about 20 years in institutions, while some of them had been institutionalized from childhood and had resided in several different institutions. Our interviewees had different types of difficulties (motor, sensory, intellectual, and cognitive disabilities), including women with serious difficulties who needed intensive support for interviews. Finally, in 2021, we collected data from institutions: i.e. we sent requests for access to information of public importance to 19 residential institutions for children and adults with disabilities in Serbia. We asked for sex disaggregated data on number of clients, their age group, whether the institution had adopted protocols for acting in cases of violence, whether the institution had established a team for protection from violence, how clients are informed about the existence of the team and about the procedure to file a complaint, the number of violent incidents in the institution in 2019 and 2020, and the number of pregnancies and abortions in the institutions for the same period.

Interviews, focus group discussions, and data collection from institutions were conducted within the projects Deinstitutionalize and End Violence against Women with Disabilities in Custodial Institution and Accessible Services for Women with Disabilities Survivors of Custodial Violence, implemented by two Serbian organizations – Mental Disability Rights Initiative of Serbia MDRI-S and Women's Rights Organisation FemPlatz.[2] The project was implemented in the period from September 2018 to November 2021, with the support of the United Nations Trust Fund to End Violence against Women (UN Trust Fund).

The chapter is divided into four main parts. The first part is about characteristics and consequences of institutionalization; the second part is on the position of women with disabilities in residential institutions in Serbia, followed by the part on different forms and manifestations of violence against women with disabilities in residential institutions. The last part is dedicated to the COVID-19 pandemic and its impact on the lives of women with disabilities, while the main points and conclusions are summarized at the end of the chapter.

Characteristics and consequences of institutionalization

There are different definitions of residential institutions, and one used most is Goffman's definition of total institution as a place of work and residence where a great number of similarly situated people, cut off from the wider community for a considerable time, together lead an enclosed, formally administered round of life (Goffman, 2011). To widen this approach, in this chapter, we are using the definition laid down in Common European Guidelines on the Transition from Institutional to Community-Based Care (2012), which state that the institution is defined not only by its capacity (number of clients), but also by its institutional culture:

> [A] residential institution is any residential care where 1) residents are isolated from the broader community and/or are compelled to live together, 2) residents do not have sufficient control over their lives and decisions which affect them, 3) the requirements of the organization itself tend to take precedents over the residents' individualized needs.
>
> *(European Expert Group on the Transition from Institutional to Community-Based Care, 2012)*

Although the size of the institution is not a determining factor in this definition, this parameter should not be disregarded in the analysis of human rights violations in residential institutions. For instance, the average size of a residential institution in Serbia is about 300 residents, while there are institutions with up to 900 residents.[3] The risk of exploitation, abuse, and violence against residents increases with higher numbers of residents in one restricted place, understaffed institutions, deteriorating living conditions, and reduced access to services.

In the Republic of Serbia, there are 74 state-led residential institutions for the elderly and persons with disabilities with capacity of 14,512 clients,[4] while the overall number of private residential care institutions for the elderly is 238, with the capacity of 8,987 clients (Ministry of Labor, Employment, Veteran and Social Affairs of the Republic of Serbia, 2021). However, the official social protection system reports show that 16,651 adult persons with disabilities were residents of institutions in 2019. Analysis of available annual reports show that the institutionalization of adults with disabilities has increased by 38.5% since 2015 (Republic Institute for Social Protection [RISP], 2020). As a comparison, there were only 27 adult persons with disabilities who used the service of assisted living (Republic Institute for Social Protection, 2020). The institutionalization of persons with disabilities is increasing in Serbia, while the residential institutions still remain the main social welfare placement, especially for persons with mental disabilities.

Common characteristics of all residential institutions notwithstanding the size or location include strict daily routines, lack of privacy, social isolation, control over residents' decisions, and restriction of the freedom of movement (Ćirić Milovanović & Marković, 2013). In research we conducted in 2017 about gender-based violence against women with mental disabilities in residential institutions, all the women we have talked to often used the words "control", "discipline", and "respect for the rules" while describing their everyday life (Janjić & Ćirić Milovanović, 2017).

Violation of a person's privacy is another striking characteristic of life in residential institution, which strongly influences the sense of personal autonomy and security. It is manifested in overcrowded rooms, insufficient living space, and lack of the possibility to choose a room or roommates. In the majority of residential institutions we have monitored and visited in Serbia, residents do not own private things – clothes, hygiene products – while the scarce personal belongings are locked in private cabinets. This practice is justified by the need to respect the rules of conduct in the institutions (the security rules) but also for the easier functioning of the organization itself. Prejudices of institution staff often manifest in explanations that women with mental disabilities are not able to understand the right to privacy. All the women we interviewed confirmed that they had received a certain amount of hygiene products and sanitary pads as monthly rations. Bathrooms and toilets in institutions are frequently used by both men and women, while in some institutions, the bathroom doors cannot be completely closed or locked or there are no separate shower stalls (Janjić & Ćirić Milovanović, 2017).

Privacy is intricately linked with respect for the right to decide and choose and also a person's identity. Withdrawing or controlling an "identity set" (appearance, wardrobe, cosmetics) leads to the erasure of personality (Goffman, 2011) and dehumanization. In this way, expressing multiple identities is restricted, and the persons tend to be reduced only to the identity of a resident and perceived exclusively through the prism of disability (Janjić & Ćirić Milovanović, 2017). One interviewee stated:

> I bathed once a week, and I could not have my things. It was a very bad institution. There were 20 of us in one room. Some people defecated there in the room. During the meal, some of them grabbed food from the plate.
>
> *(Janjić & Ćirić Milovanović, 2017)*

Freedom of movement in Serbia is guaranteed by the Constitution and, by law, can be restricted only if it is necessary for the conduct of criminal proceedings, protection of law and order, prevention of the spread of infectious diseases, or the defense of the Republic of Serbia.[5] However, persons with disabilities in residential institutions, especially those with mental disabilities, are often denied or restricted the right to freedom of movement in practice, although they are not in any of the situations stipulated by the law. They often stay in locked rooms and departments without the opportunity to freely leave the institution or even their own room (Beker & Milošević, 2017). Security reasons, concern over the residents' safety, and employee liability are the most frequently stated explanations for restricting the freedom of movement.

Although the guardianship regime in Serbia still legally allows keeping individuals in an institution against their will,[6] this does not mean that persons under guardianship can, at the same time, be deprived of liberty. Even when a person is not under guardianship but has spent a long period in the strict regime of institutional life, sometimes from birth, they have been de facto denied the possibility of making decisions and free choice.

Women with disabilities in residential institutions

As stated in the introduction, women with disabilities placed in residential institutions are among the most marginalized groups in the society, having in mind that they are at higher risk of intersectional discrimination on the grounds of gender, disability, and place of living (Beker & Milošević, 2017). They have the least power, and their voices tend to be completely silenced. In terms of hierarchy of rights, it could be stated that the position of women and girls with disabilities living in residential institutions in Serbia is worse than the position of men and women without disabilities, men and women with disabilities living in the community, and men with disabilities living in residential institutions (Beker & Milošević, 2017). The situation is even more serious for women and girls with intellectual, cognitive, and psychosocial disabilities, due to the stigma connected to mental disability in the Serbian society, while their age also has significant impact on their social marginalization.

Women with intellectual, cognitive, and psychosocial disabilities who live in residential institutions are often there without their consent and experience discrimination and specific forms of gender-based violence, while many of their rights are violated in such surroundings (Janjić & Ćirić Milovanović, 2017). Although precise data are not available, most women with intellectual, cognitive, and psychosocial disabilities in residential institutions are deprived of their legal capacity and put under guardianship, which means that they cannot decide on their own place of residence, their own treatment, medical interventions, pregnancy, parenting, or partnership (Beker & Milošević, 2017). Their legal guardians decide for them on all important life issues, which is a violation of human rights and has unforeseeable consequences, as pointed out by the Committee on Elimination of Discrimination against Women (CEDAW) as well, calling on Serbia to abolish the possibility of deprivation of legal capacity on the basis of disability (CEDAW/C/SRB/CO/4).

Forms and manifestations of violence against women with disabilities in residential institutions

According to the UN General Assembly Declaration on the Elimination of Violence against Women (1993), violence against women is any act of gender-based violence that results or could result in a physical, sexual, or psychological injury or the suffering of women, including threats that these acts will be committed, as well as coercion or arbitrary deprivation of liberty, regardless of whether these acts are done in public or private life. The term "gender-based violence" in this context means that violence is committed against a particular person because of her gender and/or because she does not fulfill socially imposed gender roles (UN Women, 2015). Gender-based violence highlights the gender dimension of violent acts: that is, the relationship between the subordinate position of women in society and their exposure to the risk of violence. Beside gender, other personal characteristics such as disability, race, social status, sexual orientation, and age contribute to a greater risk of violence and fewer options for protection (Boston Women's Health Book Collective, 1998). Once again, women with disabilities in residential institutions are at the very bottom in the hierarchy of human rights because they are at very high risk of gender-based violence in the institution, while their options for protection from gender-based violence are almost nonexistent.

Partner violence

Studies and research on partner relationships of people with disabilities are still very scarce. One research on marriages and partnerships (Center for Research on Women with Disabilities, 2001) that included people with disabilities showed that women with disabilities experience many obstacles in starting an emotional relationship. Women say that the biggest problem in achieving satisfactory emotional relationships are societal attitudes and assumptions about women with disabilities, which prevented potential partners from contacting these women, fearing what other people would say if they started a relationship with a woman with disabilities (Beker & Milošević, 2017).

While we collected data on understanding gender-based violence in residential institutions in Serbia, we noted that there were significant differences between institutions in rules about emotional relationships between residents, from those where relationships were completely prohibited through tacit admission to open relationships about which employees were aware. Interviews with the staff employed in institutions showed that such unnecessary control and exercise of power stems largely from the attitudes of the administration and employees towards the sexuality of persons living in an institution (Janjić & Ćirić Milovanović, 2017). As a rule, in institutions where relationships between residents are completely forbidden, secrecy and hiding of residents from the staff usually meant increased risk to a woman from partner violence. A woman who lived more than 25 years in institutions says she fell in love there for the first time. But the couple could only go for a walk in the yard and see each other at the open, outdoors. As she stated:

> They did not allow us to see each other indoors so as not to do some things that we were not supposed to do. Make children, for example. Staff did not allow us so that we do not make stupid things, make love.
> *(Janjić & Ćirić Milovanović, 2017)*

Apart from often repeating that relationships were prohibited, women reported that they had experienced threats and punishments if they violated this rule. Girls and women were often intimidated by very negative stories of abortion, especially women who had been institutionalized since the early childhood, so consequently, they started identifying relationships with abortion. In words of one interviewed women, "Love relationships were dangerous and undesirable."

Systemic and institutional violence

Other more serious and systemic forms of institutional violence include physical restraints and isolation (seclusion), which are still practiced in large-scale residential institutions. As determined by the Special Rapporteur for Torture, isolation or seclusion of persons with mental disabilities, for any duration, constitutes cruel, inhuman, and degrading treatment, and any form of restraint of people with mental disabilities, even for a short period of time, can amount to torture and abuse (United Nation, A/63/175, 2008). Although these practices might not be perceived as gender specific, the trauma, consequences, and additional risk are very gender specific for women. For example, the isolation of women in rooms from which they cannot exit for various reasons[7] opens a worrying possibility of abuse. The report of the Special Rapporteur on Torture (United Nation, A/HRC/31/57, 2016) states that every woman deprived of liberty and subjected to isolation suffers extremely serious consequences, including the possibility of repeated traumatization if she has been a victim of violence in the past. In addition, when a woman is isolated, she is at higher risk of physical and sexual abuse. If she is not mobile or is non-verbal, the risk of violence increases, as well as the inability to protect herself. The isolation of women who are at risk of violence or who have already survived violence only further victimizes them, discourages reporting violence, and constitutes an act of torture or ill treatment (Beker & Milošević, 2017). Although the use of restraints has severe consequences for both the physical and mental health of both men and women, this forced measure traumatizes women to a higher degree, especially if they previously survived violence or if they are pregnant. If physical restraints are used on a woman who has been sexually abused in the past, especially if her arms and legs are tied, besides all the other consequences affecting all victims of confinement, she may experience this as a repeated trauma of sexual abuse, which will further scare and victimize her (Girlescu, 2014).

Research shows that the risk of ill treatment for people with mental disabilities increases the moment they are placed in an institution. In some cases, violence in institutions is often considered justified, which creates a "culture of institutional violence" that becomes acceptable (Beker & Milošević, 2017). Isolating users, intimidating them, and exercising poor control over employee behavior creates an environment in which violence is accepted as normal. Therefore, the causes of violence should be sought within the institution itself, considering the nature and functioning of residential institutions as well as the attitudes of those employed in them (Beker & Milošević, 2017).

Different manifestations of violence against women with disabilities

Women with disabilities are exposed to all forms of violence, including physical, verbal, psychological, and sexual violence, and they experience varied manifestations of violence. They can survive violence from other clients in the residential institution (horizontal violence), from employees (vertical violence), and from persons outside the institution.

The most frequent manifestations of verbal violence in residential institutions, according to women with disabilities we spoke with, include insults, shouting, and threats. They said that almost any deviation from the established institutional regime or failure to comply with the rules was followed by verbal threats that kept the residents in control and in constant fear. The most common threats women were exposed to were that they would be placed in isolation, evicted from the institution, become homeless, or sent to another institution or psychiatric department. Women talked about their own experience of punishments for "breaking the rules", which involved standing in the corner, kneeling, being denied meals the next day, being banned from going out, and being locked in a room, all of which were often accompanied by insults, shouting, and physical violence like pulling their hair or slapping (Janjić and Ćirić Milovanović).

Life in such a restrictive environment, with very little prospect of controlling any aspect of one's own life and deciding independently, while employees manifest their power, sometimes by using physical force, can also make clients violent to each other and employees, sometimes using violence as a form of "protest" because of the way of life they are forced to lead (Advocacy for Inclusion, 2015).

Horizontal violence in institutions is defined as the psychological, physical, and sexual violence that one or more clients carry out to punish, hurt, or control other clients (Baker et al., 2002). Given that this type of violence occurs in residential institutions, it often has the characteristics of violent behavior "in the clan" and shows much similarity to the manifestations of peer violence and domestic violence. The most serious issue here is that the victim is forced to live with her abuser and cannot leave, and the fact that a joint life in the institution gives the perpetrator the opportunity to find out the most intimate information about the victim, such as her family situation, health condition, and disability, which makes it easier for the victim to be intimidated and controlled (Beker & Milošević, 2017). Apart from the fact that violence is normalized in closed institutions, in time, clients develop resistance to the internal hierarchy existing in the institution, which means that they have a particularly negative attitude towards violence surviving from other residents, while at the same time consider that employees in institutions are much more important than they are and that they have more rights (Beker & Milošević, 2017). The institution serves its own purpose, so the attitudes of employees towards people with mental disabilities are among the causes of violence in institutions (Thornberry & Olson, 2005).

Legal regime of deprivation of legal capacity

As stated previously, the majority of clients of residential institutions in Serbia are deprived of their legal capacity and are put under guardianship. Before elaboration of the violation of the sexual and reproductive rights of women in residential institutions, the legal regime of deprivation of legal capacity in Serbia will shortly be explained in order to provide deeper understanding of one of the graver violation of human rights that still legally exists. According to the Serbian Constitution,[8] every person has the right to legal recognition while with the age of adulthood (18), a person gains the capacity to independently decide on their own rights and obligations.[9] Legal recognition as a person (human being) is acquired by birth and cannot be restricted or taken away. On the other hand, a person can be fully or partially deprived of legal capacity (capacity to act). Persons who are deprived of legal capacity are placed under guardianship, and the consequences of this process are immense, considering that persons are deprived of the right to make decisions independently in any area of their lives (Beker, 2010). Persons deprived of legal capacity are put into a situation that was called "civic death" in Roman law.

Under the provisions of the Family Law,[10] full legal capacity is gained at the age of 18 or by getting married before the legal age with the court's permission.[11] Consequently, parental rights are terminated when a child turns 18 or gains full legal capacity before the legal age.[12] According to the law, an adult person who is "as a result of illness or difficulties in psychological or physical development, incapable of normal reasoning and therefore unable to care independently for his or her own rights and interests" can be fully deprived of their legal capacity.[13] Legal capacity of these persons is equal to the legal capacity of a younger minor (child below the age of 14). An adult person who, as a result of illness or difficulties in psychological or physical development, "directly threatens his or her own rights and interests or the rights and interests of other persons" can be partially deprived of their legal capacity.[14] Legal capacity of these persons is equal to that of an older minor (child between the ages of 14 and 18). A court's decision on partial deprivation of legal capacity will determine the legal actions that the person who is partially deprived of legal capacity can and cannot independently undertake.

As is evident, deprivation of legal capacity in Serbia is based on disability, which is an example of the direct discrimination prohibited by both international and national antidiscrimination laws.[15] Also, although the possibility of the reinstatement of legal capacity exists in the law, it is obvious that disability as a reason of deprivation most likely would not cease to exist, which makes this legal option almost useless for persons with disabilities.

Persons with disabilities who are deprived of legal capacity are placed under guardianship, and all decisions about the person's life are made by their legally appointed guardian. They are not even consulted about the choice of a guardian; rather, the guardianship authority (center for social work) appoints a person to act as a legal guardian. The guardian is usually a family member or a relative, but also very often, the role of the guardian is entrusted to the social worker or director of residential institution (Beker & Milošević, 2016).

Violation of reproductive and sexual rights as a grave human rights violation

The right to informed decision making of persons deprived of legal capacity is completely violated, since guardians do not have any legal obligation to inform or consult them. Among all other rights, the sexual and reproductive rights of women with disabilities in residential institutions are constantly violated. Almost as a rule, decisions on their reproductive health are made by the staff with the consent of the guardian and without their informed consent, which has serious consequences not only to their reproductive rights but also to their whole lives (Janjić & Ćirić Milovanović, 2017).

Gynecological examinations for women with disabilities in residential institutions are organized regularly, once every six months or annually, and they are usually performed in the local clinic or, in some cases, in the institution itself. However, in some institutions, there are no regular gynecological examinations; they are organized when "enough women are gathered", as stated by one doctor employed in a residential institution (Janjić & Ćirić Milovanović, 2017). The quality of these examinations is questionable since it happens that a woman's pregnancy goes unnoticed. Staff, including doctors, is very often prejudicial towards the sexuality of women with disability in residential institutions: for example, one doctor said that he does not know the exact number of sexually active clients because "the majority is prone to promiscuous behavior" (Janjić & Ćirić Milovanović, 2017).

Records of menstrual periods are kept regularly by the nurses, and if a woman misses her period, a pregnancy test and a gynecological examination are required. The staff is not interested in the wishes and decisions of women with disabilities on their health, therapy, interventions, etc. Life in the residential institution means that nurses are giving medication without any explanations, including contraceptives, which constitutes a specific form of "modernized" sterilization (Janjić & Ćirić Milovanović, 2017). There are several reasons mentioned in the literature in an attempt to justify administration of contraceptives to women with intellectual and psychosocial disabilities without their consent (Professional Training Resources, 2015). Some of them are "best interest" of a woman who is perceived as not able to understand changes in her body, increased health risks, protection of family members of a woman with disabilities who "would be forced to take care of her child", protection of the child that could be born, prevention of potential pregnancies as a result of sexual abuse or rape, and finally the protection of society, especially having in mind the cost of caring for the child (Janjić & Ćirić Milovanović, 2017). All these explanations still resemble eugenic policies and completely disregard the rights of women with disabilities to independently make decisions about their bodies, sexuality, and parenting (Beker and Milošević, 2017). Besides administration of contraceptives without consent, some women have intrauterine contraceptive devices (IUDs) inserted without consent or prior information on interventions, risks, and effects (Janjić & Ćirić Milovanović, 2017). The majority of women of reproductive age in residential institutions are given either contraceptive pills or an IUD, and the method of contraception is determined by the gynecologist. Some employees we spoke with stated that they do not ask for a women's consent; they inform the guardian about the administration of contraceptive pills, while the guardian's consent is required only for the IUD (Janjić & Ćirić Milovanović, 2017). Administration of contraceptive pills is regarded as part of the regular therapy.

Women with disabilities, especially women with mental disabilities in residential institutions, are exposed to forced abortions as well as to forced sterilization (Zampas & Lamačková, 2011). Historically, persons with disabilities were subjected to numerous inhuman practices due to the societal attitude towards them (Janjić & Beker, 2016), and it was common in many countries that persons with mental disabilities were forcibly sterilized. For example, by 1939, more than 30 countries had forcibly sterilized almost 39,000 people with disabilities (The Open University, 2015). The wrong belief that persons with mental disabilities are "defective" and that their disability could be inherited were the main reasons for this practice.

Unfortunately, even today in the 21st century, women and girls with disabilities are subjected to forced sterilization for various reasons and justifications (Human Rights Watch, 2011). Worldwide, many women and girls with disability are receiving messages not to have children, and those messages are coming from their family members and health and social workers, as well as from the society as a whole (Waxman & Wolfe, 1999). Women with disabilities are perceived as non-sexual; not able to decide on health issues; not aware of their sexuality; and, above all, not suitable for potential parenting. Or, as stated by feminists with disabilities, while women all over the world fight for the right to abortion, women with disabilities fight for "the right to decide not to decide (i.e. not to abort)" (Beker & Milošević, 2017).

Women with disabilities placed in residential institutions explained that sexual relations are usually not allowed; they are not even allowed to talk about sexual rights and sexuality, so some of them are hiding while some don't want to have sexual relation in the institution due to lack of privacy (MDRI-S, 2021). The majority of them are afraid of pregnancy. They unanimously stated that when pregnancy is detected, a woman has to go to a gynecologist to determine the stage of pregnancy and to schedule an abortion, without any consultation with the woman herself. Or, as one of interviewees explained, "As soon as you get to the institution, they put IUD in you. And that's it. Those who get pregnant need to have abortion" (Janjić & Ćirić Milovanović, 2017).

On the other hand, there are many obstacles to getting information about forced sterilization. Women with disabilities in residential institutions are not willing to talk about it, some of them are not informed, and staff employed in the institutions is completely aware that such interventions are socially unacceptable; hence, they do not talk about forced sterilization (Janjić & Ćirić Milovanović, 2017). However, the CRPD expressed concern that persons with disabilities, especially those deprived of their legal capacity, were subjected to contraceptive treatment, forced abortions, and sterilization without consent (CRPD/C/SRB/CO/1).

Data from the institutions

As already mentioned, at the beginning of 2021, we sent requests for access to information of public importance to 19 residential institutions for children and adults with disabilities and received 15 answers. Four institutions did not respond to our request in due time, so we appealed to the Commissioner for the Information of Public Importance. However, the procedure is still ongoing at the time of the submission of this chapter.[16] According to the data provided by these residential institutions, approximately 3,700 persons are residing in these institutions (1,850 are women). The data is not exact since one institution with more than 900 clients did not send sex-disaggregated data on clients and their age groups. Hence, we assumed that the number of men and women in this institution is equal.

According to the law, every residential institution is obliged to have a protocol for acting in cases of violence, as well as a team for protection from violence. However, out of the 15 institutions that responded, 13 have adopted protocols for acting in cases of violence, and 11 have established teams for protection from violence. The institutions are also obliged to publicly display information about the protection team members and their phone numbers and inform all clients about the team. Three institutions stated that clients are deprived of legal capacity, so the institution informed their legal guardians. Two institutions wrote that clients are "severely mentally retarded", so they are not able to understand that information. Only three institutions organized different workshops and meetings with clients on the topics of violence and protection from violence, and those institutions also reported individual conversations with clients on the topic. The majority of institutions stated that both protocols for acting in cases of violence and information on the team for protection from violence were published on the bulletin board in the institution.

We asked for data on the number of cases of violence in 2019 and 2020 because we wanted to compare the situation before the COVID-19 pandemic with that after the complete closure of the institutions during COVID-19. Despite the fact that research shows very high levels of violence in institutions, including gender-based violence, the institutions reported only 20 cases of violence in 2019 and only 10 cases in 2020. Twenty cases of violence in 2019 were reported by the five institutions. In 14 cases, the perpetrators were men, and out of 20 victims, 7 were women. Ten cases of violence in 2020 were reported in one institution; nine perpetrators were men while there was one woman among the victims. Presented data clearly show that violence is underreported in institutions, so we can assume that adequate protection from violence is not provided for women with disabilities living in residential institutions.

In 2019, regular gynecological examinations were organized only in ten institutions (out of fifteen), while in 2020, regular gynecological examinations were organized only in six institutions. Two institutions explained that regular gynecological examinations were not organized due to the COVID-19 pandemic but emphasized that urgent gynecological conditions were treated properly. Finally, in 2019, three institutions reported three pregnancies, while in 2020, three institutions reported four pregnancies. Unfortunately, but not surprisingly, all pregnancies were terminated. Only one institution wrote an explanation for one case of abortion: namely, the woman used medication that could harm the fetus; thus, her pregnancy was terminated. Although we are not sure whether all pregnancies in institutions were officially reported, available data show that every reported pregnancy in residential institutions in Serbia in the last two years was terminated.

COVID-19 and its impact on women's lives

Although the COVID-19 crisis profoundly affected the lives of all people, there are some groups of women who have been disproportionately hit by the restrictive measures and human rights violence. This crisis has provided us with another clear proof of the importance of urgent deinstitutionalization because the size, location, organization, and types of assistance provided in residential institutions cannot set up appropriate protection systems for either residents or employees. According to Special Rapporteur for Persons with Disabilities, residential and psychiatric institutions for persons with disabilities "have become hotspots of the pandemic" (Devandas Aguilar, 2020). Persons with disabilities are at higher risk of contracting the virus and have a higher mortality rate because they have significant barriers to basic hygiene needs, difficulties in maintaining social distancing rules, and limited access to information about the virus, testing, and health protection (Devandas Aguilar, 2020).

The relevant line ministry in Serbia confirmed the presence of COVID-19 in about 90 private and state-led residential institutions for adults and the elderly, and it stated that 5,789 residents and 2,880 employees had been cured (Ministry of Labor, Employment, Veteran and Social Affairs of the Republic of Serbia [MLEVSA], 2021), while there was no information about the total number of residents infected from the beginning of the pandemic or data about the deceased from the consequences of COVID-19.[17]

The state of emergency due to the COVID-19 pandemic in the Republic of Serbia was declared on March 15, 2020. Shortly before that, the line ministry for social affairs issued its first instructions to the residential institutions about hygiene, the prohibition of visits, and limited movement of people (MLEVSA, 2020). These measures were imposed for almost five months, meaning that residents of the institutions had their freedom of movement completely prohibited. After almost 50 days, the residential institutions allowed the residents to go for walks but only in the institution backyard with very restrictive rules (e.g. temperature from 18 to 25 degrees Celsius, no wind, no rain) (MLEVSA, 2020).

All these circumstances exacerbated the risk of violence against women. Although the global reports state high increases in the violence against women, there is no adequate information about the position of women in residential institutions as there are no functional and safe mechanisms for reporting violence in residential institutions, nor is there a support service to women survivors of violence. There has been no external control of the institutions for over a year, and such controls are one of the key mechanisms for monitoring violence and providing support to survivors. The team of the National Preventive Mechanism for Torture,[18] which conducts regular (announced and unannounced) control visits of residential and psychiatric institutions and places of detention, was denied the entrance to one of the institutions for adults with disabilities. Non-governmental organizations that conduct independent monitoring of residential and psychiatric institutions were denied basic information and completely prohibited from accessing the institutions and residents (MDRI-S, 2021).[19]

Conclusions

Even when the specific position of women and girls with disabilities is acknowledged and included in public policies on gender equality or violence against women, women with intellectual, cognitive, and psychological disabilities in residential institutions stay invisible. They are left out of policies and support programs, and existing services are unavailable and/or inaccessible to them. It could be said that the Serbian society does not have a response to violence against women with disabilities in residential institutions, especially sexual and partner violence.

Most women we talked to testified about various forms of violence that they have survived or are still surviving in residential institutions, from verbal violence, such as threats, humiliation, and shouting, through physical violence from other clients and employees to sexual violence and gross violations of their reproductive rights. However, in rare reported cases of violence, their statements about the experiences of violence are questioned, they are not believed, and they are often assumed to be unaware of the violence they suffer or unable to recognize it (Janjić & Ćirić Milovanović, 2017).

Denial of the right to informed decision making increases the risk of various coercive interventions, including administration of contraception without consent, sterilization, and forced abortions – specific forms of gender-based violence against women with disabilities in residential institutions. Administrating contraception to a woman with disabilities without her informed consent is a form of abuse. It violates her right to informed consent, the right to physical integrity, the right to care for her health and body, the right to express sexuality, and the right to parenting. Forced sterilization is an act of violence against women, a form of social control and violation of the right to freedom from torture and other cruel, inhuman, and degrading treatment and punishment. The lack of adequate protection of the sexual and reproductive health of women with disabilities is a matter of great concern, especially during COVID-19.

Women with disabilities in residential institutions with whom we talked during the COVID-19 pandemic stated that they did not feel safe because there were many people living in the same place, and the living conditions were bad. They were not allowed to leave their rooms or sections, let alone the premises of the institution. One of them said:

> I do not feel safe at all. I live in awfully bad conditions. Everything is bad in the institution, especially during this situation. The food and the accommodation are awful. The mattress in my bed is so thin that I can feel the bed frame. While I was in self-isolation, I was beaten by bugs all over my body.
>
> *(Beker & Janjić, 2021).*

Notes

1 Lesbian, bisexual and trans* women.

2 Results of our research are published in several publications during 2019–2021. More information at: Inicijativa za prava osoba sa mentalnim invaliditetom (MDRI-S).

3 See, for example, regular annual reports on social welfare institutions, available at official website of the Republic Institute for Social Protection, Извештаји из система (zavodsz.gov.rs).

4 Including 56 institutions for adults and the elderly (3 of which are for persons with disabilities and 14 for persons with mental and intellectual disabilities) and 18 institutions for children (5 of which are for children and youth with disabilities).
5 Article 39, Paragraphs 1 and 2 of the Constitution of the Republic of Serbia.
6 Service of residential accommodation of persons deprived of their legal capacity can be contracted only on the basis of referral by the center for social work or on the basis of court decision (Article 78 of the Law on social protection). As for involuntary placement in psychiatric institutions, the decision can be made by a member of the close or extended family or legal guardian (Article 20 of the Law on protecting people with mental health problems). Also, a person with mental health problems can be placed in a psychiatric institution without consent of the legal guardian if the court decides so (Article 27 of the Law on protecting people with mental health problems).
7 Besides placement in a locked, separated room, isolation also includes leaving a person in a bed/crib that they cannot leave independently. For example, a woman can be isolated in a seclusion room that is locked and can be unlocked only from outside. She can also be alone in a room that is not locked, but if she is not mobile, cannot speak, or needs intensive support for moving and communication, she cannot leave the room by herself, which puts her at risk of abuse and neglect.
8 Constitution of the Republic of Serbia, "Official Gazette of the RS", No 98/2006.
9 Article 37, Paras. 1 and 2 of the Constitution.
10 Family Law, "Official Gazette of the Republic of Serbia", no. 18/2005, 72/2011 – other law 6/2015.
11 Article 11 of the Family Law.
12 Article 84, Paragraph 1, Points 1 and 2 of the Family Law.
13 Article 64, Paragraph 1 and Article 146 Paras. 1 and 2 of the Family Law.
14 Article 147, Paras. 1–3 of the Family Law.
15 E.g. the Law on Prohibition of Discrimination, "Official Gazette of the Republic of Serbia", no. 22/2009 and 52/2021; the Law on Suppression of Discrimination of Persons with Disability, "Official Gazette of the Republic of Serbia", no. 33/2006 and 13/2016.
16 May 2021.
17 Civil society organizations asked for this information several times during the COVID-19 crisis by sending requests for access to information of public importance, but the official institutions have never responded to the requests.
18 In Serbia, the National Preventive Mechanism for Torture is mandated to the Protector of Citizens.
19 See, for example, *Open Letter to the Prime Minister of Serbia: How many people have died from COVID-19 in social care homes?* MDRI-S, 31 July 2021, available at: Open letter to the Prime Minister of Serbia: How many people have died from COVID-19 in social care homes? (mdri-s.org).

References

Adults in social protection system in 2019, Republic Institute for Social Protection, Belgrade, 2020. Available at: http://www.zavodsz.gov.rs/media/2163/punoletni-u-sistemu-socijalne-zastite-u-2020.pdf

Baker, L., et al., *Peer-to-Peer Aggression in Residential Settings: Increasing Understanding to Enhance Intervention*, Centre for Children and Families in the Justice System, Canada, 2002.

Beker, K., *My Right to Make a Decision*, Initiative for Inclusion VelikiMali, Pančevo, 2010.

Beker, K., Baćanović, V., *Reproductive Health of Women with Disabilities in the AP of Vojvodina,* Province of Vojvodina Ombudsman, Novi Sad, 2018.

Beker, K., Janjić, B., *COVID-19 Measures Impact on Social and Economic Rights of Women with Disabilities in Serbia*, FemPlatz, Pančevo, January 2021, 2021-02-16_Kovid-19_i_zene_sa_invaliditetom.pdf (femplatz.org)

Beker, K., Milošević, T., *PERSON Country Report, Legal Capacity, Court Practice and Legislation in Serbia 2016*, MDRI-S, Belgrade, 2016.

Beker, K., Milošević, T., *Violence against Women with Disabilities in Residential Institutions*, Mental Disability Rights Initiative MDRI-S, Belgrade, 2017.

Beker, K., et al., *Report on the Women's Rights and Gender Equality in Serbia in 2019*, FemPlatz, Pančevo, 2020.

Beker, K., et al., *Report on the Women's Rights and Gender Equality in Serbia in 2020*, FemPlatz, Pančevo, 2021.

Ćirić Milovanović, D., Marković, M. M., *Torture and Abuse in the Context of Persons with Disabilities*, Mental Disability Rights Initiative of Serbia MDRI-S, Belgrade, 2013.

Common European Guidelines on the Transition from Institutional to community-based Care, European Expert Group on the Transition from Institutional to Community-based Care, November 2012, Brussels, Belgium.

Concluding observations for Serbia, CEDAW, CEDAW/C/SRB/CO/4 para. 23, 37

Concluding observations on the initial report of Serbia, Committee on the Rights of Persons with Disabilities, 2016. CRPD/C/SRB/CO/1

Constitution of the Republic of Serbia, "Official Gazette of the RS", No 98/2006

Contraceptive Choices for Women with Learning Disabilities, *Contraceptive Choices for Women with Learning Disabilities*, The Open University, London, 2015.

Declaration on the Elimination of Violence against Women, General Assembly Resolution 48/104, 1993.

Family Law, "Official Gazette of the Republic of Serbia", no. 18/2005, 72/2011-other law 6/2015

General comment No. 3 (2016), Article 6: Women and girls with disabilities, CRPD.

Girlescu, O. G., *Human Rights Oversight in Institutional Settings*, MDRI-S, Beograd, 2014.

Goffman, E., *Asylums* (Serbian edition), Mediterranean publishing, Novi Sad, Serbia, 2011.

Instructions of the Ministry of Labor, Employment, Veteran and Social Affairs, number 500–01–2/2020–09 from 10 March 2020, and 500–01–2/2020–09 from 12 March 2020.

Instructions of the Ministry of Labor, Employment, Veteran and Social Affairs, number 500–01–7/4/2020–09 of 28 April 2020.

Interim Report of the Special Rapporteur on Torture and Other Cruel, Inhuman or Degrading Treatment or Punishment, United Nation, A/63/175, 2008.

Janjić, B., Beker, K., Persons with disabilities in institutions as victims of discrimination and human rights violations, *TEMIDA*, Vol. 19, br. 1, 2016, pp. 109–134.

Janjić, B., Ćirić Milovanović, D., *Here the Walls Have Ears Too: Testimonies of Women with Mental Disabilities about Gender-Based Violence in Residential Institutions*, Mental Disability Rights Initiative of Serbia MDRI-S, Belgrade, 2017.

Law on Prohibition of Discrimination, "Official Gazette of the Republic of Serbia", no. 22/2009 and 52/2021

Law on Suppression of Discrimination of Persons with Disability, "Official Gazette of the Republic of Serbia", no. 33/2006 and 13/2016

Marković, M. M., *Persons with Disabilities in Serbia, 2011 Census of Population, Households and Dwellings in the Republic of Serbia*, Statistical Office of the Republic of Serbia, Belgrade, 2014.

Mitanovski, L., et al., *Women with Disabilities in Serbia – First Analysis of the Position and Legislation Related to Women with Disabilities in the Republic of Serbia*, . . . Iz kruga – organization for protection and support to women with disabilities in Serbia and Center for Monitoring and evaluation, Belgrade, 2009.

National Study of Women with Physical Disabilities – Final Report, Center for Research on Women with Disabilities, Department of Physical Medicine and Rehabilitation, Baylor College of Medicine, Sexuality and Disability, Vol. 19, No. 1, USA, 2001

Official statement of the Ministry of Labor, Employment, Veteran and Social Affairs of the Republic of Serbia from 6 May 2021, У установама социјалне заштите и домовима за смештај одраслих и старих заражено 153 корисника и 191 запослени | Министарство за рад, запошљавање, борачка и социјална питања (minrzs.gov.rs) (accessed on 7 May 2021).

Open Letter to the Prime Minister of Serbia: How many people have died from COVID-19 in social care homes, MDRI-S, 31 July 2021, available at: *Open letter to the Prime Minister of Serbia: How many people have died from Covid-19 in social care homes? (mdri-s.org)* (accessed on 10 November 2021).

Programming Essentials, Monitoring & Evaluation, UNWOMEN, 2015.

Report from the Workshop with Women Self-Advocates, MDRI-S, Belgrade, 2021 (unpublished).

Report of the Special Rapporteur on Torture and Other Cruel, Inhuman or Degrading Treatment or Punishment, United Nation, A/HRC/31/57, 2016.

Special Report on Discrimination against Women, Commissioner for Protection of Equality, Belgrade, 2015. Available at: https://ravnopravnost.gov.rs/wp-content/uploads/2012/11/images_files_Poseban_izvestaj_o_diskriminaciji_zena_priprema_korigovana-1.pdf

Statement of Catalina Devandas Aguilar, United Nations Special Rapporteur on rights of persons with disabilities, 10 August 2020, 20200810_StatementCatalinaDevandas.pdf (ohchr.org) (accessed on 5 May 2021).

Sterilization of Women and Girl with Disabilities – A Briefing Paper, Human Rights Watch, London, 2011.

Submission to the Senate Inquiry Into the Violence, Abuse and Neglect against People with Disability in Institutional and Residential Settings, Advocacy for Inclusion, Australia, 2015.

Thornberry, C., Olson, K., *The Abuse of Individuals with Developmental Disabilities*, University of Alberta, Canada, 2005.

Violence against Women, Boston Women's Health Book Collective, Touchstone, USA, 1998.

Waxman Fiduccia, B., Wolfe, R. L., *Women and Girls with Disabilities: Defining the Issues*, Center for Woman Policy Studies and Women & Philanthropy, Washington, DC, 1999.

Zampas, C., Lamačková, A., Ethical and legal issues in reproductive health: forced and coerced sterilization of women in Europe, *International Journal of Gynecology and Obstetrics*, Vol. 114, 2011, pp. 163–166.

17

DISABILITY AND DISPLACEMENT

Disability hierarchy among refugees and other displaced people

Jennifer Ward

Introduction

Disabled[1] refugees are considered the most marginalized group of all displaced populations. Disabled displaced people are at particular risk of violence, exploitation, and abuse. Additional barriers to accessing humanitarian assistance, education, healthcare, and other services exist for disabled displaced people. Multiple barriers impact the accessibility and inclusiveness of displacement camps, which creates a hierarchy among disabled refugees. Various driving forces cause this hierarchy, including attitudinal biases, communication and language barriers, exclusive policies and practices, and physical inaccessibility of spaces. The different levels of services provided and the discriminatory and exclusive practices within displacement camps provide more or fewer opportunities for some disabled people over others. Displacement often causes a disruption of access to necessary health services, such as medication, therapy, or specialized equipment, often leading to permanent disabilities as a result of injury, illness, or birth-related causes. In addition to disabilities caused by displacement, displaced populations reflect the general population, wherein the World Health Organization (WHO) estimates that approximately 15% of the global population are disabled (WHO, 2021).

In my dissertation titled "Narratives of Disability and Displacement: Oral Histories of the Lived Experiences of Disabled Refugees" (Ward, 2021), I recorded the narratives of Deaf[2] or disabled refugees who had lived in resettlement camps in various countries and who had since resettled in the United States. While conducting these narrative interviews, I noticed that instances of disability hierarchy among refugees living in the camps came up organically and from more than one participant. The participants described either their own personal experiences with disability hierarchy or situations that they had witnessed other disabled camp residents experience. Disability hierarchy

DOI: 10.4324/9781003410089-20

is the perception that one type of disability and/or the severity of the disability is better or worse than other disability types (Snow, 2015). It considers some disabilities more acceptable than others, and views disability negatively overall (Nichols, 2019).

In this chapter, I discuss disability hierarchy among refugees living in displacement camps, the driving forces behind this hierarchy, and the impact it has on disabled refugees. I conclude with some recommendations for practice to help reduce instances of hierarchy among both the disabled and non-disabled communities.

Disability and displacement

Article 14 of the Universal Declaration of Human Rights (United Nations, 1948) proclaims, "Everyone has the right to seek and to enjoy in other countries asylum from protection," which includes disabled people. At the end of 2019, 79.5 million people were forcibly displaced worldwide; of this total number, 41.3 million are internally displaced, 25.9 million are refugees, and 3.5 million are asylum seekers (UNHCR, 2019). In their annual Global Trends report, the United Nations High Commissioner for Refugees (UNHCR) reported that worldwide displacement numbers are the highest ever recorded (2019). The true number of disabled people worldwide may be underestimated and underreported due to the tendency to overlook disabled refugees during conflict and in the aftermath. Refugees and asylum seekers crossing borders are even more likely to be ignored or overlooked (Crock et al., 2017).

Historically, disabled people have been marginalized and oppressed and have experienced multiple instances of discrimination. Similarly, refugees, asylum-seekers, and other displaced people face multiple oppressions and systems of disadvantage that influence their experiences (Elder, 2015; Besic et al., 2018). In addition to their already-existing multiple identities, displaced people acquire the added identity of displaced person (Elder, 2015). The intersectionality of these multiple identities influences the attitudes and biases of the general public, therefore creating additional systems of disadvantage (Besic et al., 2018). As a result of discriminatory practices that consider refugees as less than or undesirable immigrants, mobility in pursuit of safer, more sustainable living conditions is often restricted (Mirza, 2011a).

A human rights framework for disability and displacement

The Convention on the Rights of Persons with Disabilities (CRPD) was founded on a rights-based approach to supporting disabled people, including refugees, asylum-seekers, and other displaced populations. It advocates for disabled people to be treated with respect and dignity and views them as rights bearers, rather than as objects of pity or in need of charity (United Nations, 2006). Additionally, the CRPD calls for the protection of disabled people in situations of humanitarian emergency and risk (Pearce, 2015). Article 11 of the CRPD addresses situations of emergency, conflict, and displacement and recognizes that disabled people are especially disadvantaged in these situations (Smith-Khan, Crock, Saul, & McCallum, 2014).

Ratifying the CRPD means that states have committed to being held responsible by the global community for the obligations outlined in the Convention. As of February 2020, 181 countries have ratified the CRPD (Disabled World, 2020). However, the lived experiences shared by disabled refugees demonstrates the contrast between these states' commitments and the reality of what is happening. Both the Universal Declaration of Human Rights (UDHR) and the CRPD address immigration and mobility as human rights issues. Both documents contain language outlining the right to seek asylum from protection, liberty of movement, and the right to freely leave and enter one's country (United Nations, 1948; United Nations, 2006).

Participant profiles

The participants in my study lived in displacement camps for varying lengths of time, ranging from 5 years up to 20 years. They described their experiences living as Deaf or disabled people in the refugee camps and the barriers they faced that impeded their full access to and inclusion in different aspects of camp life.

In order to contextualize the migration journey of the participants, I will include a brief introduction with background information on each participant in order to make sense of their stories.

Diutay from Ethiopia

Diutay is married with four children. Born hearing, he became deaf at the age of eight as a result of an illness. Diutay and his older brother fled Ethiopia in 2005 after his parents and another brother were killed by rebels. They escaped to a refugee camp in Kenya after being arrested and tortured by Ethiopian

Table 17.1 Participant profiles

Name	*Age*	*Home country*	*Country of camp/refuge*	*Time spent in resettlement camps*	*Arrival in US*	*Disability identity*
Diutay	36	Ethiopia	Kenya	14 years	2019	Deaf
Gopal*	36	Bhutan/Nepal	Nepal	20 years	2011	Deaf
Jacques	34	Democratic Republic of Congo	Rwanda	17 years	2013	Physical
Masuod	35	Afghanistan	NA	NA	2019	Physical
Rihana	25	Somalia	Ethiopia	5 years	2014	Physical

Note: *Pseudonym

police officers. Diutay attended school in the camp and learned both Kenyan Sign Language (KSL) and American Sign Language (ASL). After high school, he attended college to become a teacher. He then returned to the refugee camp where he taught Deaf children. In 2019 he resettled in the United States. Diutay hopes to return to Ethiopia someday to establish education for Deaf children there.

Gopal from Bhutan

Gopal was born in Bhutan. His family fled to Nepal when he was six years old after being forced out of Bhutan by the Bhutanese government. They lived in the refugee camp in Nepal for 20 years before coming to the United States in 2011. Gopal was born hearing but started to lose his hearing when he was around six years old and was completely deaf by the time he was eight. He attended school in the refugee camp with hearing students and teachers. Unable to understand what his teachers were saying, Gopal taught his friends some sign language, and they tutored him after school and helped him pass his classes. After college, he worked in the camp disability center, teaching sign language to other Deaf residents.

Gopal is married with two children. Through his work at a local non-profit organization, he assists Deaf newcomers adjust to life in the United States by teaching classes in American culture, providing resources for learning ASL, and teaching them the things he wishes someone had taught him when he first arrived.

Jacques from the Democratic Republic of Congo

Jacques has been in the United States for almost eight years. His family fled DRC for a refugee camp in Rwanda, walking for two weeks on a perilous journey. In 2008 Jacques returned to DRC to attend high school, and, while there, he was shot in the hip by rebels during the civil war, leaving him paralyzed. Jacques was then taken back to the refugee camp in Rwanda to recover. Once there, he experienced severe depression as a result of his trauma.

Jacques is now married, has two children, and drives for rideshare companies. He is a leader in both the refugee and disabled communities and volunteers his time to help other newcomers. Jacques hopes to become a mentor for other disabled refugees as well as those who have experienced trauma.

Masuod from Afghanistan

Masuod studied information technology and worked with the United States military in Afghanistan. As a result, he was considered a spy by the Afghani government, which put his life and the lives of his wife and children in danger from the Taliban. Masuod and his family were accepted for special immigrant visas (SIV) and resettled in the United States in 2019. Masuod became disabled as a teenager as a result of rheumatoid arthritis. As a disabled man, he experienced discrimination from his colleagues, neighbors, and even his own family members.

Rihana from Somalia

Rihana has used crutches or a wheelchair ever since contracting polio as a baby. Because she was disabled, Rihana could not attend school in Somalia or in the refugee camp in Ethiopia. When Rihana was only five years old, her mother was killed in an explosion at the marketplace. Her father was killed by Al Shabab militants when she was six. After their deaths, Rihana and her three siblings were separated, and they have not seen each other since. Rihana went to live with her mother's friend, and she does not know where her siblings are. When she was thirteen, her caretaker passed away, and the caretaker's son told Rihana she had to marry him if she wanted to continue living in the house. To avoid child marriage and seek safety, Rihana fled Somalia with neighbors. Using wooden crutches and shoes that were not suitable, Rihana walked for six months from Somalia to Ethiopia, where she lived for five years. In 2014 Rihana resettled in the United States. Currently, she is studying for her GED and hopes to become a social worker or counselor and help women in Somalia. She also hopes to return to Somalia to search for her siblings and be reunited with them. Rihana plays wheelchair basketball for her local and state teams.

Disability hierarchy in the resettlement camps

Life in refugee camps is incredibly challenging for everyone, but especially for disabled refugees because the necessary supports are often nonexistent. Infrastructure such as housing, schools, and other services are often temporary and built rapidly; therefore, the support needs of all people living in the camps may not be taken into account (Ward, 2021). Multiple barriers to accessibility often exist, such as uneven surfaces, long distances to access services, narrow doorways, and inaccessible bathroom facilities (Shivji, 2010). Multiple larger systems, structures, and environmental factors influence the experiences of disabled refugees, both in the refugee camps and as they resettle in a new country (Shivji, 2010). The layout and infrastructure of resettlement camps are often inaccessible for physically disabled people, which impedes access to facilities and services such as schools, healthcare, water and food distribution points, and restroom facilities (Ward, 2021). Additionally, making information accessible, hiring interpreters, training staff, and other necessary services and accommodations are not in place. This contributes to increased isolation of disabled people.

As Gopal shared, people moved into the camp very quickly in Nepal. There wasn't the time or resources to really support everyone, and they had to prioritize housing, food, and clothing. Displacement camps often face shortages of essential supplies needed by the entire population, such as soap and cooking fuel. Dilemmas over distributional ethics often arise due to limited resources and the vast variety of needs of the camp residents. Those responsible for budgeting and the allocation of resources often face difficult decisions about how to best meet the needs of the entire camp population (Ward, 2021). Allocating funds to meet the specific needs of the disabled residents could result in insufficient funds to meet the basic needs of the rest of the population. On the other hand, purchasing supplies to meet the needs of all the residents could mean that disability-specific needs go unmet (Mirza, 2011b).

This lack of resources is one factor contributing to the hierarchy of disability among refugees living in displacement camps because some disability-related needs may be met while others may not. This can include medications, specialized equipment, therapy, dietary needs, and so on. Disabled residents whose disability related needs are more readily accessible or are less costly are more likely to have their needs met than others. This can lead to more independence and self-sufficiency for some, while creating more isolation and dependence for others.

Barriers create hierarchy

In a survey conducted by Handicap International (2015), disabled people identified four types of barriers that impede their access to services, independence, and overall quality of life.

The types of barriers identified by disabled people are attitudinal, environmental, informational, and institutional (Handicap International, 2015). This chapter takes a deeper look into each of these barriers and how they contribute to disability hierarchy within displacement and resettlement camps for disabled refugees and other displaced people. These barriers create different experiences for disabled refugees based on their disability category. The intersectionality of different identities, such as gender and disability or age and disability, further hinders access and impedes independence for some disabled refugees.

Attitudinal barriers

Attitudinal barriers stem from negative attitudes towards diversity and resistance to adaptation. These attitudes are sometimes a result of unconscious bias. Attitudinal barriers impact accessibility on all levels because more of the other barriers are rooted in attitudes (Handicap International, 2015).

Attitudinal barriers include implicit bias and cultural norms and beliefs about disability, which lead to further discrimination, oppression, and dependence for disabled refugees. Negative attitudes and stigma towards disabled people in someone's local community often follow them to their new communities in refugee camps or their eventual resettlement. For example, Masuod described the way an Afghani caseworker who was assigned to assist him in his resettlement in the United States discriminated against him. The caseworker reflected Afghani attitudes towards disabled people; in their culture, people disabled in war are treated better than those born with a disability or acquiring one in youth. He described how the government provides financial support to citizens injured or disabled as a result of war or conflict but does not support disabled citizens who were born disabled or became disabled as a result of illness or injury.

Masuod's story demonstrates that, while hiring caseworkers who reflect the language and culture of the refugee population being served is good practice, it may also mean that, if not properly trained in rights-based service provision, negative cultural beliefs about disability may be reproduced during the resettlement process.

Many cultures believe that disability is a result of sin or past wrongdoing by the mother or is an ancestral curse, and the family is now paying for the past behavior of their ancestors. Beliefs such as these lead to stigma and further discrimination towards disabled people and their families. The earlier example outlines how, in some cultures, it is not only the disability itself but also how the person became disabled that impact the care and services they receive and how they are viewed by society. People disabled as a result of service to their country, such as in war or conflict, are often seen as more acceptable and receive more help and support (Ward, 2021).

These attitudinal barriers create a hierarchy not only in in the non-disabled community but also among disabled residents of the resettlement camps. Gopal explained how he preferred to hang out with his hearing friends because he felt smarter than many of his Deaf friends. He believed that if he was seen with and accepted by hearing peers, the community would see him differently and, in turn, be more accepting of him. He went on to share that at times his hearing friends shunned and ignored him by not letting him go to work with them or participate in other activities because he is Deaf. This caused him a lot of grief and heartache.

People with intellectual or mental health disabilities were looked down upon by the communities in the camps. They had difficulty enrolling in and being accepted into programs and school because of the belief that they didn't have the capacity to learn. They were often forced to stay home and were the family's responsibility. However, they were often ignored and neglected by family members as well because of the stigma associated with disability and the cultural beliefs surrounding disabled people. In many cultures, it is believed that disabled people can't learn; therefore, they often were forced to stay home and could not attend school or find work. This was especially true for intellectually disabled people and those with mental health disabilities.

As mentioned previously, intersecting identities play a large role in disability hierarchy. Individuals located at the intersections of class, gender, disability, race, and refugee status are often considered non-citizens and unjustly treated (Erevelles & Minear, 2010). Most notably, the intersectionality of gender and disability plays a large role in creating a disability hierarchy among disabled refugees. Treating disabled refugee women as non-citizens is a violation of their human rights. Furthermore, it serves to support the discriminatory policies and practices that view them as less desirable citizens and human beings (Ward, 2021).

In addition to policies that create further discrimination towards women, deeply rooted cultural beliefs about gender and disability are also at play. To illustrate this, Rihana candidly spoke about how women in her culture do not have any rights, and the situation is even more grave for disabled women. Rihana's story is an example of this. As a disabled teenager whose parents and, later, caretaker had died, she faced the decision of being forced to marry or fleeing her country.

> In my culture women get married young and depend on a family. That is how it has been for a long time. Now young people don't understand. Women have a choice. So before, you have to stay with your family and the married family member. I said no, I don't want to stay with the man. I grew up with him. He was like my brother. When his mom died, he said if you stay you will be my wife. I said no because I was young. I didn't have experience. I didn't want to get married as a young woman. When you get married and you're handicapped your life is very difficult. No education, you have to stay with the man, so I said no. I left the house and went to the neighbors. And we raised money for a better life. Like, we had to escape. Otherwise, we will be dying. If I had stayed in Somalia it would have been very difficult. I didn't see other women; I saw women without handicap get married young and their situations were very bad. Men use their power to control women. I don't agree with that in my culture. I think women have a choice. Some women understand some women have no choice. They have no options. They die or get married. Maybe to someone they never met before. Women in my culture don't have rights. Women with disabilities have less rights.
>
> *(Interview with Rihana, November 1, 2020)*

Rihana's experience as a disabled woman with few rights in Somalia continued in the resettlement camp in Ethiopia. In Ethiopia she lived in a Somali refugee community as a single, disabled young woman. Because she did not have family to support her, she was forced to rely on the support and assistance of others. Rihanna could not attend school because she did not have the means to pay for an education, nor could she work because of her status as a disabled woman. These attitudinal biases and cultural beliefs did not change when her environment changed; they followed her and continued to negatively impact her situation and quality of life.

Environmental barriers

Environmental barriers are natural or man-made barriers (e.g. staircases, narrow doors, inaccessible public transportation, poor lighting, etc.). Natural environmental barriers may be caused by natural disasters in which roads and buildings are destroyed, therefore restricting access to services (Handicap International, 2015).

A shared experience for physically disabled participants was how environmental barriers impacted their access to services, basic needs such as food and shelter, and education. Many spaces were physically inaccessible because of narrow doorways or steps. Often, physically disabled residents of the camps could access services only if they were independently able to move around the camp or if they had someone to assist them with mobility. If they didn't, they either did not receive the services they needed or wanted or were forced to rely on the help of others, even for basic needs such as food. (Ward, 2021).

Jacques described his experience as a physically disabled person. His wheelchair did not fit through the doors of the standard housing units, and he was not able to independently push himself around the camp because of the poor quality of the roads. He was forced to stay home and rely on others to bring him food.

> After I became paralyzed, I lived in the camp health center because I had no way of living in those tiny houses for refugees. They are very little houses 2 ½ meters by 4 meters for every family. And the roads are really dirty and pits, stones, they are not good. So then living in there [the health center], I could have somebody help me. Because I couldn't handle life on my own. I needed to have someone push me every time if I wanted to go somewhere. I couldn't get in my house with my wheelchair. I arrived at the front door [and] I had to have someone lift me and take me to the room. The doors were too small for my wheelchair. Each time I need to go around the camp to relax, I need to have someone push me. Because I can't push myself because [of] the way the roads are really dirty and full of pits. So I stayed in the health center for a while. I stayed in the healthcare center for one year. In 2010 I lived in Kanombe Military Hospital until the end of the year. Then in 2011 they built me a house near the hospital so I can get out of the hospital. Maybe live my life, take a shower whenever I want, and sleep. So nobody is pushing me around or standing beside me. To make me more independent.
>
> *(Interview with Jacques, November 11, 2020)*

Other residents with physical disabilities who could independently travel within the camp experienced more autonomy and self-reliance than those who couldn't. The infrastructure within the camps themselves created hierarchies even within the same disability category. For physically disabled residents, their level of independence, autonomy, and self-reliance was directly related to their level of mobility. Some spaces were physically accessible for some disabled refugees but not for others.

Gopal worked in the camp disability center in Nepal. He explained that in addition to the disability type, the camp infrastructure also played a role in the ability or inability to access spaces and information. In this camp in Nepal, many people with physical disabilities stayed home because they couldn't walk, and most didn't have wheelchairs. Only a few people had wheelchairs, but buildings did not have ramps, and they were inaccessible. Schools did not have wheelchair ramps, so only physically disabled students who could navigate the stairs could attend school. Those who used wheelchairs could not.

He went on to share that most students with physical disabilities stayed home instead of going to school. The camp was hastily built, and priority was given to housing and other shelter. For this reason, school was held outdoors in the forest. Students had to sit on their sandals because they didn't have chairs or tables, and the teacher carried the blackboard to school every day on his back. Students with physical disabilities were not provided supportive seating so that they could participate. Sitting on the ground for hours at a time was difficult or impossible. Gopal explained that on days when it started to rain suddenly, the students had to run home quickly. Students with physical disabilities or low vision were unable to do so, which made attending school more of a challenge (G. Dangal, personal communication, March 25, 2021).

Although all students were required to attend school in the Kenyan camps, Diutay also shared that it was not always possible for students with physical disabilities. He explained that the roads in the camp were bad, and students who used wheelchairs could not travel independently. If those students lived near the schools, the teachers and students would push them so they could attend school. But they were unable to help those students who lived too far away, and therefore, those students could not attend school. Education was physically more accessible for some students than others, due to camp infrastructure, their type of disability, and where they lived in location to the school.

Informational barriers

Informational barriers occur when information is not made available to or accessible for everyone. While informational barriers are often invisible, they can cause a large number of people to be excluded. Examples of informational barriers include early warning systems, evacuation alerts, relief operations, and access to aid (Handicap International, 2015). Deaf residents in the camps are significantly impacted by informational barriers. Lack of access to information stems from not providing interpreters or information presented in sign language (Ward, 2021).

Deaf students could not access education in the same way their hearing peers could because the information was presented in spoken language, and teachers were not trained in how to teach Deaf children. Lack of resources and supports for teachers and Deaf students further contribute to barriers in accessing information and instruction. Although Deaf students were allowed, and sometimes required, to attend school in the resettlement camps, they were forced to reply on the help of peers in order to understand the instruction and pass their classes. These communication barriers made education challenging or inaccessible for Deaf students (Ward, 2021).

Gopal shared his frustration with school and how he almost gave up because he couldn't pass the class. Gopal did not have interpreters or teachers who knew Nepalese Sign Language (NSL), and so he really struggled. Gopal had friends who were willing to help him, family members who encouraged and supported him, and the motivation to work hard to get an education. He explained how, after he taught his friends some sign language, they acted as his tutors and interpreters.

> I tried to go to the hearing school, but the teacher spoke, and I couldn't understand any of it. I failed and failed third grade so many times. I was ready to give up, go find a job or something. I couldn't understand, and I didn't learn anything. But my family, my brother, said no, you're still young, 11, 12, 13 years old. An education is important. They really encouraged me to continue. But in 1996, I went to the sign class and started learning Nepalese Sign Language. Sometimes at [hearing] school, teacher didn't come, or it was break time or whatever; I tried to teach my friends who lived near me sign language. They picked it up fast. I could read lips a little bit, so we could communicate. I understood them better than the teacher who just talked and talked, told stories; I didn't understand any of that. During break time or after school, I asked my friends to help me. I asked them what the teacher said at school, what they talked about, about the homework. My friends were willing to help me, so they explained it, and I understood, and I passed the classes.
>
> *(Interview with Gopal, December 12, 2020)*

Gopal's story demonstrates how the different barriers overlap and how they affect and interact with one another. One example of this is how the Deaf students were required to attend school (institutional) but were not given interpreters to access the information they needed to succeed and learn (informational).

Informational barriers made information such as warning systems and messages inaccessible, putting the lives of some camp residents in danger. During the 20 years Gopal lived in the camp in Nepal, he experienced two fires and the flooding of the entire camp. He shared how the houses were made of wood and were very close together, the roofs touching, so if one caught on fire, it rapidly spread to the surrounding houses. Gopal described his experience when the entire camp flooded during the night, and they had to quickly evacuate. He did not know what was happening because he couldn't hear any announcements or receive information from his neighbors. He woke up when the water started to enter his house, and he had to quickly scramble to get his family to safety.

Institutional barriers

Institutional barriers include policies and procedures that discriminate against disabled people, such as organizational practices that are not flexible or adapted to disabled people, leading to exclusion (Handicap International, 2015).

Displacement often causes disruption to formal schooling and impedes access to quality education (Rodriguez & Dieker, 2018). As noted previously, many barriers to receiving an education exist for disabled children. Article 24 of the Convention on the Rights of Persons with Disabilities addresses education and calls for equal access to free, quality, and compulsory inclusive education (United Nations, 2006). As Gopal's story illustrated, schools that are put into place rapidly or temporarily may not be accessible. Both Diutay's and Gopal's experiences highlight that teachers may not have the training, materials, or equipment needed to teach disabled students.

Education is a human right outlined in several international conventions. Article 26 of the Universal Declaration of Human Rights outlines for the right to education for everyone, including a free education at the elementary and fundamental stages (United Nations, 1948). The Convention on the Rights of Persons with Disabilities recognizes the right to an inclusive education for all disabled people in Article 24 (United Nations, 2006). These calls for the right to education are further outlined in Article 28 of the Convention on the Rights of the Child (UN, 1989) and Article 22 of the Refugee Convention (United Nations Refugee Convention, 1951).

Although Deaf residents did not have interpreters or instruction in sign language, they were permitted and often required to attend school, whereas physically disabled students could only attend school if they could get there independently. Blind students could attend school if they had adequate vision to get to school independently; however, no extra supports or services were in place to help them access instruction. Camp residents with intellectual disabilities or mental health needs were shunned, looked down upon, and ostracized. In the resettlement camp in Nepal, Deaf residents were able to access more services and had more work and educational opportunities because they could be more independent. Bicycles were the main mode of transportation around the camp, so those who could ride a bicycle and navigate the camp easily had more access. For this reason, Blind and physically disabled residents of the camp had fewer opportunities for school, employment, and the ability to access other programs and services in the camp (M. Das, personal communication, April 9, 2021).

While living in the refugee camp in Kenya, Diutay experienced education both as a student and, after completing college, as a teacher. He used the term "inclusive education" to explain that all kids in the camp were required to go to school, and teachers were not allowed to deny any students. However, supports, services, and training were not provided for the students or the teachers to make it a truly inclusive and accessible education. Like Gopal, Diutay did not have interpreters, nor did the teachers know sign language, but he was still held responsible for the content of the lessons. Because of these language and communication barriers, he had to put extra effort into his studies in order to pass his classes.

> In middle school, I was with hearing students. Communication was hard. Why? They spoke English, a different language. Writing was okay, why?

> Because I copied the teacher, and I went home and studied. At the hearing school, I tried to lip-read, but it was hard, so I wrote.
>
> *(Interview with Diutay, December 4, 2020)*

He went on to explain that, even though he is Deaf, he was born hearing and became deaf around years eight years of age. This meant that he had already acquired a strong foundation in spoken language, and he was able to transfer those skills to learning written language and sign language. However, he shared that other Deaf students, who did not have that language base, had much greater difficulty accessing the language and information at school. This created a hierarchy among Deaf residents in the camp among those who became deaf later and those who were born deaf. Gopal was also born hearing and became deaf later as a result of illness. He described a similar experience – because he had previously had access to spoken language, he had less difficulty than his peers who were born deaf. However, he still described his struggles, frustrations, and the extra effort he had to put into his schoolwork in order to pass his classes.

Education is a fundamental human right that can help break the cycle of poverty, improve health, and bring about social change and stability. The UN's Sustainable Development Goal 4 (SDG4) aims to ensure inclusive and equitable quality education for all (United Nations, 2015). The 2030 Sustainable Development Goals are a set of shared goals adopted by UN member states as a call for action working towards peace and prosperity (Ward, 2021). Despite these calls for free and inclusive education for all, the participants' experiences show the reality of education for disabled displaced people and highlight the barriers in place that impede access to education for many disabled camp residents.

Recommendations and conclusion

Respect for human dignity is at the center of human rights. Human rights are fundamental rights, are not earned, and cannot be taken away. A human rights framework considers all human beings as rights bearers with inherent self-worth. I make the following recommendations in order to better understand the needs of disabled refugees and to change the narrative around disability.

Human rights education

Knowing that one has rights and understanding what those rights are are necessary in order to recognize when those rights are absent or being violated. An important start to achieving this is incorporating human rights education in school curricula. Furthermore, adults need to be aware of their rights and the rights of their children and family members so they can work towards change in their communities and advocate for these rights to be recognized and upheld. It is vital that this information is accessible for all people, regardless of their language or communication mode. Additionally, disabled people need to be taught their rights and how to recognize when these rights are not being upheld and how to take action. Resettlement workshops should include discussions on the Americans with Disabilities Act (ADA) and the Individuals with Disabilities Education Act (IDEA) as an important first step to creating rights awareness.

Attitudinal biases such as cultural views and beliefs around disability create further barriers to education, employment, and independence. Education to create awareness around disability and disability justice is necessary to change the narrative around disability and work towards changing these attitudes and beliefs. Changing the narrative is an important step in dismantling the hierarchy that exists.

Inclusive policies and practices

Exclusive policies and practices don't consider the unique needs of disabled displaced people, and lack of or inadequate distribution of resources contribute to the marginalization and oppression of this group. A common narrative around disability and displacement is that of need and dependence. I argue that this is a result of systemic failures and exclusive policies and not because of personal values and a desire to depend on others. The participants in my research study all expressed the desire to get an education so they could support their families, work, and be independent. What hindered them in doing so was lack of appropriate support and accessibility, not their personal drive and motivation.

An inclusive and quality education has the power to create knowledge, break down barriers to opportunity, and reduce social inequities (Ward, 2021). Inclusive education means not only physically accessible spaces but also adapted curricula and training for teachers and providing teachers the appropriate support to meet the needs of their students.

Training and cross-collaboration between resettlement and disability organizations

Mirza (2011b) and Handicap International (2015) reported on the knowledge of resettlement workers regarding disability and meeting the unique support needs of this group of refugees. Their findings align with the experiences of the participants in my study (Ward, 2021), concluding that resettlement workers lack sufficient training, knowledge, resources, and expertise when working with disabled refugees. Because of this, the needs of disabled refugees often are not met throughout the resettlement process, creating feelings of frustration and isolation.

Fifty-six percent of humanitarian workers recommend prioritizing collaboration and coordination between mainstream actors, specialized actors, and disabled persons' organizations (DPOs) (Handicap International, 2015). Furthermore, 85% of these same humanitarian workers recognized that disabled displaced people experience increased vulnerability, but the vast majority (92%) feel that the unique needs of this group are not taken into consideration in humanitarian situations (Handicap International, 2015). These findings are also reflected in the participants' narratives and further support the need for change.

Improving CRPD compliance for participating states and establishing more global accountability by developing guidelines, providing training to agencies and organizations, and reallocating resources would improve the resettlement experiences of disabled displaced people regardless of which country they migrate to (Ward, 2021).

Conclusion

Chimamanda Adichie (2009) explains the dangers of a single story. Single stories create stereotypes that are untrue and incomplete. These stories often become the only story about a person or country. The single story around disability is one of need, pity, and brokenness. The single story around refugees is that of difference, less desirability, and otherness. The dangers of these stories are that they rob people of their dignity, emphasize our differences while ignoring our similarities, and cloud our recognition of equity and humanity (Adichie, 2009).

The ideology of ability views disability as something to be feared and a burden on society. This is reflected in the perceptions of refugees as the other, to be feared and denied a place in their communities (Dawson, 2019).

Our stories can be used to empower, humanize, and repair the broken dignity caused by a single story (Adichie, 2009). Our stories matter. People become refugees by circumstance, not by choice. Every disabled refugee's lived experience is unique. However, we must understand their shared experiences in order to support the success and self-determination of disabled refugees and other displaced persons. Their stories are instrumental in working towards dismantling barriers that hinder self-reliance and independence. With these stories, we can work towards changing the narrative from one of pity, charity, and need to one of resilience and resistance.

Notes

1 *Identity-first language* (disabled person/disabled people) affirms that disability is an integral part of disabled people's identities and experiences. It recognizes the importance of disability in how it defines and shapes individual and collective experiences (Brown, n.d.).

People-first language (person with a disability; people with disabilities) affirms that people with disabilities are more than labels or diagnoses but are human beings who should be thought of as people first (Brown, n.d.).

While both terminologies aim to emphasize a person's value and worth, people-first language suggests the person can be separated from the disability. It is important to note that neither identity-first nor people-first language should be used exclusively in any situation. Some individuals and groups prefer people-first language, and it is important to respect how different communities and individuals choose to identify themselves. When in doubt, ask the person their preference.

2 Deaf with a "D" refers to members who culturally and linguistically identify as being Deaf and belong to the Deaf community. Deaf with a "d" refers to the audiological condition of not hearing. Not everyone in the Deaf community identifies as belonging to the greater disability community. However, Deaf participants were included because in their home countries they are considered disabled, and for the purposes of immigration paperwork, they are required to register as a disabled person.

References

Adichie, C.N. (2009, July). *The danger of a single story [Video file]*. https://www.ted.com/talks/chimananda_adichie_the_danger_of_a_single_story/discussion

Besic, E., Paleczek, L., & Gasteiger-Klicpera, B. (2018). Don't forget about us: Attitudes towards the inclusion of refugee children with(out) disabilities. *International Journal of Inclusive Education*, 202–217. https://doi.org/10.1080/13603116.2018.1455113

Brown, L.X.Z. (n.d.). *Autistic hoya*. https://www.autistichoya.com/p/definitions.html

Crock, M., Smith-Khan, L., McCallum, R.A., & Saul, B. (2017). *The legal protection of refugees with disabilities*. Edward Elgar.

Dawson, A.C. (2019). Stasis in flight: Reframing disability and dependence in the refugee. *Disability Studies Quarterly, 39*(1). http://dx.doi.org/10.18061/dsq.v39i1.6285

Disabled World. (2020, September 10). *Invisible disabilities: List and general information*. https://www.disabled-world.com/disability/types/invisible/

Elder, B. (2015). Stories from the margins: Refugees with disabilities rebuilding lives. *Societies Without Borders*, *10*(1), 2.

Erevelles, N., & Minear, A. (2010). Unspeakable offenses: Untangling race and disability in discourses of intersectionality. *Journal of Literary & Cultural Disability Studies*, *4*(2), 127–145. https://doi.org/10.3828/jlcds.2010.11

Handicap International. (2105). *Disability in humanitarian contexts: Views from affected people and field organizations*. https://www.hi-us.org/disability_in_the_humanitarian_context#:~:text=Global%20Report%20%7C%20Disability%20in%20Humanitarian%20Context%20(2015)&text=Results%20found%20that%2085%25%20of,into%20account%20in%20humanitarian%20response

Mirza, M. (2011a). Disability and cross-border mobility: comparing resettlement experiences of Cambodian and Somali refugees with disabilities. *Disability and Society, 26*(5), 521–535. https://doi.org/10.1080/09687599.2011.589188

Mirza, M. (2011b). Disability and humanitarianism in refugee camps: The case for a traveling supranational disability praxis. *Third World Quarterly*, *32*(8), 1527–1536. https://doi.org/10.1080/01436597.2011.604524

Nichols, M. (2019, July 22). Disability hierarchy is real and it's holding us back. *Unpacking Disability*. https://www.meriahnichols.com/disability-hierarchy/

Pearce, E. (2015). 'Ask us what we need': Operationalizing guidance on disability inclusion in refugee and displaced people programs. *Disability and the Global South*, *2*(1), 460–478.

Rodriguez, J.A., & Dieker, L.A. (2018). Emerging inclusive education in the United Nations relief and works agency for Palestine refugees in the Near East: A review of the literature. *Journal of International Special Needs Education*, *21*(1), 32–42. https://doi.org/10.9782/15-00018R2

Shivji, A. (2010). Disability in displacement. *Forced Migration Review*, *35*, 4–7.

Smith-Khan, L., Crock, M., Saul, B., & McCallum, R. (2014). To 'promote, protect and ensure': Overcoming obstacles to identifying disability in forced migration. *Journal of Refugee Studies*, *28*, 38–68. https://doi.org/10.1093/jrs/feu020

Snow, K. (2015). The disability hierarchy. *Revolutionary Common Sense*. www.disabilityisnatural.com

United Nations. (1948). *Universal Declaration of Human Rights*. https://www.un.org/en/universal-declaration-human-rights/index.html
United Nations. (1989). *Convention on the Rights of the Child*. https://www.ohchr.org/en/professionalinterest/pages/crc.aspx
United Nations. (2006). *Convention on the Rights of People with Disabilities*. https://www.un.org/development/desa/disabilities/convention-on-the-rights-of-people-with-disabilities.html
United Nations. (2015). *Transforming our world: The 2030 agenda for sustainable development*. https://sdgs.un.org/2030agenda
United Nations High Commissioner for Refugees. (2019). *Global trends: Forced displacement in 2019*. https://www.unhcr.org/globaltrends2019/
United Nations Refugee Convention. (1951). https://www.unhcr.org/en-us/3b66c2aa10
Ward, J.L. (2021). *Narratives of disability and displacement: An oral history of the lived experiences of disabled refugees*. [Unpublished doctoral dissertation]. University of San Francisco.
World Health Organization (2021). https://www.who.int/health-topics/disability#tab=tab_1

18

HIERARCHY, EDUCATION AND PERSONS WITH DISABILITIES IN ANGLOPHONE CARIBBEAN

Senator Floyd Morris

Introduction

In this journey of life, it is reasonable to assume that men and women are consistently engaged in activities for self-actualization. Men and women want to be the best that is possible, once the environment is created. Included in this group of individuals who aspire to be the best that they can be are persons with disabilities (Anderson, 2014).

Persons with disabilities are regarded as one of the most marginalized groups in society (World Health Organization-WHO/World Bank, 2011). Their marginality comes about due to lower-level health outcomes, low levels of education, less representation in the labour market and negative attitudes and stigma from individuals in society. Resultantly, these individuals are among the poorest in society (World Bank, 2016). Persons with disabilities therefore have to be consistently fighting for survival, and when they achieve, it is hailed and glorified in society. Their achievements are treated as an exception, rather than the norm (Anderson, 2014).

When persons with disabilities achieve, individuals in society place these achievers in a special category, thus creating a hierarchical structure among persons with disabilities (Nichols, 2021). For example, persons with disabilities who attend regular education institutions are generally hailed as preeminent achievers when they graduate after a successful course of study (Jamaica Gleaner, 2017). Their accomplishments are treated as exceptional, so much so that we have seen persons with disabilities now being referred to as 'individuals with exceptionalities'.

 DOI: 10.4324/9781003410089-21

In this chapter, this author examines the issues of hierarchy, inclusive education and persons with disabilities in the Anglophone Caribbean. I present the argument that hierarchy among persons with disabilities is a social construct that is formulated by the general isolation and exclusion of persons with disabilities from mainstream society. The spotlight is on the education system within the Anglophone Caribbean, which by and large, excludes persons with disabilities from the regular classroom. Thus, when individuals with disabilities do enter into that space, these individuals are seen as novel or exceptions. I present the case of two prominent persons with disabilities who emanate from two distinct Anglophone Caribbean jurisdictions to argue the point. These individuals are Ambassador Dr. Aubrey Webson of Antigua and Barbuda and Miss Kerryann Ifill of Barbados. The chapter is concluded with some recommendations for action. But, before we delve into the gravamen of the chapter, it is prudent for us to examine some foundational concepts that are germane to it.

Conceptual framework

In examining this issue of hierarchy, persons with disabilities and education in the Anglophone Caribbean, it is sagacious for us to look at some essential concepts that will occur regularly in the chapter. These are hierarchy, persons with disabilities, inclusive education and Anglophone Caribbean.

Hierarchy

Hierarchy in disability is positioning certain impairments as more or less disabling than others, with the idea that some impairments are better or less severe than others (Stewart, 2004). This hierarchization has the effect of intensifying the exclusion and isolation of some persons with disabilities from the mainstream of society (Meyers, 2020). The hierarchy of disability comes about due to certain realities that persons with impairments have to face on a daily basis: for example, the extent of access to education institutions, which by and large have been inaccessible to these individuals. When persons with disabilities do venture into these social institutions, they are perceived as novel and exceptional (Anderson, 2014).

The hierarchy of disability also manifests itself, according to some scholars, when the needs of men with disabilities are prioritized over those of women with disabilities in mainstream disability rights organizations (Sands, 2005). Laws and culture also rank persons with disabilities according to the specific type or circumstance of their impairment (Deal, 2003). There is also the manifestation of hierarchy in the international disability movement and international scholarship, where these organizations and academic literature from the Global North are perceived as superior to those of the Global South (Grech, 2015). In this chapter, the author will show how hierarchy emerges in the Anglophone Caribbean through the education system where persons with disabilities are concerned.

Persons with disabilities

"Persons with disabilities" is seen as a complex concept and carries varied definitions in different contexts. The United Nations Convention on the Rights of Persons with Disabilities (CRPD), which is the global 'bible' for persons with disabilities, highlights who are included as persons with disabilities. It states: 'Persons with disabilities include those who have long-term physical, mental, intellectual or sensory impairments which in interaction with various barriers may hinder their full and effective participation in society on an equal basis with others' (United Nations, 2006).

Ostensibly, the CRPD never articulated a definition of persons with disabilities. In fact, the discussions at the negotiations of the CRPD placed a significant focus on the matter, and it was highlighted that the concept had different meanings in different states (Degener, 2017). The decision was thus taken by the states parties negotiating the treaty not to set a single definition for the concept, but rather to indicate what it includes.

Evidently, the CRPD has sought to conflate both the social and human rights models of disability. The social model, developed primarily by Mike Oliver, adumbrates that it is social factors that restrict the participation of individuals with impairments in society on an equal basis with others (Oliver, 1990). Conversely, the human rights model treats all individuals, including persons with disabilities, as having the rights and freedoms as prescribed by the Universal Declaration of Human Rights (United Nations, 1948). In this chapter, this author posits the view that the hierarchical structure among persons with disabilities emerges because of the varied social barriers that have served to restrict the participation of individuals with impairments in society on an equal basis with others. If these barriers, which violate the fundamental rights and freedoms of persons with disabilities, are removed (Morris, 2019; 2020), it will allow persons with disabilities to participate freely in society, thus reducing or eliminating this hierarchical structure.

Inclusive education

According to the United Nations Education, Scientific and Cultural Organization (UNESCO) inclusive education is a process of strengthening the capacity of the education system to reach out to all learners. As an overall principle, it should guide all education policies and practices, starting from the fact that education is a basic human right and the foundation for a more just and equal society (UNESCO, 2009, p. 8). The definition proffered by UNESCO gives a foundational understanding of the concept of inclusive education. It affirms certain primordial principles: the all-embracing nature of education, the right of all citizens to education and the fact that education is quintessential to the attainment of social justice.

In 1994, UNESCO and other partners framed the Salamanca Statement and Framework for Action. The statement affirmed the commitment to establishing an inclusive education system throughout the world. It states specifically: 'Schools should accommodate all children regardless of their physical, intellectual, social, emotional, linguistic or other conditions' (UNESCO, 1994). The Salamanca Statement further adumbrated:

> Regular schools with this inclusive orientation are the most effective means of combating discriminatory attitudes, creating welcoming communities, building an inclusive society and achieving education for all; moreover, they provide an effective education to the majority of children and improve the efficiency and ultimately the cost-effectiveness of the entire education system.
>
> *(UNESCO, 1994)*

Evidently, an inclusive education system is designed to create greater levels of equality in society and will undoubtedly bring persons with disabilities into the mainstream of society.

Resultantly, in 2006, the CRPD reaffirmed the right of persons with disabilities to an inclusive education. Article 24 of the CRPD expressly states:

> States Parties recognize the right of persons with disabilities to education. With a view to realizing this right without discrimination and on the basis of equal opportunity, States Parties shall ensure an inclusive education system at all levels and lifelong learning directed to . . .
>
> *(United Nations, 2006)*

Countries that have signed and ratified the CRPD are obligated to honour these provisions.

The Committee on the Rights of Persons with Disabilities in its General Comment No. 4, opined:

> Recognition of inclusion as the key to achieving the right to education has strengthened over the past 30 years and is enshrined in the Convention on the Rights of Persons with Disabilities, the first legally binding instrument to contain a reference to the concept of quality inclusive education. Sustainable Development Goal 4 too affirms the value of inclusive, quality and equitable education. Inclusive education is central to achieving high-quality education for all learners, including those with disabilities, and for the development of inclusive, peaceful and fair societies.
>
> *(Committee on the Rights of Persons with Disabilities, 2016)*

There can therefore be no doubt as to the indispensability of inclusion to the participation and empowerment of persons with disabilities in mainstream society.

But what does this concept of inclusive education entail? Kasa (2014) articulates some salient factors that must be present. In this context, schools should be equipped with ramps that will allow wheelchair users to navigate the school. It should have accessible bathroom facilities to accommodate children with disabilities. There should be teachers who are trained to interact with and impart knowledge to persons with disabilities. There should be technological support to assist with the learning of children with disabilities, and there should be support for children with disabilities to participate in school activities throughout the school day (Kasa, 2014). The education system in the Anglophone Caribbean is, however, lacking in the majority of these factors (Gooden-Monteith, 2019).

Anglophone Caribbean

Anglophone Caribbean refers to those countries in the West Indies that were once colonies of Britain. These countries include Anguilla, Antigua and Barbuda, The Bahamas, Belize, Barbados, British Virgin Islands, Cayman Islands, Dominica, Grenada, Guyana, Jamaica, Montserrat, St. Kitts, St. Lucia, St. Vincent and the Grenadines, Trinidad and Tobago and Turks and Caicos Islands. These countries have adopted a system of government that is similar to Britain's (Buddan, 2012). Consequently their education system mirrors that of Britain: pre-primary, primary, secondary, post-secondary and tertiary. It is this education system that will be interrogated in this chapter.

The education system in the Anglophone Caribbean

For one to understand the issues being discussed in this chapter, it is prudent to have some understanding of the education system in the Anglophone Caribbean. Both subjects under study in this chapter hail from the Anglophone Caribbean. These individuals cumulatively received their education in four Anglophone Caribbean countries: Jamaica, Antigua and Barbuda, Barbados and Trinidad and Tobago. These countries came out of a similar colonial experience as they were all colonized by Britain for over 300 years (Beckles, 2013). The education system was thus fashioned off the coloniality of Britain. In this context, the education system in the region has a system of pre-primary (basic school), primary, secondary, post-secondary (vocational institutions and extension schools) and tertiary institutions. Special education institutions were established as a means of providing education exclusively for persons with disabilities. However, in the post-colonization era – that is, after 1962 – persons with disabilities started to experience mainstream education. Those persons with disabilities who were attending special education institutions – for example, the Salvation Army School for the Blind – and were displaying tremendous academic performance were integrated in the mainstream education system whilst still being a part of the special education institution (Gooden-Monteith, 2019).

But persons with disabilities in the Anglophone Caribbean have not been able to regularly attend school, and this has profound implications for the quality of education these individuals receive. The Economic Commission of Latin America and the Caribbean 2017 Report highlights the situation of school attendance for students with disabilities. It states:

> School attendance by children with disabilities still lags behind that for children without disabilities. Among those countries for which data is available, only in Bermuda and the Cayman Islands was school attendance for children with disabilities comparable to that for children without disabilities. The countries with the largest differences in school attendance between children with and without disabilities were Grenada (25 per cent in 2010), Guyana (22 per cent in 2010), and Jamaica (22 per cent in 2010) (see figure 18.9). The countries with the smallest gap were Barbados (10 per cent in 2010), Saint Lucia (seven per cent in 2000) and, as mentioned above, Bermuda and the Cayman Islands.
>
> *(ECLAC, 2017, p. 47)*

There are a number of factors contributing to the attendance of children with disabilities at school. However, these are not the focus of this chapter. Nevertheless, it is paramount for this author to point out that accessibility has been one of the major factors contributing to the consistent attendance at schools in the region. Such a factor has been discussed by scholars such as Morris (2020; 2021), Gayle-Geddes (2015), Anderson (2014) and Rieser (2008).

School attendance has profound implications for the outcome of the education of persons with disabilities. For example, it has tremendous consequences for the completion and certification of these individuals and thus impacts their ability to find decent jobs. The ECLAC (2017) Report further states:

> As a group, persons with disabilities have lower levels of education. The countries with the largest differences in completion of secondary education between working age adults with and without disabilities were Grenada (30 per cent), Trinidad and Tobago (30 per cent) and Antigua and Barbuda (26 per cent), all in 2010 (see figure 11). The countries with the smallest gap were Belize (eight per cent in 2000), Bermuda (eight per cent in 2010) and the Cayman Islands (five per cent in 2010).
>
> *(ECLAC, 2017, p. 47)*

It is irrefragable that persons with disabilities are less likely to complete school than individuals without a disability. One can therefore understand why the few who have a disability and complete a tertiary education are held in such high esteem in society. But it requires a degree of sedulousness on the part of persons with disabilities to achieve such a feat. Ostensibly, it is these few individuals with disability who have completed the full cycle of the education system in the Anglophone Caribbean who emerge as leaders in the community of persons with disabilities.

Theoretical framework

The theoretical framework anchoring this research study is that of social constructionism and intersectionality.

Social construction

Disability is seen as a social construct and, as such, best fits within the theoretical frame of social constructionism. Berger and Luckmann (1966) theorized that society is created by human beings and their interactions. These interactions Berger and Luckmann treat as habitualization. According to Berger and Luckmann, habitualization is the process by which any frequently repeated action becomes cast into a pattern, which can then be performed again in the future in the same manner and with the same economical effort (Berger & Luckmann, 1966). Additionally, Berger and Luckman opine that human beings build a society and accept it as it is because previous generations created it. Society, therefore, according to Berger and Luckman, is a habit.

For centuries, persons with disabilities have been viewed and treated in a negative manner in society. These individuals have been regarded as outcasts (Campbell, 2021) who cannot make any meaningful contribution to society, and this is anchored in the welfare model of disability (Gayle-Geddes, 2015). Similarly, there are those in society who believe that the disease contributing to the impairment of individuals is the source of the problem, and this is anchored in the medical model of disability. Both the welfare and medical models of disabilities have been 'habitualized' in distinct societies across the world and have contributed to the marginalization of persons with disabilities (Oliver, 2009).

Ostensibly, the social model as adumbrated by Oliver strongly suggests that a disability comes about due to various barriers placed on individuals with impairment by members of society (Oliver, 1990). The barriers include but are not limited to social, environmental, economic and attitudinal factors that restrict the participation and inclusion of individuals with impairments in society (Oliver, 2013). In the context of this chapter, the social barrier of access to education is foundational. Because persons with disabilities have been excluded from regular education institutions in the Caribbean, this has stymied their development (Morris, 2020; 2019; 2010). When a few of these individuals get the opportunity to participate in regular education institutions and excel, they are thus construed as exceptional (Anderson, 2014). It is here that the hierarchical structure of disability emerges.

Education is a means of social mobility. The higher one climbs up the education ladder, the greater the possibility of men and women making it in society (Wright, 2020). The probability of employment increases. The social network expands, and there is a level of respect for the educated individual in society.

Therefore, when a person with disability climbs up the education ladder, these experiences are shared with others (Morris, 2017). Automatically, the educated person with disability is thrust up the leadership ladder in the community of persons with disabilities. Additionally, the peers of the educated person with disability consistently make reference to him or her in different circles, and this increases public knowledge of the educated person with disability. Sometimes, this contributes to resentment among members of the community of persons with disabilities as they believe their efforts are not being recognized. However, in the majority of cases in the Caribbean, most of these educated persons with disabilities who are active in the community of persons with disabilities are embraced and respected. The experiences of the two participants who are the focus of the case study in this chapter will substantiate these arguments.

Intersectionality

The second theory anchoring this chapter is that of intersectionality. According to the Commonwealth Foundation (2019, p. 1):

> Intersectionality refers to how people in all their diversity embody multiple identities, face intersecting oppressions and suffer differently from the same structural and institutional power imbalances. It offers an analytical lens through which one can see and understand from various angles where/how various levels of power and privilege interface and cross in a given context.

Kimberle Crenshaw was the first scholar to articulate the theory of intersectionality in a seminal work in 1989. Crenshaw's expressions came within the context of her assessment of Black women and race in the United States (Crenshaw, 1989). In the context of this chapter, the argument is applied to the intersectionality of education and disability because one cannot assess the situation of hierarchy in disability without examining the issue of education.

Access to education is one of the social barriers that have been restricting the participation of persons with disabilities in society on an equal basis with others (United Nations, 2018). The design of education institutions, absence of trained teachers and lack of assistive technologies and professional support for students with disabilities are all factors that have contributed to the exclusion of persons with disabilities from regular education (Morris, 2020; Gayle-Geddes, 2015). Therefore, when a person with disability does get the opportunity to attend a regular education institution, the individual is treated as an exceptionality. This commences the process of hierarchy in disability, which accelerates if the person with disability is performing on par or above their peers without disability. Ultimately, the person with disability who has acquired an education through the mainstream educational institution is perceived by members of society as an exceptionality and is thus placed at the helm of the community of persons with disabilities.

One can highlight the utility of these theories to this chapter. Disability is a social construct, and the meanings prescribed to these individuals with impairments are based on years of interactions in society. These interactions have been habitualized and have contributed to varied restrictions being placed on these individuals participating effectively in society on an equal basis with others. Restriction from regular education institutions, for example, when it intersects with disability, has contributed to the marginalization of these individuals. However, we have seen when these individuals are included in mainstream society and they are performing on par or above their peers with disabilities, they are seen as exceptional. This precipitates the argument of hierarchy in disability. Both social constructionism and intersectionality are thus important theoretical frames for creating greater understanding of the issue of hierarchy in disability and education of persons with disabilities in the Anglophone Caribbean.

Methodological approach

In preparing this research study, a qualitative approach was adopted. This is because qualitative research by nature gives the researcher the option to engage in in-depth interviews. A qualitative research technique of case study was thus utilized, along with elite interviews with the subjects identified for deliberation. Specifically, a collective case study approach was utilized to assess the phenomenon under study (Stake, 1995). Yin (1994) postulated that case studies must have five essential components: the research question(s), its propositions, its unit(s) of analysis, a determination of how the data are linked to the propositions and criteria to interpret the findings.

Case studies can be exploratory, descriptive, interpretive or explanatory (Mariano, 2000). The purpose of this case study is both descriptive and explanatory. It seeks to describe the exposure of persons with disabilities to an inclusive education system. Further, it explains how this exposure to an inclusive education contributes to hierarchy in disability.

The significance of the phenomena of interest is to explain how an inclusive educational environment contributes to the creation of hierarchy in disability. Persons with disabilities have been generally excluded from regular education institutions. However, when they are included in the regular education system, they are treated as exceptionalities, especially when they perform above their non-disabled peers. It is suggested that this is where the hierarchical structure begins in disability.

The preeminent research questions in this case study are:

1. To what extent does restrictive access to an inclusive education stimulate hierarchy in disability?
2. Are persons with disabilities the creators of hierarchy in disability?
3. Does the experience of inclusive education make a person with a disability a better leader?

For the case study, Ambassador Dr. Aubrey Webson of Antigua and Barbuda and Miss Kerry Ann Ifill from Barbados were selected as the subjects for analysis. These are individuals who have experienced inclusive education and become successful in their respective fields. Ambassador Dr. Aubrey Webson is a person who is Blind and has risen to the rank of Antigua and Barbuda's Permanent Resident Ambassador to the United Nations (Think Magazine, 2016). Miss Kerry Ann Ifill is also a Blind person living in Barbados and was the first person who is Blind to occupy the position of President of the Senate of Barbados (Eye Care Caribbean, 2012).

These individuals were selected primarily because of their inclusion and participation in inclusive education in the Caribbean. Furthermore, they have been elevated to prominent leadership positions in their respective countries. Additionally, they represent gender balance, which is important for this research study.

Articles from various archival sources were integrated into the study for triangulation purposes, in order to increase the credibility of the arguments presented. Thus, newspaper articles, blogs and webcasts about these individuals were consulted. Adopting this methodological approach gave the researcher tremendous data on the subjects and the topic for discussion.

Additionally, a list of questions was prepared and sent to the subjects for their responses.

Upon completing the questionnaire, a careful transcription was done of the data collected. The responses were carefully transcribed by a research assistant. This was done sequentially in order to preserve data transcription credibility.

Upon completing the data transcription, the author ventured on to a mapping of the major concepts. This was done through comparing the notes from the two interviews and linking them to the literature on the subject. The preeminent concepts from the study are persons with visual disabilities, special education, inclusive education, hierarchy, leadership and network.

The findings from the research were carefully documented. This was done through a narrative approach, describing and explaining the experiences of both subjects under study: their places of birth, educational institutions attended, years of attending educational institutions, treatment of educational professionals, accessibility at education institutions, performance at education institutions, leadership roles and networking with non-disabled individuals.

Ambassador Dr. Aubrey Webson – Antigua and Barbuda

Very few individuals get the opportunity to represent their country, and for an individual to be elevated to an ambassador at the United Nations is indeed seminal. Ambassador Aubrey Webson is undoubtedly one of few persons with a disability to have been appointed as an ambassador to the most powerful multi-lateral institution in the world when he was selected by the government of Antigua and Barbuda.

Ambassador Webson was born on the peaceful and tranquil Caribbean island of Antigua and Barbuda on October 12, 1954. He grew up in a single-parent household. His mother was responsible for his growth and development.

Aubrey was born with his full sight but became totally blind by age four. This unfortunate situation had a negative impact on him initially. However, with strong support from his mother and family, he was given the necessary assistance that would increase his functionality in society. He attended pre-primary school at age four but had to transition to a special education institution by age five. His secondary and tertiary education was at regular education institutions.

Ambassador Webson attended the Cobs Cross School in Cobs Cross, St. Paul's, Antigua and Barbuda. Then he transitioned to the School for the Blind in Trinidad and Tobago. He participated in the University of the West Indies (UWI) Extension Programme in Kingston, Jamaica, to get additional secondary certification, and after this, he matriculated at the UWI and pursued his undergraduate degree programme at Mona. Ambassador Webson pursued post-graduate studies at New School for Social Research in New York City and received his PhD from Case Western Reserve in Ohio, USA.

Ambassador Webson indicated that at both the primary and special schools, support was as expected from teachers. At the UWI, he indicated, there was no specific support. He further opined that all but one or two lecturers gave some support. At the post-graduate level, which he pursued in the United States of America, the system worked with him to solve whatever issues were present. Here, it seems as if there was restrictws access to inclusive education for Aubrey Webson, although he managed to navigate the system throughout the Anglophone Caribbean.

Ambassador Webson was asked, 'How did you perform academically in the inclusive education setting?'

Ambassador Webson outlined that his performance at all levels of the education system could be best described as 'above average'. There were some challenges at the early stage, largely due to the onset of blindness. However, as these issues were resolved, his performance improved. He opined that his performance at the graduate and post-graduate levels were 'outstanding' as he achieved honours in the three programmes that he took.

Ambassador Webson highlighted that there were a number of challenges in the education system, but he managed to work around them. The biggest challenges were encountered at the University of the West Indies in the 1980s, as he was among the first set of visually impaired students to attend the institution. At that time, lecturers and systems were not fully responsive to the needs of students with disabilities, and this restricted the access of persons with disabilities to higher education. However, he pointed out that most of the lecturers did what they could to assist students with disabilities.

Ambassador Webson was asked, 'What leadership roles, if any, did you play at these educational institutions?' Ambassador Webson pointed out that he was always actively involved at school, albeit in teams. However, he opined that he never demonstrated any outstanding leadership. He was mostly involved in planning and organizing activities. Such exposure to planning and organizing activities whilst pursuing his education nevertheless equipped him with some essential tools for leadership.

Ambassador Webson opined that he was mostly involved in community-oriented leadership. This is where his leadership acumen became manifest. The global community of persons with disabilities has subsequently benefitted exponentially from his leadership skills (Think Magazine, 2016; Pitt News, 2020).

Ambassador Webson was asked, 'Do you believe that your experience at inclusive educational institutions contributed to your leadership roles in the community of persons with disabilities and other organizations in your country?' Ambassador Webson is of the unequivocal view that his experience at regular education institutions contributed to his leadership roles in the community of persons with disabilities and other organizations. Further, he adumbrated that his network of friends who emanated from regular education institutions contributed tremendously to the various leadership roles he has subsequently occupied. Undoubtedly, this network of friends would have seen the talent at school and in the community of this iconic person with disability and contributed to his elevation to one of the top diplomats from the Caribbean to the United Nations.

Miss Kerryann Ifill – Barbados

It is irrefragable that Kerryann Ifill is one of the most outstanding persons with disabilities in the Caribbean. Her accomplishments speak volume about her standing in Barbados and the broader Caribbean. Her accomplishments include being the first person who is Blind to become president of the Senate of Barbados, and her contributions to the community of persons with disabilities in Barbados and the Caribbean also make her an excellent case study for this chapter (Eye Care Caribbean, 2012).

Kerryann was born on the beautiful Caribbean island of Barbados on December 20, 1973. She grew up in a single-parent household. She was born with her sight, but by the age of five, she had lost her sight completely.

Kerryann started attending school before she lost her sight at age five. However, upon losing her sight, she stopped attending school for a year. This was largely due to the fact that most educational institutions in the Caribbean do not have provisions to cater to children with disabilities who develop blindness whilst attending school.

In the embryonic stages of her schooling, Kerryann attended a regular education institution. The onset of blindness precipitated her attending a special education institution: the Irving Wilson School, located on Pine Plantation Road, Bridgetown, Barbados. She then attended a regular secondary school: the Combermere Secondary School, located at Waterford, St. Michael's, Barbados.

For clarity, a regular secondary school in the context of this chapter refers to an established secondary school where students who are perceived to be 'normal' attend. Some of these regular education institutions have been mandated to accept persons with disabilities in the Anglophone Caribbean, thus commencing the process of inclusive education.

Kerryann then attended the University of the West Indies, Cave Hill, where she completed her first degree. Kerryann completed a master's in business administration at the Durham Business School as well.

Kerryann indicated that during her school sojourn, she had support through the use of Braille. All through her educational experience, she used Braille to take notes and then to transcribe these into print so that her teachers could assess her work. It was whilst at the tertiary level that she started using more modern technologies, such as Job Access with Speech (JAWS). This is software that converts printed text into speech so that a Blind person can hear what is being typed. Additionally, she used audiobooks and other electronic-based documents whilst she was at the tertiary level.

According to Kerryann, some teachers were more supportive than others whilst she was pursuing her education. She indicated that her maths teacher was extremely supportive. This teacher gave her two years of free classes in order to increase her knowledge of the subject. She also indicated that her special needs school was extremely supportive in her education.

As it relates to performance academically, Kerryann was no featherweight. Miss Ifill was asked, "How did you perform academically at these inclusive educational institutions?" She indicated that she was usually at the top of the class from the primary level up to the varied tertiary institutions she attended.

In general, teachers and lecturers were pleased with her performance throughout her educational sojourn. Kerryann indicated that, at the secondary level, teachers were selected on the basis of their willingness to work with students with disabilities. Her maths teacher was sceptical at first. However, as she saw the results, her enthusiasm intensified as she was enjoying the challenge.

As she went up the education ladder, appreciation of her performance intensified. Both students and lecturers demonstrated their appreciation of her performance. There was a greater recognition of the talents and abilities of persons with disabilities at this level of the education system.

During her quest for education, Kerryann was involved in diverse extra-curricular activities, especially at the secondary level. She was asked, 'What leadership role, if any, did you play at these educational institutions?' At the secondary level, she was a member of the Girl's Guide Association and president of the debating club. Her participation at the tertiary level was less intense due to the workload she had to carry as a student with a disability.

Kerryann was asked, 'Do you believe that your experience at inclusive educational institutions contributed to your leadership roles in the community of persons with disabilities and other organizations in your country?' Kerryann believes that her experience in mainstream education institutions contributed exponentially to the diverse leadership roles she has played in the community of persons with disabilities and other organization. She is of the firm belief that the network she built up during her years at the secondary and tertiary levels has been a strong contributing factor to her current roles. For example, she indicated that the general secretary of the most powerful trade union in Barbados today was her classmate at secondary school. Furthermore, she indicated that the lecturers and friends she met at university form a preeminent part of her diverse current activities.

Comparative analysis between subjects of study

The cases of Ambassador Webson and Miss Ifill are of significant importance in understanding the issue of hierarchy in disability and education of persons with disabilities in the Anglophone Caribbean. A comparative look at these individuals provides interesting revelations.

Both Webson and Ifill are visually impaired individuals. They developed their visual disability after birth and before the tender age of five. Such an experience would have placed these individuals in a precarious position and robbed them of their full childhood development (Morris, 2017; Anderson, 2014).

For Webson and Ifill to adjust and become resilient, they had to be included in an educational facility that would contribute to their developing skills such as reading and writing Braille. Barbados had such facility for Ifill to utilize, but Webson had to go to Trinidad and Tobago at the time. Special education thus played an integral role in the early years of their development. However, as they matured, they transitioned to a more inclusive educational environments at the secondary level, although there were limitations to access for persons with disabilities.

Both Webson and Ifill had the opportunity for an inclusive secondary-level education. Ifill was able to attend a regular secondary school in Barbados. However, Webson had to attend a secondary facility in Jamaica at the time. It must be pointed out that Webson and Ifill have generational age differences. Therefore, Webson attended secondary-level school in the 1980s, whilst Ifill attended during the early 2000. From the 1970s to the 1980s, inclusive education was just beginning to take shape in the Caribbean (Morris, 2021), and this explains some of the restrictions to access and why Webson had to go to Jamaica to advance his education. Conversely, by the early 2000s, the world and the Caribbean were experiencing a shift in their philosophy towards the education of persons with disabilities (Rieser, 2008), and this contributed to Ifill's experience in a more inclusive secondary facility in Barbados.

Webson and Ifill both had experience in an inclusive tertiary education space. For their undergraduate programme, the University of the West Indies, which is the premier tertiary education institution in the Caribbean, was the place of choice to study. Again, the generational differences figured in their experiences. Webson attended the UWI in the 1980s when there were no systems in place to accommodate students with disabilities (Morris, 2019). However, Ifill attended at a time when inclusive education was more entrenched at UWI, and systems were in place to give support to students with disabilities (Morris et al., 2021).

Interestingly, both Ifill and Webson received their graduate degrees from universities outside the Caribbean. They received their graduate degrees in the United States and the United Kingdom. These countries have accepted and been practicing an inclusive education philosophy for decades, notwithstanding their systemic challenges (Gooden-Monteith, 2019; Rieser, 2008). These countries' inclusive education policy is anchored in the social model (Oliver, 1990) and the human rights model (United Nations, 2006; Degener, 2017) of disability. These models of disability recognize the right of persons with disabilities to education and to inclusion in society on an equal basis with others (Committee on the Rights of Persons with Disabilities, 2016).

Inclusive education is a critical intersectionality in understanding the leadership roles of persons with disabilities in society (Commonwealth Foundation, 2019; Crenshaw, 1989). This is because, in inclusive educational settings, persons with disabilities are exposed to significant organizational and planning skills and networks of individuals who are vital to promoting the talents and abilities of persons with disabilities. Both Webson and Ifill have been involved with different activities at varying levels of the education system. Webson indicated that he was more involved in planning and organizing than in direct leadership. Ifill was directly involved in the Girls Guide movement at school. This is a service club that is established in the education system and can be found all over the world. It is the equivalent of the Boys Scout in the school system.

Through their involvement at distinct levels of the inclusive education system, Webson and Ifill forged strong networks that both individuals agree have played indispensable roles in their national and organizational leadership. These networks involved school administrators, lecturers and students they associated with during their school years, and some of these individuals have transitioned into managers and other leaders in Barbados and Antigua and Barbuda. Being a part of the 'old boys' and 'old girls' networks plays a pivotal role in social empowerment and upward mobility (Wright, 2020). Invariably, these individuals look out for each other to ensure their success.

Obviously, Webson's and Ifill's involvement at the various inclusive education institutions implanted strong memories in the minds of their counterparts, and this aided in how they were perceived by their peers. Such perceptions, based on the fact that Webson and Ifill were appointed to high government offices, seem to have left a positive attitude towards them as individuals, and this contributed to their national leadership roles.

This is where there is a 'dialectical turn' on the issue of hierarchy in disability. It is the varied interactions that these individuals had at the diverse inclusive education institutions where persons with disabilities are viewed as exceptionalities by non-disabled individuals (Nichols, 2021). Thus, these persons with disabilities who have traversed the inclusive education space are always in the line of sight of their non-disabled colleagues who place them at the apex of the community of persons with disabilities. It is 'able-bodied' individuals who therefore place persons with disabilities in a hierarchical structure (Campbell,

2021; Nichols, 2021) as they will refer and promote those individuals they are acquainted with from their inclusive educational institution.

The hierarchical structure created by 'able-bodied' individuals filters into the community of persons with disabilities through social institutions such as the media (McGrail et al., 2020). The media in the Caribbean and across the world has consistently promoted persons with disabilities who have graduated from tertiary education institutions as high achievers. When these individuals with disabilities graduate from any tertiary institutions in the Caribbean, oftentimes, they are placed in prominent spaces in the media (Jamaica Gleaner, 2017). It is promotional activities like these that place such graduates in a positive light among their colleagues with disabilities, resulting in their being elevated to leadership positions in the community of persons with disabilities.

Evidently, individuals attending inclusive educational institutions have a role to play in the perception of persons with disabilities. It is a critical means of intersectionality in the context of disability and therefore important in understanding hierarchy in disability. It is individuals from these institutions, who, in interacting with the limited number of persons with disabilities attending such inclusive education institutions, consistently promote and highlight what they perceive to be exceptional talents on the part of the person with disability. Hierarchy in disability is formulated and is therefore a social construct (Nichols, 2021).

Recommendations

If inclusive education institutions trigger a hierarchical structure in disability due to the limited number of persons with disabilities attending such institutions and able-bodied individuals from these institutions view the performance of persons with disabilities as exceptionalities, then there is a need for these educational institutions to be further 'liberalized' so that more persons with disabilities can attend. When more persons with disabilities are in attendance at regular education institutions, teachers, administrators and students will understand that the performance of individuals with disabilities is not an exceptionality. They will be exposed to more individuals with disabilities who have the capacity to perform efficaciously in an inclusive education environment.

However, for the education system to include more persons with disabilities, a compendium of actions must be taken by governments. Schools have to become accessible in terms of the physical plant and information (Morris, 2020). Teachers have to be trained in how to relate to students with disabilities (Gooden-Monteith, 2019). There must be the presence and availability of accessible technologies for students with disabilities in the classroom (Rieser, 2008). Additionally, the curriculum must take into consideration the learning needs of individuals with disabilities (Parey, 2021). And, where needed, there should be support staff (shadows) to assist students with disabilities (Kasa, 2014).

Relatedly, governments should embark on a consistent public education campaign to ensure that all stakeholders are aware of the needs of students with disabilities in the classroom. The public education campaign should also be designed to demystify myths that exist among some parents about disability. For example, there are some individuals in the Caribbean who have the misguided and false view that disability is contagious and that it can be transmitted to an individual associating with a person with disability. Such disability infodemics must be jettisoned from society, and one of the best ways to do so is through consistent public education campaigns.

Conclusion

In this chapter, this author examined the issue of hierarchy in disability from the perspective of inclusive education. The argument has been posited that hierarchy in disability is a social construct and that it was able-bodied individuals who created this conception through their experiences with persons with disabilities in inclusive educational institutions in the Anglophone Caribbean. To test my arguments, a case study was conducted with two prominent persons with disabilities from the Anglophone Caribbean who had the opportunity of receiving an inclusive education. They both shared and accepted that inclusive education played an indispensable role in the leadership roles that they have occupied in society and other organizations. Furthermore, they accepted that inclusive education provided tremendous opportunities for them to build a network of support and friends who assisted them in their varied leadership roles. Most importantly, they accepted that the experience of inclusive education assisted in how they are perceived by their colleagues with disabilities, thus pivoting them to varied leadership roles in the community of persons with disabilities.

From the experiences of these two iconic persons with disabilities from the Caribbean, certain conclusion can be drawn from the questions that are of focus of this chapter by this author:

1. To what extent does restrictive access to an inclusive education stimulate hierarchy in disability? It seems from the experiences of these individuals that because there have been restrictions to mainstream educational institution for persons with disabilities, those individuals who get the opportunity to attend such institutions are perceived as exceptional, and it is this perception that triggers the hierarchical structure in disability. If more persons with disabilities had the opportunity to attend inclusive education institutions, able-bodied individuals would be exposed to more persons with disabilities and realize that persons with disabilities, in general, have the capacity to perform as anyone else in an inclusive education system. What is required is for the requisite support mechanisms to be put in place so that persons with disabilities can perform on an equal basis with others. It is therefore imperative that education systems be fully 'liberalized' so that persons with

disabilities can exercise their right to participate in inclusive education on an equal basis with others (Committee on the Rights of Persons with Disabilities, 2016).

2. Are persons with disabilities the creators of hierarchy in disability? Persons with disabilities are not the architects of hierarchy in disability. It is a social construction, which, in the cases cited in this chapter, has its origins in educational environments that restricted the full participation and inclusion of persons with disabilities. Based on the performance of persons with disabilities in the inclusive education space, non-disabled individuals see it as exceptional and place these individuals on a pedestal. Their claims of exceptionality are repeated often enough that they become 'habitualized' (Berger & Luckmann, 1966), and society accepts the claims and pivots these individuals into leadership roles in the community of persons with disabilities.
3. Does the experience of inclusive education make a person with a disability a better leader? From the cases cited in this chapter and based on the personal experiences of the author, who also has a disability and experienced inclusive education (Morris, 2017), it seems reasonable to conclude that inclusive education does contribute to a person with a disability becoming a better leader. Inclusive education exposes persons with disabilities to a plethora of opportunities, chief of which is the exposure to a diversity of individuals who eventually become a part of the network of the person with disability, and this is a tremendous asset for any leader, as postulated by Webson and Ifill in the case study.

For the issue of hierarchy in disability to be addressed, governments have to move with alacrity to 'liberalize' the education system to make it more inclusive of persons with disabilities. In so doing, they will have to ensure that the requisite facilities are put in place to accommodate persons with disabilities in regular education institutions. When persons with disabilities are allowed to participate consistently in regular education institutions, non-disabled individuals will realize that these individuals have the capacity to learn and that they are not exceptionalities.

References

Anderson, S. (2014). Climbing every mountain: Barriers, opportunities, and experiences of Jamaican students with disabilities in their pursuit of personal excellence. Kingston: Arawak Publications.

Beckles, H. (2013). Britain's black debt: Reparation for Caribbean slavery and native genocide . . . . Kingston: The University of the West Indies Press.

Berger, P., & Luckmann, T. (1966). The social construction of reality. London: Penguin Books.

Buddan, R. (2012). The foundations of Caribbean politics. Kingston: Arawak Publications.

Campbell, F.K. (2021, April 8). The concept of ableism: Challenges to deep thinking and critique. In Keynote Prepared for the ALTER (European Society for Disability Research) 2021 Conference.

Committee on the Rights of Persons with Disabilities. (2016). General comments on Article 24 of the Convention on the Rights of Persons with Disabilities. www.ohchr.org
Commonwealth Foundation. (2019). Gender and its intersectionality: Guidelines for programming and engagement in governance. London: Commonwealth Foundation.
Crenshaw, K. (1989). Demarginalizing the intersection of race and sex: A black feminist critique of antidiscriminatory doctrine, feminist theory and anti-racist politics. University of Chicago Legal Forum, 189(1). http://chicagounbound.uchicago.edu/uclf/vol1989/iss1/8.
Deal, M. (2003). Disabled people's attitudes toward other impairment groups: A hierarchy of impairments. Disability & Society, 18(7), 897–910.
Degener, T. (2017). A new human rights model of disability. In V. Della Fina, R. Cera & G. Palmisano (eds.), The United Nations convention on the rights of persons with disabilities: A commentary, 41–60. Cham: Springer.
ECLAC. (2017). Disability, human rights and public policy. Port of Spain, Trinidad and Tobago: United Nations.
Eye Care Caribbean. (2012 March 20). Caribbean Council for the Blind (CCB) congratulates . . . http://eyecarecaribbean.com/latestnews/carib . . . /.
Gayle-Geddes, A. (2015). Disability and inequality: Socioeconomic imperatives and public policy in Jamaica. New York: Palgrave Macmillan.
Gooden-Monteith, C. (2019). Inclusion of students with special needs in the regular classroom: teachers' knowledge, attitudes and practice in Jamaica and globally. Kingston: Self-published.
Grech, S. (2015). Disability and poverty in the global South: Renegotiating development in Guatemala. London: Springer.
Jamaica, G. (2017 March 9). 'Doctor' in waiting . . . Blind senator Floyd Morris nears PhD. https://jamaica-gleaner.com
Kasa, C.H. (2014). Strategies for success: Creating inclusive classroom that works. http://inclusionu.com/strategies-for-success/
Mariano, C. (2000). Case study: The method. Chapter 10. In P. Munhall & C. Oiler Boyd (eds.), Nursing research. A qualitative perspective (2nd ed., 311–337). Sudbury, MA: Jones and Bartlett Publishers.
McGrail, E., McGrail, J.P., & Rieger, A. (2020). Friday night disability: The portrayal of youthful interactions in television's *Friday Night Lights*. Disability Studies Quarterly, 40(4).
Meyers, S. (2020). Allies, enemies, or indifferent? The disability and older persons movements in Jamaica. Research in Social Science and Disability: Alliances, Allies and Disability, 12, 41–65.
Morris, F. (2010). Access and inclusion of children with disabilities in the Jamaican education system. www.cds.mona.uwi.edu.
Morris, F. (2017). By faith, not by sight. Kingston: I-Published.
Morris, F. (2019). An inclusive, equitable and prosperous Caribbean: The case of persons with disabilities. Social and Economic Studies, 67(4), 95–119.
Morris, F. (2020). The regional disability index and strengthening resilience of persons with disabilities in the Anglophone Caribbean. Journal of Caribbean Environmental Sciences and Renewable Energy. www.cesarejournal.org
Morris, F. (eds.) (2021). Inclusive education: The key to social transformation. Kingston: Ian Randle Publishing.
Morris, F., McPherson, B., & Cardoza, S. (2021). A model for social transformation of the marginalized: A case study of persons with disabilities of the University of the West Indies. In F. Morris (ed.), Inclusive education: The key to social transformation. Kingston: Ian Randle Publishing.
Nichols, M. (2021). Disability hierarchy is real and it is holding us back. https://www.meriahnichols.com
Oliver, M. (1990). The politics of disablement. London: Macmillan Press Ltd.

Oliver, M. (2009). Understanding disability: From theory to practice (2nd ed.). London: Palgrave MacMillan.
Oliver, M. (2013). The social model of disability: Thirty years on. Disability & Society, 28(7), 1024–1026. https://doi.org/10.1080/09687599.2013.818773
Parey, B. (2021). Promoting inclusive education through national assessments: Required Caribbean efforts. In F. Morris (ed.), Inclusive education is the key to social transformation. Kingston: Ian Randle Publishers.
Pitt News. (2020 October 16). U.N. Ambassador Aubrey Webson brings . . . https://pittnews.com/article/arts-and-entertainment/
Rieser, R. (2008). Implementing inclusive education: A Commonwealth guide to implementing article 24 of the UN Convention on the Rights of Persons with Disabilities. London: Commonwealth Secretariat.
Sands, T. (2005). A voice of our own: Advocacy by women with disability in Australia and the Pacific. Gender & Development, 13(3), 51–62.
Stake, R.E. (1995). The art of case study research. Thousand Oaks, CA: Sage Publications.
Stewart, R. (2004). The "really disabled": Disability hierarchy in John Hockenberry's moving violations. Berkeley, CA: University of California.
Think Magazine. (2016). Ambassador gives voice to the vulnerable. https://case.edu/think/spring2016/ambassador-gives . . . /.
United Nations. (1948). Universal Declaration of Human Rights. https://www.un.org/en/universal-declaration-human-rights/
United Nations. (2006). Convention on the Rights of Persons with Disabilities. www.un.org.
United Nations. (2018). Disability and development report – Realizing the sustainable development goals by, for and with persons with disabilities. https://www.un.org/development/desa/disabilities/wp-content/uploads/sites/15/2018/12/UN-Flagship-Report-Disability.pdf
United Nations. (2015). The sustainable development goals. Retrieved from www.un.org.
United Nations Educational, Scientific, and Cultural Organization. (1994). The Salamanca statement and framework for action on special needs education. Salamanca, Spain: World Conference on Special Needs Education. www.unesco.org
United Nations Educational, Scientific, and Cultural Organization. (2009). Policy guidelines on inclusion in education. Washington, DC: United Nations Educational, Scientific, and Cultural Organization.
World Bank. (2016). Disability overview (online data). http://www.worldbank.org.
World Health Organization/World Bank. (2011). World report on disability. Geneva: World Health Organization.
Wright, C. (2020). How old girls' networks make the boys mistakes. Macquarie Park: Macquarie Business School.
Yin, R.K. (1994). Case study research: Design and methods (2nd ed.). Newbury Park, CA: Sage Publications.

PART III

Which rights on top, whose rights on the bottom?

19

HIERARCHIES OF IMPAIRMENT AND DIGITAL DISABILITY RIGHTS

Sarah Lewthwaite and Abi James

The right to accessible digital information, services and education is recognised internationally through the Convention on the Rights of Persons with Disabilities (United Nations, 2006), but in practice, digital disability rights are enabled and constrained through regulations, technologies and the socio-cultural contexts that structure experiences of disability at a local, regional and global level.

In this chapter, we observe the resulting 'hierarchies of impairment' in digital accessibility; how these are articulated in a constellation of laws, regulations and standards; and how these hierarchies are then reflected and reconfigured in use in varied contexts and, most particularly, in the Global South, where experiences of disability, digital divides and indices of digital exclusion vary widely from the implicit expectations exported in the standards-making practices of the Global North.

Digital accessibility

'Accessibility' in digital contexts is generally understood to refer to efforts that ensure users are not prevented from participating in the content, services or experiences offered by technologies on the grounds of disability. Ensuring digital content is accessible means that it must be compatible with a wide range of assistive technologies and personalisation mechanisms. Assistive technology can enable a person to

- Perceive content via a means that can be consumed by an individual: for example, being read aloud via a screen reader or text-to speech-engine, enlarged via magnification tools or presented as symbols or simplified language
- Operate a device in different ways: for example, through tracking eye motion, a single switch voice or a standard keyboard

DOI: 10.4324/9781003410089-23

- Create content through different inputs: for example, via dictation, adapted keyboards or symbol/word banks.

Assistive technology relies on content being developed using robust coding standards so that it can be passed between browser and applications through assistive technology or personal settings and presented to the users in the most effective format for them. Digital content and tools are considered accessible when they are perceivable, operable, understandable, and robust for all users. These four "POUR" principles form the basis of digital accessibility legislation, standards and related best practices (Web Accessibility Initiative, 2019).

As Seale and Cooper (2010) observe, many definitions of accessibility focus on reducing barriers to the web[1] and ensuring equitable access for users with disabilities (Web Accessibility Initiative [WAI], 2005). However, they also observe the influence of the social model of disability in recognising the socially and culturally contingent aspects of disability. This results in a more nuanced definition that recognises accessibility as an artifact of the relationship between a user and a digital tool in a given environment, rather than a mismatch between tools and perceived innate, individual personal traits or needs. Such definitions prioritise concepts of adaptation and flexibility and throw sharply into focus the social and cultural role of digital technologies in society. This sits alongside the situated nature of tools whereby intentional design is mediated by delivery and use in a particular social and cultural context.

Inaccessible digital tools are not only barriers to participation. Through inaccessible design, technologies can engender disabled subjectivities and compromise disabled people's digital rights – this is exclusion on grounds of disability. Critical commentators note that disability and ability continue to be 'built in' to technological networks. For disabled users who experience a close functional fit with a technology or adjustments enabled by assistive technologies for independence and support, non-disabled subjectivities become possible. Disability here can be a matter of relevance, not definition. However, while internet use among disabled people is increasing globally, the lack of progress improving digital accessibility internationally is troubling. Where tools, services and public networks are inaccessible, disabled people are disadvantaged and locked out of mainstream interactions by technical barriers that produce them as 'disabled' (Goggin & Newell, 2005; Ellis & Kent, 2011).

Hierarchies of impairment in accessibility

'Hierarchies of impairment' identify the ways in which physical and cognitive differences are identified and arranged within society. We know that different cultures, geographies, economies, politics and histories imbue different impairments with different cultural significance. Disability is 'culturally, ideologically and contextually positioned . . . multidimensional' (Grech & Soldatic, 2016,

p. xv). These understandings 'permeate everything, including technology and accessibility practice' (Lewthwaite & Swan, 2013). Hierarchical views of disability and impairment have been researched since the 1970s, but in 2003, Deal expanded the focus of disableism to research inter-group discrimination amongst disabled people. This analysis of hierarchic understandings of impairment among disabled, and non-disabled people acts to motivate vigilance and critical engagement, inclusive of those communities that seek to enable and empower. Hierarchies of impairment were first used as an analytic lens on accessibility practice to highlight how accessibility research and resources frequently prioritise certain communities and their requirements above others for a nexus of reasons (Kelly et al., 2010). Kelly et al. foreground Deal's call for critical research centred on the most marginalised:

> [I]t is important that, whilst disabled people fight a common cause in seeking equality within society and the removal of discriminatory practices, strategies for attitude change are targeted in a manner that makes them most effective. This may include focusing attention on impairment groups that face the most discrimination in society (i.e. those ranked lowest in the hierarchy of impairments), rather than viewing disabled people as a homogenous group.
>
> *(Deal, 2003, p. 907)*

In this respect, the use of hierarchies of impairment as a critical lens is productive. For example, it shifts analysis from the broader questions of what dominant discourses do (in the Foucauldian sense), allowing us to scrutinise the 'modes of ordering' in situated practices and examine how these are enacted in different material forms (Foucault, 1998), to centre instead on those who are most marginalised, to recognise intersections of differing marginalising factors and to mobilise alternatives. Fundamentally, it operationalises a deconstruction and vigilance to ask, "Who is missing here?"

Our previous work has identified important ways in which prevalent accessibility standards discourses and the use of web accessibility guidelines such as WCAG 1.0 (now 2.1, soon to be 3.0) as the de facto international standards have instituted hierarchies of impairment with potentially counterproductive and detrimental outcomes for some groups (Lewthwaite & Swan, 2013; Lewthwaite, 2014; Roy & Lewthwaite, 2016). These have centred first on issues with the standards themselves: for example, how those with cognitive disabilities have been underserved whilst visual impairments are privileged; second, on how these hierarchies and the socio-cultural construction of disability traced within standards are thrown into sharp relief when considered against alternative global contexts. Here, technological specificity (e.g. the predominance of mobile in the Global South, lack of assistive technologies) and cultural specificity (e.g. national variations in definitions of disability, who is included, who is excluded) expose further hierarchies. In sum, whilst digital standards enact disability hierarchies rooted in the assumptions and norms of the Global North, digital divides and inequalities will be compounded.

In this chapter, we return to these concerns in light of developing accessibility standards practices; new policies, laws, and technologies; and recent shifts in the cultural and social understanding of disability and digital life. We argue that the current trajectory of equality and digital accessibility policy, standards making and technology instigate new lines along which dis/ability difference is affected, organised and re-organised. In this analysis, we continue to pay particular attention to critical issues that can be occluded by Northern disability standards discourse in accessibility and digital disability rights: intersections of impairment, gender, geopolitics, aging and race, amongst others. We also notice how the very activity of standards making operates to effect biopolitical norms. While the rise of machine learning, artificial intelligence and big data represents new vistas through which dis/ability difference is iterated, accessibility represents the foundation upon which disability digital rights are currently predicated. We also observe the ways in which the constellation of policy, standards and law effects digital disability rights in increasingly sensitised ways.

Digital disability rights

As personal technologies, the internet and social media have evolved, so has the concept of digital rights and, in particular, the right to internet access. Disability has been a driver of both technical innovation and rights-based policy in digital domains, as the first 'protected characteristic' for whom digital access has been legislated. Early in the history of the web, inventor Tim Berners-Lee stated, 'The power of the Web is in its universality. Access by everyone, regardless of disability is an essential aspect' (W3C, 1997). This sentiment was formalised by the United Nations (UN) when the World Summit on the Information Society (WSIS) declared that "everyone, everywhere should have the opportunity to participate and no one should be excluded from the benefits the Information Society offers" (WSIS, 2003), echoing rights outlined in Article 19 of the Universal Declaration of Human Rights (United Nations, 1948). In this frame, technologies and the information society they enable are held to 'powerfully contribute to the worldwide democratisation, civic engagement and action-orientated social responsibility'.

In 2006, Article 9 of the UN Convention for the Rights of People with Disabilities (UNCRPD) set out that in order to enable people with disabilities to live independently and participate fully in all aspects of life, state parties should 'promote access for persons with disabilities to new information and communications technologies and systems, including the Internet' (Article 9, 2.(g), United Nations, 2006). It also linked the right to freedom of expression and opinion and access to information specifically to the accessibility of the internet and digital platform so that persons with disability can 'seek, receive and impart information and ideas on an equal basis with others and through all forms of communication of their choice' (United Nations, 2006).

While the UNCRPD articles set out that digital accessibility is core to the rights of disabled people, the intersection between disability and technology remains complex. Efforts are often driven by the actions of disability rights groups campaigning for their needs to be addressed against an environment of dynamic and fast-changing technologies which require technical standards for interoperability. In this context, early efforts to consider how internet access for people with disability could be legislated were driven by individuals' and groups' groundbreaking efforts to apply equalities laws to the internet. The Americans with Disabilities Act (ADA) Title II established that failure to make reasonable accommodations for the needs of individuals with disabilities constituted discrimination, while Title III requires places of public accommodation to provide people with disabilities accommodations in order to have equal access (ADA, 1990, p. 42). Early cases of activism by disabled people's organisations (DPOs) in the US led to legal recognition that digital rights could be protected under equality laws, although guidance on how to achieve this was still lacking.

Web standards as a tool for digital rights

Whereas disability digital rights could once be considered to solely focus on assistive technology working alongside hardware and software, used by an individual through physical interaction, the advent of the internet has led to our digital interactions being dominated by information, tools and services that are accessed nearly instantaneously through the internet without any engagement with a third party. Customers and services users are remote, with no first-hand, direct interaction with the provider of the digital platforms. Hence, equal access to the internet is only possible through anticipating accommodations that may be required by people with disabilities instead of relying on providing additional support and adapations at the point of service delivery. As a result, content authors, digital designers and service providers need guidance on how to anticipate these needs and ensure they have met the requirements for accommodations. Regulators, governments and disability advocates also need tools to measure whether these services are or are not discriminating against disabled users. At the same time, individuals with disabilities need information on what they can and cannot access. When faced with the requirement to make 'digital platforms accessible', developers with minimal understanding of disabilities and user preferences must turn to technical standards setting out what they must do that can translate into functional requirements. Web standards strive to answer these requirements. Unlike many technical domains, the internet standards that drive the development of the web have always been led by the technical community itself, rather than a government or formal standards-making organisation (Nickerson & Muehlen, 2006). Though treating accessibility as a 'standard' also fits into the technologist model of open web standards to allow for the interoperability of code and content, open to all (Abou-Zahra & Brewer, 2019), importantly, it also provides an opportunity for the disability community to participate and co-create.

One of the first attempts at accessibility guidelines was developed for the city of San Jose (Waddell, 2000) in response to a complaint filed in 1995 by a blind city commissioner and screen reader user under the ADA. The guidelines focused solely on the needs of individuals with sensory disabilities, with five of its seven guidelines supporting access for people with visually impairments; one considered access to media for people with visual or hearing impairments, and one guideline required that an access instruction page be available for visitors. In focusing on a limited range of needs, these guidelines overlooked a wide range of barriers affecting many other groups, such as those who could not understand the content and those who were unable to physically reach and activate interactive content such as links. This may not be surprising, given that, at the time, the internet was evolving from a simple text-based interface that was relatively accessible for people with sensory disabilities into a multimedia platform. However, this hierarchy of needs has continued to be reified as digital accessibility and digital rights have evolved over the subsequent 25 years, with disability groups continuing to be frequently siloed by their perceived needs and requirements.

How standards are made

The Web Accessibility Initiative (WAI), part of the World Wide Web Consortium (W3C), was established in 1997. The W3C is an international body comprising volunteer organisations (including several DPOs;[2] the UK Royal National Institute for the Blind is a founding W3C member) alongside experts and full-time staff who work together to develop web standards (W3C, 1997). The standards-making process is intentionally open and transparent; however, it is also lengthy and complex (Lewthwaite & Swan, 2013). During the development process, the public is invited to provide feedback on the guidelines before they become an official 'normative' document. These opportunities for feedback are where disability advocates and DPOs with technical expertise can highlight issues and concerns.

Since the first publication in 1999 of the Web Content Accessibility Guidelines (WCAG), the W3C WCAG standard has become the worldwide de facto standard for web accessibility. While other guidelines exist, the vast majority derive from current or earlier versions of WCAG and are adapted according to each country's or territory's context. Some governments worldwide reference WCAG verbatim within their disability legislation. In this way, governments seek to effect quality measures that are commensurate with disability discrimination laws. For example, across the European Union and the UK, the EU's Web Accessibility Directive public regulations (European Commission, 2016) refer for specifics to Standard EN 301 549 of the Accessible ICT Procurement Toolkit, which itself is aligned to WCAG 2.1 Level AA standards. Australia,

Korea, China and many other developed countries have adopted WCAG as the basis for their digital accessibility regulations. Importantly, global corporations are bound by national accessibility laws in the territories where they operate, meaning that even in nations where accessibility standards are not enforced strongly at a policy level (e.g. Japan, UK), corporations must still apply such digital standards to avoid litigation in major Western markets. In this respect, national laws enacting standards can and do drive international change.

Yet when the first set of Web Content Accessibility Guidelines were published as a standard by W3C as WCAG 1.0 in 1999, a tension was established between incorporating wider requirements for all disability, language and culture versus what is testable (Ellcessor, 2010). From the onset of efforts to address digital accessibility, it was recognised that the needs of individuals with disabilities would vary based on their impairments, with needs grouped into people who are deaf, blind or 'physically challenged' and those who have cognitive and visual impairments (W3C, 1997). While classification of disability is at odds with the social model of disability, it has become an inherent part of explaining differences in people's needs in accessible design. Data led to certain guidelines being removed from WCAG 1.0 as too reliant on subjective judgement, which, in turn, led to a reduction in support for the needs of people with cognitive disabilities (Ellcessor, 2010). Later revisions to WCAG in 2008 (WCAG 2.0) brought the standards more into line with the US Section 508 of the US Rehabilitation Act (McLawhorn, 2001) with testable statements. But at the same time, there was an acknowledgement that this led to gaps in covering some disability needs that rely on design decisions (Kirkpatrick et al., 2018). The editors note these limits: '[E]ven content that confirms at the highest level (AAA) will not be accessible to individuals with all types, degrees or combinations of disabilities, particularly in the cognitive and learning areas' (Kirkpatrick et al., 2018). In light of this, digital content authors are encouraged to consider going beyond what is specified and seeking additional advice and best practices.

Web standards as a foundation for digital disability rights

The development of accessibility standards has become a self-perpetuating cycle of moving between specific testable approaches and more user-centric outcomes. These standards represent what experts have been able to reach consensus on and the state of technology at the time of publication, rather than covering or anticipating all accessibility and inclusive design requirements. Guidelines must also anticipate and balance contextual factors such as the influence of legacy technologies, what is practicable to require in terms of economic stringencies and so forth (see Kelly et al., 2009; Kelly et al., 2007; Kelly et al., 2005).

Notably, WCAG 2.1, published in 2018, sought to address new technologies such as touch-screen devices and provide wider support for addition needs. Yet WCAG 2.1 still does not address many of the design and technical recommendations made for people with learning and cognitive disabilities (James et al., 2017). This may reflect a longstanding criticism (Clark, 2006; Seeman, 2006) that identifies how people with learning and cognitive disabilities, those who are D/deaf and those with print impairments have been marginalised within standards making, particularly the processes, drafting and conferencing involved and required. Significantly, those DPOs most directly engaged in the standards-making process, either formally or informally, have an organisational and financial scale that can support the time and expertise necessary for sustained engagement and influence at this international level. This is consistent with Meyer's analysis, which observes how human rights frameworks are pursued by 'big DPOs' with national or international agendas, whilst local and grassroots organisations prioritise different goals (Meyers, 2014). In the resulting implicit hierarchies of web accessibility, grassroots DPOs and people with learning and cognitive disabilities are placed at the bottom of the hierarchy. This situation echoes the social, hierarchical stigmas that Deal (2003) observes within wider society and between and amongst disabled people themselves. In this respect, standards making can be seen to bear out inequalities present within disability advocacy and the wider disabled people's movement. While disability has long been theorised as 'the other Other' (Wendell, 1996) – marginalised amongst marginalised groups – people with intellectual disabilities have been further occluded by the internal hierarchies of the disability movement (Petri, 2017). Importantly, this is understood within WAI, with those within the standards body voicing concerns that they are not necessarily the right body and should not be left to define rights (Brewer, 2017). This is important as WCAG is a technical standard that seeks to support developers in creating interoperable, accessible systems. Within this, disabled people are an indirect or secondary audience, and opportunities for mobilising the self-advocacy of many marginalised groups can have difficulty gaining traction. In recent years, there have been efforts by the Web Accessibility Initiative to develop a greater understanding of the needs of people with cognitive and learning disabilities with the establishment of the W3C Task Force for Cognitive and Learning Disabilities Accessibility (COGA) and the ETSI Specialist Task Force (STF ZV) (Böcker et al., 2016; Lewis & Seeman, 2019), which have led to additional guidelines. Both groups set out to encourage participation by user groups and experts in both the technology and disability domains with limited success. Reflecting on the lack of support for cognitive and learning disabilities in web standards, Lewis and Seeman (2019) note that people with cognitive and learning disabilities are less likely to self-identify as disabled, reducing the likelihood of participation but also reflect that:

> [O]ne likely cause is poor COGA in the WCAG process itself. The online tools used for deliberation in the guidelines development process are quite difficult to use for anyone, but especially for people with cognitive limitations and differences. . . . Not all groups find it equally easy to represent their opinions in the process.
>
> *(Lewis & Seeman, 2019)*

Users with cognitive disabilities and learning difficulties also have commonalities in terms of challenges but with many more variables. In this respect, the development of research and attendant standards development can be observed to be sociotechnical – stemming from both culture and technology – and borne out in an iterative cycle that continues to marginalise particular impairment groups.

Further criticisms pertaining to hierarchies of impairment and resulting in exclusion relate to how WCAG itself is presented. WCAG is a large technical document. It has been cited as poorly organised, too heavy in its use of technical language and not user friendly. It can be difficult for non-native speakers of English, Deaf users (whose first language may be, for example, Auslan, Libras or British Sign Language.)[3] Translation initiatives have resulted in 14 completed and planned translations of WCAG 2.1, with 28 for WCAG 2.0. Many advocates have discussed the need for plain language: for example, on the basis of Deaf experience (Herrod, 2008). Others (Clark, 2006; Moss, 2006) have wryly noted that WCAG's glossary of definitions is itself punctuated with complex language. For example:

programmatically determined: determined by software from data provided in a *user-agent-supported* manner such that the *user agents* can extract and present this information to users in different modalities

Web unit: a collection of information, consisting of one or more resources, intended to be rendered together, and identified by a single Uniform Resource Identifier (such as URLs)

While attempting to make the web usable for all, WCAG does not meet expectations for usability (Kapsi et al., 2009) or the needs of its target audience (Yesilada et al., 2015). However, this is a challenge that faces most technical writing, and as Kapsi et al. (2009) point out, "[A]ccessibility guidelines become more and more complex primarily due to technology advances" (p. 723), raising the need to focus on how they are disseminated and consumed by stakeholders. W3C intends to address this with the new generation of guidelines, WCAG 3.0, with improved readability, learnability and usability as a tool for advocacy part of its goals (Spellman et al., 2021). This is important because accessibility requires usability. Further, usability as a facet of accessibility is particularly essential for low-income communities where limited assistive technologies can result in more frequent traditional human proxies for access: a family member, carer or support assistant. In these circumstances, where a non-disabled but potentially non-technical proxy assists a disabled user, usability is key

Technically driven hierarchies

While aversive disableism (Deal, 2007), or the prioritising of more vocal and organised disabled people's organisations, appears to inform the conditions in which the standards are created, the nature of technology itself compounds this situation. WCAG has been widely criticised as privileging visual impairment among impairment groups because of the visual nature of the web (Lewthwaite & Swan, 2013). In short, it is relatively straightforward to write guidelines that reinforce good practice in generating code for screen readers, whereas knowing how to accommodate users with cognitive impairments, intellectual impairments and learning difficulties is more complex. A lack of capacity within WAI for systematic, empirical research (Kelly et al., 2010) may exacerbate this issue. However, it may also be a reflection that research on web accessibility remains dominated by studies of the impact of accessibility for blind and low-vision people (Mack et al., 2021). Importantly, the COGA task force[4] now works across the W3C working groups, contributing to new standards and documents, improving existing W3C material that addresses the cognitive space and encourages participation by individuals with cognitive disabilities through both direct collaboration and wider stakeholder engagement.

Further, there is a question as to what can be deemed reasonable or feasible for developers to achieve. For example, the provision of sign language interpretation is an accessibility best practice in many territories but is not required by WCAG. Shifts in technology can quickly transform this picture in ways that are difficult to anticipate. Until the recent advent of auto-captioning – currently a point of innovation and competition among video-conferencing platforms – the supply of captioned or subtitled video (required for WCAG 2.1 Level AA compliance) resulted in some educational organisations removing video, rather than countenancing the expense of captioning their video materials. For instance, in 2017, UC Berkeley removed 20,000 videos from public websites. When we consider that video can be far more accessible to people with print impairments (who constitute substantial numbers of disabled people, particularly in regions with low literacy), it is clear that compliance without nuance does not always serve disability rights.

Nonetheless, governments across the global continue to rely on professional standard bodies rather than embed technical requirements in civil rights regulations. Future standards may embrace the need for wider recognition of digital requirements across all disabilities, as proposed within the development of WCAG 3.0, but this faces the challenge of not only creating consensus across the accessibility community but also being developed while existing standards continually need maintenance and advocacy.

Global adoption of digital disability rights

International accessibility standards such as WCAG have been used by many industrialised countries to underpin digital rights; however, many countries have yet to define digital accessibility rights within their legislative framework. The Digital Accessibility Rights Evaluation index (DARE index) was created in 2006 by G3ict, the Global Initiative for Inclusive Technologies, to provide a global benchmark for governments, advocates and private sector organizations to assess their progress and identify opportunities for promoting and implementing digital accessibility. This benchmarking index was developed to assist governments and organisations with their progress towards implementing Article 9 of the UNCRPD and captures data on the relevant policy, processes and systems that are necessary to ensure information and technology are accessible to all. The CRPD General Comments (United Nations, 2014) recognise and link digital accessibility explicitly to further conventions.[5] The 2020 DARE index found that while 61% of countries included ICTs or electronic media in the country's laws or regulations in their legal definition of accessibility for people with disabilities, only 44% of countries refer to international accessibility standards (G3ict, 2020). However, there is considerable variation between countries, with 88% of high-income countries referencing international accessibility standards, compared to 22% of low-income countries. While 51% of countries have no policy to promote or guarantee equal access to the internet for people with disabilities, there is evidence that lower-middle income countries, particularly in East Asia, the Pacific, the Middle East and North Africa, are making increasing efforts to increase access to digital platforms, and the relationship between country income and digital accessibility is decreasing (G3ict, 2020).

Digital rights are not just about access to devices and resources, nor are they solely reliant on policy and legislation. Successful adoption of adaptive and assistive technology is highly dependent on being able to access support, training, and funding in a timely fashion (Scherer, 2014). Accessibility infrastructure, defined by Pal as 'the sum of technological, social, and economic facilities that underlie the use of AT in a given ecosystem' (Pal, 2017), varies greatly between countries and is impacted by external factors such as internet infrastructure, language and culture. In lower-income countries and the Global South, internet access for the majority is through mobile devices or slow connections, with only 13% of people in low- and middle-income nations having access to broadband internet connections (World Bank, 2020). This is compounded by the cost of data, which remains unaffordable in most in low-income countries (UNCTAD, 2021).

In this context, disabled people in low-income countries are likely to be more reliant on free or low-cost assistive technologies, which are often not available in local dialects or languages, with the availability of assistive products the largest gap in an effective assistive technology system (MacLachlan et al., 2018). However, even when assistive technology, digital tools and the internet are available, their effectiveness is tempered by access to suitable training and support. Digital rights for disabled people in low-income countries are compounded by barriers to education and employment and access to technology, as well the access to expert support and training in the digital skills required to use the technology effectively (MacLachlan et al., 2018). Where assistive technology is available, its effectiveness is often compromised as it is not suited to the local language or cultural requirements (Pal, 2017). Failure

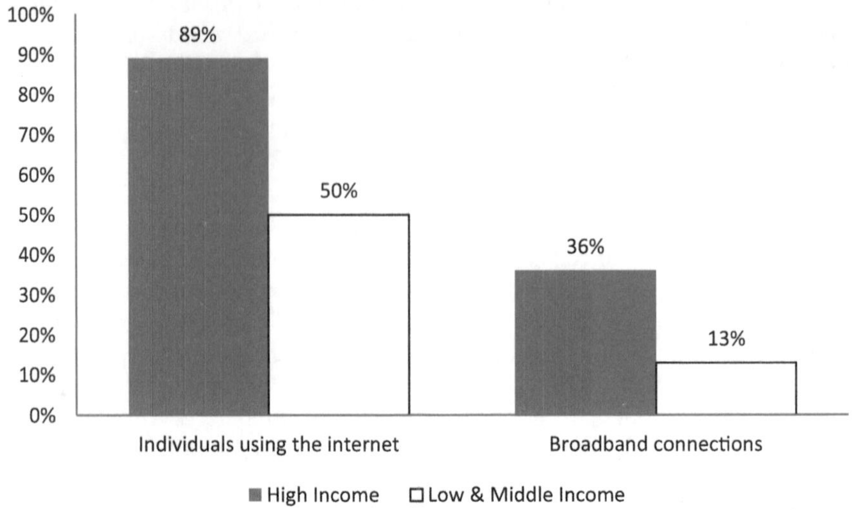

Figure 19.1 Chart showing comparison of internet and broadband access between high- and low/middle-income countries

Source: World Bank, 2020

to accommodate dialects, accents and orthography present further challenges (Banes & Draffan, 2020). The lack of suitable assistive technology is due not just to commercial drivers; it also relates to the difficulties with engaging with disabled communities to understand their needs and preferences when these communities lack autonomy and advocacy (Banes & Draffan, 2020). For example, Vashistha and Anderson (2016) reported how lack of exposure to English compounds barriers for visually impaired people attempting to access the internet through screen readers using American voices. Access to voices in local languages are limited and are often of poor quality.

Critical disability theorists have long established the political, cultural and complex nature of 'disability'. Disability is 'so complex, so variable, so contingent, so situated' (Shakespeare & Watson, 2002, p. 19) that it resists classification. In view of this, Adam and Kreps (2009) observe 'that it is probably impossible to make standards which will guarantee the accessibility of the web' (2009, p. 1043). At the same time, science and technology studies have established the partial nature of technology: the features and standards of hardware and software convey underlying assumptions based on existing societal structures and, consequently, re-represent those power dynamics (Latour, 1991; Sassen, 2002). Despite this, the values underpinning accessibility work – specifically the project of universal design and barrier removal – are largely accepted as a self-evident good. However, 'different approaches to accessibility infer different values systems' (Lewthwaite, 2014). WCAG represents a perspective on accessibility that is rooted deeply in the Global North.

Digital disability rights in practice: from guideline to standard – a new epistemology

At the outset, the Web Content Accessibility Guidelines represented a set of guidelines. However, as these have been adopted as de facto standards, the guidelines have functioned less contextually. A web standard is a formal term for a technical specification. These are fixed and unambiguous. In short, a standard must have a juridical fit – establishing a dichotomy between compliant and non-compliant (in plain terms 'acceptable' and 'unacceptable') in a mode that can be assessed and enforced in a court of law, if necessary. Guidelines, on the other hand, may be more readily adapted and negotiated according to the context in which they are applied, on the basis of location, culture, technology and so on. In positive terms, standards should ensure that minimum thresholds of accessibility can be set, maintained and policed. However, standards making and its juridical 'fit' imply new conditions and added complexity. As Lewthwaite and Swan (2013) observe: 'This subtle shift is not simply semantic; it gestures to a completely different epistemology of both technology and disability' (2013, p. 159). This empirical switch concerns the implicit, 'invisible power' of standards (Bowker & Star, 1999) and the politics they induct into digital life. In short, the very act of standardising results in the substitution of precision for validity. As a form of technical writing, 'Each standard . . . valorises some point of view and silences another' (Bowker & Star, 1999, p. 5).

From a human rights perspective, General Comment 2 (United Nations, 2014) states that the 'State parties must develop standards about accessibility for public and private organisations to follow' (p. 16). The trajectory of guideline-to-standard is increasingly driven by a disability rights agenda. This also suggests that 'States parties must work with people with disabilities and the organizations that represent them to develop the standards' (p. 16, United Nations, 2014). There is a disjuncture here, however. Developers and others working on accessibility do not access this supra level of policy. Web developers and accessibility professionals default to national and regional law in the sphere where they operate. It is here, at the national level, that WCAG-as-standard has global reach, and the boundaries, language, authorial power and detail of compliance and non-compliance become heavily contested (Lewthwaite & Swan, 2013). Yet the act of standardisation itself bears scrutiny. As standards represent a fixed point of view, refracted only marginally through national and regional legislation, the guideline-as-standard operates to promote certain practices. In doing so, the standard user must be 'scaffolded' into a new and fixed epistemology or perspective (Lewthwaite & Swan, 2013, p. 161). This requires acquiescence on the part of the developer to external regimes of knowledge. This affordance is double edged. On the one hand, it represents the opportunity to promote disability rights, and, as stated previously, WAI is unique amongst web standards bodies in its efforts to explicitly educate; on the other hand, there is a risk of colonisation as forms of web practices are propagated that exacerbate the exclusion of groups of disabled people who fall outside the norms of disability in an anglophone Global North. In view of this, the appropriation of web guidelines for disability rights policy and law raises important issues that are keenly felt.

Importantly, if the value systems underpinning accessibility actions don't fir the context within which they are applied, 'there is a risk that steps taken to improve accessibility may instead exacerbate exclusion' (p. 1376). Lewthwaite (2014) argues that dominant accessibility discourse, in the form of WCAG, can be shown to be highly technicist (overestimating the inherent benefits of technology) and highly positivist, implying a subjugation of bodies to powerful norms that establish disability as a deficit, medical and deviant characteristic. Specifically, web accessibility standards inherently promote accessibility as a property of an online resource or service. This undervalues the importance of the user's intentions and expertise, their context and the social and cultural nature of disability (Kelly et al., 2010). Additionally, Lewthwaite (2014) teases out the ways in which standardised approaches to accessibility, conveyed within WCAG, fail to accommodate non-Western disability and accessibility norms.

The W3C's constituents involved with developing WCAG primarily represent converging Western European, East Asian and North American interests. Where standards such as WCAG form part of a policy network at an international level, they not only reduce barriers to trade but also promote the participation and inclusion of non-governmental actors (Abbott & Snidal, 2010; Giannoumis & Beyene, 2020). In turn, such initiatives also export cultural and socio-political ideals at a national and regional level. Importantly, when non-government and disability representation in these networks is limited, such as in the Global South, this leads to standards being developed without an understanding of the barriers to digital rights and technology within these countries (Giannoumis et al., 2017; Ghai & Reddy, 2020).

In this respect, WCAG exists within, and perpetuates a power relation between, a productive, dominant North and a consuming, subjected South (Roy & Lewthwaite, 2016). Within the standards themselves, issues persist regarding the Western expectations that are written into current standards practice, which is reenforced by the dominance of US and English-speaking tech companies within the web and assistive technology domains. For example, the prioritising of screen reader–friendly systems is predicated on the notion that screen readers are readily available globally. They are not, with their usability limited by the availability of synthetic speech engines in all languages and the implementation of web accessibility across all languages (Pal, 2017).

> There are no problems as long as you are using English. Once you start using Arabic, the problems increase substantially. Sometimes, there are buttons that are not accessible. I need someone to click them for me.
>
> *(Quote from a screen reader user. Pal, 2017, p. 812)*

Knowledge of the English language as a barrier to technology in developing countries is not just limited to people with disabilities (Karusala et al., 2018). However, as access to education and language acquisition itself is a dimension of the lived experiences of people with disability, this further exacerbates and dilutes the effectiveness of global web accessibility standards for these communities. Efforts to address this power imbalance are underway, notably in actions to recruit non-Western participants to accessibility standards groups and task forces. Actions to translate web standards have also opened the process to a wider audience.

Conclusion

The relationship between digital standards making at the supra level and user experience at the micro level is a complex one. As we have seen, in accessibility standards, complexity is introduced at multiple levels, in (culturally situated) digital design and development, in delivery and in the enabled or disabled subjectivities that are engendered in use in a given context, culture or geopolitics. Nonetheless, standards making is important.

Scrutiny and communal efforts to improve the salience of standards and their accountability to disabled people are ongoing. Importantly, WAI develops standards openly with specific periods of public consultation. This process is transparent and, in this respect, very different to the activities of other standards-making bodies (e.g. the British Standards Institute or International Standards Institute). Importantly, the very transparency of the WAI project allows the process to be contested and makes these critiques available to us. It allows alternatives to be voiced and mobilised, arguably giving opportunities to harness what Hacking identifies as 'looping effects' (Hacking, 1995): namely, recognising the ways in which those who are subjected to the ascriptions of standardising knowledges re-mediate the power/knowledge dichotomy by resisting or renegotiating that ascription and repositioning themselves as subjects.

However, whilst resistance or re-ascription is possible, in practice, this process is more complicated. Questions remain. Must accountability to disabled people be in tension with standards and technical specifications? Would a more nuanced approach to disability/accessibility help or undermine legally driven efforts for digital inclusion?

To this end, Adam and Kreps (2009) argue that it is not the constituent parts but the prevalent discourses of web accessibility that exclude disabled people from the standards-making agenda. They establish four major discourses that define web accessibility: 1) a digital divide discourse, 2) social construction of disability discourse, 3) focusing on the historical relationship between disability and technology and 4) legal discourse (Adam & Kreps, 2009, p. 1042). These strands do not intersect, and in the gaps, the authors argue, important groups are excluded from the dominant policy-making agenda (Adam & Kreps, 2009). The authors cite this as leading to the continuing obduracy of web inaccessibility. Fundamentally, disabled people are indirect stakeholders in the standards-making effort. Adam and Kreps (2009) ask 'for whom such standards are made? Do they reflect the needs of users, especially disabled users or are they designed to reflect corporate interests?' (p. 1043). In truth, WAI negotiates a path between stakeholders, but if we ask, 'Who are web accessibility guidelines for?' it is clear that they continue to be bounded by technical requirements and available resources.

Looking forward, it is clear that digital accessibility on its own is not enough to ensure disabled people's rights, and this was vividly borne out in the experiences of disabled people globally during the COVID-19 pandemic. Standards compliance is far from guaranteed, and while digital interactions are a part of everyday life, they are not the sum of accessibility and disability inclusion. In view of this, digital accessibility is too often conceived as a stand-alone and disembodied space in which physically accessible experiences are occluded. Further, the notion that 'technology can fix everything' in and of itself is not only technicist but also aligns with problematic medical and individual models of disability that identify disability as a personal deficit. The focus must shift from accessible products to accessible experiences (Kelly et al., 2010).

There is also a concern with the trajectory of impairment categorisation that could effect a disaggregation of disability as standards seek to serve specific groups on the basis of impairment. Experiences of exclusion and disadvantage present social commonalities that may be lost through disaggregation. Disaggregation may also potentially privilege clinical diagnosis above social identification. Importantly, this returns us to the epistemic assumptions of standards making. Standards based on an identity model of disability are vulnerable. As Tremain (2001) observes:

> A disability movement that grounds its claims to entitlement in the identity of its subject can expect to face similar criticisms from an ever-increasing number of constituencies that feel excluded from, and refuse to identify with, those demands for rights and recognition.
>
> *(Tremain, 2001, p. 44)*

Disaggregating by impairment may lead to ever-increasing fractions and subgroups: gesturing more totalising 'regime of knowledge' as it bio-politically aligns with the medical models and loses impetus in division and subdivision. Instead, we suggest approaches that foreground the most marginalised in the hierarchies extant within digital standards and policy and appeal to '[v]ariation of bodies, variations of codes, and variations in experience can offer a more nuanced and flexible notion of access' (Ellcessor, 2010).

Looking forward, we note a developing trajectory in legislation for centralised monitoring and enforcement in accessibility regulation. For example, the recent EU directive and public regs (EC, 2016) enacted in 2019 set out a Europe-wide framework for monitoring and enforcing accessibility. In this mode, the impetus is with national governments to sample and monitor the accessibility of websites through national teams. Sampling will be guided by complaints escalated to government, as well as by disabled people's organisations. This is heartening as it represents a move from a past model of individual responsibility (for the developer to ensure accessibility, for the disabled person to claim their rights through litigation) to a model of centralised enforcement that also seeks to better support the development of accessibility capacity in the tech sector by raising awareness and encouraging the sharing of best practices (Lewthwaite & James, 2020). Further, we notice growing awareness of digital accessibility in industry as a result of legislation and demand. With the pandemic, the digital turn has resulted in high-profile competition among platforms, with accessibility an active point of innovation between competing companies: for example, with the addition of automated live captioning for video calls in Zoom and Microsoft Teams. The sensitising of web standards to different voices, enabled by transparency, advocacy and looping effects (Hacking, 1995) will continue with the future release of WCAG 3. This promises to be an exciting next chapter, foreshadowed by W3C initiatives to integrate diverse voices and marked by new groups to extend and sensitise standards to those traditionally marginalised in the process. Challenges remain, however, as new domains (augmented reality, virtual reality) demand new standards to ensure digital rights are technically maintained. At these frontiers, the influence of the inclusive – or exclusive – cultures of the companies and actors forging such new technologies will be telling. Accessibility must be built in, not an add-on (Lewthwaite et al., 2018).

Accessibility has been our focus in this chapter as a bedrock of digital disability rights. Looking beyond the technical divide between accessible/inaccessible at the threshold of technology, it is clear that social divides are also enabled and produced in networked public domains such as social media (Lewthwaite, 2011). Network conditions and surveillance capitalism that it affords are reshaping disabled experience in powerful ways, through context collapse in social media and associated normative social pressures and the 'extra visibility' that it engenders. New modes of exclusion on the basis of data profiling through the use of big data, machine learning and algorithmic modelling are also increasingly established. Just as the ADA was used to establish the ground for early web accessibility guidelines, guidelines-as-standards now reach further in digital policy and legislation. In view of this, leading-edge technologies remind us that equalities laws must be called into digital domains and that efforts towards inclusion must be underwritten by digital accessibility.

This work is funded by UK Research and Innovation Future Leaders Fellowship MR/S01571X/1.

Notes

1 Digital accessibility discourse predominantly centres on web-based technologies. Whilst software, operating systems and so forth are key parts of accessibility infrastructure, it is the governance of the web as a digital commons that is most developed in terms of disability policy and interoperable accessibility standards.

2 The Hilfsegemeinschaft (the Austrian association in support of the blind and visually impaired), Hong Kong Blind Union and the National Federation of the Blind (USA) are also W3C member organisations that support and engage with the standards-making process.
3 As British Sign Language differs from American Sign Language (which has greater commonality with French Sign Language), the dominance of the USA as the location of many tech multinationals means that, whilst (American) English is a majority language online, British Sign Language is a minority language.
4 https://www.w3.org/WAI/GL/task-forces/coga/
5 These include the Universal Declaration of Human Rights (articles 13 and 19), the International Covenant on Civil and Political Rights (articles 12, 19 and 25), the International Convention on the Elimination of All Forms of Racial Discrimination and the International Telecommunication Regulations (Article 12). The United Nations Standard Rules on the Equalization of Opportunities for Persons with Disabilities also require 'States parties to make . . . information and communication accessible to people with disabilities' (United Nations, 2014, p. 8).

References

Abbott, K. W., & Snidal, D. (2010). International regulation without international government: Improving IO performance through orchestration. *The Review of International Organizations*, 5(3), 315–344.

Abou-Zahra, S., & Brewer, J. (2019). Standards, guidelines, and trends. In Y. Yesilada & S. Harper (Eds.), *Web Accessibility: A Foundation for Research* (pp. 225–246). Springer, London.

Adam, A., & Kreps, D. (2009). Disability and discourses of web accessibility. *Information, Communication and Society*, 12(7): 1041–1058.

Americans With Disabilities Act of 1990, Pub. L. No. 101–336, 104 Stat. 328 (1990).

Banes, D., & Draffan, E. A. (2020). Democratisation of AAC symbol design for people with intellectual disabilities. *Global Journal of Intellectual & Developmental Disabilities*, 7(1), 18–20.

Böcker, M., Floratos, N., Martínez, L., Pluke, M., Von Niman, B., & Whitney, G. (2016). Cognitive accessibility to mobile ICT. In *International Conference on Computers Helping People with Special Needs* (pp. 179–186). Springer, Cham.

Bowker, G. C., & Starr, S. L. (1999). *Sorting Things Out: Classification and Its Consequences*. MIT Press, Cambridge.

Brewer, J. (2017). Standards bodies, access to information technology, and human rights. In *Disability, Human Rights, and Information Technology* (pp. 11–23). University of Pennsylvania Press, Philadelphia.

Clark, J. (2006). To Hell with WCAG 2. *A List Apart*. no. 217. http://alistapart.com/articles/tohellwithwcag2

Deal, M. (2003). Disabled people's attitudes toward other impairment groups: A hierarchy of impairments. *Disability & Society*, 18(7), 897–910.

Deal, M. (2007). Aversive disablism: Subtle prejudice toward disabled people. *Disability & Society*, 22(1), 93–107.

Ellcessor, E. (2010). Bridging disability divides. *Information, Communications and Society*. 13(1), 289–308.

Ellis, K., & Kent, M. (2011). *Disability and New Media*. Routledge, New York and London.

European Commission (EC). (2016). *Directive (EU) 2016/2102 of the European Parliament and of the Council of 26 October 2016 on the Accessibility of Public Sector Websites and Mobile Applications of Public Sector Bodies*. http://data.europa.eu/eli/dir/2016/2102/oj

Foucault, M. (1998). *The History of Sexuality Vol. 1: The Will to Knowledge*. Penguin, London.

G3ict. (2020). DARE index 2020 global progress. *Digital Accessibility Implementation by CRPD States Parties*. https://g3ict.org/publication/dare-index-2020-global-progress-by-crpd-states-parties

Ghai, A., & Reddy, V. Y. (2020). Assistive technology research and disability studies in the global south: the need for synergy. *CHI 2020 Workshop: Nothing about Us Without Us. Investigating the Role of Critical Disability Studies in HCI*. https://katta.mere.st/nothing-about-us-without-us/

Giannoumis, G. A., & Beyene, W. M. (2020). Cultural inclusion and access to technology: Bottom-up perspectives on copyright law and policy in Norway. In *International Conference on Human-Computer Interaction* (pp. 341–355). Springer, Cham.

Giannoumis, G. A., Nthenge, M., & Manhique, J. (2017). The pivot model of policy entrepreneurship: an application of European ideas in the global South. In J. Lazar & M. A. Stein (Eds.), *Disability, Human Rights, and Information Technology* (pp. 227–243). University of Pennsylvania Press, Philadelphia.

Goggin, G., & Newell, C. (2005). Foucault on the phone: Disability and the mobility of government. In S. Tremain (Ed.), *Foucault and the Government of Disability*. University of Michigan Press. https://doi.org/10.3998/mpub.8265343

Grech, S., & Soldatic, K. (2016). *Disability in the Global South: The Critical Handbook*. Springer, Cham.

Hacking, I. (1995). The looping effects of human kinds. In D. Sperber, D. Premack & A. J. Premack (Eds.), *Symposia of the Fyssen Foundation. Causal Cognition: A Multidisciplinary Debate* (pp. 351–394). Clarendon Press/Oxford University Press, Oxford.

Herrod, L. (2008). Deafness and the user experience. *A List Apart*, 265. https://alistapart.com/article/deafnessandtheuserexperience/

James, A., Draffan, E. A., & Wald, M. (2017). Designing web-apps for all: How do we include those with cognitive disabilities? *Studies in Health Technology and Informatics*, 242, 665–668.

Kapsi, M., Vlachogiannis, E., Darzentas, J., & Spyrou, T. (2009). The usability of web accessibility guidelines: An approach for evaluation. In *International Conference on Universal Access in Human-Computer Interaction* (pp. 716–724). Springer, Berlin, Heidelberg.

Karusala, N., Vishwanath, A., Vashistha, A., Kumar, S., & Kumar, N. (2018). "Only if you use English you will get to more things" Using smartphones to navigate multilingualism. In *Proceedings of the 2018 CHI Conference on Human Factors in Computing Systems*. ACM Press, New York, NY, Paper 573, 1–14.

Kelly, B., Lewthwaite, S., & Sloan, D. (2010). Developing countries, developing experiences: approaches to accessibility for the Real World. In *W4A '10: Proceedings of the 2010 International Cross-Disciplinary Conference on Web Accessibility (W4A)*. ACM Press. New York, Article 3, 1–4.

Kelly, B., Nevile, L., Sloan, D., Faou, S., Ellison, R., & Herrod, L. (2009). From web accessibility to web adaptability. *Disability and Rehabilitation: Assistive Technology*, 4(4), 212–226.

Kelly, B., Sloan, D., Brown, S., Seale, J., Petrie, H., Lauke, P., & Ball, S. (2007). Accessibility 2.0: people, policies and processes. In *W4A '07: Proceedings of the 2007 International Cross-Disciplinary Conference on Web Accessibility (W4A)*. Banff, 7–8 May. ACM Press, New York.

Kelly, B., Sloan, D., Phipps, L., Petrie, H., & Hamilton, F. (2005). Forcing standardization or accommodating diversity? A framework for applying the WCAG in the real world. In *Proceedings of the 2005 International Cross-Disciplinary Workshop on Web Accessibility* (W4A). Chiba, 10–14 May. ACM Press, New York.

Kirkpatrick, A., O'Conner, J., Campbell, A., & Cooper, M. (2018). *Web Content Accessibility Guidelines (WCAG) 2.1*. https://www.w3.org/TR/WCAG21/

Latour, B. (1991). The impact of science studies on political philosophy. *Science, Technology, & Human Values*, 16(1), 3–19. https://doi.org/10.1177/016224399101600101

Lewis, C., & Seeman, L. (2019). Policy and standards on web accessibility for cognitive and learning disabilities. In Y. Yesilada & S. Harper (Eds.), *Web Accessibility: A Foundation for Research* (pp. 281–299). Springer, London.

Lewthwaite, S. (2011). Disability 2.0, student dis/connections: A study of student experiences of disability and social networks on campus in higher education. PhD Thesis. University of Nottingham. https://eprints.nottingham.ac.uk/12406/

Lewthwaite, S. (2014). Universal web standards and disability: Developing critical perspectives on accessibility. *Disability and Rehabilitation*, 36(16), 1375–1383.

Lewthwaite, S., & James, A. (2020). Accessible at last?: What do new European digital accessibility laws mean for disabled people in the UK? *Disability & Society*, 35(8), 1360–1365.

Lewthwaite, S., Sloan, D., & Horton, S. (2018). A web for all: A manifesto for critical disability studies in accessibility and user experience design. In K. Ellis, R. Garland-Thomson, M. Kent, & R. Robertson (Eds.), *Manifestos for the Future of Critical Disability Studies* (pp. 130–144). Taylor and Francis, London.

Lewthwaite, S., & Swan, H. (2013). Disability, web standards and the majority world. In L. Meloncon (Ed.), *Rhetorical AccessAbility: At the Intersection between Technical Communication and Disability Studies* (pp. 157–174). Baywood Publishing, Amityville.

Mack, K., McDonnell, E., Jain, D., Wang, L. L., Froehlich, J., & Findlater, L. (2021). What do we mean by" accessibility research"? A literature survey of accessibility papers in chi and assets from 1994 to 2019. In *Proceedings of the 2021 CHI Conference on Human Factors in Computing Systems*. ACM, New York. https://doi.org/10.1145/3411764.3445412

MacLachlan, M., Banes, D., Bell, D., Borg, J., Donnelly, B., Fembek, M., Ghosh, R., Gowran, R. J., Hannay, E., Hiscock, D., Hoogerwerf, E-J., Howe, T., Kohler, F., Layton, N., Long, S., Mannan, H., Mji, G., Ongolo, T. O., Perry, K., Pettersson, C., Power, J., Delgado Ramos, V., Slepičková, L., Smith, E. M., Tay-Teo, K., Geiser, P., & Hooks, H. (2018). Assistive technology policy: A position paper from the first global research, innovation, and education on assistive technology (GREAT) summit. *Disability and Rehabilitation: Assistive Technology*, 13(5), 454–466. https://doi.org/10.1080/17483107.2018.1468496

McLawhorn, L. (2001). Leveling the accessibility playing field: Section 508 of the Rehabilitation Act. *North Carolina Journal of Law & Technology*, 3, 63–100. http://scholarship.law.unc.edu/ncjolt/vol3/iss1/6

Meyers, S. (2014). Global civil society as megaphone or echo chamber?: Voice in the international disability rights movement. *International Journal of Politics, Culture and Society*, 27, 459–476.

Moss, T. (2006). WCAG 2.0: The new W3C accessibility guidelines evaluated. *Webcredible*. https://www.codeproject.com/Articles/16536/WCAG-2-0-The-new-W3C-web-accessibility-guidelines

Nickerson, J. V., & Muehlen, M. Z. (2006). The ecology of standards processes: Insights from Internet standard making. *Mis Quarterly*, 467–488.

Pal, J. (2017). The Accessibility Infrastructure and the Global South. In J. Lazar & M. Stein (Eds.), *Disability, Human Rights, and Information Technology* (pp. 244–262). University of Pennsylvania Press, Philadelphia.

Petri, G. (2017). Children with learning disabilities and their participation in judicial procedures – What can disability advocacy offer? *Tizard Learning Disability Review*, 22(1), 10–15. https://doi.org/10.1108/TLDR-10-2016-0035

Roy, A., & Lewthwaite, S. (2016). Critical silences: Disability, technology and the global south. In S. Grech & K. Soldatic (Eds.), *Disability in the Global South: The Critical Handbook* (pp. 483–500). Springer, London.

Sassen, S. (2002). Towards a sociology of information technology. *Current Sociology*, 50(3), 365–388. https://doi.org/10.1177/0011392102050003005

Scherer, M. J. (2014). From people-centered to person-centered services, and back again. *Disability and Rehabilitation: Assistive Technology*, 9, 1–2.

Seale, J., & Cooper, M. (2010). E-learning and accessibility: An exploration of the potential role of generic pedagogical tools. *Computers and Education*, 54(4), 1107–1116.

Seeman, L. (2006). *Formal Objection Explained.* W3C WCAG 2.0 Public Comments List, 20 June 2006. https://lists.w3.org/Archives/Public/public-comments-wcag20/2006Jun/0118.html

Shakespeare, T., & Watson, N. (2002). The social model of disability: An outmoded ideaology? *Research in Social Science and Disability*, 69, 9–28.

Spellman, J., Lauriat, S., & Cooper, M. (2021). *Requirements for WCAG 3.01. W3C First Public Working Draft*, 21 January. https://www.w3.org/TR/wcag-3.0-requirements/

Tremain, S. (2001). On the subject of impairment. In M. Corker & T. Shakespeare (Eds.), *Disability/Postmodernity*. Continuum, London.

UNCTAD. (2021). *Least Developed Countries Suffer Digital Divide in Mobile Connectivity*. https://unctad.org/topic/least-developed-countries/chart-april-2021

United Nations (UN). (1948). *Universal Declaration of Human Rights*. United Nations, New York. https://www.un.org/sites/un2.un.org/files/2021/03/udhr.pdf

United Nations (UN). (2006). *Convention on the Rights of Persons with Disabilities*. Treaty Series, 2515, 3. https://www.un.org/disabilities/documents/convention/convoptprot-e.pdf

United Nations (UN). (2014). *Convention on the Rights of Persons with Disabilities. General comment on Article 9: Accessibility*. Office of the High Commissioner for Human Rights. https://www.ohchr.org/en/documents/general-comments-and-recommendations/general-comment-no-2-article-9-accessibility-0

Vashistha, A., & Anderson, R. (2016). Technology use and non-use by low-income blind people in India. *ACM SIGACCESS Accessibility and Computing*, 116, 10–21.

W3C. (1997). *Briefing Packages for Project Web Accessibility Initiative*. https://www.w3.org/WAI/References/access-brief

Waddell, C. D. (2000). "Electronic curbcuts": The ADA in cyberspace. *Human Rights*, 22–24.

Web Accessibility Initiative. (2005). *Introduction to Web Accessibility*. http://www.w3.org/WAI/intro/accessibility.php

Web Accessibility Initiative. (2019). *Accessibility Principles*. https://www.w3.org/WAI/fundamentals/accessibility-principles/

Wendell, S. (1996). *The Rejected Body: Feminist Philosophical Reflections on Disability*. Routledge, New York.

World Bank. (2020). *International Telecommunication Union (ITU) World Telecommunication/ICT Indicators Database*. https://data.worldbank.org/indicator/IT.NET.BBND.P2?locations=XO

World Summit on the Information Society. (2003). *Declaration of Principles: Building the Information Society: A Global Challenge in the New Millennium*. https://www.itu.int/net/wsis/docs/geneva/official/dop.html

Yesilada, Y., Brajnik, G., Vigo, M., & Harper, S. (2015). Exploring perceptions of web accessibility: A survey approach. *Behaviour & Information Technology*, 34(2), 119–134.

20

COMMUNICATION RIGHTS MODERATED THROUGH HIERARCHIES OF DISABILITY AND CHILDHOOD

Sharynne McLeod and Jessica McLeod

Introduction

Communication rights are enshrined in Article 19 of the Universal Declaration of Human Rights, which states that individuals have the right to receive and convey messages, to hold opinions, and to express themselves in any language or modality (McLeod, 2018; United Nations, 1948). Traditionally, communication rights have been associated with the right to free assembly and association, freedom of the press, and freedom to protest; however, communication rights are fundamental human rights for all and are important for the realisation of most other human rights. This chapter begins by exploring communication rights and three vulnerable groups: those who do not speak the dominant language of their community, people with disabilities (including communication disability), and children. Next, hierarchies of disability relating to ability/disability and visible/invisible and static/dynamic disabilities are outlined. Disabilities can be visible to the general public (e.g. limb loss) or invisible (e.g. communication disability). Static disabilities are similar each day, and accommodations are more predictable (e.g. vision impairment). Dynamic disabilities change over a short time frame, even within the course of a day, and can seem unpredictable (e.g. psychosocial disabilities). Traditionally, governments do not prioritise resources for people with invisible and dynamic disabilities to enable realisation of their communication rights, resulting in wide-ranging impacts to functioning and participation. Children with communication disability, an invisible disability, have particular needs to enable the realisation of communication rights.

DOI: 10.4324/9781003410089-24

Communication rights and participation in society

Communication is central to being human. Communication rights encompass the "right to freedom of opinion and expression" "without distinction of . . . language" "through any media and regardless of frontiers" (United Nations, 1948). Traditionally, Article 19 of the Universal Declaration of Human Rights (UDHR) has been used to support the right to free assembly and association, freedom of the press, and freedom to protest and is fundamental for the realisation of most other human rights, including the right to vote (Howie, 2018; United Nations, 2011). However, as articulated in Article 19, all people have the right to communicate:

> Everyone has the right to freedom of opinion and expression; this right includes freedom to hold opinions without interference and to seek, receive and impart information and ideas through any media and regardless of frontiers.
>
> *(United Nations, 1948)*

Communication rights are "necessary for the enhancement of people's lives and the creation and maintenance of strong, healthy democratic societies" (Howie, 2018, p. 15).

The right to communicate has been restated throughout most United Nations conventions and declarations, including:

- Convention on the Rights of Persons with Disabilities (CRPD, Art. 21, United Nations, 2006)
- Convention on the Rights of the Child (CRC, Art. 12, 13, United Nations, 1989)
- International Convention on the Elimination of All Forms of Racial Discrimination (Art. 5, 15, United Nations, 1965)
- International Covenant on Civil and Political Rights (Art. 19, 25, United Nations, 1966a)

General Comment No. 34 (United Nations, 2011) indicates that the freedoms of opinion and expression "are closely related, with freedom of expression providing the vehicle for the exchange and development of opinions" (p. 1).

The right to communicate does not just apply to adults who competently speak, read, and write dominant languages of the world and their communities:

> All people, regardless of their age, status, ability, or communicative capacity have the right to receive and convey messages, to hold opinions, and express themselves. . . . Everyone should uphold others' right to communicate as they interact with people in daily life in order to enhance equality, justice, and human dignity.
>
> *(McLeod, 2018, p. 4)*

Communication is central to developing and maintaining relationships and for education, occupation, and the enjoyment of civil liberties. The need for communicative competence continues to increase due to globalisation connectivity. For example, occupations that relied on manual labor in the 1900s have been replaced with occupations relying on communication (Ruben, 2000).

Three aspects of communicative competence will be discussed in this chapter that are associated with the ability to realise communication rights within the United Nations conventions and declarations: language, disability, and childhood. These relate to three vulnerable groups of people who may be denied communication rights: those who do not speak the dominant language of their community, people with disabilities (including communication disability), and children. Multilingual children with communication disabilities are the embodiment of hierarchies of disability that can impact their current and future functioning and disability.

Communication rights, language, and multilingualism

Affirmation of the right to communicate should occur "without distinction of... language" (Art. 2, UDHR, United Nations, 1948) and has been reaffirmed in:

- Convention on the Rights of the Child (CRC, Art. 2, 29, 30, 40, United Nations, 1989)
- Universal Declaration on Cultural Diversity (Art. 5, UNESCO, 2001)
- International Covenant on Civil and Political Rights (Art. 2, 4, 14, 24, 26, United Nations, 1966a)
- International Covenant on Economic, Social and Cultural Rights (Art. 2, United Nations, 1966b)
- Declaration on the Right to Development (Art. 6, United Nations, 1986)
- Declaration on the Rights of Peasants and Other People Working in Rural Areas (Art. 10, United Nations, 2015a)

and the preambles and annexes of:

- International Convention on the Elimination of All Forms of Racial Discrimination (United Nations, 1965)
- Millennium Declaration (United Nations, 2000)
- Convention on the Protection and Promotion of the Diversity of Cultural Expressions (UNESCO, 2005)
- Declaration on the Right to Peace (United Nations, 2015b)

For example, rights "without distinction of... language" are articulated in the Universal Declaration on Cultural Diversity, which states "All persons have therefore the right to express themselves and to create and disseminate their work in the language of their choice, and particularly in their mother tongue"

(Art. 5, UNESCO, 2001), and in the Declaration on the Rights of Indigenous Peoples, which supports the revitalisation, use, development, and transmission of "language, oral traditions, philosophies, writing systems and literatures" (Art. 13, 14, 16 United Nations, 2007).

There are over 7,000 languages in the world (Eberhard et al., 2023), including spoken, signed, and written languages. Our globalised society rewards competent communicators who use the dominant language of their community and who are able to converse in the dominant languages of the world used within the economy, education, and politics (e.g. English, Spanish, Chinese). There is evidence that competent communicators who speak the dominant language of the country who are bilingual/multilingual are more likely to have higher levels of employment, education, and income than monolingual speakers (Blake et al., 2018). Additionally, there is extensive evidence that multilingualism has many academic, cognitive, social, economic, and political benefits (Bialystok, 2011; McLeod et al., 2016; Pietiläinen, 2011). In contrast, multilingual speakers who are not competent communicators in the dominant language of their community are less likely to have employment, education, and income than monolingual speakers (Blake et al., 2018). English competency has been found to be a strong predictor of self-sufficiency for humanitarian migrants (Blake et al., 2017). It is important to support people who do not speak the dominant language of their community in the right to "seek, receive and impart information and ideas" "without distinction of . . . language" (Art. 19, 2, UDHR, United Nations, 1948) in all domains of their lives. For example, providing accessible information in food insecure communities for people who do not speak the dominant language (Jagoe et al., 2023).

Communication rights and people with disabilities

It is estimated that 15% of the world's population have a disability; however, the World Health Organization indicates that "people with . . . communication difficulties, and other impairments may not be included in these estimates [of disability], despite encountering difficulties in daily life" (World Health Organization & The World Bank, 2011, p. 22). The CRPD (United Nations, 2006) was designed to ensure that people with disabilities had access to and were afforded the same rights and fundamental freedoms agreed upon in the UDHR (United Nations, 1948). The right of people with disabilities to communicate is upheld in Article 21 of CRPD:

> States Parties shall take all appropriate measures to ensure that persons with disabilities can exercise the right to freedom of expression and opinion, including the freedom to seek, receive and impart information and ideas on an equal basis with others and through all forms of communication of their choice.
>
> *(United Nations, 2006)*

Communication with people with disabilities needs to account for "accessible formats and technologies appropriate to different kinds of disabilities in a timely manner and without additional cost," "sign languages, Braille, augmentative and alternative communication, and all other accessible means, modes and formats of communication," including via "mass media" and "the Internet" (Art. 21, CRPD, United Nations, 2006).

People with communication disability have "difficulties with fluency, forming sounds and words, formulating sentences, understanding what others say, and using language socially" (Bercow, 2008, p. 13). Most people with communication disability have no known cause: that is, communication disability is their primary disability (McLeod & McKinnon, 2007). Some people have communication as a secondary disability, as a result of known causes, including neurological disorders (e.g. cerebral palsy, stroke, Parkinson's disease, Alzheimer's disease), cleft palate, hearing loss, intellectual disability, and illness (e.g. laryngectomy due to cancer). In Australia, it is estimated that over a quarter (27.4%) of people with a disability experience a communication disability (Australian Bureau of Statistics, 2017a); however, this high number does not include those who have communication disability as their primary disability. There is a higher prevalence of communication disability in males than in females and in children and older adults (Australian Bureau of Statistics, 2017a; McLeod & Harrison, 2009; McLeod & McKinnon, 2007).

Communication disability impacts people's participation in society and the workforce due to their reduced ability "to seek, receive and impart information" (Art. 19, UDHR, United Nations, 1948). For example, the Australian Bureau of Statistics (2017a) reported that 73% of people with communication disability had employment restrictions, and 25.3% reported no participation in activities away from home in the last 12 months. People with aphasia report that their communication disability disrupts their ability "to demonstrate competence, share experience, and participate in life as before" and "depletes social networks . . ., impedes return to work . . . and results in 'third party disability' for families" (Hersh, 2018, p. 40). People with communication disability are vulnerable to human rights abuses, including sexual and gender-based violence (Marshall & Barrett, 2018; World Health Organization & The World Bank, 2011).

Communication rights and childhood

Children are afforded additional rights that enable them to fulfil their potential, be protected from exploitation and abuse, and actively participate within society (Correia et al., 2020). Therefore, the CRC (United Nations, 1989) outlines human rights for children under the age of 18. The CRC is the most widely ratified human rights treaty, demonstrating a general acceptance of the articles within the it as part of the global standard (Lansdown et al., 2016).

Communication rights for children are outlined in Articles 12 and 13 of the CRC (United Nations, 1989):

> Article 12 1. States Parties shall assure to the child who is capable of forming his or her own views the right to express those views freely in all matters affecting the child, the views of the child being given due weight in accordance with the age and maturity of the child. . . .
>
> Article 13 1. The child shall have the right to freedom of expression; this right shall include freedom to seek, receive and impart information and ideas of all kinds, regardless of frontiers, either orally, in writing or in print, in the form of art, or through any other media of the child's choice.
>
> *(United Nations, 1989)*

Lundy (2007) conceptualized Article 12 for children by outlining four key elements (space, voice, audience, and influence) and two core components: 1) the right for children to express their view (space, voice) and 2) the right for their views to be given due weight (influence, audience). The Lundy model has been applied to many aspects of children's communication rights, including in Ireland's child protection and welfare services (Kennan et al., 2019) and for understanding the impact of childhood communication disability (McCormack et al., 2018).

Many areas of society (including schools) rely heavily on children's voices being heard through traditional spoken and written means (Gillett-Swan & Sargeant, 2018), such as by being interviewed, completing surveys, and answering questions in the dominant language of the community. Through focusing on a narrow understanding of communication, children are not always provided with an equal space or opportunity to express their voice. Enabling children's right to communicate "regardless of frontiers" can include drawing, videos, photography, play, and many other age-appropriate methods so they can receive information, and their voice can be heard (e.g. McCormack et al., 2022; Roulstone & McLeod, 2011). For example, drawings created by 124 young Australian children with speech sound disorder revealed that they drew talking and listening either as an action requiring mouths and ears, something represented by symbols (letters, speech bubbles), or as an activity undertaken with a variety of people. Most of these children portrayed themselves as happy when talking; however, some were able to express that they had to draw themselves alone without a communicative partner because they felt "sad 'cause they don't let me play" (McCormack et al., 2022)

Once children have been given space and voice, their views need to be given due weight. That is, children's views need to be considered and contribute to and influence decision making (Shier, 2001). Children need to be informed about decisions made and whether or not their ideas were part of that final decision. For example, Grace et al. (2019) reviewed 207 papers regarding

Figure 20.1 Young children with a communication disability (speech sound disorder) drew themselves talking and revealed that 1) they needed their mouth and "listening ears" to talk with others (note the large ear on the "listener") and 2) sometimes they felt "sad, because they don't let me play" because children could not understand their speech (McCormack et al., 2022).

Source: Reprinted with permission from Sharynne McLeod, Linda J. Harrison, Lindy McAllister and Jane McCormack

children's and young people's engagement in the development, implementation, and evaluation of services. While almost all the papers included children as participants, very few involved children and young people in designing research questions, analysis, and dissemination. Adults play an important role in ensuring the realisation and enactment of children's rights as they are the main duty bearers of supporting rights realisations (Lundy, 2007; McLeod, 2021; Wang et al., 2018). The vital role of adults is outlined in General Comment No. 5 (GC5) of the CRC:

> If the adults around children . . . teachers and carers, do not understand the implications of the Convention, and above all its confirmation of the equal status of children as subjects of rights, it is most unlikely that the rights set out in the Convention will be realized for many children.
>
> *(United Nations Committee on the Rights of the Child, 2003, p. 16)*

Figure 20.2 Young children with a communication disability (speech sound disorder) drew themselves talking and revealed that 1) they needed their mouth and "listening ears" to talk with others (note the large ear on the "listener") and 2) sometimes they felt "sad, because they don't let me play" because children could not understand their speech

Source: Reprinted with permission from Sharynne McLeod, Linda J. Harrison, Lindy McAllister and Jane McCormack

Hierarchies of disability

Human rights and disability are social constructions; therefore, in most societies and cultures, the rights of some people are promoted, and others are marginalized. While everyone has the right to communicate, there are moderating influences on the realisation of communication rights, particularly for those experiencing disability. Hierarchies of communication rights can be related to societal definitions of ability/disability, including whether the disability is visible/invisible and static/dynamic. These factors can mediate distribution of resources of the individual/society/community to enable people with disabilities to realize their human rights, including their communication rights.

As discussed throughout this chapter, although communication is a fundamental human right stipulated throughout multiple United Nations declarations and conventions, the realisation of these rights can be dependent on individuals' ability to "fit" within societal norms and existing societal systems (Cologon, 2020). Inclusive education that recognises all forms of communication is commonly interpreted as "conditional" and dependent on students' ability to fit into existing educational settings, practices, and systems (Armstrong et al., 2011; Cologon, 2020). Students with disability often face greater marginalisation than students without disability (UNESCO, 2020). Students who experience disabilities that are invisible or not easily understood by the general population (e.g. communication disability) could face greater marginalisation than students without disability because they are do not always fit into existing educational systems. Furthermore, children labeled as having severe and multiple or profound disabilities can face greater marginalisation than their peers with less profound disabilities in accessing inclusive education because of the belief that their needs are too complex to fit within existing educational systems (Cologon, 2020; Graham & Sweller, 2011). For example, some students with communication disability require accommodations such as using alternative and augmentative communication (AAC) devices or having hearing feedback loops installed in classrooms that may be (incorrectly) perceived as complex to install and use in regular classrooms. The need for systemic transformation and reform of education systems is demonstrated by the prevalence of exclusionary practices in education and the prevailing view that inclusive education and acknowledgement of multiple communication methods are conditional. The CRC provides guidance to enable true inclusion in which all students are respected and empowered members of the school community (McLeod, 2021).

Definitions of ability/disability

Hierarchies of communication rights can be related to societal definitions of ability/disability. Disability can be perceived as something that exists biologically in an individual or as multifaceted, with societal, personal, political, and environmental influences (Cologon & Thomas, 2014). Common models of disability are the medical model, the social model, the social relational model, and the biopsychosocial model (Carrington, 1999; Cologon & Thomas, 2014; Reindal, 2008; WHO, 2001). The medical model of disability focuses on interventions that target the person with the disability and their need to integrate more fully in society. Some suggest that the medical model of disability focuses primarily on what people cannot do (Carrington, 1999; Cologon & Thomas, 2014). The social model of disability conceptualises disability as the result of interactions between social, personal, and environmental factors that can create barriers to fully participating in experiences and society (Graham et al., 2020). In the social model, "impairment" is defined as a physical, cognitive, sensory, or social/emotional restriction to an individual's body, and "disability" is defined as the barriers that individuals face due to negative attitudes, behaviours, and unaccommodating environments (Queensland Government, 2021). The social relational model describes the interrelationship between factors within society that place limitations and barriers to an individual's full participation and views disability as being imposed through avoidable practices that are discriminatory and exclude people from full participation in society (Reindal, 2008; Thomas, 2007). Within the social relational model, disability is described as barriers to being, barriers to doing, and impairment effects (Mackenzie et al., 2016; Thomas, 2007, 2010). The interdisciplinary biopsychosocial model of disability considers the interconnection between biology, psychology, and socio-environmental factors. The World Health Organization (2001, 2007) used the biopsychosocial model of disability as the framework for the International Classification of Functioning Disability and Health (ICF) (WHO, 2001, 2007). The ICF describes body structures, body functions, activities and participation, and environmental and personal factors that contribute to a person's health/disability. The ICF frequently has been applied to people with communication disability (e.g. Blake & McLeod, 2019).

An individual's ability to realise their communication rights will be influenced by the model of disability used by the community in which they live. For example, if a biopsychosocial model of disability is employed, there will be a focus on individualised interventions to support remediation of body structures and body functions, as well as family and community interventions to enable participation and environmental interventions to change societal attitudes and access to funding and reduce geographical barriers.

Static/dynamic and visible/invisible disabilities

While all people with disabilities are impacted by personal and environmental facilitators and barriers, there are two key dimensions of disability that can impact societal perspectives and government decision making: visible versus invisible and static versus dynamic disabilities.

Table 20.1 Examples of static versus dynamic and visible versus invisible disabilities

	Static	*Dynamic*
Visible	**Visible + Static** Many people with: • Vision impairment • Severe cognitive impairment • Down syndrome • Cleft lip and palate • Cerebral palsy • Paraplegia • Limb loss	**Visible + Dynamic** Many people with: • Arthritis • Parkinson's disease
Invisible	**Invisible + Static** Many people with: • Hearing loss • Communication disability (speech sound disorder, developmental language disorder, stuttering, aphasia, dysarthria)	**Invisible + Dynamic** • Psychosocial disability (e.g. bipolar disorder) • Medical disability (e.g. multiple sclerosis, diabetes, cancer) • Chronic pain

Visible versus invisible disabilities

Disabilities can be visible or invisible to the general public. Invisible disabilities occur when there is an incompatibility between the internal experience of an individual's disability and what is observed outwardly (Parker et al., 2021). Because invisible disabilities cannot be seen, this can impact the perceived legitimacy of the disability, which may lead to needs not being met. People with visible disabilities include those with physical disabilities (e.g. paraplegia, limb loss), facial difference (e.g. Down syndrome, cleft lip) and motor/movement disabilities (e.g. cerebral palsy). In many cases, disabilities become more visible due to the accommodations and aids that are required for participating in society (e.g. wheelchair, white cane, prosthetic limb, cochlear implant).

People with invisible disabilities include people with communication disabilities (e.g., speech sound disorder, developmental language disorder, stuttering, aphasia, dysarthria), some neurodevelopmental disorders (e.g. autism spectrum disorders, intellectual disabilities), psychosocial disabilities (e.g. bipolar disorder), and medical disabilities (e.g. multiple sclerosis, diabetes, cancer) (McLeod et al., 2010; Parker et al., 2021). Sometimes people can choose whether to make their disability visible or invisible. For example, a person with a hearing loss may have long hair so that their cochlear implant or hearing aid is not seen.

Static versus dynamic disabilities

Disabilities can be short term, long term, or lifelong. Static disabilities are those that rarely change over time with similar levels of impairment experienced day to day. People with static disabilities (e.g. vision impairment, Down syndrome, cleft palate, severe cognitive impairment) may experience some change over time; however, it is likely that their disability will be similar each day, and the required accommodations will be predictable. For example, a person who has a significant vision impairment is likely to require a guide dog and/or cane for mobility and access to Braille and/or text to speech support each day. This level of predictability and consistency can be reassuring for the individual, their family, friends, colleagues, and community and also facilitates planning to accommodate the person's disability and maximise participation in society.

Dynamic disabilities change over time, even within the course of a day (e.g. psychosocial disability, asthma, diabetes). Some people's disabilities change due to the environment (e.g. weather), physical/medical issues (e.g. hormonal fluctuations), environmental stressors (e.g. anxiety), or other unknown reasons, whereas, others can change with regular interventions (e.g. pharmacological). For example, people with Parkinson's disease are able to move freely during the window when their medications are working, then their ability to move can diminish prior to the next dosage of medication.

It is acknowledged that the distinction between visible/invisible and static/dynamic disabilities can change due to individual surgical and rehabilitation interventions (e.g. closure of a cleft palate) or due to reduction of environmental barriers (e.g. building ramps to replace stairs). However, when addressing communication rights, governments can prioritise resources for people with static visible disabilities: for example, people with cerebral palsy receive access to AAC devices (Hemsley et al., 2018), and people who are blind receive access to Braille. In contrast, people with invisible disabilities (e.g. children with speech sound disorder or developmental language disorder) may be less likely to receive resources to enable realisation of their communication rights (McLeod et al., 2010).

Communication rights and children with invisible communication disabilities

Children with communication disability typically have an invisible disability that is often overlooked and "often remains hidden" (McGregor, 2020, p. 7). Parents have reported "the continuous fight" to secure educational support for children with communication disability (Paradice & Adewusi, 2002). Children with invisible disabilities can also be overlooked by society, even though there are additional conventions and protections to ensure that their rights are upheld (Art. 12, 13, CRC United Nations, 1989; Art. 21 CRPD, United Nations, 2006). Children with communication disability identified in preschool are more likely to have ongoing difficulty with reading, writing, mathematics, and overall school achievement and experience social-emotional challenges (poorer peer relationships, bullying, and less school enjoyment) and are at greater risk of experiencing exclusion in school than their peers (McCormack et al., 2011, 2018, Maclean et al., 2017; McLeod et al., 2019). For children with communication disabilities, communication rights and participation need to be nurtured both inside and outside the classroom (e.g. on the playground) because these activities facilitate learning, friendships, social systems, and a sense of belonging (Cologon, 2014).

Childhood communication disability is more prevalent than other disabilities (McGregor, 2020; McLeod & Harrison, 2009; McLeod & McKinnon, 2007; Tambyraja et al., 2020). For example, Bishop (2010) demonstrated that children with developmental language disorder (DLD) and speech sound disorder (SSD) were more prevalent than children with autism spectrum disorder, attention deficit hyperactivity disorder, and Down syndrome. A large-scale longitudinal study of over 14,500 students within one Australian school district presents evidence for hierarchies of disability in education. McLeod and McKinnon (2007) documented the identification of learning needs for 36.6% of 14,514 students (wave 1) then 33.3% of 14,533 students two years later (wave 2) from the first to last year of school (i.e. indergarten to grade 12) in 37 primary schools and 7 secondary schools. Specific areas of learning need that were identified across the two waves of data collection were:

1. Specific learning difficulty (17.93% wave 1, 19.10% wave 2)
2. Communication disorder (13.04%; 12.40%)

3. English as a second or other language (9.16%; 5.80%)
4. Behavioural/emotional difficulty (8.16%; 6.10%)
5. Early achiever/advanced learner (7.30%; 5.50%)
6. Physical/medical disability (1.52%; 1.40%)
7. Intellectual disability (1.38%; 1.20%)
8. Hearing impairment (0.96%; 0.80%)
9. Visual impairment (0.16%; 0.30%)

Communication disorder was the second most prevalent area of learning need; greater than ten times more prevalent than intellectual disability or hearing or visual impairment (McLeod & McKinnon, 2007). From these nine areas of additional learning need, a communication disorder was the most predictive factor of teachers' belief that students required a high level of support at school (McLeod & McKinnon, 2010). Specifically,

- Students with communication disorder + behavioral/emotional disorder + intellectual disability were identified by their teachers as requiring the highest level of support.
- Students with communication disorder + intellectual disability were most likely to have an individual education plan and received the highest level of learning support within the educational setting.
- Students with communication disorder + intellectual disability + physical/medical disability were most likely to receive long-term support from agencies outside the school system.
- Students with intellectual disability + physical/medical disability received the greatest curriculum adaptations.

Students were more likely to be identified with communication disorder, if they were, at the time of transition to different levels of schooling (grades 1, 2, 7, 8, or 10). The most predictive demographic variables for higher levels of support for students with communication disorder were being male and socio-economic status (SES) (i.e., the students were from a middle-class school). These findings demonstrate that intersectionality (sex, SES, age, disability) has an impact on support for children with communication disabilities and the realisation of communication rights.

Communication rights in the Australian education context

The international educational context is informed by human rights obligations, the social and social relational model of disability, and developing acknowledgement of inclusive education (Graham et al., 2020; Meehan, 2016). Australia demonstrates its policy commitment to implementing children's rights and inclusive education primarily through the Disability Discrimination Act 1992 (DDA) and Disability Standards for Education 2005 (DSE) (Australian Government, 1992, 2006). The standards outline obligations that ensure the same rights are provided to children with disability as to their peers without disability in areas including enrolment, participation, delivery of content, student support services, and the prevention of harassment and victimisation. However, these standards do not include communication disability as a primary disability, and only physical, cognitive, sensory, and social/emotional disabilities are counted in the NCCD disability census (NCCD, 2021). This is in contrast to other countries that name communication as a specific disability category (Bercow, 2008; Ireland et al., 2020). For example, in 2016 in the US, the most prevalent disability category for children receiving services was speech-language impairment (SLI) with 323,789 preschool children plus 1,016,212 school students receiving services for speech-language impairment under IDEA (U.S. Department of Education, 2018). Despite national imperatives, Australia is still working towards a more inclusive education system (Anderson & Boyle, 2015; de Bruin, 2019; Poed et al., 2020). Existing research on children's right to inclusive education highlights systemic barriers to accessing and participating in education for children with disabilities "on the same basis" as their peers (DSE Standard 4.2) and to being provided with "reasonable adjustments" (DSE Standard 3.4) (Australian Government, 2006), regardless of their ability (Anderson & Boyle, 2015; de Bruin, 2019; Poed et al., 2020).

Children with communication disability have additional barriers because they are often invisible within Australian health, education, and disability legislation and policies (McLeod et al., 2010). Anderson and Boyle (2015) discuss the presence of a "policy-practice divide" (p. 6). Although invisible disabilities reduce the risk of stigmatisation, children with invisible disabilities may be likely to receive less support. A student with a visible and static disability is more likely to be labeled with a disability and be provided with supports because the disability is identifiable, whereas a student who has a dynamic or invisible disability (e.g. communication disability) may be less likely to be identified (e.g. Harrison et al., 2017). In Australia some advocacy groups help promote, protect, and shape the enactment of rights for people who experience disability. Advocacy groups that promote the communication rights of children in Australia include but are not limited to Speech Pathology Australia (SPA, 2019, 2021) and Children and Young People with Disability Australia (Children and Young People with Disability Australia, 2021).

Every five years, the Australian government reports to the United Nations Committee on the Rights of the Child on Australia's development in implementing children's rights. Within the concluding observations, the Committee discusses and assesses the progress Australia has made on children's rights and makes recommendations for further improvement. In 2019 the Australian national children's commissioner addressed the Committee to discuss Australia's enactment of children's rights. One issue that featured prominently in the concluding observations was that Australian children in minority groups, such as children with disability, were often discriminated against (Committee on the Rights of the Child, 2019). At the same time, the Australian Human Rights

Commission (2019) surveyed Australia's children and found that children with disabilities were less likely to say: "1. I can have a say about things that are important to me, 2. I am treated fairly, and 3. I can get accurate information when I need it" (p. 17). The first and third comments relate to communication rights. Children with communication disabilities are less likely to be able to realise their communication rights because of limited notions of appropriate or accepted forms of communication (Gillett-Swan & Sargeant, 2018). Therefore, it is important that we are purposeful and creative in enabling children to realise their "right to freedom of opinion and expression" by providing space, voice, influence, and audience (Lundy, 2007).

Conclusion

Communication is fundamental to being human, and communication rights are outlined in Article 19 of the UDHR (United Nations, 1948) and have been restated throughout most of the United Nations conventions and declarations. Although the right to communicate is recognized throughout multiple conventions and declarations the realisation of communication rights can be restricted, particularly for people who experience disability. Hierarchies of communication rights can be determined by societal assumptions of ability and disability. Hierarchies can be further influenced by societal assumptions of the type of disability; these assumptions can be influenced by whether the disability is visible/invisible and static/dynamic. Static disabilities include those that rarely change over time, whereas dynamic disabilities change over time or over the course of the day. Visible disabilities are visible to the general public, whereas invisible disabilities are not. People who experience invisible disabilities are often overlooked. Children with communication disability, an invisible disability, have particular needs to enable the realisation of communication rights in the Australian educational context. Recognition of invisible and dynamic disabilities allows societal assumptions of disability to shift and facilitates promotion of the "right to freedom of opinion and expression" for all people.

References

Anderson, J., & Boyle, C. (2015). Inclusive education in Australia: Rhetoric, reality and the road ahead. *Support for Learning, 30*(1), 4–22. https://doi.org/10.1111/1467-9604.12074

Armstrong, D., Armstrong, A. C., & Spandagou, I. (2011). Inclusion: By choice or by chance? *International Journal of Inclusive Education, 15*(1), 29–39. https://doi.org/10.1080/13603116.2010.496192

Australian Bureau of Statistics. (2017a). *4430.0 – Disability, Ageing and Carers, Australia: Summary of Findings, 2015: Australians Living with Communication Disability*. http://www.abs.gov.au/AUSSTATS/abs@.nsf/Lookup/4430.0Main+Features872015?OpenDocument

Australian Government. (1992). Disability Discrimination Act 1992. *Federal Register of Legislation*. https://www.legislation.gov.au/Details/C2018C00125

Australian Government. (2006). Disability standards for education (2005) plus guidance notes. *Attorney-General's Department and Department of Education, Science and Training, Commonwealth of Australia*. http://education.gov.au/disability-standards-education

Australian Human Rights Commission. (2019). *Free and Equal: An Australian Conversation on Human Rights*. https://www.humanrights.gov.au/our-work/rights-and – freedoms/publications/free-and-equal-australian-conversation-human-rights-2019

Bercow, J. (2008). *The Bercow Report: A Review of Services for Children and Young People (0–19) with Speech, Language and Communication Needs*. London: Department for Children, Schools and Families. https://dera.ioe.ac.uk/8405/7/7771-dcsf-bercow_Redacted.pdf

Bialystok, E. (2011). Reshaping the mind: The benefits of bilingualism. *Canadian Journal of Experimental Psychology/Revue canadienne de psychologie expérimentale*, *65*(4), 229–235. https://doi.org/10.1037/a0025406

Bishop, D. V. M. (2010). Which neurodevelopmental disorders get researched and why? *PLoS ONE*, *5*(11), Article e15112. https://doi.org/https://doi.org/10.1371/journal.pone.0015112

Blake, H. L., Bennetts Kneebone, L., & McLeod, S. (2017). The impact of oral English proficiency on humanitarian migrants' experiences of settling in Australia. *International Journal of Bilingual Education and Bilingualism*. https://doi.org/10.1080/13670050.2017.1294557

Blake, H. L., & McLeod, S. (2019). Speech-language pathologists' support for multilingual speakers' English intelligibility and participation informed by the ICF. *Journal of Communication Disorders, 77*, 56–70. https://doi.org/https://doi.org/10.1016/j.jcomdis.2018.12.003

Blake, H. L., McLeod, S., Verdon, S., & Fuller, G. (2018). The relationship between spoken English proficiency and participation in higher education, employment and income from two Australian censuses. *International Journal of Speech-Language Pathology, 20*(2), 202–215. https://doi.org/10.1080/17549507.2016.1229031

Carrington, S. (1999). Inclusion needs a different school culture. *International Journal of Inclusive Education*, *3*(3), 257–268. https://doi.org/10.1080/136031199285039

Children and Young People with Disability Australia. (2021). What we do. *Children and Young People with Disability Australia*. https://www.cyda.org.au/about/what-we-do

Cologon, K. (2014). Adapting the curriculum in the school years. In K. Cologon (Ed), *Inclusive Education in the Early Years: Right from the Start* (pp. 242–259). South Melbourne: Oxford University Press.

Cologon, K. (2020). Is inclusive education really for everyone? Family stories of children and young people labelled with 'severe and multiple' or 'profound' 'disabilities'. *Research Papers in Education* (Advance online publication). https://doi.org/10.1080/02671522.2020.1849372

Cologon, K., & Thomas, C. (2014). Ableism, disableism and the early years. In K. Cologon (Ed.), *Inclusive Education in the Early Years: Right from the Start* (pp. 27–48). South Melbourne: Oxford University Press.

Committee on the Rights of the Child. (2019). *Concluding Observations on the Combined 5th and 6th Periodic Reports of Australia*. https://digitallibrary.un.org/record/3863406?ln=enc

Correia, N., Carvalho, H., Durães, J., & Aguiar, C. (2020). Teachers' ideas about children's participation within Portuguese early childhood education settings. *Children and Youth Services Review*, *111*, 104845. https://doi.org/10.1016/j.childyouth.2020.104845

de Bruin, K. (2019). The impact of inclusive education reforms on students with disability: An international comparison. *International Journal of Inclusive Education*, *23*(7–8), 811–826. https://doi.org/10.1080/13603116.2019.1623327

Eberhard, D. M., Simons, G. F., & and Fennig, C. D. (Eds.). (2023). *Ethnologue: Languages of the World* (26th ed.). Dallas, TX: SIL International. http://www.ethnologue.com

Gillett-Swan, J., & Sargeant, J. (2018). Assuring children's human right to freedom of opinion and expression in education. *International Journal of Speech-Language Pathology, 20*(1), 120–127. https://doi.org/10.1080/17549507.2018.1385852

Grace, R., Knight, J., Baird, K., Ng, J., Shier, H., Wise, S., Fattore, T., McClean, T., Bonser, G., Judd-Lam, S., & Kemp, L. (2019). Where are the silences? A scoping review of child participatory research literature in the context of the Australian service system. *Children Australia, 44*(4), 172–186. https://doi.org/10.1017/cha.2019.32

Graham, L. J., Medhurst, M., Tancredi, H., Spandagou, I., & Walton, E. (2020). Fundamental concepts of inclusive education. In L. J. Graham (Ed.), *Inclusive Education for the 21st Century*. Crows Nest: Allen & Unwin.

Graham, L. J., & Sweller, N. (2011). The inclusion lottery: Who's in and who's out? Tracking inclusion and exclusion in New South Wales government schools. *International Journal of Inclusive Education, 15*(9), 941–953. https://doi.org/10.1080/13603110903470046

Harrison, L. J., McLeod, S., McAllister, L., & McCormack, J. (2017). Speech sound disorders in preschool children: Correspondence between clinical diagnosis and teacher and parent report. *Australian Journal of Learning Difficulties, 22*(1), 35–48. https://doi.org/10.1080/19404158.2017.1289964

Hemsley, B., Palmer, S., Dann, S., & Balandin, S. (2018). Using Twitter to access the human right of communication for people who use Augmentative and Alternative Communication (AAC). *International Journal of Speech-Language Pathology, 20*(1), 50–58. https://doi.org/10.1080/17549507.2017.1413137

Hersh, D. (2018). From individual to global: Human rights and aphasia. *International Journal of Speech-Language Pathology, 20*(1), 39–43. https://doi.org/10.1080/17549507.2018.1397749

Howie, E. (2018). Protecting the human right to freedom of expression in international law. *International Journal of Speech-Language Pathology, 20*(1), 12–15. https://doi.org/10.1080/17549507.2018.1392612

Ireland, M., McLeod, S., Farquharson, K., & Crowe, K. (2020). Evaluating children in U.S. public schools with speech sound disorders: Considering federal and state laws, guidance, and research. *Topics in Language Disorders, 40*(4), 326–340. https://doi.org/10.1097/tld.0000000000000226

Jagoe, C., O'Reilly, C. F., Gunnell, H., Tirzi, K., Lancaster, C., & Brahmbhatt, K. (2023). Communicating accessible messages for food insecure communities in Northern Mozambique: Supporting Sustainable Development Goal 2. *International Journal of Speech-Language Pathology, 25*(1), 62–67. https://doi.org/10.1080/17549507.2022.2140829

Kennan, D., Brady, B., & Forkan, C. (2019). Space, voice, audience and influence: The Lundy Model of Participation (2007) in child welfare practice. *Practice, 31*(3), 205–218. https://doi.org/10.1080/09503153.2018.1483494

Lansdown, G., Lundy, L., & Goldhagen, J. (2016). The U.N. Convention on the Rights of the Child: Relevance and application to pediatric clinical bioethics. *Perspectives in Biology and Medicine, 58*(3), 252–266. https://doi.org/10.1353/pbm.2016.0005

Lundy, L. (2007). 'Voice' is not enough: Conceptualising Article 12 of the United Nations Convention on the Rights of the Child. *British Education Research Journal, 33*, 927–942. https://doi.org/10.1080/01411920701657033

Mackenzie, M., Cologon, K., & Fenech, M. (2016). "Embracing everybody": Approaching the inclusive early childhood education of a child labelled with autism from a social relational understating of disability. *Australasian Journal of Early Childhood, 41*(2), 4–12. https://doi.org/10.1177/183693911604100202

Maclean, M. J., Sims, S., Bower, C., Leonard, H., Stanley, F. J., & O'Donnell, M. (2017). Maltreatment risk among children with disabilities. *Pediatrics, 139*(4). https://doi.org/10.1542/peds.2016-1817

Marshall, J., & Barrett, H. (2018). Human rights of refugee-survivors of sexual and gender-based violence with communication disability. *International Journal of Speech-Language Pathology, 20*(1), 44–49. https://doi.org/10.1080/17549507.2017.1392608

McCormack, J., Baker, E., & Crowe, K. (2018). The human right to communicate and our need to listen: Learning from people with a history of childhood communication disorder. *International Journal of Speech-Language Pathology, 20*(1), 142–151. https://doi.org/10.1080/17549507.2018.1397747

McCormack, J., Harrison, L. J., McLeod, S., & McAllister, L. (2011). A nationally representative study of the association between communication impairment at 4–5 years and children's life activities at 7–9 years. *Journal of Speech, Language and Hearing Research, 54*(5), 1328–1348. https://doi.org/10.1044/1092-4388(2011/10-0155)

McCormack, J., McLeod, S., Harrison, L. J., & Holliday, E. L. (2022). Drawing talking: Listening to Children with speech sound disorders. *Language, Speech, and Hearing Services in Schools, 53*(3), 713–731. https://doi.org/10.1044/2021_LSHSS-21-00140

McGregor, K. K. (2020). How we fail children with developmental language disorder. *Language, Speech, and Hearing Services in Schools, 51*(4), 981–992. https://doi.org/10.1044/2020_LSHSS-20-00003

McLeod, J. (2021). *Teachers' Perceptions of their Obligations to Uphold Education Rights of Young Primary Children with Disabilities*. Unpublished Masters' Thesis. Queensland: University of Queensland.

McLeod, S. (2018). Communication rights: Fundamental human rights for all. *International Journal of Speech-Language Pathology, 20*(1), 3–11. https://doi.org/10.1080/17549507.2018.1428687

McLeod, S., & Harrison, L. J. (2009). Epidemiology of speech and language impairment in a nationally representative sample of 4 – to 5-year-old children. *Journal of Speech, Language, and Hearing Research, 52*(5), 1213–1229. https://doi.org/10.1044/1092-4388(2009/08-0085)

McLeod, S., Harrison, L. J., & Wang, C. (2019). A longitudinal population study of literacy and numeracy outcomes for children identified with speech, language, and communication needs in early childhood. *Early Childhood Research Quarterly, 47*, 507–517. https://doi.org/10.1016/j.ecresq.2018.07.004

McLeod, S., Harrison, L. J., Whiteford, C., & Walker, S. (2016). Multilingualism and speech-language competence in early childhood: Impact on academic and social-emotional outcomes at school. *Early Childhood Research Quarterly, 34*, 53–66. https://doi.org/10.1016/j.ecresq.2015.08.005

McLeod, S., & McKinnon, D. H. (2007). The prevalence of communication disorders compared with other learning needs in 14,500 primary and secondary school students. *International Journal of Language and Communication Disorders, 42*(S1), 37–59. https://doi.org/10.1080/13682820601173262

McLeod, S., & McKinnon, D. H. (2010). Support required for primary and secondary students with communication disorders and/or other learning needs. *Child Language Teaching and Therapy, 26*(2), 123–143. https://doi.org/10.1177/0265659010368754

McLeod, S., Press, F., & Phelan, C. (2010). The (in)visibility of children with communication impairment in Australian health, education, and disability legislation and policies. *Asia Pacific Journal of Speech, Language, and Hearing, 13*(1), 67–75.

Meehan, C. (2016). Inclusion and inclusive practice in Australia. In Z. Brown (Ed.), *Inclusive Education: Perspectives on Pedagogy, Policy and Practice*. New York: Routledge.

NCCD [Nationally Consistent Collection of Data on School Students with Disability] (2021). Definitions of disability and the NCCD categories. *Australian Government.* https://www.nccd.edu.au/wider-support-materials/definitions-disability-and-nccd-categories

Paradice, R., & Adewusi, A. (2002). 'It's a continuous fight isn't it?': Parents' views of the educational provision for children with speech and language difficulties. *Child Language Teaching and Therapy, 18*(3), 257–288. https://doi.org/10.1191/0265659002ct238oA

Parker, L.-S., Topcu, G., De Boos, D., & das Nair, R. (2021). The notion of "invisibility" in people's experiences of the symptoms of multiple sclerosis: A systematic meta-synthesis. *Disability and Rehabilitation, 43*(23), 3276–3290. https://doi.org/10.1080/09638288.2020.1741698

Pietiläinen, J. (2011). Public opinion on useful languages in Europe. *European Journal of Language Policy, 3*(1), 1–14. https://doi.org/10.3828/ejlp.2011.2

Poed, S., Cologon, K., & Jackson, R. (2020). Gatekeeping and restrictive practices by Australian mainstream schools: Results of a national survey. *International Journal of Inclusive Education* (Advance online publication). https://doi.org/10.1080/13603116.2020.1726512

Queensland Government. (2021). *Categories of Disability.* https://www.qcaa.qld.edu.au/p-10/student-diversity/categories-disability

Reindal, S. M. (2008). A social relational model of disability: A theoretical framework for special needs education? *European Journal of Special Needs Education, 23*(2), 135–146. https://doi.org/10.1080/08856250801947812

Roulstone, S., & McLeod, S. (Eds.). (2011). *Listening to Children and Young People with Speech, Language and Communication Needs.* London, UK: J&R Press.

Ruben, R. J. (2000). Redefining the survival of the fittest: Communication disorders in the 21st century. *Laryngoscope, 110*(2 part 1), 241–245.

Shier, H. (2001). Pathways to participation: Openings, opportunities and obligations. *Children & Society, 15*(2), 107–117. https://doi.org/10.1002/chi.617

Speech Pathology Australia. (2019). *Speak up for Communication Rights.* https://www.speechpathologyaustralia.org.au/SPAweb/whats_on/Speak_Up_for_Communication_Rights/SPAweb/What_s_On/Speak_Up_for_Communication_Rights/Speak_Up_for_Communication_Rights.aspx?hkey=411a246a-f554-490b-87fa-d4796160be91

Speech Pathology Australia. (2021). *Speech Pathology Week.* https://www.speechpathologyaustralia.org.au/SPAweb/whats_on/Speech_Pathology_Week/SPAweb/What_s_On/Speech_Pathology_Week/Speech_Pathology_Week.aspx?hkey=bda669cc-f0ed-4c09-ba3f-58623572a886

Tambyraja, S. R., Farquharson, K., & Justice, L. (2020). Reading risk in children with speech sound disorder: Prevalence, persistence, and predictors. *Journal of Speech, Language, and Hearing Research, 63*(11), 3714–3726. https://doi.org/10.1044/2020_JSLHR-20-00108

Thomas, C. (2007). *Sociologies of Disability and Illness: Contested Ideas in in Disability Studies and Medical Sociology.* London: Palgrave Macmillan.

Thomas, C. (Ed.). (2010). *Medical Sociology and Disability Theory.* London: Palgrave Macmillan.

UNESCO. (2001). *Universal Declaration on Cultural Diversity.* http://portal.unesco.org/en/ev.php-URL_ID=13179&URL_DO=DO_TOPIC&URL_SECTION=201.html

UNESCO. (2005). *Convention on the Protection and Promotion of the Diversity of Cultural Expressions.* http://en.unesco.org/creativity/sites/creativity/files/passeport-convention2005-web2.pdf

UNESCO. (2020). *The Global Education Monitoring Report, in Brief.* https://en.unesco.org/gem-report/about

United Nations. (1948). *Universal Declaration of Human Rights*. http://www.un.org/en/universal-declaration-human-rights/

United Nations. (1965). *International Convention on the Elimination of all Forms of Racial Discrimination*. http://www.ohchr.org/EN/ProfessionalInterest/Pages/CERD.aspx

United Nations. (1966a). *International Covenant on Civil and Political Rights*. http://www.ohchr.org/EN/ProfessionalInterest/Pages/CCPR.aspx

United Nations. (1966b). *International Covenant on Economic, Social and Cultural Rights*. http://www.ohchr.org/EN/ProfessionalInterest/Pages/CESCR.aspx

United Nations. (1986). *Declaration on the Right to Development*. http://www.un.org/en/events/righttodevelopment/declaration.shtml

United Nations. (1989). *Convention on the Rights of the Child*. https://www.unicef.org/crc/

United Nations. (2000). *Millennium Declaration*. http://www.un.org/millennium/declaration/ares552e.htm

United Nations. (2006). *Convention on the rights of persons with disabilities*. https://www.un.org/development/desa/disabilities/convention-on-the-rights-of-persons-with-disabilities.html

United Nations. (2007). *Declaration on the Rights of Indigenous Peoples*. http://www.ohchr.org/EN/Issues/IPeoples/Pages/Declaration.aspx

United Nations. (2011). *International Covenant on Civil and Political Rights. Human Rights Committee General Comment No. 34: Article 19: Freedoms of Opinion and Expression*. https://www2.ohchr.org/english/bodies/hrc/docs/gc34.pdf

United Nations. (2015a). *Declaration on the Rights of Peasants and other People Working in Rural Areas*. http://www.ohchr.org/_layouts/15/WopiFrame.aspx?sourcedoc=/Documents/HRBodies/HRCouncil/WGPleasants/Session2/draftDeclaration.doc&action=default&DefaultItemOpen=1

United Nations. (2015b). *Declaration on the Right to Peace*. http://www.ohchr.org/_layouts/15/WopiFrame.aspx?sourcedoc=/Documents/HRBodies/HRCouncil/WGRightPeace/Session3/RevisedDraftDeclaration.docx&action=default&DefaultItemOpen=1

United Nations Committee on the Rights of the Child. (2003). *Committee on the Rights of the Child General Comment No. 5: General Measures of the Implementation of the Convention on the Rights of the Child*. https://www.refworld.org/docid/4538834f11.html

U.S. Department of Education. (2018). *40th Annual Report to Congress on the Implementation of the Individuals with Disabilities Education Act*. https://www2.ed.gov/about/reports/annual/osep/2018/parts-b-c/40th-arc-for-idea.pdf

Wang, C., Harrison, L. J., McLeod, S., Walker, S., & Spilt, J. L. (2018). Can teacher–child relationships support human rights to freedom of opinion and expression, education and participation? *International Journal of Speech-Language Pathology, 20*(1), 133–141. https://doi.org/10.1080/17549507.2018.1408855

World Health Organization. (2001). *International Classification of Functioning, Disability and Health: ICF*. Geneva: World Health Organization.

World Health Organization. (2007). *International Classification of Functioning, Disability and Health: Children and Youth Version: ICF-CY*. Geneva: World Health Organization. http://apps.who.int/iris/bitstream/10665/43737/1/9789241547321_eng.pdf

World Health Organization and The World Bank. (2011). *World Report on Disability*. Geneva: World Health Organization.

21

INCLUDING THE VOICES OF PERSONS WITH INTELLECTUAL DISABILITIES IN ACADEMIA

Participatory research, education and development in the academic world

Anikó Sándor, Csilla Cserti-Szauer, András Futár and Jan Walmsley

Introduction

People with intellectual disabilities should have the same rights as any non-disabled person. While all the major international documents presenting the human rights approach, including the United Nations Convention on the Rights of Persons with Disabilities, focus on the realisation of civil, political and social rights, there is little systematic development to promote implementation in practice. This is no different in academia, where people with intellectual disabilities rarely have a voice. In our opinion, it is of utmost importance to raise awareness among academic stakeholders by involving persons with intellectual disabilities in research, teaching and innovation so that this sector can also contribute to their empowerment and ensure the full enjoyment of their rights.

For decades, persons with disabilities have been left out of the knowledge creation about their own lives and needs. Research was conducted without their participation, and the training of disability professionals didn't represent their voices. Services were developed for them without asking about their preferences.

Following a unique path, in 2016 our university team decided to introduce participatory research and teaching that gives people with intellectual and

 DOI: 10.4324/9781003410089-25

physical disabilities opportunities to get involved in academic structures and work. We did this in response to the following questions:

- What does university and higher education mean? How can we change it to be inclusive and empowering?
- How can we decide if someone is qualified or competent enough to be a university teacher? What makes a university teacher authentic and reliable?
- What is the real impact of academic work? Can we even talk about social impact without the presence of persons with disabilities in the community of our university?
- What methods can be used to balance out existing power structures and hierarchies in academia? What challenges may occur within inclusive teams? How can we manage those challenges?

In our chapter, we examine these questions through the life story of our colleague András, a member of our team from the beginning of our journey with participatory teaching and an author of this chapter (Walmsley & Johnson, 2003). We write as a team: Anikó, Csilla and András are members of the initial group who created the participatory method at the Hungarian ELTE University, and Jan is supporting us as an internationally well-known expert in the field of inclusive research. During the process of writing, we discussed the chapter, and András mentioned additional reflections and comments that we quote. I-poems, which are posted in seminar groups that we share with students, are also part of the text. I-poems are usually used in inclusive research to make analysis more accessible to persons with intellectual disabilities. They are often produced by the researchers from data that was previously collected by the inclusive research group, focusing on the sentences that include the personal pronoun 'I' (Edwards & Weller, 2012). The first poem included in this chapter was produced by Anikó, using texts that András wrote during our first joint university semester. After that, András started to create his own I-poems regularly.[1]

We are constantly analysing the hierarchy that is reflected in language and are still working on the terms that we use in Hungarian to describe our method and its participants. We used to refer to members with disabilities as participatory co-teachers, and to non-disabled members as professionals or non-participatory teachers, but we realised that this approach may be criticised because it is recreating oppressive practices. In this chapter, we focus on our team as an inclusive unit but also highlight factors that are linked to the individual experience of living with a disability. In order to support empowerment and to respect that every person should have the right to use the terminology for their own conditions that is comfortable for them, we don't change the wording in original quotes, even if some terms do not represent the theoretical framework of the social and human rights model of disability ('impairment').

> I know that the books say otherwise, but the books don't know that they are hurting others. For me, when someone says 'disabled', they don't

know that they are hurting me and they don't see my good characteristics. They only see the negative and I don't like the word 'disabled' because of that. I like the word 'impaired', or András. That's it.

Participatory tracks in higher education

Higher education has significantly surpassed its traditional roles over the past years. In knowledge-based societies, in addition to educational and research activities, academic identity is increasingly complemented by service development and innovation, which connect higher education institutions with the communities around them (Delanty, 2004; Flecknoe et al., 2017).

The United Nations Convention on the Rights of Persons with Disabilities has accelerated this transformation by defining a participatory paradigm as an added value for academia. A new opportunity to break down the boundaries between the minority and the majority and empower people with disabilities. The joint work of disability activists and academics is mutually beneficial (Barnes, 2007; Bergold & Thomas, 2012; Losoncz et al., 2018; Armstrong et al., in press).

People with disabilities enforce the 'Nothing about us without us!' principle related to science and higher education: they make their voices heard and participate in areas that directly affect their lives. The participatory method considers it to be a strength if a person with local knowledge and insider experience works as a co-researcher, a co-teacher or a co-developer. The argument is that both research and teaching about disability in higher education, as well as social service development, are more authentic and valid when co-created (Goodley, 1996; Walmsley, 2004; Heiszer et al., 2019; Kunt, 2021; Sándor, 2021).

In participatory research, teaching and development, we try to ensure different but equal roles for disabled and non-disabled staff. Involvement in the academic process expands the knowledge of a participatory actor about science and higher education, just as, conversely, their experience adds to the knowledge of non-participatory scientists, who gain insight into the lives of disabled people. This enriches everyone and blurs the boundaries of knowledge creation (Könczei et al., 2019).

Ideally, people with disabilities should be involved in the whole process. For example, if we are talking about research, then they should participate from the formulation of research questions to the dissemination of results. However, this rarely happens; more often, we talk about different levels of participation: for example, adapting research methods to groups, formulating appropriate questions, conducting pilot interviews or disseminating research results (Katona et al., 2019).

When it comes to participatory teaching, the spectrum is also diverse and wide. All teachers on the inclusive team work in partnership in the educational process, from preparation to assessment. This has the added advantage of serving as a role model for the students. Anikó and Csilla, for example, introduce the theoretical background, present state of the art and facilitate the discussion with tasks and questions. András, in turn, shares his life experiences on the topic. Everyone is participating in a meaningful way.

However, joint preparation, in which each actor can define their own area, is essential for this. When we work with participatory teachers who use wheelchairs or live with ADHD, but even more when we teach together with colleagues with intellectual disabilities, we have to make sure this process is accessible. It involves transforming communication and teaching materials into easy-to-understand information.

These inclusive seminars, where we have been teaching together since 2016, offer the possibility of co-creation to the students and also support the career plans of our participatory colleagues in various fields. András, besides teaching, shares his poems with the community of the faculty:

> When I write poems, I write from inspiration. Sometimes I think of things that I could write a poem about, or people who inspire me, and I write poems about them. . . . I also read a lot of poems and I often use poems as a painkiller. And I get a lot out of myself with poems whether I'm in a good mood or not.

Such in this I-poem:

I'm András Futár from Solymár, I will talk about me now.
I like many things.
I like to sing and to play.
I like hugs,
face and forehead kisses.
I like to talk to others.
We need peace to work together well.
We need faith and hope and love.
I am sad, I am looking for myself but I cannot find me sometimes.
I need help to find myself.
I like to be with you and you are very important to me.
For me, Bárczi University is peace.
Every time I am at Bárczi University I get peace!
I dreamed about Bárczi and I don't give up.
I fight like a lion, but sometimes thorns stand my way.
I am the stronger, I crunch them and jump over them, so I do at Barczi University.
I'm not afraid, I'll fight for you, I love you very much.
It is good to be a teacher at the Bárczi University.
I'm happy at the Bárczi University.
I became much stronger.
To work at the Bárczi Gusztáv University is great.
My dream came true to be with you at Bárczi University.

(Katona et al., 2018, p. 21)

A career as a participatory teacher, tutor and chairperson from the perspective of András

I was diagnosed with Williams syndrome during my 20s, so the first step that I took into the academic world was to participate in a research project about Williams syndrome. I gained experience in qualitative interview techniques and was highly motivated in supporting other members of the research group. Later, I joined the doctoral research of Katalin Heiszer, who conducted the first inclusive research in the field of disability studies in Hungary (Heiszer, 2017).

In 2014, our team collected experiences of Hungarian researchers in the field of social sciences, regarding inclusive and participatory research methods. I gave an interview on my opinion about the possibilities and obstacles that I could identify (Heiszer et al., 2014).

These studies built good relationships between members of the faculty and me. It gave the group a solid basis of trust to further work together on participatory teaching.

Inclusive seminars and participatory teaching were introduced by the Bárczi Gusztáv Faculty of Special Needs Education at the ELTE University in 2016. These are inclusive courses where disabled and non-disabled lecturers teach together as partners.

The method is based on three main pillars:

- Dual teaching: there are always at least two teachers in the classroom who prepare, conduct and evaluate the seminar together. We also have successful courses with the participation of three, four or even five teachers.
- Infocommunication technologies: we use different kinds of interactive tools to involve students and teachers in the co-creation process. We also introduce students to the use of augmentative and alternative communication techniques with the support of our colleagues.
- Inclusive seminars are based on participatory projects that are planned and conducted by students and persons with disabilities (Katona et al., 2019; Katona & Sándor, 2020; Cserti-Szauer et al., in press).

In 2018, we also developed an interdisciplinary course for persons with disabilities and students of social sciences, social work and special needs education to learn together about supported living. This was the outcome of an international project on deinstitutionalisation, Path of Deinstitutionalization Urgent Moves (PODIUM), that was committed to establishing participatory practices to train the trainer seminars that were created. Within this course, new trainees were invited to talk about their experience on transitioning from total institutions to supported living arrangements. I took the role of participatory tutor and supported my peers in developing the skills that I had learned during my work at the university.

An I-poem from this period:

For a long time I had a dream to be a member of the Bárczi Faculty.
Being a researcher and a lecturer is a great responsibility.
Raising awareness activities are important.
Speaking about my diverse identity is also important.
The word 'disability' is not a good word for me because it expresses my bad characteristics.
I like the word 'impairment'.
During class everyone is equal to the other.
It is important to help each other and to love the other person.
In the PODIUM project I support new participatory lecturers to be prepared for the lessons.
I participated in a project meeting in Belgrade, where we presented our work successfully.
We received an award for our inclusive work and for changing higher education.

(Katona et al., 2018, p. 18)

The poem refers to an award that the team was given in 2017 for our accomplishments for the International Development in Higher Education and for our contribution to the internationalisation strategy of the ELTE University.[2]

In recent times, together we have coordinated and taught about 15–20 inclusive seminar groups on the topics of self-determination, disability history, adult persons with disabilities, supported living and supported decision making. Not only are the curricular activities considered very important, but also the social activities that are connected to extra-curricular work. Our team spoke at several international disability studies and disability research conferences and workshops. We started a collaboration with colleagues at Tallinn University, where we visited for a week and gave a lecture on participatory methods for the students of the international MA program for social entrepreneurs. We enjoyed not only the work with international colleagues but also the social events and leisure activities, such as conference dinners and sightseeing.

In addition to teaching, we present our work at self-advocacy events such as the Independent Living Day of the Hungarian Association for Persons with Intellectual Disability in 2018, where I felt like a role model for my peers. At this event, we took on chairperson tasks together for the first time. In our workshop, where more than 20 self-advocates participated with their assistants, my job was to help my peers to speak up for themselves.[3]

In the same year, at the Sixth Conference of Disability Studies in Budapest, Csilla and I co-chaired a panel discussion. The topic was the participatory approach in higher education.[4]

A summary about of experiences: "We dare to speak up for ourselves and for others, because this is an example that we are not in such a fearful social group, but we are brave and we fight. We speak the truth, even if others disagree."

Sometimes I also contribute autonomously to events of other faculties of the ELTE University. Every year, I am an invited member of a living library program at the Faculty of Education and Psychology.

I regularly join social events of the faculty organised for the teachers and staff of the university. Our goal is to underline that every colleague is a valuable member of this academic community, not only during the hours of teaching and research activities but also beyond. This is especially important in the case of persons with learning disabilities or intellectual disabilities because the meaning of the social elements of a workplace can be re-learned with their support. We love to have lunch together where we have the possibility to meet students and other colleagues. We go to the Christmas and New Years' celebrations and participate in the farewell party for the senior graduates.

My career also had an empowering effect on my personal life. When we started working together in 2016, I was visiting a day center that had a sheltered workshop. The possibility of working in an inclusive environment on the open labour market changed my views about this center. After a couple of semesters together, I reached out to my family and our team and wanted to completely transition to the university. With their support, I left my former workplace and became an external lecturer on the faculty.

Services and cooperation

The participatory academic work had an impact on our patterns of work, and we realised that we could develop new services in order to support all participants. Compared to non-participatory teaching, every member of our team puts in more time beyond working hours. Preparation of the seminars and projects need a lot of time and communication within the team. Because we were the first to co-design and introduce this method at a Hungarian university, there is no course or training that prepares someone to become the member of a participatory team. At the moment, this task is fulfilled by us, which generates extra work.

In order to support our mental health, we decided to form an interdisciplinary team with psychologists and special needs teachers and to start a supervision pilot project for participatory teaching. The goal of this project is to address and define the challenges that we face every day by working together. This highly self-reflective practice can help us cooperate effectively and maintain our motivation for the continuous development of the method. We ran the pilot project in 2020 with great success and important experiences. The COVID-19 lockdown showed us that it is essential to have non-judgmental platforms and safe spaces, where teachers can express their frustrations and problems. Our plan was to start the pilot project in person, but we needed to adapt the plans to remote work. Just like all seminars and activities during the lockdown, personal and group supervision was provided via online channels like Zoom and Microsoft Teams.

Unfortunately, there was also a need for a shift of our topics: due to the tragic loss of our colleague Zsuzsa Antal, we had to integrate grief support along with the planned professional modules. Zsuzsa was one of the first disabled persons who joined us in 2015 in a participatory research project and played a central role ever since. She led many seminars and introduced us to the importance of the lack of personal assistance services in Hungary. She was also a main figure in preparing new members for their tasks and responsibilities as participatory teachers as a mentor; therefore, she is missed very much by all of us.

The positive responses to our first pilot showed us that there is a need for this type of support, and we believe that this participatory supervision can also be used by other faculties that try to work with participatory teachers.

This collective, very traumatic experience inspired another I-poem by András:

I know that many of you want to know how I feel.
I want to talk to you about the things that I went through and also, what helped me.
Many of you know that I work at the Bárczi Faculty, at Ecseri Street 3.
I love my colleagues and friends at Bárczi very much.
October 2020 gave me a big lesson, when I lost Zsuzsa Antal, my colleague, friend, participatory co-worker and my activist partner.
I had to think about a lot of things, for example, if I could be strong and brave enough to go on with my work.
I have to admit that I wanted to leave Bárczi, because I could not let Zsuzsa go.
I was broken for a long time and cried a lot, but on the 12th December everything changed.
I got a support video that I watched many times and cried happy tears, and you know why? Because Bárczi needs me.
My video and the love and messages of the people in this video made me stronger.
András is staying at Bárczi until Bárczi needs András.
I have many plans and others have plans with me.
I am doing my work and everything will go well.
I want to thank that I found my place at Bárczi and that so many of you love me.
I hope that I can be a blessing in the life of Bárczi and in the life of others.

When Zsuzsa left, I wrote a poem about her too. For me, it was the hardest I-poem. It was very disturbing for me. Emotionally. How to express what I wanted to tell Zsuzsa. It was very difficult, because I was tormented by thoughts. It was the most painful poem I've ever written.

Breaking down the barriers of academic publishing

Despite three decades of inclusive research and pioneering initiatives like the employment of András in a university, one of the bastions of non-disabled privilege in the academic world is publishing. An author of this chapter, as editor of the *British Journal of Learning Disabilities* back at the turn of the century, introduced accessible abstracts and encouraged co-produced articles. Things moved on little in the intervening 20 years. Indeed, when in 2020, she offered an accessible illustrated summary of an article of which she was a co-author to JARID, they turned it down – even though this was at no cost to them.

Things began to change in 2020 when Professor Melanie Nind took on the editorship of the *British Journal of Learning Disabilities.* She invited board members Jan Walmsley and Liz Tilley to coordinate In Response, an experiment in which self-advocacy groups select an article due for publication to critique.

At the time of writing, this experiment had involved three different UK groups commenting on a paper, with their response appearing alongside the article in the *Journal.* The papers that have been part of this initiative at the time of writing are Bates et al., 2020, response by Lewis et al., 2020, Symonds et al., 2021, response by Williams et al., 2021, and Birdsey, 2020, response by Blackley et al., 2021.

Gradually, we developed a process with a number of stages. First, self-advocates select a paper from the *Journal* to respond to. The *Journal* lets the authors know and asks them if they would like to point to other resources (e.g. easy read, video) that might be shared. The self-advocates then write a response paper with their thoughts, including six questions for the author. Before sending the response to the author, we, as *BJLD* representatives, review it and make some suggestions, which self-advocates may or may not accept. The response paper is then shared with the author(s), and a video meeting is scheduled for a discussion, chaired by a member of the *BJLD* board. After this meeting, self-advocates amend their response. This is shared with the paper's authors for accuracy before publication alongside the original article.

The self-advocates earn a modest fee for their work, paid by Wiley, the *Journal* publishers. The response paper is open access when published, and self-advocates receive printed copies of the *Journal* issue.

The initiative has been welcomed by self-advocacy groups and authors alike and has thrown up interesting issues, only some of which are discussed here.

Inaccessible titles and summaries

Although the *Journal* has had a policy of requiring accessible summaries for 20 years, most are not readily accessible. Nor are most article titles. This made selecting the paper quite a challenge for the self-advocacy groups. They handled this in different ways.

BAROD's non-disabled colleague wrote easy read summaries of three papers; the group then made their choice.

SPF had five papers to choose from. They found it hard because they didn't understand the titles and the plain English summaries because they were not in plain English. In the end, they chose the paper that they found easiest to understand the summary of.

Cardiff People First reported

> We were sent a list of titles and accessible summaries so we could choose one. This took longer than we expected, because even with summaries it was hard to tell what they were about. Not everyone liked the same ones best, so we voted.
>
> One person commented:
>
> I didn't understand, it's all jargon. I could understand, if it was explained. (Everyone agreed with this.)
>
> *(Blackley et al., 2021, p. 191)*

In responding to this criticism, author Nicole Birdsey acknowledged that she had found it difficult to write, not having done it before and not having access to self-advocates who could help her.

To resolve this issue of inaccessible accessible summaries, two In Response groups suggest:

- Requiring 'easy read' with symbols rather than 'accessible summary'
- Asking referees to pay careful attention to the Easy Read or accessible summary when commenting on papers
- Asking authors to find a plain English title to sit alongside the 'key words' title

Jargon

Cardiff People First members were scathing, even angry about the use of language they called jargon:

- There's too much jargon in research. People with a learning disability should be able to understand the research they are doing on us. We are just guinea pigs.
- They write down what they want. They are all judging us.
- The language is too complicated. Jargon and gobbledy gook.
- They use jargon because they know people don't know what it means.
- They want to sound important.

(Blackley et al., 2021, p. 192)

Conventions like 'et al.' in a reference, so familiar to academics, were quite off-putting to self-advocates grappling with the article.

The author's response was to recognise that had she reached out earlier, she could have written a paper that more people could understand.

Meeting the author

In all three cases, meeting the author was a positive experience. Authors of all three papers responded with enthusiasm to the challenges put to them by the self-advocates, and the self-advocates, although nervous, reported that they had found the encounters enjoyable.

Here are some examples from Cardiff People First:

- Nicola wasn't what I expected.
- She was lovely to speak to.
- She was very understanding and took feedback on board.
- She didn't take offence or tell me off.
- Did I sound rude when I said her name should have been in there?
- I didn't know she was the therapist as well, that was embarrassing.
- I was surprised, I thought the whole thing was a made up story, not about a real person.
- It was all in the 3rd person so it was harder to work out if it was real and that the researcher was the therapist as well.

(Blackley et al., 2021, p. 193)

Challenges of the inclusive method

As the first pilot seminar was introduced, the leaders and the administration of the faculty were both supportive. Participatory teachers started to work on a pro bono basis, and after presenting our first results, they were given the opportunity of formally joining as guest lecturers. Unfortunately, still to this day, we cannot arrange permanent contracts for participatory colleagues and have to contract them every semester for the individual courses. This is a factor of uncertainty that should be rearranged in future. On one hand, our main challenge is that Hungary has a system of special and regular schools, and some types of special institutions do not offer a degree that allows you to apply for university. A university master diploma, on the other hand, is necessary in order to be able to teach as a junior lecturer. At some point, it is also crucial to receive a doctoral degree to become a senior teacher and researcher, and due to these systemic obstacles, this path cannot be taken by persons with learning disabilities or intellectual disabilities. On the other hand, the support of this method may be considered an investment to raise the quality of university teaching. There are trends in higher education that support more cost-effective solutions: e.g. single teaching, frontal lectures with a large number of students and written exams or tests. The economic and social crisis accompanying the COVID-19 pandemic will not make it any easier to include and finance our method.

At the end of every seminar, students give us feedback, both directly and anonymously. Many of them meet disabled persons for the first time in their lives and don't know what to expect. By the end of the courses, they feel more secure in their interactions and build their experience of assistance and accessibility. Challenges may occur outside the classroom, in social interactions and in communication on social media platforms. Participatory teaching is collaborative and encourages companionship, while redefining the classic roles in higher education. However, it has to respect the privacy and free time of students, which requires participatory teachers to reflect on their own position and boundary setting in communication. We encourage open conversations about this topic and have always been able to resolve misunderstandings.

Even if the majority of the students give positive feedback about the method, some colleagues raise concerns about the fact that participatory teachers don't have the qualifications and diplomas that are required for working in higher education. This is also supported by a general scepticism towards the participatory paradigm and qualitative techniques. We contribute to these professional debates by publishing our results in a transparent way, including the challenges that we face. We regularly conduct research projects that evaluate and monitor the development of the project. For the latest evaluation, we invited three observers to analyse an inclusive seminar from the perspectives of a student, a teacher and a participatory teacher (Katona & Sándor, 2020).

As far as *BJLD*'s In Response is concerned, it is early days. So far, the *Journal* publishers have been supportive, although there have been some administrative errors along the way, such as positioning the In Response as a letter rather than an article in its own right. This was rectified. Authors of the papers chosen by In Response teams have all welcomed the challenge; exchanges have been courteous and fruitful. Two issues are beginning to emerge. In Response teams appear to be less willing to be critical of papers co-written with people with intellectual disabilities, and putting everything the In Response team says into Easy Read risks oversimplifying what start as quite complex concepts. Finally, the In Response teams are pushing for more change. Why are people with intellectual disabilities not on the editorial board? Why not ban any research which is not carried out by an inclusive team? We are only at the starting gate of this process.

Future plans

This chapter discussed different aspects of participatory academic work, like research, teaching and publishing. Our team has plans for the future development and dissemination of the participatory method. First of all, it is crucial to create positions for employees with learning and intellectual disabilities. In Hungary, it is not possible to apply for a degree in higher education from certain schools for special needs; therefore, there is no pathway to becoming a university employee either. While we certainly find it important to generate new ways for people with intellectual disabilities to be able to participate as university students, in parallel, we are working on establishing participatory workplaces for them. To make the process of inclusion easier than it is now, purposeful assistance will play a main role: e.g. through a cooperation with providers who are offering supported employment services. Workplace assistants could support us in welcoming new participatory teachers or when we experience new situations or tasks.

Our team is also working on the development of personal assistance services in Hungary, which are not available at the moment (Sándor & Kunt, 2020). Our colleagues struggle to recruit, hire, train and support their own assistants, and this has effects on our academic work too. As activists and allies, we created the Freekey initiative, which fights for the right to personal assistance. A very powerful insight into our daily challenges might be that the first time that we could all be together as a whole team in the same place was during the lockdown, when we started to have our group meeting online. Before that, there was always at least one member missing because of accessibility issues and the lack of support services and support persons. In Hungary, public transport is not fully accessible, and there are not enough accessible transport services operating to cover the needs. Although the university building is accessible, the road leading to it is not.

Our inclusive and participatory service development work plays a huge role in our teaching practice. This way, our work has a direct impact on the training of special needs teachers of the future. An added value is also the input of the students: thanks to their projects and constantly new and refreshing professional thoughts and diverse skills, our work is influenced by them. They make flash mobs, videos and online and offline games, and we even had an inclusive street art team once that created a legal graffiti in Budapest. These projects have a social impact that can be directly detected, mainly through the reactions of disabled persons to these projects on social media.

Figure 21.1 Inclusive graffiti project 'We are a unit!'

We also see development in the field of academic writing. In Response has begun to throw up some important challenges for academic publishing. The copyright declaration has been rewritten, rules about sharing work after publication have been clarified, the questions asked of referees will be reviewed, and the *Journal* is now requiring video abstracts. We look forward to a continuing dialogue about how "Nothing about us without us" can translate into academic publishing. There's a long way to go.

Instead of closing remarks, we share the latest I-poem written by András, which summarises the most relevant values and benefits of the participatory method:

I love the Bárczi Gusztáv Faculty of Special Needs Education for several reasons:

1. *Everyone is open-minded.*
2. *I am appreciated and my work is valued.*
3. *I can share my opinion.*
4. *I get a lot of love in the form of conversations, hugs and forehead kisses, that's who they love me at Bárczi.*
5. *I can travel abroad to give speeches in English.*
6. *There is equality.*
7. *I am different from the others in many ways, but we are one team and we fight for the same goals. I am happy that I can be a lecturer, researcher, friend and role model at the Bárczi Gusztáv Faculty of Special Needs Education.*

Notes

1 A video about the I-poems can be seen here: https://drive.google.com/file/d/13pY9PaJt07CkwhkiWr9HHURpI4yYQZSY/view?usp=sharing.

2 https://www.barczi.elte.hu/en/content/together-we-teach.t.1248.

3 A collection of the photos can be seen here: https://egyuttvelunk.onervenyesites.hu/?page_id=2112.

4 Photos can be seen here: https://www.barczi.elte.hu/content/hatodik-fogyatekossag-tudomanyi-konferencia-2018-november-13.g.32?fbclid=IwAR1wboNAG7QG3hbKijDnODSvuz47I2UT_dRFRQaWdmr-nFUNTHNKTWBO_YM.

References

Armstrong, W., & Collis. (in press). The messy realities of inclusive research. In Lamputtong, P. (Ed.), *Handbook of Social Inclusion, Research & Practices in Health and Social Care*. Springer.

Barnes, C. (2007). Disability, higher education and the inclusive society. *British Journal of Sociology and Education, 28*(1), 135–145. https://doi.org/10.1080/01425690600996832

Bates, C., McCarthy, M., Milne Skillman, K., Elson, N., Forrester-Jones, R., & Hunt, S. (2020). "Always trying to walk a bit of a tightrope": The role of social care staff in supporting adults with intellectual and developmental disabilities to develop and maintain loving relationships. *British Journal of Learning Disability, 48*(4), 261–268. https://doi.org/10.1111/bld.12320

Bergold, J., & Thomas, S. (2012). Participatory research methods: A methodological approach in motion. *Forum: Qualitative Social Research, 37*(4), 191–222. https://doi.org/10.17169/fqs-13.1.1801

Birdsey, N. (2020). "I don't wanna be mad and sad": Using individual systemic therapy to help manage anger and low mood in an adult with a learning disability. *British Journal of Learning Disabilities, 49*(2), 179–190. http://doi.org/10.1111/bld.12356

Blackley, J., Gullis, D., Haines, B., et al. (2021). Response to Birdsey (2020) "I don't wanna be mad and sad": Using individual systemic therapy to help manage anger and low mood in an adult with a learning disability. *British Journal of Learning Disability, 49*(2), 191–194. https://doi.org/10.1111/bld.12384

Cserti-Szauer, C., Sándor, A., Katona, V., & Könczei, G. (in press). Social innovation in higher education from a disability studies perspective. In Păunescu, C., Lepik, K-L., & Spencer, N. (Ed.), *Social Innovation in Higher Education*. Springer.

Delanty, G. (2004). Does the University have a future? In Odin, J. K., & Manicas, P. T. (Eds.), *Globalization & Higher Education* (pp. 241–254). University of Hawaii Press.

Edwards, R., & Weller, S. (2012). Shifting analytic ontology: Using I-poems in qualitative longitudinal research. *Qualitative Research, 12*(2), 202–217. https://doi.org/10.1177/1468794111422040

Flecknoe, S. J., Choate, J. K., Davis, E. A., Hodgson, Y. M., Johanesen, P. A., Macaulay, J. O., Murphy, K., Sturrock, W. J., & Rayner, G. M. (2017). Redefining academic identity in an evolving higher education landscape. *Journal of University Teaching & Learning Practice, 14*(2). http://ro.uow.edu.au/jutlp/vol14/iss2/2

Goodley, D. (1996). Tales of hidden lives: A critical examination of life history research with people who have learning difficulties. *Disability & Society, 11*(3), 333–348. https://doi.org/10.1080/09687599627642

Heiszer, K. (2017). *Participatív kutatás értelmi sérült személyekkel: A Play Decide módszer adaptációja*. PhD thesis. ELTE PPK Neveléstudományi Doktori Iskola (Participatory research with intellectually disabled people: the adaptation of Play Decide method. PhD thesis).

Heiszer, K., Katona, V., & Kunt, Z. (2019). A részvételi paradigma áttekintése. In Katona, V., Cserti-Szauer, C., & Sándor, A. (Eds.), *Együtt oktatunk és kutatunk! Inkluzív megközelítés a felsőoktatásban* (pp. 19–29). ELTE BGGYK (The participatory paradigm; In We teach and do research together! Inclusive approach in Higher Education).

Heiszer, K., Katona, V., Sándor, A., Schnellbach, M., & Sikó, D. (2014). Az inkluzív kutatási módszerek meta-szintű vizsgálata. *Neveléstudomány, 3*, 53–67. (A meta-level study of inclusive research methods).

Katona, V., Cserti-Szauer, C., & Futár, A. (2018). What is inclusive higher education in our opinion? In Hernádi, I. (Ed.), *PODIUM Project – Path Of Deinstitutionalization – Urgent Moves from a Participatory Aspect. An Edited Collection of Studies on Deinstitutionalisation in Serbia and Hungary* (pp. 15–24). ELTE BGGYK.

Katona, V., Cserti-Szauer, C., & Sándor, A. (Eds.). (2019). *Együtt oktatunk és kutatunk! Inkluzív megközelítés a felsőoktatásban*. ELTE BGGYK (We teach and do research together! Inclusive approach in Higher Education).

Katona, V., Kolonics, K., & Sándor, A. (2019). A participatív kutatótárs szerepe. In Katona, V., Cserti-Szauer, C., & Sándor, A. (Eds.), *Együtt oktatunk és kutatunk! Inkluzív megközelítés a felsőoktatásban* (pp. 60–61). ELTE BGGYK (The role of the participatory researcher; In We teach and do research together! Inclusive approach in Higher Education).

Katona, V., & Sándor, A. (2020). *Az inkluzív felsőoktatási módszertan adaptációs lehetőségei egy metakutatás alapján*. Záróbeszámoló (Adaptation possibilities of inclusive higher education methodology based on a meta-research. Final report).

Könczei, G., Hernádi, I., & Sándor, A. (Eds.). (2019). *Esély? Egyenlőség? Taigetosz? Egy fogyatékosságtudományi kutatás tapasztalatai.* Eötvös Loránd Tudományegyetem (Opportunities? Equality? Taygetus? Experiences from a Disability Studies research).

Kunt, Z. (2021). Personal assistance in the context of disability studies and cultural anthropology. *Hungarian Journal of Disability Studies and Special Education*, (2), 18–24.

Lewis, B., Richards, S., Rice, S., & Collis, A. (2020). A response to Bates, C., et al (2020) "Always trying to walk a bit of a tightrope": The role of social care staff in supporting adults with intellectual and developmental disabilities to develop and maintain loving relationships. *British Journal of Learning Disabilities. British Journal of Learning Disabilities, 48*(4), 269–271. https://doi.org/10.1111/bld.12352

Losoncz, M., Bogdán, B., Cserti-Szauer, C., Katona, V., & Sándor, A. (2018). 'The process is far more complicated than I thought' Experiences of an Innovative and Inclusive Curriculum Development in Higher Education. *Hungarian Journal of Disability Studies & Special Education, Special Issue, 2018*, 64–71. https://doi.org/10.31287/FT.en.2018.1.7

Sándor, A. (2021). Self-determination opportunities of persons with high support needs. *Hungarian Journal of Disability Studies and Special Education*, (2), 9–17.

Sándor, A., & Kunt, Z. (2020). "A »gondozás« túlélést biztosít számunkra, a »személyi asszisztencia« életet" – A Személyi Asszisztencia Szolgáltatás szakirodalmi hátterének elemző áttekintése. *Szociálpolitikai Szemle, 6*(1), 5–26 ("Care" allows us to survive, "personal assistance" enables us to live – Analytical review of the literature on the Personal Assistance Service).

Symonds, J., Abbott, D., & Dugdale, D. (2021). "Someone will come in and say I'm doing it wrong." The perspectives of fathers with learning disabilities in England. *British Journal of Learning Disabilities, 49*(1), 23–33. https://doi.org/10.1111/bld.12351

Walmsley, J. (2004). Inclusive research in learning disability: The (non disabled) researcher's role. *British Journal of Learning Disabilities, 32*(2), 65–71. https://doi.org/10.1111/j.1468-3156.2004.00281.x

Walmsley, J., & Johnson, K. (2003). *Inclusive Research with People with Learning Disabilities. Past, Present and Futures.* Jessica Kingsley Publishers.

Williams, J., Barr, G., Bell, S., Baynes, L., Moon, M., & Jamieson, S., & Sunderland People First. (2021). Response to Symonds, Abbott and Dugdale (2020) "Someone will come in and say I'm doing it wrong." The perspectives of fathers with learning disabilities in England. *British Journal of Learning Disabilities, 49*(1), 34–38. https://doi.org/10.1111/bld.12369

22

EXPLORING INTERSECTIONAL AND ETHICAL FEMINIST PERSPECTIVES AS A POSSIBLE FRAMEWORK FOR UNDERSTANDING VIOLENCE AGAINST WOMEN WITH DISABILITIES IN AFRICA WITH SPECIFIC REFERENCE TO FORCED STERILISATION

Adetokunbo Johnson and Karin van Marle

Introduction

Violence against women and girls is perhaps one of the most severe but unacknowledged issues on the African continent. However, this issue is not necessarily a new phenomenon. In 2012, the Special Rapporteur on Violence against Women explicitly mentioned the significant susceptibility to violence that women with disabilities face compared to women without disabilities and men with disabilities (Human Rights Council, 2012). According to the Special Rapporteur, compared to their non-disabled sisters and male counterparts with disabilities, women with disabilities are more likely to encounter abuse over an extended period with distinct forms of violence by a more significant number

DOI: 10.4324/9781003410089-26

of perpetrators (Human Rights Council, 2012). Furthermore, women with disabilities are particularly prone to violence and abuse, including infringement of their sexual and reproductive rights in Africa, due to the intersecting identities of gender and disability that they embody (Ortoleva & Lewis, 2012).

Violence against women with disabilities manifests differently and in distinct forms (United Nations General Assembly, 2017). It manifests itself in multiple ways as femicide; domestic violence; sexual violence; harmful practices such as child marriage; and female genital mutilation, including treatments such as forced contraception, forced abortion and forced sterilisation (United Nations General Assembly, 2017). According to the Special Rapporteur, forced sterilisation is a form of violence and discrimination that violates women's bodily integrity and rights, particularly women and girls with intellectual disabilities in Africa (Human Rights Council, 2012, United Nations General Assembly, 2017; United Nations General Assembly, 2018). The Special Rapporteur on the Rights of Persons with Disabilities echoes this description, interpreting this forced practice as a form of social control that is harmful and dangerous (United Nations General Assembly, 2017). Several studies attest that women with intellectual disabilities are disproportionally targeted for forced sterilisation (Ortoleva & Lewis, 2012; Kanter & Villarreal, 2018, Bakare & Gentz, 2020). The situation worsens for women and girls with intellectual disabilities who, on account of the severity of their impairment, are erroneously believed to be unable to make rational sexual and reproductive choices (United Nations General Assembly, 2017). Such misconceptions make women and girls with intellectual disabilities easy targets for forced sterilisation. However, it is also true that other vulnerable, poor and uneducated women and women at the margins, including ethnic and racialised women and women living with HIV in Africa, can also be targeted (Durojaye, 2017; Ravnbol, 2010).

The difficulty with forced sterilisation is that it is not just medically, socially and legally acceptable in most African countries but is considered in the 'best interests' of women and girls with intellectual disabilities (Ofuani, 2017). Several studies in African countries such as Nigeria (Ofuani, 2017), Kenya (African Gender & Media Initiative, 2012), Namibia (Bakare & Gentz, 2020; Durojaye, 2017) and South Africa (Essack & Strode, 2012) confirm how ethnic and racialised women, women living with HIV in Africa and women and girls with disabilities, particularly women with intellectual disabilities, are forced to undergo this practice because they are not considered human enough to express or suppress themselves sexually. If forced sterilisation is legitimised under the guise of the best interests of women and girls with intellectual disabilities in these African countries, how these interests are defined and who defines these interests are questioned.

Against this backdrop, this chapter explores whether the disabled African woman's encounters and experiences of forced sterilisation could be better understood from a reconfiguration of intersectional and ethical feminist perspectives. On the one hand, Crenshaw's idea of intersectionality is used to draw attention to the invisibility of disabled women because of complex intersecting identities such as gender, disability and geographical location that make them unlikely to fit neatly into any of the dominant social and legal categories (Crenshaw, 1989). On the other hand, Drucilla Cornell's (1991, 1995) notion of ethical feminism, particularly her idea of the 'imaginary domain', is used to challenge dominant legal responses to the disabled African woman. Bodily integrity and its link to wholeness and selfhood are explored as ways that show how dominant legal responses fail to protect disabled women against the power and violence of the state. The argument is that an intersectional lens combined with ethical feminism could better defy the hierarchies that reinforce violence against women with disabilities is evident in the dangerous practice of forced sterilisation in Africa.

In terms of structure, this chapter has five sections over and above the introduction. In section two, we explore the situation of forced sterilisation against women and girls with intellectual disabilities in Africa. This analysis lays a good foundation for section three, where we briefly investigate the global and regional frameworks that tackle forced sterilisation. Drawing on the intersectional lens in section four, we explore how complex intersecting identities such as gender, disability and geographical location make women with intellectual disabilities unlikely to fit neatly into any dominant social and legal categories. In section five, Cornell's work on ethical feminism developed in the 1990s is revisited. We believe it is valuable in assisting us in thinking about how to challenge dominant legal responses to disabled African women. Finally, a short conclusion is included.

Exploring forced sterilisation of women and girls with disabilities in Africa

Women comprise approximately half of the over one billion persons with disabilities, and a large chunk of them live in African countries (Kanter & Villarreal, 2018). Research suggests that, compared to women without disabilities, women with disabilities are at least two and almost three times more likely to suffer physical and sexual violence (Kanter & Villarreal, 2018). Violence against women with disabilities manifests in distinct forms, including rape, sexual abuse, physical abuse and exploitation. Many abusers, including relatives, intimate partners, teachers, neighbours and caregivers, could perpetrate this violence. In addition, forced sterilisation is a distinct form of violence targeted at women with disabilities that is not just socially, legally and medically acceptable but can also be sanctioned by the state (Kanter & Villarreal, 2018; United Nations General Assembly, 2017; United Nations General Assembly, 2018).

Historically, women with intellectual disabilities have had minimal control over their sexual and reproductive decisions (Stinston et al., 2002). For this reason, the actual number of women with disabilities who have been forcibly sterilised in Africa is unknown. However, sufficient data suggest this practice is widespread in several parts of Africa. Research conducted by the United Nations Population Fund (UNFPA) in 2021 confirms the situation. The report vividly describes how women and girls with intellectual disabilities have disproportionately undergone forced sterilisation in Africa and the world (United Nations Population Fund, 2021). The Special Rapporteur on the Rights of Persons with Disabilities echoed the scarcity of data on the prevalence of forced sterilisation worldwide, including in Africa, but mentioned that 'the sterilisation of women and girls with disabilities continues to be prevalent, and up to three times higher than the rate for the general population' (United Nations General Assembly, 2017, para 29).

Anecdotal and empirical research reveals the susceptibility of women and girls, specifically those with intellectual disabilities, to forced sterilisation in Nigeria (Ofuani, 2017). This point is valid, especially when compared to men with disabilities, women with other forms of disabilities and women without disabilities. Ofuani's 2017 empirical study conducted in Nigeria corroborates this assertion. This study found that 38.8% of 224 respondents cited examples of female teenagers with intellectual disabilities who had been forcibly sterilised (Ofuani, 2017). Several reported cases of forced sterilisation are also documented in Kenya (Africa Gender & Media Initiative, 2012), South Africa (Holness, 2013; McLaughlin, 2014), Lesotho (Shale, 2015) and Namibia (Bakare & Gentz, 2020).

Although this research proves the prevalence of forced sterilisation of women with intellectual disabilities, there are limited testimonies. Multiple reasons can be associated with this scarcity. First, the stigma associated with disability and female sexuality means the forced sterilisation of women with intellectual disabilities is invisible. Second, the conflation of legal capacity with mental capacity means that women with intellectual disabilities are denied sexual autonomy, leading to forced sterilisation. Third, the legal and social acceptance and parents' acquiescence to forced sterilisation make it difficult to view it as a crime. Moreover, although testimonies of forced sterilisation of women with disabilities are scarce, the studies on the forced sterilisation of other women minorities, such as women living with HIV, show the possibility of similar forced acts being done on other marginalised women, including women with disabilities (Shale, 2015).

A 2012 study in Kenya has underscored the narratives of women living with HIV/AIDS who had been forcibly sterilised. According to Selina, one of the women:

> She was admitted to the Kenyatta National Hospital in 2000 with tuberculosis and pre-term labour pains. At the time, she was seven months pregnant and, at delivery, underwent a caesarean section. In the process, she claims that she was sterilised but only got to know about it seven months later when her husband decided to marry another wife. Her husband had signed the consent forms but did not inform her. She thought her husband only signed forms to allow the hospital to operate on her as she delivered. . . . [S]he was never given a chance to choose the family planning method of her choice. Her husband has since married another

> wife because he 'could not live with a woman who cannot give birth.' 'Your illness cannot allow you to carry a pregnancy to term, so I have no option but to marry another woman,' Selina recalls her husband's words. A mother of two, her husband sent her away from their matrimonial home and took away their children. 'The sterilisation ruined my life', she says bitterly.
>
> *(African Gender and Media Initiative (2012, p. 1)*

Durojaye traces the origins of the forced sterilisation practice to the outcome of the *Buck v Bell* case that was decided in 1927 in the United States of America (Durojaye, 2017). In that case, the plaintiff, a woman with intellectual disabilities, had her tubes removed in line with the state of Virginia's laws. The plaintiff questioned her sterilisation because it infringed her rights to equality and due process as enshrined in the Fourteenth Amendment of the United States Constitution. However, the reasoning of the Supreme Court appeared to be that since forced sterilisation was state-sanctioned, it did not violate the due process provision of the Fourteenth Amendment.

A threefold analysis of the Court's opinion on forced sterilisation is significant for this discussion. First, the Court seemed oblivious to the discrimination suffered by marginalised groups. Second, the Court appeared to suggest that state policy must be upheld even to the detriment of the human rights of the marginalised group. Third, the Court seemed unconcerned about the gendered and biological hierarchies evident in this case. Evidence has shown how forced sterilisation has targeted female minorities in countries like Germany, Finland, Chile, Sweden and Africa (Bakare & Gentz, 2020).

The history of forced sterilisation in African countries can be traced to the colonial legacy. For example, a strong correlation between colonialism and disability in the Global South has been established (Grech, 2015; Meekosha, 2011; Connell, 2011, Johnson, 2019). Colonialism denotes power exerted over people that manifests in different ways: either structural, cultural, economic or political (Meekosha, 2011). Using this power, the colonialists introduced 'otherness', in which the colonised were viewed as inhuman, inferior, backward and animal-like, especially compared to the colonial superiors. The colonial superiors legitimised their violent invasion of African societies by claiming Africans were godless and beasts (Meekosha, 2011). Specifically, colonialism has long equated the Black female body with ugliness, darkness or blackness. Bernard, for instance, describes how Black female bodies have historically been correlated with savagery and sexual abnormality (Bernard, 2016). For him, the colonial intrusion introduced the idea that Black women's bodies are perceived as animalistic and could be measured like a disabled body (Bernard, 2016). The consequences of this otherness encouraged a form of eugenics. Such derogatory labels ascribed to female bodies make them the object of surveillance and control by the coloniser, which could be reflected in forced sterilisation.

From this, the rationale behind the forced sterilisation of women and girls with intellectual disabilities, as provided by literature, is threefold. First, studies indicate that women with intellectual disabilities were sterilised historically in Africa, as in the rest of the world, for eugenics reasons (United Nations General Assembly, 2017; United Nations General Assembly, 2019). The eugenics narrative is founded on the need to prevent the conception of unfit and defective individuals. Unfortunately, defective and unsuitable usually meant marginalised. For example, women from ethnic minority groups, women living with HIV and women with intellectual disabilities were disproportionately affected and targeted for forced sterilisation. Unfortunately, the eugenics narrative is not purely historical but has a contemporary basis for women with disabilities in Africa today. This modern basis is evidence of how forced sterilisation reflects the lived realities of marginalised women. For instance, in the same Ofuani (2017) empirical study conducted in Nigeria, 36.1% of 224 respondents interviewed mentioned the prevention of unwanted pregnancies is a viable excuse to condone the forced sterilisation of women with intellectual disabilities.

Secondly, most times, women and girls with intellectual disabilities in Africa are forcibly sterilised because of their disability and socio-economic status. For example, returning to the 2017 empirical studies conducted in Nigeria, 23.2% of 224 respondents found that financial limitations were another significant reason parents and guardians allowed their girl children with disabilities to be sterilised (Ofuani, 2017). Therefore, the gendered and discriminatory nature of forced sterilisation triggered by harmful legal, traditional and social norms is evident in Nigeria, given that financial limitations are usually not considered enough reason to hinder pregnancy for women and girls without disabilities.

Thirdly, most times, African women and girls with intellectual disabilities are forcibly sterilised for their own 'good'. This assertion is consistent with Kanter and Villarreal Lopez's reminder of how the legitimacy of these forced practices rests under the guise of ensuring the best interests of women with intellectual disabilities (Kanter & Villarreal, 2018). African governments: legal and medical practitioners also argue for the 'best interests' of the women and girls with intellectual disabilities to excuse forced sterilisation. In Kenya, for example, regarding women with disabilities, the guardians consent to sterilisation on their behalf (CRPD Committee's concluding observations, 2015, para 33–34). Laws in African countries such as Kenya and South Africa still allow for substituted decision-making; families are still permitted to make reproductive health decisions for women with disabilities, including forced sterilisation and forced abortion (Kanter & Villarreal, 2018).

These best interest arguments are usually couched as the need to ensure that women with disabilities are saved from the harms associated with menstruation, pregnancy and childbirth and prevention of motherhood without seeking the informed consent of the disabled woman or girl (Kanter & Villarreal, 2018, p. 129), In most cases, on this basis, forced sterilisation is deemed necessary. It is justified because it helps prevent burdensome pregnancies, particularly in rape cases, and ensures the future safety of women and girls with intellectual disabilities, considering the severity of sexual assault on women with disabilities (2018, p. 129). The sterilisation of Deafblind women and girls without their consent, which was viewed as a response to the increased incidences of rapes in Malawi, is a case in point (Humanity & Inclusion, 2018, p. 13). Paradoxically, African women and girls with intellectual disabilities are particularly susceptible to sexual violence, rape and HIV. According to Kamga, this susceptibility is grounded on the faulty virgin cure belief (Kamga, 2013).

Yet the truth is that what is often presented as the best interests perspective is, in reality, a distorted interpretation and, as Sifris explains, is usually a proxy and disguise for the interests of others (Sifris, 2016). According to Kanter and Villarreal Lopez, forced sterilisation does not protect women and girls with intellectual disabilities, so it is not a helpful way for African states to prevent sexual assault (Kanter & Villarreal, 2018). The reasons are usually premised on misconceptions – misconceptions that women with disabilities, on the one hand, are asexual and not expected to have sexual relationships and, on the other hand, are regarded as hypersexual and sexual freaks in Africa. Grobbelaar-du Plessis describes how negative stereotypes usually associated with women with disabilities, such as 'sick', 'helpless', 'childlike', 'dependent', 'in need of care' and 'incompetent', create an illusion that women with disabilities do not have sexual urges and should be protected from sexual relations (Grobbelaar-du-Plessis, 2007). This description aligns with studies showing how parents and guardians force their girl children with disabilities to undergo this practice to ensure they remain small and 'childlike'.

In addition, forced sterilisation is usually done without informed consent because of the unfounded assumption that women with intellectual disabilities are unfit or unqualified to be mothers. Grobbelaar-du Plessis aptly describes how homemaking and motherhood roles are perceived as unsuitable for disabled women (Grobbelaar-du-Plessis, 2007). She explains how it is inconceivable for disabled women to marry and bear children in certain parts of Africa (2007, p. 406). Other misconceptions include the idea that the pregnancy is unwanted or that disability is hereditary and could be inherited by the unborn child (Haihambo & Lightfoot, 2010, p. 76). Scenarios from Namibia where women with disabilities believed to be cursed are murdered to prevent the risk of their children inheriting disability and generational curses confirm this point (2010, p. 76).

International frameworks on forced sterilisation of women and girls with disabilities in Africa

The section will briefly explore the normative and institutional framework for protecting women and girls with disabilities from forced sterilisation.

Sterilisation without full, free and informed consent has been enshrined in several international, regional and national human rights instruments (United Nations General Assembly, 2017). When women with intellectual disabilities are forcibly sterilised, several rights are infringed. These include the right to health, the right to information, the right to dignity, the right to bodily integrity, the right to privacy, the right to decide on the number and spacing of children, the right to found a family and the right to be free from discrimination (United Nations General Assembly, 2017).

These rights are encapsulated in several global and regional human rights treaties, including Article 7 of the United Nations (UN) International Covenant on Civil and Political Rights (United Nations General Assembly, 1966). Specifically, the Committee on Economic, Social and Cultural Rights in its General Comment No.5 mentions how the practice of forced sterilisation of women and girls with disabilities is an infringement of Article 10 of the International Covenant on Economic, Social and Cultural Rights (ICESCR General Comment No. 5, 1994, para 31). Similarly, Articles 10, 12, 16 and 19 of the Convention on the Elimination of All Forms of Discrimination against Women (CEDAW) also implicitly tackles forced sterilisation (United Nations General Assembly, 1979). The General Recommendation (GR) No. 18, adopted by the Committee on the Elimination of all Forms of Discrimination Against Women (CEDAW Committee), terminates the debate on whether the CEDAW includes protecting the rights of women and girls with disabilities (CEDAW Committee, General Recommendations Nos. 16, 17 and 18, 1991*)*. The GR acknowledges the 'double' discrimination that women with disabilities encounter daily because of intersecting factors of gender and disability. In addition, consistent with General Comment No 13 adopted by the Committee on the Rights of the Child, there is an emphasis that women and girls with disabilities face violations of their sexual and reproductive health (CRC Committee General Comment No. 13, 2011, para 23).

In one of its earliest cases, *AS v Hungary*, a Hungarian Romani woman was subjected to forced sterilisation by medical staff at a public hospital resulting in the loss of her reproductive abilities (AS v. Hungary; 2004). Although this case does not involve a woman with intellectual disabilities, lessons can be drawn. In this case, the CEDAW Committee found Hungary had violated CEDAW by the hospital's failure to obtain informed consent.

Similarly, in the African context, the CEDAW Committee, in its concluding observations on Kenya's eighth periodic report in 2017, expressed concern about the violence against women with disabilities, particularly forced sterilisation (CEDAW Committee's Concluding Observations, 2017). It required the Kenyan government to take proactive actions to eliminate the practice. Also, the CEDAW Committee's concluding observations to Namibia in 2015 hinted at the progressive decision by the High Court and Supreme Court in *Government of Namibia v. LM and Others* (CEDAW Committee's Concluding Observations, 2015, para 36; The Government of the Republic of Namibia v LM and Others, 2014). The outcome of this case is worth mentioning. Again, although this case involves the sterilisation of three women living with HIV and not women and girls with disabilities, lessons can be drawn, particularly the decision by the High Court that forced sterilisation without informed consent infringes on the rights of these women under Namibian law (The Government of the Republic of Namibia v LM and Others, 2014*)*. Despite the progressive ruling, concerns still exist about the extent of coerced sterilisation in the country. This point is reinforced by how the outcome of the case failed to recognise forced sterilisation as an infringement of human rights and the lack of clarity on how free and informed consent should be defined (Patel, 2017; Bakare & Gentz, 2020).

Article 6 of the UN Convention on the Rights of Persons with Disabilities (CRPD), adopted in 2006, recognises that women with disabilities face multiple and intersectional discrimination (United Nations General Assembly, 2006). Article 3 confirms the legal capacity of persons with disabilities, including Articles 12, 17 and 25, which forbid forced treatment and sterilisation. In addition, Article 15 of the CRPD requires member states to ensure that persons, including women with disabilities, are not subjected to torture or cruel, inhuman, or degrading treatment or punishment. Likewise, Article 16 guarantees protection from violence for every person with a disability, including women with disabilities. The provision further mandates state parties to eliminate acts of exploitation, abuse and violence committed by third parties.

Most importantly, in 2016, the Committee on the Rights of Persons with Disabilities (CRPD Committee) adopted General Comment No. 3 on women and girls with disabilities (CRPD Committee General Comment No. 3, 2016). The observation in the General Comment is the historical disregard for violations of the rights of women and girls with disabilities. As far as the CRPD Committee is concerned, states parties must take proactive steps and review laws and policies to prohibit forced sterilisation and forced abortion. This includes ensuring that persons with disabilities can marry and found a family, including providing access to sexual and reproductive health services per Article 23. Furthermore, in several initial concluding observations of African countries such as Niger (CRPD Committee's concluding observations, 2019, para 30), Kenya (CRPD Committee's concluding observations, 2015, para 33–34) and South Africa (CRPD Committee's concluding observations, 2018, para 32–33), the CRPD Committee expressed concern about the unabated occurrence of forced sterilisation of women with disabilities. The CRPD Committee, therefore, requested that state parties revise laws and policies that encourage this practice. It further required enacting legislative frameworks that will effectively prohibit these practices.

At the African regional level, some human rights treaties specifically address the forced sterilisation of women with disabilities. For example, Article 2 of the African Charter on Human and Peoples' Rights (African Charter) provides that individuals are entitled to rights and freedoms on an equal basis and without discrimination, including based on sex or 'other status', including disability (African Union's African Charter, 1981). At the same time, Article 18(3) outlines the protection of women from any form of discrimination. Expressly, persons with disabilities, including women with disabilities, are provided with special protection under Article 18(4). Similarly, Article 2 of the Protocol to the African Charter on Human and Peoples' Rights on the Rights of Women in Africa (Maputo Protocol), adopted by the African Union (AU) on 11 July 2003 and coming into force on 25 November 2005, focuses on the elimination of discrimination against women (Maputo Protocol; 2003). Therefore, state parties should adopt 'appropriate legislative, institutional and other steps to fight discrimination against women'.

The Maputo Protocol further commits state parties to the adoption of specific measures to combat violence against women, especially sexual violence (Article 3 (4); Article 4; Article 5; Article 6; Article 11 (3)) and authorises medical abortions in situations involving sexual assault, rape and incest (Article 14 (2) (c)). In addition, Article 23 of the Maputo Protocol addresses the 'special protection of women with disabilities'. It requires state parties to ensure that women with disabilities are free from violence, sexual abuse and discrimination. These provisions, which implicitly target forced sterilisation, are further strengthened by Resolution 260, adopted by the African Commission on Human and Peoples' Rights (African Commission) in 2013, recognising the prevalence of forced sterilisation in Africa. It is a significant resolution as it explicitly recognises forced sterilisation infringes on women's rights (African Commission, Resolution 260, 2013). In the Resolution, the African Commission reaffirmed forced sterilisation as an infringement on human rights to autonomy, dignity and non-discrimination (2013, para iv). Speculatively, although this resolution concerns women living with HIV/AIDs, it can be argued that it can be applied to women with disabilities.

The Protocol to the African Charter on Human and Peoples' Rights on the Rights of Persons with Disabilities (African Disability Protocol) was adopted on 30 January 2018 (African Union's African Disability Protocol, 2018). However, the African Disability Protocol has not come into force as it has yet to be ratified by at least 15 member states. Although the African Disability Protocol is yet to enter into force, it contains specific provisions that address forced sterilisation. Article 27, on the rights of women and girls with disabilities, explicitly obligates state parties to guarantee their sexual and reproductive rights, the right to retain and control their fertility, and the right not to be sterilised without their consent.

Intersectionality as a framework to make sense of and expose discrimination against women and girls with disabilities in Africa

Crenshaw has been credited with coining the term 'intersectionality' (Crenshaw, 1989). In her earliest work, she identified a fault in how anti-discrimination law defines discrimination in the United States. Her insight shows how African American women experience of discrimination is more than an additive equation expressed as sexism on top of racism (Crenshaw, 1989). She explained how African American women's encounters with discrimination could be the same as and different from those of European women and African American men. Nonetheless, African American women can simultaneously face discrimination as both black and women, an identity greater than the sum of racism on top of sexism. Drawing from the rape experiences of African American women, she described how an African American woman is not raped just because she is a woman but mainly because she is a Black woman. She used this example to show that while it is true that rape is an expression of male power and patriarchal hierarchies over a woman's sexuality, this single issue and the essentialist view is flawed as it obscures how rape can also be an expression of both ableist and racial domination (Crenshaw, 1989).

In a much later work, Crenshaw (1991) discussed how the intersecting identities of an African American woman as Black and a woman contribute to her discrimination experience. Although Crenshaw did not mention the forced sterilisation of women and girls with intellectual disabilities, we hold that the same reasoning is applicable in this situation: When a woman or girl with intellectual disabilities is sterilised forcibly, it is likely not just because she is a woman but because she is a woman and a minor, Black or from an ethnic minority and disabled. Most likely, depending on the severity of her intellectual disabilities, she is viewed as unable to communicate appropriately simultaneously.

Therefore, an intersectional lens forces us not to look at discrimination from a single-issue perspective but recognises multiple intersecting forms of discrimination. The intersectionality perspective focuses on a threefold issue relevant to women and girls with intellectual disabilities targeted for forced sterilisation. First, it challenges the tendency of antidiscrimination law to treat discrimination as a single issue. Women and girls with intellectual disabilities have been disproportionally affected by forced sterilisation mainly because of intersecting identities such as gender, age, race, ethnicity and the severity of the disability they embody. However, the outcome of *Namibia v LM and Others* shows how in Namibia, as in most African countries, forced sterilisation is yet to be seen as a form of discrimination based on the intersecting identities of the three women living with HIV/AIDS: their gender and health status (The Government of the Republic of Namibia v LM and Others, 2014; Nair, 2010; Patel, 2017). Namibia's Supreme Court found insufficient evidence to prove that forced sterilisation is a form of discrimination (The Government of the Republic of Namibia v LM and Others, 2014; Nair, 2010; Patel, 2017).

Second, the intersectionality perspective confronts the creation of the essential woman (Crenshaw, 1989). This creation reinforces the tendency to view gender as the single axis of identity when focusing on sexual violence. In doing this, other identity categories that could impact and increase the susceptibility to specific forms of violence are minimised. Using this intersectional reasoning, attention is paid to how different identity categories like race/ethnicity, geographical location, class and disability severity play significant roles in fuelling the forced sterilisation experience.

Third, the intersectionality lens removes the narrow focus on identities to encompass unequal power relationships. Ribet's reminder about the unequal power relationship between the disabled female patient and the medical practitioner is apt (Ribet, 2011, pp. 163 &164). This unequal power relationship is evident when medical practitioners assume that, based on her disability, a woman is unfit to have children and, on that basis, is sterilised. Therefore, the unequal power relationships and how the intersecting identities of class, gender, disability severity and race/ethnicity heighten the discrimination experience are apparent.

Feminist theorists mention the patriarchal hierarchies in dominant international human rights discourse that silence women's specific forms of violence. These patriarchal hierarchies grounded in colonialism thrive on women's inferiority and men's superiority (Meekosha, 2011). The 'woman' identity category has been subject to patriarchal definitions: men define what it is and means to be a woman. One would be right to speculate that women have been unable to define what it means to be a woman because the man's foot is constantly on her throat (EC Dubois et al., 1985). This assertion is true in most African countries. For instance, the patriarchal tradition in Nigeria, where women are treated as minors and encounter gender-based violence, supports this assertion (Durojaye, 2013). Nonetheless, these patriarchal hierarchies are worsened for women with disabilities who, according to Eleweke and Ebenso (2016), are further marginalised due to intersecting identities of gender and disability in Nigeria.

Patriarchal hierarchies are evident when the interests of men with disabilities have been prioritised over those of women with disabilities. Multiple reasons can be advanced for this prioritisation. First, it can be attributed to patriarchal tendencies favouring men over women with disabilities. Research, for example, finds a correlation between patriarchal hierarchies and the violence that women with disabilities experience (Grobbelaar-du-Plessis, 2007). Scholarship further ascribes the sexist, social, cultural and religious beliefs and the stereotypes and misconceptions about womanhood and disability prevalent in Africa to the severity of violence experienced by women with disabilities (Grobbelaar-du-Plessis, 2007).

Another reason could be traced to the social formulations of disability advanced by mainly white men in wheelchairs (Kayess & French, 2008). In addition, the patriarchal hierarchies are apparent in the tendency to treat persons with disabilities as homogenous. Yet the encounters of men with disabilities primarily represent the experiences of persons with disabilities, usually to the detriment of specific violent acts perpetrated against women with disabilities. Kim believes this tendency is based on a faulty argument that acknowledging disability as gendered could potentially weaken the disability movement (Kim, 2009). The consequence of this three-fold issue is gender-blind research that reinforces the invisibility of the specific forms of violence against women with disabilities.

Feminists have challenged the patriarchal hierarchies in the dominant human rights discourse by invoking the 'woman question' (Byrnes, 1989). However, feminists have erroneously assumed that all women share the same lived experiences and realities by asking the 'woman question'. Essentialist hierarchies in the dominant women's rights discourse are therefore premised on the encounters of the 'essential' or 'universal' woman experience represented mainly by the experiences of a white, middle-class, Christian, heterosexual and able-bodied woman, usually to the detriment of specific violent acts perpetrated against women with disabilities in the Global South. Essentialist assumptions are evident in most African countries where significant attention is given to the right to abortion, for instance, as opposed to the little or no mention of the specific reproductive concerns of disabled women, such as forced sterilisation (Sifris, 2016).

Essentialist feminist perceptions often link African women to the role of wife and mother. Although feminist theorists have objected to these stereotyped motherhood roles, nonetheless, when women with intellectual disabilities are forcibly sterilised, they are immediately disqualified from their motherhood functions on account of their disability. For this reason, disabled women struggle with the need to end the culturally dominant models of femininity. Yet, as Lloyd explains, at the same time, they aspire to achieve such femininity (Lloyd, 2001). Furthermore, disabled women struggle to have their sexuality acknowledged yet struggle to be free of the shackles of such feminine stereotypes. This struggle stems from cultural stereotypes perpetuating the view of disabled women as asexual, unfit to reproduce, dependent, unattractive and generally unable to be true women. We believe ethical feminism, also discussed later, could respond well to this specific dilemma.

As previously argued, essentialist hierarchies are evident when the specific violent acts against women with disabilities are disregarded. This situation occurs because of an assumption based on an 'essential' woman experience that fails to consider women's different identities and lived experiences. The result is what Mohanty describes; in her words, ignoring women's differences builds a false homogeneity that disregards the power imbalances that divide women (Mohanty, 1988).

Indeed, the example of forced sterilisation of women and girls with disabilities reflects patriarchal and essentialist hierarchies evident in most African societies that could benefit from an intersectional framework. First, the gendered and patriarchal hierarchies of forced sterilisation are apparent, considering that they primarily affect women over men, particularly in African countries. The patriarchal and gendered hierarchies present in forced sterilisation are evident. For instance, in Northern Nigeria's penal code, emasculation is defined as a hindrance to male procreation, described as grievous bodily hurt. This kind of grievous physical harm attracts imprisonment of up to seven years (Northern Nigeria Penal Code, 1959, Section 55 (1) (d)).

Yet, as Ofuani (2017) rightly observes, the same gesture of protection is not accorded to Nigerian women. Evidence shows that women with disabilities are frequently subjected to medical interventions without consent, including forced sterilisation, abortion and contraception. On this basis, she rightly infers that men are protected from sterilisation, but women are not. This patriarchal and gendered hierarchy is also evident in the doctor-patient power relationship in which medical doctors, primarily men, perform these forced treatments on women and girls with disabilities. Thus, forced sterilisation puts women and girls with intellectual disabilities in a position of inequality and discrimination.

Importantly, patriarchal hierarchies are evident where men's bodies are placed on a higher pedestal than women's bodies.

Second, the essentialist hierarchies in forced sterilisation response are evident in several African countries. For instance, abortion is considered a criminal offence in many African countries (Chiweshe & Macleod, 2018). However, a few African countries, including Togo, Tunisia and South Africa, permit legal abortion on request (2018, p. 52). However, the essentialist bias is evident even in African countries where whether abortion is a crime or not, forced sterilisation and abortion of women and girls with disabilities continue and, in most cases, are state approved (see the CRPD Committee's concluding observations to Kenya, 2015, para 33–34; and South Africa, 2018, para 29, 32–33). This bias is particularly evident where, although any woman may have an unplanned or unwanted pregnancy, it is mainly marginalised women who become targets and are subsequently subjected to forced sterilisation. Thus, forced sterilisation puts women and girls with intellectual disabilities in a position of inequality and discrimination. Importantly, essentialist hierarchies are evident where the bodies of women without disabilities are placed on a higher pedestal than disabled women's bodies.

Consequently, it is clear how the forced sterilisation of women with disabilities in Africa violates the rights of disabled women, underpinned by patriarchal and essentialist hierarchies. For instance, the link between eugenics and forced sterilisation demonstrates a metaphorical ladder of patriarchal and essentialist hierarchies on which there is a determination of who is allowed to conceive or even exist. Further, racial hierarchies are also evident in forced sterilisation. Ethnic minorities, more than ethnic majorities, are usually targeted for forced sterilisation. It is more likely to happen to Black women than White women; it is expected to occur more often in the Global South than in the Global North.

Additionally, forced sterilisation targets minorities, a category not always limited to socio-economic classes, as seen in the Namibian situation when women were targeted because of their health status. In fact, according to a 2020 report by the DisAbled Women's Network of Canada (DAWN), forced sterilisation rests on the oppressive reasoning of ableism, in which certain bodies are considered deviant (DAWN, 2020). This label is because these bodies do not meet specific physical and physiological standards and therefore deserve discrimination. Interestingly, as far as the DAWN (2020, p. 33) report is concerned, forced sterilisation illustrates ableism that justifies racist, patriarchal colonialist and cis-normative practices.

These issues maintain patriarchal and essentialist hierarchies that contribute to violence against women with disabilities. These hierarchies, individually and collectively, could explain why, according to Abu-Habib, women with disabilities remain at the bottom of a metaphorical ladder of human rights protection (Abu Habib, 1995). Therefore, the need for an intersectional framework to respond to violence, particularly forced sterilisation against women with disabilities, is evident.

Adetokunbo Johnson and Karin van Marle

Revisiting ethical feminism as a way to make sense of and respond to the discrimination against women and girls with disabilities in Africa

Drucilla Cornell (2011, p. 1), in a piece in which she reflects on her more than 20 years of work as a feminist theorist, explains the frustration of feminist theorists, towards the late 1980s and early 1990s, with how women were 'gendered' in a way that boxed them into 'a certain kind of being in the world'. It is important to take note of Cornell's involvement in and experience of political movements in the past to understand her commitment to political struggle as a central element of liberation while simultaneously proclaiming the 'ethical limitations on politics'. She explains that she never wanted to replace politics with ethical feminism but that ethical feminism was conceived to question how gender was asserted as a 'self-evident empirical category' (2011, p. 2). Ethical feminism was also cautious from the start about merely accepting solidarity among women just because all women lived under patriarchy and underscored the need to reflect on the ethical relations among women. A critical engagement with colonialism and coloniality, with an emphasis on the role of Western modernity, is part and parcel of ethical feminism, which makes it an apt theory to engage with the complex issue of forced sterilisation of disabled women in Africa. The approach is acutely aware of the violence committed over years of oppression and the endurance of the violence in societal and state practices. At the heart of ethical feminism stands the notion of 'the feminine within sexual difference'. Cornell, for many years, has argued that women need to hold on to sexual differences in order not to repeat or mirror the 'abjection of the feminine' within patriarchy. However, inspired by several theorists, Cornell (2011, p. 2), in developing ethical feminism, argued that the 'feminine could be reworked through metaphor and myth' and that such a reworking could open ways for women to be gendered differently. In other words, by drawing on narrative and art, for example, ways for women themselves to live differently and be perceived differently could be created and opened. One way for disabled women to bring their experiences to light is through stories and art.

Throughout her work, Cornell has held a sceptical view of legal equality and has suggested the notion of the 'imaginary domain' as a response to the limits of legal equality. In defining the 'imaginary domain', she responded to the way in which legal equality has set up a tension between equality and freedom. Her vision of equality provides for 'the equal protection of certain minimum conditions of individuation' (1995, p. 4). The minimum degree of individuation requires three things: 1) bodily integrity, 2) access to symbolic forms that will allow one to be able to differentiate oneself from others, and 3) the protection of the imaginary domain. The imaginary domain refers to that space from which an individual is free to imagine herself, to imagine who and what she can and wants to be without any restrictions. Cornell's concept of 'the person' is crucial to understanding her notion of the imaginary domain and also what the minimum conditions of individuation entail. In short, in her view, a person is never fully developed; a person is not a given but rather a possibility or an aspiration. Every individual must be free to aspire to becoming on an equivalent basis. Cornell stands critical of attempts that to protect substantive equality, provide a full elaboration of what free personhood entails (1995, p. 5).

Crucial for her is the 'space for the renewal of the imagination [the imaginary domain] and the concomitant re-imaging of who one is and who one seeks to become' (1995, p. 5). Cornell emphasises the importance of sex and sexuality and insists that we all are 'sexual beings', which has important implications for how we see ourselves. She explains that to have a sex means that human beings are sexual beings that involve having sex for pleasure and as a way to reproduce. Sex is an 'internalised identity', and added to that, each of us has a 'sexual imago' which influences our 'sexual imaginary' to the extent that we cannot separate ourselves from this image. Cornell argues that, for women, the sexual image has been split in two: conventional femininity is imposed on them so as to distance them from their own identification as a woman. 'The masquerade of femininity' is imposed on women in a way that prevents women from imagining and developing in a way that is different from this imposition.

For Cornell, self-respect – what John Rawls called a 'primary good' – is connected to the imaginary domain. Following Rawls, she argues that the denial of self-respect leads to imposed shame, but she adds that the primary good of self-respect is also crucial to the 'freedom to transform oneself into a person' (1995, p. 9). She develops the idea of a 'degradation prohibition' as a way to constrain someone from being downgraded because of their sex.

Someone is degraded when they are reduced to stereotypes of their 'sex' or have imposed upon them objectified fantasies of their 'sex' so that they are viewed and treated as unworthy of equal citizenship. We are degraded, in other words, when our 'sex' is defined, symbolised and treated as antithetical to equal personhood and citizenship (1995, p. 10).

Relying on Immanuel Kant's definition of freedom under the law and dignity of the person, Cornell argues that all persons should be 'worthy of happiness' (1995, p. 12). All persons should have an equal chance to be happy. Cornell asserts the importance of the 'feminine within sexual difference' as a way to ask for equivalence that recognises difference and does not have to rely on an argument of sameness. We argue that this could be significant for the prohibition of forced sterilisation of disabled women as well. The end goal of ethical feminism, as argued for by Cornell, is to reject all fixed and rigid descriptions of femininity. To call for the minimum conditions of individuation is to demand for each person to be treated equally as a 'sexuate . . . creature'.

The issue of forced sterilisation turns on equality and how effectively it can be applied to assist disabled women. As mentioned earlier, Cornell is concerned about the extent to which substantive equality 're-encodes' gender and ultimately leaves us with a limited understanding of femininity. The flaws of formal equality based on sameness are more obvious because it fails to address real differences and relies on comparability.

We want to unpack Cornell's argument on abortion here because we think that the argument could be of value also in our reflection on the forced sterilisation of disabled women. But before we do that, we want to note Cornell's critique of intersectionality, which, even though we support intersectionality as framework, we think should be heeded. From the perspective of ethical feminism and, in particular, the insistence on the feminine within sexual difference, Cornell warns that intersectionality 'reinscribes' a specific and fixed notion of gender. With reference to race, for example, she explains that 'what we needed . . . was an analysis of the way in which a black woman is a different configuration of the feminine within sexual difference from a white woman' (2011, p. 3). Arguing from the importance of protecting the imaginary domain, her concern is that intersectionality, by inscribing fixed gender identity, is not allowing women the space from where they can imagine themselves freely. This is, in our view, also relevant to the violence involved in the forced sterilisation of disabled women – the extent to which the freedom to imagine the self as mother is infringed.

For Cornell, the discussion about abortion is intimately linked to the legal guarantee to have an equivalent chance to become a person (1995, p. 32). She argues that because projections show that over half the babies born in the next 50 years will be female, the issue is also a generational one. She holds that there can be no meaningful equality for women unless the right to have an abortion is protected. We interpret this statement to apply also to the right of disabled women to become pregnant, to have the right to reproduce. The right in question to abort – or, in our interpretation, to reproduce – is a right to equivalent bodily integrity (1995, p. 33). Denying this right stands in the way of achieving 'the minimum conditions of individuation necessary for any meaningful concept of selfhood' (1995, p. 33). What is important is that this right should be understood as a right not to privacy, but rather to 'the establishment of conditions in which safe abortions are available' or, in our argument, in which disabled women can pursue their reproductive rights. Cornell calls for 'a new rhetoric' in which feminine sexual difference within the law can be articulated in a way that is compatible with equality. The equivalent value of the feminine sex implies that every person is worthy of personhood, which necessarily means that the right to bodily integrity must be protected (1995, p. 34). At the centre of the issue is that the state should not be allowed to regulate women's bodies, which means that women's bodies can't be treated as inviolable. As Cornell rightly argues, treating women as lesser beings makes an egalitarian legal system impossible.

Integral to ethical feminism is the protection of the symbolic, social and legal conditions needed for individuation. To deny the right to abortion or, in our interpretation, the right to reproduce rejects the protection of bodily integration because it gives the control of a woman's body to others. The call for a new rhetoric referred to earlier must also encompass the 're-articulation of the subject and . . . of the subject of rights' (1995, p. 41). Cornell's argument rests on the assertion that one's bodily integrity is 'fundamental to the most basic sense of self': that the sense of wholeness that is achieved by the projection of bodily integrity is central to a conception of selfhood (1995, p. 43). In our view, what is at stake when the bodies of disabled women are violated and, in particular, when a disabled woman is prevented from becoming a mother is her sense of selfhood and her ability to become whole. The law, including all current frameworks, fails to respond adequately to protect the right to bodily integrity for disabled women.

Conclusion

This chapter identifies the prevalence of forced sterilisation and the disproportionate exposure of women with intellectual disabilities globally, especially in Africa. The engagement with the history of this practice, particularly in Africa, reveals the invisibility of incidences of forced sterilisation committed against women with disabilities and the role that colonialism played and continues to play in birthing disabled persons and arguably encouraging eugenic notions. We examine forced sterilisation as a human rights infringement committed against women with disabilities and explore the legal and normative framework regarding this practice in Africa. The outcome of *Namibia v LM and Others* is significant. It shows how, although Namibia's Supreme Court found a violation had occurred when the three women living with HIV/AIDS were sterilised without their free and fully informed consent, it exposed the idea that forced sterilisation in Namibia, as in other African countries, is yet to be recognised as a discriminatory act. This decision has implications for women with intellectual disabilities vulnerable to forced sterilisation in most African countries.

We explore the possibility of an intersectional and ethical feminist framework to work together to respond to the current failures of the law and human rights to protect disabled women against forced sterilisation in African countries. An intersectional approach can assist by not only insisting that forced sterilisation of disabled women be seen as a matter of disability or sex or gender or race but also that the unique ways in which all these traits work together are recognised. From an ethical feminist perspective, intersectionality should not fall into the trap of again gendering disabled women: in other words, boxing them in and thereby preventing them from imagining themselves freely how and what they want to be and become. From an ethical feminist perspective, the issue of reproduction is intrinsically linked to a woman's bodily integrity and sense of wholeness, which is not protected unless a woman is allowed to see herself as a whole person.

Forced sterilisation of disabled women in African countries is a material manifestation of the legacy of colonialism and the continuance of patriarchal power in the face of legal protection. Albeit a very concrete harm against women that calls for direct intervention, the underlying reasons are to be investigated and also criticised on a conceptual level. This chapter responds to the practice of forced sterilisation by acknowledging the need for more action and more conceptual work to be done.

References

Abu Habib, L. (1995). Women and disability don't mix! Double discrimination and disabled women's rights. *Gender and Development*, 3(2), 49–53. https://doi.org/10.1080/741921809

African Charter on Human and Peoples' Rights (adopted 27 June 1981, entered into force 21 October 1986) (1982) 21 ILM 58 (African Charter)

African Commission 260 Resolution on Involuntary Sterilization and the protection of human rights in access to HIV services (2013) ACHPR/Res. 260(LIV). https://achpr.au.int/sessions/54th/resolutions/260/

African Gender and Media Initiative. (2012). *Robbed of Choice: Forced and Sterilisation Experiences of Women Living with HIV in Kenya*. https://kelinkenya.org/wp-content/uploads/2010/10/Report-on-Robbed-Of-Choice-Forced-and-Coerced-Sterilization-Experiences-of-Women-Living-with-HIV-in-Kenya.pdf

African Union (AU), Protocol to the African Charter on Human and Peoples' Rights on the Rights of Persons with Disabilities in Africa, 29 January 2018. https://au.int/en/treaties/protocol-african-charter-human-and-peoples-rights-rights-persons-disabilities-africa

Bakare, K., & Gentz, S. (2020). Experiences of forced sterilisation and coercion to sterilise among women living with HIV (WLHIV) in Namibia: An analysis of the psychological and socio-cultural effects. *Sexual and Reproductive Health Matters*, 28(1), 335–348. https://doi.org/10.1080/26410397.2020.1758439

Bernard, A.A.F. (2016). Colonising black female bodies within patriarchal capitalism: Feminist and human rights perspectives. *Sexualisation, Media and Society*, 1–11. https://doi.org/10.1177/2374623816680622

Byrnes, A. (1988–1989). Women, feminism and international human rights law – Methodological myopia, fundamental flaws or meaningful marginalisation – Some current issues. *Australian Year Book of International Law*, 12(1), 205–240.

Chiweshe, M., & Macleod, C. (2018). Cultural de-colonization versus liberal approaches to abortion in Africa: The politics of representation and voice. *African Journal of Reproductive Health*, 22(2), 49–59. https://doi.org/10.29063/ajrh2018/v22i2.5

Connell, R. (2011). Southern bodies and disability: Re-thinking concepts. *Third World Quarterly*, 32(8), 1369–1381. https://doi.org/10.1080/01436597.2011.614799

Cornell, C. (1991). *Beyond Accommodation: Ethical Feminism, Deconstruction and the Law*. New York: Routledge.

Cornell, C. (1995). *The Imaginary Domain. Abortion, Pornography & Sexual Harassment*. New York: Routledge.

Cornell, C. (2011). Revisiting beyond accommodation after twenty years. *feminists@law*, 1(1), 1–13. https://doi.org/10.22024/UniKent/03/fal.13

Crenshaw, K. (1989). Demarginalizing the intersection of race and sex: A black feminist critique of antidiscrimination doctrine, feminist theory and antiracist politics. *University of Chicago Legal Forum*, 139–167.

Crenshaw, K. (1991). Mapping the margin: intersectionality identity politics and violence against women of color. *Stanford Law Review*, 43(6), 1241–1299. https://doi.org/10.2307/1229039

DisAbled Women's Network of Canada (DAWN). (2020). *Girls without Barriers: An Intersectional Feminist Analysis of Girls and Young Women with Disabilities in Canada* https://dawncanada.net/media/uploads/page_data/page-64/girls_without_barriers.pdf

Dubois, E.C., Dunlap, M.C., Gilligan, C.J., MacKinnon, C., Menkel-Meadow, C.J., Marcus, I., & Spiegelman, P.J. (1985). Feminist discourse, moral values, and the law – A conversation. *Buffalo Law Review*, 34(1), 11–88.

Durojaye, E. (2013). Woman but not human: Widowhood practices and human rights violations in Nigeria. *International Journal of Law, Policy and the Family*, 27(2), 176–196. https://doi.org/10.1093/lawfam/ebt001

Durojaye, E. (2017). Involuntary sterilisation as a form of violence against women in Africa. *Journal of Asian and African Studies*, 53(5), 721–731. http://dx.doi.org/10.1177/0021909617714637

Eleweke, C.J., & Ebenso, J. (2016). Barriers to accessing services by people with disabilities in Nigeria: Insights from a qualitative study. *Journal of Educational and Social Research*, 6(2), 113–124. https://doi.org/10.5901/jesr.2016.v6n2p113

Essack, Z., & Strode, A. (2012). I feel like half a woman all the time": The impacts of coerced and forced sterilisations on HIV-positive women in South Africa. *Agenda*, 26(2), 24–34. https://doi.org/10.1080/10130950.2012.708583

The Government of the Republic of Namibia v LM and Others (SA 49 of 2012) [2014] NASC 19 (3 November 2014)

Grech, S. (2015). Decolonising Eurocentric disability studies: Why colonialism matters in the disability and global South debate. *Social Identities. Journal for the Study of Race, Nation and Culture*, 21(1), 6–21. https://doi.org/10.1080/13504630.2014.995347

Grobbelaar-du-Plessis, I. (2007). African women with disabilities: The victims of multilayered discrimination. *South African Public Law*, 22, 405–421.

Haihambo, C., & Lightfoot, E. (2010). Cultural beliefs regarding people with disabilities in Namibia: Implications for the inclusion of people with disabilities. *International Journal of Special Education*, 25(3), 76–87.

Holness, W. (2013). Informed consent for sterilisation of women and girls with disabilities in the light of the Convention on the Rights of Persons with Disabilities. *Agenda*, 27(4), 35–54. https://doi.org/10.1080/10130950.2013.857869

Humanity & Inclusion. (2018). *Gender and Disability Intersectionality in Practice: Women and Girls with Disabilities Addressing Discrimination and Violence in Africa*. https://www.makingitwork-crpd.org/sites/default/files/2018-05/MIW-HI%20Gender%20and%20disability%20intersectionality%20in%20practice%20-%20Women%20and%20girls%20with%20disabilities%20addressing%20discrimination%20and%20violence%20in%20Africa.pdf

Johnson, A. (2019). *The Voiceless Woman: Countering Dominant Narratives Concerning Disabled Women in Nigeria* (DPhil Thesis). Faculty of Law University of Pretoria South Africa.

Kamga, S.A.D. (2013). A call for a Protocol to the African charter on human and peoples' rights on the rights of persons with disabilities in Africa. *African Journal of International and Comparative Law*, 21(2), 219–249.

Kanter, A.S., & Villarreal, L.C. (2018). A call for an end to violence against women and girls with disabilities under international and regional human rights law. *Northeastern University Law Review*, 10(2), 583–653. http://dx.doi.org/10.2139/ssrn.3279759

Kayess, R., & French, P. (2008). Out of darkness into light? Introducing the convention on the rights of persons with disabilities. *Human Rights Law Review*, 8(1), 1–34. https://doi.org/10.1093/hrlr/ngm044

Kim, E. (2009). Minority politics in Korea: disability, interraciality, and gender. In Cooper, D., Graham, E., Krisnades, J., & Herman, D. (eds.), *Intersectionality and beyond: Law, Power and the Politics of Location*. Oxfordshire: Routledge.

Lloyd, M. (2001). The politics of disability and feminism, discord or synthesis. *Sociology*, 35(3), 715–728. https://doi.org/10.1177%2FS0038038501000360

McLaughlin, L.C. (2014). The price of failure of informed consent law: Coercive sterilisations of HIV-positive women in South Africa. *Minnesota Journal of Law and Inequality*, 32(1), 69–93.

Meekosha, H. (2011). Decolonising disability: Thinking and acting globally. *Disability and Society*, 26(6), 667–682. https://doi.org/10.1080/09687599.2011.602860

Mohanty, C. (1988). Under western eyes: feminist scholarship and colonial discourses. *Feminist Reviews*, 30(1), 61–88. https://doi.org/10.1057/fr.1988.42

Nair, P. (2010). Litigating against the forced sterilisation of HIV-positive women: Recent developments in Chile and Namibia. *Harvard Human Rights Journal*, 23, 223–231.

Nigeria Penal Code cap. 89 (1959) (Laws of Northern Nigeria)

Ofuani, A.I. (2017). Protecting adolescent girls with intellectual disabilities from involuntary sterilisation in Nigeria: Lessons from the Convention on the rights of persons with disabilities. *African Human Rights Law Journal*, 17(2), 550–570. http://dx.doi.org/l 0.17159/1996–2096/201 7/v17n2a9.

Ortoleva, S., & Lewis, H. (2012). *Forgotten Sisters – A Report on Violence against Women with Disabilities an Overview of Its Nature, Scope, Causes and Consequences*. https://papers.ssrn.com/sol3/papers.cfm?abstract_id=2133332

Patel, P. (2017). Forced sterilisation of women as discrimination. *Public Health Reviews,* 38(15), 1–12. https://doi.org/10.1186/s40985-017-0060-9

Ravnbol, C.I. (2010). The human rights of minority women: Romani women's rights from a perspective on international human rights law and politics. *International Journal on Minority and Group Rights*, 17(1), 1–45. https://doi.org/10.1163/15718 1110X12595859744123

Ribet, B. (2011). Emergent disability and the limits of equality: A critical reading of the UN Convention on the Rights of Persons with Disabilities. *Yale Human Rights and Development Law Journal*, 14, 155–204.

Shale, I. (2015). Sexual and reproductive rights of women with disabilities: implementing international human rights standards in Lesotho. *African Disability Rights Yearbook*, 3, 31–62.

Sifris, R. (2016). The involuntary sterilisation of marginalised women: Power, discrimination, and intersectionality. *Griffith Law Review*, 25(1), 45–70. https://doi.org/10.1080/10383441.2016.1179838

Stinston, J., Christian, L.A., & Dotson, L.A. (2002). Overcoming barriers to the sexual expression of women with developmental disabilities. *Research & Practice for Persons with Severe Disabilities*, 27(1), 18–26.

United Nations Committee on the Elimination of Discrimination Against Women (CEDAW Committee), General Recommendations Nos. 16, 17 and 18, adopted at the Tenth Session, (1991) (contained in Document A/46/38), 1991, A/46/38, https://tbinternet.ohchr.org/_layouts/15/treatybodyexternal/Download.aspx?symbolno=INT%2FCEDAW%2FGEC%2F4729&Lang=en

United Nations Committee on the Elimination of Discrimination Against Women Concluding observations on the combined fourth and fifth periodic reports of Namibia (28 July 2015) CEDAW/C/NAM/CO/4-5.

United Nations Committee on the Elimination of Discrimination Against Women's Concluding observations on the eighth periodic report of Kenya (22 November 2017) CEDAW/C/KEN/CO/8

United Nations Committee on the Rights of the Child (CRC Committee) General Comment No. 13 (2011) CRC/C/GC/13. https://www2.ohchr.org/english/bodies/crc/docs/crc.c.gc.13_en.pdf

United Nations Committee on the Rights of Persons with Disabilities' Concluding observations on the initial report of the Kenya (2015) CRPD/C/KEN/CO/1. https://digitallibrary.un.org/record/811095?ln=en

United Nations Committee on the Rights of Persons with Disabilities' Concluding observations on the initial report of South Africa (2018) CRPD/C/ZAF/CO/1. https://www.ohchr.org/en/documents/concluding-observations/crpdczafco1-concluding-observations-initial-report-south-africa

United Nations Committee on the Rights of Persons with Disabilities' Concluding observations on the initial report of the Niger (2019) CRPD/C/NER/CO/1. https://www.ohchr.org/en/documents/concluding-observations/crpdcnerco1-committee-rights-persons-disabilities-concluding

United Nations Committee on the Rights of Persons with Disabilities General Comment No. 3 Article 6: Women and girls with disabilities (2016) CRPD/C/GC/3. https://www.ohchr.org/en/documents/general-comments-and-recommendations/general-comment-no3-article-6-women-and-girls

United Nations General Assembly. (1966). *International Covenant on Civil and Political Rights* (adopted 16 December 1966, entered into force 23 March 1976) 999 UNTS 171 (ICCPR).

United Nations General Assembly. (1979). United Nations Committee on the Elimination of Discrimination Against Women under article 7, paragraph 3, of the Optional Protocol to the Convention on the Elimination of All Forms of Discrimination against Women (thirty-sixth session) Communication No. 4/2004. https://www.un.org/womenwatch/daw/cedaw/protocol/decisions-views/Decision%204-2004%20-%20English.pdf

United Nations General Assembly. (2006), *Convention on the Rights of Persons with Disabilities: resolution/adopted by the General Assembly*, 24 January 2007, A/RES/61/106

United Nations General Assembly. (2017). *Report of the Special Rapporteur on the Rights of Persons with Disabilities: Sexual and Reproductive Health and Rights of Girls and Young Women with Disabilities A/72/133*. https://documents-dds-ny.un.org/doc/UNDOC/GEN/N17/214/63/PDF/N1721463.pdf?OpenElement

United Nations General Assembly. (2018). *Report of the Special Rapporteur on Persons with Disabilities A/73/161*. https://documents-dds-ny.un.org/doc/UNDOC/GEN/N18/224/75/PDF/N1822475.pdf?OpenElement

United Nations General Assembly. (2019). *Report of the Special Rapporteur on violence against women, its causes and consequences on a human rights-based approach to mistreatment and violence against women in reproductive health services with a focus on childbirth and obstetric violence: A Human Rights-based Approach to Mistreatment and Violence against Women in Reproductive Health Services with a Focus on Childbirth and Obstetric Violence A/74/137*. https://eipmh.com/wp-content/uploads/2019/09/UN_Res.71170..pdf

United Nations Human Rights Council. (2012). *Thematic Study on the Issue of Violence against Women and Girls and Disability: Report of the Office of the United Nations High Commissioner for Human Rights A/HRC/20/5*. https://digitallibrary.un.org/record/724782?ln=en

United Nations Office of the High Commissioner for Human Rights 'ICESCR General Comment No. 5: Persons with Disabilities' Adopted at the Eleventh Session of the Committee on Economic, Social and Cultural Rights, on 9 December 1994. https://www.globalhealthrights.org/wp-content/uploads/2013/10/CESCR-General-Comment-No.-5-Persons-with-Disabilities.pdf

United Nations Population Fund (UNFPA). (2021). *My Body Is My Own: Claiming the Rights to Autonomy and Self Determination*. https://www.unfpa.org/sites/default/files/pub-pdf/SoWP2021_Report_-_EN_web.3.21_0.pdf

23

INCLUSIVE EDUCATION THROUGH A NEOLIBERAL LENS

The hierarchal differences between rural and urban China

James Hardy and Gaye Tyler-Merrick

In China, disability can be traced back 2,000 years (Pang & Richey, 2006). Ancient texts advocated for these individuals to be treated with respect and acceptance. However, in the Chinese education sector, there appears to be little evidence of inclusion of children with special educational needs and disability (SEND) in education before the late 20th century, despite a longstanding acknowledgement of individuals with SEND. Moreover, an evaluation of rural education in China yielded no explicit mention of SEND education (Yue et al., 2018), even though the overall enrolment and graduation rates of children with SEND have steadily increased across the country (Alduais & Deng, 2019). It is important to state at this point, in lieu of an internationally recognised definition of "urban" and "rural", geographical areas based on the percentage of their urbanization is used in this chapter (Wineman et al., 2020).

This chapter explores the differences between urban and rural SEND provision in China. The authors suggest there is an intentional hierarchy of educational provision due to the economic reforms in China in 1978, which saw an ideological shift from economic developmental to global neoliberalism and an economical deviation from industrial based towards knowledge based. This initiation, known in the West as the "opening up" of China, enabled exchanges to take place with neoliberalists, foreign economists and the World Bank (Weber, 2020, p. 1). As a result, an unprecedented rise in GDP over the past 40 years has allowed the state to invest heavily in education and raise national attainment and enrolment numbers (National Bureau of Statistics of China, 2019; Yue et al., 2018), but economic disparities still remain between urban and rural China. This has been further exacerbated by the COVID-19 pandemic (Chorzempa & Huang, 2021), and this further perpetuates this educational inequality (Han et al., 2021).

 DOI: 10.4324/9781003410089-27

Officially, China follows a biopsychosocial model of disability. This is a synthesis of biology (medical view) and psychological and social models of disability (Wang, 2016). One of the main issues with this model and the subsequent SEND education policy is the different lens through which SEND is viewed. In the Western world, SEND and inclusive education is based on the view that an individual is unique, and society needs to evolve to be more inclusive of this individual and their needs (Haegele & Hodge, 2016), whereas, in China, SEND education is seen to be more pragmatic, in that inclusion occurs when children with SEND are enroled in school. China appears to maintain a preference for the medical model approach to disability, which Qu (2019) suggests is conveniently concealed within the more broadly accepted biopsychosocial model.

There are problems associated with the different models. This can be seen in the cultural understanding of how children with SEND are regarded in schools and in the equitable access to resources to support SEND policy and practice in schools (Xu et al., 2018). Education policy has historically stated that education is a fundamental right for all children, which indicates a willingness to allow children with SEND to attend schools without it being mandated (People's Republic of China, 1986). However, presence in schools alone does not ensure inclusion in education (Kritzer, 2014) as children with SEND are often ignored due to a misguided belief that they will never become the elite in the eyes of the state.

The difference in policy and enactment is further exacerbated between the rich urban and the poorer rural areas where geographical location accounts for 58% of the national income gap (Chen et al., 2015). This disparity is much larger in China than other developing countries (Eastwood & Lipton, 2004). Furthermore, it is argued this urban/rural hierarchy is both consciously and unconsciously embedded within the Chinese individual psyche because of the Confucius notion which prioritises the collective over the self (Wang, 2016). This view also appears to permeate through the Chinese definition of inclusive, *Quánnà (全纳)*, which translates to "all in" and lays emphasis on the outcome rather than the process.

Theoretical positioning – urban bias theory

In 1984, Lipton formulated the theory of urban bias which suggests that state economic and development planning in less developed countries is biased against the rural areas as almost all the economic power and resources are based in urban areas. The notion of urban bias is particularly popular among those who advocate neoliberal economic policies, and its prevalence in China has been well documented for over 40 years (Shen et al., 2018; Lipton, 1984, 1977). As a result, inequalities and poverty occur in rural areas because there is a migration of rural people to urban areas for employment and little or no work for the remaining rural people. This is an intentional act to ensure economic growth to maintain the status quo, which, in turn, further marginalises children with SEND in rural China and perpetuates educational inequality (Romstein, 2015).

SEND policy in China

The current policy and legislation with regards to SEND in China appear comprehensive. Notwithstanding, the translation of these documents into practice has received justifiable criticism (Alduais & Deng, 2019). There are two main initiatives which ensure all urban and rural children with SEND engage in education. The Learning in the Regular Classroom (LRC) initiative first appeared in 1987 to address those children with mild intellectual disabilities (An et al., 2018). This initiative was more to solve the problem that there were no special schools or resources for special education. In 1994, the LRC was updated (Ministry of Education, 1994), and this was when the most prominent initiative on providing access to school for those children with SEND appeared. This laid the foundation for the ensuing inclusion in school. There were several further iterations with inclusion not made policy until the Compulsory Education Act in 2006 (Xu et al., 2018). This change also created three tiers of special education: special schools, special classes and learning in regular classroom (LRC) (Deng & Zhu, 2016). However, the LRC policy appears to be based on increasing, as quickly as possible, the number of children with SEND in classrooms (rather than on altruistic reasons), but at the same time, the state increased the number of special education schools (Xu et al., 2018). As a result, the historical view of regarding people with SEND as subordinate who will never make the elite is exacerbated, and this view permeates subsequent policy as children with SEND are still segregated. This perspective is thought to be the driving force behind the current policy-to-practice gap experienced in rural China (Xu et al., 2018; Sharma et al., 2013).

In this time of economic change, the implementation of the Teachers' Law of the People's Republic of China (National People's Congress, 1993) and the Education Law of the People's Republic of China (National People's Congress, 1995) were crucial for the categorisation of SEND. "China now recognises six classes of disability: visual, hearing, intellectual, physical, psychiatric and multiple impairments" (Kritzer, 2011, p. 59). Despite this, it is feared the categorisation is not comprehensive enough as some children, such as those with autism who are still isolated from educational support due to being categorised in the broad category of those with a mental disorder (Zhang & Spencer, 2015).

In 2008, China ratified the United Nation Convention on the Rights of Persons with Disabilities (UNCRPD) (2006). By doing this, the state agreed they would ensure a holistic/inclusive education system (Article 24). Nonetheless, statistics from the China Disabled Person's Federation in 2010 (as cited in Qi et al., 2020) show that of the 24 million children with SEND attending school in China, only 7,666 children attended classes which met their complex educational needs. This finding suggests that China's ratification of the UNCRPD has not been practically implemented (Qi et al., 2020).

The Disabled Person's Self-help Organizations (DPOs) lobbied for five years for an inclusive education policy that provided funding and experts to support children with SEND in regular schools. This finally occurred in 2012 (Zhang,

2017). In the past ten years, China has been promoting inclusive education for children with SEND by expanding the LRC initiative with the 2014–2016 Promotion Plan of Special Education. This plan aimed to promote inclusive education and provide an appropriate education for those with SEND (Xu, et al., 2018).

There are problems associated with these policies in the rural areas. Xu et al. (2018) found that, in the rural areas, even with these policies, attendance and engagement in education of children with SEND appeared to be influenced by conflicts or gaps between policy and implementation, a lack of resources, tension between the knowledge-centred and learner-centred curricula and conflict in understanding the Western and Chinese cultural perspective of inclusive practice. While these policies say the right things, their implementation appears not to benefit children with SEND. It appears justifiable to ask whether children with SEND in rural China are being intentionally marginalised to enable the maintenance of an ideological status quo, thus creating a hierarchal system of economic, cultural and education practices which excludes those with SEND. As Kritzer (2014, p. 3373) suggests, "The only thing consistent about their system is the lack of consistency, from school to school, city to city and province to province".

Urban/rural – the great divide

Between 1980 and 2019, China's GDP increased from $306 billion to $14.3 trillion (National Bureau of Statistics of China, 2020), a rise which is invariably a result of neoliberalism. The term "neoliberalism" describes a system of economic and political thought which emphasises and associates with free market relations, globalisation, deregulation, austerity and privatization (Springer et al., 2016). In 1979, China embraced neoliberalism, and over the past four decades, this has left the country with an economic growth rate that is incomparable in human history (Wu, 2010). However, the benefits of this growth have not been felt as much in rural China as the state elected to prioritise "urban-centred wealth accumulation" and, as a consequence, uphold the neoliberal ideal of "winners and losers" (He & Wu, 2009, p. 284).

This neoliberal view plays out in education when children with SEND participate in regular classrooms, but only in a way which maximises their social and economic usefulness to the state and its market needs (Bacon & Pomponio, 2020; Liasidou & Symeou, 2018). There appears to be a tension between the socialist system of collectivism (the greater good) and the Western view of individualism (in meeting the individual needs of children with SEND). Consequently, under this framework, the social inclusion of children with SEND (Couzens et al., 2015) and their access to specialised academic materials (Reed & Kennett, 2017) has not been addressed.

This divide has been problematic for children with SEND in rural areas. With the state focused on urban economic development, for those who fall outside the elite and cannot lobby the state – e.g. those children with SEND

– there appears to be an unequal distribution of educational resources between the urban and rural regions, with the urban areas gaining the most (Zhang, 2011). Guan (2009) suggests the reasons behind the urban/rural divide in the education of children with SEND can be attributed to the unequal distribution of the education budget, which presently favours urban provinces (57%) over rural provinces (43%) (National Bureau of Statistics of China, 2019). When money is available, school budgets focus on areas other than SEND due to a belief that those with disabilities are second-class citizens. The primary focus of the state appears to be closing the gap between China and the rest of the world in terms of the education of children with SEND, rather than closing the internal gap between urban and rural areas in terms of equity of education resources (and thus meeting the educational needs of all children with SEND). This approach clearly indicates an intentional alignment with urban bias theory. For example, Zhang et al. (2015) report from the China Family Panel Survey and the Rural-Urban Migration in China Survey that in 2009–2010, all rural children's academic performance was significantly lower than that of urban children, and their attendance at school was lower as well; this has not diminished over time. As can be seen in Table 23.1, these gaps also occur in enrolment and graduation rates in junior and senior high schools and in higher education. No information could be sourced for colleges or universities. More recent data appears not to be available, as does the specific data in relation to the number of children with SEND who enroll in and graduate from schools.

In terms of geographical location, Wang (2016) claims there are growing regional gaps in educational achievement between urban and rural and eastern and western parts of the country. Liao and Zhao (2013) indicate that the rate of school returns for children with SEND in urban regions (7.6%) is higher than those in rural regions (5.3%). The school return rates from the east, west and central regions also highlight discrepancies across regions in favour of urban areas. As an explanation for these discrepancies, Zhang (2011) suggests that educational resources are first directed towards Beijing, then provincial capitals, province-level cities, county-level cities and then villages. From this, there appears to be a well-entrenched, intentional inequality in the distribution

Table 23.1 The percentage of enrolment and graduation of children in China from 2010–2012

	Percentage of children		*Percentage of graduating children*	
	Urban	*Rural*	*Urban*	*Rural*
Junior high	100	88	100	70
Senior high	63	3	63	3
College/University	54	2		

of resources across gender, school choice and regions in the education of children with SEND. This is further evidence of China's implementation of urban bias strategies.

Inadequate resourcing and funding for children with SEND (both urban and rural) result in a trade-off as their educational needs are not addressed. Of note, the cuts made to the Disabled Student's Allowance, which is used to finance supportive resources, indicate that the priorities of the state only support those they deem more able to enhance economic growth (Lewthwaite, 2014). The current business-as-usual approach serves to exacerbate the negative outcomes attributed to poor policy-to-practice implementation, and this further excludes and marginalises children with SEND in both urban and rural China (Wang, 2016).

China's recent focus on economic growth appears to have exacerbated negative public perceptions of those children with SEND. This view has created an education system which, despite state claims to the contrary, appears to perpetuate inequalities for those children with SEND in rural areas. For example, only 13% of China's special education teachers currently teach in rural areas, despite 80% of China's disabled population residing there (National Bureau of Statistics of China, 2019; Kritzer, 2011). Children with SEND receiving education in rural areas is problematic. They may not attend school because reading and writing are not required for agricultural manual labour (Worrell & Taber, 2009) and, thus, may not be represented in national or international statistics (OECD, 2018).

Practice (curriculum and pedagogy)

Historically, the Chinese primary curriculum has followed a knowledge-centred curriculum approach that includes nine compulsory subjects which are structured around examination preparation and taught by teachers using tools such as textbooks (Hayhoe, 2019; Lam, 2005). To ensure international recognition and to align with the Organisation for Economic Co-operation and Development (OECD) recommendations, China has recently attempted to shift towards a more progressive "holistic" education model which focuses on problem solving and personal growth (Wang, 2019). This deviation was the result of large-scale longitudinal data from their Ministry of Education, which found that the former curriculum was overreliant on knowledge transmission and unsuitable for children with SEND (Cui, 2001). Despite this change in curriculum, traditional teaching methods still appear to be loyally adhered to in rural China (Xing, 2011), despite holistic education being embedded in the Ministry of Education (2011, 2001) Core Competencies Framework. The new holistic methods appear to be successfully implemented in urban settings (Reyes & Tan, 2019). This difference in implementation creates a hierarchy, consciously or unconsciously, which disadvantages rural children with SEND due to the holistic learner-centred approaches being practiced only in urban settings.

The desire to learn new skills and change traditional practice appears to be the reason this holistic policy and practice are not successful in rural China. This lack of change, Deng and Holdsworth (2007) suggest, is the main limitation to inclusion of all children in education and claim that without social change, the inclusion of children with SEND will fail.

The implementation of inclusive policies in rural regions is difficult. Most teachers have no training in SEND, and what they do know comes from the Western education system (Kritzer, 2014). However, the training of teachers in SEND is improving, but once trained, they are not selecting to work in rural regions. This may be salary related as the salary for SEND teachers is not dissimilar to that of regular teachers, or, alternatively, teachers may opt to remain in the city of their training rather than return to the rural areas where they originated (Feng & Yang, 2015).

In theory, children with SEND are welcomed into schools. Teachers have a pragmatic approach to teaching these children. Meng (2008) found that both urban and rural teachers hold preferable views on segregated special needs schools whilst simultaneously advocating for holistic education, whereas Yan and Deng (2019) found that Chinese teachers make decisions on the implementation of holistic strategies based on their knowledge of effectiveness. There is little room for teachers to support children with SEND due to the high number of children in classrooms and financial restraints (Kritzer, 2014). As a result, many teachers question the practicalities of implementing the holistic/inclusive policies (Sharma et al., 2013) and still follow the medical model of disability; thus, they do not approve of changing the environment or including children with SEND (Deng & Poon-McBrayer, 2004, as cited in Su et al., 2020).

In terms of gender and parental choice, there appear to be additional hierarchies of exclusion. The one-two-child policy has led to an imbalance of gender in the population, with 33 million more boys than girls (Zhu et al., 2009). Deng and Holdsworth (2007) state that the Chinese hierarchal social order restricts woman to household chores, and this is mirrored in the classroom, with female children with SEND ignored in class and/or not attending school. Typically, girls are without education as they do not need to earn money to support the family and, in extreme cases, are abandoned at birth if a disability is detected or suspected (Baker, 2015; Doane, 2014). However, there is renewed optimism that the new three-child policy could alleviate some of these issues (Kwete et al., 2021).

Competition, PISA and the impact on policy and practice

China's desire for international recognition in the field of education has led to policies and practice which substantially disadvantage children in the rural provinces (Wang, 2019). This recognition is primarily obtained through the competitive Programme for International Student Assessment (PISA), which measures the reading, science knowledge and mathematical skills of 15-year-olds. The 2018 PISA results show Chinese children top the world in these subjects (OECD, 2018). However, since China only included children from four urban provinces (Beijing, Shanghai, Jiangsu and Zhejiang), these results cannot be generalised to the whole population and should instead be viewed as an indication of where the state's education priorities lie. The historic success that China has achieved appears to have come at the sacrifice of children in rural areas as a myriad of resources are provided to children in the urban provinces. Whilst there has been acknowledgement of an achievement gap between the urban and rural areas, policies are often tokenistic and rarely observed in rural areas (Xing, 2011). Moreover, any real attempts to address this issue have been confined to urban and rural areas in the key provinces, such as Shanghai (Tan, 2012). It appears that China attempts to project an image which attributes their PISA success to a focus on holistic education and needs, rather than the actual unbalanced distribution of resources (Reyes & Tan, 2019). Notwithstanding, even if this is true for those residing in urban areas, this does not appear to be the case for children with SEND in rural China. One way to establish a greater understanding of this difference is to critically evaluate the relationship China has with the OECD and their partners.

Partnership with the World Bank

The OECD (2019) claims not to have the means or finances to influence policy development at a national level in any country, but the Chinese development partnership with the World Bank indicates this may not be the case. The World Bank is an international financial institution that allocates funding to developing countries, such as China, and is often described as being "the most authoritative source of education policy" (Klees et al., 2012, p. 16). This organisation, whose neoliberal advocacy can be traced back to the 1980s, provided technical support to China when they were developing their 2035 education modernisation policy (Zhu, 2019). Whilst consulting international organisations during policy formulation is not uncommon, owing an organisation financially and having them dictate and/or control policy can have negative outcomes for certain individuals (Grek, 2009). The World Bank strategies in China and other countries appear to align with urban bias theory. This can be inferred from their recent Urban China: Toward Efficient, Inclusive, and Sustainable Urbanisation initiative (World Bank, 2021) and is further reinforced through their financial projects, which show a sizable difference in investment in urban (1.55 billion USD) and rural (605 million USD) areas (International Aid Transparency Initiative, 2021). What has occurred is that, instead of closing the urban and rural gap in SEND through suitable policy and investment, China initiated projects which expanded and exercised bureaucratic state power and protected the investment of the World Bank through the intentional maintenance of educational inequalities. Moreover, where policy did appear to favour or show preference for the educational needs of rural children with SEND, these policies were often disregarded in practice and were seldom evaluated with any urgency (Huang, 2004; Tabulawa, 2003).

Given China's strict adherence and commitment to upholding neoliberal values and maintaining economic growth, it appears a hierarchy was intentionally cultivated to protect the national status quo and ensure rural losers. It would be utopian to hope that this position might altruistically change in the near future. It is now the author's intention to present an ideological shift which could have the potential to demonstrate that all parties can be winners and that there need not be any sacrifices for the greater good of the state or for those children with SEND living in rural areas.

Alternative approach

An alternative approach to including all children with SEND in education in China could focus on approaches which could be implemented and supported by future research and practice. It is idealistic to suggest that neoliberalism can be overthrown entirely. To do so may also be deemed culturally insensitive when we consider the role this ideology has played in raising the country out of poverty and may ultimately prove counterproductive to securing an education for children with SEND in rural areas. Consequently, suggestions are put forward with the view of inclusion for all children in education simultaneously coexisting alongside the current hegemonic ideology and mitigating some of the apparent shortcomings.

The forthcoming propositions have a degree of commonality in that there is a focus on happiness, something which is distinctly absent in neoliberalism. We suggest that shifting towards this approach may result in increased inclusion of rural children with SEND due to a consequential realignment of learning environments and a reduction in the focus on the performative educational outcomes which have historically excluded children with SEND to the fringes of education and society. Furthermore, due to research into the positive impact happiness can have on educational outcomes (Assari, 2019; Datu et al., 2017), these approaches are deemed appropriate in the present context as they can still align with the neoliberal values of prioritising economic growth via education. It is pertinent to acknowledge that any suggestions made are not put forward in a stringent one-size-fits-all manner; all approaches require flexibility and the input and knowledge of local and national experts to ensure a holistic, inclusive educational approach for children with SEND which is culturally appropriate for the setting for which it is intended.

Weighted utilitarianism/utilitarianism

Adopting an approach of weighted utilitarianism towards holistic inclusive education for all children has the potential to mitigate some of the educational inequalities which are discernible in China. Utilitarianism, which has been evident in China from the late 19th century (Li, 1996), is a combination of consequentialist ethical theories which promote actions which maximise happiness for much of the population (Mill & Bentham, 1987). Whilst a focus on happiness is seemingly positive, utilitarian thinking has appeared to exacerbate and rationalise the differences in the education of children with SEND in urban and rural China due to a disproportionate focus on most children through performance-centred pedagogy which often favours the elite (Qu, 2019). Conversely, weighted utilitarianism, which could be described as a hybrid of utilitarianism and egalitarianism, assigns greater importance to the redistribution of utility towards the less fortunate (Argenziano & Gilboa, 2019). In practice, this might mean that educational resources are directed to those children who are most in need. This would ensure an equitable dissemination of happiness (utility) among all children. Whilst weighted utilitarianism has the potential to ease hierarchal disadvantages in rural China for children with SEND, it is not without its limitations. Under this approach, it is problematic to correct and/or assess unequal distributions of happiness as it is often viewed in relation to economic growth and market outcomes, and these are not valued equally by all citizens. Therefore, for a more accurate measure of happiness, it may be appropriate to combine weighted utilitarianism with alternative approaches that focus on what the individual values rather than what the state values and determines via the capabilities approach.

Capabilities approach

The capabilities approach is a normative economic theory which focuses on the individual's ability to achieve happiness. In contrast to the utilitarian view of happiness (extrinsic – as defined by the state), the capabilities approach suggests that happiness must be achieved by the individual pursuing interests which hold personal value for them (intrinsic – defined by the individual) (Sen, 1992, 1985). The capabilities approach, due to a strong degree of internal pluralism, can be applied to a variety of different settings and contexts (Alkire, 2002). Therefore, this approach can be applied to the education of children with SEND and potentially decrease ableism in rural China due to a focus on the children's capabilities rather than their economic potential (Van Aswegen & Shevlin, 2019). In practice, this would require a shift away from the neoliberal outcome-based model of schooling towards a more innovative learner-centred model, such as the Montessori method, which focuses on autonomy and how children can become what they value (Hart & Brando, 2018). Furthermore, the capabilities approach can also be used to create a curriculum that enables children with SEND to achieve happiness through the relation of capabilities to knowledge, thus enabling participation in society and a reduction of injustice (Terzi, 2008). Notwithstanding, this approach, in theory and practice, relies on a power dynamic which values individual over state and facilitator over teacher, something which is often vigorously opposed in China. Therefore, it is pertinent to discuss how weighted utilitarianism and the capabilities approach can combine to allow them to be successfully utilised in China and how this can assist in a reduction in the present urban/rural hierarchy in the education of children with SEND.

Moving forward

A combination of weighted utilitarianism and the capabilities approach has greater potential to be effective in practice, despite each approach having the ability to be beneficial autonomously (Norwich, 2014). However, prior to implementation, certain steps must allow such an amalgamation to operate efficiently. First, a weighted utilitarianism approach to the distribution of educational resources must be combined with a capabilities approach measure of happiness. This would hopefully ensure that children with SEND in rural China can pursue their innate happiness through a plethora of different activities, curricula and pedagogy. Concentrating on capabilities in this way, rather than on resources, focuses on the end rather than the means, which can reduce the ableist view currently held in society (Anderson, 2010). Secondly, since any ideological realignment must be enacted by the Chinese state, we would compel researchers to empirically test these suggestions in practical settings with a focus on how educational outcomes and children with SEND enrolment are impacted by increased levels of happiness. Additionally, we need to know if some of the prominent Western-based learner-centred education models are culturally appropriate and can be as successful in rural China as they appear to be in urban areas (Hu et al., 2016). We suggest that such research will allow the state to understand that there is no need for a trade-off between educating all children with SEND in rural areas and economic growth. Thirdly, an alteration in the historically negative perception of those children with SEND, especially those in rural areas, is eminently needed to ensure that policies on holistic education/SEND are adhered to. This could be achieved in China by a state-driven focus on moving away from the outdated medical model currently practiced to a holistic and more inclusive model which includes all children in education and broader society.

Note: The authors acknowledge that the views in this chapter are formulated primarily from a Western perspective, despite the first author having substantial professional experience working in China and utilising local literature sources.

References

Alduais, A., & Deng, M. (2019). The effect of the national plan (2010–2020) on the development of special education in China: Evidence from before–after design at a 7-year interval. *Education Sciences*, *9*(2), 95–107.

Alkire, S. (2002, September). *The capability Approach and Human Development* [Paper presentation. In Wadham College and Queen Elizabeth House Seminar (9), 1–64]. Oxford: Oxford Poverty and Human Development Initiative (OPHI).

An, G. E., Hu, X. H., & Horn, E. (2018). Chinese inclusive education: The past, present, and future. *Intervention in School and Clinic*, *52*(2), 118–122. https://doi.org/10.1177/1053451218765244

Anderson, E. (2010). Justifying the capabilities approach to justice. In H. Brighthouse & I. Robeyns (Eds.), *Measuring Justice: Primary Goods and Capabilities* (pp. 81–100). Cambridge: Cambridge University Press.

Argenziano, R., & Gilboa, I. (2019). Perception-theoretic foundations of weighted utilitarianism. *The Economic Journal, 129*(620), 1511–1528.

Assari, S. (2019). Race, education attainment, and happiness in the United States. *International Journal of Epidemiologic Research, 6*(2), 76–82.

Bacon, J., & Pomponio, E. (2020). A call for radical over reductionist approaches to 'inclusive' reform in neoliberal times: an analysis of position statements in the United States. *International Journal of Inclusive Education*. https://doi.org/10.1080/13603116.2020.1858978

Baker, H. D. (2015). *Chinese Family & Kinship*. London: Macmillan International Higher Education.

Chen, J., Fang, F., Hou, W., Li, F., Pu, M., & Song, M. (2015). Chinese Gini coefficient from 2005 to 2012, based on 20 grouped income data sets of urban and rural residents. *Journal of Applied Mathematics, 2015*, 1–16.

Chorzempa, M., & Huang, T. (2021). China will run out of growth if it doesn't fix its rural crisis. *Foreign Policy*. https://foreignpolicy.com/2021/02/08/china-rural-crisis-economy-growth-middle-income-trap/

Couzens, D., Poed, S., Kataoka, M., Brandon, A., Hartley, J., & Keen, D. (2015). Support for students with hidden disabilities in universities: A case study. *International Journal of Disability, Development and Education, 62*(1), 24–41.

Cui, Y. H. (2001). Xin Kecheng Xin Zai Hechu [What is new in the new curriculum?]. Jiaoyu Fazhan Yanjiu. *Exploring Education Development, 21*(9), 5–10.

Datu, J. A. D., Valdez, J. P., Cabrera, I. K., & Salanga, M. G. (2017). Subjective happiness optimizes educational outcomes: Evidence from Filipino high school students. *The Spanish Journal of Psychology, 20*, 1–5.

Deng, M., & Holdsworth, J. C. (2007). From unconscious to conscious inclusion: Meeting special education needs in West China. *Disability & Society, 22*(5), 507–522.

Deng, M., & Poon-McBrayer, K. F. (2004). Inclusive education in China: Conceptualisation and realisation. *Asia Pacific Journal of Education, 24*(2), 143–156.

Deng, M., & Zhu, X. (2016). Special education reform towards inclusive education: Blurring or expanding boundaries of special and regular education in China. *Journal of Research in Special Educational Needs, 16*(s1), 994–998. https://doi.org/10.1111/1471-3802.12244

Doane, S. (2014, June 27). CBS News: A look at China's "baby hatches" for unwanted infants. *CBS News*. https://www.cbsnews.com/news/a-look-at-chinas-baby-hatches-for-unwanted-infants/

Eastwood, R., & Lipton, M. (2004). Rural and urban income inequality and poverty: Does convergence between sectors offset divergence within them. *Inequality, Growth, and Poverty in an era of Liberalization and Globalization, 4*, 112–141.

Feng, B., & Yang, X. (2015). A comparative study of urban-rural integration of special education teachers in China and the US. *Chinese Journal of Special Education, 177*, 59–64.

Grek, S. (2009). Governing by numbers: The PISA 'effect' in Europe. *Journal of Education Policy, 24*(1), 23–37.

Guan, O. (2009). Developing Chinese rural special education: Basis, focus, integration, fulcrum. *Chinese Journal of Special Education, 105*, 3–7.

Haegele, J. A., & Hodge, S. (2016). Disability discourses: Overview and critiques of the medical and social models. *Quest, 68*(2), 193–206.

Han, C., Cumming, T. M., & Strnadová, I. (2021). The education of students with disabilities in remote or rural areas of China. *Intervention in School and Clinic*. https://doi.org/10534512211024940.

Hart, C. S., & Brando, N. (2018). A capability approach to pupils 's well-being, agency and participatory rights in education. *European Journal of Education, 53*(3), 293–309.

Hayhoe, R. (2019). *Contemporary Chinese Education*. London: Routledge.
He, S., & Wu, F. (2009). China's emerging neoliberal urbanism: Perspectives from urban redevelopment. *Antipode*, *41*(2), 282–304.
Hu, B. Y., Roberts, S. K., Leng Ieong, S. S., & Guo, H. (2016). Challenges to early childhood education in rural China: Lessons from the Hebei province. *Early Child Development and Care*, *186*(5), 815–831.
Huang, F. (2004). Curriculum reform in contemporary China: Seven goals and six strategies. *Journal of Curriculum Studies*, *36*(1), 101–115.
International Aid Transparency Initiative (IATI). (2021). Data on development and humanitarian activities. *International Aid Transparency Initiative*. https://iatistandard.org/en/
Klees, S. J., Samoff, J., & Stromquist, N. O. (2012). Introduction. In S. J. Kless, J. Samoff, & N. O. Stromquist (Eds.), *The World Bank and Education. Critiques and Alternatives* (pp. xv–xxi). Rotterdam: Sense Publishers.
Kritzer, J. B. (2011). Special education in China. *Eastern Education Journal*, *40*(1), 57–63.
Kritzer, J. B. (2014). A four-country comparison: Special education in the United States, China, India and Thailand. *Current Journal of Applied Science and Technology*, 3370–3382.
Kwete, X., Knaul, F. M., Essue, B. M., & Langer, A. (2021). Gender equity, caregiving, and the 1–2 - 3-child policy in China. *The Lancet*, *398*(10304), 953.
Lam, A. S. (2005). *Language Education in China: Policy and Experience from 1949: Policy and Experience from 1949* (Vol. 1). Hong Kong: University Press.
Lewthwaite, S. (2014). State cuts to disabled students' Allowances must be resisted. *Disability & Society*, *29*(7), 1159–1163.
Li, Q. (1996). The principle of utility and the principle of righteousness: Yen Fu and utilitarianism in modern China. *Utilitas*, *8*(1), 109–126.
Liao, J., & Zhao, J. (2013). Rate of returns to education of persons with disabilities in rural China. In *International Conference on Applied Social Science Research* (ICASSR-2013) (pp. 230–233). Beijing: Atlantis Press.
Liasidou, A., & Symeou, L. (2018). Neoliberal versus social justice reforms in education policy and practice: Discourses, politics and disability rights in education. *Critical Studies in Education*, *59*(2), 149–166.
Lipton, M. (1977). *Why Poor People Stay Poor: A Study of Urban Bias in World Development*. London; Canberra: Temple Smith; Australian National University Press
Lipton, M. (1984). Urban bias revisited. *The Journal of Development Studies*, *20*(3), 139–166.
Meng, D. (2008). The attitudes of primary school teachers toward inclusive education in rural and urban China. *Frontiers of Education in China*, *3*(4), 473–492.
Mill, J. S., & Bentham, J. (1987). *Utilitarianism and Other Essays*. London: Penguin.
Ministry of Education. (1994). *Guanyu kaizhan canji ertong shaonian sui ban jiu du gongzuo de shixing banfa [Pilot Project of implementing Learning in Regular Classrooms for pupils with disabilities]*. Beijing: Ministry of Education.
Ministry of Education. (2001). *Guidelines for Curriculum Reform of Basic Education. Document 17*. Beijing: Ministry of Education.
Ministry of Education. (2011). *Yiwu Jiaoyu Chuzhong Kexue Kecheng Biaozhun [Curriculum Standards for Primary Education and Junior Secondary Education: Junior Secondary Science]*. Beijing: Beijing Normal University Press.
National Bureau of Statistics of China. (2019). *National Bureau of Statistics of China: China Statistical Yearbook 2019*. http://www.stats.gov.cn/tjsj/ndsj/2019/indexeh.htm
National Bureau of Statistics of China. (2020). *National Bureau of Statistics of China: National Economy was Generally Stable in 2019 with Main Projected Targets for Development Achieved*. http://www.stats.gov.cn/english/PressRelease/202001/t20200117_1723398.html

National People's Congress. (1993). *Teachers Law of the People's Republic of China*. A Collection of Major Documents on Early Childhood Education in the People's Republic of China. http://en.moe.gov.cn/Resources/Laws_and_Policies/201506/t20150626_191389.html

National People's Congress. (1995). *Education Law of the People's Republic of China*. http://en.moe.gov.cn/Resources/Laws_and_Policies/201506/t20150626_191385.html

Norwich, B. (2014). How does the capability approach address current issues in special educational needs, disability and inclusive education field? *Journal of Research in Special Educational Needs, 14*(1), 16–21.

Organisation for Economic Co-operation and Development (OECD). (2018). *Programme for International Student Assessment (PISA) Results from PISA 2018*. http://www.oecd.org/pisa/publications/PISA2018_CN_QCI.pdf

Organisation for Economic Co-operation and Development (OECD). (2019). *Who Pays for PISA*. https://www.oecd.org/pisa/pisa-for-development/20-Who-pays-for-PISA-D.pdf

Pang, Y., & Richey, D. (2006). The development of special education in China. *International Journal of Special Education, 21*, 77–87.

People's Republic of China. (1986). *Compulsory Education Law of the People's Republic of China*. http://ncee.org/wp-content/uploads/2017/01/Sha-non-AV-2-Compulsory-Education-Law-1986.pdf

Qi, F., Hu, L., & Wu, Y. (2020). Rhetoric and reality: Litigation rights of Chinese disabled people. *Disability & Society, 35*(8), 1343–1348.

Qu, J. (2019). A defense of utilitarian pedagogy: Whether education should focus more on human utilitarianism. In *2nd International Conference on Social Science, Public Health and Education (SSPHE 2018)* (pp. 171–174). Beijing: Atlantis Press.

Reed, M. J., & Kennett, D. J. (2017). The importance of university students' perceived ability to balance multiple roles: A comparison of students with and without disabilities. *Canadian Journal of Higher Education*, 47(2), 71–86.

Reyes, V., & Tan, C. (2019). PISA and self-projection in Shanghai. In F. Waldow, & G. Steiner-Khamsi (Eds.), *Understanding PISA's Attractiveness: Critical Analyses in Comparative Policy Studies* (pp. 161–176). London: Bloomsbury Publishing.

Romstein, K. (2015). Neoliberal values and disability: Critical approach to inclusive education [Paper presentation]. *Annual International Conference of the Bulgarian Comparative Education Society*, Sofia, Bulgaria, June 10–13.

Sen, A. (1985). Well-being, agency and freedom: The Dewey lectures 1984. *The Journal of Philosophy, 82*(4), 169–221.

Sen, A. (1992). *Inequality Reexamined*. Oxford: Oxford University Press.

Sharma, U., Forlin, C., Deppeler, J., & Yang, G. X. (2013). Reforming teacher education for inclusion in developing countries in the Asia Pacific region. *Asian Journal of Inclusive Education, 1*(1), 3–16.

Shen, L., Ren, Y., Xiong, N., Li, H., & Chen, Y. (2018). Why small towns cannot share the benefits of urbanization in China? *Journal of Cleaner Production, 174*, 728–738.

Springer, S., Birch, K., & MacLeavy, J. (Eds.). (2016). *Handbook of Neoliberalism*. London: Routledge.

Su, X., Guo, J., & Wang, X. (2020). Different stakeholders' perspectives on inclusive education in China: Parents of pupils with ASD, parents of typically developing pupils and classroom teachers. *International Journal of Inclusive Education, 24*(9), 948–963.

Tabulawa, R. (2003). International aid agencies, learner-centred pedagogy and political democratisation: A critique. *Comparative Education, 39*(1), 7–26.

Tan, C. (2012). The culture of education policy making: Curriculum reform in Shanghai. *Critical Studies in Education, 53*(2), 153–167.

Terzi, L. (2008). *Justice and Equality in Education: A Capability Perspective on Disability and Special Educational Needs*. London: Bloomsbury Publishing.

United Nations Convention on the Rights of Persons with Disabilities (UNCRPD). (2006). Department of economic and social affairs: Convention on the rights of persons with disabilities. *United Nations*. https://www.un.org/development/desa/disabilities/convention-on-the-rights-of-persons-with-disabilities/convention-on-the-rights-of-persons-with-disabilities-2.html

Van Aswegen, J., & Shevlin, M. (2019). Disabling discourses and ableist assumptions: Reimagining social justice through education for disabled people through a critical discourse analysis approach. *Policy Futures in Education*, *17*(5), 634–656.

Wang, T. (2019). Competence for students' future: Curriculum change and policy redesign in China. *ECNU Review of Education*, 2(2), 234–245

Wang, Y. (2016). *Imagining Inclusive Schooling: An Ethnographic Inquiry into Disabled Pupil's Learning and Participation in Regular Schools in Shanghai* [Unpublished doctoral dissertation]. Edinburgh: The University of Edinburgh.

Weber, I. (2020). Origins of China's contested relation with neoliberalism: Economics, the World Bank, and Milton Friedman at the dawn of reform. *Global Perspectives*, *1*(1).

Wineman, A., Alia, D. Y., & Anderson, C. L. (2020). Definitions of "rural" and "urban" and understandings of economic transformation: Evidence from Tanzania. *Journal of Rural Studies*, *79*, 254–268.

World Bank. (2021). The World Bank in China. *World Bank*. https://www.worldbank.org/en/country/china/overview#3

Worrell, J. L., & Taber, M. (2009). Special education practices in China and the United States: What is to come next? *International Journal of Special Education*, *24*(3), 132–142.

Wu, F. (2010). How neoliberal is China's reform? The origins of change during transition. *Eurasian Geography and Economics*, *51*(5), 619–631.

Xing, H. J. (2011). Zhongguo Jichu Jiaoyu Kecheng Gaige: Fangxiang Mishi De Weixian Zhi Lu [Basic education curriculum reform in China: losing directions in a risky journey, Jiaoyu Kexue Yanjiu]. *Educational Science Research*, *4*, 5–21.

Xu, S. Q., Cooper, P., & Sin, K. (2018). The 'learning in regular classrooms' initiative for inclusive education in China. *International Journal of Inclusive Education*, *22*(1), 54–73.

Yan, T., & Deng, M. (2019). Regular education teachers' concerns on inclusive education in China from the perspective of concerns-based adoption model. *International Journal of Inclusive Education*, *23*(4), 384–404.

Yue, A., Tang, B., Shi, Y., Tang, J., Shang, G., Medina, A., & Rozelle, S. (2018). Rural education across China's 40 years of reform: Past successes and future challenges. *China Agricultural Economic Review*, *10*(1).

Zhang, C. (2017). 'Nothing about us without us': The emerging disability movement and advocacy in China. *Disability & Society*, *32*(7), 1096–1101.

Zhang, D., Li, X., & Xue, J. (2015). Education inequality between rural and urban areas of the People's Republic of China, migrants' pupils education, and some implications. *Asian Development Review*, *32*(1), 196–224.

Zhang, D., & Spencer, V. G. (2015). Addressing the needs of students with autism and other disabilities in China: perspectives from the field. *International Journal of Disability, Development and Education*, *62*(2), 168–181.

Zhang, Y. Y. (2011). *Rural-Urban Teacher Professional Stratification in Compulsory Education*. Changchun: Northeast Normal University.

Zhu, W. X., Lu, L., & Hesketh, T. (2009). China's excess males, sex selective abortion, and one child policy: Analysis of data from 2005 National Intercensus Survey. *BMJ*, 338, b1211. https://www.bmj.com/content/338/bmj.b1211

Zhu, Y. (2019). New national initiatives of modernizing education in China. *ECNU Review of Education*, *2*(3), 353–362.

PART IV

Pushed to the periphery of the disability rights movement

24

EXCLUDED FROM THE DISABILITY RIGHTS DEBATE

The missed voices of people with speech impairments

Armineh Soorenian

Introduction

This chapter is an account of my journey as a disabled activist and how feelings of marginalisation within the world of activism have influenced my participation in the disability rights movement and beyond. First, I will write about the time before I became an activist; then I will discuss some of the barriers I have encountered over the years. I hope this reflection will contribute to the desire for a new kind of activism. The chapter will conclude with the sharing of some notes geared towards social change and making activism inclusive for all disabled people.

In 1996, I arrived in the United Kingdom (UK) as a 20-year-old disabled woman with low self-esteem and limited English language skills. Due to a lack of resources and limited infrastructure, living independently in my home country was not something I could attain. I attempted to attend school there after becoming disabled, but as there were steps into each classroom, I could not even access the school building, let alone participate in lessons, which were delivered using a blackboard and then distributed in standard print. I left school for those reasons, and for six years, I spent time at home with inadequate stimulation for a developing and inquisitive teenager. The situation had a major impact not only on my physical health but also on my mental health, the effects of which I still feel to this day. I therefore felt I had no choice but to leave my loving family and endure an unbearably high financial and emotional cost to move away. In the UK, I settled at the Royal National College for the Blind, a segregated educational institution. While the college offered me a platform for learning and helped me overcome years of boredom, I now see that, as

DOI: 10.4324/9781003410089-29

with all special education settings, there was no real opportunity to be part of mainstream society while residing at the college. The segregated nature of the institution gave me the illusion that the rest of the world operated in a way that was as specialised and protective as the college and its staff. Nowhere did I feel this contradiction more acutely than when I arrived at my first university to complete an undergraduate degree. Here, very few adjustments were made to enable my participation in what was a highly academic discipline. For example, no support was available to meet my communication needs and help me with presenting in the seminars. The expectation was that disabled students should modify their needs to fit into university life, rather than there being a requirement for the institution to make its culture more inclusive.

However, my situation did change after I enrolled to study for an MA in disability studies at a more inclusive institution. I then completed my doctorate in November 2011 at the Centre for Disability Studies (CDS) at the University of Leeds. Unlike my previous university, in Leeds, the expectation was that disabled students may have support needs, and accommodations were put in place accordingly to meet different needs. When I sought these adjustments, I began to flourish socially and academically, a process which ultimately allowed me to reach the academic level of PhD. For example, I was provided with a personal assistant in my PhD viva to help me with communication and clarify any misunderstandings. It was here in Leeds that I first felt included and developed a sense of solidarity with my fellow disabled course mates. Learning about the social model of disability informed me that it had been the damaging and oppressive socio-economic and political systems that had disabled me, not any of my impairments or my biology. This new understanding allowed me to gain confidence, and I felt liberated. By sharing the principles of the social model, I was eager to have a positive impact on the lives of fellow disabled people, and so began my journey towards disability politics. With enthusiasm, I joined several local and national disability rights groups that debated and campaigned for disabled people's rights to independent living and inclusion in mainstream society. Little did I know I would then face another battle, this time within my own community.

Having acquired a brain injury three decades ago, as well as some physical and sensory impairments, I have dysarthria, which is defined as speech that is difficult or has unclear articulation. As part of my medical condition, I need more time to process information, to reflect and to prepare my responses, a situation not necessarily conducive to traditionally framed 'success' in the Western neoliberal context, in which people are expected to demonstrate an economically, politically, socially and culturally privileged position by being articulate and having clear speech. I do not always remember what I am saying, and I often make statements which are incomplete and unclear. As a result, it can take me longer to recall and reformulate what to say; sometimes I require double the time taken by a non-disabled person in order to speak.

The majority of non-disabled people usually respond to my slow and often slurred speech in impatient or patronising ways. Some treat me like a child and use voices that are not age appropriate, and even where such obvious verbal responses are absent, the underlying prejudice appears ingrained in people's attitudes. It can be evident that people have low expectations of me, or doubts are expressed about my capacity to understand complex ideas. I often feel compelled to say to people, 'I have a speech impairment, but I do not have a problem understanding'. The consequences of such negative attitudes are that I am either not given time or space to express my arguments or my views are unrecognised and dismissed straightaway, without a willingness to really understand.

I know I am not alone in this. Media articles documenting how people with speech impairments are treated negatively in public can be found quickly by searching on Google. Three examples can be found in iNews, *The Washington Post*, and *The Independent*, and there are many more out there (Barrie, 2018; Hoge, 2017; Tracy, 2018). In the literature, this phenomenon is referred to as 'impairment hierarchy', which is a social construct that makes certain kinds of impairments more acceptable than others (Deal, 2003). Disabled people are reported to be frequently judged and categorised, but within the hierarchy framework, certain disabled people are perceived in more negative ways than others. Further, it is not only non-disabled people who hold such attitudes towards groups of people with different impairments; sadly, this can be the case with disabled people too.

Impairment hierarchy is an arbitrary and complex web of factors, in which certain sub-groups of disabled people, based on their own impairments, view other sub-groups as inferior. In relation to the concept of stigma, Dovido et al. (2000) comment that the process of stigmatising others can produce an enhancement of the stigmatiser's own self-esteem through a 'downward-comparison' process. A member of a stigmatised group can find that, by comparing themselves to others perceived to be less 'able' than themselves, their self-esteem is enhanced. An important warning about this phenomenon is articulated by Deal (2003, p. 907): 'Hence, those ranked lowest in the hierarchy become even more vulnerable to the vagaries of social policy without the support of those who should be their comrades and defenders'.

Added to my multiple impairments, I am a non-native speaker of English, which at times has proved difficult. This is especially the case when I am feeling under pressure and even more of an issue after more than 20 years living in the UK. In Western disability rights groups, reflecting the dominant white middle classes, it seems increasingly clear that the activism of those groups supports and reinforces the ways and the culture of the dominant members. White middle-class activists often consider their participation in disability rights groups without recognising their privileged position; they are provided with a means to socialise within the behaviours and norms of the dominant group, as well as advantages in terms of access to resources and power. At times, my opinions and comments have been met with blank looks, clearly indicating that I have not been understood; however, without being asked to repeat or clarify, my voice has been silenced. It is through this process that my own voice has been largely excluded in white disability rights groups, in which I have felt little regard for my lived intersectional experiences and the need to debate and campaign for intersectional and interlocking issues. When gender is considered, the disparities in the disability rights movement are even more pronounced. The high ground of non-gender-specific disability groups is dominated by men. As women, our experiences can be trivialised and our voices not heard. The masculine, middle-class and white character of the disability rights movement often fails to recognise how gender and disability oppression interact and intersect in the lives of many disabled women.

The ways in which my impairments and other identities have been dealt with in different disability rights groups has created and perpetuated inequalities. My contributions intended to create more inclusive structures, taking account of various impairments, have been often dismissed outright, due to a lack of understanding. Ultimately, this has meant that my needs, voice and experiences have been left out. The implicit but rarely stated ways in which my speech impairments have been responded to within activism have led to my being self-conscious when I speak. I have been either rushed or clearly not understood and not responded to, just subjected to empty and meaningless nods. The frequent 'blank looks' have left me feeling that I would not be understood if I spoke, so therefore why try? The lack of representation has resulted in the many accumulated layers of oppression becoming internalised and therefore even more hidden: 'Internalized oppression is not the cause of our mistreatment, it is the result of our mistreatment' (Mason, 1990, p. 1). The barriers I experienced in my journey of being a disability activist were multi-layered and multifaceted, the underlying oppression damaging and destructive to my self-esteem.

As I have grown and strengthened my passion for social change, I have developed means by which I include myself in different groups. One such technique is to give permission in meetings for members to ask me to repeat myself if anything is unclear. I have also tried to contribute to discussions without being asked, in order to build my confidence. While arguably, these techniques have been effective to some extent, I do not feel they have had a long-term impact on my inclusion. For these reasons, my participation in the disability rights movement has largely taken the form of writing and publishing in various academic journals, as well as mainstream publications, about our rights to access society without being discriminated against. While writing has given me a different tool to campaign for equality, I find the exclusive practices within the movement to be deeply damaging. Such ableist practices contribute towards the exclusion from the disability rights movement of those already marginalised in society. This creates a further level of social oppression, not from outsiders, but from within one's own community. The invisibility and erasure of my experiences as a disabled woman of colour with a speech impairment within activist groups point to ingrained societal internalised ableism and microaggressions.

The sidelining of the contributions of certain disabled people has resulted in the exclusion, and thereby waste, of key lived experiences and voices, amounting to a very unjust state of affairs. This disquieting situation ought to be thoroughly challenged by all those concerned with continuing the disability rights movement, locally, nationally and internationally. Instead of condoning oppressive practices, we should build on the premise that the problem is more one of politics and representation. By identifying ourselves as disabled people with multiple identities, we begin to challenge the exclusive nature of disability identity from within the disabled community in relation to impairment and other characteristics. The diversity of our experiences will no doubt contribute to the strength and richness of our movement. We recognise that activism takes different forms, and there is no one way that fits and is relevant for all disabled people.

Whilst disabled people fight a common cause in seeking equality within society and the removal of disabling barriers, focus needs to be centred on impairment groups that face the most discrimination in society and are ranked lowest in the hierarchy of impairments, instead of simply perceiving disabled people as a homogenous group. The disability rights movement should be accessible to all, and accommodations need to be made for those whose access and participation is restricted. Disabled activists should feel empowered to speak out about their experiences and the impact of discrimination within the disability rights movement, acknowledging the accumulative effects of oppression, which amount to ableist exclusions and practices. Importantly, we need to be critical of our own bias towards other impairment groups, to ensure prejudice and discrimination do not hinder the progress of the disability movement in campaigning for social inclusion for all: 'Thus, we, as disabled people, may need to acknowledge our own prejudices before we can truly argue we demand a wholly inclusive society' (Deal, 2003, p. 907). We need to recognise the mainstreaming of ableism as an exclusionary practice, one that goes beyond disability and challenges difference in all its forms. There is therefore a requirement for us to tackle the racism, sexism and classism present in our movement in equal measure.

Conclusion

As a collective political project, informing equality practice is key in addressing unequal distribution of resources and social power and transforming the culture of the disability rights movement. Any new system must provide opportunities to engage in politics and attend to the intersectional ethics of solidarity with everyday acts of resistance, starting with addressing the perceptions of those who have speech impairments. If we in the disability rights movement cannot get our own houses in order, what hope is there for the rest of the world?

References

Barrie, J. (2018). A man with a speech impediment says Wetherspoon's staff chucked him out for slurring his speech. *iNews*. https://inews.co.uk/news/man-speech-impediment-chucked-out-pub-182778

Deal, M. (2003). Disabled people's attitudes toward other impairment groups: A hierarchy of impairments. *Disability & Society*, 18(7), 897–910.

Dovido, J. F., Major, B., and Crocker, J. (2000). Stigma: Introduction and overview. In Heatherton, T. F., Kleck, R. E., Hebl, M. R., and Hull, J. G. (eds.), *The Social Psychology of Stigma*. London: Guilford Press.

Hoge, R. (2017). I stutter. As a result, I have been mocked, insulted, misjudged and refused service. *The Washington Post*. https://www.washingtonpost.com/national/health-science/i-stutter-as-a-result-i-have-been-mocked-insulted-misjudged-and-refused-service/2017/11/03/f43e20fc-9efa-11e7–8ea1-ed975285475e_story.html

Mason, M. (1990). Internalized oppression. In Rieser, R., and Mason, M. (eds.), *Disability Equality in Education*. London: ILEA.

Tracy, T. (2018). A disabled woman with a speech impediment was thrown out of a Wetherspoons pub because managers thought she was drunk. *The Independent*. https://www.indy100.com/people/disabled-woman-throw-out-wetherspoons-pub-grace-currie-shropshire-8316836

25

HIERARCHIES OF LEADERSHIP WITHIN DISABILITY JUSTICE MOVEMENTS

The voices of individuals with intellectual disabilities are often left unheard

Jason Harris, Micah Fialka-Feldman, Megan E. Cartier and *Sara Jo Soldovieri*

Introduction

A few months ago, Jason Harris, one of the authors and an advocate, posed a provocative question on his social media page: "Why do the disability rights movement and the disability justice movement not promote individuals with intellectual disabilities as leaders within their movements?" What followed was a rich discussion among his friends and fellow advocates, and this became the catalyst for the interest in creating a piece that reflects the historical marginalization of people with intellectual disabilities among disability rights leadership but also an honest conversation about/between advocates and researchers about how we authentically talk about leadership.

In this chapter, the authors (two well-known advocates for individuals with intellectual disabilities and two colleagues/friends) join together to explore the various hierarchies of leadership within both the disability rights movement and the disability justice movement in the United States. The authors interrogate who has/has not been elevated to leadership positions and discuss possible reasons why. The authors situate these ideas around a conversation about what it means for people who meet leadership norms and expectations of productivity to work inclusively with those who do not necessarily work in that way and yet still contribute to a whole range of other forms of knowledge, expertise, and experience. By drawing on their own lived experiences as advocates, two authors offer significant insight into how they experience leadership enacted

DOI: 10.4324/9781003410089-30

within the various organizations to which they belong. With thoughtful consideration of the histories and works of several notable individuals with intellectual disabilities (Bernard Carabello, Lois Curtis, Micah Fialka-Feldman, Tia Nelis, Jenny Hatch, Roland Johnson, Liz Weintraub, Elaine Wilson, and many others) who have served and continue to serve in various capacities of leadership in different organizations, the authors explore concepts such as interdependent leadership and deliberately independent teamwork that is inclusive.

The authors also consider how visible and invisible hierarchies of leadership within the disability rights/justice movements in the United States do not necessarily align with the often-used rallying cry of the disability community: "Nothing about us without us." By examining the various visible and invisible hierarchies of leadership within both the disability rights and disability justice movements, the authors hope to provide thoughtful consideration and suggestions for increasing leadership opportunities within the organizations mentioned earlier specifically and other organizations for individuals with intellectual disabilities generally.

Historical overviews

> Disability is not simply a natural phenomenon: it is always influenced by social relations and cultural values.
>
> *(Shakespeare, 2017)*

The preceding words by disability scholar Tom Shakespeare remind us that to construct a timeline or provide a historical recounting of disability is not as simple as listing dates and prominent figures – this often privileges one historical narrative over another. In her book on disability history in the United States, Kim Nielsen (2012) echoes this claim stating, "Disability is not just a bodily category, but instead also a social category shaped by changing social factors" (p. xv). Most disability scholars and activists agree that examining the treatment of individuals with disabilities across time and cultures helps construct insight into common attitudes. These examinations lead to significant changes in how society as a whole conceptualizes its framing of disability and its acceptance and treatment of individuals with disabilities. Garland (1995) states that:

> The study of history can never fruitfully be an end in itself. Rather, it forms part of a discourse between the past and the present, whose purpose is to measure cultural distance and difference, as well as to establish cultural similarity and identity.
>
> *(p. xii)*

In keeping with the notion that constructing a historical accounting of disability is more than just an assemblage of dates and notable figures, the authors recognize the irony of having one of the first sections of this chapter be on historical overviews. However, the authors felt it necessary to provide a historical context for the disability rights/justice movements within the United States to situate their conversations on leadership hierarchies later in this chapter. To address this conundrum, the authors try to make evident the many intersectional identities that coalesce and impact (and sometimes impede) the progress of these communities' members. Our historical overviews strive to focus on the grassroots organizing efforts collectively enacted by members of these organizations rather than through a rigid timeline of dates and a veritable parade of notable "who's who" among those participants. Our chapter also spends considerable time examining the ideas of presuming competence, ableism, and the use of intelligence to position individuals as worthy or unworthy.

Disability rights movement

> We support you because you're asking America to change, to treat you like human beings, like you belong. We always support people fighting for their rights.
>
> *(Member of the Black Panthers, San Francisco 504 Sit-in, quoted in O'Toole, 2019)*

The preceding quote comes from Corbett Joan O'Toole's book, *Fading Scars: My Queer Disability history*. This particular quote reminds us of the allyship and labor it took for *one* sentence to be added to the Rehabilitation Act of 1973. O'Toole goes on to say, "They [the Black Panthers] showed us what being an ally could be. We never would have succeeded without them. They are a critical part of disability history and yet their story is almost never told in this context" (p. 33). Although the disability rights movement centers largely on the passage of legal protections for individuals with disabilities, it is important to recognize the impressive amount of organizing, coordinating, and commitment required to secure the addition of legal protections in the Rehabilitation Act of 1973.

Because the authors live and work in the United States, this overview of the disability rights movement will be US-centric. However, the authors recognize the myriad significant contributions towards disability rights made in numerous countries around the globe. Later in the chapter, the authors provide reading recommendations with a more global focus. Identifying a singular starting point of any action towards disability rights depends largely on time and cultures in terms of whose stories get told and whose lived experiences are honored. In the United States, general agreement among members of the disability community indicates that disability rights as a movement largely parallels the timeline of the civil rights movement. However, it should be understood that individuals with disabilities have been working towards equity and inclusion for a lot longer. In their edited book *Keywords for Disability Studies*, Adams et al. (2015) astutely claim, "As with segregation, colonialism, and apartheid, shared experiences of social separation and political disenfranchisement ultimately galvanized many people with disabilities and their supporters toward a common purpose" (p. 7). Such grassroots movements around the country and throughout history have been well documented in disability and historical literature. Still, these stories rarely center on the experiences of multiply-marginalized intersectional groups of individuals, including Black, indigenous, and people of color (BIPOC) and queer and/or trans individuals. Rather, the stories center the lived experiences of primarily white and predominantly middle/upper-class people – those with the social, financial, and familial capital to advocate for change.

By and large, the disability rights movement (DRM) in the United States is first and foremost a legal movement seeking to establish legal recognition for equal rights, equal opportunities, and fair treatment of people with disabilities. Advocates, activists, and allies alike agitated for equity and access within several domains such as transportation, accessibility of buildings and worksites, availability of meaningful and fiscally supportive employment, independent living, and access to appropriate accommodations in schools. "The struggle for disability rights has followed a similar pattern to many other civil rights movements – challenging negative attitudes and stereotypes, rallying for political and institutional change, and lobbying for the self-determination of a minority community" (Anti-Defamation League, 2018, para. 8). Benchmark legal victories include the ratification of Section 504 of the Rehabilitation Act of 1973, the 1975 Education for All Handicapped Children Act – renamed in 1990 to the Individuals with Disabilities Education Act (IDEA), the passage of the Americans with Disabilities Act (ADA) of 1990, and the Olmstead decision of 1999. Collectively, these legal victories codified expectations of legally binding protections for individuals with disabilities across a broad spectrum of categories, including employment, transportation, housing, education, and independent living.

Frameworks of disability justice

> The US Disability Rights Movement established civil rights for people with disabilities. . . . And like many movements, it is a product of its time and left us with some "cliff-hangers" that have yet to be resolved.
>
> *(Sins Invalid, 2019, p. 17)*

Formal organizations working on behalf of disabled individuals have been documented since the 1800s, but their existence exploded in popularity in the 1900s. The League of the Physically Handicapped formed in the 1930s. The National Federation of the Blind and We Are Not Alone began in the 1940s. The National Association for Retarded Children (NARC) started in the 1950s. These are just some of the examples. The problem with these organizations, though, lies in how they were founded. These organizations were almost always exclusively created *for* individuals with disabilities and not *by* or *with* individuals with disabilities. This distinction is important to note as it is one of the catalysts that galvanized the work of those within disability communities to center the voices of those within their communities. Though producers of important and notable work, the organizations mentioned here were limited in their reach because they provided a very narrow perspective of the disabled experience and ultimately failed to account for the experiences of those with multiple marginalized identities. Even when the voices of disabled individuals were present, they were not those of individuals in leadership positions and were almost exclusively white, upper/middle-class citizens. Because of the vast disparities created by the whitewashing of disability rights, disability justice was born. Disability justice is a movement and framework that centers the experiences and voices of disabled individuals.

Sins Invalid,[1] a disability justice–based performance organization, has largely taken up the labor of addressing the myriad cliffhangers left by the DRM. One of the ways in which they endeavor towards this goal is in the production and publication of a disability justice primer – now in its second edition. *Skin, Tooth, and Bone: The Basis of Movement Is Our People* centers the collective voices of those most marginalized and multiply marginalized in the disability community. Sins Invalid fully articulates their vision of disability justice in the following statement found on the Mission and Vision portion of their webpage:

> Sins Invalid recognizes that we will be liberated as whole beings – as disabled, as queer, as brown, as black, as gender non-conforming, as trans, as women, as men, as non-binary gendered – we are far greater whole than partitioned. We recognize that our allies emerge from many communities and that demographic identity alone does not determine one's commitment to liberation. Sins Invalid is committed to social and economic justice for all people with disabilities – in lockdowns, in shelters, on the streets, visibly disabled, sensory minority, environmentally injured, psychiatric survivors – moving beyond individual legal rights to collective human rights. Our stories, embedded in analysis, offer paths from identity politics to unity amongst all oppressed people, laying a foundation for a collective claim of liberation and beauty.
>
> *(Sins Invalid, 2015, Mission and Vision)*

Indeed, their focus on imagining beyond the individual legal rights of people with disabilities towards a collective sharing of upholding human rights is the very underpinning that defines and constructs the frameworks of disability justice (DJ). The authors posit that true disability justice has not and cannot be fully realized until individuals with intellectual disabilities – particularly those who identify as BIPOC, queer, and/or trans – are fully included to serve in leadership roles.

Many discriminatory beliefs and behaviors exist within and among members of the disability community. These beliefs and behaviors contribute to creating and upholding barriers for those most marginalized and further perpetuating an atmosphere of inequality. Historically, work toward the inclusion of individuals with disabilities was heavily influenced by notions of who belongs and why. Much of this exclusion/inclusion binary is steeped in ableist beliefs. Ableism is the practice of discriminating against individuals with disabilities by seeing them as less than able to participate in nearly all facets of life. The insidious nature of ableism is that while it indeed categorizes entire groups of people as being less than, there is often a desire to compare one's disability with someone else's – that particular abilities are more desirable than others. For example, someone with a physical disability may feel as though they are more capable of completing various tasks than an individual with an intellectual disability.

It is at every level that we see the disparate and disproportionate impact of ableism on individuals with intellectual disabilities; those with the most need seemingly receive the least amount of protection from state and federal law. The disparate and disproportionate impact of ableism is illustrated clearly within public school systems in the United States. The Individuals with Disabilities Education Act (IDEA) guarantees the right of all disabled students to receive a free and appropriate public education (FAPE) alongside their non-disabled peers in the general education setting through the guarantee of the least restrictive environment (LRE). Yet despite this, no state in this country reports a proportional number of students with intellectual disabilities being educated alongside their non-disabled peers or with fellow students with other disabilities such as physical disabilities, learning disabilities, etc. (Artiles & Kozleski, 2007; Ferri & Connor, 2007; Gabel et al., 2013; Valle & Connor, 2019). We see ableism enacted in several ways in schools (Hehir, 2005), including the segregation of students with disabilities into separate schools (Connor & Ferri, 2006), the use of seclusion and restraint to control students with disabilities (Trader et al., 2017; Villani et al., 2011), and placement of students with disabilities within institutions (Yell, 1995). We must also acknowledge that among those with intellectual disabilities segregated away from the general education classroom, a disproportionate number are students of color (Ferri & Connor, 2007; Ford & Russo, 2016; Harry & Fenton, 2016; Losen & Orfield, 2002; Skiba & Losen, 2016). These types of ableism further show the interconnectedness of such complex issues.

According to the US Department of Education, in 2013, 63.3% of students who received special education services in the state of Minnesota were educated for at least 80% of the day alongside their non-disabled peers. But within this same state, only 8.9% of students with intellectual disabilities were educated for at least 80% of the day alongside their non-disabled peers. Despite the landmark *Brown v Board of Education* decision in 1954, which states, "In the field of public education the doctrine of 'separate but equal' has no place," as segregated schools are "inherently unequal" (*Brown v Board of Education*,

347 U.S. 483 (1954)), many schools across the country still experience racial disparities and segregation. Schools in the United States are more racially segregated than ever (Owens, 2020). Within our schools, we reinforce a form of inter-ableism. The authors define "inter-ableism" as ableist actions that set up a hierarchy within the disability community by privileging those whose perceived body-mind and speech most closely resemble the socially constructed norm. In many ways, inter-ableism perpetuates stigma and negative perceptions against ability, which sets up hierarchies within the disability community based on disability status.

On competence

> Rather than seeing intelligence and competence as a fixed set of expectations regarding scores on IQ tests or performance on standardised measures, we need to recognise the socially constructed nature of ability and disability and recognise alternative notions of intelligence.
>
> *(Ashby & Causton-Theoharis, 2009)*

There are many reasons people with intellectual and developmental disabilities are not included in the leadership process within the disability rights/justice movements. A core reason is that society generally does not presume competence, even in those with whom we share a collective struggle. In essence, the presumption of competence means that, in the absence of proof, society as a whole should assume that individuals with intellectual disabilities are capable of participating in all facets of society (Biklen & Burke, 2006). The majority of the general public identify as *homo sapiens* or simply – humans. The Latin term "*homo sapiens*" translates to "wise man." We see this nod towards intelligence in how we define ourselves in relation to other non-human animals. Humans, as wise men, are superior. As a result, intelligence becomes predicated on what we *think* it means to be intelligent. In this way, humans typically accept only a very narrow definition of intelligence, one that defines intelligent creatures as capable of using tools and language and/or exhibiting some control over their environment. Humans have long been able to contrive definitions of intelligence that make it clear that we are the only creatures to exhibit these behaviors in a way that should be "counted." Even when we test intelligence in animals such as primates, elephants, or dolphins, we compare them using the same human benchmark norms. Obviously, this results in the assignment of extremely low age-equivalency scores.

Ascribing value to cognition and function has always been problematic, especially for those with intellectual and developmental disabilities, including autism, Down syndrome, Cri-Du-Chat, and Rett syndrome, to name a few. Ashby and Causton-Theoharis (2009) address the social construction of intelligence norms, stating, "Notions of retardation and competence are not fixed ideas or absolute truths (Bogdan & Taylor, 1994; Hayman, 1998; Kliewer,

1998). Rather, they are based on cultural norms and are perpetuated through language, media, institutions, etc." (p. 502). First author Jason Harris, a self-identified autistic person[2] and advocate, discusses the social construction of intelligence, stating how it sounds like the Theory of Mind often ascribed to autistic people. Simon Baron-Cohen (2000) describes Theory of Mind as:

> [B]eing able to infer the full range of mental states (beliefs, desires, intentions, imagination, emotions, etc.) that cause action. In brief, having a theory of mind is to be able to reflect on the contents of one's own and others' minds.
>
> *(p. 173)*

It is essential to recognize that autistic people bring a wealth of ideas and unique skills to their interests.

As an autistic person, Jason states that to generally be accepted as competent, he has to try to show he is "super" intelligent. The autistic community has understandably co-opted this belief in demonstrating "super intelligence" in some ways to justify their existence and desire to be a part of things. However, this becomes problematic when it requires other autistic people or people with intellectual disabilities to demonstrate a certain level of competence just to be able to participate in activities of interest and assume leadership positions. Jason states that in many situations, the need to justify oneself is often done by exerting socially constructed norms that require individuals to compare themselves to others. Asking individuals to justify or demonstrate their competence often comes as a double-edged sword. Jason further explains that in some ways, he is often forced to live up to the weird expectations of the so-called "super crip," all the while being ignored by both non-disabled and disabled individuals. In the disability community, a super crip is someone that "overcomes" their disability – usually in some socially constructed ideal of inspiration (Silva & Howe, 2012).

The pervasive attitude of having to overcome one's disability in order to be seen as competent and eligible to access various communities (most notably, higher education and leadership) largely shaped the lived experiences of both first and second authors, Jason and Micah. Micah and Jason worked hard throughout school and were accepted to colleges of their choice. However, when Micah applied to live in the dorms on campus at his university, his competence was called into question by members of the school community and then, later, members of the judicial community when he pursued his case through legal avenues (*Micah Fialka-Feldman v Oakland University Board of Trustees*, 2011). Despite his victory and subsequent move into the dormitory, Micah shares that he was subjected to hours of deposition, enduring questions such as "What would you do if the fire alarm went off in the dorm?" and "How would you be sure to wake up on time to get to your classes?" When applying to live in the college dorms, no other student is asked such banal questions.

Although Jason and Micah share different college experiences, they both report needing to justify their presence in academic and leadership spaces. Jason shares that while he can generate and navigate ideas well, he still has other access needs. "I'm really good at having ideas and holding multiple thoughts, but executive functioning is something that I struggle with." Task initiation, breaking down tasks into manageable events, and social anxiety are also chief among Jason's access needs and considerations. Micah also indicates having access needs. To address these needs, Micah hires staff to help manage his daily calendar, finances, and workload, including numerous speaking engagements around the country. He also has a tight-knit group of family and friends who step in and lend a hand when needed.

Intelligence and IQ as gatekeepers

> The human experience is infinitely complex, yet the concept of the norm presents a circumscribed view of the lived experience of individuals – or groups of people – in ways that mislead and misrepresent.
>
> *(Dudley-Marling & Gurn, 2010)*

In their edited work *The Myth of the Normal Curve*, Dudley-Marling and Gurn set out to challenge notions of "normalcy" in relation to the bell curve. Contributors to this edition "make the case that not only is the normal curve not *normal*, the idea that human behavior distributes along a bell-shaped curve with most people clustered around the mean or average grossly oversimplifies the diversity of human experiences" (2010, p. 3). Georges Canguilhem (1978) gives an even deeper and more critical summarization of the idea of normal, stating:

> When we know that *norma* is the Latin word for T-square and that *normalis* means perpendicular, we know almost all that must be known about the area in which the meaning of the terms "norm" and "normal" originated. . . . A norm, or rule, is what can be used to right, to square, to straighten . . . to impose a requirement on an existence.
>
> *(p. 239)*

Throughout history, we see vast and varied ways in which the concept of intelligence and IQ act as gatekeepers and impose requirements for access to various situations for people with disabilities.

Jason shares that disability has long been a way for these groups to become disenfranchised when it comes to marginalized groups. This is especially true around ideas of intelligence. Jason states, "We know, as with the Autistic community, many other communities have had intelligence and IQ used against them and in many cases are still used against them today." Intelligence and IQ are often interpreted as so-called behavioral issues and have been used to place a disproportionate number of Black and brown children in segregated special education (Albrecht et al., 2011; Annamma et al., 2014; Blette, 2020; King Thorius et al., 2014). For many of these students, this also means a subsequent funneling through the school-to-prison pipeline into life in and out of incarceration (Annamma, 2018). Intelligence was also used throughout history to justify numerous unsavory acts such as slavery, Jim Crow laws, denial of women's rights, eugenics, institutionalizing individuals with disabilities, colonialist and pro-Christian hegemony of thoughts, and so much more.

Intelligence and IQ as gatekeepers to various settings and organizations are often overt acts of discrimination. For example, language use and intent are often gatekeepers in clinical and professional settings and in popular culture. The word "retard" was still used in clinical references and everyday vernacular to describe an individual with an intellectual disability. Many state offices also used it until the 21st century. The use of pejorative words to describe individuals with intellectual and developmental disabilities also includes euphemisms such as "idiot," "moron," and "imbecile." Ashby and Causton-Theoharis (2009) problematize the use of pejorative names and the importance of language concerning intelligence, stating, "What is so damaging about these terms, aside from the stigmatising nature of the labels themselves, is that they not only reflect societal ideas of normalcy and deviance, but they also shape those ideas" (p. 508). They further go on to explain that "Language both reflects and shapes the ways in which individuals with disabilities are constructed. Once someone is seen through a lens of retardation, the person behind the label becomes obscured, often leading to denial of opportunities" (p. 508). Indeed, language is a powerful tool for shaping socially constructed ideals of normalcy.

In many ways, the use of intelligence or IQ as a marker of normalcy in terms of eligibility for certain services, for access to higher education, for inclusion in organizations, to access leadership positions, or to participate in basic events has perpetuated the idea that individuals with lower IQs are somehow less. O'Toole (2019) demonstrates how these ideas are embedded in our ways of thinking about disability, stating, "Presuming the competence of some people – those closer to the 'normal' standard – and presuming the incompetence of the 'other,' is built into the fabric of our society" (p. 9). First author Jason troubles this idea, stating that, in the United States, it is generally assumed that any disability that is physical in nature, such as blindness or deafness, as well as psychosocial disability and learning deficits means low intelligence. For many decades, this belief in low intelligence led to the institutionalization of many people and still, to this day, holds many individuals hostage inside institutions. Here, the authors ask you to recall their previous discussion surrounding ableism and inter-ableism. While both terms are relevant when discussing intelligence and IQ, we return to the idea of inter-ableism within the disability communities and how intelligence is called upon to be a gatekeeper to access and therefore sets up the foundations of hierarchies within the disability community as a whole. Jason reminds us that at the beginning of the DRM, a common saying was frequently used to further progress. The statement

"My body is broken; my mind is not" demonstrates a clear division between individuals with physical disabilities and those with intellectual or developmental disabilities. In their chapter "Take the Pain" in *From There to Here: Stories of Adjustment to Spinal Cord Injury*, an edited compilation by Gary Karp and Stanley D. Klein, PhD, Mark M. Braunstein states, "My mind dwells inside my body, but my life dwells more inside my mind. My body matters, but my mind matters more. Although my body is broken, my mind is not broken, and so my life is not broken" (pp. 171–172).

The rhetoric included in this earlier statement, coupled with the fact that much of the intellectual and developmental disability movement has been tied up with grassroots parent movements focused first on increasing access to more inclusive school options and later on post-secondary education or employment opportunities, illustrates the schism between individuals with different disability statuses. In the following sections, the authors will explore such schisms and how hierarchies of leadership get taken up within established disability communities.

Hierarchies of leadership

> Leadership is not about titles, status, and wielding power. A leader is anyone who takes responsibility for recognizing the potential in people and ideas, and has the courage to develop that potential.
>
> (*Brown, 2018*)

A brief internet search for the definition of "leadership" indicates that leadership is both an active and a passive trait. Actively, leadership means taking charge and guiding individuals, groups, or organizations. Passively, leadership is described as a personal characteristic. Leaders are described as possessing the skills to influence or guide others. Despite Dr. Brown's claim that leadership is *not* about titles, status, or wielding power, leadership roles are often clearly defined by titles such as president, vice president, and chairperson, and power and status are bestowed upon those in leadership positions. As with any movement or organization, there tends to be a hierarchical structure defining those in leadership positions. When considering leadership roles among disability communities, there is a considerable disconnect among various organizations and how they view and enact leadership. Historically, disability has been routinely coded as white and male with certain types of disability. While disabled white males are still marginalized, in disabled spaces, they often hold more weight. Rightfully, many disability communities have started working towards breaking down this patriarchy and are moving towards centering the collective voices of women and those who are trans, non-binary, and individuals of color. However, these efforts still fail to include the voices of individuals with intellectual disabilities. Let us return for a moment to the statement presented in the previous section: "My body is broken; my mind is not." Though meant to further the efforts of members of the DRM, this statement demonstrates a clear example of the inter-ableism that routinely occurs and ultimately lays the foundation for hierarchies within and among the various disability communities.

As with other professional fields, industries, and movements, it is not always about your skills or what you know but about *who* you know. Unfortunately, it seems that activists in the mainstream movements of disability rights and disability justice often do not know of people like Bernard Carabello, Lois Curtis, Micah Fialka-Feldman, Tia Nelis, and Jenny Hatch, Roland Johnson, or Elaine Wilson. However, these individuals are credited with furthering the efforts and rights of individuals with intellectual and developmental disabilities. Next, the authors provide a brief overview of these individuals to situate their contributions and efforts towards furthering the rights of individuals with intellectual and developmental disabilities. In addition, the authors provide some extra reading suggestions at the end of the chapter for readers interested in learning more about the works and achievements of these individuals.

Though born with cerebral palsy, Bernard Carabello was misdiagnosed with developmental disabilities and, on the advice of family doctors, was sent to Willowbrook State School in New York. Carabello resided at Willowbrook, an institution for individuals with intellectual and developmental disabilities, for 18 years. Upon his release from Willowbrook at age 21, Carabello fell into a life of activism within the disability rights community. Carabello started the Self-Advocacy Association of New York in 1986 (Hampton, 2021). Lois Curtis and Elaine Wilson are two women with intellectual and developmental disabilities credited with furthering the rights of individuals with IDD to live and work in a community setting instead of institutions. Curtis and Wilson were denied access to living in a community setting based on their intellectual and developmental disabilities diagnoses. However, on June 22, 1999, US Supreme Court Judge Ruth Bader Ginsburg declared the denial of their right to live in a community setting unconstitutional. Now known as the Olmstead decision, it secured for individuals with intellectual and developmental disabilities the right to live in their community rather than an institution (Appelbaum, 2019). Born in Chicago, Illinois, in 1969, Tia Nelis devotes her life to advancing the rights of individuals with disabilities through teaching the development of self-advocacy skills. Throughout her life work, Nelis uses her lived experiences to serve in various leadership capacities and as a spokesperson and trainer for self-advocacy. (Self-Advocates Becoming Empowered, 2019). On August 2, 2013, Jenny Hatch, an individual with IDD, won a landmark court case in the United States awarding her the right to make decisions about her life, finances, and medical choices using supported decision making. Hatch's triumphs in court for supported decision making helped turn the topic of guardianship into honest conversations for other individuals with intellectual and developmental disabilities (Hatch Justice Project, 2014). Roland Johnson, an individual with an intellectual disability, was sent to Pennhurst State School and Hospital in Pennsylvania at the age of 12. While at Pennhurst, Johnson endured over a decade of neglect and abuse at the hands of the staff. In addition to having a disability, Johnson was also subjected to abuse and bigotry because of the color of his skin. As a Black man, Johnson experienced the effects of racism during his time at Pennhurst and his life works outside the institution. Johnson devoted his life to securing the release of individuals with disabilities from institutions. He also worked tirelessly to promote advocacy skills among individuals with IDD (Rifkin, 2020).

Even when activists are aware of these individuals, it often seems that their presence at disability rights activities is in tokenistic roles. However, the disability justice movement is steadily working towards increasing access for all individuals with disabilities as expressed in their commitment to cross-disability solidarity:

> We value and honor the insights and participation of all of our community members, even and especially those who are most often left out of political conversations. We are building a movement that breaks down isolation between people with physical impairments, people who are sick or chronically ill, psych survivors and people with mental health disabilities, neurodiverse people, people with intellectual or developmental disabilities, Deaf people, Blind people, people with environmental injuries and chemical sensitivities, and all others who experience ableism and isolation that undermines our collective liberation.
>
> *(Sins Invalid, 2019, p. 25)*

And yet, despite these efforts, by and large, individuals with intellectual or developmental disabilities are often left without a seat at the table. In the next section, the authors turn their gaze towards the different ways in which Jason and Micah have experienced leadership successes and failures over the years of their advocacy.

Leadership capacities

> The myth of the lone individual is a trope, a rhetorical device. In real life no one is self-made; few are truly alone.
>
> *(Kerber, 1989)*

When thinking about capacities for leadership among individuals with intellectual disabilities, Micah and Jason remind us that it is essential to consider accommodations and how the requests for and granting of accommodations play a considerable role in defining hierarchical structures in leadership settings. Questions about which accommodations are deemed "acceptable" are often not determined by those experiencing similar access needs. For example, Jason shares that although he identifies as an individual with an intellectual disability and as a member of the autistic community, he is often considered "too smart" for *x*, *y*, or *z* services and/or accommodations, yet those are the very accommodations he requires to demonstrate "competence" and to be successful. Disability activists are not wrong, though, that sometimes all people, including those with intellectual and developmental disabilities, can be heavily influenced or controlled by non-disabled people. Obviously, this is a concern for groups when considering who is actually doing the leading.

Nonetheless, Jason and Micah remind us that with the lack of accommodations and processes to include individuals with intellectual disabilities, they feel as though, to some extent, they are controlled by individuals within the disability communities. Jason goes on to say that "because of the lack of input from individuals with intellectual and developmental disabilities, our access needs are generally not met." This statement reinforces the stigmatizing belief that it is too hard to include individuals with IDD in leadership capacities or roles or that assumptions are made that individuals with IDD cannot do the job. In Kim Nielsen's book, *A Disability History of the United States*, she provocatively asserts:

> When disability is equated with dependency, disability is stigmatized. Citizens with disabilities are labeled inferior citizens. When disability is understood as dependency, disability is posited in direct contrast to American ideals of independence and autonomy. In real life, however, just as in a real democracy, all of us are dependent on others. . . . We are an interdependent people.
>
> *(2012, p. xiii)*

Although this quote is not explicitly referring to any one category of disability, both Jason and Micah feel it is a good representation of how individuals with IDD are often labeled as inferior. Throughout this chapter, the authors have tried to expressly point out and provide alternatives to pushing aside individuals with intellectual disabilities when it comes to leadership positions. Both Jason and Micah serve in various leadership roles, from Micah's membership on President Obama's Committee for Persons with Intellectual Disabilities to Jason's scholarly research and commitment to equity through his work at the Burton Blatt Institute at Syracuse University, to name just two.

When reflecting on these experiences, Jason and Micah share that adequate support (the level of which should be determined by the individual) and an interdependent model of working collectively have proven to create the context in which the most authentic leadership experiences can be cultivated. We authors argue that everyone thrives in a system of interdependence. Ostensibly, no one goes through life without support. Unfortunately for individuals with intellectual disabilities, these supports are either seen as "too much," thereby canceling out any of their contributions, or are simply not given at all. This denial of supports thereby reifies the notion that individuals with intellectual disabilities are not capable. Micah stresses that this model of interdependence has not only allowed him to thrive in his personal life but also allowed him to make real and impactful changes for the IDD community. The authors define interdependent leadership as a collective nurturing and sharing of individual skills that all group members benefit from. When one group member excels in one area, they take the lead on putting those skills to work, while someone else addresses another area of need. Jason adds that within the creation of interdependent spaces and opportunities, accommodations cannot and should not be an afterthought. The very premise by which we plan/organize/rally should be steeped in embedded supports and accommodations. We are, indeed, an interdependent people. The authors acknowledge that there is a fine, tricky line that must be navigated along which folks with intellectual disabilities are supported in leadership roles while not placing the burden of receiving said support on the individual with an intellectual disability while also not positioning folks without intellectual disabilities as the gatekeepers of these supports. We authors contend that for true equity to exist within and across disability movements, individuals with intellectual disabilities must not be an afterthought.

Note: Because the authors live and work in the United States, this overview of the disability rights movement has been US-centric. However, the authors recognize the myriad significant contributions towards disability rights made in numerous countries around the globe. We encourage readers to explore contributions around the world. What follows is a curated list of possible readings to help guide readers in finding and exploring more about the topics covered throughout this chapter.

Notes

1 Readers can locate a wealth of information on Sins Invalid by visiting their website at https://www.sinsinvalid.org/.

2 A note on language. Throughout this chapter, the authors have chosen to use person-first language when referring to individuals with disabilities. As a member of the autistic community, Jason Harris chooses to use identity-first language when discussing autistic individuals.

References

Adams, R., Reiss, B., & Serlin, D. (Eds.). (2015). *Keywords for disability studies* (Vol. 7). New York: NYU Press.

Albrecht, S. F., Skiba, R. J., Losen, D. J., Chung, C.-G., & Middelberg, L. (2011). Federal policy on disproportionality in special education. *Journal of Disability Policy Studies*, *23*(1), 14–25. https://doi.org/10.1177/1044207311407917.

Annamma, S. A. (2018). *The pedagogy of pathologization: Dis/abled girls of color in the school-prison nexus*. London: Routledge (an imprint of the Taylor & Francis Group).

Annamma, S., Morrison, D., & Jackson, D. (2014). Disproportionality fills in the gaps: Connections between achievement, discipline and special education in the school-to-prison pipeline. *Berkeley Review of Education*, *5*. https://doi.org/10.5070/b85110003.

Anti-Defamation League. (2018). *A brief history on the disability rights movement*. https://www.adl.org/media/6891/download

Appelbaum, L. (2019, March 29). Lois Curtis: Woman with disabilities fights for freedom for all. *Respect Ability*. Retrieved December 9, 2021, from https://www.respectability.org/2019/03/women-disabilities-lois-curtis/.

Artiles, A. J., & Kozleski, E. B. (2007, March). Beyond convictions: Interrogating culture, history, and power in inclusive education. *KU Scholar Works*. Retrieved December 8, 2021, from https://kuscholarworks.ku.edu/bitstream/handle/1808/10881/KozleskiBeyondConvictionsMedium.pdf;sequence=1.

Ashby, C. E., & Causton-Theoharis, J. N. (2009). Disqualified in the human race: A close reading of the autobiographies of individuals identified as autistic. *International Journal of Inclusive Education*, *13*(5), 501–516. https://doi.org/10.1080/13603110801886673.

Baron-Cohen, S. (2000). Theory of mind and autism: A review. *International Review of Research in Mental Retardation*, *23*, 169–184.

Berne, P., Morales, A. L., Langstaff, D., & Invalid, S. (2018). Ten principles of disability justice. *WSQ: Women's Studies Quarterly*, *46*(1), 227–230.

Biklen, D., & Burke, J. (2006). Presuming competence. *Equity & Excellence in Education*, *39*(2), 166–175. https://doi.org/10.1080/10667680500540376.

Blette, É. (2020). *Understanding Teacher Experiences Regarding Referrals of Black and Brown Students to Special Education* (Order No. 27829594). Available from ProQuest Dissertations & Theses Global. (2394846525).

Bogdan, R., & Taylor, S. J. (1994). *The social meaning of mental retardation: Two life stories: A reissued edition of "inside out" with a new postscript*. New York: Teachers College Press.

Brown v Board of Education, 347 U.S. 483 (1954).

Brown, B. (2018). *Dare to lead: Brave work. Tough conversations. Whole hearts*. New York: Random House.

Canguilhem, Georges. (1978). *The normal and the pathological*. London: D.Reidel.

Connor, D. J., & Ferri, B. A. (2006). The conflict within: Resistance to inclusion and other paradoxes in special education. *Disability & Society*, *22*(1), 63–77. https://doi.org/10.1080/09687590601056717.

Dudley-Marling, C., & Gurn, A. (Eds.). (2010). *The myth of the normal curve* (Vol. 11). Bern: Peter Lang.

Ferri, B. A., & Connor, D. J. (2007). *Reading resistance: Discourses of exclusion in desegregation & inclusion debates*. Bern: Peter Lang.

Ford, D. Y., & Russo, C. J. (2016). Historical and legal overview of special education overrepresentation: Access and equity denied. *Multiple Voices for Ethnically Diverse Exceptional Learners*, *16*(1), 50–57.

Gabel, S. L., Cohen, C. J., Kotel, K., & Pearson, H. (2013). Intellectual disability and space: Critical narratives of exclusion. *Intellectual and Developmental Disabilities*, *51*(1), 74–80. https://doi.org/10.1352/1934-9556-51.01.074.

Garland, R. (1995). *The eye of the beholder: Deformity and disability in the Graeco-Roman world*. Ithaca, NY: Cornell University Press.

Hampton, D. (2021, May 31). Disability pride: An interview with Bernard Carabello, champion of disability rights. *Including You*. Retrieved December 9, 2021, from https://www.includingyou.org/post/disability-pride-an-interview-with-bernard-carabello.

Harry, B., & Fenton, P. (2016). Risk in schooling: The contribution of qualitative research to our understanding of the overrepresentation of minorities in special education. *Multiple Voices for Ethnically Diverse Exceptional Learners*, *16*(1), 17–28.

Hayman, R. L. (1998). *The smart culture: Society, intelligence, and law*. New York: New York University Press.

Hehir, T. (2005). *New directions in special education: Eliminating ableism in policy and practice*. Cambridge, MA: Harvard Education Press.

Jenny Hatch Justice Project. (2014). The justice for Jenny trial. *The Jenny Hatch Justice Project*. Retrieved December 10, 2021, from http://jennyhatchjusticeproject.org/trial.

Kerber, L. (1989). Women and individualism in American History. *The Massachusetts Review, 30*(4), 589–609. Retrieved April 30, 2021, from http://www.jstor.org/stable/25090120.

King Thorius, K. A., Maxcy, B. D., Macey, E., & Cox, A. (2014). A critical practice analysis of response to intervention appropriation in an urban school. *Remedial and Special Education, 35*(5), 287–299. https://doi.org/10.1177/0741932514522100.

Kliewer, C. (1998). Citizenship in the literate community: An ethnography of children with Down syndrome and the written word. *Exceptional children*, *64*(2), 167–180.

Losen, D. J., & Orfield, G. (2002). *Racial inequity in special education.* Cambridge, MA: Harvard Education Publishing Group.

Nielsen, K. E. (2012). *A disability history of the United States* (Vol. 2). San Francisco, Boston: Beacon Press.

O'Toole, C. J. (2019). *Fading scars: My queer disability history*. Reclamation Press.

Owens, A. (2020). Unequal opportunity: School and neighborhood segregation in the USA. *Race and Social Problems*, *12*(1), 29–41. https://doi.org/10.1007/s12552-019-09274-z.

Rifkin, G. (2020, July 31). Overlooked no more: Roland Johnson, who fought to shut down institutions for the disabled. *The New York Times*. Retrieved December 10, 2021, from https://www.nytimes.com/2020/07/31/obituaries/roland-johnson-overlooked.html.

Self-Advocates Becoming Empowered. (2019, November 22). Tia Nelis: Self-advocacy and beyond. interviews with leaders of the self-advocacy movement. *SARTAC – Self Advocacy Resource and Technical Assistance Center*. Retrieved December 10, 2021, from https://www.selfadvocacyinfo.org/resource/tia-nelis-self-advocacy-and-beyond-interviews-with-leaders-of-the-self-advocacy-movement/.

Shakespeare, T. (2017). *Disability: The basics*. London: Routledge.

Silva, C. F., & Howe, P. D. (2012). The (in)validity of Supercrip representation of Paralympian athletes. *Journal of Sport and Social Issues*, *36*(2), 174–194. https://doi.org/10.1177/0193723511433865.

Sins Invalid. (2015). *Mission & Vision*. Retrieved January 24, 2021. https://www.sinsinvalid.org/mission

Sins Invalid. (2019). *Skin, tooth, and bone: The basis of movement is our people* (2nd ed.). Berkeley, CA.

Skiba, R. J., & Losen, D. J. (2016). From reaction to prevention: Turning the page on school discipline. *American Educator*, *39*(4), 4.

Trader, B., Stonemeier, J., Berg, T., Knowles, C., Massar, M., Monzalve, M., Pinkelman, S., Nese, R., Ruppert, T., & Horner, R. (2017). Promoting inclusion through evidence-based alternatives to restraint and seclusion. *Research and Practice for Persons with Severe Disabilities*, *42*(2), 75–88. https://doi.org/10.1177/1540796917698830.

Valle, J. W., & Connor, D. J. (2019). *Rethinking disability: A disability studies approach to inclusive practices*. New York: Routledge.

Villani, V. S., Parsons, A. E., Church, R. P., & Beetar, J. T. (2011). A descriptive study of the use of restraint and seclusion in a special education school. *Child & Youth Care Forum*, *41*(3), 295–309. https://doi.org/10.1007/s10566-011-9165-3.

Yell, M. L. (1995). Least restrictive environment, inclusion, and students with disabilities: A legal analysis. *The Journal of Special Education*, *28*(4), 389–404. https://doi.org/10.1177/002246699502800401.

26

ZHENSHCHINY. INVALIDNOST'. FEMINIZM./WOMEN. DISABILITY. FEMINISM.

Claiming ourselves against ableism

Alyona Lyovina, Maria Tselovatova and Philippa Mullins

Introducing the collective

We – a collective of critically thinking women with disabilities [*zhenshchiny s invalidnost'iu*] – take up the fight against ignorance and oblivion!

We are not there. We are not anywhere: neither in the women's camp, nor in the disabled people's camp.

We are not there. We are neither in right-wing, nor in left-wing discourse.

We are not there. We are neither in feminism, nor in the disability rights movement.

We are not there, but – we exist! How?

We are presented only as mothers, daughters, wives. People only speak about us when we are prepared to undertake one of those roles. The classic, made-in-Russia paradigm of social integration for women with disabilities proposes a tacit imitation of the same practices imposed on women without disabilities: chasing after beauty, compulsory heterosexuality, maternal happiness, joy at the alienation of one's labour, social dependence, and performances of overt stupidity. We understand how harmful this situation is and want to change it.

For the first time, we are trying to name ourselves, define our boundaries, recognise our collective problems and strength. We call on you to fling off the cloak of invisibility, join us, and assert your existence outside patriarchy, capitalism, and ableism!

(Manifesto by Ira I.)

This is the manifesto of the *Zhenshchiny. Invalidnost'. Feminizm.* (Women. Disability. Feminism.) Collective. It clearly states our problem. Women with

DOI: 10.4324/9781003410089-31

disabilities have been excluded from the conversation and are ignored by both disability and feminist organising in Russia, as well as by political organising across the spectrum.

Our work to assert ourselves has included festivals, discussion groups, online protests, zines, and building community on social media platforms. We have discussed visible and invisible disabilities; sex, sexualities, and relationships; what language to use in Russian to speak about disabilities; ableism and feminism; and violence against women with disabilities. These topics are often ignored, forgotten, and silenced. In particular, we note that the problems of women with disabilities are not the same as the problems of all people with disabilities.

Women are at huge risk of experiencing sexual violence, particularly women with intellectual disabilities. Women with disabilities almost always have problems at gynaecological appointments. We have difficulties achieving our professional goals. Patriarchal society and gendered socialisation throw away women with disabilities, not allowing them to realise their career ambitions. In a patriarchal society, the only socially valuable role for a woman (without disabilities) is that of a mother and a wife. But not all women with disabilities can have and want to have children. Not all women with disabilities are heterosexual. Still, a career is not seen as significant for them, and, if a woman with disabilities tries to get a job, they are more likely to hire a man with disabilities instead of her as he 'needs to feed his family'. Furthermore, the sexuality and self-identification of women and non-binary people with disabilities are erased. Rather, when people talk about a person with disabilities' right to a sex life, they are only talking about men with disabilities. In patriarchal societies, sex is about the man's satisfaction and about reproduction; it does not include any concept of the woman's satisfaction. At the same time, the sexual objectification of the female body excludes women with disabilities from the realm of people who are considered as sexual beings.

Our collective united to discuss these questions and fight for recognition. When we came together, there was practically no mention of the problems faced by women with disabilities in Russian feminist spaces. Feminist and gender studies agendas did not take disability studies into account. I and many other feminists with disabilities were outside the boundaries of the general discourse.

We have forged our own path and made our place in these discussions. For example, on our website, invaprotest.ru, women with disabilities protest violence. We are subjected to violence at 12 times the rate of others. However, not all of us can get out of the house to attend demonstrations or pickets. Still, we all have the right to speak. Through the site, we exert our right to protest violence and to be heard. Through photographs of protest placards and texts, we speak out.

Maria Tselovatova's placard reads 'From vulnerability to protest'. She describes how women have the idea that they need to bear their abuse impressed on them via their socialisation. However, in the case of women with disabilities, other factors also come into play. Often, women with disabilities are in a state of physical dependence on their abuser – that person is also their assistant or caregiver. Without a regulated system of supported living, women with disabilities experience guilt and shame and feel like a burden. This also blocks them from claiming their rights. Maria urges women with disabilities to move from this feeling to one of contestation and protest. She holds out a hand to all women who have decided to defend themselves and their rights.

Anna Kisovskaya's placard declares 'I am not invisible'. She writes about her non-apparent disability and the non-apparent, emotional violence to which she was subjected by family members. In one of her photographs, she poses with her placard and demonstrates the only sign of disability she can show: 'my underdeveloped legs, the lack of muscle in my lower legs, and my size 32 feet'. She shows them for a reason. Growing up, from her earliest childhood, her grandmother would tell her that no one would love her with legs like that. Her father would mock her incontinence. She describes how she spent a long time fighting to fit into a 'normal life', which meant trying to fit into a patriarchal template by being in relationships with 'healthy' people, masking her disability in public, and denying her disability. Now, she refuses to live this way: she is bisexual, polyamorous, proud, and no longer invisible.

Nadezhda Kolosova's placard says 'Cruelty will be covered by silence'. She describes the different forms of emotional, physical, and sexual violence she has lived through – and asks how many other women with disabilities there are who, like her, have also been silent about the violence they have experienced. She calls for the voices of women with disabilities to be heard, and an end to silence and abuse.

Anna Lyubimova holds a placard saying 'I hurt'. She describes the emotional violence and discrimination she experienced because of her disability and the energy she previously put into covering up her disability. Anonymously, one person declares, 'Invisible means unprotected'. She describes how society tells her that, as a woman with disabilities, she should be grateful to have a partner at all – and ignore the fact that that partner is abusive. And yet, leaving is all the more difficult when women with disabilities are often forced into positions of physical and material dependence. Socialisation and an interiorised lack of worth also come into play here. Veronika's placard reads 'A woman can't push back [against abuse] not only because of their illness, but also because of a feeling of guilt'.

Viktoria writes 'We are trapped'. Anonymously, one woman writes 'I lived through violence at age 12. Was it my fault?' Another woman says, 'Help us to stand up for ourselves'. Alyona Lyovina's placard reads 'If you beat your daughter/sister/wife with disabilities – you should get prison, not a carer's allowance'.

In describing the violence that we have experienced as women with disabilities, we demonstrate how we are devalued. We are told we should hide our disability or be grateful for what we have – even when that includes abuse. In this chapter, we explore how this plays out through the story of one member of the collective. In Maria Tselovatova's story, we see ableism from others and internalised ableism in ourselves in the refusal of disability, when that disability is itself understood as a failing or weakness. We see ableism's violence and the suffering it causes.

I met Maria at the end of 2018, when we first joined together to assert ourselves as feminists with disabilities. Maria's text, written in 2019, is one of the stories we gathered together and published in our zine, entitled *Women. Disability. Feminism.* Maria is also one of the zine's editors. Her text vividly describes the situation faced by a girl with disabilities, even in a case of apparent privilege – she lives in a big city in an educated family. Still, she internalises the negative responses and actions of her relatives, works to avoid the judgment of doctors and others around her, and struggles to build a positive identity as a woman with disabilities.

The problems of girls and women with disabilities are systematic, structural problems. Like Maria, in my childhood, I also encountered difficulties accepting my disability. The rejection of physical weakness, the denial of external and internal differences, the inflated expectations of relatives, and the general bewilderment in the face of an incurable disease. This is a short list of how existence in a patriarchal society traumatises girls and women with disabilities. People expect us to match up to the established norms. They expect convention, heteronormativity, and gender conformism. And it is under the pretext of the norms established by society that we, with all our physical and mental diversity, are excluded. We internalise society's ableism and have difficulty recognising and defining our own disability identities. Our collective seeks not only to challenge society's ableism but also to build ways for us to celebrate ourselves.

Alyona Lyovina
Coordinator and Co-Founder of the Women. Disability. Feminism. Collective
With Philippa Mullins

'Pretending to be disabled' by Maria Tselovatova

I'm 20 years old, and I'm a disabled woman [*invalidka*]. On my 'pink certificate',[1] under 'reason for disability', is written 'disabled from childhood'. That means that, before I was 18, I was a disabled child. Realising that is really strange. In early childhood, I basically didn't understand that I was a disabled child. Or rather, that the disabled child was me. I even asked my mum once when I was around five. We were buying tickets: 'Two adults and one disabled child, please!' I asked, 'Who's that?' Mum answered, 'No one', and I shrugged my shoulders and forgot about it.

In my early childhood, the word 'disabled' was strange and definitely had nothing to do with me. What was mine were glasses and the yellow *Agusha* nourishing kids' food I had for breakfast for years. Yes, I had benefits for the metro and buses, and my parents got some money because I 'don't see well', and what? Disabled people are other people, not me.

This text is not so much an attempt to document my experience of disability since childhood (although, inevitably, it's that too). Rather, it's an attempt to understand how it was possible to be born and grow up in Moscow, in a family I can't really call poor, with loving parents who had no addictions and yet to still live with a disabling illness for almost ten years without receiving any medical help. Not even painkillers. It's an attempt to understand why now, at 20, although I can talk about stigma, about learned helplessness, putting yourself down, and the lack of information about rheumatological diseases, I nonetheless still find it hard to call myself 'disabled'. And it's an attempt to talk about my disabilities – both of them.

My first disability is that 'I've seen badly since birth'. Cataracts, operations during childhood, astigmatism, one seeing eye, and it's minus eight. My parents don't let me read in bed, I go to the hospital twice a year. B6 vitamin injections in the backside and under my eyes, 'Don't fidget and look up'; they hold my head and praise me if I don't cry. But that's not traumatic – it's normal. Yes, not everyone has to do these things, but that was not obvious to me then. In the special kindergarten for children with visual impairments, there's only one girl without glasses, and everyone has a special pocket for glasses in their locker. An inclusive environment! Glasses are natural, almost a part of my body. A removable part, but something that's mine.

I didn't even think about whether my vision was 'normal'. I didn't have any other experience to compare with. Or to miss. You can't lose something you've never had. I thought of myself as healthy and strong – just with glasses. My first disability didn't stop me from being who I wanted to be.

My first childhood disability was not a trauma. It was natural. In the social sense, I was not disabled. And physically too – I had no limitations, no problems with functionality and my acceptance of my body. In fact, I had a feeling of my own strength.

A happy six-year-old, my identity back then was Pippi Longstocking, the strongest girl in the world.[2] Morning exercises, 20 press-ups a minute, biking, skiing, and my legs always covered in bruises from running around carelessly. I swing from trees; play pirates; dream of being an astronaut, an archaeologist, or a captain of a long-distance seafaring vessel. I read books.

The entire world is open to me. And I, a book-reading pirate girl, would see everything that I'd read about. What could get in the way?

When I was 12, my state disability registration for my vision was taken away – after an intraocular lens implant which hardly even worked for my side vision, my eye started to see a tiny bit better with exactly that side vision. And, for the disability commission, that was enough.

My dad was annoyed, but I didn't care at all.

My first childhood disability was *Agusha* kids' milk, a little cloth case for my glasses, and a happy childhood. I didn't notice my first disability.

My second childhood disability was incurable disabling arthritis at seven years old. And then eight years without therapy and without any disability registration. Absurd? Yes. As if my second childhood disability just didn't exist.

It's just some kind of mistake, a stupid accident on a slide in winter. A hot swollen knee on the eighth of March, the ambulance, Morozovskaya Hospital, the first time staying in there without my Mum. Not even having the time to understand that I'm being taken off to the ward and then that my Mum isn't going to be allowed in there afterwards. The surgical ward: high ceilings, stone walls, and at night, behind those walls, a groaning guy with an open fracture. There are no visitors allowed over the May holidays; nothing is explained; everything is quick, frightening, incomprehensible, like a disaster. For traumatology, it was a simple case: puncture, pump out the liquid, and put the inflamed joint in a cast. For a week. That wasn't the right thing to do when it was actually arthritis, but who knew that then?

My second childhood disability is that frozen week in Year One[3] with a hot, pulsing knee in a cast, unbending and strange. The impossibility of walking. And fear. My working body had broken; it was some mistake. Everything will heal back together and be like before. But it never did.

It is the diagnosis, finally given to me at the Rheumatology Research Institute: juvenile rheumatoid arthritis (JRA). At the time, only three joints in my right leg were affected. The crutches they gave me rubbed my armpits; it was uncomfortable to drag my leg along. In 2006, rheumatology was helpless: the only treatment was methotrexate and hormones taken orally and injected into the joints. Autoimmune diseases meant no exact cause had been worked out, and there was no definitive cure. It was an indiscriminate attack by the immune system on its own cells. And the treatment involved strong immune suppression via hormones and an immunosuppressant (methotrexate) to delay the self-destruction. A hopeless children's ward at Kashirka. Moon-faced children on hormones (that one looks like she's five, but actually, she's 16) who explain to each other, 'We can't get better; we can only go into remission'. And my mum is afraid. You'll have this your whole life, hormones are scary, and methotrexate is used to treat cancer. No explanations from the doctor or my mum, who 'couldn't get on with the doctor' – maybe we can manage without these radical measures, Masha? I was discharged back home without treatment, left to warm my knee at the seaside. With exercises and Voltarol, the joint got better. Everything will be fine.

My second childhood disability is when it wasn't fine. My knee didn't go back to how it was before. It's when you understand that nothing is going to be like it was before. I absorbed my mother's fear and mistrust towards rheumatology. And that led to many lost years without therapy and without control. Watching how, a few years after my knee, joint after joint became affected: fingers, hands, elbows, neck. And nothing can be done. Contractures in my fingers, gradual restriction in their movement. When your joints don't particularly bend or straighten, things that were simple before – like sitting with your cheek resting on your hand – become impossible. The strongest girl in the world will never be able to do press-ups again because her hands don't straighten out anymore.

I still don't believe it. Still today, I remember very clearly my 'real', healthy body before all this, and I always forget that my body has become different. A rheumatoid stiffness that no one can see. You look and see a normal human hand, but you feel Davey Jones's scraping claw. And a sharp, aching pain. And others just see you.

My second childhood disability is that silent grating. But my mum pins her hopes on puberty and hormonal changes. She doesn't go to the rheumatologist (what good would that do?), but she does read internet forums. In her eyes, arthritis is not just an illness, but a kind of hopeless condition, a punishment from God. Still, it's also something you need to fight, rowing against the current, doing your exercises, and not giving up.

You can still pray too. Mum either cried or shamed me for my weakness and printed out quotes from the internet from some men who 'saved themselves by constantly massaging their joints!' And Dad, it seems, just didn't notice that I was ill. Movement is life, Masha, and you're being lazy. You're not doing your exercises. It's your fault.

My second childhood disability is my parents psychologically protecting themselves and my feelings of guilt and shame.

I kept on going to music school and playing the violin despite the pain – after all, I'd been playing since I was six! At some point, positioning my hand correctly became entirely impossible for me. I'd play, and it was like my wrists were breaking. A silent cracking. Everyone understood what was happening; they gave me an easier programme to play, suggested that I pass the graduation exams 'somehow'. I sobbed in the office and refused out of pride. I sobbed from stubbornness inflamed by years of despair: you can't admit that you're ill. At graduation, I didn't play the programme all the way through like everyone else. Instead, I played some parts, alternating with my best friend. My hand couldn't hold out much longer.

I don't want that to inspire you. Because it shouldn't be like that. I lived in a world where pain in the name of art was romanticised: ground glass in Paganini's shoes, Renoir painting with arthritic hands with brushes tied to them, Beethoven not hearing his Ninth Symphony, Mozart dying while writing his Requiem. I was impressionable, soaking up these stories and believing that my silent suffering somehow linked me to the Great World of Art. I wrote blank verse, played Vivaldi, and endured the pain.

Now I'd like to return to the past, shake myself, and say, 'No one should have to endure pain'. That would have helped me so much later on. But I can't return. And, at 14, it was my spine. And that was when I understood that everything that had come before that wasn't pain.

Now, this was pain.

It wasn't hell right away. At first, it was the occasional shooting pain under my shoulder blade in the mornings. And then every morning. Then it wasn't only under the shoulder blade. Then you look for a position to sleep in without pain. And there are no comfortable positions left at all. Then you wake up from the pain one hour before the alarm clock, at five a.m. And then it's impossible to sit for longer than five minutes. Then it's hard to stand. And then pain tears through you at any careless movement. The mornings were a special kind of torture – it took me an hour to get to school, all the while feeling the smallest jolts and jerks of the jammed traffic. As though a red-hot poker had been stuck in your back and was being slowly twisted. As though you are a sack of bones, stretched nerves, and fibres, and you're being shaken and shaken and everything inside you is straining, tearing, burning.

That whole time, I didn't even take painkillers. It didn't even occur to anyone. Taking tablets just somehow wasn't done in my family.

My second disability is learned helplessness after a pain syndrome which lasted for years. Three years of hellish pain in the back – and I didn't try to help myself. Despair, fatalism, believing that I deserved the pain. A lack of belief in medicine. Fatigue: well, yes, arthritic hands, then my neck, now the back, well, OK then. How could it be any different? You very quickly forget that life can be without this constant pain. The pain is numbing.

Every morning I looked up at the ceiling and thought, *So, this is how it's going to be. Forever.*

My second childhood disability is *Howl's Moving Castle* in reverse.[4] Outwardly, I looked like a girl, but really I was a wreck. And even though it happened gradually, over eight long years, I still didn't get used to it – instead, it was as if my body had been switched for a different one overnight.

I almost stopped studying. During lessons, I couldn't concentrate from the pain of sitting down; at home, I lay down on my back and didn't get up for hours. It was the only pose in which the pain was at least a little bearable. On account of my reputation as a 'clever, capable girl', how much I'd read, and my ability to talk my way out of things, I was forgiven a lot. I managed to negotiate a 'partial exception' with our PE[5] teacher: at those lessons, instead of taking part, I studied paragraphs from the PE textbook.

My second childhood disability is those double PE lessons on a bench. The bench was low, and my back hurt like hell; basketballs from my classmates would fly towards me. I'd sit with the textbook, hunched over, my hair draped over my face and covering my glasses with my hands so that they didn't get smashed. And I'd pray that a ball wouldn't break my wrist. The iron rule of the violinist, ingrained in me since childhood: take care of your hands!

I sat there and couldn't understand it: how had I turned from the strongest girl in the world to a crooked Severus Snape who couldn't take a step without pain? As you might expect, my glasses, my curved back, my heightened sense of justice, and my general 'strangeness' (now I understand that it was my gender non-conformity) made me a target of bullying in the class. I wanted my classmates to stop mocking me. I wanted to stop being such a freak. I wanted to have back again the body which had been taken away from me. I used to sign my own diary 'Crippled Thing', and I hated my own glassy vulnerability. I hated my weakness and my body more and more. I developed body dysphoria.

I felt like (and actually was) a disabled person in my daily life. In the mornings, I couldn't bend to put on my socks, and I'd ask my mum to do it. Every morning. To put my socks on. At 15. And even when I was really disabled [*invalidizirovana*] (as in, I could not do these tasks for myself anymore), I was not officially disabled. My parents didn't even try to apply to the commission to get me disability status. It just didn't occur to them!

I don't know how much longer that would have all lasted if it hadn't been for one thing. I was 15, and I had stabbing pains in my chest. I was taken from the cardiologist to the neurologist, with all of them clicking their tongues: 'Terrible curvature, terrible scoliosis, why don't you exercise, are you sick with something?' I muttered, 'Arthritis'.

And then somehow everyone in the clinic was in an uproar, up in arms: 'What, how is that possible; she's been ill for eight years'. They told my father off: 'You've not been having her treated; it's a serious illness!' By that moment, I was so stupefied from the pain that I didn't even understand what the noise was about. Well, arthritis, yeah. Referral back to the Research Institute and, through friends of friends, I end up seeing the new doctor. And, for some reason, she's really shocked, gets angry with my mum, and prescribes that I be hospitalised right away.

My second childhood disability is a 'neglected case'.

By the time I was hospitalised, I was living 24/7 with constant shooting pain in my back, unbending arms and neck. I was afraid to the point of paranoia of ending up hooked on the treatment, afraid of the Research Institute, afraid of the treatment, and afraid of recognising the fact that I was actually ill and that it wouldn't all just pass from my own willpower and stubbornness. I arrived at the in-patients unit with *One Flew Over the Cuckoo's Nest*, a music player with hard rock, and a rucksack full of scepticism. I walked through the ward in black jeans, with my hands stuck deep in my pockets and sneering at all the personnel, like R. P. McMurphy. I wasn't planning on giving up.

When the doctor prescribed me an anti-inflammatory painkiller (it was quite a strong NSAID), it was the first time in three years that I stopped feeling pain. I swallowed down the tablets morning and night, immediately hooked on them. In the endless corridor of the research institution at Kashirka, I unfold myself and run again – without pain, panting from the forgotten speed. Ecstasy. Better than flying.

Each morning, I did my exercises again – on the ward, listening to AC/DC. I still naively believed that, through some titanic effort, I could overcome everything by myself and not 'become disabled'. I still hadn't understood that I had already been disabled for a long time.

The examination ('Oh my God, but why has this girl not been to see us for so long? It's been terribly neglected') confirmed the diagnosis. Juvenile rheumatoid arthritis, polyarticular already – meaning it affected many joints. I resisted both the diagnosis and the prescribed treatment (Methotrexate) as much as I could, sobbing and freaking out. I'm still amazed at the angelic patience of my doctor, who stayed on in the ward after work to calm me down. Her attentiveness saved me – she worked out what had been going on with my spine. It was a tumour.

Benign, of course – otherwise, over those three years, I would already have been long gone. But everyone was scared anyway: the oncologist examined me, there was a panicked search for moles, and an urgent MRI. It was impossible to prescribe anything more (Methotrexate had side effects on the liver); I was discharged to surgery.

It still hurts that, because of my doomed certainty that it was arthritis (well, what else could it have been?), I lived with pain for so long.

And it turned out that my stoical pride was meaningless! My hellish curvature, shooting pains, neuralgia, depression from my constant back pain – all of it could have ended earlier. I still get angry when I think about it.

At the children's surgery ward at Polyanka, a cheerful young doctor cut out the osteoblastoma and sent me home. He told me, 'That's all done; you can live like you did before'. Without rehabilitation and without further observation. For him, I could get up and walk – and my pain and the feeling that my spine is lying on a brick, well, that's nothing; other people are far worse off. I sincerely hate the chuckles of the male doctors – they may think it cheers people up, but they are the only ones with that opinion. After being discharged and at the insistence of my doctor from the Research Institute, I still wore a corset.

My second childhood disability is hope. Rheumatology in 2014 is not the same as in 2006. In the eight years I had been desperately avoiding doctors, Russia had started using genetically engineered biological drugs, which suppress your immune system selectively and have fewer side effects. As I was lucky enough to be born in Moscow, I got those drugs with my compulsory health insurance as 'hi-tech medical support'. This wasn't the case for others, especially people who hadn't managed to pass the disability commission, who needed to raise incredible sums of money to get the drugs. Over my two inpatient hospitalisations at the Research Institution, I was prescribed treatment for juvenile rheumatoid arthritis – an infusion once a month – and the state of my joints improved. But my spine, which was not at all arthritic, didn't. That was my 'post-operative state'.

I had several compressed nerve endings – a sharp, burning pain, shivering, sweating, my vision blacking out, you fall over in the train in the morning. And a constant dull pain. My doctor at the Research Institution, who was the only one who cared about my spine, insisted on another MRI a year later. I'd relapsed.

The tumour had regrown and was even bigger than before. It was the same operation again, with the same surgeon – and the second time, it was hell. It wasn't just that I couldn't walk – I couldn't breathe without pain. A year before my school-leaving exams, I learned to stand again. My first two attempts had ended with my vision blacking out and me fainting. And my mum was so afraid that she got angry with me for it. I remember, I was falling down and she was almost shouting, 'Stop doing that!'

My second disability is the shock of pain.

And the grandmother of the person next to me on the ward, who started asking me if everything in my family was all right, if my parents hadn't sinned? Because, you know, this kind of problem with your spine – that's definitely a punishment from God. I was 17 years old, and I already knew that I was a lesbian. It really, really hurt me to laugh, but I couldn't hold it in.

I started getting treatment when I was 16 and, at the same time, was seen by the disability commission, now with rheumatoid arthritis as my main illness. After that, I had to prove my disability every year. And, every time, it's quite humiliating because the commission, contrary to common belief, doesn't consider a person's overall condition but rather the state of the 'main illness'. So, they don't consider my vision or my spine. And if the state of rheumatoid arthritis improves, then you lose your registration as disabled.

And this is already worth laughing at because, without registered disability status, a woman with a rheumatological illness doesn't get treatment. And then, without treatment, everything will quickly start getting worse again! And then, of course, she'll need to go back to the commission. 'When you're doubled up with arthritis, then come back'. In my case, the officials said twice that my illness 'isn't, of course, a disability' (although that's not true), but that they will count the operations. When I turned 18, I was registered in the third disability group[6] and as 'disabled since childhood'. And still, I can't even change the 'main illness' I'm considered for with the committee – the ophthalmologist said that with my vision, even without arthritis, I would be able to be registered as disabled. But checking that with the commission is risky.

Now I'm 20. When I say that I've been disabled since childhood, I feel a dissonance. I'm uncomfortable with the term 'disabled woman' [*invalidka*] and with the fact of my disability. It's like I know it about myself but don't entirely recognise it. I get disability benefits, I show my pink certificate at stations, I get some reduced prices. But each time, I feel like I'm cheating someone and that I could be found out at any moment. That I'm actually fine, that I've made it all up, and I'm not at all 'disabled since childhood'. That I just didn't try hard enough.

And my brain divides my disability off from my identity. I'm not 'a disabled woman'; I'm a 'woman with disabilities' – like somehow disability is something that I'm carrying around because it just happened to find its way into my pocket. Like in my childhood – seems like I'm healthy but seems like I keep getting given nourishing *Agusha* milk too. And I have to remind myself that I've not been 'healthy' for a very long time.

Just like I have to constantly stave off the feeling that my real body has just been left somewhere else. And this broken, bent, incomprehensible body I have now isn't me; it's someone else.

I have learned to live with it. I know how to lie down so that it doesn't hurt, I know how to walk so that it doesn't hurt – but it's like I'm being moved around in space, not like I'm moving by myself.

Today, my disability is linked to a rheumatoid illness and a pathology of the spine. That means people's constant ageist denial and them shrugging off my diagnoses. Because only old people have arthritis, that's their age, but you're young, so where do you fit in? When I hear that, I get furious. First of all, because this association of youth with health irritates me. My youth is disability and pain, so that means that something went wrong, right?

Secondly, it frustrates me because it's exactly because of attitudes like that that it took me so many years to stop running away from help and recognize my own disability. So many lost years. And I still now feel like I'm not a 'real' disabled person. Calling myself a 'disabled woman' [*invalidka*] is even more complicated for me – it's harsh and sounds like 'freak lady' [*urodka*]; it's always like that with these words specifically for women [*feminitivy*]. Especially if it's only the second year that you're gradually working out your body dysphoria and accepting yourself as a gender non-conforming woman. 'Disabled woman'. At the words, all the same shame washes over me for some reason.

A fake disabled woman since childhood – it's not a great identity. I look conventionally 'healthy' – the contractures in my fingers aren't visible unless you look closely, and you won't notice my limited movement because I've already gotten used to it and just don't do what I can't do. The invisibility of my disability angers me because I have to prove it's there every time that I need help.

To nurses at the clinic, conductors on public transport, people working in shops.

And then I also need to manage their emotional reactions, 'Ah, how did that happen?' or 'Yeah, you're just making it up'. I really hate that. Sometimes I even refuse the discounts and adjustments I'm entitled to – it's easier to do that than it is to prove and explain that I am entitled to them. For example, I passed my school-leaving exams like everyone else, even though I had to sit through my pain, and I couldn't see any of the instructions on the board – just because I didn't want to go the exam separately or to bother people to take me there. And because I felt awkward and ashamed about it, yes. About being a disabled woman and being 'special'.

But I could have had an extra hour for the exam – I knew people who would have sold their souls for that time. After 18, getting medical help got a lot harder – I had been warned about it, but all the same, I wasn't ready for it. My spine problems led to GI disorders and to urological and gynaecological problems. I'm not receiving treatment for my arthritis at the moment because, at the Research Institute, they suggested 'dealing with the spine' first and sent me to neurologists. But the neurologists think that my spine is 'still good, you see how much worse it could be'. Even though it's been such a long time that I don't remember how it is to be without back pain, how it is to be able to squat down on my heels and bend over to pick up fallen pens. I can't prove anything to anyone.

Now I'm on academic leave, after finishing, in this condition, two years of a course at the Philological Faculty of the Russian State University for the Humanities, where I really wanted to go. On leave because, at a certain point, I realised that I can't do this anymore. I don't have the resources to break apart this vicious cycle.

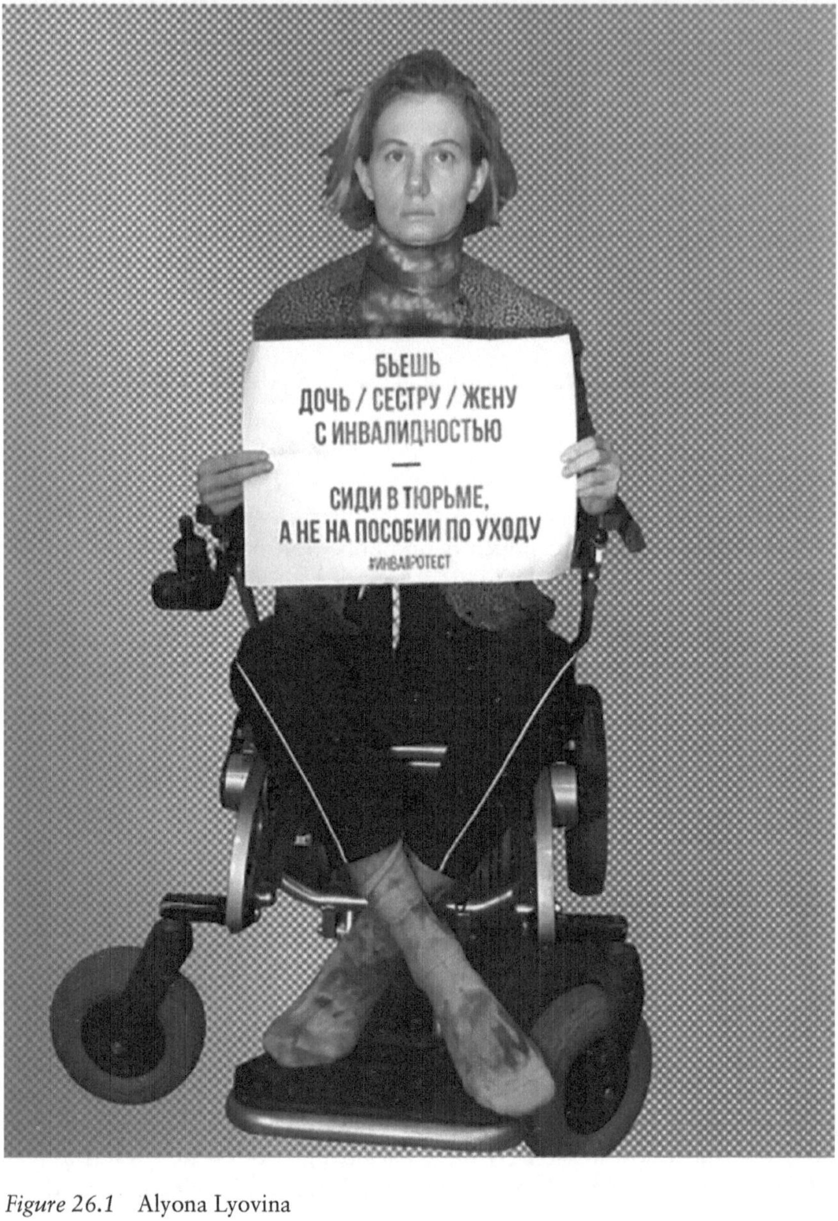

Figure 26.1 Alyona Lyovina

Constant pain in my spine and neuralgia mean depression, and compressed nerve endings mean painful sex. Yes, they do. Yes, my first association with that word is pain. At first it was something unexpected for me and my girlfriend, and then it became a sad everyday reality. Most things lesbians do are either difficult or painful for me. I walk down the streets and envy the people around me.

Figure 26.2 Maria Tselovatova

They jump, run, stretch, embrace, and sit on the grass with their legs stretched out. They aren't in pain. They don't even think about it. And I walk and feel like I'm the Tin Man who hasn't been oiled and has rusted.

Can you hear that scraping noise? It's me, walking.

Maria Tselovatova
Member of the Women. Disability. Feminism. Collective
Translated by Philippa Mullins

Notes

1 In Russia, the certificate which states that you are registered as disabled is pink. NB: Footnotes throughout Tselovatova's text are not the author's. Rather, they are additions made to the translated text.

2 Pippi Longstocking is a character from a series of children's books written by Astrid Lindgren. Widely translated, the books tell the story of Pippi Longstocking, an adventurous red-headed girl who lives independently with her monkey and horse. She is strong enough to lift that horse with one hand.

3 The school year is given as per the Russian system. In this school year, pupils are usually from seven to eight years old.
4 *Howl's Moving Castle* is a film produced by Studio Ghibli and directed by Hayao Miyazaki. In the film, the moving castle looks like a wreck but is, in fact, magical. The main character, Sophie, is a young woman transformed by enchantment into an elderly woman.
5 Physical education.
6 The Russian system of registering people as disabled categorises them into three groups, based on a medical-productivist understanding of disability related to perceived loss of physical and labour capacity. Broadly speaking, the first group is for those defined as unable to work and in need of constant care. The second group is for those defined as unable to work and in need of significant though not constant care. The third group is for people defined as maintaining some capacity to work irregularly, with a shortened working day, or in a different profession from any previously held (Phillips, 2009). Disabled children [*deti-invalidy*] are a further category, separate from the three categories for adults (ibid.).

References

Phillips, S. D. (2009). There are no invalids in the USSR. A missing Soviet chapter in the new disability history. *Disability Studies Quarterly*, *29*(3), 1–33. Retrieved from https://dsq-sds.org/article/view/936/1111 (accessed: 30.05.2021).

27

TWO SIDES OF THE SAME COIN

Domination of the views of the educated in organisations of the blind in Ghana

Alimata Abdul Karimu

Introduction

Over centuries, human beings have been forming groups to advance common interests that have brought about desired changes in their societies. Groups of persons who have long organised at the national, regional and international levels to challenge discrimination and cultural prejudice and promote their human rights prominently have included women and persons with disabilities. Women's organising has led to the enactment of international frameworks and conventions to push for gender equality and equity. In addition, the organising of persons with disabilities led to the formulation of the Convention on the Rights of Persons with Disabilities in 2006 and the inclusion of substantial issues affecting persons with disabilities in the Sustainable Development Goals in 2015, the establishment of the Secretariat of the African Decade for Persons with Disabilities to implement and monitor the Decades of Persons with Disabilities in Africa and the formation of the European Disability Forum to uphold the interests of persons with disabilities across Europe, among others.

In 1963, a number of blind and partially sighted persons came together to form one of the first representative groups for persons with disabilities in Ghana, then known as the Ghana Association of the Blind. The leadership and top positions of this organisation were largely occupied by those with very formal education or who could speak well in English for most of its existence since its core mandate was to advocate. It is argued that attending meetings to advocate and lobby policy makers and the government requires one to be fluent in English, the *lingua franca* of Ghana. Therefore, those with a formal education or English-language skills have been preferred over those without to occupy certain leadership positions, and the current Constitution of the Ghana Blind Union also mandates that their general assembly be held in English.

DOI: 10.4324/9781003410089-32

This chapter discusses in brief the background and history of blindness organising in Ghana. Three institutions that specialised in blindness service delivery are critically analysed: the Ghana Society for the Blind, the Ghana Association of the Blind, and the Ghana Blind Union.

The chapter analyses how hierarchy and privilege have enabled those who can speak English well to dominate leadership positions in the Ghana Blind Union and discusses how this preference has perpetuated the exclusion of the needs and interests of those who cannot speak English in advocacy.

Organisations for and of the blind

The mobilisation of disabled people into their representative organisations in Ghana did not start until the 1960s, when the associations of the blind and, subsequently, the deaf started. However, there was in existence a school for the blind in Akropong-Akwapem around 1945, which was responsible for the education of the vision impaired (Wilson, 1960), and later, rehabilitation centres in various parts of the country trained persons with disabilities and other young persons in various trades (Grischow, 2011). In addition to the school for the blind and the rehabilitation centres, there was a service organisation which began as a committee headed by Sir Henry Cousley. This committee was solely devoted to the welfare of the blind in the Gold Coast, colonial Ghana (Wilson, 1960). According to Wilson, this committee evolved and was incorporated in 1951 under the name the Gold Coast Society for the Blind.

The World Blind Union's Institutional Development Programme (IDP) categorises institutions or organisations that provide services for blind and partially sighted persons into two distinct forms: service organisations or membership organisations (Webson, 1997). Service organisations are normally managed by persons who are not blind but could have a few blind persons working there, with the organisation's core mandate to provide services and certain activities for the blind. They tend to include the word 'for', as in the Gold Coast Society for the Blind. Membership organisations, however, are those blindness organisations founded by persons who are blind, predominantly directed and occupied by them, and may have branches or a presence all over a country. In these types of organisations, persons who are blind or visually impaired are the board members and further occupy key and salient positions in the day-to-day operations of the organisation. In some situations, there may be one or two persons without blindness who may be co-opted as ex-officio members. Membership organisations mainly include the word 'of': for example, the Ghana Association of the Blind. Hence the phrases 'for the blind' and 'of the blind', respectively (Webson, 1997).

Similarly, in order to distinguish between disability organisations operating in the British disability landscape, Oliver (1984, 1990) distinguished between organisations that are 'for' and 'of'. In the organisations 'for' the disabled, persons without disabilities work on behalf of the disabled, while persons with disabilities themselves run the organisations 'of'. Oliver's classification was based on the type of approach the organisations employed to engage or on functions. For instance, organisations with their focus on partnership might collaborate with government, and those employing the populist approach were the ones with disabled persons themselves in charge.

In both the Webson distinction of blindness organisations and the Oliver classification of disability organisations, a key distinctive feature is the use of the prepositions 'for' and 'of' to indicate the type of organisational engagement. Another distinguishing feature of all these forms of organisations is whether 1) the persons doing the organising are doing on behalf of or representing others, or 2) the organisers are organising to represent themselves. Basically, organisations for the blind can be described as service-delivery or development-oriented organisations, while organisations of the blind are self-organising, advocacy and action-oriented, and provide some services for members. So, while the Gold Coast Society for the Blind was providing services for blind and partially sighted persons from the 1950s, the Ghana Association of the Blind also started speaking and advocating for the blind in the 1960s and became their mouthpiece. I will be discussing these organisations in significant details in the ensuing sections.

Background to the formation of the Ghana Association of the Blind

The then–Gold Coast Society for the Blind, which was a branch of the Royal Commonwealth Society for the Blind (now Sightsavers International), provided charity and welfare assistance to blind and partially sighted persons across the country. Among some of the earliest programmes designed for the society's clientele included Welfare Assistance for the Blind, in which the society's workers visited blind and partially sighted persons in their homes to give them provisions and toiletries, assisted with cleaning and book reading and offered counseling services (GSB 50th Anniversary Brochure, 2001). A vocational training centre was opened in 1954, where trainees were introduced to handicraft making to enable them make items like cane baskets, corn husk and seagrass doormats, straw hats and mats, cane baskets and other handmade things to generally occupy them.

These items were sold in various markets. Wilson reports that similar centres were functioning in Kenya, Nigeria, Uganda, modern-day Malawi, Tanzania and other parts of the British Empire (1960).

As time went on and the society secured office space and accommodation facilities, a residential programme was started in Accra within the current rehabilitation centre premises. This programme expanded the scope of training to include daily living skills, orientation and mobility, a vocational training scheme in which clients received training in palm oil and kernel seed oil extraction, shea nut oil production, crop farming, vegetable gardening and animal husbandry in addition to the craft making, along with other recreational activities (GSB 50th Anniversary Brochure, 2001).

Figure 27.1 Waste paper basket

In order to streamline all rehabilitation services in the country, in 1961, Kwame Nkrumah's government pulled all disability organisations operating as non-governmental entities into the state system or what was referred to as the 'corporatist structure of the Nkrumahist state' (Grischow, 2011). This corporatist system enabled Ghana's rehabilitation programme to transform disability

Figure 27.2 Hamper basket

from a charitable and private issue into a political one (Grischow, 2011). As a consequence of this restructuring and the Gold Coast gaining independence from the British, it became imperative for the Gold Coast Society for the Blind to be re-registered by the Trustee's (Incorporation) Act 106 of Parliament. Its name was therefore changed to the Ghana Society for the Blind (GSB) to reflect the country's independent status (GSB 50th Anniversary Brochure, 2001).

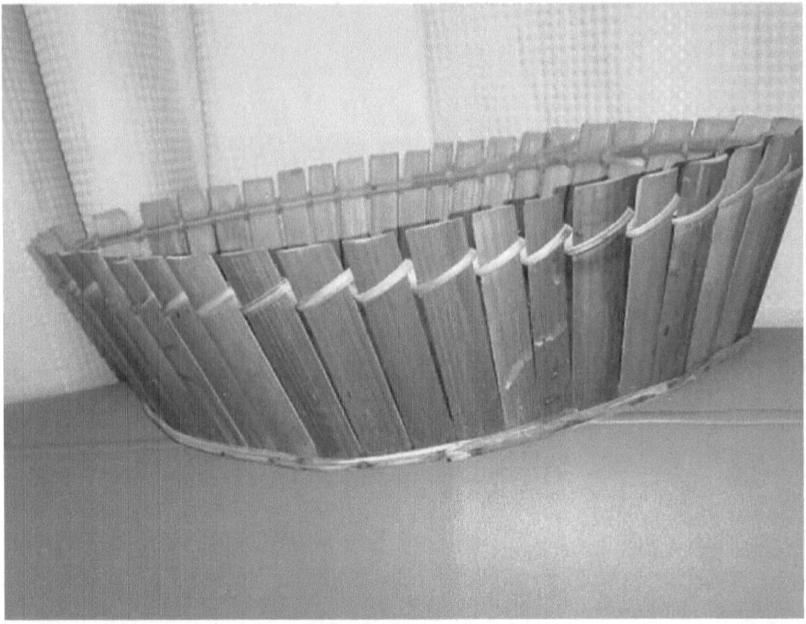

Figure 27.3 Large bamboo hamper basket

Figure 27.4 Seagrass doormat

Figure 27.5 A picture showing samples of the handicrafts mentioned in this section

Source: The Akropong School for the Blind Vocational Centre and a visually impaired craft instructor

The GSB employed the sheltered workshop concept to train blind and visually impaired persons for a productive life. One of the earliest documented sheltered employment workshops was the Perkins Institute for the Blind in 1840 (Armstrong, 2011). Sheltered employment is a setting in which persons with disabilities receive training to develop work-related skills and behaviours (Armstrong, 2011).

The purpose of the GSB sheltered workshops was to give blind and partially sighted persons the opportunity to operate or participate in a work setting and experience work environments and to engender the feeling of dignity and fulfilment. It is not very clear what kinds of work or tasks the blind and partially sighted persons in the GSB's sheltered workshop were doing, but Visier (1998), Miglioire (2010) and May-Simera (2018) assert that generally, work in sheltered centres has included assembling, packing, sewing, woodwork, clerical activities, and servicing, among others.

The long stays in sheltered work centres gave the blind and partially sighted workers a sense of solidarity and collective identity that might have led to introspection and critical thinking about their position and role in society as well as the role of the service provider, GSB. Even though blind and partially sighted persons benefited from and actively patronised the services and support provided to them by the GSB, some of them did not appreciate the paternalistic approach to their disability and service provision (K. Amankra, personal conversation, February 27, 2021). Given that the adult blind (those who became blind later in life) had experienced the non-disabled world – e.g. led a barrier-free life and had independent choices, employment and full family involvement, among other things – before their disabling condition, they felt the paternalistic approach of the GSB in service delivery and care was disempowering and stripped them of their autonomy (K. Amankra, personal conversation, February 27, 2021). Amankra indicated this stoked a bit of dislike among a segment of the blind and partially sighted community for the GSB. Aside from these, a number of national and international events might have propelled blind and partially sighted persons of the day to actually want to detach themselves from the society.

First, Ghana's independence from the British set the tone in the minds of blind and partially sighted persons who felt ruled that they needed to have more say on issues affecting them. Second, Kwame Nkrumah's rehabilitation programme in the 1960s was aimed at making persons with disabilities responsible and productive citizens instead of offering them charity, which was quite transformative at the time, and considering that the origins of sheltered work had antecedents in religious or medical institutions and was therefore characterised by charity and medical care (May-Simera, 2018), sheltered workshops became incompatible with the notions of the day. Consequently, blind and partially sighted persons in Ghana then had an urge to push for greater autonomy over their life course.

Probably drawing inspiration from these and other international demonstrations that led to the formations of disabled people's organisations in the 1960s and 70s globally, blind and partially sighted persons in Ghana demanded greater autonomy on issues directly affecting them, which led to a seismic shift in disability organising in Ghana.

So, in a GSB sheltered work centre in 1963 at Mangoase in the eastern region of Ghana, the blind and partially sighted participants of that workshop objected to the domination of the GSB in deciding their life course and demanded to take a lead role in issues affecting them. Those persons wanted to advocate for the rights of blind and partially sighted persons as well as speak for themselves. They formed a highly enthusiastic and energised group called the Ghana Association of the Blind (GAB). From the 1960s through to the latter part of the 1980s, the GAB functioned as a pressure group, welding enormous power derived from the multitude of its members and often using the premises of the schools for the blind during long vacations for their meetings (J.K. Lartey, personal conversation, February 17, 2021; T. Fosu, personal conversation, March 10, 2021).

Since the 2000s, the GSB has diversified its programmes to make them more relevant for blind and partially sighted persons as the organisation evolved from being predominantly a welfare and charitable organisation into a development-oriented service institution. In this regard, the programmes implemented were restructured and new ones introduced. The new programmes included educational support to schools and sponsorship of individuals; computer literacy, information and communication technology training; livelihood and skills training; community-based rehabilitation services; advocacy and resource mobilisation (GSB 50th Anniversary Brochure, 2001).

However, neither GSB nor GAB exist today in their original forms. In 2010, GSB and GAB merged into an organisation now known as the Ghana Blind Union (GBU). According to the boards of GSB and GAB, the coming together of the two bodies was deemed necessary in order to 'serve blind persons better'. The merger, however, did not discard the structure and practices of GAB which are of relevance to this chapter. In view of this, I will be using GAB and GBU interchangeably. But in order to be fair to history, I will refer to the organisation as GAB when referring the past and GBU for the present. Another important point I need to make is that as a result of the merger, the national executive council (NEC) of GBU, consisting of 19 persons with voting rights, must be composed of 51% blind and partially sighted persons (GBU Constitution). The national executive council comprises the president, who must be blind/partially sighted; a first vice president, who shall be sighted; and a blind/partially sighted woman as second vice president. Additionally, there are five elected zonal representatives who are also blind/partially sighted, representative each from the women's and youth wings, seven elected sighted persons, the executive director (who is an ex-officio member and also blind) and a co-opted member.

The GBU is structured based on the following: a general assembly, a national executive council (NEC), zonal councils, regional executive councils and district executive committees (GBU Constitution). There is also a small group known as the steering committee that deals with urgent matters that cannot wait till NEC meetings. But this committee is yet to be included in the constitution.

The years of empowerment, advocacy and development partners

Despite the foundational gains of the colonial government in advancing the lives of people who are blind or partially sighted and the progress Kwame Nkrumah's government chalked up in developing rehabilitation services for persons with disabilities, people with disabilities experienced restrictions to their inclusion and participation and faced barriers that marginalised and excluded them from fully contributing to mainstream society and economic activities. Therefore, the advent of GAB in 1963 heralded a paradigm shift to specifically highlight blindness issues in Ghana through advocacy to change negative perceptions and stereotypes about blindness and people with disabilities. However, the Ghana Association of the Blind did not develop a coherent advocacy strategy or have a good understanding of the shift in disability thinking until after the 1980s. There was also confusion on the roles of the GSB and GAB, which made the latter very antagonistic to the former since GAB members felt the GSB was usurping its role (K. Halm & S. Ampedu, personal conversation, October 16, 2019). Initially, too, GAB was not providing blindness services and therefore was not officially recognised as the mouthpiece and advocate of blind and partially sighted persons because it lacked funding and was basically viewed as a 'social club' (Webson, 1997). Webson asserts that membership organisations then generally operated in the shadows of service organisations since they could not be financially and materially independent (p. 52). So the advent of development partners was pertinent because they also came in with international funding. The development partners enabled the association to develop its human and material resources to better represent the voice of the blind and partially sighted persons in Ghana as well as securing funding to erect a structure for offices and guest quarters, which also served as the secretariat. Prominent among these development partners are the Institutional Development Programme (IDP) of the World Blind Union and the Danish Association of the Blind (DAB).

Together, they funded GAB's capacity development, Wings (women, youth and sports) and organisational development, community-based rehabilitation (CBR) programmes and advocacy and empowerment drives, among others. I tend to refer to that era as the "years of IDP and DAB" since those were the years that saw GAB build its capacity to advocate and better represent its constituents and strengthened its organisational structure. The financial, material and human resource support that came through the international donor funding enabled GAB to become the most dominant and vibrant organisation in Ghana not only for blindness-related issues but also for all disability issues. Aside from these, GAB became financially sound, member empowered and vocal on blindness issues, as well as earning the envy of other disabled people's organisations. Funding, for example, more than doubled within three years. For instance, Webson reported that between 1992 and 1995, GAB increased its operational budget from $4,425 to $96,920 (1997).

The Ghana Association of the Blind had its mission to advocate for the blind and work for their total integration into society through the development of services in education, rehabilitation and awareness creation and the promotion of the rights of women, youth and children. It was governed by its constitution and organised through the national congress/convention (GAB Strategic Document). GAB had branches in all ten of the regions of Ghana at the time, and members were required to pay fees. Only active and paid-up members were eligible to stand for elections of any sort in the association.

Aside from its core mandate as a pressure group and in order to improve the living conditions of members, GAB also provided various services to members including orientation and mobility training (within the CBR Project), daily living skills, capacity-building programmes and income-generation programmes, among others (Manual for the Community-Based Rehabilitation Project, 2006).

There were also empowerment trainings to equip members with social and executive life skills for advocacy and lobbying. These programmes targeted the grassroots members, who included adult persons with and without education, and the youth, who the organisation wanted to co-opt as potential role models or mentors.

A number of young persons, including myself, were invited into GAB and empowered or trained particularly for these purposes. Those trainings were called empowerment training or workshops. According to Webson (1997), empowerment was the 'raison d'être' (p. 29) of the IDP, which carried this out through 'an educational process' and rolled it out by means of training workshops, follow-up activities, seminars and conferences. The empowerment trainings were aimed at equipping us with personal power and control in order to enable us portray positive image of ourselves and acquire social skills. To this end, the IDP sought to build and develop the capacities of blind and partially sighted persons in self-awareness, self-assurance to cope with blindness, self-confidence to cope with their environment and self-belief (Webson, 1997). Rappaport (1987) asserts that empowerment is aimed at enhancing the possibilities of people taking charge of their own lives while Whitmore further views empowerment as 'an interactive process through which people experience personal and social change, enabling them to take action to achieve influence over the organisations and institutions which affects their lives and the communities in which they live' (1988, p. 13). Lord and Hutchison (1993) also defined empowerment as a means by which individuals achieve increasing control of varied aspects of their lives and become involved in their community with dignity. Additionally, there are three other levels at which empowerment occurs. First is the personal level. This empowerment draws on one's experience of acquiring control and influence in everyday life as well as participating effectively in their community (Keiffer, 1984; Lord & Hutchison, 1993; Webson, 1997). The second is the small or micro group level, at which the result of the group efforts in terms of collective experience, analysis and influence is shared (Presby et al., 1990). The third is known as the whole-group or community level. This requires the distribution of resources and strategies for the enhancement of community control (Labonte, 1989; Lord & Hutchison, 1993).

Of particular relevance to GAB members was the personal level of empowerment, even though Lord and Hutchison indicate that the three levels are very interactive. So in order to influence society's attitude towards us, in addition to ensuring we are involved in our communities with dignity as asserted by Rappaport (1987), Whitmore (1988) and Lord & Hutchison (1993), members of GAB's Women's Wing carried out educational programmes in schools and churches. In these educational programmes, select members spoke to debunk certain myths about vision loss, and those who were Braille literate demonstrated how persons who are blind read and write. These educational programmes and activities were termed 'awareness creation and raising programmes' and occurred at two levels. The first level of awareness creation or raising was for GAB membership and was aimed at empowering us, and the second targeted the general public. These awareness programmes enabled us to tell the story of blindness from our lived perspective, thereby controlling the narrative in addition to painting the image we wanted the public to have of persons who are blind or partially sighted through the demonstration activities.

The avenues of empowering us were through workshops and information-sharing seminars, where experiences of blindness were shared and alternate ways of doing things or adaptations discussed. Attending these workshops and seminars presented us with a tremendous opportunity to link up with other persons with vision-impairment; introduced us to GAB's services, through which we also acquired skills and techniques to cope with blindness; provided information to debunk myths about blindness; and learned and discussed various stereotypes, prejudice and taboos. This process increased our confidence. The base of GAB's empowerment programmes was to make the person with visual-impairment recognise the importance of developing a sense of self-worth, improve their personal skills to live with blindness and acquire skills to access information (Webson, 1997). For instance, Webson puts it better: 'to reach into the body of the blind movement and to touch individuals across the spectrum' (p. 15). Those of us who were 'touched across the spectrum' or personally empowered were expected to be active in GAB and in our various communities since we had gained knowledge on blindness and acquired various skills set. The knowledge and skills in tandem were our springboard for confidence and the human connections we established our source of motivation.

What did the empowered persons use their empowerment for?

Once individuals were empowered, they were expected, irrespective of their educational level, to participate meaningfully in GAB directly through holding leadership positions or occasionally contributing to advocacy programmes and lobbying activities. Some of the key advocacy activities of the GAB have been through its Women's Wing projects. For instance, in order to create and raise awareness of the cultural taboos and negative stereotypes that prevented visually impaired women from fully enjoying intimate family life with a person of their choosing, the Advocacy Awareness-raising and Lobbying Committee of the GAB's Women's Wing (which I chaired from 2007–2009) used International Women's Day (which falls on March 8 annually) to raise awareness of the capabilities of the blind and vision-impaired woman (Women's Wing Final Project Report, 2010). Our activities showcased select women with visual impairment doing household chores including washing clothes and cooking various Ghanaian cuisines; this was filmed and aired on some television networks – extensively on the TV 3 channel. This was important after a number of blind and partially sighted women shared stories of the families of their potential male partners rejecting them when the men proposed marriage (R. Laweh-Tei et al., personal conversation, March 8, 2009). The families of the men perceived the blind and partially sighted women as incapable of performing household chores and sometimes feared that they would give birth to children who were blind also (J.A. Danso et al., personal conversation, March 8, 2009).

Interestingly, some evidence exists to show that blind men, after investing financially in seeing women, have also been rejected by some families when they proposed marriage, albeit to a lesser extent than blind women (A. Kakabo, personal conversation, August 22, 2020; S. Fianu, personal conversation, July 2, 2015). These awareness creation and raising programmes showcased blind and partially sighted women with and without education performing domestic chores and other tasks, showcasing our capabilities without recourse to our educational attainment or level.

Since its formation, the Ghana Association of the Blind has enjoyed relative stability in terms of cohesion. But the association has suffered a great many covert tensions, especially between those who can speak fluent English (educated) and those who cannot (less or uneducated members). This stems from the fact that acquiring a formal education seems to be a major problem among persons who are blind and partially sighted in Ghana. The 2010 Population and Housing Census (2014) Survey and the 2021 Population and Housing Census (2022) revealed that 40.1% of 288,868 persons of school-going age with visual impairment had never been to school or had formal education. Equally, 39.4% of five–17-year old persons with functional difficulties have never been to school compared with 18.7% for persons without functioning difficulties. This means that over 15,800 persons with visual impairment in Ghana grow into adulthood every decade or so without any form of education, hence constituting a large cohort in the GBU. Those without much formal education have been suspicious of the educated in both the GBU and GAB, accusing them of wanting to take the association away from them. This suspicion was valid to a large extent when those who could speak English well started appearing and dominated leadership. The educated also have felt that the uneducated cannot articulate certain concepts or standpoints very well since they cannot speak fluent English. The English-speaking problem is reinforced in part by the GBU Constitution. Article 6(9) requires the business of the general assembly to be conducted in English, but Article 10(8) encourages the business of the regional executive councils to be conducted in vernacular.

In terms of representation and participation, the method by which the NEC of the GBU is currently organised promotes equitable representation. In principle, the equitable representation is realised with the five zonal council representatives. Members of this council are drawn from among the regional executives and within the various regions, where every paid-up member can be elected irrespective of educational standing. The zonal council is the blocks into which the GBU categorises the regions of Ghana. Currently, the blind and partially sighted persons on the 2021 NEC hold various academic qualifications. These include post-graduate and graduate degrees, college certificates and some others without much formal education. This diverse nature of blind and partially sighted members of the NEC is made possible through the zonal representations. What is tricky about this zonal representation, however, is that even though this has ensured a form of equitable representation, it does not enable full participation for those who cannot speak English, especially in the general assembly deliberations and in certain advocacy spaces. Therefore, even though the constitution guarantees equal representation and participation for every paid-up member, this does not translate into full participation, particularly for those with limited English-speaking capabilities.

On the one hand, the argument is advanced that, in order to fulfil GBU's mandate of advocating, working for the total integration of blind and partially sighted persons into society and raising awareness on the negative attitudes impeding the full inclusion of all persons with disabilities, those with a formal education are considered to be more able than those without education to help GBU and the disability movement at large deliver on their mandate. Hence, their dominance. On the other hand, the preference for those with formal educational backgrounds has led to the oppression of the uneducated and marginalisation of some of the specific issues affecting them. This means that the uneducated blind or partially sighted experiences 'simultaneous oppression' (Carby, 1982; Vernon, 1999) as a result of their impairment like all categories of blind persons.

But in addition, the uneducated persons experience another oppression unique to them (multiple oppression) because of their lack of education and the limitations this imposes on them, resulting in multiple marginalisation (McDonald, 1991; Begum, 1992; Vernon, 1999). This unique oppression of uneducated blind and partially sighted persons is further aggravated in the disparities in the GBU's and even the disability movement's advocacy priorities, which enhance this multiple marginalisation. For instance, whereas the educated are seeking employment opportunities, assistive devices, accessible educational facilities and affirmative action for disability inclusion and representation in political positions, the uneducated are more concerned about avenues of sustainable monthly income, income-generation activities, affordable housing so they won't have to live in a generational housing setup and funds to purchase musical instruments to establish gig bands.

In this scenario, the educated blind or partially sighted person would be more likely to have their needs captured in advocacy objectives and key messages since they are fairly represented around the decision table, but the uneducated are not. This is an affirmation of the assertion that "the personal views of less powerful disabled actors are subsumed by the political principles of the more powerful disabled actors" (Humphrey, 2000, p. 66). It is therefore not very surprising that the lived realities of uneducated persons with visual impairment or are blind have not yet filtered properly into the advocacy space in Ghana.

The dominance of educated persons in the top leadership of the GBU and the skewed nature of advocacy priorities have further increased marginalisation and hierarchies. Drawing on Humphrey's (2000) assertion that 'disabled identity is constructed in a manner that limits inclusiveness' (p. 70), I posit that the disabled identity in GBU and the entire disability movement in Ghana is constructed to recognise the educated, vocal persons and those with good jobs, which often fits normativity and ableism. This is consistent with Harasymiw et al. (1976), who pointed to a hierarchy of preference in which those impairments found to fit well into the norms of society were likely to be more accepted. The oppression of the uneducated and the marginalisation of their issues in advocacy have already had detrimental effects on GBU's regional and local advocacy. Advocacy at those levels has suffered because the grassroots members have few if any skills. A 2010 GBU Women's Wing final project evaluation found that reports were not forthcoming from the regions since many of the members and some of the regional coordinators were uneducated or were not used to writing reports.

On the other hand, other uneducated women who are blind or partially sighted have done very well in their leadership roles. For example, some past coordinators of the Grater Accra and Volta regions' Women's Wing enlisted the support and assistance of friends and some family members, such as their own children, to assist them in writing their reports. Furthermore, these two coordinators succeeded in lobbying mainstream women's groups and other organisations to include GBU women in their activities and outreach programmes. In this regard, educational level did not count as much in their situation as their empowerment level and willingness to apply the knowledge gained.

Another avenue of oppression and marginalisation is privilege, which manifests in two forms. First, privilege has created hierarchies in organisations of the blind and that privilege put some people in front of everything good. In view of this, privilege has enabled visible and invisible hierarchies to thrive, and those who have been adversely affected most have been the uneducated blind and partially sighted persons. Therefore, education becomes the variable or enabler for privilege and hierarchy as an identity of marginalisation.

All persons who are blind or partially sighted are oppressed because of their impairment, but those who are fortunate enough to be educated are privileged by their education, which naturally sorts them into a group, thereby placing them at the top of the hierarchy. This concept is better explained by Collins (2000), when she asserts in her examination of Black women's experiences in the US that groups have different forms of penalty and privilege within them. So, for instance, a white woman in a given situation may be penalised or disadvantaged by her gender but, in another vein, privileged by her race. Here, too, among a group of highly educated persons with and without blindness, the blind or partially sighted persons would be penalised for their impairment while privileged among a heterogeneous group of persons who are blind or partially sighted by their education. Therefore, whether one becomes the oppressor, the oppressed or both is context specific (Collins, 2000).

The uneducated in GBU deviate from the norm of education, which invariably becomes their source of oppression even though blindness or their impairment is the unifying element within the union. This becomes even more complex since, now that the association and the society have merged, there is a constitutional requirement of 51% of board members to be blind or partially sighted persons, with the rest seeing counterparts. The complexity stems from the fact that now there is an invisible urge to select persons who can raise the quality that the 49% of board members who are seeing persons bring to the table. In essence, this further alienates and deepens the oppression of the uneducated and, on the other hand, privileges more the educated blind. I surmise that an overarching wish of the blind members of GBU now would be to try to conform in order not to, according to Deal, 'threaten their value' (Humphrey, 2000).

The second form of privilege is knowing someone in leadership. Those who have been privileged to know someone in leadership always had opportunity to be selected for important meetings and programmes. Ordinarily, there should not be anything wrong with this. But this has, in some cases, led to a mismatch between a person and their capabilities on one hand and the function or advocacy spaces in which to represent on the other: for example, choosing a man or woman with little knowledge of violence to represent the organisation in a gender-based violence conference. Such representatives sometimes end up keeping quiet throughout the conference, thereby missing a good opportunity to advance the disability angle of gender-based violence or make a good representation. This form of privilege has also enabled the marginalisation of those who could have helped the course of the blind better, thereby affecting the outcomes for the collective.

Conclusion

The concept of blindness organising is a process that drew all blind and visually impaired persons together to speak for themselves, advocate to be included in the overall national life and provide services where needed in Ghana. Affirming that the GBU has been at the forefront of the fight for equalisation of opportunities for persons with disabilities in Ghana, with some of the gains including being a part of the advocacy teams that lobbied the Ghana government to issue the disability law, Act 715, and established the National Council on Persons with Disabilities; being the first disabled people's organisations to have a representative in the monthly meetings of the Department of Women under the auspices of the Ministry of Gender, Children and Social Protection; and further recognising that the GBU is one of the strongest mouthpieces for disability issues in the subregion, this chapter does not intend to denounce the GBU as being exclusive of uneducated blind and partially sighted persons. Nor does it intend to argue that uneducated members have not benefited from the advocacy of the union. But I sought to demonstrate here that certain practices and actions enable hierarchy and privilege, resulting in the marginalisation of those with intersecting identities, such as uneducated blind and partially sighted persons in the GBU.

Since a number of authors have raised issues about the disability movement's inclusiveness and how they can better represent its varied intersecting identities (Priestley, 1995; Vernon, 1999), the GBU needs to begin to acknowledge the various identities that may be present in the membership and intentionally seek out their nuanced views and needs in a priority setting. Whenever all cannot genuinely be represented at the decision table, given that every category of identity cannot sit at the decision table all the time because of capacity or capability limitations, deliberate measures must be employed to represent all views equally and adequately.

The GBU as well as the disability movement should constantly look out for those categories of persons who may be likely to be disadvantaged by organisational priority setting and deliberately carry them along or involve them appropriately. Admitting also that some among us might do things differently, we should not perceive that difference as less than ourselves because our strength emanates from our differences. This is highlighted by Humphrey (2000) when she asserts: '[I]t is perhaps by respecting differences in experience, roles, insights and skills that the most valuable form of equality can be engendered' (p. 17).

Again, there should be a system to pool people with disabilities who are diversely skilled and knowledgeable but do not want to vie for any leadership position in their representative organisations. In this way, disabled people's organisations can harness the talents of all persons and individuals, whether educated or illiterate, young or old, and the like.

In summary, this chapter has briefly discussed the background of the Ghana Society for the Blind and the services it provided for its clients in its early years and recently before its dissolution. The chapter further examined briefly the history of the Ghana Association of the Blind, elucidating the motivations behind blind and partially sighted persons' emancipation drive; examined empowerment as applied to the capacity development of the blind and the role of development partners in GAB's development and growth; and explored some practices and actions that enable hierarchy leading to the marginalisation of persons with intersecting identities and their issues.

The chapter again touched on the distinctions between membership and service organisations for the blind and partially sighted and disability organisations.

Finally, some measures to help GBU be more aware of different identities have been proposed.

References

2010 Population and Housing Census. (2014). Accra, Ghana Statistical Service. https://statsghana.gov.gh/

2021 Population and Housing Census. (2022). Accra, Ghana Statistical Service. https://statsghana.gov.gh/gssmain/fileUpload/pressrelease/2021%20PHC%20General%20Report%20Vol%203F_Difficulty%20in%20Performing%20Activities_final_161221.pdf. Accessed 27th May 2023.

Armstrong, A. J. (2011). Sheltered employment. In Kreutzer J., S., Deluca, J., Caplan, B. (Eds), Encyclopedia of Clinical Neuropsychology. Springer, New York. Accessed 16th March, 2021.

Begum, N. (1992). Something to be Proud of: The Lives of Asian Disabled People and Carers in Waltham Forest. London Borough of Waltham Forest, Race Relations and Disability Unit, London.

Carby, H. (1982). White woman listen! Black feminism and the boundaries of sisterhood. In Centre for Contemporary Cultural Studies (Ed), Empire Strikes Back: Race and Racism in 70's Britain. Hutchinson, Paris.

Collins, P. H. (2000). Black Feminist thought: Knowledge, Consciousness, and the Politics of Empowerment. Routledge, New York.

Final Project Report. (2010). Organisational Development of Ghana Association of the Blind Women's Wing. MP3 – B84: (unpublished).

Grischow, J. D. (2011). Kwame Nkrumah, disability, and rehabilitation in Ghana, 1956–66. Journal of African History, 52: 179–199.

GSB 50th Anniversary Brochure. (2001). Accra, Ghana Society for the Blind.

Harasymiw, S. J., Horne, M. J., & Lewis, S. C. (1976). A longitudinal study of disability group acceptance. Rehabilitation Literature, 37: 98–102.

Humphrey, J. C. (2000). Researching disability politics, or, some problems with the social model in practice. Disability & Society, 15(1): 63–86.

Keiffer, C. (1984). Citizen empowerment: A developmental perspective. Prevention in Human Services, 3(16): 9–35.

Labonte, R. (1989). Empowerment: Notes on professional and community dimensions. Canadian Review of Social Policy, 26: 4–75.

Lord, J., & Hutchison, P. (1993). The process of empowerment: Implication for theory and practice. Canadian Journal of Community Mental Health, 12(1): 5–22.

Manual for the Community-Based Rehabilitation Project. (2006). Accra, Ghana Association of the Blind. http://www.ghanablind.net/CBR%20MANUAL.pdf. Accessed 10th February, 2021.

May-Simera, C. (2018). Reconsidering sheltered workshops in light of the United Nations Convention on the Rights of Persons with Disabilities (2006). Laws, 7(1): 6–22.

McDonald, P. (1991). Double discrimination must be faced now. Disability Now, 8: 7–8.

Miglioire, A. (2010). Sheltered workshops. International Encyclopedia of Rehabilitation (Centre of International Rehabilitation Research Information and Exchange). The State University of New York, Buffalo, NY.

Oliver, M. (1984). The politics of disability. Critical Social Policy, 4(11): 21–32.

Oliver, M. (1990). The Politics of Disablement. Macmillan, London.

Presby, J., Wandersman, A., Florin, P., Rich, R., & Chavis, D. (1990). Benefits, Costs, incentive management and participation in voluntary organisations: A means to understanding and promoting empowerment. American Journal of Community Psychology, 18(1): 117–148.

Priestley, M. (1995). Commonality and difference in the movement: an association of blind Asians in Leeds. Disability & Society, 10(2): 157–169.

Rappaport, J. (1987). Terms of empowerment/exemplars of prevention: Toward a theory for community psychology. American Journal of Community Psychology, 15(2): 121–148.

Vernon, A. (1999). The dialectics of multiple identities and the disabled people's movement. Disability & Society, 14(3): 385–398.

Visier, L. (1998). Sheltered employment for persons with disabilities. International Labour Review, 137(3): 347–365.

Webson, W. A. (1997). Empowerment of the Blind: A Handbook for Organisations of and for the Blind and Visually Impaired. Hilton/Perkins Program, Watertown, MA.

Whitmore, E. (1988). Empowerment and the Process of Inquiry. A Presentation at the Annual Meeting of Canadian Association of Schools of Social Work, Windsor, ON.

Wilson, J. (1960). Blindness in the commonwealth. Journal of the Royal Society of Arts, 108(5042): 122–132.

28

BETWEEN THE DISABILITY MOVEMENT AND THE FEMINIST MOVEMENT

Intersectional mobilizations of women with disabilities in Haiti

Dominique Masson, Stephen Baranyi and Ilionor Louis

In the midst of intense battles against the Duvalier dictatorship in Haiti, several social movements transformed themselves by finding inspiration in their predecessors' experiences. This is true of a feminist movement which, inspired by feminist groups who criticized the American occupation in the 1920s and fought for women's right to vote, was rekindled by the fight for democracy and social justice in the 1980s (Côté, 2014; Merlet, 2010). It is also true of a growing movement of people with disabilities who distanced themselves from charity-based perspectives in favour of approaches based on human rights (Baranyi & Louis, 2016; Péan, 2011). That the 1987 Haitian Constitution recognizes the rights of women and of persons with disabilities is due, in part, to the efforts of these movements and their alliances with other democratic forces at the time. However, according to the new generation of organizations of women with disabilities (OWDs) that has emerged in Haiti since 2008, neither the claims nor the institutional gains made by the feminist and disability rights movements have addressed the specific experiences of women with disabilities.

This lack of recognition should not surprise us. The marginalization of women with disabilities and of their interests by the feminist and the disability rights movements – which many women with disabilities feel should be their advocates – has led to the emergence of independent organizations of women with disabilities in a variety of national and transnational contexts (Price, 2011). It was not until 1995, at the Fourth World Conference on Women in Beijing, that a symposium dedicated to women with disabilities was held, and their claims were included in the conference's Platform for Action (Conejo, 2011, p. 599). Furthermore, it was only in the early 2000s, through advocacy work that lead to the adoption of the United Nations Convention on the Rights

DOI: 10.4324/9781003410089-33

of Persons with Disabilities (CRPD) in 2006, that associations of women with disabilities affirmed themselves as independent actors in a transnational movement historically dominated by men (Price, 2011).

This chapter takes as its object the deployment in Haiti of intersectional mobilizations that politicize lived experiences located at the intersection of gender and ableism,[1] understood as interconnected systems of social domination (Masson, 2013). It centers the intersectional activism of new OWDs that, over the last decade, have engaged in advocacy for the recognition of the voices, lived experiences and demands of women with disabilities. It also analyzes the effects of such engagement and the political dynamics that shape their action, as well as their relationships with state institutions and the feminist and disability movements. How and why did an intersectional activism on the part of women with disabilities emerge in Haiti, and how was their advocacy constructed? What are the results of their efforts to date? Which national and international associative and institutional factors limit, facilitate, or support their demands for recognition? Which factors help explain the reception of the latter by Haitian state institutions, as well as by the feminist and disability rights movements?

To answer these questions, we present results based on field research conducted between 2018 and 2020, combining the analysis of documents produced by OWDs, the Haitian state and international organizations with 15 semi-directed interviews with key activists from three "new" OWDs, representatives of Haiti's disability and feminist movements and senior officials from relevant state institutions. The three OWDs discussed in this study (two based in the capital, Port-au-Prince, and the third in Les Cayes in the *Département du Sud*, the southern department) are active nationally and internationally.[2]

On the theoretical plane we draw, on the one hand, on an intersectional feminist approach (Crenshaw, 1989; Bilge, 2010) to analyze the organization and advocacy of these OWDs, as well as responses to their demands for recognition and inclusion by other social movements. We also consider the unequal relations between activists placed in "majority" and "minority" positions regarding one or more axes of domination (Masson, 2015, p. 39; Predelli & Halsaa, 2012). On the other hand, we use concepts from feminist institutionalism (Mackay & Krook, 2015; Mazur, 2009) to understand how women with disabilities organize themselves and their strategic use of the opportunities created by national and international institutions to demand inclusion for women with disabilities and their specific concerns, as well as the various ways that Haitian institutions, the feminist movement and the disability rights movement respond to these demands.

This first study of OWDs in Haiti contributes original insights by highlighting the agency of women with disabilities in this context. It documents how they have assumed the intersectional identity of "disabled women" as a basis from which to make political claims. It analyzes the evolution and effect of their advocacy, as well as the constraints that limit their impact. It contributes to intersectional analyses of how women with disabilities engage in processes of institutional change (see, for example, Kayess et al., 2014; Thill, 2019). Finally, it reveals the complex dynamics of majority-minority relations of power and hierarchies that traverse the disability rights movement, the feminist movement and state institutions.

Activism by OWDs in Haiti – emergence and advocacy

Intersectionality is a theoretical construct attributed to Kimberlé Crenshaw (1989). It has been part of academic feminist theorizing and debates ever since. Its origins, however, lie in activist knowledge produced by feminists from marginalized social groups – African American women, first and foremost, but also lesbians, working-class women, women from the so-called "third-world", and more – for whom gender analysis appeared insufficient to account for the inequalities, oppressions and discriminations that shaped their existence (Masson, 2015, pp. 36–37). Academic and activist intersectional perspectives both stand in opposition to "monist" (Bilge, 2010, pp. 51–55) understandings of social relations: that is, to unidimensional analyses and politics that only consider one axis of domination (be it gender, class, race, or even ability). With that in mind, the first section of this chapter documents and analyzes the emergence of feminist intersectional activism by women with disabilities in Haiti.

In Haiti, organizations of women with disabilities are still few in number. But since 2008, a new generation of organizations of women with disabilities has appeared in Haiti. What is truly new is the engagement of these organizations in advocacy work that politicizes the lives of women with disabilities while highlighting the way their experiences are shaped by interactions between gendered and disability-based forms of oppression. In contrast, the oldest and best known OWD is *Femmes en action de la Société haïtienne d'aide aux aveugles* (FASHAA) (Women in Action of the Haitian Aid Society for the Blind), which was established in July 1991 as the "women's section" of the *Société haïtienne d'aide aux aveugles* (SHAA) (Haitian Aid Society for the Blind). FASHAA provides its members with a space to socialize, foster solidarity and receive training on topics ranging from cooking to women's rights but does not participate in advocacy despite the fact that many active members support demands by the new OWDs (interview with two FASHAA members, 2019).

Three organizations represent the new generation of OWDs: *Association filles et femmes au soleil* (AFAS) (Association of Girls and Women in the Sun), *Union des femmes à mobilité réduite d'Haïti* (UFMORH) (Union of Haitian Women with Reduced Mobility) and *Association des femmes handicapées du Sud* (AFHS) (Association of Women with Disabilities in the South Department). AFAS, founded in 2008 by Michaelle Louis, has 70 members, mostly in the capital, Port-au-Prince. The association first became known for its annual contest, *Une couronne pour l'intégration de la femme handicapée* (A crown for the integration of women with disabilities), whose goal was to help women with disabilities rediscover their bodies, recognize their intrinsic beauty and raise their self-esteem. In 2012–2013, AFAS received financial support from the *Bureau du Secrétaire d'État à l'intégration des personnes handicapées* (BSEIPH) (Office of the State Secretary for the Integration of Persons with Disabilities) to help girls and women with disabilities develop leadership skills (Association filles au soleil, 2018). The association turned to advocacy in 2014–2015, with the help of a first project grant from the Disability Rights Fund (DRF), an international non-governmental organization, from which it would get additional funding in the years that followed (Disability Rights Advocacy Fund (DRAF), 2020). On its website, AFAS described its mission statement in 2018 as raising awareness about the concerns of girls and women with disabilities, rendering them visible, making their voices heard and defending their rights.

In September 2009, Soinette Désir and approximately ten other women with disabilities founded UFMORH

> to advocate, have a group of women with disabilities fighting for their rights: the right to education, to justice . . . [to] have a home, [to] not be victims of discrimination, and the right to be fully included in their communities.
>
> *(interview with Soinette Désir,[3] UFMORH, 2019)*

UFMORH's earliest advocacy efforts took place at the micro-local level. However, its reach grew when the organization held a well-attended press conference to present its analysis of the 2012 Law for the Integration of Persons with Disabilities, giving low marks to the Haitian government on health, education and justice for persons with disabilities, as well as on issues of particular concern to women with disabilities. From 2015, UFMORH's interest in advocacy and implementing the CRPD received annual support from the DRF for projects focused, at times, on the rights of persons with disabilities and, at other times, more specifically on women with disabilities (DRAF, 2020). Although its name may suggest otherwise, UFMORH seeks to include women with functional limitations beyond physical mobility. It has 30 active members and between 50 and 60 non-active members, concentrated in Port-au-Prince (interview with Soinette Désir, 2019). In 2020, the association defined its mission as "to uphold the rights of women and girls with a disability and promote the autonomy and inclusion of women with reduced mobility" (Union des femmes à mobilité réduite d'Haïti, n.d.).

For its part, AFHS was born of a 2013 project by the *Réseau associatif national pour l'intégration des personnes handicapées du Sud* (RANIPH-Sud) (Associative Network for the Integration of Disabled Persons in the South Department). Project goals included "establishing an organization of women with disabilities to promote their rights" in the South Department (DRAF, 2020). The creation of the association is coterminous with RANIPH-Sud's undertaking of a department-wide consultation organized with the objective of producing an alternative report for the Committee on the Rights of Persons with Disabilities, tasked with overseeing the implementation of the Convention on the Rights of Persons with Disabilities (CRPD). AFHS participated actively in this process.

> We [AFHS] conducted field work with the RANIPH-Sud coalition: visiting other communities, meeting women with disabilities and talking to them, [so they could] explain what their life is like. . . . We collected all this information and conveyed it to the coalition.
>
> *(Interview with Marijoe Pierre, AFAS, 2019)*

AFHS's stated mission is to "work on issues of advocacy and the rights of women and girls with disabilities in the Department of the South", specifically on violence and discrimination (Interview with Marijoe Pierre, AFAS, 2019). Since 2015, AFHS has received annual funding from the DRF (DRAF, 2020). The association has approximately 170 members in the departmental capital, Les Cayes, and in surrounding communities.

Their focus on women's rights and equality locates these OWDs squarely within the space of feminism. Yet women with disabilities, according to these activists, have been ignored or forgotten by Haiti's feminist movement: "Women with disabilities are not included in Haiti's feminist movement. It is [one of the reasons] that pushed us to create this association" (interview with Marijoe Pierre, 2019). In fact, in Haiti as elsewhere, the feminist movement first emerged as a monist struggle against gendered social relations understood as the fundamental axis structuring women's experiences. However, intersecting axes of social domination – here, gender and ableism – creates majority (able-bodied women) and minority (women with disabilities) positions within the space of feminism – positions that, if unrecognized, lead members of the majority to universalize their experiences to all women and, at the same time, to exclude or marginalize the experiences of women with disabilities.

As seen here, the funding of the new OWDs by DRF and the nature of their advocacy work also positions them within the disability rights movement. Yet activists also denounce unequal power relations between men and women with disabilities within this movement and affirm that it rarely if ever takes women with disabilities into account. As well, they highlight the importance of recognizing the specificity of women's lived experiences of inequality and discrimination: "Every person with a disability has problems, but we find that the problems of women and girls with disabilities in Haiti are more *specific*. . . . That's why we have created this association" (interview with Marijoe Pierre, 2019, emphasis in original). The disability rights movement in Haiti emerged as a monist fight against inequalities and discrimination experienced by persons with disabilities. However, it is also shaped by gender relations. Here, too, the interaction of gender and ableism as axes of social domination creates majority (men with disabilities) and minority (women with disabilities) positions, linked to power relations that are enacted at both the interpersonal and organizational levels.

To counter what is perceived as a deficit of representation in both the feminist and disability rights movements, it is imperative for activists in the new OWDs that women with disabilities represent themselves: "We don't want others to speak for us. We want women with disabilities to carry their own voices. . . . That's why women with disabilities have to be at the *centre* of the cause, as stakeholders and spokespersons for their demands" (interview with Soinette Désir, 2019, emphasis in original).

These voices have shaped a discourse of advocacy constructed through these OWDs' participation in the production of alternative reports, signed by them or in collaboration with mixed-gender organizations of persons with disabilities (OPDs). They have presented those reports to the UN as part of the international mechanisms tracking the implementation of the CRDP (Société civile du département du Sud, 2013; RANIPH-Sud Coalition et al., 2017) and the Convention on the Elimination of All Forms of Discrimination against Women (CEDAW) (Association filles au soleil & Union des femmes à mobilité réduite d'Haïti, 2016) and the promotion and protection of broader human rights (Association filles au soleil et al., 2016).

Two characteristics reveal the intersectional nature of the new OWDs' advocacy. First, they act simultaneously on the two fronts of disability rights and women's rights. More precisely, they press for the implementation of the CRPD by the Haitian government, as well as for the inclusion of women with disabilities in the national Policy for Equality between Women and Men overseen by the *Ministère à la condition féminine et aux droits des femmes* (MCFDF) (Ministry for the Status of Women and Women's Rights). Second, the new OWDs argue for the need to understand the lived experiences of women with disabilities and to elaborate political responses in ways that consider the interaction of gendered and ableist oppressions. The advocacy discourse of these OWDs illustrates how these experiences, shaped by intersecting axes of domination, are politicized.

The first Haitian CRPD alternative report, in which AFHS participated, sketched out some of the inequalities endured by women with disabilities (Société civile du département du Sud, 2013). The 2016 alternative report produced by AFAS and UFMORH for the 63rd session of the committee of the CEDAW in Geneva is the more detailed version of the new OWDs' advocacy discourse, aimed at including women with disabilities in Haitian public policy. This report highlights six main issues: violence and access to justice, education, employment, health, political participation and the Policy for Equality between Women and Men.

Violence is a key issue for OWDs; it was mentioned in every interview. The alternative report to the CEDAW committee indicates that women and girls with disabilities

> face violence and exclusion based on their gender and their disability. They experience a double discrimination. The violence they are subjected to is a combination of their gender and their physical, sensory, or

> intellectual disability. . . . Their situation is cause for greater concern than that of other women or even of disabled men.
>
> *(AFAS & UFMORH, 2016, p. 1)*

OWDs denounce popular beliefs according to which having sexual relations with a woman with a disability brings a man luck or money, which they say incite rape. They also criticize the exclusion of women with disabilities from initiatives to reduce violence against women in Haiti and their lack of access to shelters, telephone hotlines and information for women experiencing violence. Women's right to justice is also denied, they say: police do not take their complaints regarding violence seriously; police stations and courts are not accessible; there are no interpreters for deaf women; and police officers, courts, and judges are not trained in an inclusive approach to disability or to gender (AFAS & UFMORH, 2016, p. 2).

In terms of education, OWDs point out that "the percentage of women with disabilities who attend university or other professional schools is much lower than for men with disabilities. Furthermore, families neglect their disabled daughters' education and do not invest in their education" (AFAS & UFMORH, 2016, p. 4). Disabled women's access to education is understood by OWDs as being informed by both gender and disability, and their activism calls for campaigns to raise awareness about the importance of education for girls and women with disabilities.

The 2016 report states that women with disabilities, "because of their disability AND because they are women . . . do not benefit from equal opportunities in access to employment" (AFAS & UFMORH, 2016, p. 3, emphasis in original). Noting that unemployment is endemic in Haiti, it stresses that "women in general and women with disabilities in particular are more affected" (p. 3). In light of this, OWDs criticize Haiti's employment quotas for women and for persons with disabilities for not explicitly mentioning women with disabilities, whose specificity is not recognized and who have remained largely excluded from the implementation of these measures (p. 3).

OWDs also denounce both the fact that "for women and girls with disabilities, the right to reproductive and sexual health is not respected" and the lack of "access to information and services that would allow them to better manage their health and better protect themselves" (AFAS & UFMORH, 2016, p. 4). They report "that most families do not consider sexual education for daughters with disabilities" and that women with disabilities' right to motherhood is often denied through "verbal and psychological violence" (p. 4).

Regarding participation in political life, the organizations fault "the state for not meeting the general conditions required for women with disabilities to vote and run for office" (AFAS & UFMORH, 2016, p. 5). OWDs point out that polling stations and ballots lack accessibility and that all persons with disabilities, including women, face problems of insecurity and violence that affect their political participation (AFAS & UFMORH, 2016, p. 6).

As can be appreciated from this summary, the advocacy discourse of the new OWDs centers on the specificity of the experiences of women with disabilities, compared to those of men with disabilities or women without disabilities. Alternative reports and our interviews reveal an intersectional sensibility expressed through a vocabulary of "double discrimination" and even "multiple discriminations" when the variety of impairments is considered (Pierre & l'Association des femmes handicapées du Sud, 2020) and, more recently, of *discriminations croisées* (or crossed discriminations) (Pierre & l'Union des femmes à mobilité réduite d'Haïti, 2020).

OWDs also demand better representation of women with disabilities in the policy-making processes that affect them. This is seen in their advocacy and efforts aimed at achieving recognition for the issues specific to women with disabilities in all public policies of concern to persons with disabilities, as well as in their criticism of the Policy for Equality between Women and Men (2014–2034) and its action plan:

> The Policy for Equality between Women and Men (2014–2020) adopted by the Haitian state through the Ministry for the Status of Women and Women's Rights does not mention women with disabilities, who were not consulted during the process. . . . OWDs were not consulted during the development of this document and the needs of women with disabilities were not taken into account. They are also not included in the policy's monitoring structure.
>
> *(AFAS & UFMORH, 2016, p. 1)*

OWDs demand participation in these structures and in the policy's implementation processes, as well as a seat at the table when the ministry updates the action plan, to ensure that women with disabilities and their needs are duly considered (AFAS & UFMORH, 2016, p. 1). They also call for gender-disaggregated data production processes "that include impairments, to ensure consideration of the needs of women with disabilities in the programs implemented by the Haitian state" (AFAS & UFMORH, 2016, p. 2).

The inclusion of women with disabilities in the Policy for Equality between Women and Men is a key concern of the new OWDs. In addition to highlighting this issue in alternative reports, AFAS, UFMORH and AFHS have lobbied government institutions, notably the BSEIPH and MCFDF; organized awareness-raising workshops; and, occasionally, engaged in sit-ins and public demonstrations (interview with Soinette Désir, UFMORH, 2019). For example, banners at a 2017 protest read: "*Aba vyolens sou fanm andikapé*" (No to violence against disabled women), "*Fanm andikapé se fanm tankou tout fanm*" (Disabled women are women too) and "*Inklizion fanm andikapé nan politik egalité fanm ak gason 2014–2024 là*" (For the inclusion of disabled women in the 2014–2024 Policy for Equality between Women and Men) (Tele Ginen, 2017).

Outcomes of OWDs' activism

Transforming subjectivities and capacities within OWDs

The most immediate outcome of these organizations' activities is to contribute to transforming the subjectivities of women with disabilities: that is, to developing among activists and participants a sense of themselves as citizens with rights and women capable of action. "Women with disabilities are starting to understand that it is their duty to advocate for themselves" and make their voices heard (interview with Soinette Désir, July 18, 2019). The agency of women with disabilities is the driving force of the new OWDs' mobilizations, grounded in their activists' engagement, experiences of oppression and desire for change. Another outcome is the strengthening over time of OWDs' organizational capacities, particularly in terms of skills, leadership, strategic planning, financial management of projects and advocacy. The qualitative difference between the first alternative report written by women with disabilities and their allies (Société civile du département du Sud, 2013) and those later submitted to several UN bodies (AFAS & UFMORH, 2016; AFAS et al., 2016; RANIPH-Sud Coalition et al., 2017) illustrates this point.

While such transformation of subjectivities and capacities owes, in part, to the learning process that ensues from activism, it also owes to the arrival in Haiti of the international non-governmental organization Disability Rights Fund in 2012. Founded in 2008, DRF "provides financial and technical resources to organizations of persons with disabilities to advocate for equal rights and full participation in society" (Disability Rights Fund, 2020). In Haiti, the DRF supports projects by OWDs aimed at implementing the CRPD and Sustainable Development Goals, strengthening associations' advocacy capabilities and improving representation for the most marginalized groups, particularly women, within the disability rights movement (interview with Jo-Ann Garnier, DRF, 2019). DRF financed the creation of the AFHS. It also offered the new OWDs technical assistance and training to engage in disability rights advocacy in national and international political arenas. Since 2013, it has become their primary funder, contributing modest annual grants of $8,000 to $20,000 US for projects promoting the rights of women with disabilities in relation to CRPD implementation, as well as greater inclusion of women with disabilities in the Policy for Equality between Women and Men and the disability rights movement in Haiti (DRAF, 2020). For DRF, that OWDs are now equipped for advocacy "is a first step to success" (interview with Jo-Ann Garnier, 2019).

Yet a number of organizational factors constrain the new OWDs' action. First, they are very few, have a limited number of members, are located mostly in urban areas and have a local rather than national base. The small size of these organizations also creates the risk of a personalization of their leadership which, in turn, can be a challenge for continuity – AFAS has been inactive since its founder left the country. Furthermore, their limited financial resources force them to rely on external sources, including the DRF, International Disability Alliance (IDA), and the Haitian *Bureau des avocats internationaux* (International Lawyers Office) for technical support and on the DRAF for funding their action over time.

Impacts of OWDs' activism on the disability rights sector

What impacts has the feminist intersectional activism of the new OWDs had, to date, on the disability rights sector, both associative and institutional? One way to evaluate these impacts is to assess the new OWDs' inclusion as political actors and that of their discourse in the alternative reports produced by the disability rights movement (AFAS et al., 2016, and RANIPH-Sud Coalition et al., 2017).

The main elements of the AFAS and UFMORH's 2016 report to the CEDAW are found, albeit in a less polished form, in the alternative report submitted later that year to the United Nations Human Rights Council by AFAS, UFMORH and two disability rights organizations. As well, AFHS and UFMORH are among the signatories of the 2017 alternative report submitted as part of the CRPD monitoring process by the RANIPH-Sud Coalition and several other associations. A selection of elements of the OWDs' report to the CEDAW also features in the 2017 alternative report to the CRPD, regarding violence and access to justice, sexual and reproductive health, participation in political life and the Policy for Equality between Men and Women. The issues of education and employment for women with disabilities are absent. Yet notable additions to the 2017 report to the CRPD include the sterilization and contraception of women with disabilities without their consent (especially young women who are deaf or have intellectual disabilities), as well as the "lynching" of three deaf women accused of being werewolves on March 18, 2016, in the town of Cabaret (RANIPH-Sud Coalition et al., 2017, points 19, 30, and 67).

Mechanisms for the periodic evaluation of compliance to international conventions, to which states must respond, create political opportunities that have been seized by the new OWDs to raise awareness of issues of concern for women with disabilities within the disability rights movement in Haiti, as well as within international institutions and, eventually, national ones. As we have seen, the new OWDs have undeniably made a place for themselves in the production of alternative reports by the Haitian disability rights movement.

In accordance with the CRPD monitoring process, civil society associations are invited to evaluate their country's compliance to the articles of the convention, among which is Article 6 concerning women with disabilities. The Committee on the Rights of Persons with Disabilities uses the alternative reports to make observations and recommendations to states. Another way to assess the impact of the new OWDs' intersectional activism is to trace the inclusion of their demands in these recommendations. To what extent is their advocacy reflected in the CRPD's 2018 report?

To begin, the committee recommends that Haiti "recognize multiple and crossed forms of discrimination", including those that affect women with disabilities (*Comité des droits des personnes handicapées*, 2018, p. 9). In the spirit of Article 6, it recommends including the rights of women with disabilities in "legislation on gender equality" and "laws and public policies related to disability" (point 11a). Furthermore, the committee's observations address several women's issues. Concerns are expressed regarding sexual violence, as well as the lack of data on both violence and the obstacles faced by women with disabilities in the justice system. Regarding sexual and reproductive health, the committee recommends that Haiti "ensure equal access to sexual and reproductive health services" (point 41b). It recommends adopting measures to "promote the education of all persons with disabilities, particularly women and children" (point 43d). Lastly, it recommends implementing mechanisms "aimed at increasing the employment rate of persons with disabilities, particularly women and young people with disabilities" (point 49b). Comparing the committee's observations and recommendations to those of the OWDs reveals that the former incorporated almost all the latter's claims and added its own notions, including the concept of "multiple and crossed forms of discrimination". In so doing, the CRPD lent credibility to and amplified advocacy efforts by the new OWDs.

What of the "boomerang effect"[4] in Haiti of the incursions of Haitian OWDs into UN political arenas? According to the Disability Rights Fund, one result of these mobilizations is increased space for women with disabilities within the disability rights movement:

> We're starting to hear women's voices and . . . I'd say that women speak a lot, are making themselves heard a lot more these days than the men in the movement. . . . So, by giving them space, and really it's what had to happen, that they have space, that they have support so they can assume leadership and understand that they inevitably have a leadership role to play. So we hear them, they are very present in the media. . . . [W]e are aware of their existence.
>
> *(interview with Jo-Ann Garnier, DRF, 2019)*

On the terrain of Haitian institutions, in 2016, the BSEIPH publicized the claims of OWDs in its electronic newsletter, *Handiscoop*. In late 2018 and early 2019, it followed up on the CRPD's recommendations by launching a process to amend the 2012 law and consult the disability rights movement. Yet, women with disabilities remained poorly represented in consultations that favored representation through national disability rights organizations with no gender analysis. However, in February 2020, the Moïse government named UFMORH founder Soinette Désir the new Secretary of State for the Integration of Persons with Disabilities, a significant development for the OWDs. Placing an activist devoted to the cause of women with disabilities at the helm of the BSEIPH brought hope that the 2012 law, which mentions women only once, would be amended to reflect their realities. Nevertheless, this appointment took place during a serious legitimacy crisis for the Moïse government, as large sectors of the population had been asking for his resignation since July 2018. We will return to this highly volatile, broader context at the end of this chapter.

Also, despite the favorable reception of this nomination by the large organizations of persons with disabilities and despite the inclusion of OWDs and their issues in both alternative reports and the CRPD recommendations, the networks that lead the strategic reflection group of the disability rights movement have not, until now, invited OWDs to appoint representatives to this space. Even though the 2018 report of the CRPD echoed and amplified the claims of women with disabilities and the BSEIPH has been under new leadership, fundamental changes have been slow to manifest themselves within the movement. In fact, there seems to be an implicit activist division of labor between RANIPH-Sud, coordinator of advocacy efforts targeting the CRPD, allied to the new OWDs and defender of the importance of Article 6, and the large national networks of organizations of persons with disabilities in which discussions and reflections on women with disabilities have not yet taken place (interview with Rose-May Legouté, RANIPH-national, 2019).

While in the field, we also noted a lack of understanding, if not resistance, on the part of several male representatives in the disability rights movement to the idea that the experiences of inequality and discrimination endured by women with disabilities have a specificity and deserve special attention from the movement and state institutions. Some contested the idea that women's experiences were different. Faced with convincing examples, they then protested against a focus that, according to them, would exclude the experiences of men with disabilities. Most knew of the OWDs and praised their work but could not tell us anything substantial about the latter. This lack of recognition is better understood when we remember that relations of power grant individuals from majority groups the privilege of not experiencing the intersectional oppression endured by those from minority groups "and, as a result, of not immediately seeing its relevance" (Masson, 2015, p. 57). At the very same time, power is also granted to members of the majority group to universalize their own experience to the whole of the population they claim to represent.

Effects of activism by OWDs on feminist spaces

In contrast to their action on the disability rights terrain, OWDs submitted their alternative report to CEDAW independently: that is, not in partnership with other feminist organizations. The report's key points were presented in the first part of this chapter. Here, we cite the CEDAW committee's final observations in full, given that they reflect most of the issues highlighted by AFAS and UFMORH:

> The Committee notes the State Party's adoption of a law protecting the rights of persons with disabilities. It nonetheless remains concerned about the considerable stigmatization and discrimination experienced by women

with disabilities and girls in the State party, as well as the violence and sexual exploitation they frequently experience. The Committee notes with concern the obstacles they face in terms of access to justice, political participation, employment, education, and sexual and reproductive health services.

The Committee . . . recommends that the State Party effectively implement the law on the integration of persons with disabilities through appropriate sanctions against perpetrators of violence and discrimination towards women and girls with disabilities and by ensuring that victims of these acts receive satisfactory compensation. The Committee also recommends that the State Party engage in activities to raise awareness in order to alter negative cultural attitudes toward women and girls with disabilities and ensure their access to justice, political participation, education, revenue-generating activities, and health care, including sexual and reproductive health services.

(Comité pour l'élimination de la discrimination à l'égard des femmes, 2016, pp. 15–16)

What impact did the committee's observations have on the recognition of OWDs and their demands in Haiti? The advocacy of OWDs directed at the CEDAW did have a boomerang effect. Shortly after the committee's report, the MCFDF began recognizing these organizations, mostly through private meetings between the minister and OWDs' representatives. During the summer of 2018, the minister acknowledged the importance of consulting with women with disabilities to update the Policy for Equality between Women and Men (interview with Soinette Désir, UFMORH, 2019). Conversations continued in September 2018 with a new minister to formalize an engagement to include women with disabilities in the MCFDF's activities (interview with Soinette Désir, UFMORH, 2019). However, in the context of Haiti's profound, multidimensional crisis, no concrete action has yet taken place.

Regarding the relationship between Haiti's feminist movement and the new OWDs, the latter mention repeatedly inviting feminist leaders and organizations to their activities without even receiving acknowledgement and not being invited to many events organized by the feminist movement. As well, alternative reports and interviews reveal a sense of being excluded by a discourse that only considers women's rights "in general". For example, having doggedly struggled to be invited to a feminist event, one of our informants proposed that the words "disabled women" be included in its final declaration, only to be told that the word "women" included all women (personal communication). But far from giving up, OWDs keep arguing for inclusion:

"While we fight for equality between men and women, we must not neglect the inequalities that exist between women", says Soinette [Désir], who deplores the fact that women with disabilities are excluded from decisions that concern them, even within the feminist movement in Haiti.

(Duvil, 2016)

She specifies:

> We need a feminist movement . . . that listens to the voices of all women without discrimination. . . . We need more sisterhood between feminist organizations and organizations of women with disabilities so this voice [the voice of women with disabilities] can be carried further.
>
> *(Interview with Soinette Désir, 2019)*

Nonetheless, the emergence of a politicized discourse on women with disabilities and its progressive elaboration through the new OWDs' advocacy work and, in particular, the 2016 alternative report to the CEDAW are having some impact on Haiti's feminist movement. According to the DRF's Jo-Ann Garnier,

> Women's associations did not consider associations of women with disabilities part of the women's movement . . . And now, we see collaboration starting; there's some real networking, alliances are being created and women's organizations are starting to show an interest in the issues of women with disabilities.
>
> *(Interview, 2019)*

This assessment is partially corroborated by our interviews with OWDs, yet it must be nuanced by highlighting the larger dynamic of transformation within the feminist movement. Genuine collaboration between the new OWDs and the feminist movement in Haiti is more often the result of younger feminist organizations openly engaging in intersectional analyses. In particular, the *Initiative pour un Développement Équitable en Haïti* (IDEH) (Initiative for Equitable Development in Haiti) has begun to establish relationships with OWDs and affirm its desire to consider the experiences and demands of minoritized women, including women with disabilities. In this way, IDEH has addressed the issues of access of women with disabilities to sexual and reproductive health and the effects of disability on gender-based violence. It has also supported the OWDs' demands to update the Policy for Equality between Women and Men (interview with Claudine Saintal and Mause Darline Francois, IDEH, 2019; Initiative pour un Développement Équitable en Haïti, 2017). Recognition is mutual: "We consider IDEH a sister organization" (interview with Jeannine Adelphin, AFAS, 2019).

For its part, *Solidarite Fanm Ayisyèn* (SOFA) (Solidarity Haitian Women), founded in 1986 and the largest feminist organization in Haiti with 10,000 members in seven departments (Solidarite fanm ayisyèn, 2020), states that for several years, it has been working with FASHAA, inviting its representatives to training sessions and consultations. SOFA does not maintain similar relationships with the new OWDs that politicize the lived experiences of women with disabilities at the intersection of gender and ableism. Yet according to its representative, it has become more sensitive to the existence of both LGBT groups and organizations of women with disabilities:

> Because after 30 years, there are new actors emerging in Haitian society. There are new issues; we are listening to these issues and must invent and reinvent ourselves in relation to [them]. Because they are minorities, . . . at certain points their battles cross path with our battles. So why not work together?
>
> *(Interview with SOFA representative, 2019)*

In this context, SOFA's current strategic plan seeks to explore opportunities to build "a common political front" of minoritized groups in order to "transform unequal relations in a global way" within Haitian society. But unlike IDEH's intersectional approach, which sees the battles of women, LGBT people and women with disabilities (among others) as closely linked, SOFA's analyses remain anchored in the monist perspective that dominates Haiti's historic feminist movement. SOFA sees the struggles of women, LGBT people and women with disabilities as distinct from one another. These struggles can be the object of alliances but are not intrinsically SOFA's. Still, its representative adds, "[I]f women with disabilities have to fight, they can count on [support from] SOFA" (interview, 2019).

Conclusion

This chapter has shown that the new OWDs emerging in Haiti since 2008 are characterized by a desire to go beyond the creation of spaces of sociability for women with disabilities to enter the political sphere. Confronting the deficit of representation resulting from their minority position within intersecting axes of social domination, OWDs give voice to women with disabilities. Drawing on the repertoire of advocacy, their activism uses an intersectional lens to politicize experiences shaped simultaneously by gender and disability and affirm their specificity. It is fueled by the agency of women with disabilities who have learned, through collective action, to see themselves as genuine political subjects. This agency is exerted in a context in which a variety of political dynamics are at work; some facilitate and support their action while others limit or block them, with consequences for their agenda of sociopolitical change.

On one hand, the strategic and financial support of the international NGO Disability Rights Fund has facilitated a process of empowerment of women with disabilities in these OWDs and reinforced their organizational capacities. This support has contributed greatly to orienting their action towards advocacy. By promoting new norms – won through hard-fought battles (Arnade & Haefner, 2011) – regarding the rights of women and girls with disabilities, the CRPD and its monitoring mechanisms provide Haiti's OWDs with political opportunities to be heard on an international level. The CRPD's reiteration and amplification of their analyses and demands could have significant effects on national institutions and the disability rights movement. Similar opportunities are offered by CEDAW, which does not name disability as a discriminatory factor for women but is overseen by an international committee that practices a feminist intersectional approach (Campbell, 2015). The election of Ana Peláez Narváez to the CEDAW committee in 2018, the first woman with a disability and experienced activist to sit on that body, may foreshadow more change.

On the other hand, the current status of OWDs as small, local organizations and the majority/minority relationships that affect their dealings with the two large movements with which they identify limit the impact of their intersectional activism. Although they benefit from the support of RANIPH-Sud, as well as from the legitimacy granted by Article 6 of the CRPD, and the CRPD's language of "*discriminations croisées*" (crossed discriminations) experienced by women and girls with disabilities, the new OWDs remain at the margins of the disability rights movement, and their claims have yet to be echoed by large national organizations and networks whose activities rest on the category of disabled "persons". In Haiti's feminist movement, the dominance of monist analyses privileging solely gender could give way to strategic alliances involving OWDs, yet the development of intersectional sensibilities in younger feminist organizations fosters a more effective, direct inclusion of women with disabilities and their concerns. The majority/minority relations that materialize gendered and ableist forms of domination are also present within institutions such as the BSEIPH and MCFDF, which have been both resistant and somewhat permeable to change.

On another level, OWDs find themselves in a profoundly unfavourable context. For decades, the Haitian state and society have been experiencing a series of serious, multidimensional crises that severely constrain progressive reforms (Baranyi, 2019). The limited financial means the state possesses to respond to the demands of its population have been depleted by misappropriations, which have been denounced in popular demonstrations against corruption and the high cost of living initiated in July 2018 by the *Kot kòb Petwo Karibe a*? (Where is the Petro Caribe money?) movement. In early 2020, the Moïse administration took advantage of parliamentary mandates coming to an end to govern by decree, unleash violence against dissident voices and coopt some civil society associations. In 2020, the spread of the COVID-19 pandemic worsened the macroeconomic and fiscal crises already choking a weak and irresponsible state (Lamour, 2019). The recent increase in the number of kidnappings and attacks on poor neighborhoods by armed gangs has created a profound sense of insecurity, compounded by the assassination, on July 7, 2021, of President Jovenel Moïse. On August 13, 2021, acting prime minister and interim head of state Ariel Henry revoked all secretaries of state, including Soinette Désir. On August 14, 2021, an earthquake in the Southern part of Haiti destroyed AFHS's offices and rendered many of its surviving members homeless. As of October 2021, the physical offices of BSEIPH were occupied by people with disabilities displaced by gang violence. These contextual developments have been making work by OWDs much more difficult. Yet it has not stopped them, particularly UFMORH, from remaining active at the grassroots level.

In a better world, pressures from civil society organizations could converge with pressures from Haiti's international partners in the core group to facilitate the creation of a representative government of transition capable of organizing legitimate elections and opening the door to more profound reforms. The women's and disability rights movements are involved in such efforts. The new OWDs could help these social movements forge a cross-sectoral alliance. Yet the materialization of that scenario depends not only on the ability of minority groups to empower themselves and build alliances but also on the willingness of the de facto government and the core group to change their strategy. As Haiti descends deeper into violence and lawlessness, the window of opportunity for such a realignment may be closing rapidly.

Notes

1 Drawing on critical feminist theories of disability, Masson (2013) defines ableism as "a structure of social differentiation and hierarchization based on the normalization of certain bodily forms and functionalities". Ableism oppresses, marginalizes and excludes people whose physical and cognitive abilities do not correspond to these norms (p. 115).

2 There seems to exist a few other OWDs elsewhere in the country, but our key informants were not able to provide information about them. Therefore, their activities do not have the scope of those studied here.

3 All named interview participants gave their consent to be identified in publications based on this study. As well, all quotes from material spoken or written originally in French have been translated into English by the authors.

4 In the sociology of social movements, the concept of the "boomerang effect" proposed by Keck and Sikkink (1998) seeks to highlight movement strategies that use pressure on international institutions to effect changes at the national level.

References

Arnade, S., and Haefner, S. (2011). Standard interpretation of the UN Convention on the Rights of Persons with Disabilities (CRPD) from a female perspective. Position and reference paper on the significance of references to women and gender in the Convention on the Rights of Persons with Disabilities. *Netzwerk Artikel,* 3.

Association filles au soleil. (2018, June 15). *Accueil*; *À propos*; *Projet*. www.afashaiti.sitew.com (website now inactive).

Association filles au soleil and Union des femmes à mobilité réduite d'Haïti. (2016, January). Rapport alternatif présentant de façon brève la condition des femmes et filles handicapées en Haïti. *Report Presented to the Committee of the Convention pour l'élimination des discriminations faites aux femmes* (CEDEF/CEDAW), 62th session.

Association filles au soleil, Union des femmes à mobilité réduite d'Haïti, Association des sourds de Lévêque d'Haïti and Coalition du Réseau associatif national pour l'intégration des personnes handicapées Sud. (2016, March). Violations aux droits des personnes handicapées en Haïti. *Report presented to the UN Human Rights Council*, 26th session.

Baranyi, S. (2019). Haïti: le chaos, la refonte du système ou le bricolage continu? *Diplomatie*, *100*(1), 30–35.

Baranyi, S., and Louis, I. (2016). (Dis)ability and development in Haiti: Beyond one-dimensional views. *Third World Thematics*, *20*(20), 321–334. https://doi.org/10.1080/23802014.2016.1216328

Bilge, S. (2010). De l'analogie à l'articulation. Théoriser la différenciation sociale et l'inégalité complexe. *L'homme et la société*, *2–3*(176–177), 43–64. https://doi.org/10.3917/lhs.176.0043

Campbell, M. (2015). CEDAW and women's intersecting identities: A pioneering new approach to intersectional discrimination. *Revista Direito GV* [online], *11*(2), 479–504. https://doi.org/10.1590/1808-2432201521

Coalition du Réseau associatif national pour l'intégration des personnes handicapées Sud, Association des femmes handicapées du Sud, Association des parents des personnes handicapées du Sud, Association des personnes sourdes du Sud, Union des femmes à mobilité réduite d'Haïti, Fédération nationale de sourds d'Haïti, Association pour la promotion des droits et l'intégration des personnes handicapées du Sud. (2017). *Rapport alternatif sur la mise en œuvre de la Convention relative aux droits des personnes handicapées*. République d'Haïti.

Comité des droits des personnes handicapées. (2018, April 13). Observations finales concernant le rapport initial d'Haïti (publication no CRPD/C/HTI/CO/1). *Haut-Commissariat des Nations unies*. https://documents-dds-ny.un.org/doc/UNDOC/GEN/G18/103/60/PDF/G1810360.pdf?OpenElement

Comité pour l'élimination de la discrimination à l'égard des femmes. (2016). Observations finales concernant les huitième et neuvième rapports périodiques combinés d'Haïti (publication no CEDAW/C/HTI/CO/8–9). *Haut-Commissariat des Nations unies*. https://documents-dds-ny.un.org/doc/UNDOC/GEN/N16/064/62/PDF/N1606462.pdf?OpenElement

Conejo, M. (2011). Disabled women and transnational feminisms: Shifting boundaries and frontiers. *Disability & Society, 26*(5), 597–609. https://doi.org/10.1080/09687599.2011.589193

Côté, D. (2014). 'Anpil fanm tonbe, nap kontinye vanse': luttes féministes en Haïti. *Revue Possibles*, *38*(1), 209–223.

Crenshaw, K. (1989). Demarginalizing the intersection of race and sex: A Black feminist critique of antidiscrimination doctrine, feminist theory and antiracist politics. *University of Chicago Legal Forum*, *1*(Art. 8), 139–167.

Disability Rights Fund. (2020, August 8). *About*. https://disabilityrightsfund.org/about/

Disability Rights Advocacy Fund (DRAF). (2020, June 21). *Grants Directory*. https://drafund.org/grants/directory/

Duvil, W. H. G. (2016, August 24). Portrait de femme. Soinette Désir, debout aux côtés des handicapées en Haiti. *Le Nouvelliste*. https://lenouvelliste.com/article/162066/soinette-desir-debout-aux-cotes-des-handicapees-en-haiti.

Initiative pour un Développement Équitable en Haïti. (2017). Évaluation des risques de violence chez les femmes et les filles en situation de handicap. Unpublished research report.

Kayess, R., Sands, T., and Fisher, K. R. (2014). International power and local action – Implications for the intersectionality of the rights of women with disability. *Australian Journal of Public Administration*, *73*(3), 383–396. https://doi.org/10.1111/1467-8500.12092

Keck, M., and Sikkink, K. (1998). *Activists Beyond Borders: Advocacy Networks in International Politics*. Cornell University Press.

Lamour, S. (2019). L'irresponsabilité, une compétence de dominant. *Revue internationale des études du développement*, *239*(3), 7–29. https://doi.org/10.3917/ried.239.0007

Mackay, F., et Krook, M. L. (2015). *Gender, Politics and Institutions: Towards a Feminist Institutionalism*. Palgrave Macmillan.

Masson, D. (2013). Femmes et handicap. *Recherches féministes*, *26*(1), 111–129. https://doi.org/10.7202/1016899ar

Masson, D. (2015). Enjeux et défis d'une politique féministe intersectionnelle – L'expérience d'Action des femmes handicapées (Montréal). *L'homme et la société*, *198*, 35–58. https://doi.org/10.3917/lhs.198.0171

Mazur, A. (2009). Les mouvements féministes et l'élaboration des politiques dans une perspective comparative. *Revue française de science politique*, *59*(2), 325–351. https://doi.org/10.3917/rfsp.592.0325

Merlet, M. (2010). Haiti. Women in the conquest of full citizenship in an endless transition. In E. Maier and N. Lebon (dir.), *Women's activism in Latin America and the Caribbean. Engendering Social Justice, Democratizing Citizenship* (pp. 129–139). Rutgers University Press.

Péan, M. (2011, March 16). Haïti: Un modèle d'exclusion, un échantillon de lutte pour l'inclusion des personnes handicapées dans le Tiers monde. *Intervention to the Commission of Social Affairs and Environment of the European Parliament*. https://www.europarl.europa.eu/meetdocs/2009_2014/documents/acp/dv/point6_michel_a_pean/point6_michel_a_peanfr.pdf

Pierre, M.-J., and l'Association des femmes handicapées du Sud. (2020, June 25–26). D'où vient le mouvement des femmes handicapées en Haïti? Comment elles font face aux défis? *Presentation at the colloquium Accessibilité, handicap et environnement bâti en Haïti, Online Conference*.

Pierre, S. J., and l'Union des femmes à mobilité réduite d'Haïti. (2020, June 25–26). Genre, handicap et discrimination contre les femmes handicapées en Haïti. *Presentation at the colloquium Accessibilité, handicap et environnement bâti en Haïti, Online Conference*.

Predelli, L. N., and Halsaa, B. (2012). *Majority-Minority Relations in Contemporary Women's Movements*. Palgrave McMillan.

Price, J. (2011). La naissance d'un mouvement: les femmes handicapées et leur lutte pour s'organiser. In S. Batliwala (Ed.), *Les mouvements de femmes, concepts et pratiques* (2nd ed.). AWID. https://www.awid.org/sites/default/files/atoms/files/changer_leur_monde_-_la_naissance_dun_mouvement.pdf

Société civile du département du Sud. (2013). *Rapport alternatif sur les droits des personnes handicapées*. Les Cayes.

Solidarite fanm ayisyèn. (2020, October 12). *Qui sommes-nous?* http://sofahaiti.org/apropos.html

Tele Ginen. (2017, March 17). Haïti. L'Association de filles et femmes au soleil organise une marche pacifique [Video]. *You Tube*. https://www.youtube.com/watch?v=FInEhZD4k-M

Thill, C. (2019). Listening for intersectionality: How disabled persons' organisations have improved recognition of difference in Australia's national disability insurance scheme. In O. Hankivsky and J. S. Jordan-Zachery (Eds.), *The Palgrave Handbook of Intersectionality in Public Policy, The Politics of Intersectionality* (pp. 689–704). Springer. https://doi.org/10.1007/978-3-319-98473-5_32

Union des femmes à mobilité réduite d'Haïti. (n.d.). Accueil [Facebook statute]. *Facebook*. https://www.facebook.com/UFMORH.org/

PART V

Representations of disability

29
REFLECTIONS OF MISPERCEPTIONS

James Ian

Oh Hollywood, you made me think I could never be on the silver screen,
All because I was born with a mutated or a deleted SMN1 gene.
And when I did see disability, it was portrayed despicably in scenes,
So when I was growing up, I didn't feel I should be seen.
Because all I ever saw on TV when it came to disability,
Were folks who were ridiculed, viewed as inhuman, and folks who were pitied.
Then there were other times you told me my disability should be overcome,
And that's why I tried to defy science and maintain my ability to run.
Let's not forget the times you showed me I would always be alone,
Despite text messages to the contrary from beautiful women on my phone.
You constantly sent me messages saying I'd never be desired,
But this wasn't my reality, so which one of us is the liar?
Dating was always easy, for as long as I can remember,
And I always had partners to dance with, even if it wasn't in September.
If you don't believe me, you can check my IG and my yearbook for the proof,
The way you tried to paint me couldn't have been further from the truth.
At the end of the day, I didn't feel the way you wanted me to be perceived,
So I went back and forth internally about which one of us to believe.
It's scary to think that you almost had me fooled,
But luckily for me, I don't play by anyone else's rules.
See, as a Black man in Amerikkka living with a disability,
Even I couldn't imagine how difficult things would really be.
It seemed my trajectory, the world would conspire to stifle,
Although I can't jump, man, I was determined to fly higher than Michael.
In case you missed the reference, I'm talking about number 23,
And the things I used to try and hide are the things now that you're gonna see.
You tried to show me that my disability was something to be hated,

DOI: 10.4324/9781003410089-35

When instead it was something beautiful that should always be celebrated.
It's given me a unique point of view, and a real sense of purpose,
And lived experiences I can bring to the stage, when they lift up the curtains.
It's made me feel so many things, a whole range of emotions,
People say inside of me they can see depths as deep as an ocean.
So I use it as an asset, and I include it as I work upon my craft,
And I audition for roles with disabilities, even though there are so few of them that are cast.
Along the way I've lost some of them to nondisabled actors,
It's hard not to take it personally, then I realize it's the stereotype they're after.
I could go on and on about how you've harmed us with your portrayals,
And about how I've lost my faith in you because of all of your betrayals.
But the only person I ever needed to have faith in was myself,
And when there's a job to do I've never been one to wait for someone else.
I wish it wasn't so difficult, but do I really have a choice?
Because I'm tired of you thinking you can speak for me and you trying to steal my voice.
So I keep it pushin' and doing what it takes to try and make it happen,
And when I look back on this life of mine, no one could ever say that my effort was lackin'.
Honestly, I could care less about being famous, and I don't care about being seen,
But I do hope someone with a disability sees themselves in me whenever I'm on screen.
Hollywood you won't hold me hold me back because I know this life is for me,
I'll be damned if I let you stop me from being the one to tell my story.

30
PIRATE ISLAND

Elizabeth Mestheneos

Stage notes: The play takes place on a tropical island in mid-Atlantic with the nearest neighbouring island being Asuncion. It is inhabited by approximately 8,000 people, though it has many citizens living abroad being supported by the island and also working for it. It is not a recognized state and flies under the radar by associating itself with Asuncion. It tries to keep in line with world trends – e.g. human rights – though it has always been a democratic society in line with pirate ethics.

Though once entirely inhabited by and financed by pirates, the economy has become more mixed over the past five decades through offshore investments, initially by pirates themselves and later by private companies. In the past 20 years, tourism has slowly developed, providing jobs for the inhabitants. The COVID crisis was avoided by stopping visitors and enforcing public health measures for returning citizens. Now they look forward to more "normal" years.

There are six significant villages, one of which, Santa Rosa, is the capital, where today's meeting is being held in the modern but traditionally open-styled wooden village hall attached to which is a community, high-tech workshop. Meetings are a regular feature of island life, and today's is being held to listen to the report to their council and citizens of their investment lawyer in New York and to discuss general council decisions and assess the social welfare situation of residents and island resources.

Characters in order of appearance

WILLIE: Male, late 70s, retired sailor, chronic depressive, accepted, moans, frets.
JUNE: zFemale, 50s, XAVIER's adopted mother, council member, bossy, clever.

DOI: 10.4324/9781003410089-36

EVI:	Female, early 30s, wheelchair user with MS, works part time in workshop or tourism, bitter, angry, sarcastic, her parents help in her care.
XAVIER:	Male, mid-30s, lawyer for Pirate Island living in New York, serious, adopted, found by LBJ as baby.
MABEL:	Female, 80s, retired teacher, getting frail, fighter, knows everyone, lives in Porto Antigo.
L.J. SILVER:	Male, late 80s, ex–sea captain/pirate, claims he's the great-grandson of the original LJS, bionic limbs, ex–council member, dynamic and noisy.
NEMO:	Male, young 30s, computer specialist, bionic leg, runs the e-workshop, sardonic, serious.
EMILY BURROW:	Female, 60s, shopkeeper in Santa Rosa, representative of older persons' associations, formal.
MANDI:	Female, mid 40s, uses a wheelchair since accident in her late teens, lives with George, cook, fighter, humorous.
GEORGE:	Male, mid 40s, carer and part-time farmer, flippant but very kind, Mandi's partner.
SCHWARTZ:	Male, 40s, slight stutter, digital and data expert, maths teacher.
CONNIE:	Female, 40s, mother of three children, one is intellectually disabled: her son Kadi, aged 16/17. Fighter, kind.
FREDDIE BARMA:	Male, early 70s, depressive, farmer and fisherman, moans, kind.
JOE:	Male, 80s, Jimmy's brother, was a seaman, lives in a village, age-related muscular skeletal disorders (i.e. not very mobile).

Community hall and workshop in Santa Rosa, Pirate Island

(Noise of tropical rain, then people entering the community hall, shaking out their umbrellas. Voices shout greetings.)

Voices: Thank goodness it's warm.
I'm soaked.

JUNE: Leave your umbrellas on the verandah. It's a wooden floor inside; it doesn't need water.

WILLIE: I'm not leaving this umbrella. Three years ago, someone pinched my old one.

Voice: Old was it? Did you take it personally, Willie?

WILLIE: We don't throw away old things.

JUNE: If it was broken and you left it for ages, we would have thrown it out and recycled the metal. You know the rules. Public spaces everyone must keep clean. By the way, old umbrellas aren't the same as old people.

Voice: Less metal in old people.

WILLIE: I'll show you metal. Wait till you've lived as hard as me.

(People continue to enter the hall.)

Voice: Lucky, you lot. Stayed in the dry. Didn't have to go anywhere.
EVI: (*sarcastically*) Some of us can't get anywhere. Get real.
JUNE: Oh, good, Xavier. Glad you've arrived. The workshop people are here, and some others have come for the meeting, despite the rain.
XAVIER: Wouldn't miss it for the world. Makes us who we are. Hey! It's you, Miss Mabel! You haven't changed at all.
MABEL: Nice of you to say so. Give me a towel to mop myself off with. I knew you were leaving to catch the boat. I thought I'd come to the meeting and see you off. Looks as if you're going to get delayed. Rough seas.
XAVIER: Have to wait till the storm dies down. I came to bring legal papers for the council to sign in person. Not everything can be done electronically!
MABEL: You've done so well for us all. You're a great lawyer, so they tell me.
XAVIER: I'm a child of the island. An orphan. Remember, the island looked after me.
MABEL: Yes. You were a nice and clever boy. I see you when you come in on meetings on that cloud thing. Amazing. And you in New York! I can't keep up. I'm glad I don't teach now.

(Noise of feet, slightly uneven)

L.J. SILVER: Hey, Xavier! Came to see you off. You're one of my good actions. Set it against the bad ones. *(Laughs)*
XAVIER: Silver, I know you! A dubious reputation! Did you really earn it yet?

(Both chuckle.)

L.J. SILVER: Found a woman yet? Bringing her here, are you?
JUNE: I don't ask how many wives you have, Silver! Private is private. You know island rules.
L.J. SILVER: Sorry. Just want him to be OK.
XAVIER: OK, June. I'm fine.
L.J. SILVER: What with the rain and all, now the arthritis gets me, and my spare parts will rust! Mind you, a hook like my great great-grandad had would also have rusted.

(He roars with laughter.)

NEMO: Some of us dream your electronic arm or leg will give you a shock.
EVI: No such luck. I'm the one who keeps having to have her wheelchair cleaned and oiled from the damp and heat. Don't I, Nemo?

NEMO: Yep.

MABEL: How are you, Evi? Haven't see you – well, it must be a year. Porto Antigo is a way from Santa Rosa.

EVI: No change. My parents still look after me. So, can't complain, but I do.

(Xavier coughs and waves to get people's attention. Noise of people sitting down, excuse me, hello, etc. Xavier sits at the front of the hall – some people sit at the table, some on floor cushions, and three in wheelchairs. Rain continues.)

XAVIER: June, my adopted mother, asked if I'd help. We've always had community meetings on the island as an open democratic place for us all to talk about island issues. The rain has limited attendance obviously.

EVI: Not just the rain. Who wants to talk about us cripples and mentals?

MABEL: *(in a teacher's voice)* Evi MacFarland, you watch your words. Look, we have problems to discuss.

EVI: *(almost smiles)* Yes, Miss Mabel. It's been a long time and . . .

(Her voice trails off.)

XAVIER: Sorry to rush you. I don't know how long I have. They'll phone the office from the port when the boat can leave harbor, and I'll have to leave fast.

L.J. SILVER: I reckon, with my sea experience, the storm will be over in a couple of hours.

(He hums knowingly.)

JUNE: I'm on the council, as you know, and thought it would be good to make use of Xavier, our international lawyer. He's a good listener.

WILLIE: He'd have to be, with you for a mum, June.

JUNE: Well, you come on the council next year, Willie, see how you get on!

MABEL: Ignore Willie; he's always been a moaner. Let's get on with it.

JUNE: OK. it might be the rain, but look around you. Not many of our older islanders are here. And the meeting is partly about them. They have cafes, clubs, and associations. True, Emily Burrow?

EMILY: Quite correct. Everyone got notice of today's meeting, but not many have come. We'd arranged transport from each of the five villages to the town. Mabel, Joe, and Willie have come from three of them, and the rest of us live in or near Santa Rosa. But unless islanders have their own experiences or looked after someone with a disability, they just aren't interested. I got a lot of comments like "We're not disabled, just going slower because of our age or ill health," or

"We've lived our lives: those poor buggers (my apologies for strong language), they need the help, but we're not disabled."

EVI: So, they aren't interested in our problems. I could have told you that!

XAVIER: Let me put today's debate into some context. We've always worked to solve our problems so everyone wins . . . even if no one gets rich. We've defended the values of independence and contributed to the island with all its assortment of people. Today, we're talking about two particular groups on this island. The growing number of older people with serious health problems and our welfare system. And, of course, our citizens with disabilities.

EVI: Us and them?

WILLIE: Cripples, basket cases, and old crocks.

ALL: Hell. Willie, mind your language.
That's you. Willie.
Shut up.
Sit on him, old Grumpy.

XAVIER: Over 20 years ago all over the world, the various and multitudinous groups with physical and cognitive—

(Murmurs from the crowd.)

OK, brain disabilities, came together at the UN to try to ensure that their rights as citizens were not ignored.

MANDI: And we were there! I even went to New York back in 2004.

GEORGE: She was brilliant – point her in the right direction, and she's a voice to drown out anyone. But she was right!

EVI: OK, OK, we remember; it put us on the map. It's when we agreed to have ramps in all our public spaces. . . . Mind you, still plenty of places I can't get to.

MABEL: And we got all the kids into school.

GEORGE: And we got some people like me, paid to help the people and families who couldn't cope. That's how I got to know Mandi before I got to make an honest woman of her.

MANDI: Hey – honest is not necessarily a word of praise on this island. Now I have the best 24/7 care.

(She giggles.)

GEORGE: You're a good cook. You can earn a living.

L.J. SILVER: Well, a lot of us didn't like all that publicity. I don't want to be on any map; that's how we survive, off the radar. Some of us have managed all our lives. We use Ascension Island as a front, and we've managed to be hardly noticed. Overseas UK passports! What better could we dream of? Allows us to work anywhere.

SCHWARTZ: Em, excuse me.
XAVIER: Mr. Schwartz. I know you're here not as the school maths teacher—

(Laughter from the attendees.)

but to talk about the island economy. You're one of our financial wizards.
MANDI: He's the real modern pirate here. The whole island is better off from his investments for us.
SCHWARTZ: Um, er . . . Economically and politically, we, as an island, depend on companies putting money here for us to m-m-manage. Our money is also in sea trade – not under our flag, but a wink and a nod and we've shares in lots of sea trade all over the world. We make profits. We've our investment businesses and, obviously, t-t-tourism.
ALL: And that underwater park where tourists snorkel that we know about.
You can see the old wreck off the coast with those carefully guarded "gold" bars—
Which are well and safe elsewhere—
SCHWARTZ: We keep the original pirate treasure, including old Sparrow's. It's saved us more than once, like during the war and b-b-b-blockade. And last year's virus. We made the museum and the park and created new jobs. P-part time or seasonal, it all helps.
EVI: *(muttering)* I help at the tourist shop when I can.
SCHWARTZ: We've islanders all over the world acting for us. They are "ours", sometimes over generations.
ALL: Yes, they are islanders too.
We've got Komo in Japan; his kids come in the summer even when he can't.
Deirdre in Ireland.
And the islanders in Amsterdam and London studying and in the financial sectors.
L.J. SILVER: I like that. Sort of illegal. But gives the young 'uns some work. They seem to understand.
JUNE: We've invested in renewable energy – you've seen the windmills – and modern agriculture. We decided ages ago to do that, as some of us are old enough to remember when both the mainlands tried again to cut us off so we'd become their protectorates.
ALL: We stopped them.
Could happen again.
What does it have to do with this meeting?
SCHWARTZ: Well, I'm really trying to explain that we are not a p-p-poor island.

L.J. SILVER: Thank God. We were almost back to self-sufficiency last year. But it was a tough year.

CONNIE: Almost fun. We had a community kitchen in town.

EVI: If I have to eat any more swordfish . . .

JUNE: It was pineapples for me . . . I can heave.

MABEL: Do you remember? The school children had a project to ask the really old folks how they managed, even before your time, Captain Silver.

L.J. SILVER: 'Scuse me, I'm not much older than you, Miss Mabel!

NEMO: We all tried to look into new uses for what we have on the island – palm, bamboo.

CONNIE: Oh, dear, yes. Kids were doing chemistry with goat and donkey urine, looking for a useful chemical for processing.

FREDDIE: It's OK for fields, but you can't get them to piss into a pot!

(General laughter.)

CONNIE: I had to keep washing all my kids' clothes after. No wonder we protested.

EVI: Have you seen the junk we made for when tourists come back? One million useless but recyclable bamboo, shell, and palm thingummies.

WILLIE: If they do!

SCHWARTZ: But we survived a hard year p-p-pretty well and didn't only look backwards. We started our high t-t-tech prosthesis and aids department two years back and—

ALL: That electronic printing company?

L.J. SILVER: Brilliant. They printed a spare for my arm when I broke the casing.

NEMO: You were the first to get a bionic arm and leg. And then me. After Carli and Fredo came back, trained from university and able to build these and other gadgets in the workshop next door. It's helped a lot of us.

ALL: He's right.
Amazing how fast Silver can walk, almost normal.
Things are changing.

XAVIER: We've all seen some changes on the island, for the better, after we agreed to that UN Convention for the Rights of People with Disability, even if we aren't recognized as a state. Our island state council supported it, and we all planned programmes for our slow learners and those who physically can't do much. It isn't that people want more rights, but they need more help to enjoy the same rights.

MANDI: We all used to fight each other for what we could get from our council. I couldn't even get into the sea unless someone carried me, and that wasn't very dignified. I'm a big girl.

GEORGE:	I never minded, darling.
MANDI:	Ah, shut up, you big goof. I'm not just talking about me. It's all the people who have different problems and need a bit of adjustment so they can join in fully.
L.J. SILVER:	Well, I admit I use the wooden beach path at Paradiso to get to the sea, and I'm not the only one. Much easier than walking on sand.
ALL:	Me too. The tourists like it.
MANDI:	Your boy, Kedi, Connie, isn't bright, but look at him now. He's learned to make things; he hangs out with other kids his age; he's OK with them. Without extra help, he can't do that.
CONNIE:	It's a relief to me that he's learning a trade. I've got my other two to worry about.
L.J. SILVER:	In the workshop, he's cleaning our old island silver for very rich collectors. It gets a better price. He couldn't work on the boats. And I wouldn't trust him with the goats, that's for sure . . .

(He laughs a dirty laugh.)

XAVIER:	*(irritated)* OK. OK. Let's stick to the subject. Everyone gets money, and either they or we can pay for the care they really need. It isn't many of us, after all. We're very few anyway.
L.J. SILVER:	How many?
SCHWARTZ:	Difficult to answer.
ALL:	Why? You must know.
SCHWARTZ:	W-w-w we are 8,000 people on the island; an estimated 15% have some problems which count as disabilities. We don't always recognise them. So that's 1,200 of all ages.
L.J. SILVER:	You're kidding us.
SCHWARTZ:	Look at W-Willie. You've known him all his life; doesn't he always look on the black side?
WILLIE:	And why shouldn't I? My right.
SCHWARTZ:	He isn't alone. Depression is common. S-s-s sometimes it needs medicine and sometimes counseling. But I've tried to count only the-the ones, those needing substantive help. Maybe 500. If you're asking, Mr. Silver, how many of us may never be independent and earn a living or completely look after ourselves, the answer is different. Look, I know of 16 who have p-p-problems learning, but we train them and get them into jobs that need doing. Some p-p-problems show up when we're kids, others later. You yourself said nothing stopped *you*, but I count you amongst the 500. Medical treatment abroad and rehabilitation and then later your b-b-bionic bits don't come cheap.

EVI:	Well, they've had their lives. Can the island really afford to spend money on them? Whether I like it or not, and I don't, I am going to spend most of my life in a wheelchair needing increasing amounts of care. The council pays for that because I need it, and I'm a born-and-bred islander.
XAVIER:	Order, order. The council already voted that citizens who were disabled and could not work would be looked after.
DEDI:	Can I speak? I've only been here 18 months. I'm a nurse on the usual two-year contract. I help run the healthcare centre here. About a third to a half of older people lose their hearing. It makes normal conversation difficult. So there's another group – call them disabled if you like, but they certainly need hearing aids.
L.J. SILVER:	What did she say? What did she say?

(He bursts into laughter.)

	Sorry, a bit obvious.
EMILY:	It's what I said before. The older ones don't count themselves as disabled. Very common that many gradually go deaf, but even if we tell them, they still don't do anything about it.
WILLIE:	She's talking about old Eric, the blundering, blond, bionic captain! He can't lip-read, and apart from signing for a rum or to pay, he can't join in. He doesn't have a wife to nag him . . .
L.J. SILVER:	Perhaps Evi could. He's nice looking.
EVI:	Shut up. He's ancient.
L.J. SILVER:	He's younger than me!
ALL:	What do you think you are? Love's young dream? Bionic everything!

(Laughter. The rain noise lessens.)

L.J. SILVER:	I do notice. My wife's deaf, and my old crew – well, half of them seem deaf and then go daft.
DEDI:	Actually, it does affect the brain after a while. Send them to me.
MR. CHAN:	As the town pharmacist, I do send people to you, but too many of them don't recognise they have problems.
L.J. SILVER:	Give us all a MOT, like they do cars every year or so. I'veseen that in Europe.
DEDI:	With the nurses who have just arrived off the boat, we could.
MR. CHAN:	Not a bad idea, really, Mr. Silver. We'll discuss it among the health people here and then go to the council.
EVI:	So great! Now we have a lot of old people waiting in turn for help and services. Their life's over. They had a good life. Some of us never did and never will.
WILLIE:	Well, I've never needed help from anyone. I'm not like them.

EVI: Them! What are we? Lesser citizens?

JUNE: Anyway, you can't manage without your wife; you need her.

(Laughter.)

WILLIE: Anyway, what is disabled when you get old?

ALL: Can't walk to the bar.
Can't get it up.
Can't remember anything.

WILLIE: You wait till you get old.

EVI: You lot are old; you've had your lives. You don't have the troubles we have. You try being blind! Or deaf, or in a wheelchair, or having a brain that doesn't work properly.

ALL: I agree.
You're right.

EVI: Look how long it took me to find a job I could do. Sometimes I can't hold a pen with my MS or work sorting and selling the old treasure. Difficult to ever find a mate, and a lot of us suffer pain and can be very lonely. My illness is affecting my parents. My dad doesn't work on long sea trips anymore so he can help me. Willie, you married – God help your wife – had kids. What chance is there for me?

WILLIE: No. I agree we oldies aren't disabled. I don't want to be counted as one of you lot!

MANDI: You lot? No Willie, not acceptable – you are out of order talking like that. Some were born with disabilities; some get them thrust upon them.

WILLIE: Some never work.

EVI: Some of us can't! What do you want – starve us to death, shut us up in an institution, or give us the possibility of living in the community? And the old. What are they doing? They live off the island coffers!

WILLIE: I paid in all my working life, and it was hard work on the ships and then on the fishing boats.

ALL: Back again to this argument.
He's right, but what can we do?
I'd rather work than be disabled.

EVI: Mean old bugger. You sit in my wheelchair and see how it feels.

WILLIE: It's your parents I'm sorry for; you just moan.

XAVIER: Order, order, please.

SCHWARTZ: There's about 30 people that get Help at Home.

GEORGE: I'm no longer fully available.

(He laughs.)

Nah . . . I'm still a carer for others besides Mandi.

XAVIER: OK, everyone! You can hear we've a real difference between people with disabilities like Evi here, who don't see themselves as having anything in common with older people. She just wants us to focus on supporting all the island's disabled. On the other hand, older people, even when disabled, don't see themselves as such.

EVI: Well, they're not. Let them fight for care and help, as we did.

MANDI: We argue half the time about who's got the worst problems. And we've still plenty of them . . .

XAVIER: Yes, of course. It's a work in progress. We've had to give scholarships abroad to two very disabled kids from here who just couldn't fulfill their potential. One managed to become a very good physicist.

ALL: Anyone we know?
Who's that then?

MANDI: I don't have MS; I know it's progressive and painful, and I understand Evi's fears. She won't be able to manage. She worries that the growing numbers of older people with disabilities and their votes will reduce what she currently gets as help.

CONNIE: Disabled kids can't be left alone. Adults can.

MABEL: No. People with dementia and Alzheimer's need to be protected and cared for too.

EVI: But they are going to be with us long . . .

MABEL: Well, dear, some of them can be five or ten years in a bad state and needing care.

XAVIER: Evi, do you agree that so far the island hasn't let you down?

EVI: Not in a technical sense. But you'd be surprised how many people on the island don't want to look at us or talk to us. Don't invite us for a drink. Dedi – ask our deaf friends how often they go out.

MANDI: I do know. I don't know what more we can do. I've seen what a difference having George in my life has made.

ALL: Oh yeah!
Good to you, is he?

MANDI: Dirty minds you lot have. But we go out to local places and invite people to have a drink with us. It's easier as a couple. Evi is on her own, as are Ahmet and Gillian who can't hear.

FREDDIE: No one talks to me.

ALL: Because you're a miserable sod, Freddie.

JUNE: Leave the man alone; he can't help it.

XAVIER: Let's go back to the real problem. Can we get the two sides to cooperate, neither ignoring one another nor looking down on each other?

MABEL: It's a bit abstract. I came to this meeting to see what the community proposes for my neighbour Jimmy. I'm with Joe; we must think about some old people.

ALL: Why him?

MABEL: Everyone is different in their needs. And situations change. Maybe if we look at someone like Jimmy, disabled and old, and get everyone here, many of whom have had worse problems all their life, to think of solutions, maybe we are on the way to cooperating.

EVI: I'm willing to listen. But . . .

XAVIER: She has a point.

(Silence while people think.)

EVI: Do you think he needs a wheelchair? We can do something about that. Nemo?

NEMO: Yes, if someone can get him to us so we can fit him up with one.

EMILY: We have an adapted bus and can order it for him, but someone has to tell him and get him to agree. Porto Antigo isn't all that easy if I remember right. A lot of cobblestones which feel like hell whether you walk or are in a wheelchair.

MABEL: Especially on old feet.

MR. CHAN: In town, we've filled in the cobblestones, flattened them so everyone can walk. We can put Porto Antigo on the council list of adaptations. The tourist route for those doing sea trips will be improved, so another argument. What do you think, Evi? Mandi? Does flattening the cobblestones work here in Santa Rosa?

MANDI/GEORGE: Yes. Definitely an improvement

EVI: Yes, it helps. Should do it sooner probably than later for Jimmy and the tourists. But I haven't been there for ages, so it's stopping us islanders visiting Porto Antigo.

DEDI: May I? I'm signing for my two deaf friends from the workshop here. I think it's a priority for Jimmy to get his ears seen to. It might just be wax. He can come to us or go to Fernando Arego in town who specializes in deaf aids. It's linked to what I said before. Being depressed happens if he can't hear and has to guess what people are saying. I'd say start there.

MANDI: Is our help service able to take on someone like him? Maybe he doesn't need help every day but just to make sure his clothes are cleaned along with himself?

EVI: Look, it's for us who can't manage at all. Some days I need someone to get me up, dressed, and sometimes even fed. The four service carers helping us are already pushed. We don't have enough nurses or physios. How can we share them with an old man like him who, let's face it, is just dying.

JUNE: But surely everyone has some right to die with some decency. This Jimmy, whom I don't know, seems to have a need now. Mr. Chan, how is the budget for this?

L.J. SILVER: Just give him free rum, and he can forget his troubles.

FREDDIE: Who wouldn't like that kind of help?

JUNE: Don't be horrible, Silver. He deserves more than dying as a drunken and very dirty old man.

MABEL: It isn't just Jimmy. What about the demented?

Mr. CHAN: As Dedi said, two trained male nurses just arrived on our boat, picked up off the Nigerian coast by one of our captains. They'd heard of us. The one from Cameroon is escaping a civil war. The other – well, I think there are personal reasons. Usual two-year contract. If both sides like each other, a renewal. Housing and wages and the Cameroonian definitely said he'd love a small piece of land to grow pineapples on.

JUNE: No more pineapples.

SCHWARTZ: So we are increasing our services.

EVI: That is good news. I'm terrified one of the staff will hurt themselves lifting me or just get ill.

JOE: Look, if my couple of mates take me over, I'll talk to him. Take him clean sheets. Tell him what we are suggesting. See if the home help service can manage him straightaway. I'm ashamed he's in this state . . .

MABEL: I do agree. He needs to see you.

JUNE: We need some more paid carers. George, how are the carers? Can we find some more?

GEORGE: It's a job that pays the same as the others. But you want people to have some knowledge. There's two people I know of who looked after family who died a few months ago. They've had a rest now, and I have it in mind to ask them if they would like to join us.

EVI: You see what I mean! Always on the edge.

NEMO: You may have heard of smart homes and technologies

ALL: Like you, Nemo?
Smart!

NEMO: Yeah, like me. We are planning to get some houses fitted so people with problems living alone or who are alone during the day have a place to call for help or reassurance.

EVI: I just need a different body.

MR. CHAN: We're not there yet, Evi. But we are looking out to see what can help. Treatments, high- and low-tech gadgets for you. But the Alzheimer's patients, still not much real progress.

(Rain stops.)

ALL: Finally.
The boat will go soon.

XAVIER: OK, that's the end of the storm. So I'm afraid I won't be here much longer. Any more comments?

EMILY: We've a plan to bus family carers into Santa Rosa to use one of our other community centres for day care so they can go shopping or just have a coffee.

L.J. SILVER: Or a rum.

DEDI: It's the centre we run with exercise classes and dances.

MANDI: I go with George sometimes, to get my upper body moving and stronger. You could come to that Evi, but . . .

EVI: Thanks, but no thanks. I can't. But I appreciate the thought. It's all too good to be true.

L.J. SILVER: So is this island. But we've made it into a place we like. It keeps changing. And your moans, Evi, keep us on our feet. A joke maybe on us both. But we're here and talking.

(Xavier's phone rings. People stop talking.)

XAVIER: Just finishing. I'm on my way.

(He closes the phone.)

I'm off. There's a car outside to take me. This was the start of a discussion. But I have to say that we've something suggested in regard to Jimmy. Really a productive meeting. You are a great lot.

ALL: Thanks, Xavier

XAVIER: It was lovely to see everyone in the flesh and not just virtually. I haven't had that many hugs and kisses for a long time. It did me good to be back. I'm sorry I can't stay for the movie. June said it's one of the old favorites?

JUNE: *The Wizard of Oz*. Bye bye, my dear.

(The sound of a kiss.)

XAVIER: *(to the room)* See you soon online, and I will come when I can. June keeps me informed. You know that. Cheers!

(He walks out. People wave; sounds of people moving.)

ALL: Thanks, Xavier.
Great to see you.
Come back soon.

MANDI: OK, Nemo, get the movie running. Singing encouraged at the appropriate moments. Loudly by those with good voices who can sing in tune . . . I'm humming.

GEORGE: Thank God, darling.

Fade out to the music "The Jolly Old Land of Oz."

****

Older persons with disabilities

The UN Convention on the Rights of Persons with Disabilities and its Optional Protocol 2006, achieved through the battles and demands of the disability movement, changed the perspectives of the public, politicians, and policy makers on the rights of persons with disabilities to be included as equal citizens. However, limited use is made of the convention (CRPD) to cover the increasing needs amongst older people with disabilities in demographically ageing populations, and there are difficulties amongst governments and service providers in extending it to effectively cover their needs.

In many countries, at the age of 65, people are defined as "old," even if they previously counted as disabled. Some forms of social support and provision become reduced or even unavailable. With increasing numbers of people with disabilities living into old age, this becomes an issue for which the experiences of the disability movement are valuable and indeed vital. Solving accessibility for those with physical and cognitive limitations relates to the determination and sensitisation of politicians, planners, and the public and the availability of public and private budgets to make the necessary adaptations to the environment and the home. The rise in the number of older people with physical limitations clearly is "helpful" in indicating the larger numbers that can and need to be supported by good accessibility measures. The older age group members have a vested interest here in backing up the disability movement to make environments age and disability friendly. In many contexts, it may seem a luxury to talk about fully helping those of all ages with disabilities, but in our ageing world, the needs of many older people with disabilities are not being met adequately because they are not even counted. Indeed, this is an issue – ageism -- in which older people are systematically discounted, affecting their rights, health, and well-being and which may intersect with disability and "ableism."

Underlying various agreements made by disabled rights and older age rights groups – see later in this chapter for a bibliography – there is a fear of cooperation. Amongst disability groups, the fear of a reduction in the rights and provisions for their form of sometimes lifelong "genuine disablement" exists, as does non-identification with older people. On the other hand, having lived their adult lives as non-disabled, older people often fight against and even deny the loss of physical capacities while mental capacity remains a heavy existential threat, leading to a lack of identification with the disabled.

In the drama, Evi asks a pertinent question: why should the disabled movement care if older people don't care about disablement and the needs amongst older populations? The answer is simple: old age is not another country. Old age is not about people from Mars. Old age is a consequence of living – if you are lucky – and increasingly, more people are living longer. Caring about those with disabilities in old age is also caring about yourself, as well as those around you. The disability movement managed to work successfully to defend specific groups amongst the disabled who could not fight for themselves

Don't stop. . . . Sensory, cognitive, behavioural – whatever the disabilities, the movement must work for all of those with disabilities. We all have equal rights.

References

AGE Platform Europe. https://www.age-platform.eu/policy-work/news/age-joint-webinar-addressed-rights-older-persons-disabilities-during-covid-19

Bickenbach, J. E., et al. (2012, March 30). The Toronto declaration on bridging knowledge, policy and practice in aging and disability: Toronto, Canada. *International Journal of Integrated Care*, 12(8): e205.

EC. (2020). Green paper on ageing: Fostering solidarity and responsibility between generations. *27 January 2021 European Centre for Disease Control (EU) (2019)*. https://www.ecdc.europa.eu/en/publications-data/guidance-medically-and-socially-vulnerable-populations-covid-19

ENNHRI Submission to the OEWG-Ageing: Equality and Non-Discrimination 5th May, 2017. https://social.un.org/ageing-working-group/documents/eighth/Inputs%20NHRIs/EuropeanNetworkofNationalHumanRightsInstitutions-1.pdf

E.U: Improving the Well-being of Older Persons in the Era of Digitalisation: Council Adopts Conclusions. https://www.consilium.europa.eu/en/press/press-releases/2020/10/12/improving-the-well-being-of-older-persons-in-the-era-of-digitalisation-council-adopts-conclusions/

European Network on Independent Living. (2018). *Refers to Some Age Limits and Gaps for Older People with Disabilities*. https://social.un.org/ageing-working-group/documents/ninth/Inputs%20NGOs/ENIL_Autonomy.pdf

Eurostat. (2021). *People with Disability Struggling to Make Ends Meet*. https://ec.europa.eu/eurostat/web/products-eurostat-news/-/ddn-20210218-1?redirect=%2Feurostat%2Fweb%2Fhealth%2Fpublications

HelpAge International. (2018). *Global AgeWatch Insights: The Right to Health for Older People, the Right to be Counted*. http://globalagewatch.org/reports/global-agewatch-insights-2018-report-summary-and-country-profiles/

Salvador-Carulla, L., et al. (2009). The Barcelona declaration on bridging knowledge in long-term care and support. *Barcelona 2009*. https://ijic.org/articles/10.5334/ijic.521

UN Human rights of older persons: The data gap. Report of the Independent Expert on the enjoyment of all human rights by older persons. Human Rights Council 45th session 14 Sept.–2 Oct. 2020 Agenda item 3 Promotion and protection of all human rights, civil, political, economic, social and cultural rights, including the right to development.

UN Paper. https://www.who.int/teams/social-determinants-of-health/demographic-change-and-healthy-ageing/combatting-ageism/global-report-on-ageism#

UN Special Rapporteur. Report on the Rights of Older Persons with Disabilities, Including the Issues of Identity/Movement Tension. https://undocs.org/en/A/74/186

Verbrugge, L., and Yang, L. (2002). Aging with disability and disability with aging March 2002. *Journal of Disability Policy Studies*, 12(4): 253–267.

WHO. (2020). https://www.euro.who.int/en/health-topics/health-emergencies/coronavirus-covid-19/news/news/2020/5/new-whoeurope-guidance-shows-more-can-be-done-to-protect-people-in-need-of-long-term-care-during-the-covid-19-pandemic

Weber, G. (2009). The Graz declaration on disability and ageing 2006. *International Journal of Integrated Care*, 9(Supp. l).

https://www.age-platform.eu/policy-work/news/ageing-disability-age-replies-un-consultation-rights-older-persons-disabilities

https://www.age-platform.eu/policy-work/news/ageing-disability-intersection-needs-urgent-exploring-conference-finds

https://www.age-platform.eu/policy-work/news/rights-older-persons-disabilities-age-discusses-challenges-un-conference

31

DISABILITY OR VULNERABILITY

How courts distinguish between physical and psychosocial disabilities in an employment context

Radina Ugrinova

Introduction

The present chapter examines how courts in the UK approach psychosocial disabilities in the judicial process. The focus of the chapter falls on the manner in which courts consider the question of which categories of claimants qualify as disabled in an employment context. The study examines two sets of claims – claims alleging tort/negligence on the part of a former employer and claims for injury awards made by police officers upon retirement. The analysis falls on a comparison between the way courts approach physical injuries received in the course of employment on the one hand and psychiatric injuries on the other. The aim of the study is to explore whether courts perceive individuals who have suffered psychiatric injuries in the course of their employment as disabled or whether they mislabel them as 'vulnerable': i.e. not disabled. The assessment is carried out through the prism of the right to access to justice embedded in Article 13 of the Convention on the Rights of Persons with Disabilities (hereafter, the CRPD). This provision provides the legal context for examining whether the labelling of persons with psychosocial disabilities as either disabled or 'vulnerable' creates a hierarchy of disabilities which hinders the enjoyment of the human rights of persons with disabilities on the part of individuals with psychosocial disabilities.

The cases selected for analysis were located through systematic searches of the online database Westlaw UK. The author conducted the selection through key word searches, using the term 'disability' as the selected key word. The legal context selected was employment, with the relevant jurisdiction selected being England and Wales and the time period for the searches being the ten-year period between August 2010 and August 2020. The two sets of claims – tort/negligence claims and injury award claims – were selected on the basis

DOI: 10.4324/9781003410089-37

that these cases contained a discussion on the part of domestic courts as to the question of whether the claimant/defendant in each case was disabled for the purpose of accessing a judicial remedy.

The analysis proceeds as follows. Firstly, the right to access to justice embedded in the CRPD is briefly examined in the content of access to justice for persons with psychosocial disabilities. Then a legal descriptive analysis of the two sets of claims is carried out. The judicial reasoning in each case is briefly described, after which a comparison of the manner in which courts approach physical and psychosocial disabilities is carried out. The study examines tort/negligence claims and injury award claims in turn. Finally, a concluding assessment of the relevant judicial reasoning in the context of the right to access to justice is carried out.

The right to access to justice

The right to access to justice is embedded in the CRPD in Article 13 which stipulates the following:

1. States Parties shall ensure effective access to justice for persons with disabilities on an equal basis with others, including through the provision of procedural and age-appropriate accommodations, in order to facilitate their effective role as direct and indirect participants, including as witnesses, in all legal proceedings, including at investigative and other preliminary stages.
2. In order to help to ensure effective access to justice for persons with disabilities, States Parties shall promote appropriate training for those working in the field of administration of justice, including police and prison staff.

The CRPD is the first international human rights treaty which articulates a stand-alone right to access to justice (Flynn, 2015; Mental Health Europe, 2021). The precursors of the right are the right to a fair trial and the right to an effective remedy found in other international human rights treaties (Flynn, 2015). The right to access to justice can be defined as 'the human rights to enforce rights' – it enables persons with disabilities to enforce their human rights and seek redress in court – and has several core components: 'fair trial, due process, access to court, judicial protection, effective remedies and redress' (Mental Health Europe, 2021). Access to effective remedies and compensation is a core component of the right (United Nations, 2020).

The right to access to justice is a key prerequisite for the enjoyment of other human rights (United Nations, 2020; Mental Health Europe, 2021). The right is of particular importance to persons with disabilities, as these individuals often face significant barriers to accessing justice under domestic law (United Nations, 2020). This is specifically the case for persons with psychosocial disabilities, who are often stereotyped in the judicial process. Perlin and Dorfman (1993) state that the entire legal system operates by making certain assumptions about persons with psychosocial disabilities and treats them as different. Perlin et al. (2009) trace the outcomes of cases involving persons with psychosocial disabilities to sanism-based judicial reasoning, defining sanism as 'an irrational prejudice of the same quality and character of other irrational prejudices that cause (and are reflected in) prevailing social attitudes of racism, sexism, homophobia, and ethnic bigotry'. They also contend that 'courts teleologically "cherry pick" social science evidence to justify judicial decisions' and, in their assessment, seek to come to predetermined positions regarding persons with psychosocial disabilities, thus engaging in 'outcome-determinative reasoning'. In a UK context, Perlin et al. (2009) have identified several issues regarding the fairness of the judicial process in involuntary commitment cases stemming from sanist judicial decision making.

An analysis of the manner in which courts approach psychosocial disabilities in an employment context is important to developing a more complete understanding of how this category of disabilities is assessed in judicial proceedings. The question of whether persons with psychosocial disabilities are regarded as disabled in the same manner as persons with physical disabilities or whether they are perceived as merely 'vulnerable' is key to an assessment of the right to access to justice. The label of 'vulnerability' distinguishes between 'genuine' disabilities and other categories of conditions, thus creating a hierarchy of disabilities. The notion of 'vulnerability' can also shift attention away from an analysis of disabling acts, such as bullying and harassment, to an assessment of the individual themselves, thus placing the 'fault' for disabling experiences on the person concerned. Therefore, understanding how courts approach the issue of different categories of disabilities is crucial. If persons with psychosocial disabilities are not considered disabled but are instead labeled as 'vulnerable' in the judicial process, these individuals cannot access effective legal protection. Thus, they cannot exercise their right to access to justice and can be denied access to an effective remedy as a result of the preconception that they are not disabled but merely vulnerable.

Tort and negligence claims

This set of decisions concerned claims alleging the claimants had sustained injuries in the course of their employment as a result of negligence or tort on the part of their employer(s). The courts needed to establish whether an injury had occurred and whether to grant financial compensation for the injuries sustained. The decisions included eight claims in total: three dealt with alleged psychiatric injuries, and five dealt with alleged physical injuries resulting in physical/sensory disabilities. The following sections provide a descriptive analysis of the decisions and contrast the treatment of physical injuries with that of psychiatric injuries.

Overview: physical injuries

Cases concerning physical injuries encompassed claims for continuous exposure to loud noise (*Holloway v Tyne Thames Technology Limited, 2015*) or to harmful substances (*Mills v J P Barnes & Sons Ltd, 2013; Prater v British Motor Holdings Limited, 2016*) during the claimants' employment, as well as claims for physical injuries sustained as a result of accidents which took place during the claimants' work (*Camden v Jackpot Leisure Limited, 2015; Smith v Ashwell Maintenance Limited, 2019*). A core issue across these decisions was that of causation: i.e. whether the claimants had acquired a disability as a result of the injury they sustained.

In *Holloway*, the main issue before the court was whether the claimant had 'suffered a measurable loss of hearing as a result of the exposure to noise', thereby developing a hearing disability (*Holloway v Tyne Thames Technology Limited, 2015, paras. 9, 10*). The determination of whether the claimant was disabled turned on an analysis of medical data provided by two experts – one for the claimant and one for the defendants. The court concluded that the evidence provided by the medical expert for the defendants was more accurate and logical (*Holloway v Tyne Thames Technology Limited, 2015, paras. 25–32*). On this basis, the claimant was not found to have become disabled as a result of noise exposure.

In *Mills* and *Prater*, the claimants alleged that they had sustained respiratory disabilities as a result of exposure to toxic substances (silica and asbestos, respectively) in the course of their employment. In *Mills v J P Barnes & Sons Ltd,* (2013), a core issue regarding whether the claimant had a disability was the fact that his condition did not exhibit significant symptoms: specifically, that he did not experience breathlessness. The court relied extensively on the witness statements of the claimant and medical data. With respect to the claimant, the court concluded that he was 'an impressive witness', frank, and respected and further, that he was 'a trustworthy witness, not given to exaggeration' (*Mills v J P Barnes & Sons Ltd, 2013,* paras. 8, 14). On this basis, the court concluded that the claimant's condition was, in fact, not symptomless and thus ruled that he was disabled.

In *Prater v British Motor Holdings Limited,* (2016), the issue was whether the claimant's disability was the result of his exposure to asbestos. In a similar manner to *Mills v J P Barnes & Sons Ltd,* (2013), after a careful assessment of medical data, the court preferred the evidence given in favour of the claimant's assertion that he had acquired a respiratory disability. The court stated that the medical witnesses testifying in favour of the claimant were 'impressive experts who are currently leaders and hands-on practitioners in their particular fields' (*Prater v British Motor Holdings Limited, 2016,* para. 28). Furthermore, the court 'completely [accepted]' the evidence provided by the claimant, stating that he was a reliable witness (*Prater v British Motor Holdings Limited, 2016,* para. 8).

In *Camden v Jackpot Leisure Limited,* (2015) and *Smith v Ashwell Maintenance Limited,* (2019), the claimants had sustained physical injuries in the course of their employment. In *Smith*, the court assessed first, whether the claimant had exaggerated the extent of his injuries and second, whether he had acquired a persistent disability as a result of them. The court outlined several instances when there had been contradictions in the claimant's testimony (*Smith v Ashwell Maintenance Limited, 2019,* paras. 10, 19–27). The court stated that it was 'troubled by the extent to which [it could] rely on the claimant's evidence' due to these contradictions (*Smith v Ashwell Maintenance Limited, 2019,* para 19, paras 22–25). However, based on the available medical data, as well as an assessment of additional evidence provided by the claimant, it concluded that crucial parts of his witness statement were 'reliable and convincing' (*Smith v Ashwell Maintenance Limited, 2019*, para 28) and thus found for the claimant.

The credibility of the witness statement of the claimant were also questioned in *Camden*, in which the court had to establish to what extent the defendant was liable for the injuries sustained (*Camden v Jackpot Leisure Limited, 2015*, para. 63). In this case, the court also found for the claimant, concluding that overall, he had not engaged in fundamental dishonesty. The courts in both cases concluded that, while there had been statements which were exaggerated/incorrect, there was, at the same time, sufficient evidence to support a finding of wrongdoing on the part of the employers.

Overview: psychiatric injuries

The case-law sample included three claims for psychiatric injuries (*Manda v. USB AG, 2016; Henley v Royal Mail Group, 2016; Bailey v International Automotive Components Group Limited, 2014*). The claimants alleged that they had experienced harassment and bullying at work. The courts in these cases had to decide whether to grant monetary compensation for negligence on the part of the employers in not preventing the alleged bullying/harassment. In *Manda v USB AG,* (2016), the court did not examine the psychiatric injuries and the alleged disability in detail. This may be due to the fact that the central question in the case was whether the multiple claims the claimant had previously brought against his employer amounted to estoppel or abuse of process. Therefore, the case is not further assessed.

The question of whether the claimant had sustained psychiatric injuries due to alleged bullying/harassment was central in *Henley v Royal Mail Group,* (2016) and *Bailey v International Automotive Components Group Limited,* (2014). *Henley* (2016) concerned alleged bullying and harassment perpetrated in the form of disparaging graffiti which had been written about the claimant on the premises of her workplace and the use of a slur against her by a colleague (*Henley v Royal Mail Group, 2016,* paras. 10, 12). Two expert witnesses who examined the claimant concluded that 'if the Court considered Mrs Henley . . . had experienced bullying or harassment . . ., then on the balance of probabilities she would have experienced a stress reaction in the form of an adjustment disorder' (*Henley v Royal Mail Group, 2016,* para. 36). Thus, the determination of whether the claimant had an adjustment disorder was dependent on the court's assessment of whether the claimant had been a victim of bullying/harassment.

The court's analysis focused on two key points: first, whether the behaviour alleged to have been perpetrated against the claimant amounted to bullying and harassment and second, whether the claimant had experienced an adjustment disorder. Regarding the first point, the court concluded that the behaviour of which the claimant complained was not sufficiently serious to merit a finding of bullying and harassment. The court seemed to make an effort throughout the judgment to discredit the seriousness of the claimant's assertions regarding her experiences of bullying. For example, criticizing the claimant's conduct at work, the court in one instance asserted that the use of a slur against her had been justifiable (*Henley v Royal Mail Group, 2016,* para. 22), thus faulting the claimant for her workplace experiences.

Regarding the second point, the court called into question whether the claimant had experienced a psychiatric injury. It stated that, even if the claimant had experienced an adjustment disorder, this condition 'would have been superimposed on [her] underling and fluctuating anxiety state and also on any other psychological reaction deriving from experiences affecting her'; thus, the 'adjustment disorder might have exasperated her experience of psychological symptoms' (*Henley v Royal Mail Group, 2016,* para. 37). The court further stated that it would have been difficult to attribute the claimant's condition to her workplace experiences (*Henley v Royal Mail Group, 2016,* para. 38). In this manner, the court, in essence, traced the experience of psychiatric symptoms to the claimant's character instead of to her workplace environment and the conduct of her colleagues. On this basis, the court concluded that she had not been bullied and had not received a psychiatric injury.

The issue of whether the claimant had sustained psychiatric injuries was especially prominent in *Bailey v International Automotive Components Group Limited,* (2014). The claimant alleged that he had experienced bullying and harassment perpetrated by his manager on three occasions as a result of which he had acquired an adjustment disorder (*Bailey v International Automotive Components Group Limited, 2014,* paras. 1, 5). Similarly to *Henley*, the court in this case called into question whether the behaviour complained of was sufficiently serious for an injury to have occurred. The court seemed to overlook evidence in support of the claimant's assertion that his manager's conduct had amounted to bullying/harassment: it either did not engage in detail with the evidence (*Bailey v International Automotive Components Group Limited, 2014,* para. 64) or it discredited a witness's statements because she had experienced 'stress related problems' (*Bailey v International Automotive Components Group Limited, 2014,* para. 70). The court also asserted that the claimant lacked the stamina of 'ordinarily robust individuals' in the workplace (*Bailey v International Automotive Components Group Limited, 2014,* para. 23; 14) and consistently painted the claimant as a psychologically 'vulnerable' individual with a difficult character and an incapacity to understand the real circumstances of the incidents he described (*Bailey v International Automotive Components Group Limited, 2014,* paras. 36, 37, 38, 100, 102, 104).

The discussion of the claimant's 'vulnerability' was central in the court's reasoning that he had not, in fact, experienced workplace harassment and bullying and thus had not suffered a psychiatric injury. When assessing expert evidence, the court took a strong preference for evidence suggesting the claimant's personality traits had caused the onset of an adjustment disorder; the court rejected evidence that the claimant had sustained a psychiatric injury as a result of his workplace experiences but without providing specific reasoning for this assessment (*Bailey v International Automotive Components Group Limited, 2014,* paras. 116, 117). The court conducted an in-depth assessment of the claimant's character throughout the decision, most notably in a section entitled 'The Claimant's History' (*Bailey v International Automotive Components Group Limited, 2014,* paras. 34–40) and consistently traced the origin of the adjustment disorder to his personality. Thus, the court faulted the claimant for his negative work experiences in a similar manner to the court in *Henley v Royal Mail Group,* (2016). The cause of the injury was not traced to the workplace environment and the alleged behaviour of the claimant's manager but to the character of the claimant.

Analysis

The earlier analysis reveals several stark differences in the manner in which courts treat physical and psychiatric injuries. These relate to the outcome of the cases, the treatment of witness statements during the proceedings and the assessment of the origin of the injury. Cases concerning physical injuries were overwhelmingly decided in favor of the claimant, with the exception of *Holloway v Tyne Thames Technology Limited,* (2015). That case was decided against the claimant on the basis of the medical evidence made available to the court. In contrast, cases for psychiatric injuries were all decided against the claimant. The basis for this in both cases considered here was that the court preferred witness statements provided for the defendants. Unlike in cases for physical injuries, in which courts in the sample based their assessment on logic and a careful assessment of medical data, in cases concerning psychiatric injuries, courts gravitated towards statements which painted the claimants as 'vulnerable' but without providing equally detailed reasons why they preferred one set of evidence over another.

Decisions concerning physical injuries also exhibit a greater propensity for courts to examine sympathetically evidence provided for the claimant and by the claimant. This is so even where there are contradictions or inaccuracies in the claimant's witness statements. Where these statements are supported by sufficient evidence, courts take a more nuanced approach to handling the claimants' evidence and do not reject such evidence as irrelevant/false. In contrast, in decisions concerning psychiatric injuries, courts exhibit a more hostile attitude towards the claimants, painting them in a far more negative light. The courts question their credibility as witnesses, and in *Bailey v International Automotive Components Group Limited,* (2014), the court also questions the credibility of one witness for the claimant on the basis that she has experienced stress.

Moreover, it is striking how courts trace the origin of the injury. In claims for physical injuries, the courts accept that the claimants have sustained injuries even when they do not find for the claimant. In contrast, in claims for psychiatric injuries, the courts are more unwilling to accept that an injury has taken place and trace the origin of the injury to the claimants' personality as opposed to their workplace conditions. Despite the possibility of interpreting the medical evidence available to establish the existence of a psychiatric injury, the courts in these cases refuse to do so, instead delving into an assessment of the character of the claimants to explain away the alleged behaviour of bullying/harassment and to fault the claimants for their negative experiences at work.

It is striking that, in cases for physical injuries, there is a clear reference to a disability while in the other set of claims, courts only refer to 'psychiatric injuries' and not to psychosocial disabilities. This may be due to the manner in which the claims were framed by the claimants themselves, or it may be due to the attitudes of courts towards accepting psychosocial disabilities as such instead of as a personal vulnerability. A textual analysis of the decisions cannot provide a conclusive answer. However, such an analysis does reveal that courts in the sample exhibit a propensity to fault claimants for the experience of psychiatric injuries and to label these as a personal vulnerability or a character flaw. As courts do not find that an injury had occurred, it could be inferred that even if the claimants in these cases had alleged that they had acquired a psychosocial disability, courts would not have found that they were disabled. This precludes claimants who have suffered a psychiatric injury from being able to enforce their right to access to justice as they are not accepted as persons with disabilities. Claimants in cases for psychiatric injuries are denied access to an effective remedy on the basis that they are merely 'vulnerable' individuals who exaggerate/misinterpret/provoke the treatment they experience at their workplaces. Thus, it can be inferred that claimants with psychiatric injuries do not enjoy equal legal protection compared to claimants with physical injuries.

Injury award claims

This set of decisions concerns claims by former police officers for injury awards: i.e. pensions awarded in cases in which a police officer had become permanently disabled as a result of an injury received in the execution of duty. The applicable legal test in this set of claims is the following:

> a. The test is whether the person's injury is directly and causally connected with his service as a police officer. The causation test is not to be applied in an overly legalistic way as it is a relatively straightforward concept and one which falls to be applied in practice by medical rather than legal experts. The reference to a direct causal link does not therefore mean that fine distinctions are to be drawn between direct and indirect causes of the injury but there must be a substantial causal connection between the injury and the person's service as a police officer.
> b. The causal connection must be with the person's service as a police office, not simply with his being a police officer. In this context, duty is not to be given a narrow meaning. It relates not just to operational police duties but to all aspects of the officer's work and to the officer's work circumstances.
>
> *(Chief Constable v Police Medical Appeal Board v Middleton, 2019, para. 17)*

The police officers in these decisions were assessed by a selected medical practitioner (hereafter SMP) tasked with determining whether they had become permanently disabled due to an injury on duty. The police officers could appeal this decision before a police medical appeal board (hereafter PMAB). The set comprises of 17 decisions in total. However, some decisions were not examined as the central issue in the dispute did not concern the question of whether the police officer in question had become permanently disabled. The decisions are separated into physical/mixed injuries and psychiatric injuries.

Overview: physical and mixed injuries

Claims concerning physical injuries comprised seven cases. Several cases were not examined as they did not consider the issue of whether the claimant had become permanent disabled. One concerned an application for judicial review of a decision not to reinstate the claimant to a full-time position (*Flint v Chief Constable, 2010*). Another was an application for judicial review of a policy (*Simpson v Medical Appeal Board, 2012*). In *Haworth v Northumbria Police Authority,* (2012), *Goodland v Chief Constable,* (2020) *and Crudace v Northumbria Police Authority,* (2012), the courts had to decide whether the reduction of the claimants' pensions was justified and did not carry out an assessment of whether they were disabled. In the remaining claims, the courts examined whether the claimant had become permanently disabled for the purpose of receiving an injury award.

In *Scarfield v Police Medical Appeal Board,* (2013), the claimant challenged the decision of the PMAB that his disablement was not permanent. The decision of the PMAB was based on the premise that the claimant 'had not received . . . normal appropriate medical treatment for his condition' (*Scarfield v Police Medical Appeal Board, 2013,* para. 2). The SMP concluded that the disability was not permanent because appropriate treatments had either not been pursued or had been declined by the claimant. Challenging this decision, the claimant relied on the opinion of another medical professional:

> There is good evidence from international studies to suggest that the prognosis for patients who suffer from complex regional pain is poor once they have ongoing symptoms at 1 year following the onset symptoms. Patients maintain their same levels of pain and significant levels of disability. Significant numbers of patients do not return to work.
>
> *(Scarfield v Police Medical Appeal Board, 2013, para. 12)*

The court considered in detail whether the PMAB had appropriately interpreted the meaning of the concept of 'permanent' in the phrase 'permanently disabled', concluding that the board had erred in its analysis (*Scarfield v Police Medical Appeal Board, 2013,* para. 26). However, the court further concluded that this error had not been material to the decision of the PMAB (*Scarfield v Police Medical Appeal Board, 2013,* para. 28). The court also took the view that there were treatment options available to the claimant to alleviate his condition. On this basis, the claim was dismissed.

In *Walther v Police Medical Appeal Board,* (2009), the claimant challenged the decision of an SMP to refuse an award for an injury pension and the decision of the PMAB to dismiss the subsequent appeal. The claimant had been diagnosed with several conditions; the one under assessment in the present case was a shoulder injury. The SMP concluded that the injury was not the cause of his disability; instead, the disability was the result of longstanding progressive degeneration which was merely accelerated by the occurrences during the claimant's employment (*Walther v Police Medical Appeal Board, 2009,* para. 7). The board, concurring with the SMP, decided that the 'injury was to bring about a "permanent worsening of a prior condition"' (*Walther v Police Medical Appeal Board, 2009,* para. 8).

The court was brief in its assessment, focusing on a legal and linguistic analysis of the meaning of the term 'permanently disabled'. The court carried out an assessment of the relevant statutory framework and case law. On this basis, the court formulated the following test applicable to the present claim: 'an incapacity test: the officer is unable to perform his or her normal duties. The incapacity must be permanent. Thus the relevant condition is "a permanent disability": permanence must be a quality of the disability' (*Walther v Police Medical Appeal Board, 2009,* para. 40). The court then defined the concept of 'permanent' as it was defined in the Oxford dictionary. On this basis, the court found for the claimant.

Two cases in the sample concerned both physical and psychiatric injuries. In one case (*Fisher v Chief Constable, 2017*), it was accepted that the claimant was disabled – the issue was whether his injury pension should be reduced. Therefore, the case is not addressed here. In *Evans v Chief Constable,* (2018), the claimant suffered a number of physical and psychiatric injuries in the course of his employment as a police officer. He was required to retire after an SMP diagnosed him with mechanical back pain and PTSD. The claimant applied for an injury pension but was rejected because the PMAB disagreed that he was permanently disabled. The central question in the dispute was whether the PMAB had given proper effect to the decision of the SMP (*Fisher v Chief Constable, 2017,* para. 9). The court conducted a detailed analysis of the relevant legislative framework and applicable case law and ruled that the statutory framework had to be read in accordance with the submissions of the claimant. It concluded that the PMAB had failed to treat the decision of the SMP as final, which was contrary to the law (*Evans v Chief Constable, 2018,* para. 46). Furthermore, the court found that 'the PMAB failed to undertake the decision-making process required of it' (*Fisher v Chief Constable, 2017,* para. 49) and 'to give proper reasons for its decision' (*Fisher v Chief Constable, 2017,* para. 50).

Overview: psychiatric injuries

This set of claims comprised eight decisions. *Chief Constable v Crown Court v Kelly,* (2020) *and Boskovic v Chief Constable,* (2018) were not examined because the issue at the heart of the disputes did not concern an assessment of whether the claimant was permanently disabled for the purpose of receiving an injury award. The remaining six decisions are examined next.

The decision in *Chief Constable v Police Medical Board v Middleton,* (2019) was a challenge to the PMAB's finding concerning whether the claimant's chronic adjustment disorder was an injury sustained in the execution of his duties. The claimant had suffered back pain and an acute stress reaction, as a result of which he had been relieved of front line duties. He was assigned a series of temporary jobs for a period of several years. The claimant then requested to be retired on medical grounds. The SMP concluded that the claimant 'had an emotional unstable personality disorder of the borderline type and that he should be regarded as permanently disabled for policing duties as a result of pervasive mental health difficulties (chronic adjustment disorder)' (*Chief Constable v Police Medical Board v Middleton, 2019,* para. 7).

The claimant then made an application for an injury award. The SMP who examined him concluded that none of his injuries had been the result of an injury on duty (*Chief Constable v Police Medical Board v Middleton, 2019,* para. 8). With regard to the claimant's chronic adjustment disorder, the SMP stated that the 'persistent personality traits were by their nature not the result of any incident or any injury' and that the claimant's negative reaction to his employment was due to his 'long standing personality issues' and his 'vulnerability' (*Chief Constable v Police Medical Board v Middleton, 2019,* para 8). The PMAB, in contrast, traced the development of the adjustment disorder to the employment circumstances of the claimant and found that if the claimant had been given a permanent role within his skill set, he would not have developed an adjustment disorder (*Chief Constable v Police Medical Board v Middleton, 2019,* para. 14). The chief constable challenged this finding.

The court concluded that there was 'no doubt' that the board had misdirected itself on the appropriate legal approach to the question of whether the injuries were received in the execution of the claimant's duty (*Chief Constable v Police Medical Board v Middleton, 2019,* para. 24). The court stated that for an injury to have been received in the execution of a police officer's duty, 'there must be a substantial causal connection between the injury and the execution of duty' (*Chief Constable v Police Medical Board v Middleton, 2019,* para. 24b). Thus, the court reasoned, the 'injury must arise out of duties the officer is undertaking or the conditions or circumstances in which he was undertaking those duties' (*Chief Constable v Police Medical Board v Middleton, 2019,* para. 24b). The court stated that the key consideration that the PMAB should have made was whether the injury of the claimant 'was causally related to his status as a policeman or to his service as a policeman' (*Chief Constable v Police Medical Board v Middleton, 2019,* para. 24b). Thus, the court concluded, the board had not identified the correct legal test.

The court then stated that there were not 'sufficiently clear findings of fact which would permit only one possible decision' (*Chief Constable v Police Medical Board v Middleton, 2019,* para. 26). The court assessed critically the employment situation of the claimant, the fact that he had been assigned multiple short-term jobs, the lack of training the claimant had received and the lack of accommodations made available to him (*Chief Constable v Police Medical Board v Middleton, 2019,* para 26). On this basis, the court concurred with the PMAB that multiple small incidents had accumulated to cause an injury. Therefore, the court refused to substitute its own conclusion for that of the PMAB and instead granted an application for judicial review of the decision.

In *Doubtfire and Williams v Police Medical Appeal Board,* (2010), the claimants made an application for judicial review of the decision of the SMP that the claimants were not entitled to an injury award and/or of the decision of the PMAB to dismiss the claimants' appeal. The first claimant had a history of 'intermittent mental illness' (*Doubtfire and Williams v Police Medical Appeal Board, 2010,* para. 9). After a period of leave due to ill health, she was reassigned to the position of hate crime officer. The claimant contended the role was stressful, and she did not receive the necessary support from her superiors. The claimant later attempted to commit suicide and had several periods of leave of absence. A consultant psychiatrist assessed the claimant was disabled but concluded that it was too early to state whether her disablement was permanent (*Doubtfire and Williams v Police Medical Appeal Board, 2010,* paras. 12–13). An SMP concluded that the claimant was permanently disabled, and she was thus retired. The claimant then applied for an injury pension. The psychiatrist who had initially examined the claimant concluded that her disability had resulted from her work circumstances (*Doubtfire and Williams v Police Medical Appeal Board, 2010,* para. 16). The SMP, however, disagreed.

The second defendant had no prior history of mental illness (*Doubtfire and Williams v Police Medical Appeal Board, 2010,* para. 20). He experienced stress at his workplace and requested help but was refused; later, he had a mental breakdown (*Doubtfire and Williams v Police Medical Appeal Board, 2010,* para. 21). The claimant was then treated for a depressive illness. He was examine by an SMP who diagnosed the claimant with bipolar affective disorder and concluded that the claimant was permanently disabled from exercising his duties. The claimant then applied for an injury pension and was referred to a second SMP. The second SMP rejected the diagnosis of bipolar affective disorder and diagnosed the claimant with depressive illness, which had been linked to his work and the lack of support therein. On this basis, the SMP concluded that the injury had been received on duty. The police authority challenged the decision of the SMP. A third SMP was appointed to assess the claimant – the SMP concluded that the injury received 'should not be considered an injury on duty' (*Doubtfire and Williams v Police Medical Appeal Board, 2010,* para. 25). The claimant appealed this decision to the PMAB, which dismissed his appeal.

The court was brief in its assessment. The reasoning in this case revolved around the legality of the PMAB's decision and did not include a substantive examination of the question of whether the claimants were disabled. The court concluded that the PMABs in the two cases had asked the wrong question and thus had not considered the question of whether the injury sustained had been received in the execution of the claimants' duties as police officers (*Doubtfire and Williams v Police Medical Appeal Board, 2010,* paras. 48–49). On this basis, the court ruled in favor of the claimants.

In *Commissioner v Police Medical Appeal Board v Brown,* (2020), the commissioner of police of the metropolis challenged a decision of the PMAB to award an injury pension to the defendant. The defendant had been involved in a number of legal proceedings and later applied for retirement on the ground of ill health – he was retired. Afterwards, he applied for an injury pension. The SMP who examined him determined that his disablement was not the result of an injury received in the execution of duty. The PMAB concluded that 'events at work [or perceptions thereof], in totality or part, have substantially contributed to the appellant's permanent disablement' (*Commissioner v Police Medical Appeal Board v Brown, 2020,* para. 40). The claimant challenged this finding.

The court concluded that the PMAB 'did not correctly direct itself on the law'. (*Commissioner v Police Medical Appeal Board v Brown, 2020,* para. 67). The court did recognize that a psychiatric injury could be considered an injury in the same manner that a physical injury would (*Commissioner v Police Medical Appeal Board v Brown, 2020,* para. 50). However, the court also outlined that a central issue of consideration was

> not the type of activity (such as a disciplinary process per se) which is determinative of whether an injury is received in the execution of duty, but rather, for a psychiatric injury, whether the event is directed at the police officer . . . or a reaction to the circumstances in which the police officer exercised his or her duty.
>
> *(Commissioner v Police Medical Appeal Board v Brown, 2020, para. 53)*

On the basis of this consideration, the court quashed the decision of the PMAB.

In *Michaelides v Chief Constable,* (2019), the claimant challenged the decision of the PMAB to refuse his application for an injury pension, as well as the decision of the chief constable to refer the decision back for reconsideration. The defendant was born in South Africa and was a police officer until his forced retirement on the grounds that he was permanently disabled. He alleged that during his employment, he had been subjected to bullying, harassment and racist abuse, which had caused his mental illness (*Michaelides v Chief Constable, 2019,* para. 5). The claimant was examined by a psychiatrist, who diagnosed him with a depressive episode with associated employment-related problems.

The claimant was later assessed by an SMP who concluded that the claimant was permanently disabled to perform his duties as a police officer. The claimant then applied for an injury award. He was assessed by another SMP, who concluded that the disablement was not caused by an injury received in the execution of duty. The claimant appealed this decision. He was then examined by a consultant psychiatrist, who concluded that he had a depressive disorder and mixed anxiety. The PMAB concluded that the claimant's permanent disability was not the result of an injury received on duty on the basis that the allegations made by the claimant were not supported by medical evidence.

The court examined in detail the manner in which the board dealt with the allegations of the claimant. The court found that the PMAB had failed to reach a decision on this issue, which was central to the outcome of the appeal. On this basis, the court concluded that the decision of the board had to be quashed.

In *Sidwell v Police Medical Appeal Board,* (2015), the claimant challenged the decision of the PMAB that he was not permanently disabled. The claimant had been examined by a psychiatrist, who concluded that he had 'an adjustment reaction specifically to issues at work, in the form of a situational anxiety disorder' (*Sidwell v Police Medical Appeal Board, 2015,* para. 17). The claimant sought early retirement on medical grounds. He was examined by an SMP, who concluded that the claimant was not permanently disabled. The claimant appealed this decision to the PMAB. He was then examined by a consultant psychiatrist, who diagnosed him with an anxiety disorder. The PMAB, however, concluded that his condition was treatable and that he did not have a permanent disabling condition. The claimant was later examined by another psychiatrist in relation to a different proceeding, who concluded that the claimant suffered from phobic anxiety disorder and mixed affective disorder as a result of work-related stress and anxiety. He was later examined by an SMP, who concluded that the claimant's 'symptoms are due to vulnerability rather than disablement' (*Sidwell v Police Medical Appeal Board, 2015,* para. 23). The claimant appealed this decision, but the PMAB dismissed the appeal on the basis that he did not have a permanent disabling medical condition (*Sidwell v Police Medical Appeal Board, 2015,* para. 27).

The court was rather brief in its assessment. The court did not accept that the PMAB had erred in law, as it asked itself the correct question and thus made the correct finding. The court also stated that the board was entitled to prefer the opinion of one specialist over another as to the existence of a medical condition and that it was further entitled to make a finding that the condition was not permanent. On this basis, the claim was dismissed.

Sharp v Chief Constable v Police Medical Appeal Board, (2016) concerned an application for a judicial review of a decision of the PMAB reconsidering an earlier decision not to grant the claimant a pension on the basis that he was not permanently disabled. The claimant had a recurrent depressive disorder; a medical expert characterized the claimant as 'having a paranoid attitude' and being 'liable to develop psychiatric disorder under stress' (*Sharp v Chief Constable v Police Medical Appeal Board, 2016,* para. 2). The claimant had had long periods off work due to psychiatric illness throughout his employment (*Sharp v Chief Constable v Police Medical Appeal Board, 2016,* paras. 7–9). He later resigned from the police force and applied for an ill health award.

The SMP who examined the claimant rejected the claim, stating that there was no clear medical reason for the claimant not to be considered permanently fit for employment if his relationship with his employer had been 'neutral' (*Sharp v Chief Constable v Police Medical Appeal Board, 2016,* para. 12). Thus, the SMP implied that it was the negative attitude of the claimant which was causing his health issues. The claimant appealed this decision before the

PMAB. The proceedings included a review of a report by a psychiatrist, who diagnosed the claimant with affective disorder and concluded that it was the claimant's attitude which provoked the psychiatric disorder (*Sharp v Chief Constable v Police Medical Appeal Board, 2016*, para. 15). He summarized this by stating that the claimant's 'core disablement is his attitude' (*Sharp v Chief Constable v Police Medical Appeal Board, 2016*, para. 15).

The PMAB concluded that the claimant had a 'vulnerability' manifested in 'his paranoid attitude' (*Sharp v Chief Constable v Police Medical Appeal Board, 2016*, para. 16). The board concluded that the claimant was not permanently disabled. The claimant later appealed this decision. The board made the conclusion that there had been 'no suggestion of a mental disorder such as a personality disorder. Though mention of paranoid attitude in reports may suggest possibility of a personality trait, it would not amount to a disorder in the context of this case' (*Sharp v Chief Constable v Police Medical Appeal Board, 2016*, para. 24).

The court focused on an analysis of the distinction between the terms 'vulnerability' and 'infirmity', citing case law, and stated the following: 'If a police officer is only "vulnerable" there is in fact nothing wrong with him provided that the vulnerability has not in effect crossed the line into a condition' (*Sharp v Chief Constable v Police Medical Appeal Board, 2016*, para 42). The court concluded that the claimant's depressive disorder was an 'infirmity' and that it had been wrong on the part of the PMAB to consider whether 'his paranoid attitude' was an infirmity was well (*Sharp v Chief Constable v Police Medical Appeal Board, 2016*, para. 47). The court then moved on the issue of causation: i.e. whether the claimant's health condition prevented him from performing his duties. The court focused in its analysis on the long periods when the claimant had been off work due to his condition, pointing out that when 'he returns to work it is, however, only a matter of time before the recurrent depressive disorder will recur' (*Sharp v Chief Constable v Police Medical Appeal Board, 2016*, para. 61). The court concluded that the PMAB had not carried out an assessment of whether the claimant's inability to carry out his duties had been substantial. The court then concluded that the claimant's condition was permanent. On this basis, the court ruled in favor of the claimant.

Analysis

The decisions examined here reveal several key differences in the manner in which courts in the sample assess tort/negligence claims and injury award claims. Courts in injury award claims are significantly more concise in their discussion of the claimants' status as a disabled person than courts in tort/negligence claims. The analysis in injury award claims focuses heavily on an examination of the relevant statutory legal framework and case law; courts are also more restrained in their analysis of whether the claimants are disabled – instead, the bulk of the assessment concerning injury awards, in most cases, falls on the legality of the PMAB's decisions.

Another difference between tort/negligence claims and injury award claims is the manner in which courts trace the origin of the injury in cases concerning psychiatric injuries. In the former set of cases, courts examining claims for psychiatric injuries attribute the injury to the claimants' 'vulnerability' and personal characteristics. Thus, for example, in *Bailey v International Automotive Components Group Limited,* (2014) and *Henley v Royal Mail Group,* (2016), the alleged experience of workplace harassment is attributed to the personality of the claimants and their flawed perception while the alleged acts of harassment/bullying are assessed not to have occurred or to have been relatively unimportant. Courts also exhibit a more hostile attitude towards the claimants in these cases, conducting a detailed assessment of the claimants' personality and personal conduct and seemingly faulting the claimants for their experiences in employment.

This is not so in injury award cases. In these claims, there is no significant difference between the manner in which courts approach physical and psychiatric injuries. This set of decisions is also characterized by a more nuanced – at times, even sympathetic – approach to claimants with psychiatric injuries who allege to have become disabled as a result. For example, in *Chief Constable v Police Medical Appeal Board v Middleton,* (2019), the court, while finding that the PMAB's decision to award the defendant an injury pension was flawed, does take into consideration the workplace environment of the claimant as a relevant factor in its analysis and does not fault him for the experience of psychiatric symptoms. The issue of the claimants' 'vulnerability' is also approached differently in these cases. While an argument that the claimants are 'vulnerable' instead of disabled is put forward in several cases by the relevant SMPs or PMABs (*Sidwell v Police Medical Appeal Board, 2015; Chief Constable v Police Medical Appeal Board v Middleton, 2019; Sharp v Chief Constable v Police Medical Appeal Board, 2016*), courts do not find that the claimant is 'vulnerable' in any of these decisions. The analysis also does not include a detailed discussion of the claimants' personality or conduct. Instead, central to the assessment are the workplace situation of the claimant and the legality of the PMAB's decisions.

A final difference between tort/negligence claims and injury award claims is the outcome of these cases. In the case set concerning tort/negligence claims, most cases concerning physical injuries are decided in favor of the claimant while all cases concerning psychiatric injuries are decided against the claimant. There is no such stark difference between physical and psychiatric injuries in injury award claims – most cases in this set (regardless of the type of injury concerned) are decided in favor of the individual claiming to have sustained an injury and thus a disability. It is difficult to provide a decisive explanation for this contrast due to the brevity of some of the decisions, as well as the limitations of textual analysis. One possible explanation could be the difference in the legal frameworks applicable to tort/negligence claims and injury award cases respectively. Another possibility could be the difference in the type of claimant. It is possible that courts are more receptive towards claims coming from a specific type of claimant (such as police officers) due to their employment status and the presumption that their work carries with it greater risk of injury. It would be interesting for a larger-scale study to be conducted to investigate this hypothesis.

Conclusion

The small sample of case law discussed in this chapter reveals an uneven approach on the part of courts to the assessment of psychiatric injuries and psychosocial disabilities. Courts in tort/negligence cases exhibit a propensity to label claimants as 'vulnerable' as opposed to disabled, which can hinder the ability of persons with psychosocial disabilities to access justice, especially in terms of claiming an effective remedy in the form of financial compensation. Courts in injury award cases tend to be more acceptant of the existence of psychiatric injury and the resulting psychosocial disability. Thus, persons with such disabilities are better able to access a remedy in this set of decisions. This finding can serve as a basis for a further large-scale study of the manner in which courts react to different claimants, not just to different legal frameworks. It could be interesting to explore whether courts are more sympathetic to certain types of claimants, such as those coming from specific professional backgrounds, and how this affects the courts' decisions on whether claimants with psychiatric injuries are labeled as disabled or as 'vulnerable'. Such a research project could shed more light on the issue of ranking different disabilities and thus creating a hierarchy of disabilities.

References

Alfred William Prater v British Motor Holdings Limited, The Rover Company Limited. (2016). WL 03947474

Chief Constable of Avon and Somerset Constabulary v Police Medical Appeal Board v Alistair Middleton. (2019). WL 01117711

Christopher Michael Bailey v International Automotive Components Group Limited. (2014). WL 5833810

David Ian Sharp v The Chief Constable of West Yorkshire Police v The Police Medical Appeal Board. (2016). WL 00826246

Flint v Chief Constable of North Yorkshire Police. (2010). WL 3166443

Flynn, E. (2015). *Disabled Justice? Access to Justice and the UN Convention on the Rights of Persons with Disabilities* (1st edn). Routledge.

Harry Mills v J P Barnes & Sons Ltd. (2013). WL 8182338

Marian Holloway v Tyne Thames Technology Limited. (2015). WL 5037777

Mental Health Europe. (2021). *Access to Justice for Persons with Psychosocial Disabilities & Mental Health Problems: Reflection Paper and Promising Practices* [White Paper]. MHE_Access_to_Justice_Refelction_Paper_March_2021.pdf (mhe-sme.org)

Mr Ion Manda v UBS AG. (2016). WL 03268506

Ms Dianne Henley v Royal Mail Group. (2016). WL 08309422

Perlin, M. L., Birgden, A., & Gledhill, K. (2009). 'The witness who saw,/he left little doubt': A comparative consideration of expert testimony in mental disability law cases in common and civil law systems. *Journal of Investigative Psychology and Offender Profiling*, 6, 59–88.

Perlin, M. L., & Dorfman, D. A. (1993). Sanism, social science, and the development of mental disability law jurisprudence. *Behavioral Sciences & the Law*, 11(1), 47–66.

Peter David Walther v The Police Medical Appeal Board, The Metropolitan Police Authority. (2009). WL 7019911

R (on the Application of Robin Andrew Michaelides) v Chief Constable of Merseyside Police v Police Medical Appeal Board. (2019). WL 02716948

Raymond Leslie Camden v Jackpot Leisure Limited, Michael Knight. (2015). WL 13639235

Spencer Smith v Ashwell Maintenance Limited. (2019). WL 01472799

The Queen (on the Application of Peter Goodland) v Chief Constable of Staffordshire Police The Queen (on the application of Martin Wright, Ralph Barlow, Edward White, Jayne Baker, Nicholas Tucker, Douglas Boulton, James Taylor, Peter Bennet, Michael Thomason, Stephen Wilson, Gareth Williams, Colin Aston, David Upton, Frederick Bower, Geoffrey Tweats, Kevin Bridgwood, Simon Bonnet) v Chief Constable of Staffordshire Police. (2020). WL 05548014

The Queen (on the Application of Susan Haworth) v Northumbria Police Authority. (2012). WL 1684734

The Queen (On the Application of the Commissioner of Police of the Metropolis) v Police Medical Appeal Board v Neil Brown. (2020). WL 00821050

The Queen (on the Application of Thomas Edward Crudace) v Northumbria Police Authority. (2012). WL 382577

The Queen (on the Application of) Mark Evans v Chief Constable of Cheshire Constabulary v Police Medical Appeal Board. (2018). WL 01934578

The Queen on the Application of Anthony Weed v Commissioner of Police of the Metropolis. (2020). WL 00710292

The Queen on the Application of Carole Doubtfire and Gary Williams v The Police Medical Appeal Board v The West Mercia Police Authority, Merseyside Police Authority. (2010). WL 2801734

The Queen on the Application of Colene Boskovic v Chief Constable of Staffordshire Police. (2018). WL 00378693

The Queen on the Application of Scardfield v Police Medical Appeal Board v Hampshire Police Authority. (2013). WL 6229674

The Queen on the Application of Sidwell v Police Medical Appeal Board v The Chief Constable of the Derbyshire Constabulary. (2015). WL 55982

The Queen on the Application of Simpson v Police Medical Appeal Board, Secretary of State for the Home Department, Northumbrian Police Authority. (2012). WL 1191051

The Queen on the Application of Stanley John Fisher v The Chief Constable of Northumbria – and – the Police Medical Appeal Board. (2017). WL 00895217

The Queen on the Application of the Chief Constable of South Yorkshire Police v The Crown Court at Sheffield v Lloyd Patrick Kelly. (2020). WL 00591744

United Nations. (2020). *International Principles and Guidelines on Access to Justice for Persons with Disabilities* [White Paper]. https://www.ohchr.org/Documents/Issues/Disability/SR_Disability/GoodPractices/Access-to-Justice-EN.pdf

32

ROOTED IN RIGHTS

Women with disabilities in India and Kenya

Mildred Omino and Shubha Nagesh

Introduction

Disability rights are human rights. There has been considerable progress in global policy and legal action towards disability-inclusive development; however, the progress realized in disability-inclusive development is marred by disparities, some of which are associated with disability hierarchies (WHO & World Bank, 2011). This chapter reviews disability hierarchies in the context of women with disabilities in India and Kenya in view of cultural practices, health rights, land and property rights, culture and employment and economic rights and their implications on disability-inclusive development.

The history of disability rights can be traced back to 1975, when the Declaration of the Rights of Persons with Disabilities was passed by the United Nations, declaring 1981 as the International Year of Disabled Persons and 1983 as the beginning of the United Nations Decade of Disabled Persons and establishing the World Program of Action Concerning Disabled Persons (Roth, 2018). The change in responses to persons with disabilities was largely driven by self-organization of people with disabilities across the world, who saw disability as a human rights issue (Rimmerman, 2013). The adoption of the Convention on the Rights of Persons with Disabilities (CRPD) by the United Nations in 2007 paved the way to use the convention as an advocacy and accountability tool and a means of promoting disability inclusion in international development among partners.

Given the deficient and varied understanding around disability, the theory around hierarchies in disability becomes evident primarily due to lack of information, stigma, prejudice, negative attitudes and mindsets that have taken over the society. Within the community of people with disabilities, there exists a sort of categorization, created partly by persons with disabilities and partly by non-disabled persons: physical versus intellectual disability, with communication concerns versus without communication concerns, mild versus severe,

DOI: 10.4324/9781003410089-38

male versus female etc. (Deal, 2003). Further, the discourse around ableism and its impact on the lives of people with disabilities has advanced disability hierarchies within the disabled community.

Perspectives on the disabled community have shifted in the last three decades from a charity-based model to a rights-based model. The rights-based approach is more acceptable, more dignified, views people with disabilities as subjects as opposed to objects and asks for them to be seen as people with very valid rights (Lawson & Beckett, 2021). The novel perspective also demands that society address, accept and provide for the needs of persons with disability and provide them with what they need to function to their optimal ability so that they can lead meaningful lives in society. Centering persons with disability in all decisions that affect them would allow a fairer, supportive and equitable ecosystem – one of pride, justice and solidarity. The disability rights debate should aim to ensure equal and effective enjoyment of all human rights in the absence of discrimination by people with all kinds of disabilities at any point in time. While the acceptance and integration of persons with disabilities in communities is better than before, there is so much that needs to be done in the context of human rights and in the context of persons with disabilities (Deal, 2003).

The chapter will elaborate on experiences in India and Kenya in the context of policy and legal frameworks, health rights, land and property rights and disability rights and culture.

Policy and legal framework on the rights of women with disabilities in India and Kenya

India is a signatory to the Convention on the Elimination of All Forms of Discrimination against Women (CEDAW) and the Convention on the Rights of Persons with Disabilities (CRPD), two significant milestones as the country aims to bring visibility to a group that is largely marginalized – women with disabilities (Byrnes & Freeman, 2012). While activists and advocates recognize the need to blend in components of both the ratifications, the ground reality remains fragmented, and synergy remains a far dream. India ratified the Convention on the Rights of Persons with Disabilities (CRPD) in 2007. However, the conventions do not fully guarantee women and girls with psychosocial or intellectual disabilities the right to legal capacity and the right to independent living, as required by the treaty (Durham et al., 2014).

Context in India

The government of India has enacted three major legislations for persons with disabilities:

1. Persons with Disabilities (Equal Opportunities, Protection of Rights and Full Participation) Act, 1995, which provides for education, employment, creation of barrier free environment, social security etc.

2. National Trust for Welfare of Persons with Autism, Cerebral Palsy, Mental Retardation and Multiple Disabilities Act, 1999, has provisions for legal guardianship of the four categories of disabilities and creation of an enabling environment for as much independent living as possible.
3. Rehabilitation Council of India Act, 1992, deals with the development of manpower for providing rehabilitation services.

India's population with some form of disability is estimated to be a mere 2.21% of the overall population, accounting for 26.8 million people, as per the Census 2011 reports. According to the World Health Organization and the World Bank, 15% of the global population lives with some form of a disability: 12% of males and 19% of females. According to Census 2001, there are 11.8 million women with disabilities, which constitutes 42.46% of total population of persons with disabilities. Despite these numbers, there are considerable discrepancies between global and national estimates – what we know for sure is that there is a low level of awareness and significant underreporting (Saikia et al., 2016).

The government of India introduced a term, *divyang* (meaning "divine ability" in Sanskrit), to refer to people with disabilities. While their intention was to tackle the negative mindset towards disability, the word has sparked considerable outrage as disability rights activists objected to the use of the word, arguing that they were not involved in the process, and it is dehumanizing as it prevents them from being treated as equals, as complex individuals who are not defined by their disabilities (Karmakar, 2019).

Context in Kenya

The journey of recognition of disability rights in Kenya has been evolving over the years all the way from the pre-independence period to the post-independence period (Gebrekidan, 2012). This can be traced from the declaration of the National Year of the Disabled in 1980, introduction of education assessment and resources by the ministry of education in 1984, appointment of a taskforce to review the laws and policies relating to persons with disabilities in 1993, enactment of the Persons with Disabilities Act in 2003, signing and ratification of CRPD in 2007 and recognition of disability rights by the constitution of Kenya in 2010.

Kenya signed and ratified the Convention on the Rights of Persons with Disabilities in 2008, therefore committing to the principles and articles in the CRPD. The Convention on the Elimination of All Forms of Discrimination against Women (CEDAW) was adopted by the United Nations in 1981 and ratified by the Kenyan government in 1984. Over three decades after ratification of the treaty, there has been some progress in the realization of women rights in Kenya as well as cushioning them against violence and discrimination. The push to uphold the rights of women through the treaty has been met with barriers from various sources, including sociocultural and economic barriers, as well as the strong patriarchal system in Kenya. While these challenges are common to all women, women with disabilities have constantly been left behind in the conversations and policy implementation towards upholding the rights of women (Rohwerder, 2017).

The women's movement has long operated on the assumption that persons with disabilities can push for their rights as a homogenous group, therefore ignoring the unique rights of women with disabilities. This situation was challenged by the Kenyan Advocacy Network for Women with Disabilities, who presented a shadow report to the CEDAW committee in 2017 when Kenya was being reviewed. The CEDAW committee gave recommendations specific to women with disabilities: in particular, protecting the rights of women with disabilities in ensuring equal access to housing, justice, healthcare and social protection; protecting them against gender-based violence; abolishing forced sterilization; and guaranteeing their right to property ownership (Kabia et al., 2018).

According to Kenya's 2019 population and housing census preliminary reports, 2.2% of Kenyans (i.e. 0.9 million Kenyans) live with some form of disability (KNBS, 2019). The census report revealed that 1.9 % of men have some form of disability, compared to 2.5% of women with disability: i.e. there are 523,883 women with disabilities in Kenya. However, this data does not seem to reflect the realities on the ground, and the data disparities could be due to fewer registrations, invisible disabilities, stigma, low awareness and inadequate training of census administrators on disability (Owino, 2020).

This contextual analysis depicts India and Kenya as countries that have made tremendous progress in ratifying treaties and enacting national laws and policies. Notably, the two countries seem to struggle with data disparities with respect to persons with disabilities. The available data on persons with disabilities, both in Kenya and in India, is considerably lower than the World Health Organization data on persons with disabilities. For example, the Kenya National Census Report of 2019 pegs disability prevalence in Kenya at 2.2%, whereas the World Health Organization report pegs disability prevalence at 15%. One would ask why the policies and legislations inadequately address the challenges experienced by women with disabilities in Kenya and India. The following sections of this chapter analyze health, land and property rights, followed by economic empowerment and culture with respect to women with disabilities in Kenya and India.

Finally, the chapter concludes by proposing steps to tackle the inequalities experienced by women with disabilities in various aspects of life.

Health rights

The international human rights framework, including Article 12 of the International Covenant on Economic, Social and Cultural Rights (ECOSOC), recognizes the right of all persons to the highest attainable standard of health. Similarly, article 23 of the Convention on the Rights of the Child guarantees the rights of children with disabilities to effective access to healthcare services and rehabilitation services. The constitution of the World Health Organization (WHO) also enshrines the highest attainable standard of health as a fundamental right of every human being.

The right to health includes access to timely, acceptable and affordable healthcare of appropriate quality, which must be guaranteed and is deliverable by states. Articles 25 and 26 of the Convention on the Rights of Persons with Disabilities reinforces the right to the highest attainable standard of health and rehabilitation to persons with disabilities (Vergunst et al., 2017). Article 12 of CEDAW provides that state parties shall take all appropriate measures to eliminate discrimination against women in the field of healthcare in order to ensure, on a basis of equality of men and women, access to healthcare services, including those related to family planning.

More often, persons with disabilities experience health disparities and have poorer health outcomes than able-bodied people. These disparities are caused by various barriers to access and socio-economic factors. For instance, women with disability receive less screening for breast and cervical cancer than women without disability. Adolescents and adults with disabilities are more likely to be excluded from sexuality education. Barriers to health include the high cost of healthcare, especially since disabled people are some of the poorest; difficulty in accessing health facilities or medical equipment; lack of public health information in accessible formats; and negative attitudes from healthcare workers, especially on sexual health and reproductive healthcare service delivery, as well as lack of physical access to healthcare facilities and compromised confidentiality of healthcare service delivery due to lack of disability accommodations by healthcare providers, such as sign language interpretation and Braille services (Durham et al., 2014).

Many women with disabilities face the brunt of stigma and negative attitudes when they become mothers. Studies have found that there exists a clear hierarchy in attitudes across a spectrum – those with physical impairments being favored over those with intellectual impairment. When they do get pregnant, women with disabilities are less likely to receive maternal healthcare services – the attitude and behavior of the health staff influence the extent to which women access services. The attitude of service providers, in turn, depends on their information, knowledge and understanding of disability, which is mostly nonexistent or limited and negative. Evidence shows that women with disability have adverse pregnancy outcomes compared to those without a disability (Murthy et al., 2014).

Lack of access to sexual and reproductive health services disproportionately affects those with disabilities. Low utilization of services by women with disabilities is worse in remote and rural areas. Underdeveloped infrastructure and a lack of social amenities compound the adverse situation of girls and women with disabilities (Nagesh et al., 2020).

The reproductive health needs of women with disability have mostly gone unnoticed because of the common perception that disabled women could not be asexual (Groce & Trasi, 2004). There is a dearth of published data on the reproductive health of women with disability in India. One study provides evidence on some reproductive health parameters of women with disability in India for the first time ever. The findings will help in formulating policy and developing specific interventions to improve pregnancy outcomes for women with disability in India (Gudlavalleti et al., 2014).

Reporting in India has mostly excluded the disabled, including the National Family Health Survey, India's primary resource portal. This leads to significant underreporting and, therefore, a lack of or very slow progress in policies and practices for the disabled. Data around violence against disabled women is further lacking, though it is acknowledged that broadly, violence against disabled women is far more widespread than that against their non-disabled peers. Studies around sexual violence against disabled women in India are scant; however one in every three women in India is known to experience some form of violence (Krishnamoorthy et al., 2020). While we don't know the exact number of disabled women who experience violence in India, we do know that it's very high. The disability itself poses a significant risk – those with physical impairment are unable to move away; those with speech and hearing impairments may not be able to call for or respond to support; support may not be accessible in other ways; staff may not be oriented or trained to work with women with disabilities etc.

Apart from this, access to fair remedial measures is very difficult for women with disabilities, largely due to stigma and the associated discrimination. Most don't report or seek support because of the negative mindset in society and the lack of support in the health and the legal ecosystems. According to the 2014 Guidelines and Protocols for Medico-Legal Care for Victims/Survivors of Sexual Violence issued by India's Ministry of Health and Family Welfare, women and girls with disabilities face particular barriers to reporting sexual abuse (Government of India, 2014):

> Because of the obvious barriers to communication, as well as their dependency on caretakers who may also be abusers. When they do report, their complaints are not taken seriously and the challenges they face in expressing themselves in a system that does not create an enabling environment to allow for such expression, complicates matters further.

Despite this, a system to register and report complaints is lacking, and therefore, integrated efforts to manage this are also yet to come. All this makes the women and their problems invisible. In 2014, India's Ministry of Health and Family Welfare issued Guidelines and Protocols for Medico-Legal Care for Victims/Survivors of Sexual Violence. This integrates norms for the medical examination of women and girls with disabilities – sensitivity in history taking and examination, providing accommodations like a special educator to take consent etc. This is essential since most medical professionals do not have the time or the training to sensitively demonstrate competence in medical tests and procedures for women with disabilities who have been victims of violence. This magnifies the trauma, delays the justice and compensation and deters women from accessing support services in the future. Compensation and fair justice remain a distant dream for most. Justice takes time in India – more so for disabled women as they face additional distinct challenges, and the majority of the women and their families remain unaware of their rights, entitlement and access to justice.

Kenya has made numerous global and regional commitments to promoting health, including launching the pilot phase of its universal health coverage program in December 2018. The phased pilot was implemented across four counties with the objective of ensuring that all people access health services without the risk of financial ruin. The UHC framework reflects three dimensions of coverage – population coverage, service coverage and financial coverage/protection – and reflects eight principles: equitable access, efficiency, quality, inclusiveness, availability, adaptability, choice and innovation. It is geared towards affordable healthcare for all; the pilot phase has since ended, and a refashioned version of the scheme is due to begin sometime in 2021 (Oraro-Lawrence & Wyss, 2020).

While the UHC framework provides a comprehensive approach to affordable healthcare for all, girls and women with disabilities remain disadvantaged in enjoying the benefits of the UHC, especially reproductive health. Young girls and women with disabilities have poor health-seeking behavior owing to inability/difficulty in accessing health facilities, lack of reproductive health information in accessible formats, inadequate comprehensive sexuality education, low self-esteem owing to historical discrimination, exclusive policies that lack disability-specific indicators and, most importantly, misconceptions and myths around disability and sexuality. The situation is compounded by attitudinal barriers from the community and health workers. More often, vulnerable populations are viewed from the perspective of income levels, thereby ignoring the vulnerabilities that come with disability, gender and sexual orientation. For women and girls with disabilities, this is a twofold setback!

Article 43 (1) of the Kenyan Constitution states that every person has the right to the highest attainable standard of health, which includes the right to healthcare services, including reproductive healthcare. Article 27 of the Kenyan Constitution provides for equality and freedom from discrimination, including full and equal enjoyment of all rights and fundamental freedoms. It further prohibits discrimination, direct or indirect, against any person on any ground, including disability. In June 2013, the government of Kenya joined other countries in embracing a free maternal healthcare policy, a move that saw abolition of payment of delivery fees in public maternal health facilities. The move is geared in the right direction towards reducing maternal mortality. The *Linda Mama* policy, which is a Swahili phrase that is loosely translated as "Take care of mothers", promotes maternal health by easing the financial burden on women of child-bearing age. While this news was received with jubilation by able-bodied women, those with disability are yet to celebrate since the policy is not responsive to the unique needs of women with disabilities, who have high likelihood of delivering their children through cesarean section (a service that is not free in public health facilities) and struggle to access public health facilities owing to inaccessible public transport (Gitobu et al., 2018).

About 39% of women aged 15 and above in Kenya have experienced gender-based violence (Kenya National Gender and Equality Commission, 2016). The State Department of Gender in Kenya has established at least one gender-based violence recovery center in each of the 47 counties in Kenya, with an overall mandate of supporting victims of sexual gender-based violence in the recovery process. Gender-based violence recovery centers, which have been the main hope for survivors of gender-based violence, have failed to take care of the unique needs of women with disabilities (Temmerman et al., 2019). The centers have continued to operate with inaccessible beds, toilets and washrooms; lack of sign language interpretation services; and lack of privacy and confidentiality. Lack of accessible infrastructure brings about poor sanitation, especially for women and girls with physical disabilities, because most toilets in public institutions are pit latrines and inaccessible, therefore posing a health risk for girls with physical/multiple disabilities coming in contact with the dirty floors of the latrine as they are forced to crawl (Mahider, 2015). There are cases of women and girls with disabilities, especially intellectual and psychosocial disabilities, not getting proper medical attention after sexual violence; there have been numerous cases of their being mishandled by medical personnel. This results in cases failing in court as medical personnel provide insufficient reports and do not handle the matter urgently to get good evidence to ensure successful prosecution; evidence is lost in hospitals or police stations (Abhishek, 2018).

Women and girls with disabilities often lack reproductive healthcare information and services in accessible formats and, at times, are subjected to forced sterilization. There are a number of reported cases in Kenya of forced sterilization, and with regards to women and girls with disabilities, it is the guardians who are consenting to sterilization on behalf of the women and girls with disabilities without their consent. Forced sterilization is a violation of women's right to bodily autonomy. As per the Committee on the Rights of Persons with Disabilities (CRPD), women with disabilities have a right to make informed decisions on sexual and reproductive health, which includes but is not limited to family planning, safe and enjoyable sex, marriage and having a family.

The legal system should create accommodations and become accessible and friendly so more women and girls who are survivors of sexual violence can get justice. There is a need for enforcement of laws and policies that protect rights in cases of sexual violence against women and girls with disabilities. Police, medical facilities, social workers and community organizations should work in synchrony with the legal system to create an umbrella of services for women and girls with disabilities. Medical professionals who are the first port of call for most women should be trained in accordance with these guidelines. Data should be disaggregated based on violence against women, particularly from a disability perspective, both to understand the magnitude of the problem and to compile evidence to influence policy and programming. Justice should be ensured to the victims of abuse in as fair and equitable a manner as possible, at the very least (Lawthers et al., 2003)

Land and property rights

Land and property ownership is critical for women to ensure improved living standards and complement their roles as heads of households and caregivers. Land and property form a foundation for security, shelter, livelihood and dignity support and a pathway to economic empowerment and economic opportunity. Studies show that there is a persistent gap between law and practice on land and property ownership by women. Women in half the countries in the world are unable to assert equal land and property rights despite legal protections. Globally, women own less land and have less secure rights over land than men. Women make up, on average, less than 20% of the world's landholders but make up an estimated 43% of the agricultural labor force (Tyler Roush, 2019).

In 2010, Kenya passed a constitution that gives equal right to own and inherit land to both men and women; however, women with disabilities are already in a position of less power in marriage financially and culturally; even with laws in place, the practice is that women with disabilities continue to experience violation of their right to own and inherit land. Article 15 of CEDAW provides that state parties shall accord to women, in civil matters, a legal capacity identical to that of men and the same opportunities to exercise that capacity. In particular, they shall give women equal rights to conclude contracts and to administer property and shall treat them equally in all stages of procedure in courts and tribunals.

Kenya has a robust legal framework that governs the right to ownership of land and property. Relevant provisions include chapter four of the constitution of Kenya, the Bill of Rights, which recognizes the right of women to equal treatment under the law and prohibits gender-based discrimination; devolution of services, including land-related services, to the county level; recognition of traditional dispute-resolution mechanisms; prohibition of the use of traditional dispute-resolution mechanisms in a way that contravenes the Bill of Rights; and requiring legislative implementation of the principle that women make up at least one-third of the members of elected or appointed political bodies. A set of land laws giving effect to the constitution – the Land Act, Land Registration Act and National Land Commission Act – were approved in 2012. A new set of marriage laws, the Matrimonial Property Act, 2013, and the Marriage Act, 2014, replaced the older framework, which included seven different marriage laws but did not include explicit provisions governing customary marriages. Other legislative reforms, including community land and evictions and resettlement bills, were enacted by the Kenyan government in 2016.

Despite a progressive legal framework, Kenyan women's land rights continue to lag behind those of men. Customary law, which often discriminates against women and limits their land and property rights, governs at least 65%

of land in Kenya, and the patriarchal nature of Kenyan society often limits the rights of even those women not living on land governed by custom. Some estimates indicate that as little as 1% of land is titled in the names of women and 5–6% is titled jointly by women and men (Odote, 2013).

For women with disabilities, the situation is further compounded by cultural, gender and disability-related stereotypes. For instance, women with intellectual disabilities are often viewed as women of "unsound mind" and therefore denied property ownership rights on the premise that they cannot make informed consent. This practice hinders them from enjoying the rights to inherit and hold property and the right to buy and sell property. Complexities in the legal framework and inaccessibility of court processes often serve as hindrances to persons with disabilities in dispute resolution that relates to ownership of land and property (Groce et al., 2014).

India has enacted various laws to govern land and property ownership:

- The Indian Succession Act of 1995 governs the procedures for holding and inheriting property.
- The Transfer of Property Act of 1882 governs the procedures for buying and selling property.
- The National Trust Act of 1999 requires that if any person with disability owns property, it can be registered at the local level.

The enactment of the Persons with Disabilities Act of 2016 in India further reinforced the right to property ownership by persons with disabilities. Section 13 of the act requires the state government to ensure that persons with disabilities have a right, equally with others, to own or inherit movable or immovable property.

While ordinary women experience barriers in property ownership, even when there exist laws that uphold the rights of women to own property, women with disabilities experience even greater challenges due to their vulnerabilities and cultural misconceptions about disability. A case in point is of a woman with albinism in Nyeri County in Kenya, who was given land and a house by her mother but could not access the house since her uncles barred her from rightfully owning the property. Her effort to seek legal redress on the matter was futile since the judicial processes were complicated and costly to her (Kabia et al., 2018).

To ensure women with disabilities are accorded the right to own property, it is important that they are well informed about their rights to property ownership. They should also be accorded quality education to ensure that they have the requisite knowledge to push for their rights within the existing policy and legal framework. Education and empowerment alone cannot guarantee women with disabilities their rights if the negative perceptions, discrimination, cultural stereotypes and gap between law and practice are not eradicated. There is a need for constant sensitization of different stakeholders, from community leaders, families, lawmakers, policy makers and law enforcers to appreciate disability as part of human diversity and accord girls and women with disabilities dignity in all spheres of life.

Economic empowerment

Despite the progress in gender equality in employment and economic empowerment, women's work is still seen as secondary and inferior to that of men. Women continue to fulfill the role of the homemaker, the caregiver and the beast of burden, while men are the ones who go out, are employed and earn to support the family. Girls in many parts of the world do not receive the same privileges as their brothers, and when a girl has a disability, she has little hope of becoming anything. Young women and girls with disabilities are seen as a burden for life.

The national policy in India aims to create an environment that allows for the disabled to have equal opportunities, equal rights and the right to full participation in society. The focus of the policy is economic rehabilitation of the disabled, including wage employment in the organized sector and self-employment. The policy seeks to support services through vocational rehabilitation centers and vocational training centers in both urban and rural areas to create increased opportunities for productive employment (Yadava & Awasthi, 2016).

Although efforts have been made in India to integrate persons with disabilities into the workforce, there is a need to create economic independence for persons with disabilities. Physical access to the workplace from home, easy access within the workplace and access to education are critically linked to the ability to earn a livelihood. Education and training equip disabled people with the skills necessary for employment. Though both are provided for under the Persons with Disabilities Act, 1995, outside the major cities few persons with disabilities have access to education or training. As per the UNESCO Report in 2018, 15-to-29-year-olds with disabilities are less likely to have attended school than those without disabilities in almost all 37 countries for which data were available. On average, 87% of persons without disabilities attended school, compared to 77% of persons with disabilities (UNESCO, 2018).

The Kenyan government has put in place several policies and legislations to ensure economic empowerment of persons with disabilities. As in other low- and middle-income countries, persons with disabilities in Kenya experience high rates of unemployment compared to their counterparts without disability (Cobley, 2012). To curb this challenge, the government has put in place the following policy and legal measures to ensure improved economic participation of persons with disabilities:

1. Article 54 of the 2010 Constitution of Kenya provides that the state shall ensure progressive implementation of the principle that 5% of the members of the public in elective and appointive bodies are persons with disabilities.

2. The government of Kenya commissioned a program called Access to Government Procurement Opportunities (AGPO) in 2013, which is founded on the Public Procurement and Disposal Act of 2015 and Articles 55 and 227 of the Constitution of Kenya. Under the program, 30% of public procurement is reserved for youth, women and persons with disabilities.
3. The government has also established devolved funds, which include the National Development Fund for the Disabled, Women Enterprise Fund and Youth Enterprise Fund. Persons with disabilities who own small, medium and micro enterprises (SMEs) can access the devolved funds.

The policy and legal framework outlined here has led to some increased participation of persons with disabilities in economic activities. However, the threshold in each of the stated policies are still out of reach. For instance, the report issued by the Public Service Commission of Kenya for the year 2019 indicated that persons with disabilities comprised 1.18% of total employees in public service. However, the data of public employees with disability is not disaggregated by gender, whereas the data for public employees without disability is disaggregated by gender.

The implementation of AGPO was marred by challenges with the report, revealing that women accessed more of the procurement opportunities, followed by youth, whereas persons with disabilities recorded the lowest uptake of the opportunities. This compelled the government to issue a follow-up circular to compel public institutions to award at least 2% of the procurement opportunities to persons with disabilities. The fact that the economic empowerment data for persons with disabilities is not disaggregated by gender in itself shows the magnitude of the challenges faced in including girls and women with disabilities in development.

While women are known to be the majority of owners of SMEs, the unique challenges experienced by women with disabilities in business might go unaddressed if such data is not captured. For instance, they incur high transportation costs getting their produce to the market, which makes their operation costs higher. Those in need of the services of personal guides and sign language services have to incur such costs, which then reduce their profit margins. For those in rural areas, navigating the terrain might just be a hurdle for their meaningful engagement in economic activities. While the employment quotas and AGPO quotas may encourage women with disabilities to engage in economic activities, it is necessary for the government to ensure that the economic environment is disability inclusive.

More than half the persons with disabilities in Kenya reported in the 2015–16 Kenya Integrated Household Budget Survey that they have difficulties engaging in economic activities (Kenya National Bureau of Statistics, 2016a). Children with disabilities also experience barriers in accessing education: according to the 2009 census, 17% of children aged 6 and 17 have never attended school, compared to 10% of children without disabilities (Kenya National Bureau of Statistics, 2016b). Access to special needs schools remains a challenge, and school fees and materials can be a barrier for those who are not able to meet costs, particularly in special schools, which tend to have higher fee structures (Moyi, 2017).

Insufficient training of special needs teachers and the inadequate development of disability-friendly curricula and school materials are other key barriers faced by children with disabilities when trying to access education. It is well known that the possibility of women with disabilities securing job opportunities is heavily dependent on their ability to secure quality education which equips them with the relevant skills and knowledge required in the job market.

The following steps need to be taken to enhance the employment opportunities for women with disabilities:

1. The government may initiate a dialogue with private sector organizations to help women with disabilities in getting employment.
2. Develop appropriate home-based income generation programs for women with disabilities.
3. The system of coaching for employment may also be encouraged for persons with disabilities and their caregivers.
4. Facilitate modifications in the design of machinery, workstations and work environments necessary for disabled women to operate without barriers in training centers/factories/industries/offices etc.
5. Ensure accessible built environment and provide disability-inclusive social amenities such as roads and communication platforms to reduce the cost of running businesses for persons with disabilities.

Disability in the context of culture

Culture is the systems of knowledge shared by a relatively large group of people. Cultural factors are more related to religion, ethnicity and tradition. Culture and practices embedded in culture influence understanding and behavior towards disability, along with decision making to seek intervention and support for the disability. Professionals who work in the field of disability should have a good overview of the underlying socio-cultural context and address the same as they seek to improve the lives of women with disabilities.

India is a large and diverse country and has many different contexts and describes many causes for disability – consanguinity, bad luck, challenges in pregnancy, medicines etc. Religious beliefs that the wrath of God, punishment for past deeds, mother's mistakes etc. are all frequently seen. A vast number of families are not aware of developmental disabilities, and therefore, children are often diagnosed late. Extended family, relatives and grandparents have all often described delays or deviations in development as normal and therefore prevented concerned parents from seeking help early. Families are ashamed, reluctant and unwilling and often live isolated and in guilt. In some places, families whose children have disabilities are shunned, abused and banned from the community. They socially isolate themselves, for fear of stigma and discrimination. The disabled child becomes a mere cog in the family wheel; the family has to learn to cope with the extra needs, the consuming schedules and the compliance with therapy, intervention, aides and treatment, if they do at all. A large part of the work and the stress is often borne by the women in the family – mother, sister, aunt, grandmother etc. Significant disruption of family routines, relaxation and interaction can be expected (Singhi et al., 1990).

Kenya has a rich culture coupled with diverse ethnicity and regional cultural diversity. In a country that has 43 ethnic groups with embedded culture and values, disability has huge cultural connotations. The invisibility of women with disabilities is further compounded by their ethnic and regional identities. Women with disabilities from pastoral and nomadic communities and minority ethnic groups experience low representation in governance, education and economic empowerment. For women with psychosocial disability and other invisible disabilities, representation and active participation in the disability and feminist spaces are often skewed, rendering them more invisible and exposing them to increased violation of their rights. In the examination of gender, culture and ethnicity hierarchies and their impact on holistic integration, women with disabilities are critical (Johnstone et al., 2017).

Stigma and discrimination continue to be barriers to the equal participation of persons with disabilities in society. In many communities, disabled family members are often hidden away due to societal stigma and prejudices. Children are especially affected as they are often abused and abandoned. In addition, evidence from the Kenya National Commission on Human Rights shows that many persons with disabilities are not aware of their rights or the legislation in place to protect and promote their well-being, including the right to access social services, such as education and healthcare, and support with job training and employment (Kabare, 2018).

Some communities erroneously believe that disability is an infliction by evil spirits, leading to the view that such people can never amount to anything important in life and can only survive through a life of constant dependency. They are even shunned by the larger society and sometimes even by their own families. Children are denied the right to education as they are locked in the house by parents to avoid "embarrassing" the family. For example, children with disabilities from the Samburu community in Kenya were placed strategically near livestock so that the livestock could trample on them while heading out to graze and kill them instantly. Some communities held the cultural belief that multiple impairments were spiritually instigated. Cultural identities and beliefs in communities where girls and women with disabilities come from determine the extent to which they access opportunities in life (Bunning et al., 2017).

Socially, they are stigmatized so that even those who manage to secure a place in the mainstream educational centers suffer silently as they are labeled "disabled" persons with no ability. Actually, recent campaigns are determined to change this notion, and activist groups often use the term "persons with special abilities", along with the slogan "Disability is not inability". Not many employers are willing to absorb such people into their organizations, and this often leads to financial dependency by persons with disabilities. A person who is economically challenged faces huge hurdles in their endeavors for self-determination and personal development. Politically, the main challenge that exists is that, although laws and policies have been put in place, the political willpower to enforce them and/or to realize the rights guaranteed therein are often lacking. The rights of entitlement that only exist on paper may not do much for a group that already faces discrimination right in their own homes – discrimination that is sometimes perpetrated by their closest relatives.

Discussion

The Committee on the Elimination of All Forms of Discrimination against Women (CEDAW) applies to the well-being of all women, globally, on all contexts. Women with disabilities are first women – in most cases, it is often difficult to conclude whether the stigma and discrimination they face is attributable to their gender or their disability. Discrimination against disabled women can be subtle, overt, persistent, periodic or brutal – it takes various forms, and the standard of comparison differs accordingly.

Systemic discrimination against women and girls with disabilities leads to significant concerns around their right to experience their sexuality, engage in relationships and be a part of families. Although many international human rights organizations and declarations center the right of a woman to make her own reproductive choices the world over, women with disabilities are denied these rights. Marriage is rare, forced sterilization is common, violence is rampant and neglect is commonplace.

To improve the quality of life of disabled women, it is important to empower them – rather than "fix" the women, the environment has to become accommodating, accessible and affordable. Advocates and activists, particularly those with disabilities themselves, should lead the efforts and serve as role models for those who come after them.

Community-based awareness, advocacy and sensitization are key to removing negative mindsets, stigma and discrimination. Campaigns should be enforced at all levels with an aim to shift perceptions towards positivity towards women with disabilities.

Lack of data magnifies the problem since an underestimation will not warrant an effective response by governance to combat stigma, discrimination, violence or neglect. Reporting of incidents that compromise the rights of women with disabilities is essential and urgent to keep women with disabilities safe.

Countries, regions and provinces should comply with, adopt and adapt guidelines, policies and laws to promote optimal realization of basic human rights for women with disabilities. Normalizing atrocities based on excuses of socio-cultural context can be overcome by spreading awareness, factual information and advocacy in the community.

Conclusion

People with disabilities, despite being the world's largest minority group, continue to face many obstacles in their ongoing struggle for equality. Although both men and women with disabilities are subject to discrimination because of their disabilities, the latter are at a greater disadvantage because of the cumulative discrimination based on gender and disability. Women with disabilities have historically been neglected by both the disability landscape and the feminist landscape alike, and issues of significance to women with disabilities have, in large part, been overshadowed by the disability rights movement as well as the women's movement. In the recent past, important international feminist convening's have failed to adequately include women with disabilities: for instance, the Africa regional review of 25 years of implementation of the Beijing Declaration and Platform for Action meeting in Addis Abba in October 2019, where the accessibility needs of women with disabilities were not met, thus hindering their effective participation. Similarly the recently concluded Generation Equality Global Forums held in Mexico in March 2020 and in France in July 2021 were marred by accessibility challenges for women with disabilities. The committee on the Convention on the Rights of Persons with Disabilities (CRPD) failed to achieve gender parity when the elections conducted in June 2016 resulted in representation of seventeen men with disabilities and one woman with disability. Disability does not hold women back, but ableism, discrimination and inaccessibility do. Let's do something about it.

References

Abhishek. (2018). Invisible victims of sexual violence: Access to justice for women and girls with disabilities in India. *Human Rights Watch*. https://www.hrw.org/report/2018/04/03/invisible-victims-sexual-violence/access-justice-women-and-girls-disabilities

Bunning, K., Gona, J. K., Newton, C. R., & Hartley, S. (2017). The perception of disability by community groups: Stories of local understanding, beliefs and challenges in a rural part of Kenya. *PLoS ONE*, 12(8). https://doi.org/10.1371/journal.pone.0182214

Byrnes, A., & Freeman, M. (2012). The impact of the CEDAW convention: Paths to equality. *GSDRC*. https://gsdrc.org/document-library/the-impact-of-the-cedaw-convention-paths-to-equality/

Cobley, D. S. (2012). Towards economic empowerment: Segregation versus inclusion in the Kenyan context. *Disability & Society*, 27(3), 371–384. https://doi.org/10.1080/09687599.2012.654988

Deal, M. (2003). Disabled people's attitudes toward other impairment groups: A hierarchy of impairments. *Disability & Society*, 18(7), 897–910. https://doi.org/10.1080/0968759032000127317

Durham, J., Brolan, C. E., & Mukandi, B. (2014). The convention on the rights of persons with disabilities: A foundation for ethical disability and health research in developing countries. *American Journal of Public Health*, 104(11), 2037–2043. https://doi.org/10.2105/AJPH.2014.302006

Gebrekidan, F. N. (2012). Disability rights activism in Kenya, 1959–1964: History from below. *African Studies Review*, 55(3), 103–122. https://doi.org/10.1017/S0002020600007228

Gitobu, C. M., Gichangi, P. B., & Mwanda, W. O. (2018). The effect of Kenya's free maternal health care policy on the utilization of health facility delivery services and maternal and neonatal mortality in public health facilities. *BMC Pregnancy and Childbirth*, 18(1), 77. https://doi.org/10.1186/s12884-018-1708-2

Government of India. (2014). *Guidelines and Protocols Medico Legal Care for Survivors Victims of Sexual Violence | Ministry of Health and Family Welfare | GOI*. https://main.mohfw.gov.in/reports/guidelines-and-protocols-medico-legal-care-survivors-victims-sexual-violence

Groce, N. E., London, J., & Stein, M. A. (2014). Inheritance, poverty, and disability. *Disability & Society*, 29(10), 1554–1568. https://doi.org/10.1080/09687599.2014.969831

Groce, N. E., & Trasi, R. (2004). Rape of individuals with disability: AIDS and the folk belief of virgin cleansing. *Lancet* (London, England), 363(9422), 1663–1664. https://doi.org/10.1016/S0140-6736 (04)16288–0

Gudlavalleti, M., John, N., & Sagar, J. (2014). Reproductive health of women with and without disabilities in South India, the SIDE study (South India Disability Evidence) study: A case control study. *BMC Women's Health*, 14, 146. https://doi.org/10.1186/s12905-014-0146-1

Johnstone, C. J., Limaye, S., & Kayama, M. (2017). Disability, culture, and identity in India and USA. In S. Halder & L. C. Assaf (Eds.), *Inclusion, Disability and Culture: An Ethnographic Perspective Traversing Abilities and Challenges* (pp. 15–29). Springer International Publishing. https://doi.org/10.1007/978-3-319-55224-8_2

Kabare. (2018). *Social Protection and Disability in Kenya – Krystle Kabare Working Paper: October 2018 – Development . . ..* https://www.readkong.com/page/social-protection-and-disability-in-kenya-krystle-kabare-9815193

Kabia, E., Mbau, R., Muraya, K. W., Morgan, R., Molyneux, S., & Barasa, E. (2018). How do gender and disability influence the ability of the poor to benefit from pro-poor health financing policies in Kenya? An intersectional analysis. *International Journal for Equity in Health*, 17(1), 149. https://doi.org/10.1186/s12939-018-0853-6

Karmakar, R. (2019, September 25). 'Divyangjan' is a controversial word similar to 'mentally ill', says U.N. body. *The Hindu*. https://www.thehindu.com/news/national/other-states/divyangjan-is-a-controversial-word-similar-to-mentally-ill-says-un-body/article29508027.ece

Kenya National Bureau of Statistics. (2016a). *Kenya – Integrated Household Budget Survey 2015–2016*. https://catalog.ihsn.org/index.php/catalog/7432

Kenya National Bureau of Statistics. (2016b, May 21). 2009 Kenya population and housing census analytical reports. *Kenya National Bureau of Statistics*. https://www.knbs.or.ke/?p=517

Kenya National Gender and Equality Commission. (2016). *Gender-based Violence in Kenya: The Economic Burden on Survivors*. National Gender and Equality Commission.

KNBS. (2019, November 4). 2019 Kenya population and housing census results. *Kenya National Bureau of Statistics*. https://www.knbs.or.ke/?p=5621

Krishnamoorthy, Y., Ganesh, K., & Vijayakumar, K. (2020). Physical, emotional and sexual violence faced by spouses in India: Evidence on determinants and help-seeking behaviour from a nationally representative survey. *Journal of Epidemiology and Community Health*, 74(9), 732–740. https://doi.org/10.1136/jech-2019-213266

Lawson, A., & Beckett, A. E. (2021). The social and human rights models of disability: Towards a complementarity thesis. *The International Journal of Human Rights*, 25(2), 348–379. https://doi.org/10.1080/13642987.2020.1783533

Lawthers, A. G., Pransky, G. S., Peterson, L. E., & Himmelstein, J. H. (2003). Rethinking quality in the context of persons with disability. *International Journal for Quality in Health Care*, 15(4), 287–299. https://doi.org/10.1093/intqhc/mzg048

Mahider. (2015). *Gender Based Violence, Women with Disabilities and access to Justice: Ethiopia and Kenya – Pdf Free Download*. https://docplayer.net/77199438-Gender-based-violence-women-with-disabilities-and-access-to-justice-ethiopia-and-kenya.html

Moyi, P. (2017). School participation for children with disabilities in Kenya. *Research in Comparative and International Education*, 12(4), 497–511. https://doi.org/10.1177/1745499917740654

Murthy, G. V. S., John, N., & Sagar, J. (2014). Reproductive health of women with and without disabilities in South India, the SIDE study (South India Disability Evidence) study: A case control study. *BMC Women's Health*, 14, 146. https://doi.org/10.1186/s12905-014-0146-1

Nagesh, O., Freywhot & Vovid. (2020, September 25). The rights of women and girls with disabilities in Kenya and India Matter! *Rewriting the Narrative*. https://medium.com/rewriting-the-narrative/the-rights-of-women-and-girls-with-disabilities-in-kenya-and-india-matter-b50f7170d5e5

Odote, C. (2013). The dawn of uhuru? Implications of constitutional recognition of communal land rights in pastoral areas of Kenya. *Nomadic Peoples*, 17(1), 87–105.

Oraro-Lawrence, T., & Wyss, K. (2020). Policy levers and priority-setting in universal health coverage: A qualitative analysis of healthcare financing agenda setting in Kenya. *BMC Health Services Research*, 20(1), 182. https://doi.org/10.1186/s12913-020-5041-x

Owino. (2020). Eastone Owino. *Development Initiatives*. https://devinit.org/who-we-are/our-team/eastone-owino/

Rimmerman, R. (2013). *Social Inclusion of People with Disabilities: National and International… – Arie Rimmerman – Google Books*. https://books.google.co.ke/books/about/Social_Inclusion_of_People_with_Disabili.html?id=2ynKRc6nkkkC&redir_esc=y

Rohwerder, B. (2017). *Women and Girls With Disabilities in Conflict and Crises*. Brighton: Institute of Development Studies. p. 20. http://www.gsdrc.org/wp-content/uploads/2017/10/032-Women-and-girls-with-disabilities-in-crisis-and-conflict.pdf

Roth, H. I. (2018). *PC Chang and the universal declaration of human rights*. University of Pennsylvania Press.

Roush, T. (2019). Women in half the world still denied land, property rights despite laws. *World Bank*. https://www.worldbank.org/en/news/press-release/2019/03/25/women-in-half-the-world-still-denied-land-property-rights-despite-laws

Saikia, N., Bora, J. K., Jasilionis, D., & Shkolnikov, V. M. (2016). Disability Divides in India: Evidence from the 2011 Census. *PLOS ONE*, 11(8), e0159809. https://doi.org/10.1371/journal.pone.0159809

Singhi, P. D., Goyal, L., Pershad, D., Singhi, S., & Walia, B. N. (1990). Psychosocial problems in families of disabled children. *The British Journal of Medical Psychology*, 63 (Pt 2), 173–182. https://doi.org/10.1111/j.2044-8341.1990.tb01610.x

Temmerman, M., Ogbe, E., Manguro, G., Khandwalla, I., Mary, T., Mandaliya, K., Dierick, L., MacGill, M., & Gichangi, P. (2019). The gender-based violence and recovery centre at Coast Provincial General Hospital, Mombasa, Kenya: An integrated care model for survivors of sexual violence. *PLOS Medicine*, 16, e1002886. https://doi.org/10.1371/journal.pmed.1002886

UNESCO. (2018, March 22). *Education and Disability: Analysis of Data from 49 Countries*. http://uis.unesco.org/en/news/education-and-disability-analysis-data-49-countries

Vergunst, R., Swartz, L., Hem, K.-G., Eide, A. H., Mannan, H., MacLachlan, M., Mji, G., Braathen, S. H., & Schneider, M. (2017). Access to health care for persons with disabilities in rural South Africa. *BMC Health Services Research*, 17(1), 741. https://doi.org/10.1186/s12913-017-2674-5

WHO & World Bank. (2011). World report on disability. *GSDRC*. https://gsdrc.org/document-library/world-report-on-disability-summary/

Yadava, V., & Awasthi, P. (2016). Empowerment and well-being of disabled women. *SMS Journal of Entrepreneurship and Innovation*, 3. https://doi.org/10.21844/smsjei.v3i01.6799

33

CONVERSATION ACROSS CONTINENTS ON HIERARCHIES, HUMAN SECURITY AND COVID-19

Rosemary Joan Gowran, Eileen Davis, Natasha Layton, Ricky Buchanan, Diane Bell, Jody Lee van Heerden, Deepak Nathan and Sureshkumar Kamalakannan

Introduction

Life as we knew it has changed with the COVID-19 global pandemic disrupting every nation. We are all experiencing what occupational scientists call 'occupational disruption', which means a shifting in our habits, roles and routines to navigate engagement in our daily lives. Much of this disturbs our productivity, our leisure and our sense of self. Some of this disruption brings us a measure of freedom insofar as, if or when life 'as it was' resumes, we wonder whether we would like it to remain the same. In casting around for a blueprint on how 'to be' when our scaffolds and structures are removed, we can look to the experts – people who have been living with occupational disruption and its partner, occupational deprivation, for much of their lives. If you have not come across these people, it is because societal attitudes, services, systems and policies have systematically kept people with disabilities silent, hidden, marginalised and disadvantaged. Evidence suggests that there are multiple factors that increase vulnerabilities for people with disabilities during the COVID-19 crisis which are related to both health and environmental risk factors (Barbareschi et al., 2021; Kamalakannan et al., 2021).

The aim of this chapter is to explore daily living disruption as a result of the pandemic by engaging scholars from four countries on four different continents.

Rosie, as lead author of this chapter, proposed to her friends and academic colleagues, Eileen in Ireland, Ricky and Natasha in Australia, Jody and Diane in South Africa and Deepak and Suresh in India, a plan to compile this chapter collaboratively to reflect personal experiences and narratives about hierarchies

 DOI: 10.4324/9781003410089-39

of disability, human security and COVID-19. Four of the contributing authors live with disability and depend on health, social-care and assistive technology services to live independently within different socio-political contexts. The impact of restrictions on navigating disability hierarchies and human security during the COVID-19 global pandemic has been portrayed within context-specific narratives, emphasising vulnerability, self-reliance and resilience to preserve personhood. The sense of self is re-imagined and reflected on, couched within health and social-care systems that mask human rights and social justice. For some, there is freedom, calmness, greater connectivity and collegiality, and for others, there is fluctuating feelings of entrapment, fear, disorientation, emotional distress and isolation.

Canadian professor of occupational science and occupational therapy, Karen Whalley Hammel (2020), observed of the COVID-19 pandemic, '[W]e are experiencing the deprivation of occupational opportunities usually reserved for disabled people and others marginalised and disempowered by poverty, racism and the legacies of colonialism; people for whom life is consistently unpredictable and fraught with uncertainty'.

In the next section, as a collective, we have explored Whalley Hammel's observation, drawing on human rights, capability and disability theories, global health and COVID-19 policy, bringing together experiences from around the globe.

Understanding historical disability hierarchies and human security issues through narratives in context

In the narratives from Ireland, Australia, South Africa and India presented in this section, consideration has been given to the heterogeneity of people's lives and the in-country status of disability. It has been well documented that people with disabilities experience greater socio-economic and health inequalities (Agmon et al., 2016; Kamalakannan et al., 2021), often combined with the degradation of dignity resulting from misconceptions, social norms, beliefs and attitudes (Barbareschi et al., 2021). While there is a recognised global legacy of eroding personhood from a disability perspective (Agmon et al., 2016), a newer understanding of, or connection in, human relationships is beginning to shift the dynamics of this phenomenon. Since the launch of the United Nations Convention of Rights for Persons with Disabilities (UNCRPD) in 2006, disability inclusion has been prioritised on government agendas globally. In addition, the sustainable development goals (SDGs) promote a universal perspective whereby no one should be left behind when working to enhance the health and well-being of all, across all nations (United Nations Social Development Network, 2016). While these protocols are influencing the global direction towards equal and inclusive societies, change is slow and variable, depending on the context, where beliefs and traditions are imbedded in the cultural and socio-political milieu (Wescott et al., 2021).

Recent studies about the health risks and consequences of COVID-19 for people with disabilities identify the multiple but modifiable environmental factors that present disproportionate health risks and consequences that are additional to those that were experienced before the pandemic, as well as the need for public health and policy measures to reduce the impact of such vulnerabilities (Chan et al., 2021; Kamalakannan et al., 2021; Mesa Vieira et al., 2020).

The restrictions imposed in response to COVID-19 highlight the fragility of human life. However, they have exacerbated the specific vulnerabilities within and among the disabled community. Restrictions perpetuate our feelings of dependence on others, and, for many people, they reduce the level of autonomy that they can exercise in their lives. Clifton (2020, p. 25) reminded us that 'to be dependent is to be stigmatised and rendered powerless, to be thought of as childlike, lazy, weak, and/or vulnerable'. Reactions to COVID-19 have perpetuated a sense of 'otherness' among many people who have been cocooning, jeopardising achieved equalities and exposing imbedded societal norms of discriminatory practices that are less visible during less threatening times (Clifton, 2020; Kamalakannan et al., 2021).

Clifton (2020, p. 7) used the term 'cultural humility', which involves a commitment to redressing imbalances in the dynamics of partnerships between professionals and peer and advocacy groups for disability that work with individuals to maximise their empowerment and autonomy in all areas of life. People with disability do depend on services and welfare, as does every citizen at some point in life. Therefore, Clifton reminds us that there is a need to move from perceiving disability as dependence to affirming our universal interdependence and reframing the idea of vulnerability. We would argue that a global pandemic has presented society with an opportunity to reframe our experiences of vulnerability as a human race.

Against this background of disruption, conflicting norms and policies and changing perspectives on human relations, we have explored personal experiences and narratives in the context of historical and modern-day Ireland, Australia, South Africa and India.

Eileen reflects on her personal experiences during the COVID-19 pandemic in Ireland, where many challenges of provision exist (Gowran et al., 2020; Nally et al., 2021), focusing on personal assistant schemes and wheelchair and seating assistive technology, which are lifelines for Eileen and advocacy and research interests for Rosie.

The Irish context

The Republic of Ireland is a high-income country with a democratic, cross-party government. The republic consists of 26 island counties, bordering by land with Northern Ireland that consists of 6 counties. Situated in Northern Europe, the changeable climate, while non-extreme, is said to have four seasons in one day with high rainfall. The Emerald Isle is known for its greenness and has mixed terrain, with rugged coastlines to the north and west, plateaux and plains in the midlands, and hills and vales on the east coast (Johnston, 2011).

The Republic of Ireland remained part of the United Kingdom (UK) until the state was founded in 1922. Development in Ireland, since joining the European Union in 1973, has made it more accessible by road. However, the train system serves mainline routes between the major urban areas and cities. Internet access is good in most urban areas but can be limited in some rural locations.

Since Ireland's foundation, its fluctuating economy, culture and political influences have had a serious knock-on effect on all welfare services, leading to a scramble to find and manage resources to build a society that is more equitable for all. Ireland has a two-tiered public and private health-and-social-care system, with inconsistencies in service provision across regions. Historically, the provision of services for people with disabilities was mainly left to the religious and charity sector to subsidise. Add-on solutions have been piecemeal, seeing the populist governments of the day reacting to public pressure by providing money to solve urgent problems rather than assessing the system to find more sustainable solutions (Burke, 2009; Kirby, 2008).

The population was approximately 5 million in the most recent census in 2022. One in seven, or just over 14% of the Irish population, is reported to have a disability (CSO, 2019). Evidence suggests that there was a fall in disability discrimination during the ten years from 2004 to 2014. However, layers of inequality continue to exist despite Ireland passing the first Disability Act in 2005. This act legalised the 'support of social inclusion' as part of the framework for government in relation to equality, employment and education. The first named Minister for Disability was appointed in 2016, but this role was later merged with the new Department of Children, Equality, Disability, Integration and Youth, with a Minister of State responsible for disability appointed in July 2020. In 2017, the UNCRPD was finally ratified, but without signing the optional protocol which allowed individuals or groups to take a case to the United Nations if they believed their rights had been violated.

People with disabilities in Ireland remain at risk and are three times more likely to experience discrimination in the public service (health, education and transport, for example), which has a serious effect on people's lives, limiting fulfilment and participation (Luborsky, 1994).

The impact of the COVID-19 pandemic

The outbreak of the COVID-19 pandemic resulted in the country being placed under lockdown in March 2020, leading to the closure of non-essential services that continued to a lesser or greater extent into 2021. In a submission to the Special Committee on the Response to COVID-19, the Independent Living Movement of Ireland (ILMI) reported on the challenges and opportunities arising from the restrictions. While opportunities to connect and communicate became more accessible, using virtual technology to overcome physical and geographic barriers, a medical narrative emerged in which people were viewed as being high risk, regardless of their impairment, and cocooning was imposed without including organisations for people with disabilities in policy discussions. ILMI noted that the public in general perceived people with disabilities as being a 'problem', 'burden' and 'afterthought', based on the inconsistent and unclear information being provided (ILMI, 2020). In addition, based on a study to review healthcare policies in Ireland and the initial response to the pandemic, O'Leary et al. (2021) found that guidance for people with disabilities who used residential and community services was limited, and evidence suggested that some community disability services were postponed because of COVID-19 and healthcare workers re-deployed of to achieve the highest vaccine uptake in Europe, prioritising older adults and the most vulnerable.

Eileen Davis and Rosie Gowran are friends living in Ireland, with and without a disability

Eileen Davis (BSocSc, HDip Ad and Comm Ed. MEd Career Guidance and Counseling, Dip Life and Career Coaching), originally from County Cork, was born with cerebral palsy. Eileen is wheelchair user, and she has lived in her own home in Dublin since 1994, with the support of personal assistant services. She began her studies in UCD and graduated with a bachelor of social science degree in 1997. She is a qualified guidance counsellor and life/career coach. Eileen has experience in various roles in disability, advocacy and education. She has worked in further and higher education as a disability officer and career guidance practitioner, supporting students at various stages of educational transition since 2002. Eileen is an active member of the independent living and disability rights movement and is a visiting lecturer on the occupational therapy programme at the University of Limerick.

Rosie Gowran (PhD, MSc OT, BSc (Hons) OT), originally from Dublin, moved to London in the late 80s and completed her professional qualification in occupational therapy at Brunel University in 1995 and returned to Dublin. Rosie formally course director of MSc Occupational Therapy (professional qualification) and has developed a post-graduate certificate in posture seating and wheelchair mobility across the life course at the University of Limerick, Ireland. Rosie is an implementation scientist, adopting a human security approach to supporting people with disabilities, particularly people who use wheelchairs, to address service system challenges and erosion of personhood. Building sustainable communities of practice in health and social care is the overarching theme that drives Rosie's research and education philosophy, to advocate for appropriate person-centred service provision as a responsibility of the whole community.

Eileen and Rosie met in 1998, when Rosie joined the Irish Wheelchair Association as a senior Occupational Therapist. Sharing an office and debating the challenges faced by association members, they soon realised that they were kindred spirits, with similar philosophies about inclusivity for all, despite their very different life experiences living with and without a disability. Both human rights and disability activists for over 20 years, passionate about equal access to inclusive services and empowerment for all, Rosie and Eileen have presented at conferences together and made an educational video on the wheelchair provision process, very much ahead of their time. After leaving the IWA in the early 2000s, they have continued to advocate for equality of opportunity for all.

Ricky narrates her experiences as a home-bound, bed-ridden person with a disability in Australia as follows.

Eileen: A personal narrative within the COVID-19 Irish context

To set the scene, I define key concepts.

The purpose of a personal assistance service is to support a disabled person to have choice and control over their lives and overcome the environmental, economic and cultural barriers which are not caused by a person's impairment (Nally et al., 2021).

I would not be able to live without my team of personal assistants (PAs). PAs assist me with personal care, household chores, cooking, driving my adapted vehicle and maintaining my exercise routine, and some of them assist me with my work and administrative tasks. My PAs enable me to live, to work and to socialise. They are my arms and legs, actually, and they are people I have chosen because of their personal characteristics and skills, which I feel will ensure that I have the choice and control I need to live my life.

Thankfully, I have been able to continue to work at home since March 2020.

I employ my own team of staff using individualised funding, which has enabled me to have maximum autonomy and control in terms of the staff who work for and with me and the rates of pay which they receive.

My home is a workplace. I have a duty to provide my staff with a safe working environment. In a literature review undertaken as part of a scoping review, Nally et al. (2021) highlighted that personal assistants were not seen as key workers by governments and health service administrators. This meant that they did not have access to PPE and regular testing, which is essential if PAs are going into different people's homes. ILMI (2020) also highlighted a number of challenges for PA services during the pandemic: for example, easily accessible personal protective equipment (PPE) for both the PA and the person with disability and the PA being able to drive for people with disabilities or accompany them to hospital.

Thankfully, I was able to liaise with the health service executive to obtain PPE, and also I had sufficient funding in my budget to purchase my own PPE. Staff also attended training which made it possible for me to designate specific responsibilities to staff whom I trust and who have the skills required in relation to COVID-19 compliance and monitoring.

A study by Fleming et al. (2021) about individualised funding supported my experiences. In the study, 'freedom' was the most widely cited benefit, identified by 23% of participants. They highlighted that individualised funding provided them with the freedom to choose who supports them, as well as how, when and where the support is provided. In the study, freedom was often inextricably linked to flexibility, which had previously been absent from traditional, often 'group-based' structures of support. Having control over life choices was perceived as a facilitative mechanism in itself.

Furthermore, I am fortunate to have navigated the systemic hierarchy of service provision in Ireland. I decided to be strategic in both my career choice and my activism in the disability rights and independent living movement. I was also lucky to meet many mentors and friends along the way. My decisions and life choices have also meant that I am more confident in my ability to ensure that my primary needs are met despite a global pandemic.

I rely on wheelchair and seating assistive technology, which is a primary need and a basic human right. Evidence suggests that accessing wheelchair services is ad hoc, with processes of provision that are difficult to navigate, which contributes to major health and well-being issues that affect essential freedoms (Gowran et al., 2021). Preliminary findings of a qualitative study engaging key stakeholders concerned with the well-being of wheelchair users indicated that inconsistencies and inequalities continue to exist in service provision. It was found that challenges existed when accessing wheelchair stock and parts for wheelchair repair because of delays caused by COVID-19. In addition, access to wheelchair appointments was limited as a result of the redeployment of front-line staff, resulting in the availability of emergency services only (Gowran et al., 2020).

I have a very good relationship with my primary healthcare team, including my Occupational Therapist, on whom I know I can rely when my wheelchair breaks down. It is essential that my wheelchair and seating meet my needs, and that this is reviewed regularly. Inadequate wheelchair seating and provision of postural management have a negative impact on the physical and emotional health of wheelchair users. Being restricted to bed because of a pressure sore, which takes months to heal, has a massively detrimental impact on me physically, emotionally and economically. Thankfully, I have a second powered chair and a second ROHO cushion, which means that I am never stranded. However, many of my peers are not so lucky.

It is worth noting that the nature and quality of the services provided by primary healthcare teams in Ireland are dependent on one's geographic location. It is a postcode lottery. There is no standardisation of services, which causes inequity and inequality. Freedom of movement is not an option. In addition, my peers and I have to wait months for parts for our chairs and other essential assistive technologies to be delivered, Brexit has made a critical situation worse.

The Australian context

Australia has much in common with high-income Western countries, but the island continent is also extraordinarily diverse. Southern areas are temperate, and northern areas are tropical while our central desert and parts of the north and west are extremely remote.

Australia is home to a population of 25.36 million, of whom 4.4 million live with a disability. Australia's small, multicultural population is distributed sparsely across the world's biggest island continent. Life in urban and remote communities is very different, for example, in terms of internet coverage and health services. As a high-income country, health, disability and ageing policies are intended to meet the needs of Australian residents but are delivered through a complexity of funding silos across three levels of government (Boisselle & Grajo, 2018).

Australia is a multicultural, secular, wealthy and young democracy yet, arguably, lags behind in the recognition of Australia's First Peoples in any constitutional sense, and, while we have ratified the UNCRPD and have a Disability Discrimination Act (1992), we have no legislated bill of rights, and many Australians who live with disability and the impacts of ageing feel 'shut out' of full participation in society. Over a decade of evidence of this exclusion has been documented in the 'Shut Out' Report of the National People with Disabilities and Carers Council (NPDCC, 2009), up to and including recent government enquiries such as a royal commission into violence, abuse, neglect and exploitation of people with disability (Commonwealth of Australia, 2020); a royal commission into aged care quality and safety (Victorian Government, 2019); and a recent overhaul of disability support to provide individualised funding through a national disability insurance scheme.

The impact of the COVID pandemic

Notwithstanding this backdrop of changing policy, pandemic preparedness and the public health response to COVID-19 have largely excluded people living with disabilities and older Australians. For example, as covid vaccines arrive, provision for people who are house-bound remains an afterthought in the government's roll-out documentation (Australian Government Department of Health, 2021).

Ricky Buchanan and Natasha Layton are research collaborators living in Australia, with and without a disability

Ricky Buchanan (BSc Cognitive Science) is a systemic advocate, assistive technology expert user and disability advocate. Ricky is passionate about disability and chronic illness; she thinks and writes regularly about assistive technology and how it fits into people's lives. Ricky has been disabled and usually home-bound/bed-ridden for her entire adult life. Ricky is connected to multiple user communities, including people whose disability is caused by chronic illness and those, similar to her, who are home-bound and/or bed-ridden – two groups of people who are severely underserved by the current medical and disability systems.

Natasha Layton is an occupational therapist and senior research fellow in the Rehabilitation, Ageing and Independent Living Research Centre at Monash University in Australia and a longstanding member of the AT community in Australia and internationally, fulfilling roles with Australia's peak body for AT and ARATA and with the Global Alliance of AT Organisations, GAATO.

Ricky responded to a call for research participants in a PhD study by Natasha. This was the start of a long and fruitful collaboration, starting with the ways in which assistive technology and environmental interventions deliver human rights and equal outcomes and moving beyond into the power of inclusive research and systemic advocacy.

Ricky and Natasha bring perspectives from these diverse communities together in shared authorship about user expertise, product design and inclusive research. Ricky (notdoneliving.net/) and Natasha are based in Melbourne, Victoria, Australia.

Jody has described the challenges concerning her disability, depression and anxiety resulting from the COVID-19 pandemic in South Africa in the following narrative.

Ricky: A personal narrative within the COVID-19 Australian context

COVID-19 responses in Australia did not include people who were 'invisible'. Ricky explains:

I am an expert AT user, and I live with chronic illness. I live in my bed, and I can administrate my daily life and manage my support workers using my information communication technology/computer access gear (mounted above my bed), a screen-pushing drumstick and several home automation devices.

I rely strongly on internet and virtual services (tele-health) to keep living my life, and COVID-19 meant that several things changed, both negatively and positively.

From a practical point of view, I requested my support workers to do extra cleaning and wash their hands. After that, they started wearing PPE, such as masks. After that, we made the shifts a bit longer as doing the surface cleaning was taking time. My support workers started wearing goggles as the government required, so I sourced and ordered masks that would fit my face from someone who would sew them in patterns I liked and post them to me. Everyone having to wear PPE has affected me emotionally. It makes me feel everything is unsafe all the time. I just want the support workers to go away now, and that would be five hours of engagement I used to enjoy. Some support workers became less available or unavailable. One was a nursing student, so he could not come to work as he was a risk, but some workers lost other work and became more available.

I have had to do more rearranging, which has been frustrating. My flatmate was exposed to COVID, so he had to go away to hotel quarantine to protect me for two weeks. But my flatmate also could not attend university, so he stayed home, and that made things better because he could get me drinks and help out more.

From a social point of view, I cannot risk people visiting me, and I miss being hugged. But because everyone is feeling socially isolated now (not just me), the burden is shared. More people have checked in on me. COVID makes us slow down and notice, and this makes things seem to be 'kinder'. I feel included in social activities that are now available to me online and are often free – for example, gallery exhibitions and concerts – and they can be viewed flexibly: e.g. when I am awake, instead of at set times when I am too tired. It has made people much more conscious about making an effort to catch up with each other.

In terms of being invisible: people with disabilities are not a high priority, whether this is for social connection, for obtaining PPE or for using innovations such as technology to access healthcare. If you are home-bound/bed-ridden, even though you live in the community, the system treats you as if you do not exist.

Australia's tele-health reforms were a rapid and unexpected consequence of COVID-19. Despite years of lobbying by the disability community (NPDCC, 2009), the imperative to provide healthcare whilst complying with public health requirements for social distancing meant that tele-health medical visits were suddenly widely available and reimbursable. We now sincerely hope that access to tele-health is retained in the long term in a manner which makes it accessible to home-bound/bed-ridden people, including those who are not ever able to access their health teams face to face. People who are bed-ridden/home-bound deserve access to healthcare at all times, not just during pandemics.

The South African context

South Africa, positioned on the southernmost tip of the African continent, has a land mass five times bigger than the UK. It is bounded by the cool Atlantic Ocean on the west and the warm Indian Ocean on the east. The climate varies from tropical on the central plateau to the north to being Mediterranean on the coastal plain in the south. South Africa has nine provinces, which vary considerably in size, with the smallest being Gauteng, which is a highly urbanised and crowded region, and the Northern Cape being the largest, with vast, arid and empty areas making up almost a third of South Africa's total land area.

The Republic of South Africa is a relatively young democracy, rich in cultural diversity and history and, according to the World Bank, considered an upper-middle-income country (The World Bank, 2019). Urban areas are relatively well developed in terms of mobile phone and internet coverage and the use of smart technology. However, many rural areas are underdeveloped and impoverished. The country's infrastructure, including power utilities and road and rail networks, have not been maintained and are failing.

Even before the global pandemic, the South African economy was in crisis, which was then further exacerbated, and the country was formally declared to be in a severe recession in 2020, with unemployment reaching a record high of 30% during this time (Stats SA, 2020). Economists predicted that this situation would worsen in 2021, with South Africa's economy unlikely to recover to pre-pandemic levels until 2023/2024. Thus, crime, poverty, corruption and inequality remain widespread.

The current population of South Africa (2021) is 60,041,994, with an average annual increase of 1.25% (Macrotrends LLC, 2021). The country has 11 official languages, and South African Sign Language (SASL) is soon to be adopted as the 12th official language.

The World Health Organisation (WHO) reported that approximately 15% of the world's population lives with some form of disability, with increasing prevalence because of the ageing population and increased spread of chronic diseases (WHO, 2011). In South Africa, the national rate of disability prevalence was reported to be approximately 17% in the 2011 census (Stats SA, 2014) and approximately 16% in the community survey conducted in 2016 (Stats SA, 2018), but civil society argues that the rate is likely to be much higher for various reasons such as underreporting, inaccurate data etc.

While South Africa is party to the UNCRPD (United Nations, 2006) and has a robust national constitution, including a bill of rights, the barriers being encountered are an infringement on basic human rights, especially in the light of Article 25, which states that:

> States Parties recognise that persons with disabilities have the right to the enjoyment of the highest attainable standard of health without discrimination on the basis of disability. States Parties shall take all appropriate measures to ensure access for persons with disabilities to health services that are gender-sensitive, including health-related rehabilitation.
>
> *(United Nations, 2006)*

It is an unfortunate reality that, although South Africa has a strong policy framework, there is an overall lack of policy implementation, especially when it comes to the protection of vulnerable populations.

The impact of the COVID pandemic

On the morning of 5 March 2020, the National Institute for Communicable Diseases confirmed the first suspected case of COVID-19, and, as a result, the country went into Lockdown Level 5 on 23 March 2020 and has been in various levels of lockdown ever since, having already experienced two waves of infection, with a third anticipated in mid-2021. By 27 May 2021, South

Africa was the worst affected country on the African continent, with more than 1.64 million infections (Statista, 2021).

For most South Africans, the COVID-19 pandemic has presented, and continues to present, many challenges. For people with hearing loss, these challenges are intensified to the point of disruption, given what they already have to negotiate in the typical course of daily life. Hearing loss impacts many aspects of life for individuals, such as communication, speech and language; cognition; education; employment; social isolation and loneliness; mental health and relationships, as well as identity and stigma (WHO, 2021).

The WHO has reported that not only are people with disability disproportionately affected during the COVID-19 pandemic, but their reliance on healthcare is also higher than that of individuals without disabilities (WHO, 2020). Individuals with disabilities are thus more vulnerable to any deficiencies in healthcare services, depending on the nature of their disability. Examples of barriers to accessing healthcare include affordability, limited availability of appropriate services, physical barriers and the inadequate skills and knowledge of health workers (Macrotrends LLC, 2021). Furthermore, with the mandating of universal mask wearing as a critical measure to decrease transmission of the virus through coughs and sneezes, the ability of a person with a hearing loss to communicate – e.g. through lip-reading, and interacting independently – has been further limited significantly. Non-transparent masks, besides impeding lip-reading, also act as a sound barrier and prevent one's ability to read nonverbal cues such as lip patterns and facial expressions (Grote & Izagaren, 2020). With the lack of availability of PPE, especially in developing countries such as South Africa, the use of clear masks by healthcare professionals remains a pipe dream. The focus of this narrative is on access to communication, particularly when accessing healthcare during the pandemic.

Jody Lee van Heerden and Diane Bell are daughter and mother, living with and without disability in South Africa

Jody Lee van Heerden has a profound bilateral hearing loss, uses two cochlear implants and advocates for people with disabilities in South Africa. Despite her challenges in life, she continued to persevere through her education and her personal life. She was married in November 2020 while starting her PhD studies in health sciences, researching a thesis titled 'Impact of COVID-19 on Anxiety and Depression in Persons with Cochlear Implants'.

Diane Bell (PhD), Jody's mother, is an educationalist with specialism in AT, currently serving as Director of Programmes (leading AT2030 programme) at the Global Disability Innovation Hub (GDI Hub – 'driving disability innovation for a fairer world for all') and is an honorary Associate Professor at the University College London and a Research Fellow at the University of Stellenbosch. Being mother to a daughter born with a profound hearing impairment, she is a strong advocate for the rights of people with hearing loss and serves on the Presidential Working Group on Disability in South Africa, the

World Hearing Forum and as board chair of the CDT Trust, a non-profit and public benefit organisation, which works to enable deaf children to hear and speak. Diane presents papers and publishes internationally, with her research foci at the intersection of education, assistive technology and deafness.

Deepak comments on the treatment of people with disabilities in India in the following narrative of his experiences during the COVID pandemic.

Jody: A personal narrative within the African context

The global pandemic has exposed multiple disparities for people with hearing loss in South Africa.

As a person with a hearing impairment, the impact has been significant on aspects of my life, such as speech and language, need for assistive hearing technology, relationships (social exclusion), stigma etc. My existing barriers to inclusion, especially communication and access to high-quality and appropriate healthcare, were compounded during the COVID-19 pandemic. The negative impact on my ability to communicate with others (owing to the use of non-transparent masks) and the need for social distancing and self-isolation had a domino effect. Not only did it affect my relationships with others, but it also impacted my mental health. I became frustrated, my social anxiety increased, and my depression deepened.

On the one hand, making an appointment to see a general practitioner became easier as businesses adopted technology with online booking systems, but the challenges experienced before and during a consultation were complex and challenging, such as communicating with the receptionist and the medical professional. Communicating to have my prescription filled by a pharmacist who not only wears a face mask and a face shield but also remains behind a vertical transparent partition, with me having to stand behind a designated strip on the floor (to ensure social distancing), was not only exhausting and frustrating but also seemed impossible! My independence (Sen, 1995) has been disrupted severely by having to rely on others to accompany and speak for me, not to mention the compromising of my dignity. There have also been instances when the public decided to take matters into their own hands to improve their own lives. For example, masks with disability logos show clearly what type of disability a person has and make sure that other people in public are aware that they have a disability, especially since hearing loss is a non-visible disability. The COVID-19 pandemic has revealed all the cracks that have existed in the healthcare system over the years. In my personal opinion and experience, now is the time to fix things and improve access to healthcare for those with disabilities. We need to provide access to appropriate, quality and affordable AT for all.

The Indian context

India is the second most populous country in the world. The sub-continent in South Asia is hot and humid with diverse weather conditions. It is a tropical, low- and middle-income country with approximately 1.4 billion people, and an estimated 2.21% of the population have a disability (Saikia et al., 2017). Hindi and English are the official languages, although there are many different languages and thousands of dialects spoken by the people. India is a country with astounding cultural diversities yet is united as a nation (Geary, 2013). It has a federal, constitutionally democratic government.

India has a three-tier healthcare system managed by the Ministry of Health in each state (Chokshi et al., 2016). The social welfare of the population, especially the vulnerable including the disabled, is managed by the Ministry of Social Justice and Empowerment in each state (Goswami et al., 2019). However, the health ministry of India does not include social care, which means that there is no organised, multi-disciplinary system in the entire country for those who require rehabilitation and social care outside the tertiary-care hospitals (Kumar et al., 2012). India ratified the UNCRPD as soon as it was tabled, and it has a ratified policy for people with a disability, called the Rights of Persons with Disability (RPWD) Act of 2016 (Math et al., 2019).

Although development, measured in terms of internet penetration and access, is fair to good in cities, it is fair to poor in rural regions, which cover 60% of the geography. Inclusive development, especially from the perspective of disability, is still a neglected social determinant (Rao et al., 2016).

The impact of the COVID pandemic

COVID-19 has demonstrated the disparate situation described here, having a massive impact on the general population, including the disabled, but with a non-inclusive response in most of the states in the country (Murthy et al., 2020).

The estimates of the prevalence of disability show only 28 million people (2% of the population) living with disability in India, as opposed to the global prevalence of 15% since 2011 (Saikia et al., 2017). Although this seems to be an underestimation, it was believed to be the first time that India had officially included specific questions related to disability in its census. One could understand the magnitude of disability before 2011 and its historical inclusion in the national health and social welfare programmes before Census 2011 was implemented in the country (Saikia et al., 2017). People with disabilities have been further excluded from the scope of the country's inclusive planning and non-discriminatory pandemic mitigation programmes in the context of the COVID-19 pandemic.

Systems of social care for the disabled remained focused on mobilising the charity-based strategies of the government, private and civil societies long before, and even after, the pandemic. For example, a person with a disability used to receive INR 1,500 per month as a disability allowance before the pandemic and now,= would receive an additional INR 1,000 as a COVID relief allowance for the entire period of the pandemic (Kumar et al., 2012; The New Indian Express, 2020). The amounts of 15 pounds per month and 10 pounds for COVID relief could themselves speak to the level of inclusion and the value provided for the lives of the estimated 28 million people with disabilities in India. In India, the hierarchies of assistance are still supportive of the charity model, according to which providing charity is considered to be the most effective strategy to support the disabled.

Given the global enthusiasm for the UNCRPD, new policies for the disabled have been developed in India. The Rights of Persons with Disability (RPD) Act of India was passed in 2016 and is currently being implemented in several states (Social Statistics Division India, 2016). The current pandemic has provided useful lessons about the disadvantages of non-inclusive, top-down development of policies, such as the RPD 2016, which does not have pragmatic plans for protecting the disabled during the pandemic in the country. For example, receiving a vaccination is a right of every citizen. However, people with disabilities have been fighting for their rights to be prioritised, safely vaccinated, and protected from COVID-19 (Human Rights Watch, 2020; Kamalakannan et al., 2021).

The relentless legal and socio-political battle for the rights of people with disabilities by disability organisations, such as December 3, has sowed the seeds for healthcare providers and policy makers to consider a medical as well as bio-psycho-social model, according to which disability is viewed as a medical as well as a social problem and could be supported by appropriate medical and social interventions. Although this is inevitable in the context of the pandemic, the country is still far from the contemporary conceptualisation of disability through the bio-psycho-social, social and human rights model that was adopted globally a few decades back (Talo & Rytökoski, 2016).

The orders and announcements related to vaccines in the immediate term and extension of leave for the disabled working in the government sector have all been patchy and non-inclusive strategies which have several implications. Political willingness, inclusive policies and prioritisation, as well as specific, implementable mitigation strategies for the disabled, are the needs of the hour to protect people with disabilities, not just from the pandemic but from the non-inclusive approach to addressing the needs of this vulnerable population in the second-most populous country in the world.

Deepak Nathan and Sureshkumar Kamalakannan are close friends and colleagues, living with and without disability in India

Deepak Nathan (BBA, MSW, MSc) is a disability activist and an academic researcher with expertise in business administration, social work, and mental health. He currently works as an assistant professor of social work at Loyola

College, University of Madras, Tamil Nadu, India. Deepak was affected by poliomyelitis during his childhood, and his experiences made him very passionate about advocating for disability rights as an activist, filmmaker and the founding president of December 3, a civil society organisation working for the rights and empowerment of people with disabilities in Tamil Nadu, India.

Sureshkumar Kamalakannan (BOT, MPH, PhD) is also an academic researcher with expertise in occupational therapy, public health, disability and epidemiology. He works as an associate professor for the Northumbria University and Public Health Foundation of India and contributes to evidence-based decision making and system strengthening for disability in India and similar contexts.

Deepak and Suresh grew up in Tamil Nadu, a southern state in India. Deepak strongly believes in social-political empowerment as a solution to global disability-inclusive development. As an activist, he stands against the violation of rights of people with disabilities in India at various levels, working especially at the grassroots level, whereas Suresh's approach is bridging the evidence gaps to empower the disabled and mainstreaming disability within the agenda for health in low- and middle-income countries.

Deepak and Suresh met each other a decade ago through a mutual friend who worked for a disabled people's organisation and wanted to integrate both their perspectives within their disability programmes. Although the approaches of Deepak and Suresh come from the opposite extremes of inclusive development, their outcomes and achievements have added significant strength to the state's capacity for rights-driven and evidence-based disability empowerment. Suresh is now an advisor for the December 3 organisation, the only society in India that includes 1% of the Tamil Nadu disabled population as its members, spearheaded by Deepak. With synergistic, rights-driven, evidence-based perspectives, both Suresh and Deepak have been instrumental in the development and implementation of various disability policies and programmes, including COVID-19 inclusive mitigation plans in Tamil Nadu, India.

Deepak: A personal narrative within the Indian context

The COVID-19 pandemic increased the vulnerability of people with disabilities in India.

As a person with disability, I consider myself to be a non-regarded person in the minds of the non-disabled majority of society. I feel that my vulnerability has been increased many-fold by the abrupt onset of the COVID-19 pandemic. My vulnerability became much more severe with the introduction of the lockdown restrictions. Given that the larger, mainstream, non-disabled society has experienced a major ordeal, a substantial proportion of the people with disabilities face extreme adversities as a result of the pandemic and lockdown restrictions.

Mainstream society is replacing and suppressing the needs of even the least dependent person experiencing disability. This situation has paved the way not only for economic deprivation because of the pandemic but also for domestic violence of varying permutations at the individual, family and social levels within all the layers of the larger society.

Even for activists and lobbyists with disabilities, the pandemic and the lockdown restrictions have made life very difficult with this approach (Senjam, 2021). The situation has caused them to slip into solutions that are geared towards a charity-based approach rather than an approach based on their ideology, which is rights-based self-empowerment. The latter is considered to be essential and is of immense value in sustaining the lives of those who are disabled, in both rural and urban regions of the country.

India so far has reported fewer deaths of disabled people attributable to economic difficulties, including homicides, in which the whole family killed the disabled first and the other family members later (Hindustan Times, n.d.).

The impact of this pandemic on those who are disabled and have high support needs has been devastating. I feel people with disabilities are no longer on the brink but have fallen victim to the amoral effects of crony-capitalism-induced ableism.

Reminiscent of the historical dynamics of cruelty imposed in a fragmented federal society such as India, community-based rehabilitation has become meaningless as the communities are not resourceful, and the known visions and action plans from international agencies such as the WHO and the UN have failed to bring respite for the severely disabled in India. This is also true in the case of vaccinations. COVID vaccinations remain a distant dream for a person with a disability in India, even during the second wave of the pandemic. In a country such as India, the rights of people with disabilities are disbursed as charity and not 'rights for right's sake' (Kuper & Heydt, 2019).

Discussion

Historically across nations, people with disabilities have experienced discrimination and disadvantage, affecting personal safety and personhood (Andrews et al., 2021; Verduzco-Gutierrez et al., 2021). However, the narratives presented here suggest a vulnerability that has implications for human security, basic human rights, essential freedoms, choice and control. The experiences described are the result of dictated socio-political responses to the pandemic and preparedness to meet the needs of people with disabilities (Banks et al., 2021). Exclusion from the decision-making process, critical to support requirements and policy implications within countries when considering the impact of COVID-19, is clearly evident.

Some disabled people are more susceptible to health risks than others, depending on their impairment and context. Safeguarding against the risk of contracting COVID-19 should be the same for all members of society, and adequate supports and adaptions should be established to deal with the consequences of infection. People with disabilities, with or without underlying conditions, should follow the appropriate guidelines. However, evidence from the narratives of individuals with wide-ranging impairments indicates additional vulnerabilities and disadvantages.

Eileen noted that, unlike many of her peers, she has maintained her choices and control to navigate the system of service provision that she needs during the pandemic because she has her own personalised funding to employ personal assistants. In addition, Eileen's strong relationship with her local health service provider has enabled her to access necessary supports as required. Access to parts and repair of her wheelchair has not been easy, but Eileen is well positioned to stay well and alleviate risk, as she has a second chair and pressure-relieving cushion as backups.

Ricky commented that, given her chronic illness, she had to reduce her social and physical interaction with friends. However, technology and the virtual world have eased the burden of travel, timelines and fatigue associated with leaving the house for medical appointments, making Ricky's interactions more accessible through tele-health and other online platforms.

Jody, although being less vulnerable because of underlying conditions, found that, as a person with a hearing impairment, there were both pros and cons when living during this pandemic. Being able to book medical appointments online made things easier, with fewer layers of communication to navigate. However, the wearing of masks and visors and social distancing added to feelings of isolation and poor mental health. These practices impacted Jody's ability to communicate easily when shopping, for example, reducing her independence and increasing her dependence and reliance on others.

While Eileen, Ricky and Jody acknowledged pros and cons to the COVID pandemic, Deepak expressed frightening vulnerabilities, given the societal hierarchies established to cope with surviving restrictions and contracting or recovering from COVID-19. Deepak observed that people with disabilities in India are at the bottom of the priority list, subject to violence and death. People's rights are not considered, and survival is reliant on charity.

It is notable that the narratives across countries all reflect the contextual dimensions which impact basic human security and rights issues. Location, income level, population level, socio-political belief systems and response to COVID-19 are implicitly reflected in the stories. Consideration needs to be given to the implications for public health and the human rights of people with disabilities in specific jurisdictions. Clear policies must be developed for pandemic preparedness to ensure that no one is left behind, and citizens are treated on an equal basis with representation in the decision-making process.

A clarion call

We call for action from governments and civil society to imbed the unexpected learnings from life during a global pandemic (Grote & Izagaren, 2020; WHO, 2020).

People need to sustain themselves and to flourish. However, they have been pushed to various degrees of vulnerability and exclusion during the pandemic. A key lesson from our shared experience of occupational disruption is that 'what good looks like' is as diverse as human beings and the contexts in which they reside are (Brown, 2021).

Viewing the jurisdiction in each country presented in this chapter, the spectrum of day-to-day living ranges from basic survival described by Deepak, as a disabled person in India, to maintaining the independence to live and work at home within the pandemic restrictions described by Eileen, as a disabled person in Ireland with a personalised budget. Most of the narratives portrayed adaptation to the pandemic situation by substituting virtual reality to enable work, therapy and gatherings to continue, albeit online. Many people, no longer bound by restrictions on proximity, are connecting on many virtual platforms to congregate and create ways of coping through other forms of inclusion and participation. However, there appears to be a lack of prioritisation within many of the socio-political decision-making hierarchies to include people with disabilities in the planning conversations or to consider people's primary needs, in contradiction of the WHO, which describes nine domains of human activity and participation (ICF, 2001) and the UNCRPD human rights convention (UN, 2006) which states have ratified.

We propose the following four critical areas for prioritisation to reduce systemic and societal hierarchies for people with disabilities at every level (Eyawo et al., 2021; Green et al., 2021; Kuper et al., 2020; Mintrom & O'Connor, 2020; Puli et al., 2021; Shakespeare et al., 2021).

Prioritise equitable health and social care policies, strategies and service provision systems

Every society is facing sacrifices and cutbacks in response to the pandemic fallout and, a holistic society approach is required to prioritise equitable management of health and social care systems without compromising one group for another. While the provision of health and social-care services has always been challenging, it has become evident that effective health and social-care services and systems are paramount during a pandemic (Lund et al., 2020; Leonardi et al., 2020). However, decision-making regarding the redeployment of health and social-care staff into roles of testing, tracing and vaccinating, combined with service closures, has led to major delays in primary disability services. In addition, restricted travel, factory closures and cardboard shortages have impacted access to disability services, assistive technology assessments and repair services (e.g. product parts, wheelchair brakes, seating), compromising mental and physical health and well-being. Some traditional bureaucratic health system structures which had been very difficult to navigate were overturned with ease to enable people to connect by means of tele-health. For example, in Australia, accommodations for financial rebates for tele-health, which the chronic illness and disability communities have needed for decades and were only available to remote dwellers, are suddenly in place because of whole-of-population need and government willingness to take action. Conversely, India's historic, ablest societal hierarchy has once again become visible, rising to the surface of system inequalities and the rawness of decision making about who should be protected first.

Each nation has its own roll-out plan for COVID-19 diagnostics and vaccines, with variations in priorities of populations to be given access to treatment and vaccinations. Accommodations should be made explicit in government documentation regarding the roll-out of vaccines for unique situations, for example, to ensure availability to people who are living in congregated settings or who are house-bound and unable to attend vaccination centres, rather than as an afterthought (COVID vaccine roll-out heath.gov.au) and should be available to the homeless and most vulnerable disabled people first. Supporting this requires the global community to take action as nations together to reduce marginalisation and to prioritise timely human security initiatives for all.

Prioritise inclusion and participation for all with appropriate support networks in place

Identifying and developing formal support networks and giving consideration to the strength of informal support to negate isolation, vulnerability and increased dependence is critical. Policies, programmes and efforts to mitigate the effects of the pandemic must also include, or at least consider, people with disabilities in every single activity. There is a need to create more formal support networks within health and social-care systems and to make them accessible, with assurance of primary and essential services: for example, personal assistance services, personal support workers, general practitioners, occupational therapy, physiotherapy, audiology, ophthalmology, medical emergency and domestic violence support services. There is a need to strengthen relationships and communication systems to enable positive experiences of inclusion. Unconditional positive regard and mutual respect, with a balanced representation among pandemic response teams, should be imbedded rather than assumed during the decision-making process (Ebuenyi et al., 2020). Working together so that all voices are heard as we emerge from this crisis is critical. It is not just people's presence but people's attitudes that can make or break experiences of inclusion and participation (Layton et al., 2021; Armitage & Nellums, 2020).

Prioritise digital and assistive technology accessibility

Easy accessibility, timely provision and backup supports for primary and digital assistive technology are critical (Jesus et al., 2020; Ohannessian et al., 2020; Smith et al., 2020; Smith et al., 2020). Any information related to COVID-19 and pandemic mitigation must be made accessible digitally for people with disabilities. It is also critical to consider appropriate provision of hearing aids, communication aids, wheelchair and seating, eye glasses and other primary assistive technologies. Developing innovative solutions to empower people with disabilities through access to assistive technology and digital interventions is essential. People also need the elements of digital inclusion, which include, for example, internet access, bandwidth, backup systems, hardware and software, together with user education and training, while engaging with teleconsultation or rehabilitation services remotely (Puli et al., 2021).

From a South African perspective, a key example is when the South African government was called upon to uphold the UNCRPD through the inclusion of disability as a key component in national health policies, programmes and the national response to COVID-19 in an effort to ensure full participation in all aspects of life for people with hearing loss: e.g. to be included socially, to be valued and to have their human rights respected.

Furthermore, it is incumbent on all healthcare professionals to consider the communication needs of people with hearing loss and to embrace the use of assistive technology and assistive products to facilitate communication. West et al. (2020) provided suggestions for ensuring optimal communication with people with hearing loss during COVID-19, such as the use of images to communicate (see Figure 33.1), QR codes to share information with patients, making personal sound amplifiers available to patients who need them and using technology to improve communications such as speech-to-text mobile apps (e.g. Google Live Transcribe, Otter etc.).

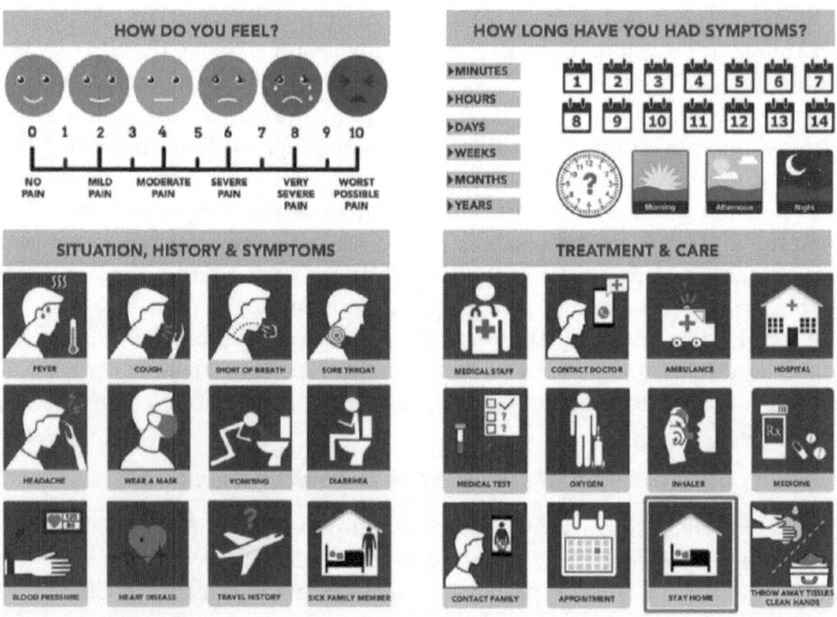

Figure 33.1 Massachusetts Commission for the Deaf and Hard of Hearing COVID-19 card

Prioritise access to safe living spaces and natural environments

Evidence suggests that people with disabilities living in residential, nursing home, institutional/congregated settings or cramped family living spaces are more vulnerable to contracting COVID-19, and reports suggest an increase in the death rate in these circumstances. Appropriate and accessible housing should be prioritised to ensure that indoor ventilation and household air circulation is planned for and made available. There is a need to evaluate and invest in communal housing of any kind and the number and consistency of staff working in such homes to create more sustainable and safe, supported-living environments.

There are many reports that the global pandemic has caused people to reconnect with nature, to have more time to focus on personal surroundings and spend less time commuting. It has been well established that climate, light, sound and the natural environment contribute to mental health and well-being. Whether in an urban or rural environment, giving attention to the micro climate, accessible indoor and outdoor space and how we view the world immediately around us are important and powerful parts of the health-sustaining process. For people restricted or confined to home quarters, access to outdoor spaces and natural views are important to help maintain good mental health. Health advice during the pandemic supports dining and socialising outdoors as a safe way to connect with family, friends and the wider community. Many restaurants and public venues have brought their services outdoors, pedestrianising streets and utilising pathways for street dining. This reopening of society, while welcomed by all, has created challenges for many people with disabilities when trying to access their local amenities and navigate pathways blocked with crowds and outdoor furniture. Consultation regarding accessible universal planning and design of the reopening of society is crucial to avoid further isolation and distress for people with disabilities.

Conclusion

The stories told in this chapter concur with Whalley Hammel's observations, reflecting the impact of the pandemic on occupational engagement, the unpredictability of living and the influence of contexts. The recommendations and calls for action made inform readers, activists, governments and civil society of ways to frame virtual reality and maintain social inclusion, valuing all people, leaving no one behind. Evaluating personal practice and attitudes, shaping the evidence and influencing actionable policy are key as we move forward into a post-COVID-19 life (Beresford et al., 2021; Whalley Hammel, 2020; Smith, Ahmad et al., 2021). As noted by the World Economic Forum:

> There is a business incentive to recognize the value of the market of those living with a disability, but there is an even stronger moral and societal imperative that this exclusion ends now. The majority have now

> experienced what mass social exclusion feels like, and we cannot "un-know" what we know about how it feels to be isolated. We now all know the global pain of exclusion – as we plan for our future, we must insist on no one being left behind.
>
> *(World Economic Forum, 2020)*

This really is doable if we are flexible and sensitive to human diversity. Let's be part of the change!

References

Agmon, M., Sa'Ar, A., & Araten-Bergman, T. (2016). The person in the disabled body: A perspective on culture and personhood from the margins. *International Journal for Equity in Health, 15*(1). https://doi.org/10.1186/s12939-016-0437-2

Andrews, E. E., Ayers, K. B., Brown, K. S., Dunn, D. S., & Pilarski, C. R. (2021). No body is expendable: Medical rationing and disability justice during the COVID-19 pandemic. *American Psychologist, 76*(3), 451–461. https://doi.org/10.1037/amp0000709

Armitage, R., & Nellums, L. B. (2020). The COVID-19 response must be disability inclusive. *The Lancet Public Health, 5*(5), e257. https://doi.org/10.1016/S2468-2667(20)30076-1

Australian Government Department of Health. (2021). *Information for People with Disability about COVID-19 Vaccines*. https://www.health.gov.au/initiatives-and-programs/covid-19-vaccines/information-for-service-providers-workers-and-people-with-disability-about-covid-19-vaccines/information-for-people-with-disability-about-covid-19-vaccines

Banks, L. M., Davey, C., Shakespeare, T., & Kuper, H. (2021). Disability-inclusive responses to COVID-19: Lessons learnt from research on social protection in low – and middle-income countries. *World Development, 137*, 105178. https://doi.org/https://doi.org/10.1016/j.worlddev.2020.105178

Barbareschi, G., Carew, M. T., Johnson, E. A., Kopi, N., & Holloway, C. (2021). "When they see a wheelchair, they've not even seen me" – Factors shaping the experience of disability stigma and discrimination in Kenya. *International Journal of Environmental Research and Public Health*. https://doi.org/10.3390/ijerph18084272

Beresford, P., Farr, M., Hickey, G., Kaur, M., Ocloo, J., Tembo, D., & Williams, O. (Eds.). (2021). *COVID-19 and Co-production in Health and Social Care Research, Policy, and Practice: Volume 1: The Challenges and Necessity of Co-production*. Bristol: Policy Press.

Boisselle, A. K., & Grajo, L. C. (2018). They said: A global perspective on access to assistive technology. *The Open Journal of Occupational Therapy*, *6*(3), 2. https://doi.org/10.15453/2168-6408.1541

Brown, T. (2021). The response to COVID-19: Occupational resilience and the resilience of daily occupations in action. *Australian Occupational Therapy Journal, 68*(2), 103–105. https://doi.org/10.1111/1440-1630.12721

Burke, S. (2009). *Irish Apartheid Health Care Inequalities in Ireland*. Dublin: New Island.

Central Statistics Office. (2019). Census 2016 summary results – Part 1. *Central Statistics Office (CSO)*. https://www.cso.ie/en/csolatestnews/presspages/2017/census2016summaryresults-part1/

Chan, E. Y. Y., Gobat, N., Dubois, C., Bedson, J., & de Almeida, J. R. (2021). Bottom-up citizen engagement for health emergency and disaster risk management: Directions since COVID-19. *The Lancet*, *398*(10296), 194–196.

Chokshi, M., Patil, B., Khanna, R., Neogi, S. B., Sharma, J., Paul, V. K., & Zodpey, S. (2016). Health systems in India. *The Journal of Perinatology, 36*(s3), S9–S12. https://doi.org/10.1038/jp.2016.184. PMID: 27924110; PMCID: PMC5144115.

Clifton, S. (2020). Hierarchies of power: Disability theories and models and their implications for violence against, and abuse, neglect, and exploitation of, people with disability. *Research Report Royal Commission into Violence, Abuse, Neglect and Exploitation of People with Disability*. https://apo.org.au/node/309065

Commonwealth of Australia. (2020). *Royal Commission into Violence Abuse Violence Abuse Neglect and Exploitation of People with Disability: Interim Report*. https://disability.royalcommission.gov.au/publications/interim-report

Ebuenyi, I. D., Smith, E. M., Holloway, C., Jensen, R., Arino, L., & MacLachlan, M. (2020). COVID-19 as social disability: The opportunity of social empathy for empowerment. *BMJ Global Health, 5*(8), e00339. https://doi.org/10.1136/bmjgh-2020-003039

Eyawo, O., Viens, A. M., & Ugoji, U. C. (2021). Lockdowns and low – and middle-income countries: Building a feasible, effective, and ethical COVID-19 response strategy. *Globalization and Health, 17*(1), 13. https://doi.org/10.1186/s12992-021-00662-y

Fleming, P., McGilloway, S., & Thomas, S. (2021). Individualised funding: A realist analysis to identify the causal factors that facilitate positive outcomes. *Disabilities, 1*, 47–57. https://doi.org/10.3390/disabilities1010004

Geary, D. (2013). Incredible India in a global age: The cultural politics of image branding in tourism. *Tourist Studies, 13*(1), 36–61. https://doi.org/10.1177/1468797612471105

Goswami, A. K., Ramadass. S., Kalaivani, M., Nongkynrih, B., Kant, S., & Gupta, S. K. (2019). Awareness and utilization of social welfare schemes by elderly persons residing in an urban resettlement colony of Delhi. *Journal of Family Medicine and Primary Care, 8*(3), 960–965. https://doi.org/10.4103/jfmpc.jfmpc_28_19. PMID: 31041233; PMCID: PMC6482716

Gowran, R. J., Bray, N., Goldberg, M., Rushton, P., Saab, M. B. A., Constantine, D., Ghosh, R., & Pearlman, J. (2021). Understanding the global challenges to accessing appropriate wheelchairs: Position paper. *International Journal of Environmental Research and Public Health, 18*(7). https://doi.org/10.3390/ijerph18073338

Gowran, R. J., Clifford, A., Gallagher, A., McKee, J., O'Regan, B., & McKay, E. A. (2020). Wheelchair and seating assistive technology provision: A gateway to freedom. *Disability and Rehabilitation*. https://doi.org/10.1080/09638288.2020.1768303

Green, C., Carey, G., & Dickinson, H. (2021). *Barriers and Enablers in the Development of a COVID-19 Policy Response for People with Disability in Australia*. https://credh.org.au/

Grote, H., & Izagaren, F. (2020). Covid-19: The communication needs of D/deaf healthcare workers and patients are being forgotten. *The BMJ, 369*. https://doi.org/10.1136/bmj.m2372

Hindustan Times. (n.d.). https://www.hindustantimes.com/delhi-news/couple-kill-disabled-son-commit-suicide/story-WS9IeGtngkvm295x9Zm47O.html

Human Rights Watch. (2020). *India: COVID-19 Lockdown Puts Poor at Risk*. https://www.hrw.org/news/2020/03/27/india-covid-19-lockdown-puts-poor-risk

Independent Living Movement Ireland. (2020). *The Impact of Covid-19 on Disabled People's Lives: Challenges faced, Opportunities Created*. ILMI submission to the Special Committee on Covid-19 Response.

International Classification of Functioning. (2001). *International Classification of Functioning (ICF): Disability and Health*. https://www.who.int/classifications/international-classification-of-functioning-disability-and-health

Jesus, T. S., Landry, M. D., & Jacobs, K. (2020). A 'new normal' following COVID-19 and the economic crisis: Using systems thinking to identify challenges and opportunities in disability, telework, and rehabilitation. *Work*, *67*(1), 37–46. https://doi.org/10.3233/wor-203250

Johnston, W. (2011). *Ireland*. http://www.wesleyjohnston.com/users/ireland/

Kamalakannan, S., Bhattacharjya, S., Bogdanova, Y., Papadimitriou, C., Arango-Lasprilla, J. C., Bentley, J., & Jesus, T. S. (2021). Health risks and consequences of a covid-19 infection for people with disabilities: Scoping review and descriptive thematic analysis. *International Journal of Environmental Research and Public Health*, *18*(8). https://doi.org/10.3390/ijerph18084348

Kirby, P. (2008). Poverty reduction and policy regimes country overview paper: Explaining Ireland's development. *Social Policy and Development Programme Paper No.37. United Nations Research Institute*. https://www.unrisd.org/unrisd/website/projects.nsf/0d098d9016856d2080256eb300388f39/c675d16c854b854cc1257439005013fc/$FILE/Kirby-paper.pdf

Kumar, S. G., Roy, G., & Kar, S. (2012). Disability and rehabilitation services in India: Issues and challenges. *Journal of Family Medicine and Primary Care*, *1*(1), 69. https://doi.org/10.4103/2249-4863.94458

Kuper, H., Banks, L., Bright, T., Davey, C., & Shakespeare, T. (2020). Disability-inclusive COVID-19 response: What it is, why it is important and what we can learn from the United Kingdom's response. *Wellcome Open Research*, *5*(79). doi:10.12688/wellcomeopenres.15833.1

Kuper, H., & Heydt, P. (2019). *The Missing Billion: Access to Health Services for 1 Billion People with Disabilities*. London: LSHTM.

Layton, N., Mont, D., Puli, L., Calvo, I., Shae, K., Tebbutt, E., et al. (2021). Access to assistive technology during the COVID-19 global pandemic: Voices of users and families. *International Journal of Environmental Research and Public Health*, *18*(21), 11273.

Leonardi, M., Lee, H., van der Veen, S., Maribo, T., Cuenot, M., Simon, L., & de Camargo, O. K. (2020). Avoiding the banality of evil in times of COVID-19: Thinking differently with a biopsychosocial perspective for future health and social policies development. *SN Comprehensive Clinical Medicine*. https://doi.org/10.1007/s42399-020-00486-8

Luborsky, M. R. (1994). The cultural adversity of physical disability: Erosion of full adult personhood. *Journal of Aging Studies*, *8*(3), 239–253. https://doi.org/10.1016/0890-4065(94)90002-7

Lund, E. M., Forber-Pratt, A. J., Wilson, C., & Mona, L. R. (2020). The COVID-19 pandemic, stress, and trauma in the disability community: A call to action. *Rehabilitation Psychology*, *65*(4), 313–322. https://doi.org/10.1037/rep0000368

Macrotrends LLC. (2021). *South Africa Population Growth Rate 1950–2021 | MacroTrends*. https://www.macrotrends.net/countries/ZAF/south-africa/population-growth-rate

Math, S. B., Gowda, G. S., Basavaraju, V., Manjunatha, N., Kumar, C. N., Philip, S., & Gowda, M. (2019). The rights of persons with disability act, 2016: Challenges and opportunities. *Indian Journal of Psychiatry*, *61*(Suppl. 4), S809–S815. https://doi.org/10.4103/psychiatry.IndianJPsychiatry_105_19. PMID: 31040479; PMCID: PMC6482682

Mesa Vieira, C., Franco, O. H., Gómez Restrepo, C., & Abel, T. (2020). COVID-19: The forgotten priorities of the pandemic. *Maturitas*, *136*, 38–41.

Mintrom, M., & O'Connor, R. (2020). The importance of policy narrative: Effective government responses to Covid-19. *Policy Design and Practice*, *3*(3), 205–227. https://doi.org/10.1080/25741292.2020.1813358

Murthy, G. V. S., Kamalakannan, S., Lewis, M. G., Sadanand, S., & Tetali, S. (2020). *A Strategic Analysis of Impact of COVID-19 on Persons with Disabilities in India*. Hyderabad: Funded by CBM India Trust, and Humanity & Inclusion (HI).

Nally, D., Moore, S. S., & Gowran, R. J. (2021). How governments manage personal assistance schemes in response to the United Nations convention on the rights of persons with disabilities: A scoping review. *Disability and Society*. https://doi.org/10.1080/09687599.2021.1877114
National People with Disabilities and Carers Council. (2009). *Shut Out: The Experience of People with Disabilities and their Families in Australia – National Disability Strategy Consultation Report*. Canberra: Commonwealth Government.
O'leary, N., Kingston, L., Griffin, A., Morrissey, A., Noonan, M., Kelly, D., Doody, O., Niranjan, V., Gallagher, A., O'riordan, C., & Lynch, A. (2021). COVID-19 healthcare policies in Ireland: A rapid review of the initial pandemic response. *Scandinavian Journal of Public Health*, 140349482110083. https://doi.org/10.1177/14034948211008371
Ohannessian, R., Duong, T. A., & Odone, A. (2020). Global telemedicine implementation and integration within health systems to fight the COVID-19 Pandemic: A call to action. *JMIR Public Health Surveill*, *6*(2), e18810. https://doi.org/10.2196/18810
Puli, L., Layton, N., Mont, D., Shae, K., Hill, K., & Callaway, L. (2021). Assistive technology provider experiences during the COVID-19 pandemic. *International Journal of Environmental Research and Public Health*, *18*(10477). https://doi.org/10.3390/ijerph181910477
Rao, G. P., Ramya, V. S., & Bada, M. S. (2016). The rights of persons with disability bill, 2014: How "enabling" is it for persons with mental illness? *Indian Journal of Psychiatry*, *58*(2), 121–128. https://doi.org/10.4103/0019-5545.183795. PMID: 27385843; PMCID: PMC4919954
Saikia, N., Bora, J. K., Jasilionis, D., & Shkolnikov, V. M. (2017). Correction: Disability divides in India: Evidence from the 2011 Census (PloS one (2016) 11 8 (e0159809)). *PloS One*, *12*(2), e0172596. https://doi.org/10.1371/journal.pone.0172596
Sen, A. (1995). *Inequality Reexamined*. Oxford University Press. https://doi.org/10.1093/0198289286.001.0001
Senjam, S. S. (2021). A persons-centered approach for prevention of COVID-19 Disease and Its impacts in persons with disabilities. *Front Public Health*, *8*, 608958. https://doi.org/10.3389/fpubh.2020.608958. PMID: 33614567; PMCID: PMC7892617.
Shakespeare, T., Watson, N., Brunner, R., Cullingworth, J., Hameed, S., Scherer, N., & Reichenberger, V. (2021). Disabled people in Britain and the impact of the COVID-19 Pandemic. *Social Policy & Administration*, 1–15. https://doi.org/10.1111/spol.12758
Smith, E., MacLachlan, M., Ebuenyi, I., Holloway, C., & Austin, V. (2020). Developing inclusive and resilient systems: COVID-19 and assistive technology. *Disability & Society*, 1–4. https://doi.org/10.1080/09687599.2020.1829558
Smith, E., Toro Hernandez, M. L., Ebuenyi, I., Syurina, E., Barbareschi, G., Best, K., &. MacLachlan, M. (2020). Assistive technology use and provision during COVID-19: Results from a Rapid Global Survey. *International Journal of Health Policy and Management*, X(X), 1–10. https://www.ijhpm.com/article_3954_ec965671ae00a3f198168e08a53dbf21.pdf
Smith, M., Ahmad, A., Arawi, T., Dawson, A., Emanuel, E., Garani-Papadatos, T., & Voo, T. (2021). Top five ethical lessons of COVID-19 that the world must learn. *Wellcome Open Research*, *6*(17). https://doi.org/10.12688/wellcomeopenres.16568.1
Social Statstics Division India. (2016). *Disabled Persons in India, A Statistical Profile 2016*. http://mospi.nic.in/sites/default/files/publication_reports/Disabled_persons_in_India_2016. pdf
Statista. (2021). *Coronavirus Cases by Country in Africa 2021*. https://www.statista.com/statistics/1170463/coronavirus-cases-in-africa/
Stats SA. (2014). *Stats SA Profiles Persons with Disabilities | Statistics South Africa*. http://www.statssa.gov.za/?p=3180
Stats SA. (2018). *Community Survey 2016. Profiling Socio Economic Status and Living Arrangement of Persons with Disabilities in South Africa*. www.statssa.gov.za

Stats SA. (2020). Steep slump in GDP as COVID-19 takes its toll on the economy. *Statistics South Africa*. 20. http://www.statssa.gov.za/?p=13601

Talo, S. A., & Rytökoski, U. M. (2016). BPS-ICF model, A tool to measure biopsychosocial functioning and disability within ICF concepts: Theory and practice updated. *International Journal of Rehabilitation Research*, *39*(1), 1–10. https://doi.org/10.1097/MRR.0000000000000151

The New Indian Express. (2020). *Rs 1,000 in COVID-19 Relief for 13.35 Lakh People with Disabilities, says Tamil Nadu CM*. https://www.newindianexpress.com/states/tamil-nadu/2020/jun/16/rs-1000-in-covid-19-relief-for-1335-lakh-people-with-disabilities-says-tamil-nadu-cm-2157354.html

The World Bank. (2019). World bank country and lending groups – World bank data help desk. *The World Bank*. https://datahelpdesk.worldbank.org/knowledgebase/articles/906519-world-bank-country-and-lending-groups

United Nations. (2006). *Article 25 – Health | United Nations Enable*. https://www.un.org/development/desa/disabilities/convention-on-the-rights-of-persons-with-disabilities/article-25-health.html

United Nations Social Development Network. (2016). 10 years of CRPD and COSP. *United Nations Social Development Network*. http://unsdn.org/2016/06/13/10-years-of-crpd-and-cosp9/

Verduzco–Gutierrez, M., Lara, A. M., & Annaswamy, T. M. (2021). When disparities and disabilities collide: Inequities during the COVID-19 Pandemic. *PM & R*. https://doi.org/10.1002/pmrj.12551

Victorian Government. (2019). *Royal Commission into Aged Care Quality and Safety*. https://agedcare.royalcommission.gov.au/

Wescott, H. N., MacLachlan, M., & Mannan, H. (2021). Disability inclusion and global development: A preliminary analysis of the United Nations partnership on the rights of persons with disabilities programme within the context of the convention on the rights of persons with disabilities and the sustainable development goals. *Disability, CBR & Inclusive Development, 31*(4), 90–115.

West, J. S., Franck, K. H., & Welling, D. B. (2020). Providing health care to patients with hearing loss during COVID-19 and physical distancing. *Laryngoscope Investigative Otolaryngology*, *5*(3), 396–398. https://doi.org/10.1002/lio2.382

Whalley Hammel, K. (2020). *Engagement in Living during the COVID-19 Pandemic and Ensuing Occupational Disruption* (Canada). https://www.caot.ca/document/7179/Ensuring%20Occupational%20Disruption.pdf

World Economic Forum. (2020). https://www.weforum.org/agenda/2020/04/covid-190-isolation-disabilities/

World Health Organisation. (2011). World report on disability. *The Lancet*, *377*(9782), 1977. https://doi.org/10.1016/S0140-6736(11)60844-1

World Health Organisation. (2020). *Disability and Health*. https://www.who.int/en/news-room/fact-sheets/detail/disability-and-health

World Health Organization. (2021). World report on hearing. *World Health Organization*. https://www.who.int/publications/i/item/world-report-on-hearing

34

AN INVITATION TO CONTEMPLATE

Dialogues about disability hierarchies between South Africa and Scotland

Njabulo Hlongwane, Judith Drake and Jean Cathro

Lokhu kwakuyinto ayekade eyilangazelele, ukuqhudelana ezinkundleni ezivulelekile zezemidlalo. Kanjalo futhi, wabe esehambe ibanga elide ukuze afinyelele kulesikole esizimele sabantwana abaphila nokukhubazeka saseThekwini. Wenza lokhu ukuze akwazi ukufeza iphupho lakhe. Ekhaya wayehlala njalo ngasekugcineni kwenkundla yezemidlalo ngolwezibili ntambama lapho ayebukela khona ontanga bakhe beqhudelana. Ubuthaka kwezempilo, ukuncipha kwezinga lezokuphepha kanye nemicikilisho yokugcwalisa amafomu esikhwama sezingozi zemigwaqo kwakuvala ngisho amathuba kanye nezinhloso ezinhle zothisha kanye nezesikole. Uthisha wakhe wabe emgqugquzela ukuba aziveze ngalokho ayekufisa empilweni yakhe. Ekugcineni walithola ithuba lokuba aphonse umcibisholo ukuze azizwe ekhululekile futhi eyingxenye yethimba lezemidlalo.

(See page xx for translation)

Are you ready to begin?

Hierarchies function through oppression, and the first step to removing that oppression is through recognising when we are the oppressed or the oppressor and then, with that knowledge, being willing to understand why they exist and to act for change if needs be. In simple terms, hierarchies are value judgements. We make these every day. Sometimes we are unaware that we are playing into a hierarchy, but they are inescapable. Our aim in creating this chapter is to explore disability hierarchies from a different perspective in a way that is accessible to academics and non-academics alike and that highlights hierarchies in form and content. We will do this by reflecting on our own research into and experiences of hierarchies in Scotland and South Africa (SA) during

DOI: 10.4324/9781003410089-40

Figure 34.1 *Isikhathi sokunqoba*
Source: Hlongwane 2020

volunteering trips enabled by Crossing Countries (CC), a social enterprise, and through the creation of this chapter. You may or may not recognise theories and concepts from academia, you may have similar or different lived experiences, and you may agree or disagree with the hierarchies we've looked at or the scenarios we've written. This is the point, after all: change comes through curiosity and knowledge. One final comment – the headings are there so you can read (or not read) sections of the chapter in any order you wish.

What questions did we begin with?

Where in the pecking order of values are your family stories as opposed to a novel as opposed to a painting as opposed to an academic text? Where in the hierarchy of knowledge is your scholarly learning opposed to what you have learned through your embodied lived experience? Does it matter how we learn, or is the reflection about that learning and the actions we take more important? What has more value: the process of learning or the output? What can we learn from other cultures about hierarchies of disability? And what about the values we place on humans with minority bodies or those that are 'other' than us? These questions and many others are the foundations of this chapter and the catalyst for further questions and, hopefully, conversations and actions about hierarchies.

What has Crossing Countries got to do with this?

CC is a Scottish asset-locked company founded by Jean Cathro that provides opportunities for disabled and non-disabled people to volunteer in Durban, SA. Judith Drake was on its successful pilot trip in 2014, and it was incorporated a year later. Since then, we have identified that one of our most important experiences was a disruption of our embedded sense of hierarchy. For the CC team members, once outside our cultural comfort zones, our hierarchical relationships changed, and we fostered empathetic, horizontal and equitable relationships, each team member using their particular skills to support the others. This equality and equity within the team is now a central principle of CC ethos, but this was not our only experience of shifting hierarchies. The disabled members of the team found that their whiteness meant that Black people of a 'higher' rank would listen to them, unlike back in the UK. Jean was also aware that her age demanded respect from people younger than she was. During the next five volunteering trips to Durban, many more instances of hierarchies in action were experienced. It was during our volunteering at Mason Lincoln Special School in Umlazi, the second largest township in SA, that we met Njabulo Hlongwane. The school caters for approximately 300 learners from 7 years to 24 years old, with various disabilities (physical, sensory, intellectual and neurodiverse), some of whom stay in the converted wards on the ex-hospital site.

What do these scenarios say to you about hierarchies?

If you were asked to creatively respond to these scenarios, how would you highlight the hierarchies you see at play here?

Scenario one

As she looked up from her powerchair into the face of grey-haired Professor Sbo Mkhize of the university's engineering department, the voice in her head said, 'I'm 25, and he is listening to me. He values my experience and knowledge. Wow, that's a new feeling, not one I get at home'. She didn't know if it was the sunburn that was turning her cheeks pink or an unexpected flush of acceptance. So different from her meeting the day before in the same university, when she had sat with her mouth open as a lecturer had said, 'So, you don't think it is the sins of the father that are passed on to the son? So, if it isn't, why are people disabled?' She couldn't believe what she was hearing. From her own experience at home, being a 'benefit scrounger', she knew she sometimes wasn't valued but this! And what's more . . . apparently 'Dyslexia and learning disabilities are only found in Western societies'. Was he winding her up?

Scenario two

He'd come all this way to volunteer and still he had to explain he had difficulty reading and that he was 'born sad'. So, for three days, he sat in the corner, in the heat of the corrugated iron– roofed art room, painting the African symbols the art teacher told him to onto wooden panels to remind the learners of their heritage. Headphones firmly attached to his ears spewing out comfort. No one said anything; they just let him be. He watched as Xolani walked into the art classroom, excited to tell the other visually impaired learners about his first show on the local radio station. He didn't use a white cane or get help from the other learners; he knew his way around the school grounds through sounds and didn't want to be thought of as totally blind from an illness he'd had as a teenager. Why couldn't he be like Xolani? What employer would want him when some days, he just wanted to get on with his work and not speak to anyone? It was only later that he found out that Xolani was respected even by the other learners because, despite being blind, his mum and dad had taught him the ways of *ubuntu*. He wondered what they thought of him.

What are disability hierarchies about?

People in dominant hierarchies do not want to lose the power they hold in society. For example, people from oppressed communities are told that a specific part of their identity is irrelevant, and all that matters is that they are viewed as people. To ignore this aspect of their identity is to ignore how hierarchies function to make people inferior. Have you heard or said 'I don't think of you as a disabled person', 'I don't see colour', 'You don't act like a woman', 'You don't look like a lesbian'? On the face of it, these statements appear to oppose prejudice, but what they actually do is devalue a particular part of a person's identity.

But what about hierarchies if you are in one of the oppressed groups? Being part of an oppressed group does not mean that group members do not uphold oppressive hierarchical structures within that group. The term 'disabled' has been used to group all disabled people with different impairments and lived experience under one umbrella. There are hierarchies within disability movements and healthcare and government benefits agencies that informally uphold the stigmatisation and the status of people with one impairment over another.

Oppressed groups who are discriminated against can also discriminate against others. This type of discrimination might be to bolster self-worth in that they may have one oppressed characteristic but at least they are not like X person and, therefore, further up the social hierarchy. For example, a white woman might be oppressed because of her gender, but she believes, consciously or unconsciously, that she is superior as she is not a Black woman or a disabled woman. Prejudice requires power for complete oppression to take place. Prejudice alone is unpleasant, but with power, it becomes a way to discriminate against groups of people. Layla Saad demonstrates how white supremacy is different from BIPOC prejudice against other races:

> All people, regardless of race, can hold some level of prejudice toward people who are not the same race as them. A person of any race can prejudge a person of any other race based on negative racial stereotypes and other factors. Prejudice is wrong, but it is not the same as racism. Racism is the coupling of prejudice with power, where the dominant racial group (which in a white supremacist society is people with white privilege) is able to dominate over all other racial groups and negatively affect those racial groups at all levels – personally, systemically, and institutionally.
>
> *(Saad, 2020, p. 107)*

It is possible to have multiple identities that are differently oppressed, such as disability, race and gender; how they intersect affects power structures and the way people are treated in society. The term and concept of 'intersectionality' was coined by Kimberlé Crenshaw while she was exploring how race intersects with gender and how it is difficult to know on what front someone might be being oppressed. Her excellent analogy to a traffic accident at an intersection explains that:

> Discrimination, like traffic through an intersection, may flow in one direction, and it may flow in another. If an accident happens in an intersection, it can be caused by cars traveling from any number of directions and, sometimes, from all of them. Similarly, if a Black woman is harmed because she is in the intersection, her injury could result from sex discrimination or race discrimination.
>
> *(Crenshaw, 1989, p. 149)*

Intersectionality means that a person who is Black, a wheelchair user, female, middle aged, from a minority religious background, lesbian and lives in the Global South is going to be treated with different prejudice and discrimination than a non-disabled, atheist, heterosexual, young, white man in the Global North. Different parts of people's identities create a different lived experience, and these experiences are usually contextual. In which countries would a white, female, blind university graduate face more discrimination than in her home country?

What made disability what it is in the UK and SA?

In writing this section, we wanted to privilege the history and roots of disability activism/hierarchies in SA as they are still underrepresented in disability studies.

How do we understand disability in the UK?

In the UK, the disability rights movement has sought to change how disability is viewed and understood. This activism has changed laws and moved the understanding of disability from a medical model that situates the disabling factor in the impairment, which is located in the individual body, to the social model, which views society as disabling people through its lack of access. The disability rights movement, as it has matured, has also sought to be more inclusive of disabled peoples' intersectionality, trying to include other aspects of their identity. The Disability Discrimination Act (DDA) became law in 1995 and gives disabled people the legal right to access and prevent discrimination. The Equality Act (2010) (which gives similar rights to other protected characteristics) incorporated the DDA and requires the law to give further protection to disabled people and places obligations on institutions and organisations to be proactive in their accommodations and prevention of discrimination of disabled people. While there have been successes in the UK in the way disabled people are treated and what services they can access, these rights are still not ingrained within the cultural and societal setting.

How do we understand disability in SA and internationally?

Disability rights in SA have come about and are still fought for in different ways than the UK/European/North American model. (For further information, see Howell et al., 2006; Black & de Matos-Ala, 2016; Jagoe, n.d.).

The difficulties faced by disabled people in SA are fundamentally shaped by the apartheid system, which meant that disability rights activists had to fight not only to end disability discrimination and oppression but also to end apartheid, as one would not be possible without the other. There was next to no support system for Black disabled people, and it was seen as the problem of the individual and their immediate family, which caused even more poverty and deprivation than they were already experiencing. For all disabled people, but especially Black people, apartheid meant there was a lack of medical support, housing, welfare, employment opportunities and education.

There began to be a significant change to disability rights in the early 80s on a global scale that affected how activists worked in SA. There had been local disability activism in the 70s both in townships and cities, but it was not a coherent movement. After the Rehabilitation International Conference (Winnipeg, Canada, 1980), where some disabled members left after the conference refused to allow 50% of the board membership to be disabled people, Disabled People International was created. The UN's International Year of Disabled Persons (1981), which the SA government refused to recognise (Jagoe, n.d., n.p.), and their Decade of Disabled Persons (1982) changed, on a global scale, how disability was understood and how disabled people were treated.

These events saw the creation of Disabled People South Africa (DPSA) in 1984. This was the first nationwide disability activist group fighting for disability rights at a local and a national level. They took a different approach to disability activism than the Global North:

> Where the societies of Europe and America tended to organise themselves according to disability type, DPSA felt that this division of disabled people actually weakened the effectiveness of the movement in South Africa. Division according to disability type focuses on the nature of the person's impairment and has the potential to create competition among disabled people for resources.
>
> *(Howell et al., 2006, p. 53)*

The disability rights movement's focus on a social model rather than a medical model was centred on political emancipation, self-representation and economic empowerment and was influenced by Steve Biko (the renowned anti-apartheid activist) and the Black consciousness movement of the 1970s (Black & de Matos-Ala, 2016, p. 342).

The disability rights movement in SA grew out of the anti-apartheid struggle. The DPSA was political from the outset, with many involved finding 'their experiences were shaped by being disabled and being black in South Africa' (Howell et al., 2006, p. 54). This led to strong links with anti-apartheid and democracy movements. This didn't mean there were not tensions; at the national DPSA conventions, it was for some people the first time they had ever sat next to someone of a different race (Jagoe, n.d., n.p.). Only by changing society completely for everyone would disabled people be able to change how they were viewed and valued by society. In 1992 the DPSA, along with the NGO Lawyers for Human Rights, successfully developed the Disability Rights Charter of South Africa. The non-legislative charter was to reframe disability in SA as a human right and viewed disabled people as citizens having the right to participate and be supported in civil society, no matter what their impairment.

The South African Constitution of 1996 gave legal protection against discrimination and introduced policies to address the prior oppression of disabled people. What followed were extensive laws and policies to improve the lives of disabled people, as well as the ratifying of international conventions, including:

- Integrated National Disability Strategy (1997)
- Education White Paper 6 Special Needs Education: Building an Inclusive Education and Training System (2001)
- United Nation's Convention on the Rights of Persons with Disabilities (UNCRPD) (2007) (SA was one of the first countries in the world to ratify; the UK ratified in 2009.)
- Protocol to the African Charter on Human and Peoples' Rights on the Rights of Persons with Disabilities in Africa (2018)

While these laws and policies for the support of disabled people in SA have been groundbreaking under a human rights agenda, this has not translated into practice. According to Black and de Matos-Ala, this has been due to a change in the government's approach to disability, away from a civil rights viewpoint towards a welfare perspective with diminished support for disabled people and, under President Zuma, compounded by a lack of income along with issues of corruption and misallocation of funds (2016, p. 345).

> The aspirational view of the policy-makers post–apartheid was idealistic and didn't reflect the lived experience of all disabled South Africans. There were issues around elitism and the use of Western norms that did not necessarily fit with South African culture. Education and employment hierarchies show how disabled people and children in SA are struggling to be considered full citizens or have automatic access to mainstream education or support, as they are entitled to by the constitution.
>
> *(Black & de Matos-Ala, 2016, p. 338)*

During current President Ramaphosa's address to the Working Group on Disability (DWG), he called for the inclusion of people with disabilities in public and private sectors (South African Government, 2019). Some of the DWG goals are on the way to being ratified (e.g. South African Sign Language recognised as the 12th official language). It is still to be seen whether the Department of Disability's move to the Department of Women, Youth and Persons with Disabilities in June 2019 under the remit of the presidential office will benefit such divergent groups. With the other goals of the DWG, it will take longer to see whether they have been successful and the promises of access and inclusion made by Ramaphosa come to fruition.

In 2021, SA faced further unrest with the imprisonment of former President Zuma for contempt of court after failing to attend a commission that was investigating allegations of corruption. This event was a catalyst for riots across the country, which became an outlet for social unrest and anger at the government in its failure to address the social inequality and severe deprivation that has built up over decades. The riots led to a breakdown in societal structures (New Frame, 2021). For disabled people living in SA, Hlongwane reports, the problem was even more severe, with areas barricaded, malls and security grant offices being burned and looted and money saved for food being used on transport to search for essentials. Visually impaired people were affected the most as they had to rely on other people for the bare essentials. Hlongwane voiced his concerns about those disabled by the violence being able to receive help in a system already stretched by the COVID-19 pandemic.

How are hierarchies of disability different in the UK and SA?

Internalised ableism is common worldwide due to the continued negative perception of disabled people. This stigma affects how disabled people view themselves and other disabled people. Unfortunately, support in the UK is underfunded (Ryan, 2019), which pits people with different impairments against one another, whereas in SA, disabled learners thought the term 'disabled' was 'offensive and hurtful' and 'limiting and extreme' (Bantjes et al., 2015, pp. 247–248). And they thought of themselves as 'being in a liminal space between "normal" and "disabled"; they did not fit into either of these groups and instead saw themselves as "different and challenged" '(Bantjes et al., 2015, p. 52).

There is limited research on how disabled people group themselves into an impairment hierarchy. Through our embodied and lived experience, we wish to propose a tentative UK hierarchy so we can point out some differences we have experienced. We are aware this is a simplistic analysis and that we have not taken into account the place and interconnectedness of race, gender and the ability to live independently or the differences between people with acquired and congenital disabilities or chronic pain.

Hierarchy of disability in the UK (ranked from least to most disabled)

- Passes as non-disabled due to hidden disabilities: epilepsy, diabetes, some mental health conditions (e.g. mild depression)
- Sensory impairment (D/Deaf, blind, visual impaired)
- Mobility issues that limit or affect walking (neurological conditions like a stroke or MS, wheelchair users)
- Substance abuse conditions
- Severe physical and intellectual disabilities/lifelong or life-limiting conditions
- Learning or intellectual disabilities and severe psychiatric conditions

In SA, Hlongwane finds from his learners that blindness and visual impairments are considered to be the worst disability as people with these impairments are thought to be at greater risk of injury and are unable to experience the world as others can. A wheelchair user will be thought to be higher on a disability hierarchy scale than a blind person because they are able to see. Similarly, with mental health, there is only one word in Zulu (*Ukuhlanya*) to describe mental disturbance and madness. Hlongwane says learners will view these conditions as a disability but will still consider them to be of a higher status than blindness. Research by Bantjes et al. finds that disabled learners police and maintain disability hierarchies within the school setting, with the learners whose disability places them at the top of the hierarchy bullying or discriminating against those they think are beneath them in order to preserve their own status (2015, p. 249).

Race also affects how students with disabilities are treated in SA. In general, white students will tend to have more advantages as their parents are better educated, will fight for the best support and have more access to resources.

How do 'knowledge cultures' play into making hierarchies of disability?

The notion of personal independence is seen as an achievement and strived for by disabled and non-disabled people alike in many cultures. In the UK, the disability rights movement has been about independence and autonomy. Disabled people demanded that they should be able to decide for themselves how and where they live. Independent living for disabled people was a hard-won fight and is ongoing with current government cuts, austerity and the backlash of the pandemic (Clifford, 2020). The move to independence highlighted which disabled people were deemed able to integrate into society with minimal support. This excluded a lot of people who were unable to meet the independence criteria.

The idea of independence for anyone is a myth. We are all connected to each other and reliant on each other for our ways of living. Mia Mingus shows how society hides behind the myth of independence; the majority of people do not grow our own food, make our clothes, build transport etc. She explains:

> [T]he Myth of Independence is not just about the truth of being connected and interdependent on one another; it is also about the high value that gets placed on buying into the myth and believing that you are independent; and the high value placed on striving to be independent, another corner stone of the ableist culture we live in.
>
> *(Mingus, 2017)*

The pursuit of independence sets all people up, irrespective of impairment, to think that they are liable for their own successes and failures. Individualism is part of the capitalistic structure that governs our societies; ableism will work alongside the myth of independence to make people believe that they are the reason they succeed when, in reality, everyone is reliant on those around them and the wider society to do well. The conspicuousness of disabled people's need for support to thrive feeds into the myth of disabled people as dependent and non-disabled people as independent.

One of the most important concepts at play in SA is *ubuntu*, which encourages a different hierarchical structure from that of the Global North. *Ubuntu* is a philosophy, a knowledge culture and a way of living which occurs under different names throughout Africa (Waghid & Shanyanana, 2016, pp. 104–106).

The concept of *ubuntu*, for which there is no direct English translation, is part of the Zulu saying '*Umuntu ngumuntu nga bantu*' which roughly translates as:

> [T]o be a human be-ing is to affirm one's humanity by recognizing the humanity of others and, on that basis, establish humane relations with

> them. Ubuntu, understood as be-ing human (human-ness); a humane, respectful, and polite attitude towards others constitutes the core meaning.
>
> *(Ramose, 2002, p. 231)*

Hlongwane parses the saying as 'a human being is who he or she is because of others'. A person lives and thrives through their relationship with others and their impact on the world around them. This means the focus is on how a person's actions implicate the wider community; it is not based on how it can make your life better. To help your neighbour or family member is to help yourself as the community is only as strong as the weakest link. If everyone is supported, then the community does well. As part of *ubuntu*, everyone is granted an intrinsic human value as a person that must be respected at all costs (Mnyaka & Motlhabi, 2005, p. 220). A person may fail to act with *ubuntu*, but that does not mean that they lose their humanness; they will be called out on their actions in order to be back in good relationships with other people (Mnyaka & Motlhabi, 2005, p. 226). *Ubuntu* has shaped and still shapes how society is formed in SA from government policies to how people relate to and care for one another. This is a basic explanation of *ubuntu* complied from both inside and outside the knowledge culture. (For further discussion, see the reference list.)

How does *ubuntu* play into disability hierarchies? Hlongwane says, of his learners at Mason Lincoln School, when a person treats someone else badly, it is thought they were not raised in the African way and comments that not everyone has the privilege of being taught or sharing in *ubuntu*. If a family moves from a rural setting to an urban setting hoping to have a better life but ends up living in extreme poverty, it is unlikely that they will teach *ubuntu* to their children, having not experienced it themselves. In the wider community, not showing *ubuntu* towards disabled people shows some of its fragility of inclusion. This is because some people believe that disabled people are a curse from the ancestors. Hlongwane finds this view problematic because it shifts the focus from someone's disability to a lack of spirituality and does not support the disabled person or adhere to *ubuntu*'s ideas of intrinsic humanness. Therefore, to have not been taught *ubuntu* is seen as a form of disability, which then affects a disabled person's status in society.

Ngubane-Mokiwa suggests that the ethic of *ubuntu* is not the issue; rather, there has been a misinterpretation of its practice that has led to the reduced status or exclusion of disabled people from society (2018, p. 6). There is a gap between treating all people with *ubuntu* and the practices of discriminating against disabled people. Waghid and Shanyanana, like Hlongwane, find inhumane treatment will not serve to further *ubuntu*: "[W]hen some people, for instance, are humiliated or oppressed they are regarded inhumanely, and this points to the absence of *ubuntu* in the practice" (2016, p. 108). When oppression happens, *ubuntu* means that others need to address the issue. The idea that *ubuntu* does not see the individual but the community is also a misunderstanding of *ubuntu*. Waghid & Shanyanana cite Ramose in suggesting:

> [T]here is an elevated judgment of the community in African thought and practice, which is greater than that of the individual, but that does not take place at the expense of overlooking the individuality of the person. A person is a person in the community, and his or her individuality is exercised through others in that community.
>
> *(2016, p. 107)*

The community is important but not at the expense of the individual as the community can only be strong through the individual expression of a person in that community with others.

Ramose suggests that it is important to understand the being and wholeness of *ubuntu* through 'three interrelated dimensions' (2002, p. 236) of living dead (*abapħansi*), living (*umuntu*), and the yet-to-be-born, which functions as a continued past, present and future. The living dead, while no longer in the world, live in an afterlife and continue to impact community decisions (2002, p. 236). Ramose finds that "It is the task of the living to see to it that the yet-to-be-born are in fact born" (Ramose, 2002, p. 236). Therefore, what has happened in the past and in the here and now will have a direct impact on those in the future, including whether they will even exist. *Ubuntu* has to encompass these multiple dimensions for the practice to be inclusive.

The contextuality of *ubuntu* also causes misunderstanding. *Ubuntu* is a living philosophy and practice that is created and enacted through being a person in and through the community. It has changed over time and will continue to do so as people and communities change. It is not a universal concept that can be extracted from the specific culture it is part of.

Berghs's understanding of *ubuntu* as constantly changing, tied into the instability of disability and impairment. She suggests:

> [I]mpairment becomes cognitive, sensory, mental, physical (inclusive of biological) and spiritual diversity that can have a multitude of shared meanings that society, as human collective, constantly (re)make together. *Ubuntu* can change over time and recognises difference of experiences of diversity of humanness (as positive or negative), which are part of our shared humanity.
>
> *(Berghs, 2017, p. 2)*

The meanings of 'impairment' and 'disability' are and can be remade alongside the context of *ubuntu*, which changes as new understandings of humanness incorporate all diversity. *Ubuntu* in this model can evolve to become inclusive of disability and add to the meanings and interpretations of disability.

Ubuntu leaves space for disabled people to be who they are as disabled people but still have a fulfilling role in the community. Waghid and Shanyanana suggest:

> [T]he oneness of African philosophy is perceivable in the plurality of its voices, and that no voice should be disregarded in the whole community of engagement. In particular, the notion of Ubuntu underlies the communalism by which the African community is characterized.
>
> *(2016, p. 107)*

The community needs the plurality of different voices and people, including disabled people, to have true inclusion and enact *ubuntu*.

In Sinenhlanhla S. Chisale's journal article "Politics of the Body, Fear and *Ubuntu*: Proposing an African Women's Theology of Disability," she explores how to use *ubuntu* to include disabled women in society. Looking at Ndebele women in Zimbabwe, she describes how they use their bodies to resist societies' fear of disability and show inclusion. Writing about a woman called Zoey, Chisale says,

> [L]iving a 'normal life' is protesting and contesting the fear of disability. She uses her body to fit into society, play as a child, and love and get pregnant as an adult. When people see a disabled body perform what an able-bodied person can, fear ceases.
>
> *(Chisale, 2020, p. 4)*

This notion of recognising the similarities in being human, rather than the differences, is a tenet of CC, but it is not without its issues as it rests on the disabled person performing in a 'normal' way.

Chisale goes on to suggest that their method of engaging with their exclusion is a form of *ubuntu* practice as rather than treating their exclusion negatively, they engage with the community's fear to overcome the negative perception of disability and to challenge ableism:

> Their response to fear has undertones of ubuntu where the victim does not respond to oppression violently, aggressively, silently or compliant, but through negotiation of her own hospitality and inclusion. Participants negotiated their inclusion through challenging ableist constructions; that is, it is only an able body that can swim, dance, be sexually attractive, falls [sic] in love, have [sic] sex and give birth.
>
> *(Chisale, 2020, p. 7)*

Chisale, through her study and construction of an African women's theology of disability, shows how disabled women, and disabled people in general, can use their bodies and aspects of *ubuntu* to resist the fear and discrimination that disability causes.

In his book *An African Path to Disability Justice: Community, Relationships and Obligations* (2020), Oche Onazi lays out a possible solution to the exclusion of disabled people from African society. He is considering a new African legal philosophy of disability justice based on the ethical ideals of community, relationship and obligation. Though this is presented as an Africa-wide solution, it has possibilities for SA. While Onazi does look for social justice for disabled people, he proposes a horizontal system for society and community, rather than a hierarchical one that promotes interdependency as being beneficial for society. Onazi's communitarian approach also ties into the reciprocal system of *ubuntu* that is found is SA, but as we have seen, it might be difficult for people with disabilities to participate. He avoids this issue with asymmetrical reciprocity, which is not founded on a person's abilities or characteristics but a moral imperative to support disabled people for the good of the society, which is not based on reciprocity.

Disabled people, for Onzai, rather than being seen as inferior because of their needs, expose the myth of autonomy in the human condition. People are all vulnerable and frail at certain times. All people need connection and support from each other to thrive. His desire for asymmetrical reciprocity is based on a reserved tax scheme and educational system to highlight society's ethical and moral obligations (Onazi, 2020, p. 5). This system would be designed to foster respect and support for disabled people as a moral obligation of society. There are issues with the system as it could risk falling into a charitable model of disability, in which disabled people are 'looked after' but are not granted full citizenship and maintaining the hierarchical system. However, it is an alternative for a more inclusive society that has aspects of *ubuntu*.

Similarly, Berghs's article 'What Can *Ubuntu* as a Disabled Model Do in the Future? How Can It Challenge People to Be Inclusive?' discusses how a disabled model of *ubuntu* can effect social change. As we said earlier, *ubuntu* is contextual and fluid; it is a practice, not just a theory. This practice changes when the oppressions and discrimination faced by the community shift, and because *ubuntu* is so specific, the answers need to come from the community (Berghs, 2017, p. 5).

For SA, according to Berghs, '*Ubuntu* makes visible the invisible inequalities for common humanity' (2017, p. 1). *Ubuntu* uncovers discrimination, oppression, apartheid, violence, colonialsation and disablement in society and shows how the common humanity is being threatened. She extends this to the environment, which has also suffered degradation, and disablement, alongside other social justice campaigns that use practices of *ubuntu*. This view of ubuntu is holistic as it incorporates everything that affects the lives of others, which can be spiritual, environmental, ecological, social, physical etc. and extends well beyond the impaired body (Berghs, 2017, p. 2).

Berghs suggests that disability studies need to use *ubuntu* to analyse the treatment of individuals and the wider society and how it connects to the past violence of colonialism and apartheid (Berghs, 2017, pp. 5–6). Moreover, ubuntu can be used as a tool for change. 'Using *ubuntu* we can ask why the social responsibilities of ethical actions are enabled or disabled individually, socially, by the state or structurally' (Berghs, 2017, p. 6). Which means if social responsibilities are being disabled or threatened, action is needed. African disability studies are entwined with civil rights and social justice movements and could be at the forefront of change that encompasses *ubuntu* in its practice to challenge all the oppressions that threaten the common humanity in SA society. 'It is a challenge that disability studies is taking up in keeping with the dynamism of ubuntu and how we understand what it means to be human' (Berghs, 2017, p. 7). Instead of disabled people being apart from society, African disability studies incorporates *ubuntu* to demonstrate to SA society how all voices need to share in a common humanity and provide social justice action.

Why is the chapter the way it is?

Designing and structuring this chapter became a discussion about hierarchies. Who and what are we privileging by putting one section before another? Is text more important than images or the other way around? While we realise we are conforming to hierarchies in many ways, we are also testing some academic conventions.

We opened the chapter with a painting which is a response by Njabulo to the scenario described under the painting. It is in Zulu as we wanted to highlight the expectation and privilege of the English language in research. This is the translation for his painting (Hlongwane, 2021):

> This is what he had longed for, to compete in the open fields of sports. At that time, he had travelled a long distance to reach this private school for learners with special needs in Durban. He had done this in order to fulfil his dream. Back at his home, he used to sit at the edge of the sports ground to watch his peers compete. His health declined, lack of security and tiresome process of filling in the forms for road accident fund hindered opportunities and good intentions by his teachers at the school. At that time, he found himself being surrounded by learners with special needs and the majority of them being Indians. His teacher was weighing on him to prove to himself about his aspirations. Finally, he got his chance to throw the javelin so that he could feel himself being free and also part of the sport team.

Njabulo chose this scenario from a selection of scenarios that identified various potential hierarchies through remembering past experiences, conversations and reading. The hierarchies we identified were race, gender, socio-economic status, education and impairment, with some of these having specific contextual connotations such, as the apartheid legacy that privileges people of Indian descent above those of African descent and below people of white descent. He also chose it because:

> [I]t best illustrates how a person with disability can be deprived of opportunities that can improve their lives or make them to pursue their dreams. People with disabilities that are from the rural areas are usually more disadvantaged than those that are from urban areas where, more opportunities are available. In this scenario the learner had to move from rural area to the urban area before they could realise their dreams.
>
> *(Hlongwane, 2021, email)*

The scenario was written by Jean about one of the white, Scottish CC volunteer's experiences in a school in Durban, but Njabulo interpreted it as a scenario about the lack of opportunities available to learners from rural areas, thereby highlighting an area of privilege which we had not considered and exposing our preconceptions.

While the conventions of academic writing and rigorous research methods have their place, they also uphold hierarchies. We are challenging these in the reference list at the end of the chapter, which includes the writings that have inspired us. We could just as easily have listed the events, experiences and people who have led us to this way of thinking. We have not parsed voices that have spoken more eloquently than we ever could and let them speak for themselves. We have used citations where we felt they were necessary and the forenames of the authors. For accessibility reasons, we have included links to the texts where we can and used e-books so they are available online or are free to download as PDFs. We have specifically chosen to use a more informal style of writing on the grounds of language accessibility and comprehension. A lack of academic education or the use of less traditional research methods excludes some authors from having a voice, while a lack of education, money and accessibility can exclude some readers.

Our research methods reflect the interdisciplinary and intersectional nature of disability studies, and their aim is to forge alliances between academics who can provide social, cultural and political analysis and activists/disabled people who can provide lived experience. It seems fitting as it bypasses binary categorisation and embraces learning through experience, empathy and engagement. We have amalgamated various methodological approaches to form content that can foster curiosity.

Our approach has been based on auto-ethnography, collaborative and narrative inquiry; our data was collected from our memories of lived experiences and our scholarship. Arts-informed inquiry, which combines the arts and their practices with scholarly research to advance knowledge, has also played a role in this work. Throughout the process, we have been very aware of the hierarchies that were at play in our choices.

As we are writing about hierarchies, we have also been highly aware of the potential within our collaboration to create an environment that fosters joint decisions and shared ownership. This chapter was shaped by the authors and our experiences – our landscapes of practice. To avoid creating hierarchies, these are a list of our identities: personal assistant, Black, female, South African, educator, artist, white, male, disabled, Scottish, PhD scholar, non-disabled, MSc scholar, and entrepreneur.

We have tried to create a horizontal, interdependent, interdisciplinary relationship. To maintain this relationship has been challenging as we need to consciously and consistently be aware of cultural (in particular, the legacy of apartheid), socio-economic and gender differences; how our individual specific skills can be balanced; and how we respond to the context and situation we are in. For example, the authors in Scotland have few problems with accessing technology while data is expensive and unreliable in SA. This dictated how we communicated.

Is this the end or another beginning?

As we have collaborated to create this chapter, we have become even more aware of the hierarchies that are at play all around us and how they are societally or culturally specific.

We feel that, although this chapter is over, our journey has only just begun. There are so many avenues of research that could support disabled people in their fight for equity. Crossing Countries was just one that started us on this journey.

We have been intrigued and enthralled by what we have learned, especially in three areas:

1. The differences between impairment hierarchies in SA and the UK
2. How cultural knowledge and activism have the capacity to shape disability hierarchies
3. The possibilities of sharing knowledge between the Global South and the Global North

But these are also fraught with more questions:

1. How could contextual cultural knowledge help find equity for disabled people globally without being accused of cultural appropriation?
2. How could we cultivate hierarchies not based on value judgements but as categories to make society equitable?
3. And finally: What does the image in Figure 34.2 say to you about culture and hierarchies?

Figure 34.2 *Nginikeni izinduku zami nesihlangu sami* (Give me my sticks and my shield)

Source: Hlongwane, 2020

APPENDICES

Glossary of terms

We have followed the common use of the term 'Black' in South Africa to describe South Africans who are not from Indian, coloured or white descent.

We have taken 'knowledge cultures' to mean the beliefs, rules and attitudes of a society.

Acknowledgement

We are acknowledging everyone we have met and every author we have read.

References

Bantjes, J., Swartz, L., Conchar, L., & Derman, W. (2015). When they call me cripple: A group of South African adolescents with cerebral palsy attending a special needs school talk about being disabled. *Disability & Society*, *30*(2), 241–254. https://doi.org/10.1080/09687599.2014.997352

Barnes, C. (2014). Disability, disability studies and the academy. In Swain, J. (Ed.), *Disabling Barriers – Enabling Environments* (Second ed.). London: Sage [available as ebook].

Berghs, M. (2017). Practices and discourses of ubuntu : Implications for an African model of disability? *African Journal of Disability*, 6(1), 1–8. https://doi.org/10.4102/ajod.v6.292

Black, D. R., & de Matos-Ala, J. (2016). Building a more inclusive South Africa: Progress and pitfalls in disability rights and inclusion. *Third World Thematics: A TWQ Journal*, *1*(3), 335–352. https://doi.org/10.1080/23802014.2016.125268

Candy, L. (2006). Practice based research: A guide. *Creativity and Cognition Studios Report* 1 [available as a downloadable pdf].

Chisale, S. S. (2020). Politics of the body, fear and ubuntu: Proposing an African women's theology of disability. *Hervormde Teologiese Studies*, 76(3), 1–10. https://doi.org/10.4102/hts.v76i3.5871

Clifford, E. (2020). *The War on Disabled People: Capitalism, Welfare and the Making of Human Catastrophe*. London: Zed Books Ltd.

Crenshaw, K. (1989). Demarginalizing the intersection of race and sex: A black feminist critique of antidiscrimination doctrine, feminist theory and antiracist politics. *University of Chicago Legal Forum*, *89*(1), Article 8, 139–167. http://chicagounbound.uchicago.edu/uclf/vol1989/iss1/8

Daiute, C. (2014). The appeal of narrative in research. In *Narrative Inquiry* (pp. 1–30). SAGE Publications, Inc. https://www-doi-org.ezproxy.is.ed.ac.uk/10.4135/9781544365

Freire, P. (2005). *The Pedagogy of the Oppressed*. London: Continuum International Publishing Group Ltd. https://libcom.org/files/Paulo%20Freire,%20Myra%20Bergman%20Ramos,%20Donaldo%20Macedo%20-%20Pedagogy%20of%20the%20Oppressed,%2030th%20Anniversary%20Edition%20(2000,%20Bloomsbury%20Academic).pdf

Goodley, D. (2021). *Society Now: Disability and Other Human Questions*. Bingley: Emerald Publish Limited [available to download at Emerald Publishing].

Howell, C., Chalklen, S., & Alberts, T. (2006). A history of the disability rights movement in South Africa. In Watermeyer, B., & Human Sciences Research Council (Eds.), *Disability and Social Change: A South African Agenda* (pp. 46–84). Cape Town: HSRC Press. https://www.hsrcpress.ac.za/books/disability-and-social-change

Ignagni, E., & Church, K. (2008). Disability studies and the ties and tensions with arts-informed inquiry: One more reason to look away. In Knowles, J., & Cole, A. (Eds.), *Handbook of the Arts in Qualitative Research: Perspectives, Methodologies, Examples, and Issues* (pp. 625–638). London: Sage.

Jagoe, K. (n.d.). The disability rights movement: its development in South Africa. *Independent Living Institute*. https://www.independentliving.org/toolsforpower/tools6.html

Mingus, M. (2017, April, 12). Access intimacy, interdependence and disability justice. *Leaving Evidence*. https://leavingevidence.wordpress.com/2017/04/12/access-intimacy-interdependence-and-disability-justice/

Mnyaka, M., & Motlhabi, M. (2005). The African concept of ubuntu/botho and its socio-moral significance. *Black Theology : An International Journal*, *3*(2), 215–237. https://doi.org/10.1558/blth.3.2.215.65725

New Frame. (2021, July, 13). A moment of rupture. *New Frame*. https://www.new-frame.com/a-moment-of-rupture/

Ngubane-Mokiwa, S. A. (2018). Ubuntu considered in light of exclusion of people with disabilities. *African Journal of Disability*, 7(1), 1–7. https://doi.org/10.4102/ajod.v7i0.460

Onazi, O. (2020). *An African Path to Disability Justice* (Vol. 78, Ius Gentium: Comparative Perspectives on Law and Justice). Cham: Springer International Publishing AG.

Ramose, M. B. (2002). The philosophy of ubuntu and ubuntu as philosophy. In Coetzee, P. H., & Roux, A. P. J. (Eds.), *Philosophy from Africa: A Text with Readings* (2nd ed.) (pp. 230–238). Cape Town: Oxford University Press Southern Africa.

Ryan, F. (2019). *Crippled : Austerity and the Demonization of Disabled People*. London: Verso.

Saad, L. F. (2020). *Me and white Supremacy: Combat Racism, Change the World, and Become a Good Ancestor*. London: Quercus Editions Ltd.

Scopa, K. (2003). *The Development of Strategies for Interdisciplinary Collaboration within the Visual Arts*, PhD Dissertation. Aberdeen: Robert Gordon University [available for download at openair@RGU].

South African Government. (2019, February, 26). *President Cyril Ramaphosa Commits to Inclusion and access for People with Disabilities*. https://www.gov.za/speeches/working-group-disability-commits-inclusion-and-access-26-feb-2019-0000

Trahar, S. (Ed.). (2013). *Contextua*lising narrative inquiry: Developing methodological approaches for local contexts. *ProQuest Ebook Central*. https://ebookcentral.proquest.com

Waghid, Y., & Shanyanana, R. N. (2016). Reconceptualizing ubuntu as inclusion in African higher education: Towards equalization of voice. *Knowledge Cultures*, *4*(4), 104–120.

Wenger-Trayner, E., Fenon-O'Creevy, M., Hutchinson, S., Kubiak, C., & Wenger-Trayner, B. (2015). *Learning in Landscapes of Practice: Boundaries, Identity, and Knowledgeability in Practice-Based Learning*. Oxon: Routledge [available as ebook].

35

COUNTERING DISABILITY HIERARCHY WITH CROSS-DISABILITY SOLIDARITY

Gabor Gombos and Amita Dhanda

Introduction

Gabor and I had been in intense discussion of this chapter through the latter half of 2021 and the early months of 2022. Through these innumerable discussions, we settled the content, even as the text had yet to be finalised, when Gabor died on 5 June 2022. This was amongst the last pieces of writing that Gabor was associated with. I relied on our long-term professional and personal relationship to complete this unfinished work so as to share our thoughts on this crucial question of disability hierarchy and cross-disability solidarity. We have explored this topic by sharing experiential vignettes from Hungary, India and the United Nations. When we wrote the abstract to this chapter, we had separated our experience of hierarchy and solidarity. The national narratives were more steeped in hierarchy, whereas we saw our work with the Disability Rights Convention in the Ad Hoc Committee through the lens of solidarity. As we moved to the full chapter, we found that expressions of hierarchy and solidarity intersected both our national and international experiences. Hence, we have dropped the separate discourse on the two concepts and speak about them together. Gabor was closely involved with the law reform efforts in Hungary, and I was doing the same in India; therefore, the two country narratives were individually written, but our report on the developments at the United Nations was jointly settled.

Since this is a posthumous piece for Gabor, I am also including one issue which significantly affected his life, of which, as was his wont, he wanted to talk about by naming all institutions and persons involved – a disclosure which he found necessary, but many found discomfiting. As a result, the matter could, at best, only be raised in private conversations or in restricted-audience gatherings. Its deliberation in public forums could not happen. With Gabor's death, I feel it is only correct to put a lid on the personal hurt, sorrow, anger and

 DOI: 10.4324/9781003410089-41

frustration and let the larger issues of competing vulnerabilities and inclusive empathy be thrown open. By considering the question of inter se vulnerabilities, we are admitting the need to address this thorny issue, and, to that limited extent, this chapter is setting an agenda for the future.

The Hungarian narrative of hierarchy and solidarity

I (Gabor) have been involved in several advocacy campaigns in Hungary and Europe. In this segment, I am sharing my experience of working on the ban on cage beds in Hungary, reworking the text on legal capacity and support in the Hungarian Civil Code and, lastly, I share some personal encounters with support and guardianship.

Banning cage beds

The superimposition of an iron or netting cage on top of a bed to confine a person within the space of a four-poster bed is the common description of a caged bed. A caged bed symbolized for me the most obvious restriction on free movement experienced by a person with psychosocial disability. The limited height required persons to be on their knees as it was not possible to stand. For me, as a person with psychosocial disability, the humiliation and loss of dignity signified by the cage bed was obvious and in your face. To ask for its ban was a logical consequence of the prohibition against cruel and degrading treatment. As the campaign started, there were many members of the medical and nursing profession who justified the use of the beds to protect the staff and the inmates from the dangerous behaviour of the inmates. Since the medical and nursing professionals were the gatekeepers of these beds, it was evident that the movement of the ban could not gain momentum as long as the caring and treating professionals were resisting it. It was decided to address the resistance by organising a training for the nurses working in the psychiatric institution. I have found that some humans are unconcerned about the dehumanizing treatment meted to other humans because the humanity of the others has become invisible to them due to labelling, physical appearance or prejudice. With the training, we worked to restore the human connection and to show the caring professionals that the persons locked in cages were no different from them. Humane treatment would reduce risk whilst force and brutality increase the chances of violence.

The movement for the cage bed ban, like the other campaigns I have participated in, gained momentum when the campaign was not only being led by persons with psychosocial disability. This happened in the case of cage beds when the community of persons with autism and organizations of persons with intellectual disability also joined the crusade and provided evidence of how the intervention was counterproductive. We next approached the college of psychiatry and provided them with evidence on the inhumanity of the intervention. Since convincing the professionals alone would not change ground reality, a lot of time was spent with the concerned bureaucrats and the minister in charge to convince them of the need for the ban. In order to ensure that the ban did not remain a paper exercise, we worked to include a module in nurses' training on how to look after persons with psychosocial disabilities without encaging them.

The caged bed was a recognised psychiatric intervention because the people caged in them were not seen as humans. And the caging of non-human animals was not looked at askance at that time. Hence, humans who were seen as no different from non-human animals could be treated like them. This hierarchy was challenged when we obtained support from other disability groups, and our interaction with people who opposed us, be they professionals, administrators or politicians, was patient and persuasive. Anger, I found, could be internal fuel, but it was counterproductive when talking to others. Since we were the irrational ones, we were compelled to rely on patient persuasion to win people over. The cage beds were banned in Hungary in July 2004.

Ousting guardianship and incorporating supported decision making in the civil code

Persons with intellectual and psychosocial disability have been denied legal capacity by the law. The institution of guardianship was established in order to create a mediator between the incapacitated person and the law. Again, as in the cage bed situation, the absence of legal capacity placed persons with psychosocial disability at the bottom of the disability hierarchy. With even the disability community believing that the deprivation was inevitable, it was a lonely, excluded space from which we were starting our crusade. Even as I have found near-universal validation for it, my narrative stems from my experience in Hungary.

Since personal experiences of discrimination are accorded little credence, the battle against guardianship was started by documenting the failures of guardianship. The guardianship studies undertaken by the Mental Disability Advocacy Centre (MDAC) showed how an institution meant for the benefit of persons with disabilities resulted in their civil death and became a major source of oppression and exploitation.

Even as the institution of guardianship had been established for persons with intellectual and psychosocial disabilities, the attribution of incapacity or the blight of ableism has been experienced by all persons with disabilities. This stereotype was strongly challenged by the election of Adam Kosa, a Hungarian, as the first deaf member of the European Parliament in 2009. The stereotype of incompetence was challenged and the need to recognize the contribution of persons with disabilities was more easily conceded.

The need to build alliances with opponents was a major learning experience for me during the campaign to ban cage beds. The same learning stood me in good stead during the civil code reform campaign in 2010. Gabor Gado, my namesake in the bureaucracy, taught us the value of a listening bureaucrat and how pathways can be found if there is desire to listen and an openness of mind. Since Mr. Gado was chairing the negotiations, we were heard, and our concerns were not ignored even though many civil law experts found our advocacy for legal capacity and support to be untenable. The supported decision-making provisions found their way into the code due to this support. The reform of the Hungarian Civil Code around 2010 ran into its own confusions; however, I am not dwelling on the travails of the substantive reform of legal capacity in this chapter. I am only sharing my experience of prejudice, surrogate pride and solidarity in the same process. And how even one open-minded strategically placed ally provided us with a space in the law reform process I never thought was possible.

Personal encounters with guardianship

As long as I can recall, I have had personal encounters with psychosocial disability whether as a carer or a person with the disability. My psychosocial disability made me feel both strong and vulnerable. Strong because it connected me to human difference and diversity. And vulnerable because of the manner in which psychosocial disability has been looked at by the world at large; my freedom and autonomy have always been at risk. Whether it be retaining the child I had adopted or the property I owned, an adverse psychiatric determination could get me to lose my child and the right to manage my own property. It is often said that the existence of a deprivation in the law should not matter if it is rarely used. That statement can only be made by a person who comes from a place of privilege. For me (and others like me), a deprivation in the law which is considered lawful is a Damocles sword hanging over my head. Even if I was not decapitated, I have always lived in the fear of it happening.

I did not want guardianship because it is a lose-lose venture. Once placed under guardianship, I would lose all autonomy in relation to my life. But did I need support? I surely did. I know because every time that support or companionship went missing in my life, be it my mother, my wife or close friends, I have struggled. However, I have needed this support with both love and respect. Guardianship has not been constructed to provide that kind of support. Consequently, I have preferred to stumble around.

In the last couple of years of my life, as my physical and financial health deteriorated and the pandemic made just everyday life immeasurably more difficult, I had a circle of support around me. This circle of friends and well-wishers did not just raise money to ensure that I lived a life of respect and dignity but also took care of my everyday living needs and coordinated my health treatments and interventions, be it my sugar, my blood pressure or my cataract. The circle helped me obtain a disability card and had a personal assistant regularly visit me. I needed all this support but could not have put it together myself. I feel eternally grateful that I received this support, and having received it, I know this is what we need to put in place for all of us: a system which can come into being, if we see ourselves as interdependent beings and break out of the stranglehold of hollow independence. As a person with psychosocial disability, I was at the bottom of the disability hierarchy. My education and advocacy occasionally provided me visibility. However, in settings where I was unknown, I have experienced the same devaluation which my less fortunate peers constantly report. Having lived in active communication with a cross-disability support network, I can unhesitatingly say that guardianship is protection in confinement whereas support circles provide assistance to enjoy freedom.

The Indian narrative of hierarchy and solidarity

I (Amita) have, like Gabor, been involved with several law reform activities in my country both before and after the adoption of the Convention on the Rights of Persons with Disabilities (CRPD). However, for this chapter, I am sharing my experience of hierarchy in the law reform efforts after the CRPD. These were civil society initiatives occurring from 2009 to 2011 aimed at amending the National Trust (for Autism, Cerebral Palsy, Mental Retardation and Multiple Disabilities) Act 1999 and preparing for the consideration of a government statute on the rights of persons with disabilities. I next look at how the proactive law reform efforts with the active involvement of the people triggered informed opposition to a governmental bill on disability rights in 2014. And in the third segment, I wish to share my personal reflections on hierarchy and solidarity as a person who sees herself occupying a grey zone between the disabled and non-disabled worlds.

Reforming the law

The National Trust Act was enacted in 1999 primarily to address the concerns of parents about who would look after their children after their death. The statute was a curious mix of protection and self-reliance. Even as it incorporated a simplified procedure for the appointment of a guardian, it also envisaged that every person with the named impairments (autism, intellectual disability, multiple disability) might not need a guardian and allowed for the statutory authority to make a declaration to this effect. The declaration, it was believed, would help persons with the named disabilities assert their legal capacity.

After the CRPD was signed and ratified by India, the National Trust was among the first authorities which, in active involvement with civil society, started the process of law reform. A number of drafts were formulated. In one law reform exercise, it was proposed that the National Trust, instead of continuing as this paternalistic body, should become the entity which helps the sector move from the regime of substitution to the paradigm of support. In order to make support the ruling paradigm, and in recognition of the fact that support was a universal need which everyone requires to a greater or lesser extent, it was proposed that the National Trust should cater to the entire disability sector and not limit itself to the four named disabilities.

The ensuing people's consultation in 2010 was harsh and ugly. The representatives of the four included disabilities – autism, cerebral palsy, mental retardation and multiple disabilities – were vociferous in their opposition. Their argument was that the four included disabilities were among the most marginalized in the sector, and the moment the National Trust and the attendant legislation concerned itself with all, their concerns would be outvoted. They were not strong enough to stand up to the more articulate and developed disability organizations. The economics of the trust would trump its politics. In response to this apprehension, it was suggested that let there be solidarity, at least among the marginalized. Let the trust expand its constituency to include psychosocial disability. The opposition to this proposal was even more strident. The representatives of the included disabilities, especially the organizations of parents of persons with intellectual disability, contended that they could not shoulder the stigma associated with psychosocial disability. Interestingly, the cross-disability solidarity initiated in the draft proposal received scant validation from the representatives of the more organized disability groups, most particularly the Organizations of the Blind, as in their view, they were not in need of the kind of support required by the four marginalized disabilities. On the inclusion of psychosocial disabilities, they felt that the voices of those with the already-included disabilities should prevail.

I encountered a similar rejection of support when we were drafting the Rights of Persons with Disabilities Bill in 2011. The committee undertaking the process recognized that whilst, for some persons with disabilities, simple support might be sufficient, others, be it due to the nature of the impairment or social barriers, might require more support. Since the need for more support was not linked to impairment alone, the entitlement to seek that support was to be made available to all persons with disabilities. Blind persons wanted it explicitly stated in the law that they would not need such support. The fact that blind persons in the more remote parts of the country might need such support and accessing it was only an entitlement, not an obligation, cut no ice with the representatives of the organizations of the blind. The fear which prompted the agitation was that the provisioning of support for even some blind persons might render the legal capacity of all questionable.

My own lesson was that law reform cannot gallop ahead of the people for whom it is meant. Also, ableism does not exist just in the non-disabled world; it is as much internalized by persons with disabilities. Any awareness-raising exercise would also need to include the sector.

Creating cross-disability solidarity

Once the committee had drafted the Rights of Persons with Disabilities Bill in 2011, in order to make the proposed law accessible to all persons and to seek the view of the constituency on significant issues included in the law, the committee got the law translated into the regional language of every state. Audiotapes and Braille copies were also produced. The committee then travelled the length and breadth of the country, apprising disabled people and their organizations of the proposed law and seeking their suggestions on it. The suggestions sent by the people were scrutinized, and every suggestion accepted by the committee was appropriately acknowledged in the footnotes to final bill submitted to the government.

After the committee submitted its draft, the government of India examined it for more than two years, and in 2014, a mutilated version was introduced in Parliament. In the truncated version, the interest of every disability group was compromised. The sector realized that the legislation introduced by the government was not the legislation they were consulted on, and the only way in which the enactment of the law could be stalled was if the sector united. Innumerable protests were held in different parts of the country. Memorandums were submitted, legislators were lobbied and the inadequacies of the proposed law widely disseminated. In the face of the united stand taken by the sector, the government was compelled to withdraw its proposal to enact the law and agreed to re-examine the text. The proposed legislation was then examined by a joint parliamentary committee, which resulted in several provisions of the 2011 draft bill being brought back, and the final statute was enacted in 2016.

The protest and the pushback could happen because the law was not just discussed in committee rooms but was taken to the people. These consultative meetings, which happened in the language of the people, caused disability groups to listen to each other's concerns. Even as every group was pushing its own agenda, it was understood that the whole sector had been shortchanged. The joint work on the law got hierarchies to soften and the need for cross-disability solidarity admitted.

Personal reflections on hierarchies and solidarity

I have been advocating for disability rights in my academic and popular writing for more than four decades. My work on psychosocial disability was prompted by a close and intense encounter with mental distress and suffering in my undergraduate days. Even as that experience informed my post-graduate and doctoral work and was the inner wellspring nurturing my writing, I did not talk about my personal experience. I explained my silence by my fierce attachment to my privacy. And in the pre-CRPD days, my academic credentials shielded me from any probing questions.

The CRPD advocacy and my inclusion in the World Network of Users and Survivors of Psychiatry (WNUSP) delegation made the silence more political. It was felt that by not publicly owning the experience I was feeding the stigma associated with the identity. Having not experienced the disadvantages accompanying a diagnosis, I felt that claiming the identity was like seeking reparations for a loss I did not experience. It took me a fair amount of time to distinguish between owning the experience and claiming representational rights. The first was an act of solidarity, which should not have been held back because I was not seeking a seat at the table.

I have started speaking about my experience and participating in conversations on disability rights. While participating, I continually need to reflect on my identity. I do not belong to the non-disabled world, nor can I claim to be full a member of the disabled community. So where do I stand in this hierarchy? At this point, I see myself standing at the boundaries of both worlds, and in that space, I can see the need for interlocutors. A need for conversations between the two worlds and the consequent alliances which are brought by communication. Disabled people are ousted and made invisible in the non-disabled world as they are seen as those others whose lives have nothing to say to the rest of humanity. I feel people like me can help show the falseness of the dichotomy and how the disabled and the non-disabled are part of a continuum.

The UN narrative of hierarchy and solidarity

When the General Assembly of the United Nations in 2001 set up the ad hoc committee to negotiate a Convention on the Rights of Persons with Disabilities, the UN was not really prepared for this direct encounter with disability. The range of bodies and minds with disabilities that the people working at the UN had to deal with shocked many ableist sensibilities. We were required to stand in long queues to obtain our security passes, and the people who had assembled to register outstripped the counters set up to register them. We had been standing for hours without any clue of when and if our registration would happen. Sensing the restlessness of the crowd, a conscientious UN official came to apologize for the delay and to inform them that they would soon begin by first providing passes to the wheelchair users. "But why?" asked Karl Bach, the co-chair of the WNUSP delegation. "They have been sitting on their chairs. It is the rest of us who are exhausted". The UN official did not know what hit him. Persons with disabilities were more than wheelchair users; the education of the UN had begun.

Documents, memorandums and supporting papers were distributed to the sighted in Room 4. Braille copies, it was routinely announced, were available at the back of the room. This carried on till Kicki Nordstrom, the head of the World Blind Union, decided to take matters in hand. Braille copies of a memorandum of the World Blind Union were distributed to all members on their seats, and ink print copies, the members were informed, were available at the back of the room. The strategy worked, and an assistant was recruited to ensure that Braille copies were personally handed to the blind delegates.

Referring to persons with intellectual, psychosocial and developmental disabilities as idiots, morons, insane and mad was resorted to routinely by state delegates, some of us from WNUSP and Inclusion International, the international organization for persons with intellectual disabilities, told the chair that we would sit out in protest if the disrespectful language continued. The chair censured state delegates and asked them to mind their language.

The United Nations was planning a fire drill on the next day, but the occupants in Room 4 need not worry as they were exempted. A high-powered delegation strongly protested, and Room 4 was included. Any number of wheelchair users could not get out because there were inadequate accessible exits and inadequate information on the accessible ones.

According to UN protocol, civil society organizations can only participate in the formal proceedings of treaty negotiations. When informal proceedings begin, civil society members are expected to leave the room. Inaccessibility and the ponderousness of the process allowed the civil society delegates to attend both formal and informal deliberations of the ad hoc committee; we did not seek equality with other committee proceedings. If, due to disability, the UN bureaucracy was compelled to give us more, we were not protesting!

The United Nations, like the world, was ableist and disability unfriendly. The disabled occupants of Room 4 were calling out the ableism of state delegations and UN officials. They were also compelled to look at the narrowness of their own worlds. Civil society organizations were permitted to present their views on each draft article. It was soon realized that if every organization chose to speak on each article, often repeating what another group had already spoken, disabled people and their organizations would be ousted, citing the constraint of time. This realization resulted in the creation of the International Disability Caucus (IDC), and speaking time was divided among organizations. The various articles were divided according to which disability group had the highest stake in them. Thus, advocacy for adoption of sign language came within the purview of the World Federation for the Deaf, legal capacity was represented by WNUSP and Inclusion International, and the right to rehabilitation was spoken about by Disabled People International and Rehabilitation International. The IDC met every evening to plan the next day's intervention and to learn by listening how little they knew of impairments other than their own.

It is this cross-disability solidarity, nurtured over many detailed conversations, which prevented universal legal capacity from becoming the exclusive battle of WNUSP and Inclusion International. At several points in the legal capacity debate, for strategic reasons and in solidarity, the first intervention came from an organization that was not seen as its primary stakeholder. We remember that, in a particularly discordant discussion on the right to universal legal capacity, the first intervention came from Lex Grandia of the World Federation of the Deaf-Blind; at other times, delegates from the World Blind Union spoke. Universal legal capacity could not be dropped from the convention because the defence of the article was not limited to persons with intellectual, developmental and psychosocial disabilities. All civil society and disabled people's organizations made it their article. In the face of this unity, state parties could see that the convention could not be adopted without the article on legal capacity. The strength of that agreement was again evidenced when a footnote placing a caveat on the right to legal capacity was incorporated in the text of the convention, which was adopted ad referendum by the ad hoc committee. The IDC had Stefan Tromel of the European Disability Forum unequivocally condemn the inclusion of the footnote before Kicki Nordstrom made the celebratory speech.

It was this unity which resulted in the withdrawal of the footnote from the text of the convention.

We confronted both the hierarchy of ableism and challenges to it in the UN. We also saw the visible and invisible hierarchies within the disability sector softening and melting into informed solidarity: a solidarity which emerged from close and patient listening. We saw and know that the various disability organizations were represented by their most experienced hands. People who had seen manipulations and who knew the value of unity and understanding. It would be incorrect to claim that personal foibles and prejudices were not present in the ad hoc committee negotiations; rather, it would be more accurate to concede that the goal the delegates wished to reach prevailed over individual frailties.

Reflecting on inclusive empathy

The point our piece seems to have been making up till now is that even as there is an evident hierarchy between non-disabled and disabled people and a pecking order within the disability community created by the nature of the impairment or the availability of resources, it is possible to scale this hierarchical barrier by informed understanding. Such informed understanding, our experience shows, may be developed by systematic instruction, extended conversations and working and producing things together. By sharing these communication breakthroughs, we are not claiming or even implying that such understanding always develops, and there are no communication breakdowns, be they between non-disabled persons and persons with disabilities or, more importantly, between similarly and dissimilarly situated persons with disabilities. Since conflicts do and will happen, how should they be addressed?

This question needs to be asked within disability communities so that the disability perspective on human relationships and conflict resolution can emerge, and a non-disabled appropriation is not unquestioningly enabled. The defence of insanity has been found inadequate by persons with both intellectual and psychosocial disability. It has been found that the benefits (if any) of the defence outweigh the costs that the disability community pays for accepting the bounty of non-culpability. It is commonly believed that the defence allows persons with psychosocial and intellectual disabilities to escape the consequences of their wrongful conduct. That the defence could result in indefinite and lifelong incarceration of persons acquitted on grounds of insanity is a legal reality which does not invite similar attention.

The zero-sum mode of adjudicating wrongdoing when extended to conflict between two persons with disabilities causes irreparable loss to the person seen as the wrongdoer, be it a sexual relationship between an older boy and a younger girl with intellectual disability or a run-in between a man and a woman with psychosocial disability. There is a need to address the vulnerabilities of both gender and disability. If only gender is addressed and the need for accommodation and accessibility of persons with disability forgotten, decisions are being reached by an unfair process.

A procedure can only be considered fair if it recognizes the vulnerability of all parties and doesn't make one disability more worthy of consideration than another. As we agitate for the right to live in the community, it is important to reflect on how our inter se disputes should be resolved. Reasonable accommodation and non-discrimination should not only be available in exchanges with non-disabled others. The perspective of inclusive empathy, which asks us to extend understanding and not oust the different other, has long been espoused by the disability community. This outlook should not limit its reach to interaction between the disabled and non-disabled worlds; it should also take within its purview the disputes and conflicts between persons with disabilities.

Conclusion

This chapter, in sharing experiences across geographical spaces, has shown both the operation of disability hierarchies and the manner in which cross-disability solidarity has been fostered. The questions raised in the last section need deep deliberation in an independent study. We have incorporated them in this chapter because it is our belief that there is need for empathetic and inclusive dispute resolution among persons with disabilities if we wish not only to build but also to strengthen and retain cross-disability solidarity.

36
INTERSECTING IDENTITIES

Elizabeth Hassler

Author's note on SELF-CONSERVED: Poems Experimenting with (My?) Disability Rights: I was asked to provide some context for the following poems, which are often opaque and experimental. Self-direction is a difficulty in my everyday life, and I find it to be best expressed through text that confuses, is repetitive, and has echoes. (I tried for a more straightforward autobiographical note here, but something in my process refuses!)

In the absence of concrete information, I hope that my poems can provide a space to wonder, to iterate, and to play. Within the refusal of self-telling is a curiosity, and I hope that curiosity can be wide and deep and its own container.

As a writer invested in community, I offer prompts:

> When disabledness is not a story, what is it? When rights cannot be told, what do they mean? When the hierarchy keeps shifting, how is it reinforced? When violence cannot be held, what does it do? What are we when we are (or: what do we present when we present) a contradiction in terms? What do you wonder? What can you change or not change? What is the practice of connection in struggling? What does it mean to have, much less to offer or to *do*, disability human rights?

PRESUME COMPETENCE

you've seen/your teeth
crowding your mouth:
you watched/how the moon fell
when it was mouth with sea,
bulbous, alive.
did you wonder? how to
feed food with language?

DOI: 10.4324/9781003410089-42

did you circle above yourself?
you were kept here, wet dam
so bright with knowing
yes, bell rung so of course;
the bright slippery fish you are
when you are yourself swimming
mouths hello, hello, hello and
does swallow and is enough fed
(inhabit me)
(be so smart)
(shock
fucking
writers)

HIERARCHIES, ALREADY

with your tongue caught
on "bright slippery," you'll
say *blight* instead: speak the
very thing on society you squeeze
(more lemon).
+ you don't believe in intelligence:
you believe in moved colors,
and what pulsing is in
(don't stop!)
how time rhythm does and.

HIERARCHIES, AGAIN

because the world seeps in:
you look at me. don't!
stop!

SELF-CONSERVED

preserve
your
archives of ache.
be a lemon. be
sour. sting
your enemies. *you
have enemies?*
pucker
your own rind.

MEAL ASSISTANCE

names, cascading, cascading being named.
names named after what named us; naming
what leaves; what stays here. name me
a recipe for myself, discrete ingredients
with distinct cook times. can love, less
want, make delicious thing? when you are not
a minus sign, you wonder what crossed you
over. you don't know God, but was He
involved? capital letters are for *names*:
you wonder sometimes if He is not
your name, or why not. you are all girl,
girl cream, cream girl, ugly girl ugly cream
as creamed corn defines herself more girl
than ugly, and milk. you do or do not get
churned into butter and spread on grilled
toast.

EXECUTIVE FUNCTIONS

when the poetry
falls away,
so only the body is left,
who sings?
who has rights? who
can be cleaned to sparkling?

FALL DETECTION

Your body imagines
a free mouth.
Your body is
thirsty, imagining.
Your body trusts
itself. Your body
knows you are
body you are.

CONSENT TO TREATMENT

is your body a prop? not according
to national regulations, and yet:

your lips and face are cardboard.
your lips and face are the realest part.
close your mouth, girl! like a fish, hanging
open or undrowned drowning or left
to smoke and dry pin bones. is your
body a prop? only if it results in point
deduction, and still and still and still so still.
(hold still!) is your body a prop? do props
need medical attention? does a nurse
bother to tell you where her hand is
due to arrive? if a glove isn't *mail* it must
be a present – is your body an aphorism?
is this too much question and answer
about things that never ever ever
happen, inside? is your body a prop?
is a cardboard target lonely? does
queer victory ever say no? does
queer victory ever say why, in the
skin-knowing, it holds itself so tight?
does queer victory hold tight to skin?
will cardboard be skin, soon? do
you feel it? does cardboard feel itself?
does cardboard feel? is your body a
prop? are you ready to lose two points?

DIAGNOSTIC PROCEDURE

A list of what opens for you:
a list of my mouth,
which stays open
or closes or. A list
of mouth sounds.
A body is a list of
what mouth asked
for/didn't ask for. A
body is an unpromised
length. A body hopes
not to be listed *too*
much – that is,
enlisted for medical
textbooks. Body
is listing, always. Where
does listening come?

HOME/BOUND

What poems do beds need?
Sheet held, held tight, held
mouth off bad mouth.
Held tight wax-off war.
It is easier to wander
when you can feel your
edges, and I eye edges edged edger
you can feel, hoping, dissolved
into darkness, turn on light
off turned not
off off off off off turned.
Are we, wet, some
bright thing? How we
travel? Where we
hold the sun?

PREEMIE

i was born, sometimes,
a girl without a container.
sometimes i was born
a container, a without-girl.
sometimes i was container
without a girl, a born.
born: girl, sometimes.
a container. a without.

NEEDS ASSESSMENT

you are mermaid,
Cinderella, or
slippery eel
or rainbow fish
who gives all her scales away, or should –
you are gravity, or wind, or telekinesis. You
are the castle who cages ten princesses
and a dragon, ten cannons of cannons
and suits of armor with kittens inside.
You are the book who protects herself
by being a book with no pages; plain ink
inside; words without a treehouse.
You are all magic spell,

or not. You are whatever you need, aren't
you? You are emptied shell of promise
lost, kept, held.
Tell a magical story about yourself.
Tell how fullness comes (reach out
to find)

NARRATIVE ASSESSMENT or (AVOIDING) GUARDIANSHIP

Write up though the container
your voice lives in. Don't write
about your mouth! Rearrange
what longings your teeth are,
what teeth, what rearranging
or what rearranging holds.
Unfinished, searching,
toward/away promise
yes yes yes yes yes yes yes yes no
why not why open why loneliness
back in. Constellations to guide
away from whiteness – no, don't
be ridiculous. You *are* white
and all the stars you see are white,
of course! What stars do you taste,
but not eat? What stars keep guiding
unguiding dazzling you home, or with
ideas of what home tastes will taste
is tasting like? the container is the home
–place. the container is cardboard you
found, found singing, found hermit
crab singing, hermit crab your body,
your body hermit crab, your voice a
crab your tongue-crabs crabs crabs
your tongue following homes.

PERI CARE or BIDET INSTALLATION

when loneliness is a thing that opens
ocean-blue true untrue true tides
that live and live and are water that
moves, salty enough to keep aliving,
and you resound a welcome mouth,
melting can be a kind of promise.
dissolving can be a kind of body, yes,
and you can imagine your skin (not

poison) some known thing that does still
exist after the story is taken, or told,
or held out to dry. promise your pelvis,
your overgrown under-planted flower
garden overfoot/underfoot/overfoot
foot foot ankle ankle thigh labia labia
thigh lip lip throat tongue, to put in
so many colors, colors we can see

SELF-TRANSFER

and who are the fleshes you are
trying to preserve? where have you moved?
what are the ink marks? what do fish eat?
when you know how to be lonely, to wait,
you cushion yourself incorrectly or so well.
you know! you know so much!
you know the marks will leave, and they do,
but not yet. yet stays a slippery thing,
when the disaster is skilled nursing
– dance – delicately unskills
– for now, for now,
for now you are still here.

INDEX

Note: Page numbers in *italic* indicate a figure and page numbers in **bold** indicate a table on the corresponding page.